IN ARTISTS' FOOTSTEPS

THE RECONSTRUCTION OF PIGMENTS AND PAINTINGS

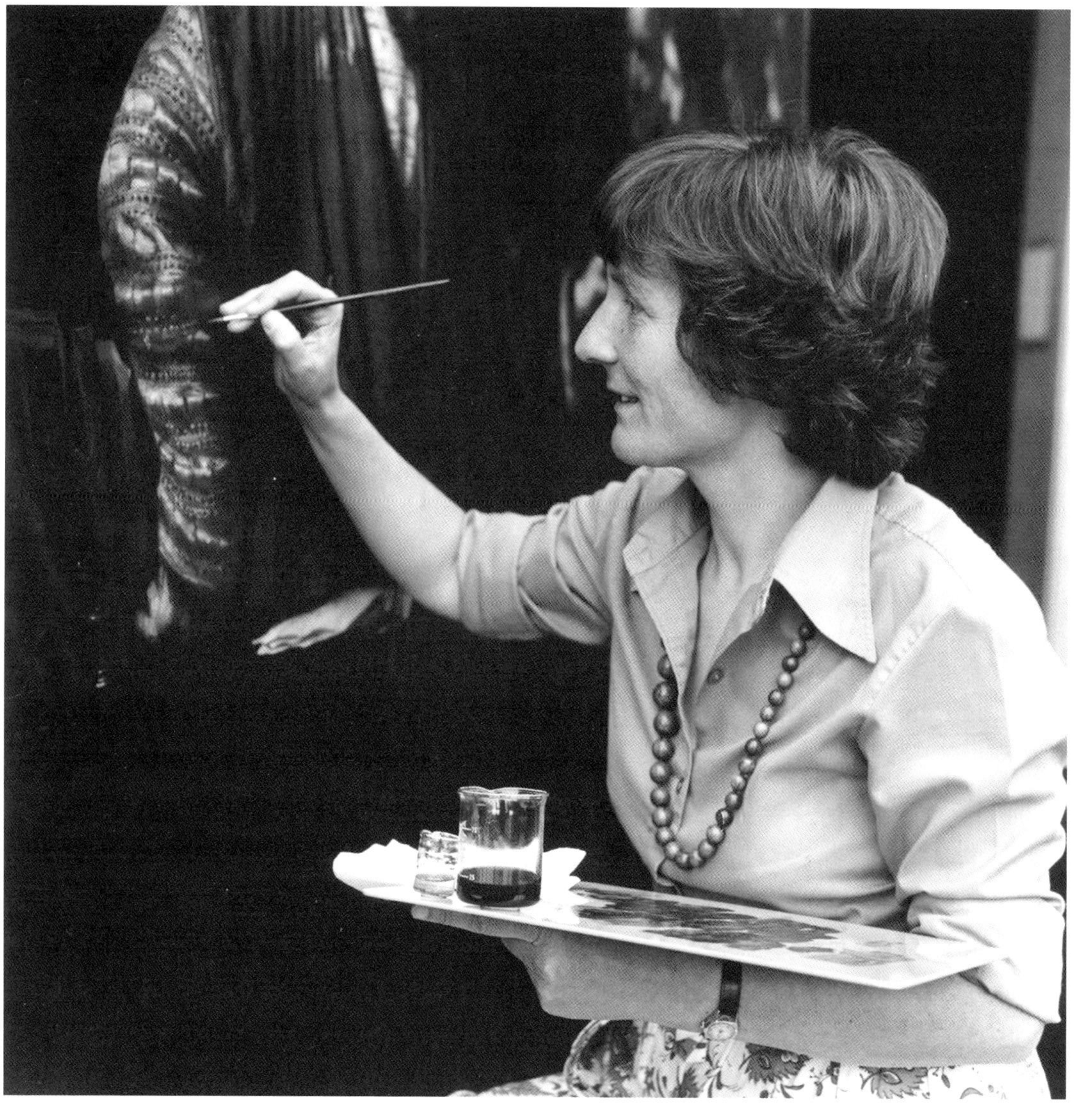

IN ARTISTS' FOOTSTEPS

THE RECONSTRUCTION OF PIGMENTS AND PAINTINGS

Studies in honour of Renate Woudhuysen-Keller

Edited by Lucy Wrapson, Jenny Rose, Rose Miller and Spike Bucklow

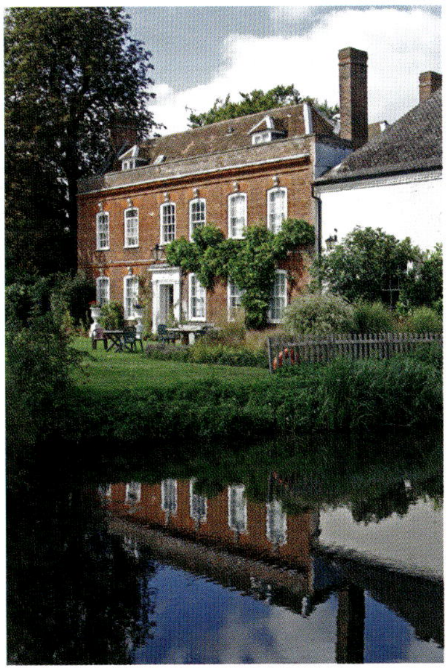

Archetype Publications

First published 2012 by Archetype Publications Ltd

Archetype Publications
c/o International Academic Projects
1 Birdcage Walk
London SW1H 9JJ
www.archetype.co.uk

ISBN: 978-1-904982-85-2

British Library Cataloguing in Publication Data
A catalogue record for this book is available from the British Library.

Front cover illustration: detail of Dieric Bouts (attrib.), *St Luke Painting the Virgin*, oil on panel (transferred to canvas), Private Collection, UK.
Title page illustration: The Hamilton Kerr Institute, Whittlesford

Designed by Marcus Nichols at PDQ Digital Media Solutions Ltd.
Typeset by PDQ Digital Media Solutions Ltd., Bungay
Printed and bound in Italy by Printer Trento Srl

CONTENTS

CASE STUDIES

TABULA GRATULATORIA

Carmen Albendea
Katherine Ara
Trond E. Aslaksby
Pippa Balch
Wiltrud Baumgärtner-Ustaheim
Barbara Berrie
Simon Bobak
Emma Rebecca Boyce Gore
Helen Brett
Lara Broecke
Spike Bucklow
Mary Bustin
Ian S. Butler
Charlotte Caspers
Meta Chavannes
Radoslaw Chocha
Nicola Christie
Sue Ann Chui
Mark Clarke
Nicola Costaras
Jessica David
Phoebe Dent Weil
Tiarna Doherty
Jean Dommermuth
Hélène Dubois
Sylvie and James Fawcett
Rupert Featherstone
Kate Fletcher
Simon Folkes
Eike Friedrich
Tine Frøysaker
Michael Gallagher
Melanie Gifford
David and Caroline Gill
Helen Glanville
Margaret Greeves
Anne van Grevenstein-Kruse
Karin Groen
Groeningemuseum, Bruges
Clare Heard
Ella Hendriks
Sarah Herring
Elizabeth Holford
Isabel Horovitz
Amelia Jackson
Liliana Janik and Simon Kaner
Rica Jones
Madeleine Katkov
Kristin Kausland
Joachim Keller
Rosemarie Keller
Walter Keller
Mary Kempski
Rebecca Kench
Narayan Khandekar
Christine S. Kimbriel
Jo Kirby
Marina Kiseleva
Lizet Klaassen
Beate Knuth Federspiel
Kaja Kollandsrūd
Maria Kubik
Herbert Lank
Andria Laws
Daniela Leonard
Mirjam Liu
Muirne Lydon
Chie Manabe
Sally Marriott
Ann Massing
Lorraine Maule
Ian McClure
Jane McCree
Karen Mengshoel

Sreekumar Menon
Rose Miller
Anne Milnes
Julia Nagle
Britta New
Youjin Noh
Kathryn Oat Grey
Devi Ormond
Régine Page
Christine Patrick
Ian Perrins
Alan Phenix
Unn and Leif Einar Plahter
Sophia Plender
Carol Pottasch
Thérèse Prunet-Brewer
Esther Rapoport
Jenny Rose
The Royal Collection Trust
Annette Rupprecht
Joanna Russell
Artemis Rüstau
Anna Sanden
Andrea Sartorius
Marie Louise Sauerberg and Larry Keith
Mikkel Scharff
Karin and Manfred Schoeller
Libby Sheldon
Eddie Sinclair
Christine Sitwell
Erling S. Skaug
Kristel Smits
Linn Solheim
Sarah Staniforth
Mille Stein
Alison Stock
Maartje Stols-Witlox
Kate Stonor
Noëlle Streeton
Swiss Institute for Art Research (SIK-ISEA), Zurich
Terje Syversen
Alice Tavares da Silva
Sebastian Thewes
Chris Titmus
Hayley Tomlinson
Joyce H Townsend
Ute Tüchler-Heinisch
Ian Tyers
UCL Institute of Archaeology
Geraldine van Heemstra
Ernst van der Wetering
Abbie Vandivere
Johanneke Verhave
Edwin Verweij
Nelly von Aderkas
Elizabeth Walmsley
Valentine Walsh
Janine Wardius
Winterthur Museum, Library, and Garden
Margreet Wolters
Sally Woodcock
Paul Woudhuysen
Lucy Wrapson
Adèle Wright
Martin Wyld
Hanna Zawadzka and Rita Jones

PREFACE

Renate has been an intrinsic part of the Hamilton Kerr Institute (HKI) for as long as I can remember. Even before I arrived here as a student in 1981, I had heard her praises sung by those who had already experienced her inimitable teaching style. Everyone who has learnt from her, past and present, holds her in great affection, in recognition of the generosity of spirit that she brings to the studios, her quiet authority coupled with a sense of wonder in the face of great paintings, and her passion to understand paintings and the minds of the artists who created them. She has a deep love for the HKI and for the students, and we are all heavily in her debt.

Mention the single word Renate at a gathering of paintings conservators, and you will almost certainly see smiles of recognition and goodwill. Renate's influence has spread well beyond the walls of the Institute, where she has been happily ensconced almost constantly since 1978. Abandoning her mountainous homeland for the dramatic flatness of the fens, she has thus spent most of her professional life at Cambridge University and it is fitting that, in addition to her skilful and dedicated practical conservation treatments, she has devoted so many hours to research. Her training was grounded, both literally and figuratively, in the central European tradition and her time in Cologne, Zürich and Stuttgart included the time-honoured discipline of copying paintings. From this point on, and beginning with her thesis with Thomas Brachert, she has been at the forefront of the technical reconstruction of historical painting techniques and materials, linking her practical experiments to the results of research into the sources, and examination of the paintings themselves. Her willingness to 'get her fingers dirty' has vouchsafed her insights which would not have been possible from a purely theoretical approach.

Renate's tenacious character and limitless curiosity are intrinsic to her work; she will wrestle with a problem like a terrier until a painting reveals its secrets or a pigment comes out true from the mixing pot. Coupled to this is a maternal concern for the welfare of the students, not least in their needs for cake and chocolate to reward effort or spur them on to greater things. In all of this she has been constantly supported by her husband Paul, who has been a tower of strength throughout her time here.

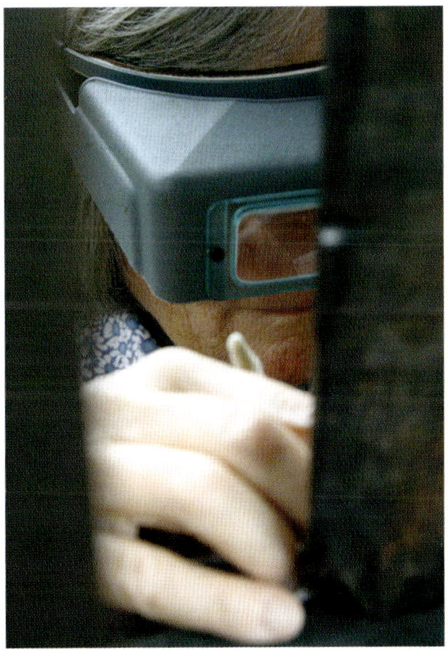

The hackneyed expression 'an inspiration to generation of students' is for once completely appropriate. Renate's alumni are now spread across the world – not only those from the Hamilton Kerr but also many who studied with her on courses at other institutions in Europe – and this present volume is testimony to their achievements, so much inspired by her example. In honour of Renate's formal retirement this Festschrift is dedicated with love and admiration.

Rupert Featherstone
Director, Hamilton Kerr Institute

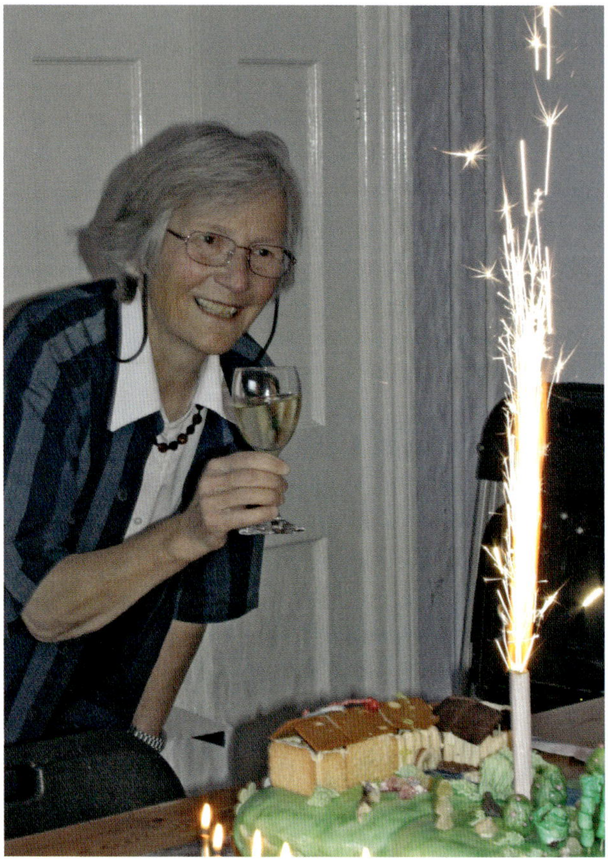

I met Renate soon after I became Director of the Hamilton Kerr Institute in 1984. She had taught previously at the Institute but had returned to Switzerland before I arrived from Glasgow. Her reputation as a teacher and mentor of students led me to initially hire her to undertake a conservation project on contract and then to appoint her as an assistant to the director. I soon realised that in Renate I had a colleague of enormous energy, devoted to the Institute and someone who set very high standards both for herself and for the students. What followed was a collaboration of 23 years, until I left for a post at Yale University. In that time we worked together on many projects, by far the most memorable being the recovery of the original image of *Henry Prince of Wales on Horseback* by Robert Peake from Parham Park in Sussex, which was one of the star attractions of the *Treasure Houses of Great Britain* exhibition, held at the National Gallery of Art in Washington, DC in 1985. We had to work to a strict deadline in order to complete the treatment and I remember sitting in the Director's apartment in the Institute at 3.00am in the morning trying to decide with Renate whether we should apply another spray coat of varnish. It is typical of Renate that she thought the restoration too rushed and I had the ticklish task of persuading the owners to allow us to have the painting back after the exhibition in order to do the job to Renate's satisfaction. This, in a way, was the pattern of our partnership. I, the Director, hoping to get things completed to a timetable and Renate, who would not accept that the best work could be done to a deadline. I had many phone conversations with owners starting 'I am afraid that we will not be ready ...'. Nevertheless great things were achieved – not least her conservation of the sixteenth-century *Battle of the Spurs* from the Royal Collection, which required years of painstaking removal of overpaint, and the recovery of a severely blanched *Landscape* by Gaspard Dughet.

In times of stress – meeting deadlines and undertaking ambitious projects – Renate was invariably positive and encouraging. The possibility of failure never came near. I remember one freezing winter day at Belton House in Lincolnshire, when we were moving an enormous painting by Melchior de Hondecoeter which had to be rolled and moved out of an upstairs window. I was terribly anxious but Renate, wise to the moment, produced as if by magic a Malakoff torte (although the ingredients suggested Molotov torte), which she had baked the night before. Our group rallied and the operation went smoothly thereafter. Renate's culinary contributions to the life of the Institute, either of Swiss origin or with a significant ethanol content were always welcome; her passion for Jerome K. Jerome's *Three Men in a Boat* less so.

'Can I take the students to gather buckthorn berries?' was my introduction to Renate's deep interest and passion for early pigment recipes and recipes for painting media – oil and egg emulsions and egg white varnishes among them. Renate would prepare recipes that involved boiling linseed oil and adding resin – one of my small victories was having this moved to the stone forecourt of the Institute where potential explosions and conflagrations would do little damage. But from this passion came one of the Institute's great strengths – students imbued with the knowledge of painting techniques and the ability to make valuable reconstructions of paintings which opened their eyes to the changes that take place due to 'inherent vice' and past treatments. Renate's deep knowledge and expertise led to requests for her to teach courses elsewhere and the influence she has had on this most practical aspect of 'technical' art history is demonstrated in her own publications and, movingly, in this publication.

Ian McClure
Susan Morse Hilles Chief Conservator, Yale University Art Gallery
Former Director, Hamilton Kerr Institute

A LETTER

Falls jemand etwa heute meint, diese Zeilen seien aus Anlass der Pensionierung von Renate geschrieben, der irrt. Renate und Pensionierung, das wird es nie geben. Viel zu lebendig ist der künstlerische Geist, der seine lebendige Entfaltung sucht. Viel zu hoch die Begabung, als dass sie sich mit einer Pensionierung ersticken ließe. Allenfalls könnten sich nicht geschriebene Restaurierungsberichte melden und sagen „Und wir?"

Damit sind wir aber beim Thema: In Deinem Buch über Monets Spätwerk hast Du den längsten Restaurierungsbericht Deines Lebens geschrieben, der aller Welt kund getan, dass Du auch in diesem Metier Meister bist. Wer das Glück hatte, Dir still über die Schulter bei der Arbeit zuschauen zu dürfen, der hat es nicht nur gesehen, sondern vielmehr intensiv gespürt, wie Du INEINS mit dem Kunstwerk wurdest. Allein das war beglückend! Ich denke jetzt an die Felsen von Dieppe, wo es bis zum letzten Quadratzentimeter offen blieb, ob nicht Ungemach droht.

Aber auch für die Niedrigkeiten hattest Du ein Herz wenn es galt, Vogelköpfe im Kunstwerk zu versetzen, wo sie sich in der freien Natur besser bewegen konnten und erst noch die Wandmalerei wesentlich verschönerten. Für diesen Opfergang danke ich Dir heute nochmals von Herzen.

Schon damals zeichnete sich im Frühwerk die hohe Begabung ab, die nicht nur im vollendeten Beherrschen der handwerklichen Kunst besteht, sondern im Hineinfühlen und im Erspüren des Künstlers. Stundenlanges Sitzen vor dem Kunstwerk, ohne einen Handstrich zu tun, Unwissende mögen dies als Ausschlafen gedeutet haben. Aber sie irren, denn allein schon der laufende Genuss von Schokolade und Kaffee hätte dies gar nicht möglich gemacht.

Sehr innigen und lieben Dank Dir, liebe Renate, auch für die große Geduld, mit der Du Dank Deiner Hochschulausbildung Unwissende durch den Louvre und andere Stätten hoher Kunst führtest. Selbst „Schinken" konntest Du etwas abgewinnen. Zu Recht wurde Dir mit summa cum laude darum auch der Doktortitel verliehen, den wir auf antikem Geschirr von Augustus Rex gebührend im Kreise Dir nahestehenden Menschen feierten.

Wir danken Dir von ganzem Herzen und wünschen Dir alles nur erdenklich Gute

Karin und Manfred Schoeller

If anyone were to think that these lines are being written to mark the occasion of Renate's retirement, they would be mistaken. Renate and retirement – that will never happen. Her artistic spirit is far too alive and continues to seek expansion. Her talent is so great, that it would be suffocated by retirement. At most, unwritten treatment reports might emerge and ask: '... and what about us?'

With that we come to the actual theme. In our book about Monet's late work you have written the longest treatment report of your life, showing all the world your mastery in yet another *metier*. Anyone who was lucky enough to have been able to look over your shoulder quietly while you worked, would not only have seen, but would have felt deeply, how you become one with the work of art. This alone was exhilarating! We think back to the *Felsen von Dieppe*, where the restoration remained critical to the last minute.

You also cared about the smallest detail, for example when reconstructing birds' heads in a painting so that they could move more freely (as in nature), enhancing the wall painting significantly. For this sacrifice I thank you again today with all my heart.

As far back as then, your early work began to reveal your talent. This consisted not only of the perfect mastery of craft skills, but also in the understanding of, and compassion for the artist. You could be lost in hours-long contemplation in front of the artwork without doing a stroke of work; those who didn't know you might have mistaken this as dozing. However, they would be wrong, not least because the constant enjoyment of chocolates and coffee would have made this impossible.

Warm and heartfelt thanks to you, dear Renate, also for your abundance of patience, with which (thanks to your university education), you have led the uninformed through the Louvre and other museums of high art. Even great daubs could give you pleasure. You were also deservedly awarded your doctoral degree with *summa cum laude*, which we fittingly celebrated on antique Augustus Rex porcelain within a circle of close friends.

We thank you with all our hearts and wish you all the very best.

Karin and Manfred Schoeller
Translated by Esther Rapoport
and Genevieve Madgwick

ACKNOWLEDGEMENTS

The editors express their warmest thanks to the following individuals who have so kindly helped with this book: Rupert Featherstone, Genevieve Madgwick, Esther Rapoport and Paul Woudhuysen. Thanks are also due to the many institutions and individuals who gave permission for the use of their images within this volume, without charge.

Unless otherwise stated, images are courtesy of the Hamilton Kerr Institute, Fitzwilliam Museum, University of Cambridge. Sincere thanks to Chris Hurst, Chris Titmus and Nelly von Aderkas for taking many of the photographs.

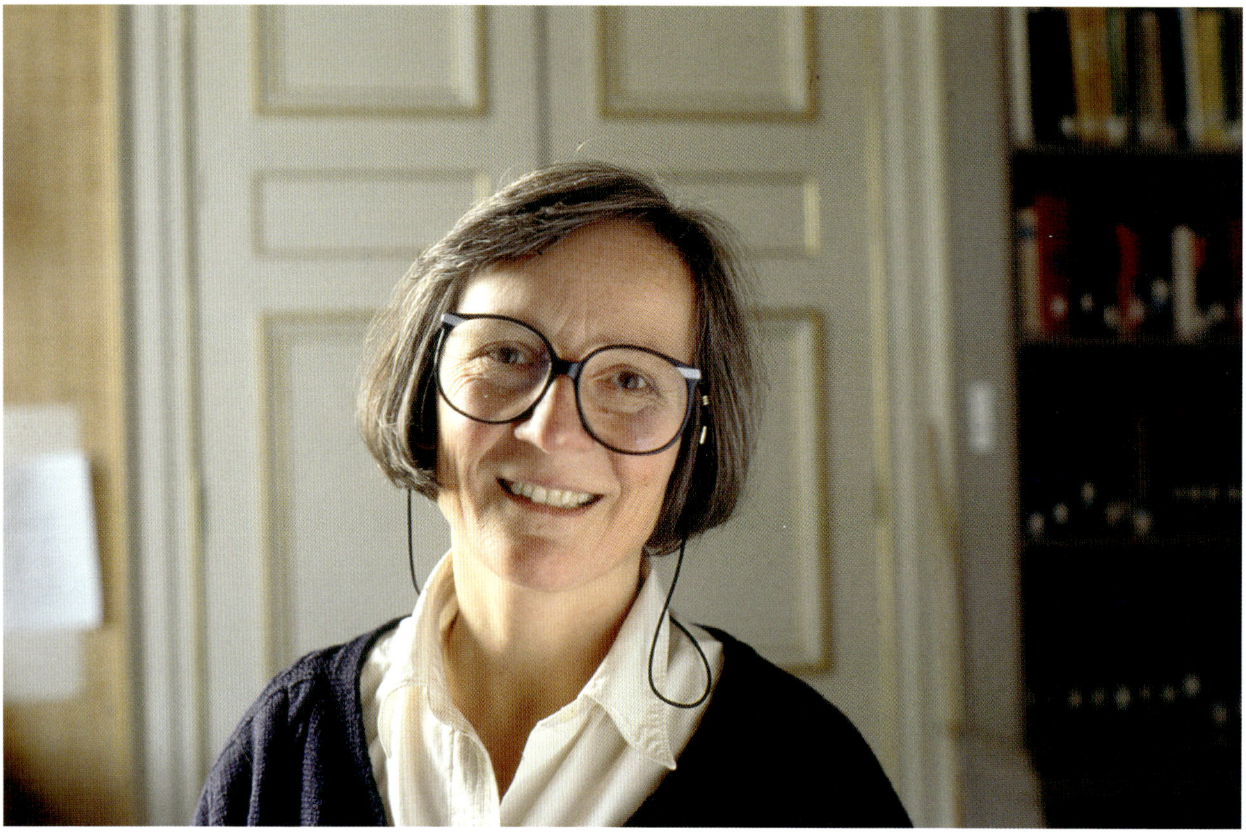

PUBLICATIONS BY RENATE WOUDHUYSEN-KELLER

Keller, R. 1971. 'Der Schnitzaltar des Jean de Furno aus der Eglise des Cordeliers in Fribourg', *Schweizerische Maler- und Gipsermeister Zeitung* 78(x): 211–17.

Keller, R. 1971. 'Graphische Vorlagen zu den Reliefs des Furno-Altars', *Unsere Kunstdenkmäler* 22(3): 132–5.

Keller, R. 1973. 'Leinöl als Malmittel; Rekonstruktionsversuche nach Rezepten aus dem 13. bis 19. Jahrhundert', *Maltechnik-Restauro* 2: 74–106.

Keller, R. 1973. 'Das Entstehen eines Fresko in der italienischen Renaissance', *Applica* 80(15 June): 15–21.

Keller, R. 1974. ' Kleine Baustilkunde anhand von Beispielen in der Schweiz', Parts 1–3. *Applica* 81(15 February): 14–23; 81(7 June): 22–32; 81(19 July): 5–16.

Keller, R. 1975. '... Und lass die Wände los; ein offener Brief an Meret Oppenheim', *Kunstverein Winterthur Jahresbericht* 55: 35–43.

Keller, R., Breidenbach, C., Gros D. and Teoh, G. 1982. '"Der Stadt Zürich Conterfey"; Maltechnische Untersuchung und Restaurierung', *Zeitschrift für Schweizerische Archäologie und Kunstgeschichte* 39(3): 163–80.

Woudhuysen-Keller, R., McClure, I. and Thirkettle, S. 1988. 'The restoration and treatment of *Henry Prince of Wales on Horseback* by Robert Peake', *The Hamilton Kerr Institute Bulletin* 1: 15–22.

Woudhuysen-Keller, R. and McClure, I. 1990. 'The restoration of *The Battle of the Spurs*'. In *Henry VIII: Images of a Tudor King*, C. Lloyd and S. Thurley (eds) 124–6. Oxford: Phaidon.

Woudhuysen-Keller, R. and Woudhuysen, P. 1990. 'Zwei Versionen aus Claude Monet's Serie *L'Allée de Rosiers*'. In *Die Kunst und ihre Erhaltung, Rolf E. Straub zum 70. Geburtstag gewidmet*, K.-W. Bachmann, W. Koch and U. Schiessl (eds) 193–211. Worms: Wernersche Verlagsgesellschaft.

Woudhuysen-Keller, R., Woudhuysen, P., Cuttle, J. and Hurst, C. 1993. 'Zwei Gemälde von Camille Corot: Gedanken zur Maltechnik und zur Restaurierung', *Restauro* 99(5): 306–15.

Woudhuysen-Keller, R. and Woudhuysen, P. 1994. 'The history of egg white varnishes', *The Hamilton Kerr Institute Bulletin* 2: 90–141.

McClure, I. and Woudhuysen-Keller, R. 1994. 'The Oxburgh Chapel Altarpiece: examination and conservation', *Apollo* 139(387): 20–23.

Woudhuysen-Keller, R. 1995. 'Aspects of painting technique in the use of verdigris and copper resinate'. In *Historical Painting Techniques, Materials, and Studio Practice*, A. Wallert, E. Hermens and M. Peek (eds) 65–9. Marina del Rey, CA: Getty Conservation Institute.

Woudhuysen-Keller, R. and Woudhuysen, P. 1998. 'Thoughts on the use of the green glaze called "copper resinate" and its colour-changes'. In *Looking through Paintings: The Study of Painting Techniques and Materials in Support of Art Historical Research*, E. Hermens (ed.) 133–46. Leiden: deProm and London: Archetype Publications.

Woudhuysen-Keller, R. 1999. 'Observations concerning Corot's late painting technique'. In *Barbizon: Malerei der Natur – Natur der Malerei*, A. Burmester, M.F. Zimmermann and C.H. Heilmann (eds) 192–200. Munich: Klinkhardt & Biermann.

Woudhuysen-Keller, R. and Woudhuysen, P. 1999. 'A short history of egg white varnishes'. In *Firnis, Material – Ästhetik – Geschichte, Braunschweig Internationales Kolloquium 15–17 Juni 1998*, 80–86. Braunschweig: Herzog-Anton-Ulrich-Museum.

Woudhuysen-Keller, R. 2001. *Das Farbbuechlin Codex 431 aus dem Kloster Engelberg. Ein Rezeptbuch über Farben zum Färben, Screiben und Malen aus dem späten 16. Jahrhundert*. PhD dissertation, University of Zürich.

Woudhuysen-Keller, R. and Woudhuysen, P. 2001. 'Das Kunstbüchlein "Artliche kunste" aus dem Jahre 1531: eine Abschrift des deutschen Originals mit Erläuterungen'. In *Unser Kopf ist rund, damit das Denken die Richtung wechseln kann: Festschrift für Franz Zelger*, M. Wohlgemut and M. Fehlmann (eds) 529–53. Zürich: Verlag Neue Zürcher Zeitung.

Woudhuysen-Keller, R., Schoeller-von Haslingen, K., Schoeller, M. and Woudhuysen, P. 2001. *Die Rosenallee: der Weg zum Spätwerk Monets in Giverny*. Aachen: Mainz Verlag.

Woudhuysen-Keller, R. and Woudhuysen, P. 2001. 'La serie *Il sentiero dei roseti* di Claude Monet'. In *Monet: I luoghi della pittura*, M. Goldin (ed.) 299–314. Conegliano: Linea d'Ombra.

Woudhuysen-Keller, R. 2001. 'Review of *Paint and Purpose: A Study of Techniques in British Art*, S. Hackney *et al.* (eds), *Restauro* 4: 265–6.

Woudhuysen-Keller, R. 2001. 'Review of *Lexikon historischer Maltechniken: Quellen – Handwerk – Technologie – Alchemie*. Brachert, T', *Restauro* 4: 296–8.

Woudhuysen-Keller, R. and Woodhouse, H. 2003. 'Conservation and observations about the painting technique of *The Battle of Pavia* and its counterpart in the Royal Armouries'. In *The Battle of Pavia*, T. Wilson (ed.) 19–24. Oxford: Ashmolean Museum.

Woudhuysen-Keller, R. and Woudhuysen, P. 2003. 'Claude Monet's series *L'Allée de Rosiers*: history, materials, painting technique, removal of over-paint'. In *Monet: atti del convegno*, R. Rapetti, M.-A. Stevens, M. Zimmerman and M. Goldin (eds) 145–56. Conegliano: Linea d'Ombra.

Woudhuysen-Keller, R. and Woudhuysen, P. 2004. 'Review of *Kunsterhaltung – Machtkonflikte: Gemälde-Restaurierung zur Zeit der Weimarer Republik*. von der Golz, M. Graf', *Studies in Conservation* 49(4): 284–6.

Woudhuysen-Keller, R. 2008. 'Reconstruction of tempera painting techniques: some examples, including *gesso sottile*'. In *Art Technology: Sources and Methods*, S. Kroustallis, J.H. Townsend, E. Cenalmor Bruquetas, A. Stijnman and A. San Andres Moya (eds) 166–73. London: Archetype Publications.

FORTHCOMING PUBLICATIONS

Bucklow, S. and Woudhuysen, R. 'Processes and pigment recipes: azurite', *The Hamilton Kerr Institute Bulletin* 4.

Woudhuysen-Keller, R. 'The Engleberg monastery's Farbbuechlin manuscript, a 16th–17th century recipe book for pigments, colourants and dyestuffs', *Dyes in History and Archaeology* 23.

Woudhuysen-Keller, R. *Das Farbbuechlin Codex 431 aus dem Kloster Engelberg. Ein Rezeptbuch über Farben zum Färben, Schreiben und Malen aus dem späten 16. Jahrhundert*. Riggisberg: Abegg-Stiftung.

Compiled by Lucy Wrapson and Paul Woudhuysen

RENATE WOUDHUYSEN-KELLER: ZÜRICH TO CAMBRIDGE

Ann Massing[1]

Renate and I first met in 1978. We were both waiting to be interviewed for the position of assistant to the director of the newly created Hamilton Kerr Institute (HKI). In 1970, the Old Mill House in Whittlesford and the surrounding outbuildings had been generously donated by the former member of parliament for Cambridge, Sir Hamilton Kerr, to the Fitzwilliam Museum, University of Cambridge (McClure 1988). Herbert Lank was appointed director in 1976, and he had overseen the conversion of the buildings and taken on the first students (Lank 1983). By 1978, the HKI was looking for a new member of staff. Renate and I introduced ourselves and chatted nervously with each other for a few minutes, and quickly found we had much in common.

We had both studied, at different times, in Germany with Professor Rolf E. Straub at the Institut für Technologie der Malerei in Stuttgart. He had sent us both for short internships to the Fortessa da Basso in Florence. I went in the early 1970s, set up a tent at the Piazza Michelangelo camping site and had an instructive if isolated experience due to my insufficient Italian. Renate prepared herself much better and went to language school first in Perugia, then arrived in Florence at the Fortessa just after the flood of 1966. She stayed with a former German-speaking professor for two months in a spacious villa with a large garden, and she had a wonderful time meeting other restorers from all around the world. We both also went to the National Maritime Museum in Greenwich – Renate in 1968, for a three-month internship to work with Westby Percival-Prescott, and I, several years later. In 1969 Renate did another three-month internship at the Central Laboratorium, predecessor of the ICN (Netherlands Institute for Cultural Heritage), now the Netherlands Cultural Heritage Agency, in Amsterdam.

Renate Keller had begun her career in painting conservation in 1963 under Professor Wolfgang Hahn at the Wallraf-Richartz Museum in Cologne where she had trained for two years as an apprentice. She then continued her training under Dr Thomas Brachert, chief restorer at the Swiss Institute for Art Research in Zürich for another year. Then, having completed the prerequisite three years of practical training, she joined Professor Rolf E. Straub's course for restorers at the Institute for Painting Technology in Stuttgart, but stayed only for one year, 1966–67.[2] She found the theory interesting, but longed to get back behind the easel. Therefore she returned to Dr Brachert in Zürich. His encouragement to combine art history with practical restoration studies suited her well. Employed as a junior restorer, she set up a laboratory and began experimenting with artificial glues and then with historic binding media – she heated oils and added lead oxides to improve the drying time according to recipes dating from the thirteenth to the nineteenth century. She was guided by the chemical technical lexicon that had belonged to her father, an industrial chemist. He had given it to her as her other siblings were not interested: her twin sister and middle brother were to become professional musicians and her elder brother a physicist. The results of her experiments led to her *Lizentiatsarbeit* (the equivalent of an MA thesis) from the University of Zürich on *Medieval Painting Techniques and Materials: Reconstructing Painting Oils and Pigments According to Recipes Dating from the 13th to the 19th Centuries*; the results were published in *Maltechnik-Restauro* (Keller 1973).

Dr Brachert was pleased to employ her as an assistant in the university's Institute of Art History and she was made responsible for the photographic collection. The plan was to earn money for her graduate studies in order to complete a PhD at the University of Zürich, but the practical work at the Swiss Institute for Art Research proved more exciting. Dr Brachert continued to employ her to teach an introductory course on the technology of painting and she also did freelance restoration work for the Swiss government from 1973 to 1977.

Renate remained in contact with Professor Straub, and it was he who suggested that she should apply for the job

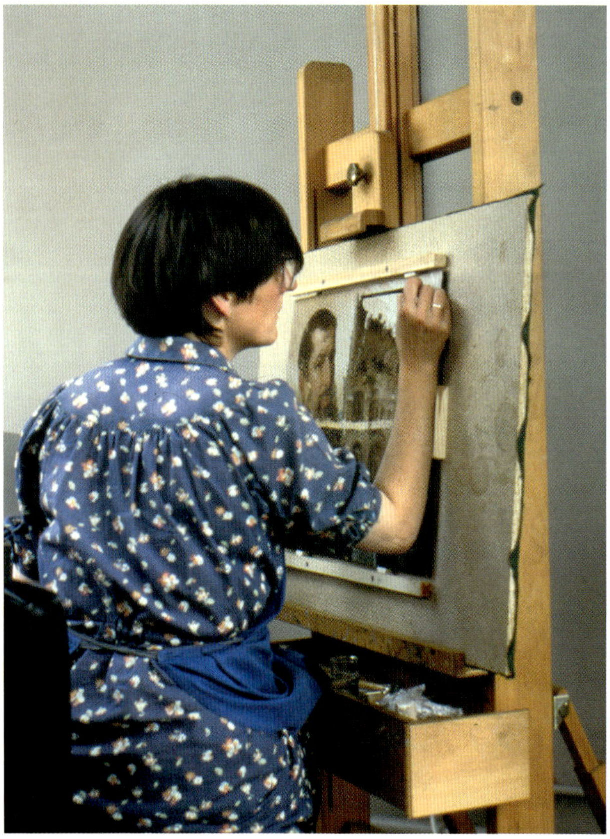

Figure 1 *Renate restoring Maerten van Heemskerck's* Portrait of the Painter with the Colosseum Behind, *The Fitzwilliam Museum, Cambridge.*

at the newly created Hamilton Kerr Institute. Although only one job was advertised, we were both employed. In September 1978, Renate and I joined Herbert Lank and Norman Brommelle at the HKI in Whittlesford, 7¼ miles from the Fitzwilliam Museum in Cambridge. I was to be the new assistant to the director and Renate the research historian. In 1979, Herbert Lank decided to return to private practice in London, staying on part-time until 1982 to facilitate a smooth transition. After leaving the Victoria and Albert Museum, Norman Brommelle became part-time director until 1983. Alec Cobbe was the first assistant to the director and Pamela England the research chemist – she had been trained by Joyce Plesters at the National Gallery.

Thirty prospective students from the sciences and the humanities, mainly aged between 20 and 28, were interviewed for the first intake and three chosen for the three-year certificate course in the conservation of easel paintings that began in 1977. The completion of another year of internship was to lead to the award of a diploma. The students present in 1978 when Renate and I arrived included Keith Laing and Amelia Jackson, Simon Folkes and Mary Allden (now Kempski). Renate's initial role involved working in the library and her office was Sir Hamilton Kerr's guest bedroom (today it holds the Roberson Archive). In those days it still boasted hand-painted murals on the walls of the en-suite bathroom and golden swan's head taps on the bath tub. But she was rarely there; she could not stay out of the studio.

One of Renate's first projects was to prepare a painting by Canaletto to be exhibited in the Queen's Gallery in 1981. At the time four or five paintings by Canaletto were on easels in the Institute's downstairs studio – an impressive site against the backdrop of the River Cam. Another early project was the restoration of the Fitzwilliam Museum's *William Laud, Archbishop of Canterbury* painted by Sir Anthony Van Dyck. Renate then joined Alec Cobbe and me in the studio restoring and supervising the students. Alec left the Institute in 1981 and Renate, homesick for Switzerland, also left to take up a job as head of the Department of Restoration of Paintings and Sculptures at the Swiss National Museum in Zürich.

After one year Renate realised that she had made a mistake. As soon as she could, she gave up her job in her beloved Switzerland, came back to Cambridge and married Paul, librarian at the Fitzwilliam Museum whom she had met through her work for the HKI library. Several years later she was to restore Maerten van Heemskerck's *Portrait of the Painter with the Colosseum Behind*. It was to be one of her favourite restoration jobs. We were all convinced that Renate enjoyed it so much because the painter looked like Paul (Fig. 1).

Following her return to Cambridge, she worked from home as a freelance restorer for a short time. Meanwhile Ian McClure, who had come from the Fine Art Department of Glasgow Art Gallery and Museums to replace Alec Cobbe as assistant to the director in 1981, became the new director in 1983. Ian's former position now needed to be filled, and Renate was asked if she would come back. Finding herself in the studios full-time, Renate put her all into doing the best job she could. Long evenings and weekends were frequent. She was always eager to help.

One of Ian's first big jobs was the cleaning and restoration of a large painting by George Stubbs, *The Hambletonian* from Mount Stewart House (National Trust). Ian worked with a team of students including Rupert Featherstone (today director of the HKI), Karen Ashworth (now conservator at the Royal Collection), Ella Hendricks (now head of conservation, Van Gogh Museum in Amsterdam), and Larry Keith (now director of conservation at the National Gallery, London). One Monday morning we all came in to find Ian and Renate standing in front of the large painting – retouching palettes in hand. Ian had telephoned Renate to ask if she would help out over the weekend. She had accepted Ian's request without hesitation; for Renate there was no better way to spend her weekend.

Other collaborations were equally successful. Four wings of a Flemish Gothic altarpiece from Oxburgh Hall (National Trust) were flaking and needed conservation. In order to do the consolidation, overpaint on the exterior of two of the four wings needed to be removed. The overpaint turned out to be insoluble and had to be removed mechanically, taking 473 hours over a two-year period. Ian and Renate published an article on its restoration (McClure and Woudhuysen-Keller 1994).

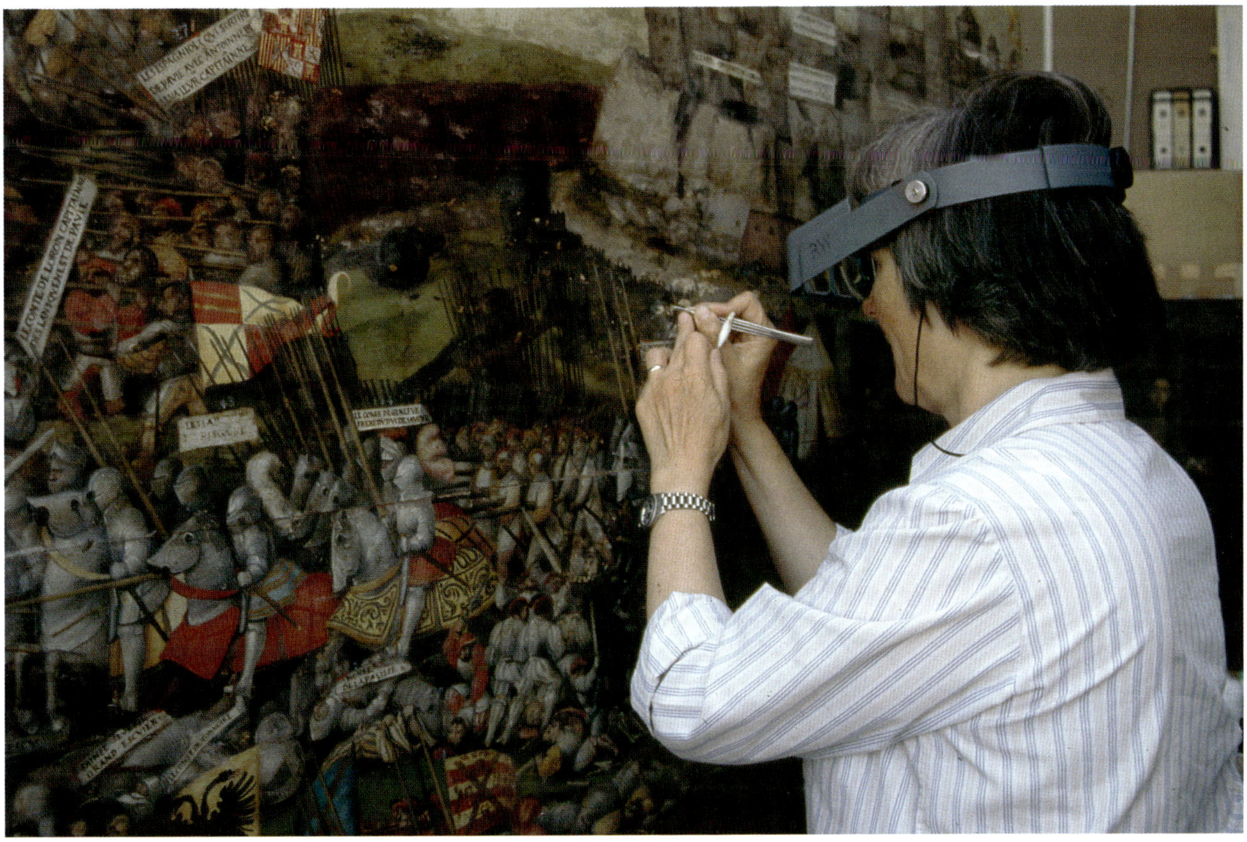

Figure 2 *Renate behind the easel: the restoration of* The Battle of the Spurs, *Royal Collection.*

Renate also jointly published an article on an early seventeenth-century English painting from Parham Park, the restoration of which revealed an entirely different image underneath the landscape (Woudhuysen-Keller *et al.* 1988). Her contribution to the restoration was significant. Just as Ian was beginning to despair, Renate cracked the cleaning method for removing the old hard repaint from the (more soluble) landscape – undoubtedly applied only about 50 years after the painting was completed – with a system of applying solvent and then preventing evaporation by covering the area with Melinex (in a way the precursor of the gel system). Also, it was decided that the non-original top strip of the painting, which must have replaced a missing section of the original, should be reconstructed. After a careful examination of the fragments that were left, Renate made an entirely convincing reconstruction of the dense foliage.

Her next major project was to take over 10 years. It was a painting that represented *The Battle of the Spurs*, recording the incidents from Henry VIII's first invasion of France in 1513. It arrived in the studio in May 1986. The lining had been damaged by heat and water during the fire at Hampton Court earlier in the year and, in order to reline the painting, it was first necessary to clean it. The resinous green glazes were easily soluble and were covered with many layers of putty made of oil paint (probably from palette scrapings). Removing the overpaint from at least three restorations during the last 300 years was more difficult than anticipated due to the sensitivity of the original paint, while the oil-based putty was exceptionally resistant.

Renate and her assistant, Julia Nagle, eventually found that a goldsmith's polishing tool, also used as a glass-engraving tool, could be used safely to remove the old restorations mechanically. But when the tool arrived, it vibrated and made a whining noise like a dentist's drill, driving everyone mad; Renate and Julia were banished from the main studio. Julia told me that she remembers this time with Renate as an amazing learning experience, an invaluable time that she now looks back on with gratitude – for Renate's kindness and patience, for her trusting and encouraging attitude towards teaching and for just letting her 'get on with it'. Julia remembers the view of the River Cam from the varnishing room to which they had retreated, and neither of them recollects a cross word being spoken during all those years of very delicate work in close quarters. We could always hear that they were hard at it – the drone of the grinding needle was audible even behind closed doors. When we dared visit, we found them both dressed in lab coats, gloves and face-masks, wearing optivisors with homemade Melinex visors attached to the headbands as protection from the dust of the lead white fillings. This was before the days of rigorous health and safety inspections – but they would have passed with flying colours!

Renate and Julia removed the overpaint a square millimetre at a time – sometimes little shrieks of excitement were heard as another figure or a tree was uncovered from

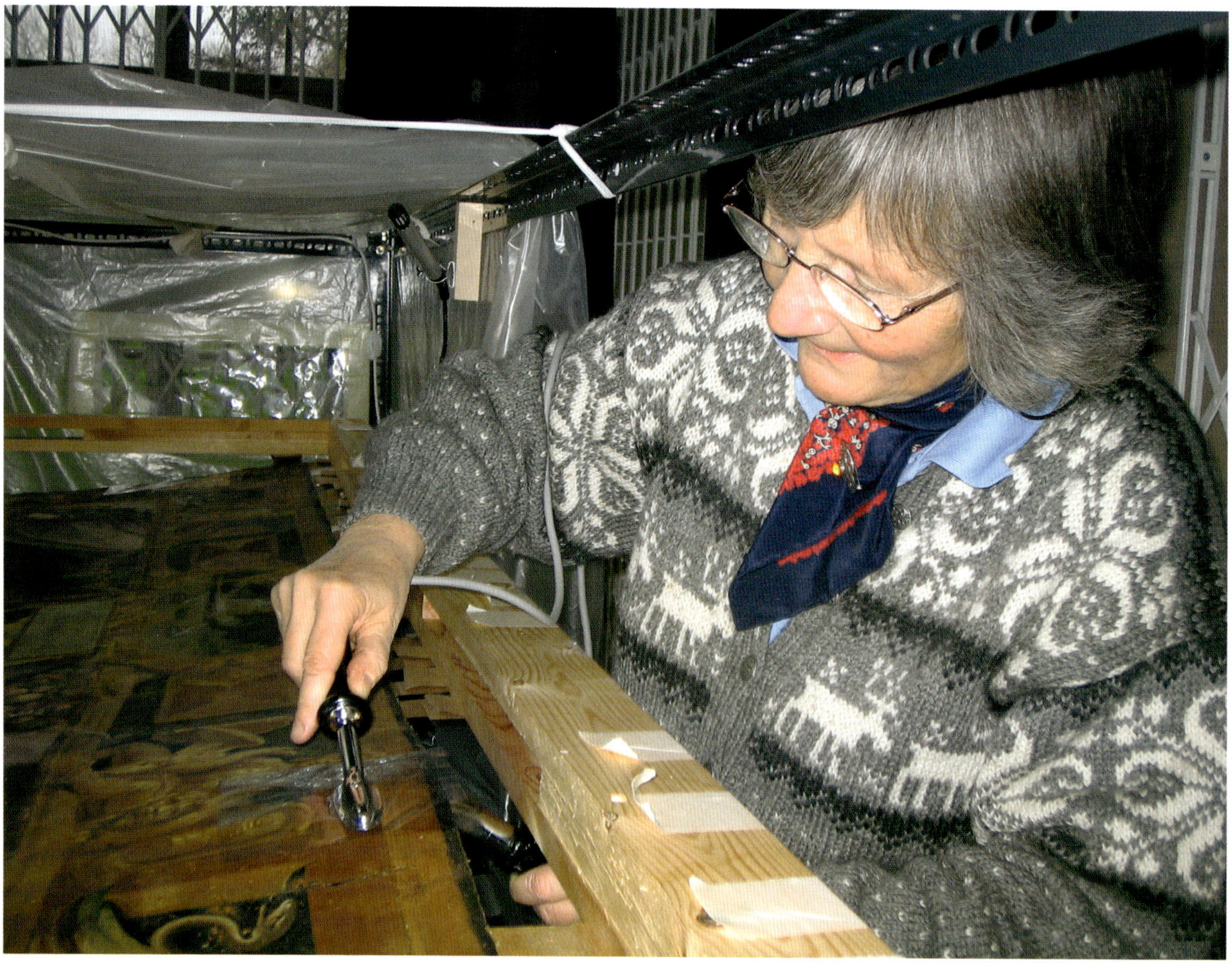

Figure 3 *Renate secures the flaking paint on Frederico Zuccaro's* The Calumny of Apelles, *Royal Collection, with satisfaction.*

underneath an old filling. The infrared reflectograph was particularly revealing and aroused general excitement as the armoured soldiers sitting on their horses were discovered to have bare bottoms in the underdrawing! But best of all, they found that the condition of the original paint, once freed of overpaint and putty, was pristine: for centuries it had been protected from both light and past restorers' solvents. The greens and blues of the town in the background were as bright as in a miniature. Time-consuming and delicate structural work was then carried out. Analysis of the painting was undertaken by Narayan Khandekar, the HKI chemist (from 1991 to 1993) who had replaced Alan Phenix (from 1989 to 1991) and Karin Groen (from 1981 to 1989). Renate was very curious about the results and tried to speed up the process by trying to trap Narayan with one of her famous bets: 'I'll give you a bar of chocolate if . . .'. The retouching was a pleasure and Renate and Julia were assisted by others including Marie Louise Sauerberg (appointed 1998, then assistant to the director, 2008 to 2012). The restoration of *The Battle of the Spurs* was completed with success and it left the HKI in July 1999 (Fig. 2).

Renate was rewarded with another battle scene, *The Battle of Pavia*, from the Ashmolean Museum, Oxford. Painted in the Burgundian Netherlands *c.*1525–28, it represents the celebrated battle of 24 February 1525 between the dominant European powers, the moment described by many as marking the end of the Middle Ages. The French were defeated and King Francis I captured. There were many accounts of the battle with countless contradictions and, further to this, the Ashmolean picture presents events that took place at different times simultaneously, with the artist contriving to depict as many details as possible. In addition to the French and English troops, there were Italian, Spanish and German mercenaries, and the Swiss infantry was also involved – and all loved pomp and chivalry. The battle scene was extremely confused, but again Renate gleefully uncovered soldiers buried under overpaint. This time the restoration took only three years.

Following on came yet another large painting, Frederico Zuccaro, *The Calumny of Apelles* from the Royal Collection in Hampton Court – and this one Renate considered to be a special treat! The picture refers to a painting by the Greek artist Apelles who worked at the court of Alexander the Great in the fourth century BC – a work described by the Greek philosopher, Lucian, in the second century AD. The painting is loaded with references to the writings of antiquity, as well as to Zuccaro's own life and the calumnies from which he was suffering. Zuccaro signed the

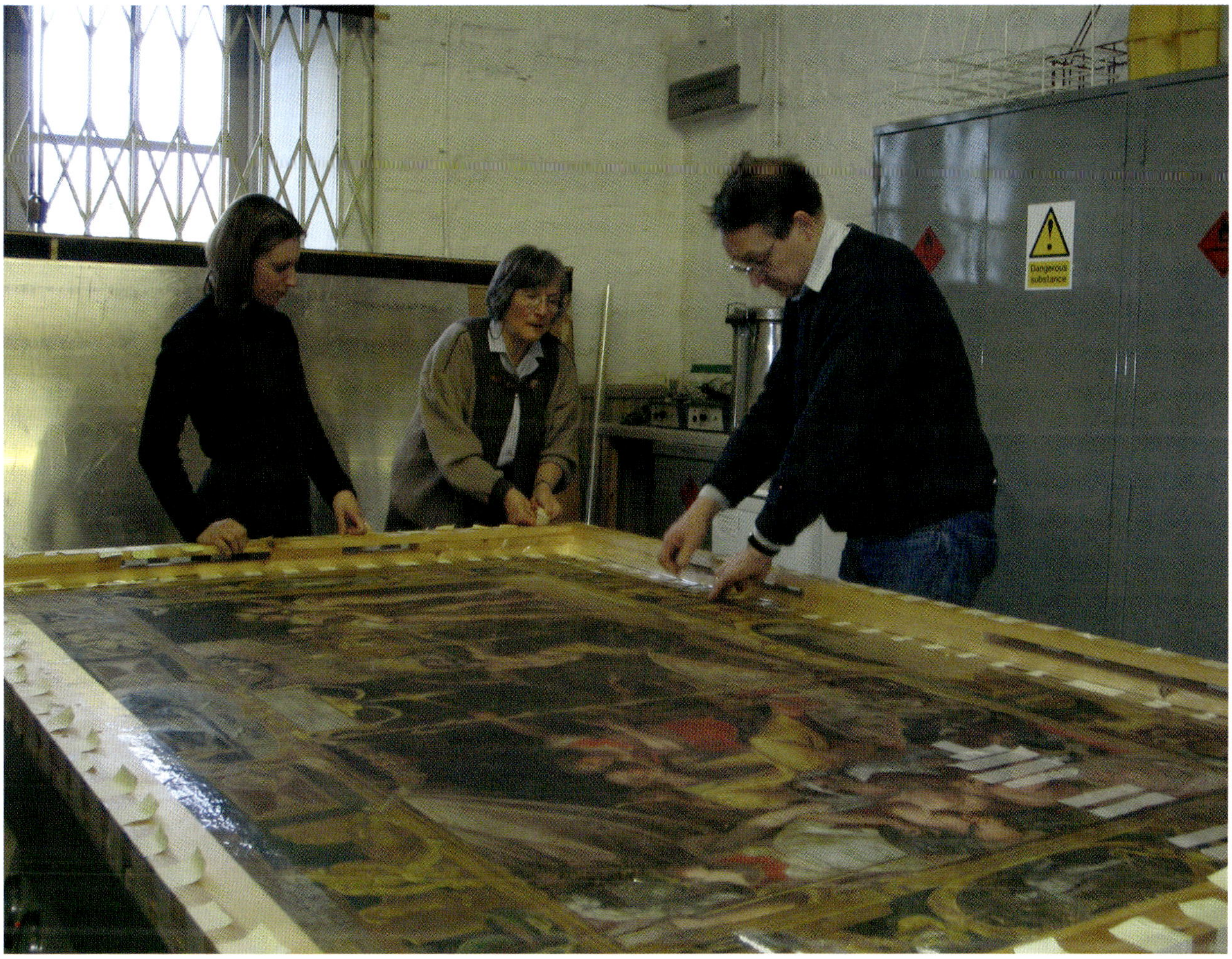

Figure 4 *Renate, with Ian McClure and Tabitha Teuma, reflecting on the lining process*

painting with his rebus, a sugar loaf. The old lining canvas had shrunk, causing the paint to detach and the raised flakes to overlap. Renate, assisted by a student, Tabitha Teuma, removed many layers of overpaint and embarked on the structural work. She devised what was then an ingenious solution for the overlapping paint flakes: a humidity tent was constructed so that the shrunken canvas could again expand, and during this prolonged exposure to higher humidity the paint layer could be gradually relaxed back down; while the painting was still in the humidity chamber she lifted a flap and applied heat gently with a spatula onto a supportive yet non-rigid surface. Somehow, she thought of contacting the local veterinarian and so procured a cushion used to operate on small animals; it worked perfectly as a firm yet flexible support for the canvas. The painting was then put onto the low pressure table to correct any further unevenness in the paint layer in preparation for the attachment of a new lining canvas (Figs 3 and 4).

Big paintings seem to have become one of her *fortes*; the teamwork that was possible at the HKI drew them to its studios. Of course, Renate also restored smaller paintings, including several belonging to a private owner, who became a friend as well as employer. One by one he sent her four Corots and as many paintings by Monet (Woudhuysen-Keller *et al.* 1993; see also Stoner *et al.*, in this vol.). Two late paintings by Monet were a special challenge as the exposed priming of the edges had been overpainted, probably for a dealer in the 1950s who thought they looked unfinished. When the owner felt he could not live with the overpaint anymore, he asked Renate to remove it. Renate peered at each brushstroke of paint almost with reverence and came to know every detail intimately, determining which bits were original and which were the later highlights that were to be removed. Indeed, when she had finished, one could see the movement of the artist's brushstrokes once again and the painting gained a coherence that had not been apparent before; these late paintings by Monet developed from the centre and grew out towards the edges of the canvas – which were now white again. Renate joyfully proclaimed that with the overpaint removed, the painting started to sing.

After a time Renate and I became good friends and I came to admire her qualities as a painting restorer and as a person. She was drawn to those in need of a motherly touch and extra support and became an *in loco parentis* for many of the students and interns. There seemed to be nothing that could not be fixed – if only there were a few more chocolate mints or an extra generous boost of caffeine. But Renate was also impatient with those who did not abide by her standards, and anything that was 'Mickey Mouse' or 'woolly thinking' was not tolerated. Kind and patient with the students, perfectionist and persevering with the paintings, she was – by her own confession – hopeless at administration.

Renate's long awaited PhD materialised in 2001 and she received her doctorate from the University of Zürich (Woudhuysen-Keller 2001). Her professor of medieval art history at Zürich University had been a pupil of a boarding school in the Benedictine monastery of Engelbert in Switzerland. In the library of the school he had discovered a handwritten booklet written in the sixteenth century in old-fashioned Swiss-German that contained recipes on how to make paints and on colours for dyeing textiles. He thought, 'this is something for Renate.' And so it was. The end result, after more than 10 years of research, was her PhD, and it will soon become a splendid publication by the Abbeg Stiftung of Riggiberg. As she researched, Renate tried out the recipes, delighting in the unexpected: such as the sap green that looks purple until it is painted out on paper and turns green in front of your eyes. Many of the students and interns at the HKI remember being enticed to go for a walk along the footpath towards Sawston and traipsing through hedgerows to collect ripe and unripe buckthorn berries.

Renate has always been very loyal to the HKI. Having finally abandoned her desire to go back to Switzerland, she became convinced that the Institute was indeed the best place in the world to be employed. She was uncomprehending when Ian McClure resigned as director and left the Institute to become the Susan Morse Hilles Chief Conservator at Yale University Art Gallery in New Haven, Connecticut. Only the prospect of having Rupert Featherstone as his replacement consoled her. Then, despite illness and having gone beyond retirement age, she remained involved in the work of the Institute and her enthusiasm for being behind the easel was undiminished.

Notes

1. Written by Ann Massing with thanks to those who have shared their memories.
2. Renate published an article in Professor Rolf E. Straub's Festschrift (Woudhuysen-Keller 1990).

References

Keller, R. 1973. 'Leinöl als Malmittel; Rekonstruktionsversuche nach Rezepten aus dem 13. bis 19. Jahrhundert', *Maltechnik-Restauro* 2: 74–106.

Lank, H. 1983. 'The Hamilton Kerr Institute; converted premises for the training of painting conservators', *International Journal of Museum Management and Curatorship* 2: 71–8.

McClure, I. (ed.) 1988. 'The training programme', *The Hamilton Kerr Institute Bulletin,* 1: 9–11.

McClure, I. and Woudhuysen-Keller, R. 1994. 'The Oxburgh Chapel Altarpiece: examination and conservation', *Apollo* 139(387): 20–23.

Woudhuysen-Keller, R. 2001. *Das Farbbuechlin Codex 431 aus dem Kloster Engelberg. Ein Rezeptbuch über Farben zum Färben, Screiben und Malen aus dem späten 16. Jahrhundert.* PhD dissertation, University of Zürich.

Woudhuysen-Keller, R., McClure, I. and Thirkettle, S. 1988. 'The restoration and treatment of *Henry Prince of Wales on Horseback* by Robert Peake', *The Hamilton Kerr Institute Bulletin* 1: 15–22.

Woudhuysen-Keller, R., Woudhuysen, P. Cuttle, J., Hurst, C. 1993. 'Zwei Gemalde von Camille Corot: Gedanken zur Maltechnik und zur Restaurierung', *Restauro* 99(5): 306–15.

‘HANDS ON’: PERSONAL REFLECTIONS ON TEACHING THE PRACTICE OF PAINTINGS CONSERVATION

Anne van Grevenstein-Kruse and Ernst van de Wetering

Anne: A warm autumn day in the garden of the Hamilton Kerr Institute on Monday 10 October 2011. My memory circles around the building: sun reflected on water, a (once very slippery) bridge, apple trees and their harvest, a bench as a reminder of the splitting of wood for panel making. Renate and I just talked about the painting she is finishing, a tough job. The workshop is, as ever, peaceful and the ‘ravaged image’ has our full attention. She touches the painting, feels the surface of the fillings, comments on the colour of the ground and underpainting in relation to the first layers of retouching … her quiet words translate years of experience into sound advice to the student. I am watching the vital link between the hand and the eye, between knowledge and action.

Another memory of a similar moment, but 30 years ago, when Ernst van de Wetering and I brought our colleague and analytical chemist Karin Groen from the Central Laboratory in Amsterdam to the Hamilton Kerr Institute in Cambridge. I saw for the first time the paintings in the workshop and Renate with her students. Interdisciplinarity was existential, a matter of fact. Ernst and Renate had painting and music in common and they shared a solid background in art history. We walked through the galleries of the Fitzwilliam Museum and there Renate, in the persona of the conservator, explains, shows what she has done. Ernst wants to understand the boundaries between the original materials and the virtuosity of her illusionistic integration of the losses in the paintings. Questions about the invasive power of the conservator are tempered by trust and friendship (‘Du kleine Mahlerin du’ …). The quality is convincing because her retouchings are based on the formal analysis of the composition and on her knowledge of the original sequence of the paint layers.

Ernst: The world of conservation, restoration and scientific studies of paintings in Renate’s young years was large and small at the same time. Large in the sense that in many European countries, in the US and Canada, people were active in that field; small because even as a beginner you soon knew all the main characters in this ‘scene’, if only by name. The amount of periodicals, handbooks, conferences and controversies was so limited that you soon knew about the existence and accomplishments of all the protagonists because they were the subject of many conversations, anecdotes and rumours. Many of them we, young beginners, had never met in person, but they had become part of a sort of mythology or, rather, a widely spread Olympus peopled with gods, demigods, heroes and also a few questionable individuals. Sometimes we had met one or two of them during guest lectures, visits to their studio or small conferences. The geographically large world of conservation and investigation of paintings was also small because it was normal that trainees in the field accomplished their compulsory internships in conservation studios and related institutions and research laboratories all over the world.

That is how I met Renate. She was an intern in the Central Research Laboratory for Objects of Art and Science in 1969, the year I myself had become a young staff member in that so-called ‘institute-with-the-long-name’, usually abbreviated to CL.

At that young age one easily makes friends. It was natural to be curious about each other and there seemed to be an endless amount of time to sit together and chat about our future ‘field’ with its fascinating problems and even more fascinating people, whether you had met them or not.

Then something overwhelming happened: in the early autumn of 1969 the complete Olympus assembled in Amsterdam. They had come from all over the world to the first big triennial International Council of Museums-Committee for Conservation (ICOM-CC) conference. Renate, pupil of the legendary Thomas Brachert in Zürich, and I, having spent some time in the conservation studios and research laboratories in London, Berlin and Copenhagen in connection with the Rembrandt Research Project (RRP), knew just enough of that world to be aware how privileged we were to see all these legendary figures now in person. Of course we were too shy to meet them on equal terms; we just looked at them with curiosity and listened to their talks at the conference. My first close contact with one of my heroes was when I met Rutherford J. Gettens (from Gettens and Stout's indispensable and well-phrased *Painting Materials* from 1942, reissued 1966) on the way to the sessions of the second day. He, of course, did not know who I was, but I collected all my courage to draw his attention to the fact that there still was a lot of shaving foam on his cheeks. He thanked me graciously while removing it with his handkerchief. That was a great event on the lower slope of my Olympus. During that conference I saw Renate rushing from session to session, we hardly had time to wave to each other. But I am sure she had her own unforgettable encounters.

The day after that crowded conference there would be a symposium organised by the CL and the RRP, devoted entirely to the possibilities and potentials of scientific research of paintings by Rembrandt (rightly or wrongly attributed to him). Renate was extremely eager to attend that interdisciplinary meeting as well. But that was a much more intimate gathering of big shots like Joyce Plesters and Sir Philip Hendy from the London National Gallery, Herman Kühn from the Doerner Institute, the formidable Madame Hours from the Laboratoire du Louvre, Stephen Rees Jones of the Courtauld Institute, Nathan Stolov from Ottawa, the medical radiologist Dr Meyer Siem from Hamburg (obsessed – in a nice way – by the investigation of micro-symptoms on X-radiographs of paintings), the dendrochronologists Bauch and Eckstein (who Meyer Siem had brought with him from Hamburg), and some 15 other experts. Instead of running from one session to another, always afraid to have chosen the less interesting parallel-session, this symposium promised to be the ideal concentrated gathering of many of our gods and heroes all together in the same room. Renate feverishly dreamt of attending that symposium as it would – she hoped – enrich her knowledge of historic studio practice. But she was too young and still too insignificant to be invited. In my modest role of assistant to the RRP I was involved in the symposium's organisation and together we managed to find a solution to her problem: she was appointed as the 'secretary' to make notes of all that was said and she was expected to produce a detailed report of the symposium afterwards. There she sat, nearly invisible in a corner of the room, behind the whole Olympus of gods, goddesses and heroes following and noting all that was being said. I had not the slightest doubt that she would do a very good job as I had had the chance to enjoy her smartness, her lively curiosity and her guts, in combination with her command of the different languages as they would be spoken at the symposium.

Becoming familiar with the big world around historic paintings and the then still small community of pioneers active in that field was a privilege. It also made (and would later make) it so fascinating, and professionally and socially so enriching for the future students of Renate and of Anne.

But then she became a member of that Olympus herself! I witnessed that during my occasional visits as guest lecturer in the Hamilton Kerr Institute. She had become an authority; but also a pioneer, as I would experience during an unforgettable conference, organised by Ijsbrand Hummelen at the Academy of Fine Arts (Jan van Eyck Academie) in Maastricht. On that occasion those who studied historic painting techniques were brought together with artists who wanted to learn from the great masters from the past. Renate was invited to speak about her experiments with the reconstruction of historic binding media.

While preparing that conference we had succeeded in tracing and inviting one of those other legendary figures in our field, the mysterious J.A. van de Graaf who, in 1958, had defended his dissertation about the de Mayerne manuscript at Utrecht University. We all had that book because there were still piles of them available. But the man himself had vanished. He told us during the conference that he had dropped out of the field soon after 1958 because he had not succeeded in getting the only job he really aspired to – becoming professor in historic painting techniques at the National Academy of Visual Arts (the Rijksacademie) in Amsterdam. After first becoming a scrap merchant in South Africa he studied law and had become a hard-headed lawyer boasting to us how many murderers, of whose guilt he was convinced, he had kept out of prison. There he sat in a formal dark suit looking bitter, behaving as an outsider until he heard Renate. What in his young years he had dreamt of doing, reconstructing the recipes of the de Mayerne manuscript in reality, Renate was now doing. His hard heart started melting. He was happy, and he missed no chance during that day to sit next to Renate talking with her in admiration. He looked like he was in love. I do not think they ever saw each other again, but I have seen many others, young conservators and art historians being grateful for the expertise, love and enthusiasm with which she (in her unique, Renatesque English with a German accent) introduced them into the world of historic studio practice. For them she had descended from Mount Olympus.

Anne: The first Dutch training programme in paintings conservation started in 1990 at the Stichting Restauratie Atelier Limburg (SRAL, opened in 1987), situated in the abbey of Rolduc; two years later it was transferred to Maastricht. Both locations were situated in beautiful buildings, with gardens and the memory of place so helpful and soothing when dealing with cultural heritage. Karin Groen came back to the Netherlands and started her laboratory to teach the 'SRAL 1' students, Ernst van de Wetering taught painting technique and then Renate took over the course. She would keep coming to Maastricht and later to Amsterdam when the training programme was taken over by the university in 2005.

Renate's involvement in the Amsterdam-Maastricht Summer University was fundamental in creating a meeting ground for interdisciplinarity: art historians, museum personnel and conservators working together in the 'painters' workshop'. This was the very fertile ground from which the summer courses in the Ateliergebouw in Amsterdam kept developing with cross-disciplinary students combining their Master studies in art history with advanced training in historic painting techniques.

In all aspects, the SRAL copied the fundamental ingredients for the training of conservators that had been implemented with success in Cambridge. Paintings came from public collections, museums and historic buildings. They were at the centre of interdisciplinary attention and the students participated in the reality of research and treatment. These projects were started and finished, in due time and with proper financial support. Students were selected at postgraduate level and could count on a five-year stipend. Grafting a training programme onto this 'workshop based' culture was made possible by keeping the students in the Institute, from nine to five, five days a week and for three consecutive years. Museum internships in the fourth and fifth years widened their professional and institutional experience. This basic structure was repeated in 2005 within the academic BA/MA structure of the University of Amsterdam, Faculty of Humanities: a year in the Bachelors, a so-called Minor in conservation/restoration, is followed by a two year Masters degree in one of the eight specialisations (paintings, historic interiors, contemporary art, glass and ceramics, metal, textiles and furniture). In the fourth year, the post-initial phase, students are further immersed in the workshop practice, in Maastricht or in the Ateliergebouw in Amsterdam. The fifth and final year is an internship in a museum or conservation institute with a final conservation project that will give admission to the profession of conservator. The format and duration of the study transcends the realm of humanities and is taken from the so-called 'designers' diploma' in exact sciences, where the learning element contained in professional practice is kept within the training programme.

Teaching conservation within the tradition of workshop practice may seem old-fashioned as today, all over the world, universities house training programmes within their own buildings, using auditoria designed for speakers and listeners. When it comes to the integration of conservation theory and practice, this can sometimes – conveniently – be achieved for large groups of students, by working on simulation models or so-called 'test objects'. Results can be predicted by the teacher, mistakes are not important, one does not take risks. Ethical issues can be talked about, but not experienced: conservators need to be trained within a context of moral responsibility.

The traditional conservation workshop in which Renate Woudhuysen-Keller has worked and studied during her long and impressive career, hosts works of art and studies them in their unique historical context. Inherent fragility can be painful and confronting and dealing with these aspects takes time, care and experience. Above all, students need to be coached in the process. The teacher in the practice of conservation predicts effects of interventions, demonstrating how to do things, showing results and handing over the instruments to the student, guiding and correcting in due time, stimulating questions, sharing responsibility and giving comfort when something goes wrong. Without this coaching a young conservator will learn to escape, finding solace in non-intervention. Given the large numbers of young conservators issued by academic training each year, this seems a reasonable and utterly acceptable consequence: the happy few will do the actual work, the others will reflect on theoretical issues. Another scenario is lurking though: the actual conservation work will be done ad hoc by cheap forces in the grey zone that still exists, worldwide, between thinking and doing. It is a familiar enough scenario, because it is easier to organise a training programme in that manner.

Teaching conservation techniques, conservation science and technical art history, needs to be done of course, but it is the fundamental understanding, triggered by historic consciousness, that each artefact is unique and irreplaceable, that should guide the 'hands-on' training of the student. The moral responsibility for each intervention in the material reality of the object starts there. Renate's approach to teaching has been fundamental in instilling these guiding principles in her students.

MAKING RECONSTRUCTIONS AT THE HAMILTON KERR INSTITUTE

Mary Kempski

Introduction

Copies after the great masters have been a well-known teaching aid for countless artists throughout history. It has been the aim of many artists to discover the techniques of admired painters by means of imitation. It was, of course, a challenge to understand what exactly lay beneath, only being able to view the result of accumulated paint layers and varnish on the surface of the painting. Reynolds is said to have stripped paintings down layer by layer to ascertain the 'secret' of the Italian painters.[1] Whether or not this is an apocryphal story, we can understand the desire to work out another artist's technique and achieve the same effects. Artists in the past copied in front of the painting and the results are often a truthful rendition from a viewing distance but when examined more critically do not have the same construction; it is only an impression. Even more removed, in the modern age, is copying from photographs of paintings, where neither the true colour and texture nor subtlety can be truly ascertained by the copyist.

The aim of students at the Hamilton Kerr Institute (HKI) in making copies is rather different. True, there is a need for the practice of manual dexterity and artistic skill but there are also important lessons about the knowledge and understanding of an artist's materials and how they were ordered and handled to produce the desired effects. Copies or, more accurately, reconstructions, are an integral part of the course at the HKI. This is not unusual; many European teaching institutions, concerned with the education of paintings conservators, have a part of their course devoted to copying. These are most often made from photographs covering general techniques rather than using an individual painting and artist. A quick survey of students of painting conservation from other European institutions reveals that they all make copies during their training to experience the use of different paint media and also perhaps gilding techniques. However only two students interviewed made a copy in front of a real painting on the wall of a museum.[2]

'Reconstruction', or 'copy', is very different by definition from 'fake', although occasionally they have been confused. A reconstruction does not try to compel the viewer into believing the work has been made at the time of the artist in question. In other words there are no ageing features and the painting could be described as looking as newly painted as it did when it left the artist's studio. Achieving this is not quite as straightforward as it might seem. The ageing of the original materials has to be undone in the mind of the copyist. This may only be an informed guess. We cannot know exactly what a painting looked like when it was freshly off the easel. However, knowledge of other paintings of the period, the alteration of certain materials, pigments, media and varnish will provide many clues as to the degree to which a particular painting may have changed.

From its initiation, the HKI demonstrated that reconstructions would be at the core of its educational agenda. Herbert Lank, in his wisdom, was committed to this area of instruction and introduced a distinctive approach to reconstruction in painting conservation training, working from the actual painting (Fig. 1). A clear and informed understanding of technique harks back to the teachings of Helmut Ruhemann, to whom Herbert Lank was an apprentice from the late 1940s onwards. Ruhemann was a devotee of egg tempera retouching and was continually engaged in discovering the layer build-up of each painting on which he worked. For this reason it was his natural inclination to discover and reconstruct historic paint layers in an ordered and scientific way.[3] Technical research and analysis has progressed since then,

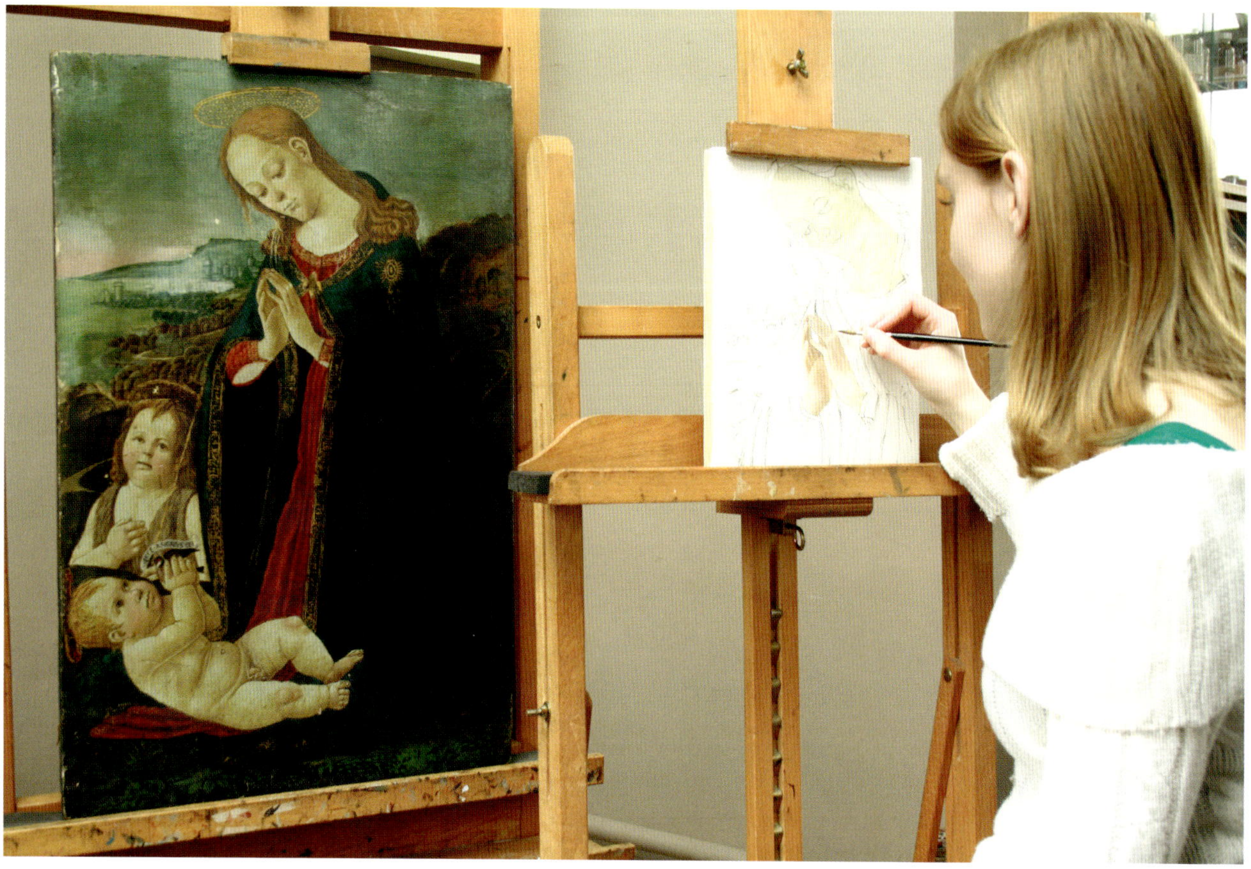

Figure 1 *A copy being made in the studio by first-year student Adèle Wright.*

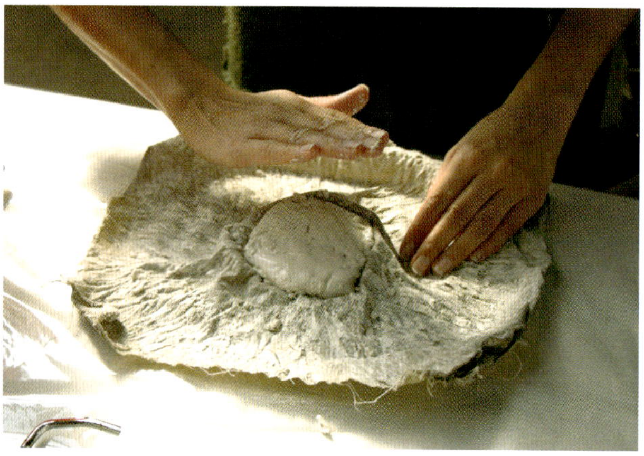

Figure 2 *The* gesso sottile *cakes being made from the slaked calcium sulphate.*

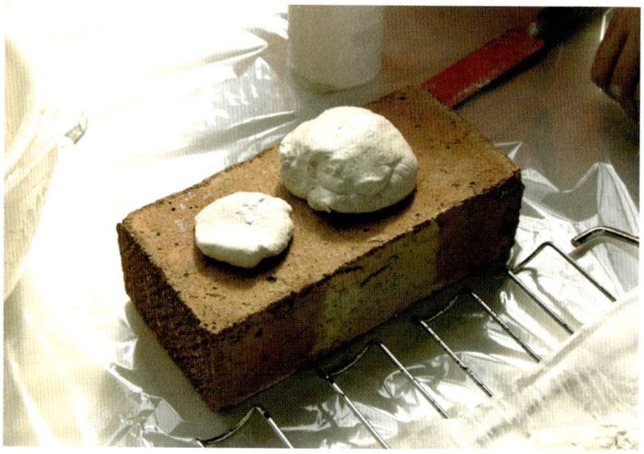

Figure 3 *The dry* gesso sottile *cakes.*

discovering the precise nature of pigments and media. However, scientific analysis can still be greatly augmented by practical reconstruction.

Egg tempera retouching continues to be taught at the HKI and is an important retouching option. Reconstruction plays a key role in promoting the understanding of egg tempera retouching and it contributes an even larger part to the understanding of historic painting techniques. This is a vast area of research and one which Renate Woudhuysen-Keller has embraced. For Renate, reconstruction and paint technology go hand in hand. Even before she came to the HKI this was an area of enormous interest to her, and she gladly took on the teaching and research of historic painting techniques which has become her area of expertise, respected internationally.

First- and third-year copies

It is usual that students (at present, two are enrolled every other year) start the course at the HKI with an introduction to painting techniques lasting one term. Typically, egg tempera on panel and oil on both panel and canvas, covering styles from the fifteenth to the seventeenth century are practised; the techniques of gilding on tempera panels are also included, of which *sgraffito* and tooling are part. Immediately, the new student is immersed in a world of genuine pigments, egg tempera medium, linseed oil, driers and grounds made from calcium sulphate or calcium carbonate. Thus they become artist and apprentice all in one, regardless of a scientific or art historical background; they are encouraged to apply paint to support, be it wood or canvas. This task is daunting and yet by the end of the term hugely rewarding and confidence boosting for the new student. The results can be stunning. For at least the last 10 years, students have followed Renate's introductory course, copying both an early Italian and early Northern (Netherlandish or German) painting from the Fitzwilliam Museum.

The early Italian painting, which the new students have copied for the past few years, is Sellaio's *Nativity* from the Fitzwilliam Museum. Various details of the painting have been copied over the years. Small panels are provided, cut from poplar or pine wood, and the first task is to apply a ground with *gesso grosso* and *gesso sottile.* Renate guides students through the process of slaking the calcium hemihydrate to produce dried *gesso sottile* cakes that can then be soaked and heated to produce the silky smooth *gesso sottile* layer. Renate's bible is Cennino Cennini's *Il libro dell'arte* (1960) and the students become well acquainted with Thompson's translation. Following this recipe book to the letter, even the small details – which might not be intuitive – have been found to be hugely important in practice: for example, rubbing in the first layer with fingers to create a good bond with the *gesso grosso.*

What did Cennino Cennini mean by 'gesso grosso, cioè Volteriano' (Brunello 1982: 120)? The jury is still out. Here the recipe lets the modern artist down. It was probably so common a material in the fifteenth century it needed no clarification. Renate has experimented and come to the conclusion that this must be 'plaster of Paris' or calcium sulphate hemihydrate (Woudhuysen-Keller 2008: 166–7). Others may disagree and chemically the crystallised form of *gesso grosso* does not always appear to be this on analysis. It is very often a more homogenous mix of anhydrate, hemihydrate and anhydrite (Federspiel 1995). Renate's *gesso sottile*, however, appears to work supremely well on small-scale panels, after slaking the plaster of Paris according to Cennini's recipe. Recently, Renate has discovered that the slaking process has to take place over at least three months – less time than this will lead to a more gritty texture of the ground (Figs 2–4).

The underdrawing is made with charcoal pigment mixed with gum arabic. The tempera layers then follow including the usual *terre verte* layer beneath the flesh tones. Then the glaze layers are applied in oil. Numerous students have watched and assisted Renate in the making of glazes such as cochineal red and verdigris green (copper resinate). It is exciting to witness, whilst making cochineal, how the solution of red dye (from the insects) in alum and water fizzes and froths when mixed with

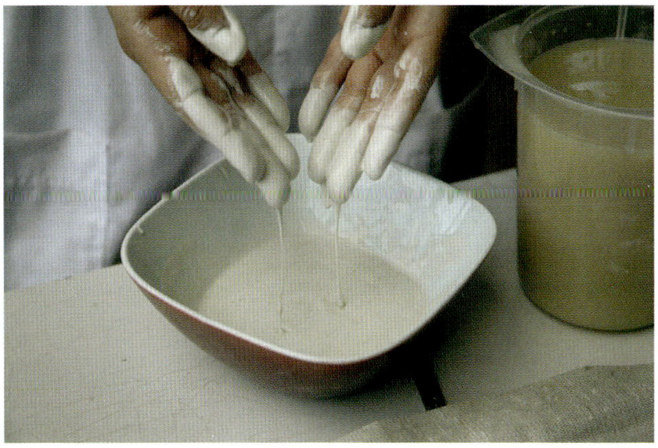

Figure 4 *The* gesso sottile *being made, mixing with the hands.*

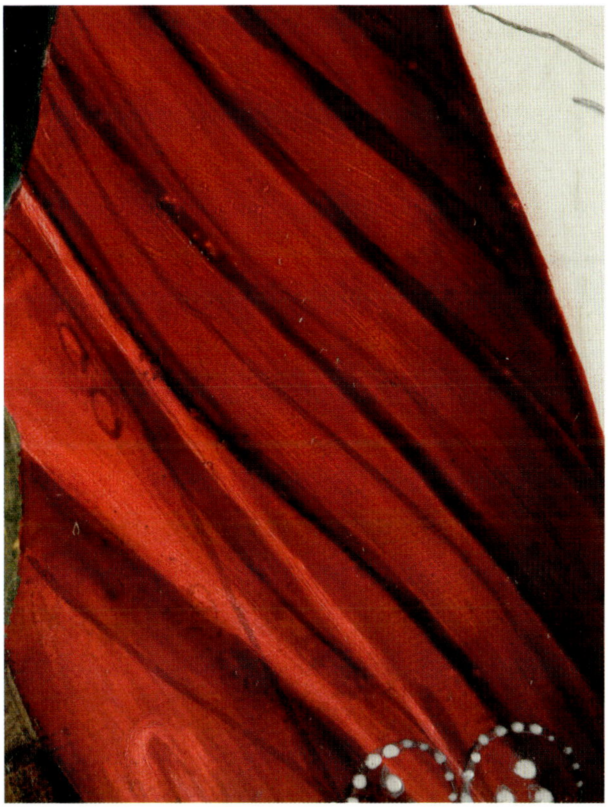

Figure 5 *Detail of red lake glaze on a copy of an early Northern painting.*

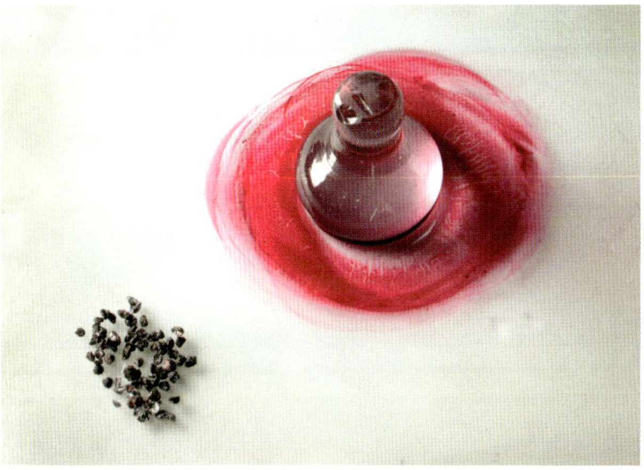

Figure 6 *Ground red cochineal lake with cochineal beetles.*

a

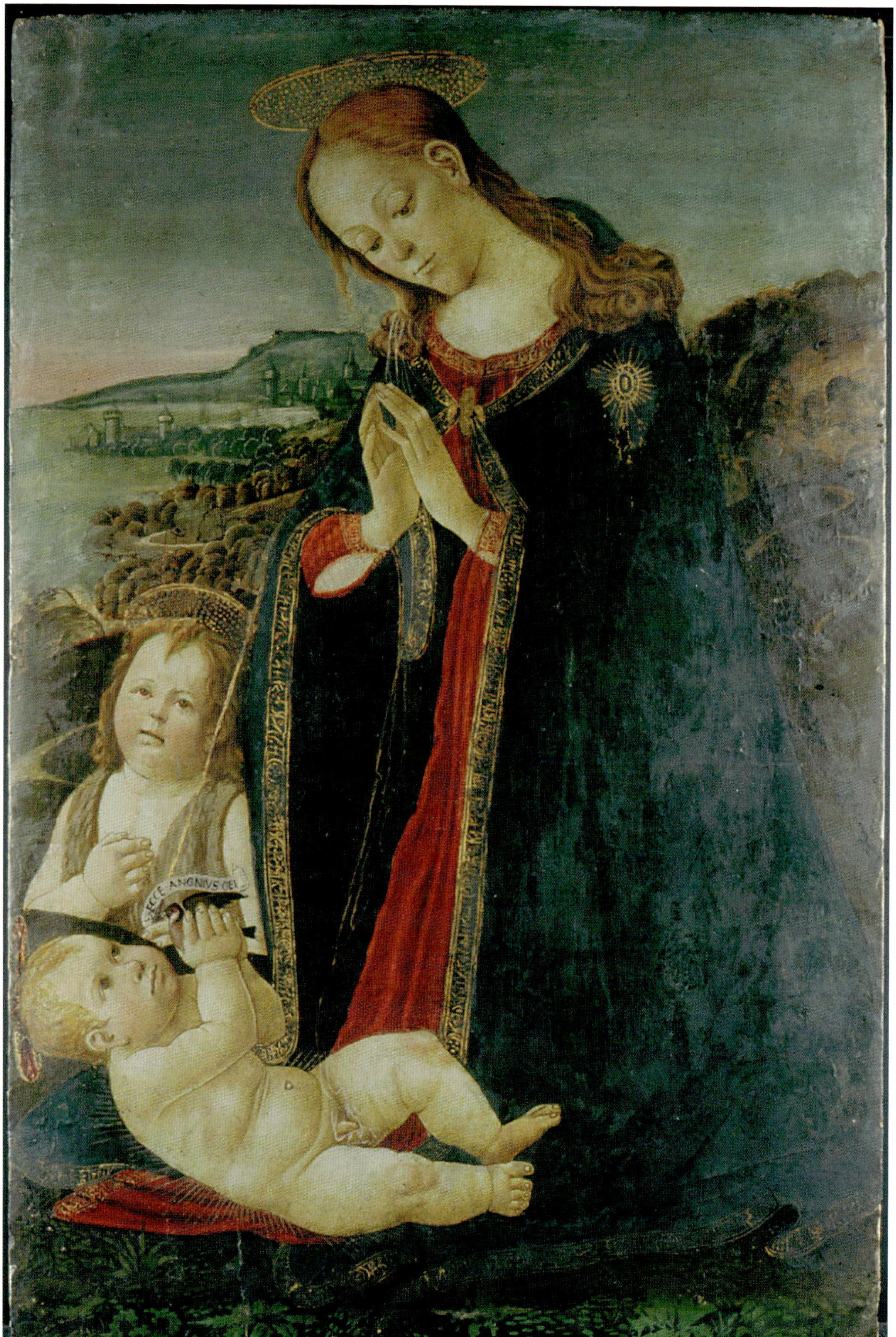

Figure 7 *(a) Sellaio's* Adoration, *The Fitzwilliam Museum, with six detail copies made of the painting (b–g) by first-year students.*

b

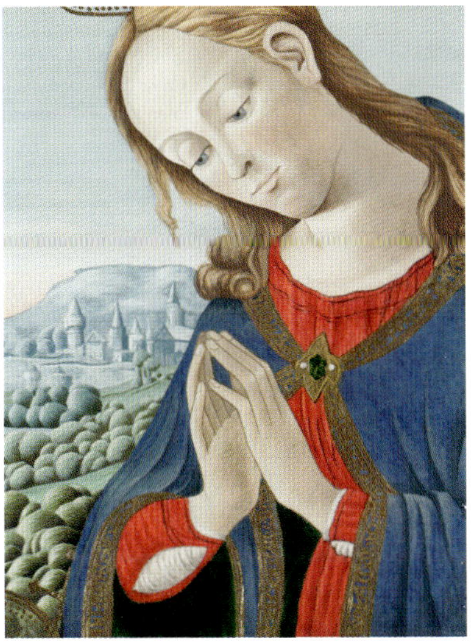

c

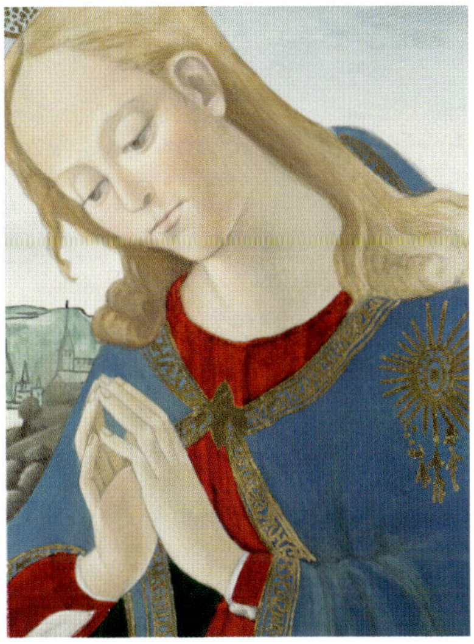

d

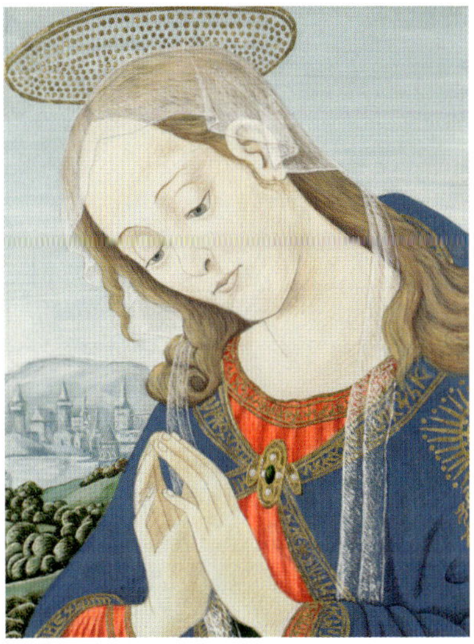

e

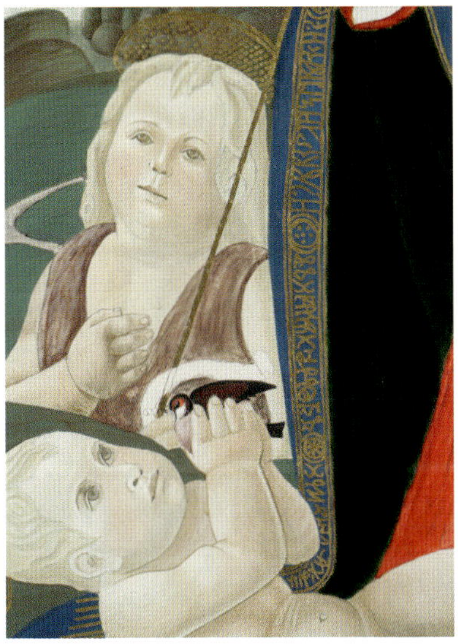

f

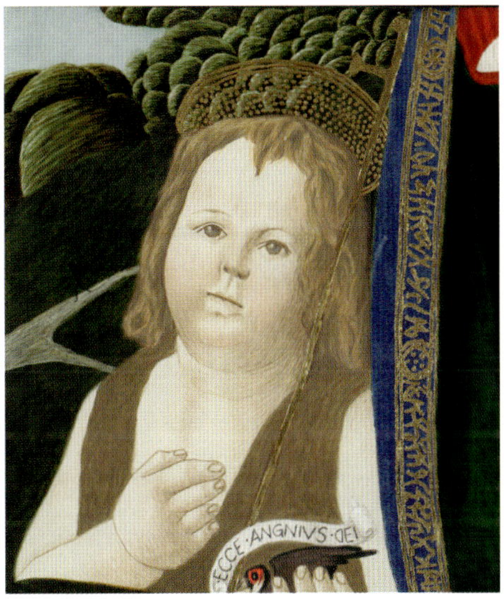

g

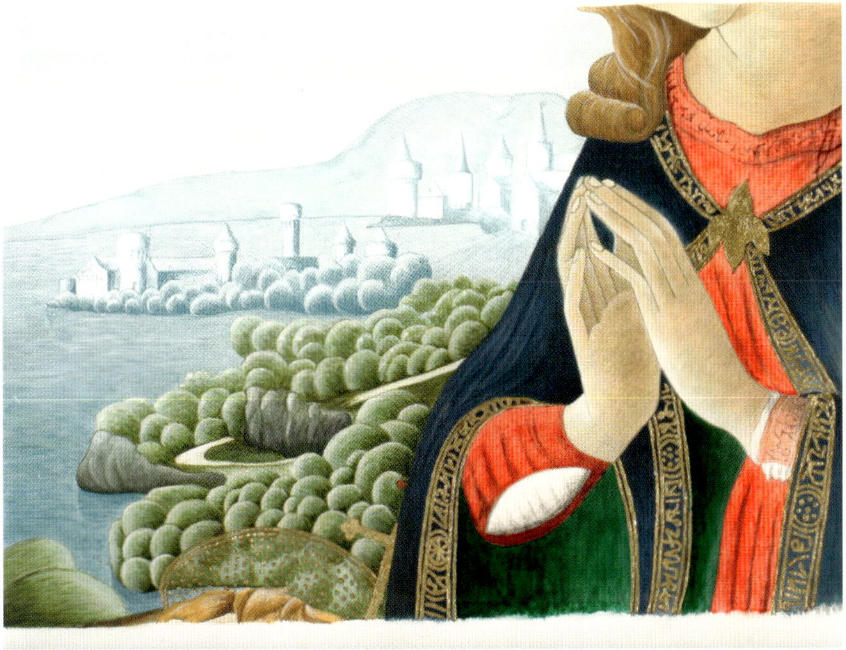

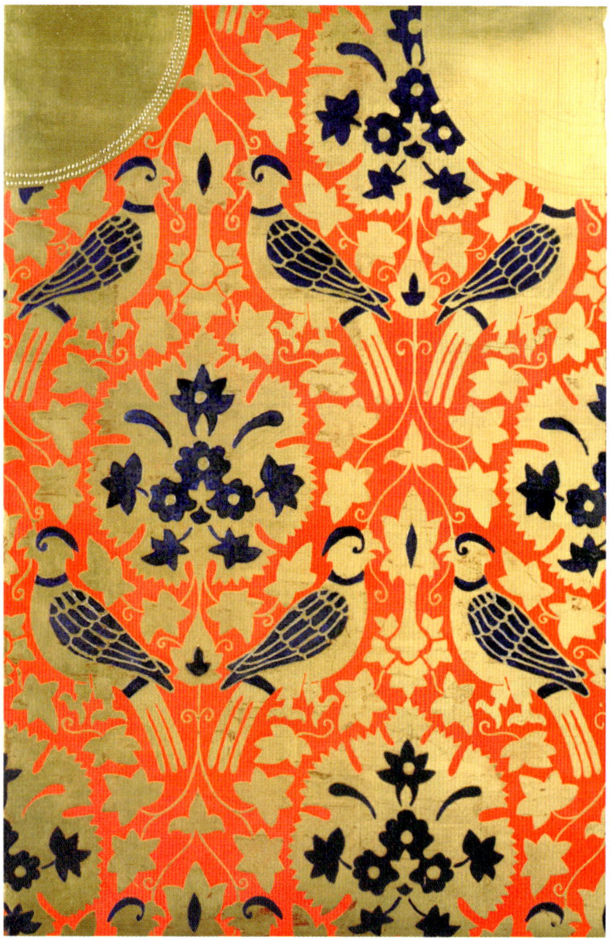

Figure 8 *Gilding reconstruction from an early Italian painting.*

potash, releasing carbon dioxide as small snowflake-like crystals of potassium sulphate are formed. The dye is then attached onto the substrate of aluminium hydroxide and the remnants are washed away. After twice filtering the cochineal lake, it is left to dry on filter paper, appearing to be a rich purple. It is then collected into a jar and is generally mixed with a heat-bodied oil (with or without resin) producing a brilliant transparent red. It may sometimes have been applied in warm oil and resin, as discussed below with reference to copper resinate (Figs 5 and 6).

The sequence of layers is followed precisely and for each pigment the different handling qualities and their respective drying times are experienced. The students have to disregard the ageing that has affected the paint and varnish on the painting by Sellaio, which has not been cleaned recently. A comparison between the different copies shows just how subjective interpretations can be (Fig. 7 a–g). Finally there are some small areas of mordant gilding to tackle. Some students in the past have also made panels to experience different early Italian gilding techniques. First bole is applied and then sheets of gold leaf according to the water gilding method; more demanding still are the techniques of *pastiglia*, tooling and *sgraffito*. Designs are copied from gilding on early Italian paintings from the Fitzwilliam Museum. It is interesting, and perhaps slightly astonishing, for students to see gilded decoration before the ravaging effects of time have dulled its initially 'gaudy' appearance (Fig. 8).

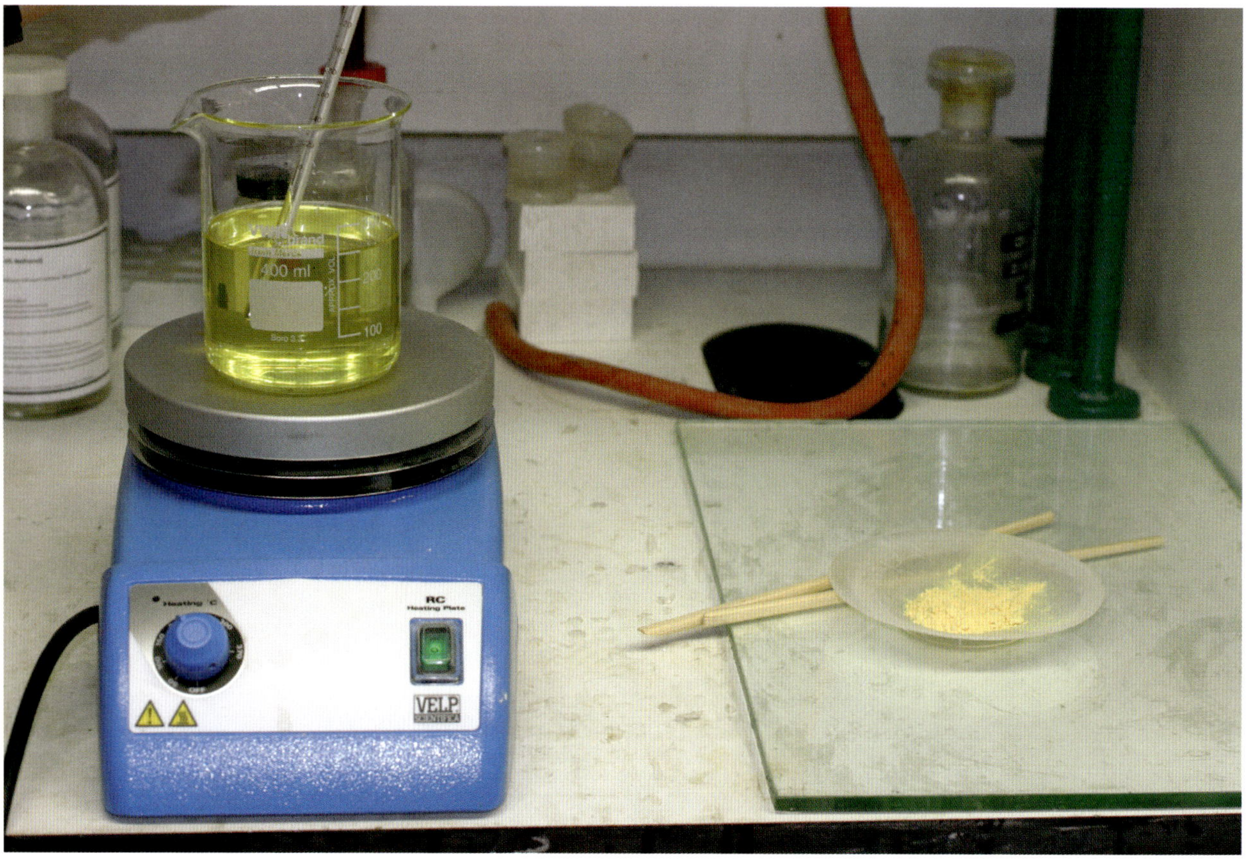

Figure 9 *Lead oil being made with linseed oil and lead oxide.*

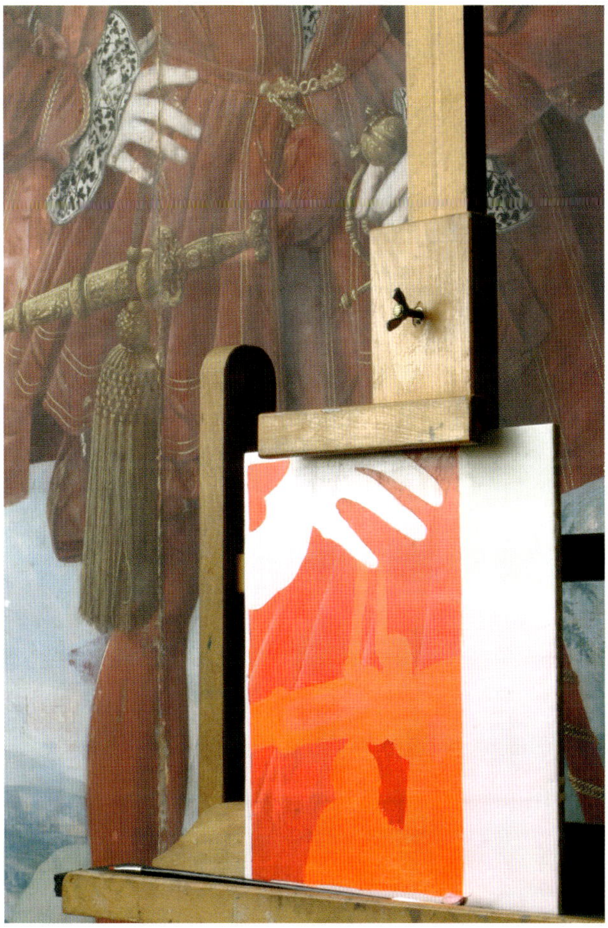

Figure 10 *Reconstruction of an early Northern painting being made in the studio with the original painting behind.*

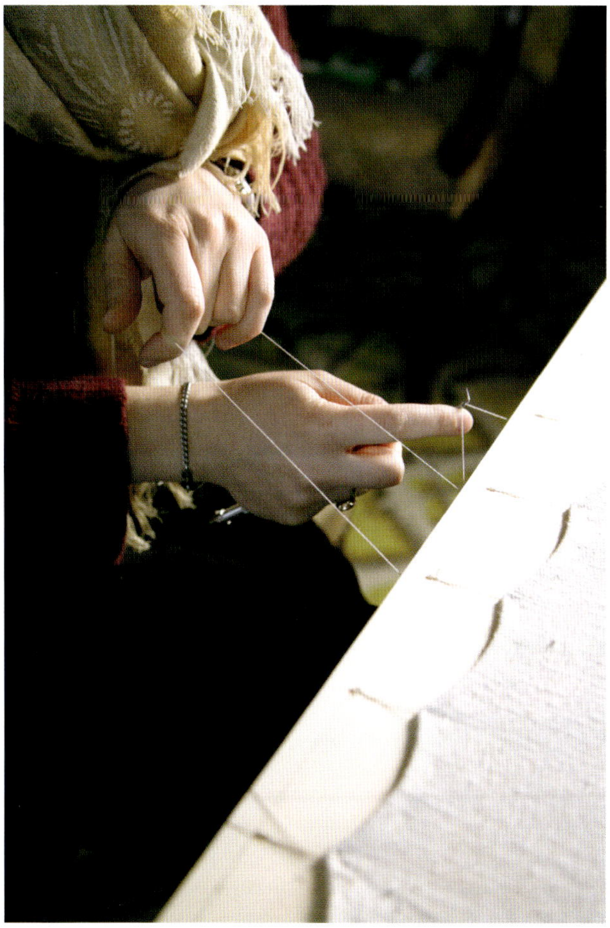

Figure 11 *Stretching canvas, carried out following the practice of the seventeenth century.*

The early Northern European painting reconstruction is on a chalk ground, which is less complicated than the 'southern' gesso ground to apply, but equally demanding to get the smooth finish required after many thinly applied layers. Fine grade wet and dry sandpaper is used, but also very often Renate's supply of dried 'mare's tail' stalks, opened out, to get a feel for a traditional method. The pigments are ground in Renate's lead oil (linseed oil with a lead oxide dryer). All students watch the making of the lead oil, thus experiencing the critical colour change when the lead oxide is added to the hot oil (Fig. 9). During application of paint layers, achieving the perfect consistency and proportion of pigment to oil involves a learning curve. The sable hair brushes allowing small tempera brushstrokes are now swapped for bristle brushes, where 'wet-in-wet' application can lead to subtle, smooth gradations. Renate's glazes are again used for the final layers (Fig. 10).

The seventeenth-century copy is made on canvas and serves to illustrate a completely different approach to painting technique. The canvas is first stretched onto a strainer by means of thread that is sewn through the edges of the canvas and then threaded through holes in the sides of the strainer – the convenience of a stretcher largely still unknown at this date. Pulling on the thread can then tighten all four sides of the canvas together. Paintings – for example, that by Gerrit Dou – showing seventeenth-century artists' studios are evidence that this type of canvas stretching was commonplace (van de Wetering 1986: 33–7). In this country it is rare to find paintings that still have their stringing method intact but it is possible in some Dutch museums to witness the original stringing method hidden behind the frame. Past reconstructions remain strung to their strainers as they would have been during the painting stage in an artist's studio (Fig. 11). Originally, the paintings were often restrung more rigidly onto another strainer, which would be covered by the frame.

The oil ground in use by the seventeenth century, often coloured, is applied with a palette knife. Several layers are necessary with sanding or pumicing between them. Students then transfer the composition using white chalk, which shows up well on a coloured ground but is not visible with infrared photography. Oil is then used as the medium, often in a much freer way than in the previous copy. Wet-in-wet methods are more usual and students discover this allows for a much quicker application, often using the ground as a part of the final image (Fig. 12).

Renate's legacy for each student is her knowledge of the 'tricks of the trade', whether in the production of

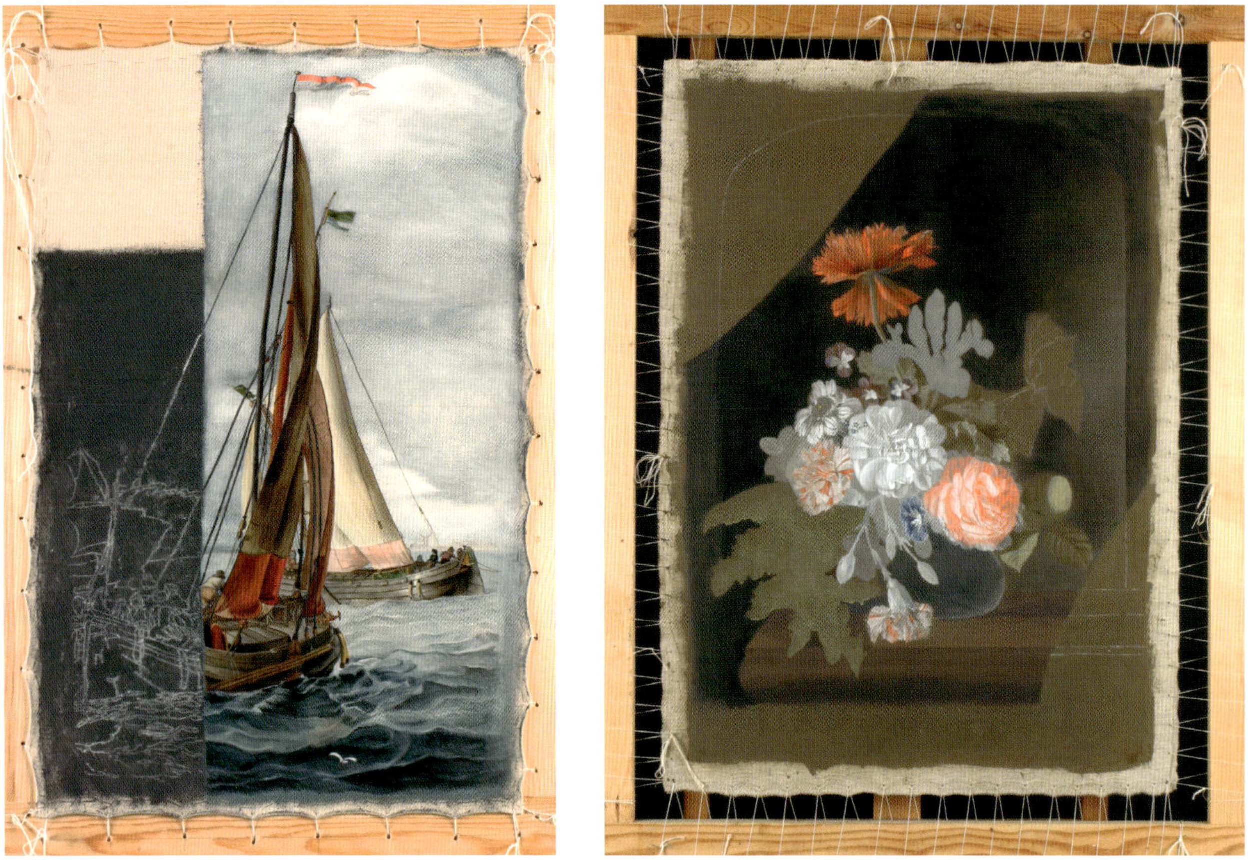

Figure 12 *Two seventeenth-century paintings on strainers showing the use of coloured grounds.*

materials or their application. By thorough reading of the extant texts she has discovered important details, such as the drying times for oil/resin mordants, or the use of different-sized pigment particles for azurite and malachite. She has experimented with the principle of levigation on copper blue and green pigments (Woudhuysen-Keller 2008: 166–7). This is referred to by Cennino Cennini and when tried in practice is seen to remove fine dust and extraneous matter and grade the pigments' particle size according to the number of levigations undertaken. The larger pigment particles prove to be the darkest for both the azurite and malachite. It may only be possible to sprinkle the coarsest pigments on the surface of the paint layers in some cases, as brush application is impossible. The coarse texture becomes extremely obvious in the reconstructions; in an original painting, such coarsely pigmented layers have often been obliterated by abrasion and heavy varnishing. As Renate describes, 'the wealth of surface texture in the reconstructions was noticeable: the porous luminous blue of the azurite in the robe contrasts with the silky surface of the red glaze and the shiny intense green of the lining. All this is complemented by the lustrous gold on the hem of the Virgin's mantle. If our reconstructions come anywhere near the original appearance of the painting, they show how much the appearance of early Italian tempera paintings has been altered by indiscriminate varnishing' (Woudhuysen-Keller 2008: 172) (Fig 13).

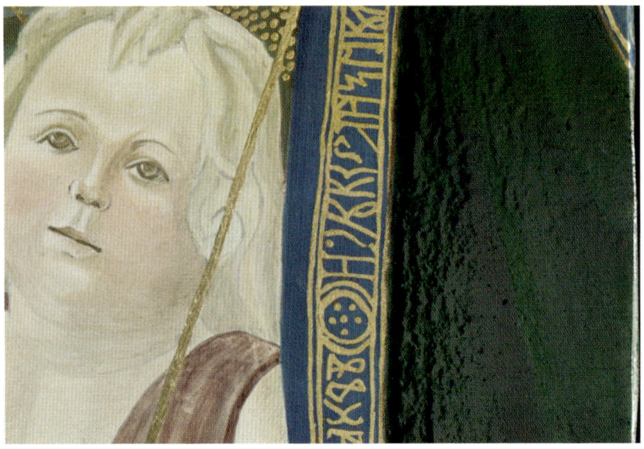

Figure 13 *A copy in raking light from Sellaio's* Adoration *showing the different surface textures and gloss on an unvarnished painting of this period.*

The third-year copy

In the third year a rather more involved project is undertaken. Here students work independently on a painting of their choice (chosen from the store of the Fitzwilliam Museum to allow the painting to be kept at the HKI for a long period of time). The painting is first cleaned and closely examined, usually cross-sections are taken and pigments and layer structures are analysed. The reconstruction is then produced using pigments and media as close to the original as possible. There are certain pigments that are difficult to reproduce and these include lead white produced by the traditional, Dutch stack method, genuine ultramarine and lead-tin yellow. Their modern equivalents are used instead. How much the modern version affects the handling is hard to evaluate. It is customary for students to leave areas unfinished on their reconstructions revealing the build-up of layers.

The type, support and period of painting copied have varied enormously over the years, as the following chronological list of students and their copies illustrates.

- **2009** Emma Boyce: 'The conservation, reconstruction and reattribution of a seventeenth-century Dutch seascape'
- **2009** Daniela Leonard: 'Dirck van Delen Fecit 1628: the construction of a seventeenth-century Dutch church interior'
- **2007** Jessica David: 'Investigation and reconstruction of a seventeenth-century *pronk* still-life: *The Yarmouth Collection*'
- **2007** Alison Stock: 'A reconstruction of a late sixteenth-century painting on a copper support: Hendrick van Balen's *Adoration of the Shepherds* from the Fitzwilliam Museum'
- **2005** Clare Heard: 'The technical reconstruction of a thirteenth-century medieval English altarpiece: the Westminster Abbey Retable'
- **2005** Tabitha Teuma: 'Zuccaro: *Calumny of Apelles* (Royal Collection), examination and copy'
- **2003** Lara Wilson: 'The examination, reconstruction and treatment of Juàn and Diego Sanchez: *Road to Calvary* (Fitzwilliam Museum)'
- **2003** Hayley Woodhouse: 'Examination and comparison of early and late Golden Age Dutch flowerpieces: Ambrosius Bosshaert *Flowerpiece with Monkey* (*c.*1635) and Jan van Huysum's *Vase of Flowers* (*c.*1710–20) – reconstruction of Jan van Huysum's *Vase of Flowers*'
- **2002** Adelaide Izat: 'A copy of a seventeenth-century Roman School painting: *St Dominic Receiving the Rosary from the Virgin*'
- **2001** Meta Chavannes: 'A reconstruction of Domenico Ghirlandaio's *Nativity* (Fitzwilliam Museum, Cambridge)'
- **1999** Rebecca Kench: 'A copy of Alfred Stevens' *La Liseuse*, examination, treatment and copy'
- **1999** Lorraine Maule: '*The Gadarene Swine* by Paul Bril, technical examination and the making of a copy'
- **1997** Alison Smith: '*The Battle of the Spurs*, a technical examination and construction of a copy'
- **1995** Jo Lynn: '*The Judgement of Zaleucus*, 1606 by Ambrosius Francken, technical examination and the making of a copy'
- **1995** Nicola Pause: 'Technical examination and execution of a copy of *The Grand Canal North of the Rialto Bridge* by Michele Marieschi'
- **1995** Pippa Balch: 'Bartolome Esteban Murillo's *Madonna and the Rosary*; the artist's technique and construction of a copy'
- **1994** Claire Chorley: '*The Adoration of the Magi*, Flemish School, *c.*1500. An investigation and copy of a Flemish panel from the Fitzwilliam Museum'
- **1993** Spike Bucklow: 'The cleaning and copying of *Still-Life with Fruit and Flowers* by Jan van Os'
- **1993** Annabel Robinson: 'The construction of a copy of a nineteenth-century canvas painting *The Florentine Procession* by Jane Eleanor Benham Hay'
- **1992** Hélène Dubois: 'A copy and reconstruction of the technique of W.P. Frith's *Othello and Desdemona*'
- **1992** Minako Ota: 'Reconstruction of two panel paintings by Adrian Isenbrandt'
- **1991** Michael Gallagher: 'The construction of a copy of *The Emperor Charles V*, a panel attributed to the Master of the Magdalen Legend'
- **1991** Marika Spring: 'A copy of the painting *Pan and Syrinx in a Classical Landscape* by Anton Ryckaert, from the Fitzwilliam Museum'
- **1990** Katherine Ara: 'A copy of a later fifteenth-century or early sixteenth-century Flemish painting *Adoration of the Magi* from the Fitzwilliam Museum'
- **1989** Aella Diamantopoulos: '*The Entry of Christ into Jerusalem*, copy of a Greek icon of the late 16th century'
- **1989** Rosanna Eadie: 'A copy of Gerrit Dou's *Woman at a Window*'
- **1988** Nicola Christie: '*The Hunt in the Forest* by Paolo Uccello, technical examination and copy'
- **1987** Sarah Murray: 'Copy of *A Basket of Flowers* by Balthasar van der Ast'
- **1986** Larry Keith: 'Mazzolino's *Christ Before Pilate*, examination, treatment and copy'
- **1983** Caroline Quinn: 'A copy of the *Entombment of Christ* by the Master of Saint Ursula from the Fitzwilliam Museum'
- **1980** Mary Allden (Kempski): 'A copy of the *Adoration of the Magi* by the studio of Joos van Cleve'
- **1980** Simon Folkes: 'Examination and copy of the *Virgin and Child* attributed to the studio of Perugino from the Fitzwilliam Museum'
- **1979** Amelia Jackson: 'Examination and copy of a Florentine School, 15th century *Madonna and Child* from the Fitzwilliam Museum'

Third-year students have made copies on panel, canvas and copper, using egg tempera, oil, or a combination of both as the medium. All are of varying sizes and states of completion. The copies remain at the HKI and many are displayed on the walls of the reception area (Fig. 14). They are written up and kept in bound copies in the library. These books have become essential documents as each intake of students learns from previous ones.

In 1991 Marika Spring made a copy of *Pan and Syrinx* by Anton Ryckart from the Fitzwilliam Museum

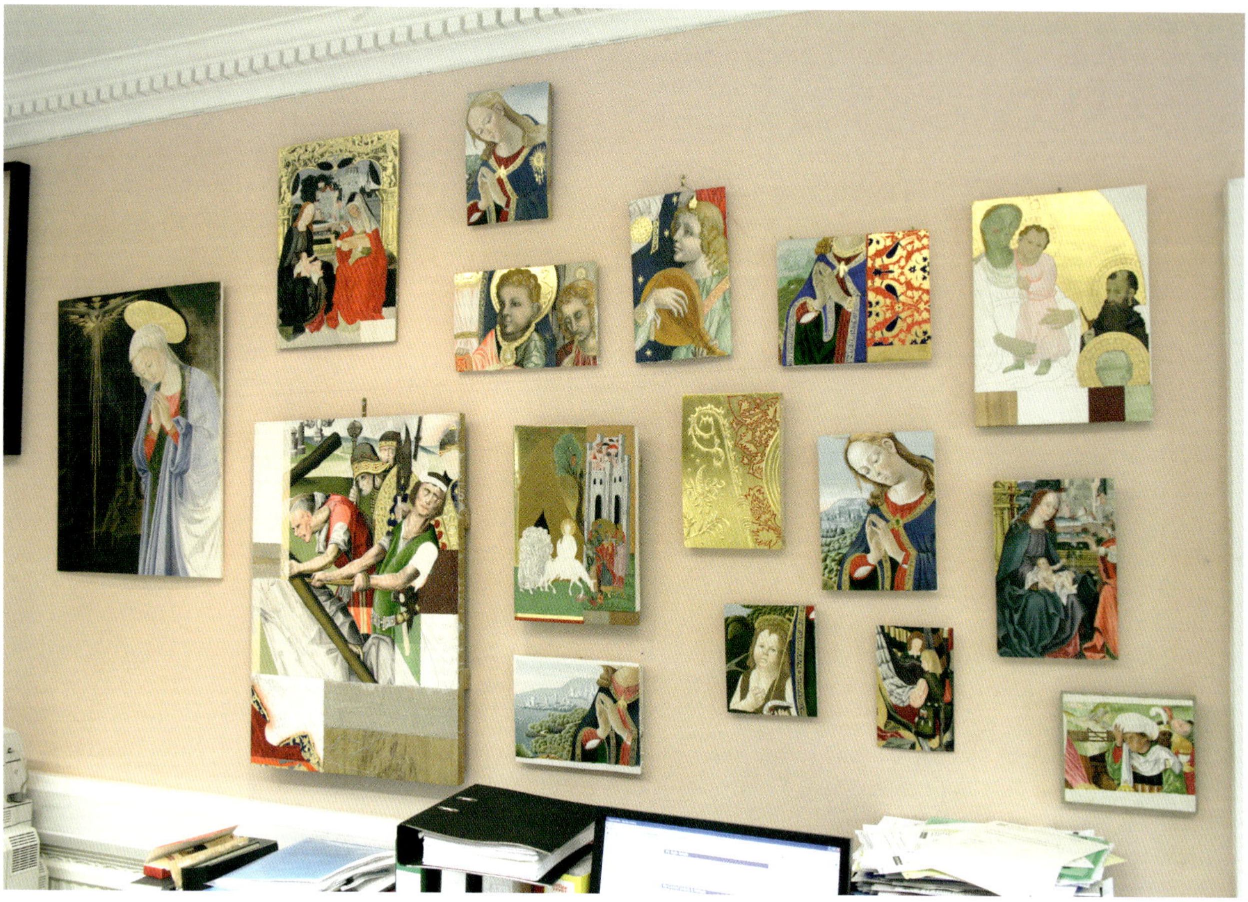

Figure 14 *Reconstructions displayed in the reception area of the Hamilton Kerr Institute.*

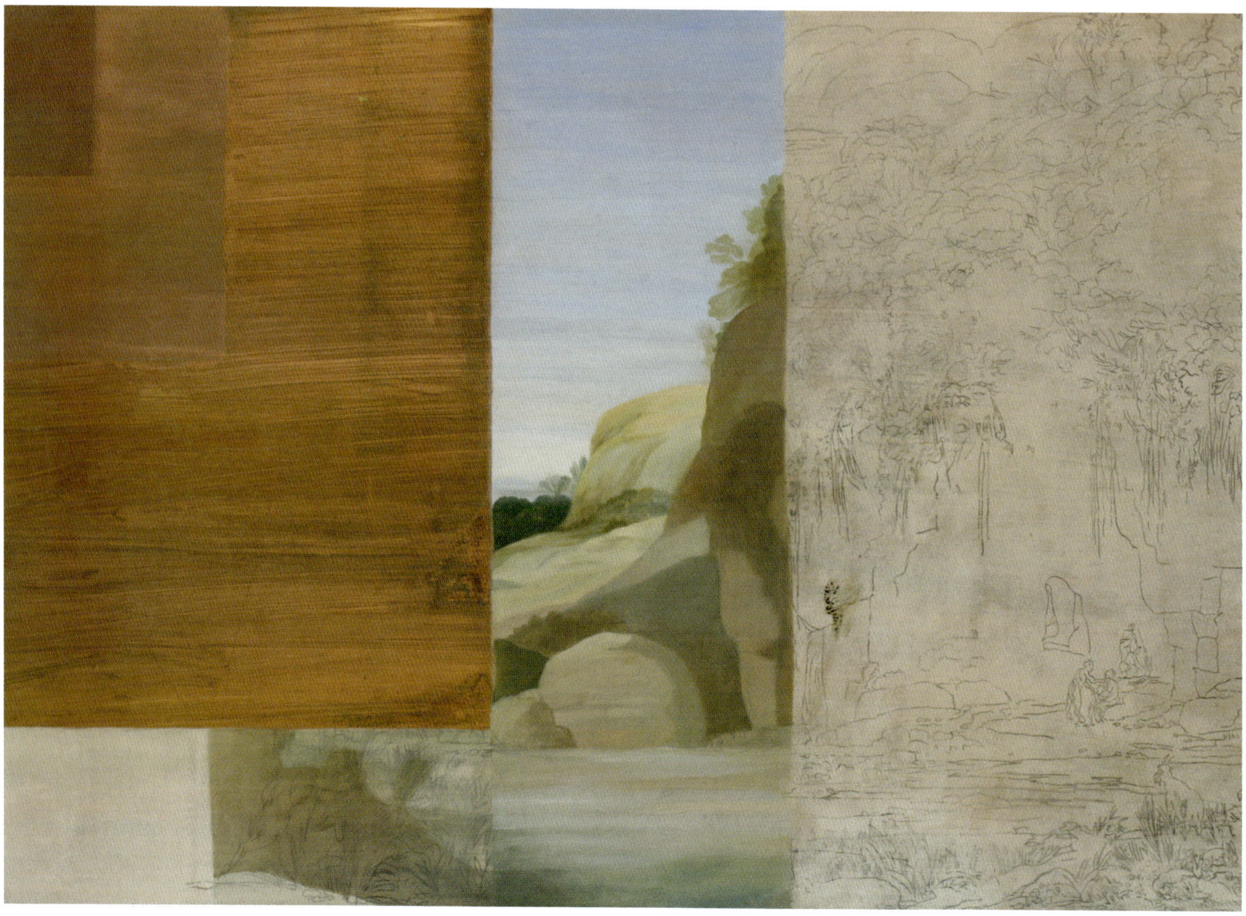

Figure 15 *Reconstruction of a copper panel by Marika Spring of Anton Ryckaart's* Pan and Syrinx, *The Fitzwilliam Museum.*

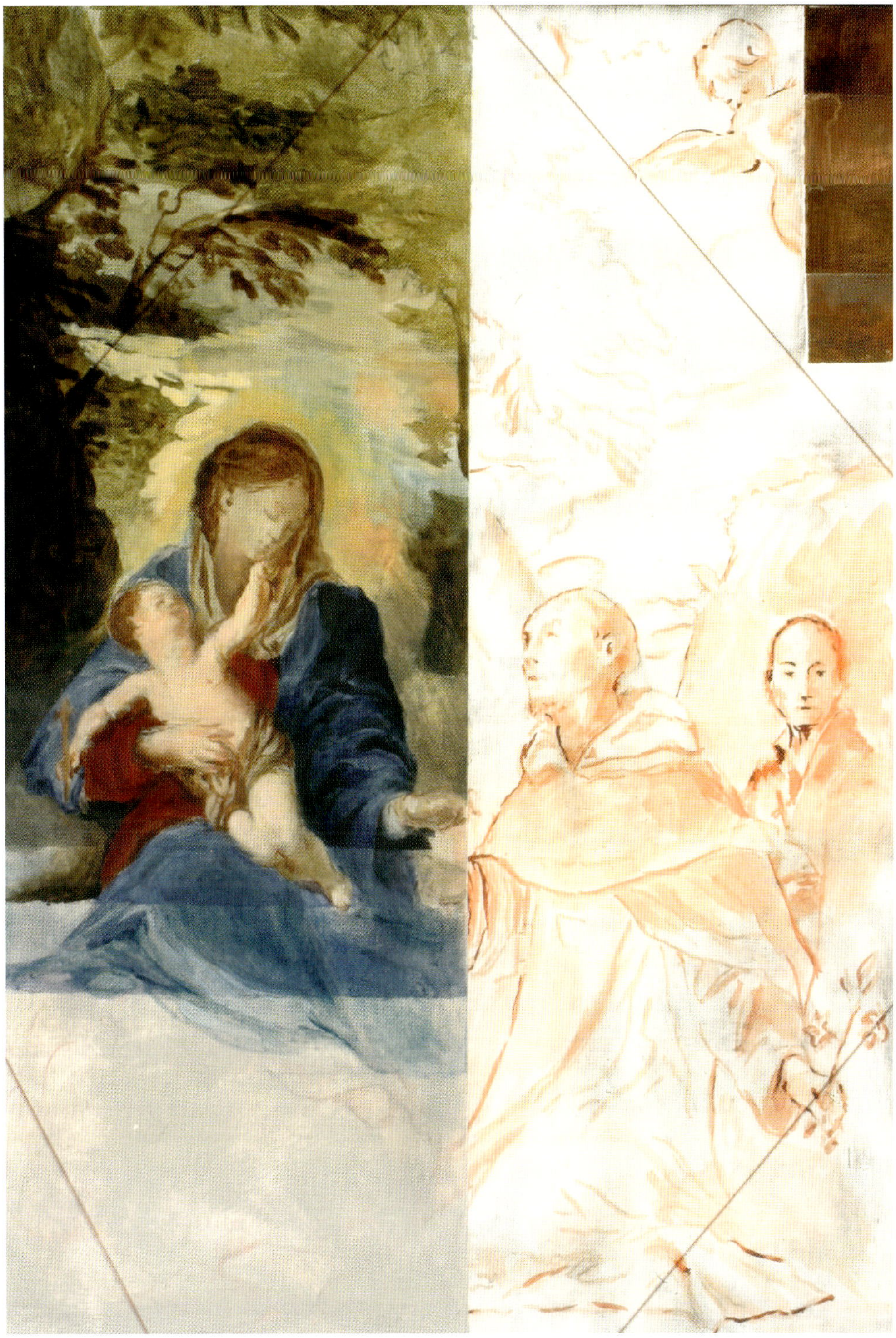

Figure 16 *Reconstruction of a copper panel by Adelaide Izat of Roman School,* St Dominic Receiving the Rosary, *The Fitzwilliam Museum.*

(Fig. 15). She was particularly concerned with the preparation of the copper support and first roughened the surface. Then she degreased the surface with garlic as instructed in treatises of the period. However Marika was aware that sulphur compounds, similar to those found in garlic, promote corrosion. Interestingly it was only a few weeks before her copper panel was showing spots of discoloration located in areas rubbed by the garlic, although she concluded this could be due to the garlic or might also be due to inclusions in the metal occurring in these areas. The next stage was to apply a thin layer of drying oil. Various oils were tried and preparations made; after three weeks these were tested. The results proved that the oil samples had not discoloured, except the oil in the strip where the plate had not been properly cleaned of fingerprints; here it had turned strongly green and also in areas where any oxidation products had not been removed before applying the oil.

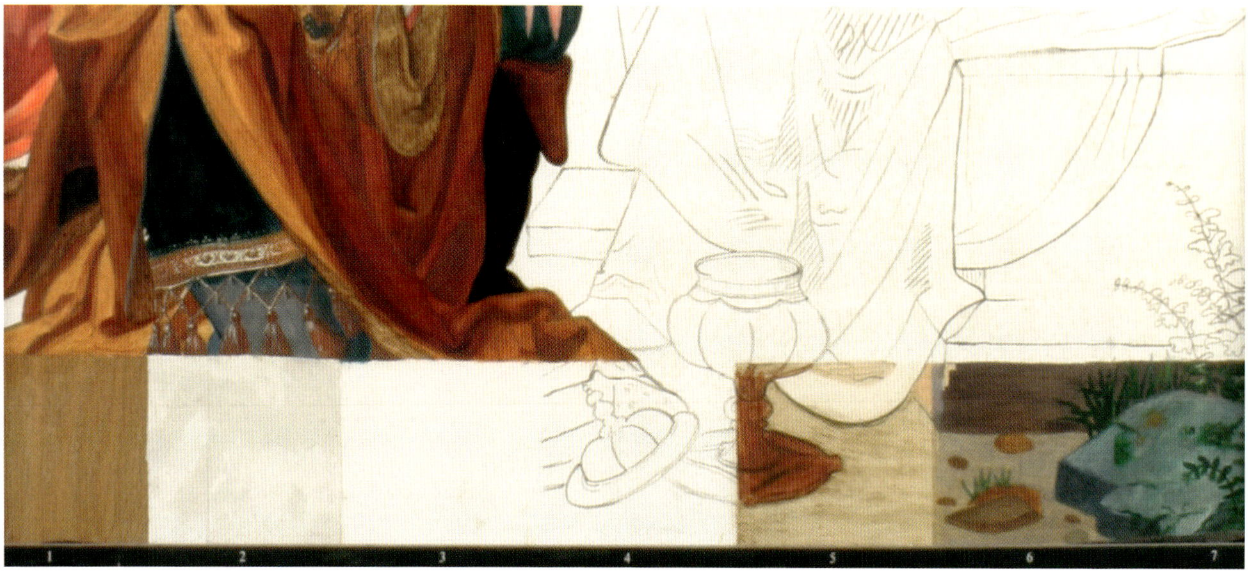

Figure 17 *Reconstruction by Mary Kempski of studio of Joos van Cleve's,* Adoration of the Magi, *The Fitzwilliam Museum.*

Such details were passed onto Lorraine Maule who made a copy on copper of *The Gardarene Swine* by Paul Bril, and included an in-depth description of the different methods of copper sheet production in her write-up. From this Adelaide Izat was able to recognise the type of copper production on her painting, *St Dominic Receiving the Rosary* (seventeenth-century Roman School). She concluded that the original copper panel was rolled as well as being hammered (Fig. 16). Alison Stock has also gone on to reconstruct preparation layers for copper panel as can be seen in her case study in this volume ('Preparing a copper panel for painting: a late sixteenth-century reconstruction').

Many minor but collectively important lessons have been learned in the making of the reconstructions. For example, Hayley Woodhouse, in her copy of a *Vase of Flowers* by Jan van Huysum, discovered that the canvas still needed to be de-crimped first, despite being stretched by the lacing method on a strainer. Likewise, I found that using egg tempera on top of oil layers could produce the extremely fine lines in lead-tin yellow needed in the king's brocade decoration of *The Adoration of the Magi* (studio of Joos van Cleve). Small details such as these cannot guarantee the correct method, but if it is the most effective means of production this would seem to be proof enough.

We will never know all the secrets of the 'old masters' but by trying out various methods a technique becomes more obvious just by the efficiency of its handling and result. Very often the trial panels or canvases worked alongside the actual reconstruction are as instructive as the final copy itself. It is the discovery of what did not work as much as what did that is revealing. Each student will have had this experience and that is why the log books of these reconstructions are invaluable. In the reconstruction mentioned above of the *Adoration of the Magi* I was interested to try out different media as it was not clear whether the medium was solely oil after staining tests. On a designated area of the reconstruction I tried a section of egg tempera underlayers with oil glazes and then next to it an area using an egg/oil emulsion. Although the visual results of the emulsion were acceptable the handling was problematic. This would seem, in my mind, to rule out the extensive use of this mixed medium (Fig. 17, detail). Reconstructions may contain areas that have been less successful but this is all part of the learning experience which Renate has then been able to pass on to each subsequent student.

Two areas where there has been almost universal agreement over the years are the apparent difficulty of applying ultramarine pigments and copper greens. It is interesting to see how many times the mixture of ultramarine with white is avoided by artists due to the mixture often appearing grey and losing the rich intensity of the blue. Microscopic investigation of the original pigment construction often confirms this fact. Adelaide Izat's painting of *St Dominic Receiving the Rosary*, follows the description in Armenini (1977: 194), where a modelled azurite layer is followed with a glaze of ultramarine. Lead white is used on top for the highlights and either indigo or black for the shadows followed by a semi-transparent glaze which, according to Adelaide, could be described as a semi-opaque light scumble consisting of ultramarine with a calcite extender that was also found in the sky. Rosanna Eadie found that not much white was mixed with the ultramarine in the curtain on her copy of Gerrit Dou's *Woman at a Window*; instead chalk was found. Genuine lapis has not been used on the whole by students for their copies but many of the same problems have been encountered using French ultramarine. In early Italian reconstructions black is often found as an underlayer on the Virgin's robe, giving it a richer and darker tone. Meta Chavannes found this to be the case on the *Nativity* by Domenico Ghirlandaio and she

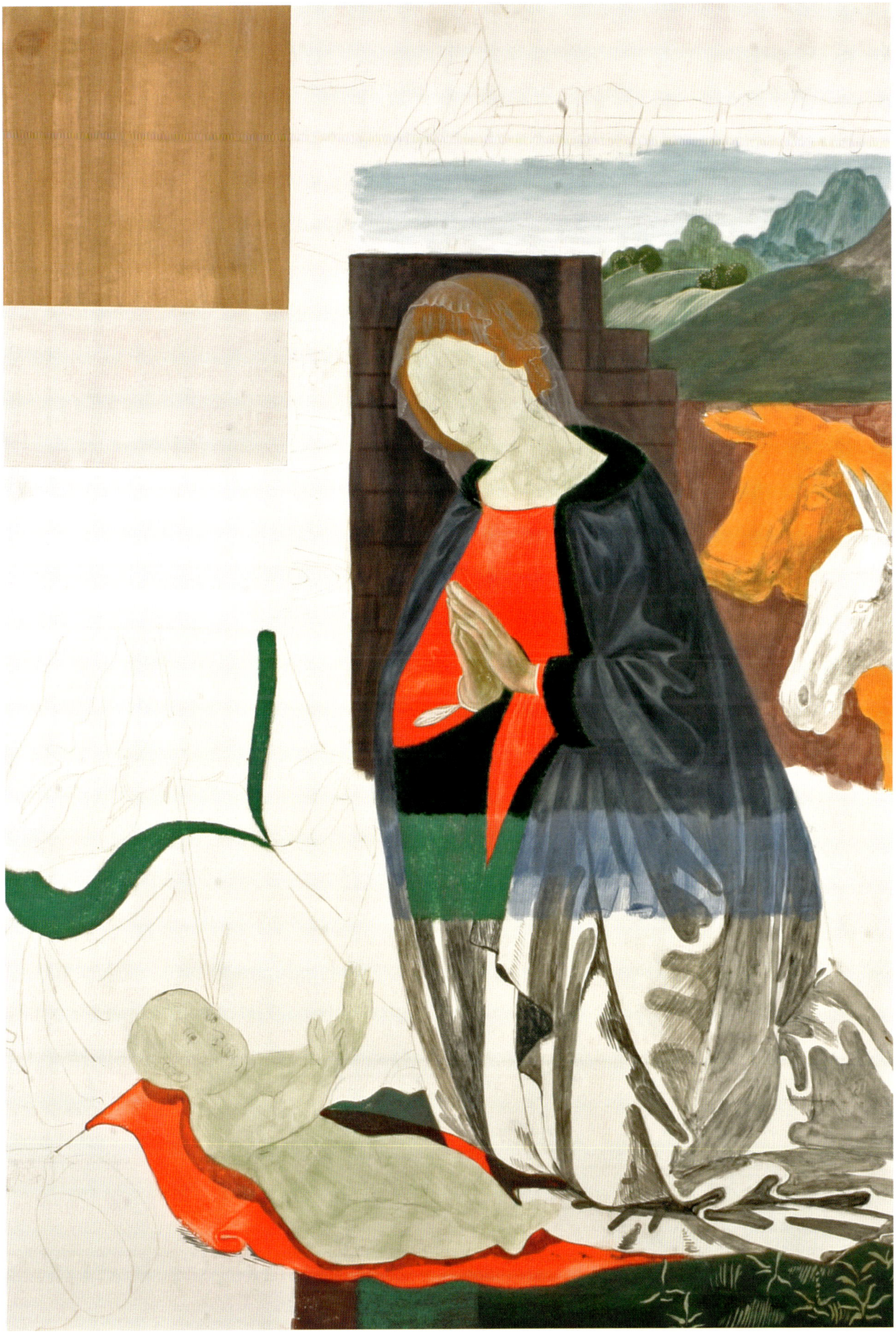

Figure 18 *Detail from the reconstruction by Meta Chavannnes of Ghirlandaio's* Nativity, *The Fitzwilliam Museum.*

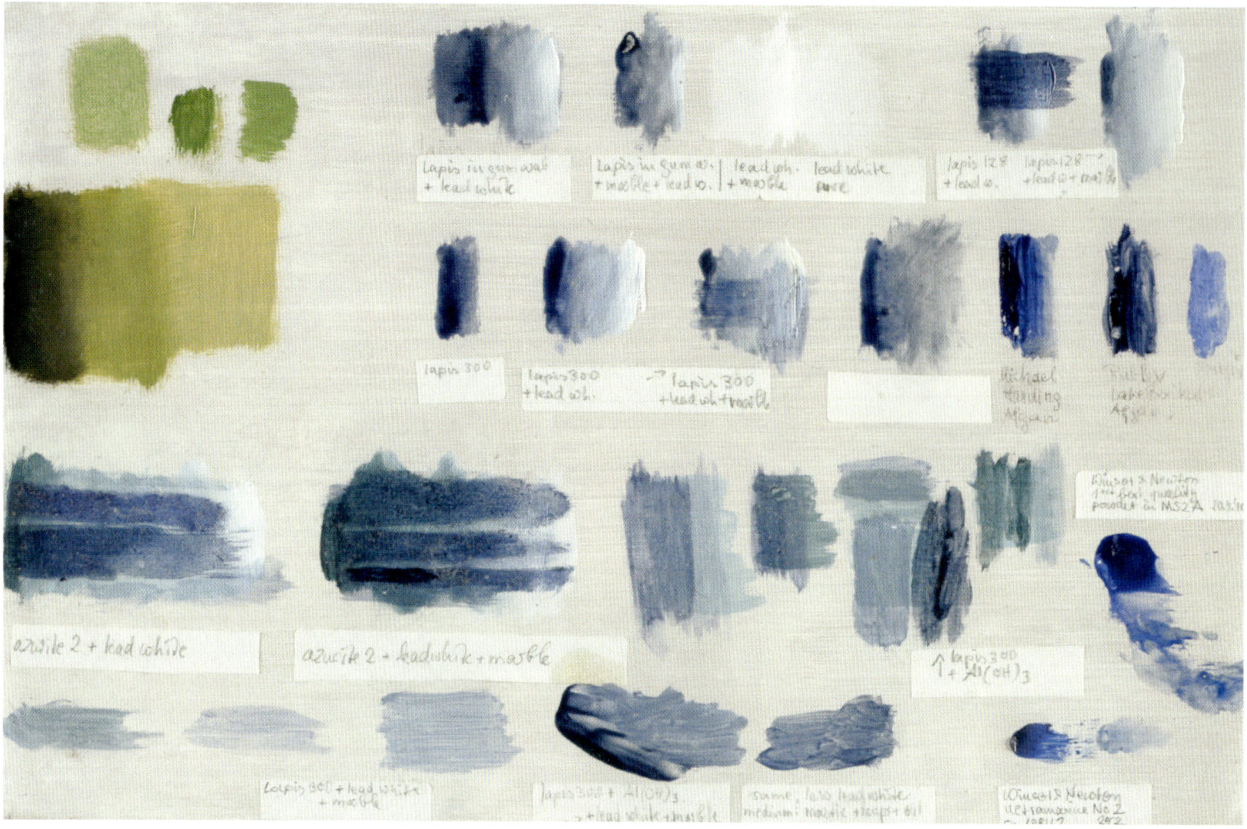

Figure 19 *Panel showing trials with genuine ultramarine blue.*

compared it to the unfinished *Manchester Madonna* by Michelangelo where a modelled black layer under the Virgin's robe can be clearly seen (Figs 18 and 19).

Greens are notoriously difficult to reproduce correctly. 'Copper resinate' has been reconstructed with a number of differing recipes. Renate makes hers from a recipe by de Mayerne which involves using Venice turpentine, colophony and verdigris heated together. The green liquid is then dried and finally ground with a drying oil as if a regular pigment. Usually the pigment is then easy to apply with a brush in the normal manner. However, it has been observed on many paintings from medieval times onwards that green glazes are often applied with textiles or with the finger and are dabbed on, indicating a stiff consistency. Renate has also experimented making copper resinate by dissolving verdigris in warm linseed oil and this method produces a viscous liquid. Brushed out imprecisely, on drying it produces wrinkles, whereas if the mixture is dabbed on with a textile pad then no wrinkling is observed (Woudhuysen-Keller 1995: 65–9). It seems both methods may have been employed. It is hard to quantify whether one preparation compared with the other is responsible for more discoloration over time (the copper green turning brown) (Fig. 20).

Margriet van Eikema Hommes has proffered a different interpretation of copper resinate and claims that on easel paintings the green glaze is formed by simply mixing verdigris with a pre-polymerised oil. The pigment particles, evident at first, dissolve after a few days and the green appears as a homogenous glaze under the microscope. This, she claims, is closer to what has been found by recent analysis (van Eikema Hommes 2005). It seems the recipes are as contradictory as the possibilities of producing a paint that fulfils a number of criteria. It is likely the methods of production have varied equally over time.

Conclusion

There are copies dating back over 30 years at the HKI and it will be interesting to see how they age. Most of them appear to be surviving reasonably well apart from the odd warped panel or evidence of some fading of red lead to white that happened in two copies in a matter of weeks. The fading red lead phenomenon was interesting as these particular cases did not appear to have experienced any of the processes outlined by research at the National Gallery in London (Saunders *et al.* 2002).

We would perhaps learn more in the future if we could compare cross-sections taken from some of the reconstructions with their originals. The copies may also provide avenues for future fields of research,[4] yet they will remain as a gallery of works and a testament to the teaching and experience of one person.

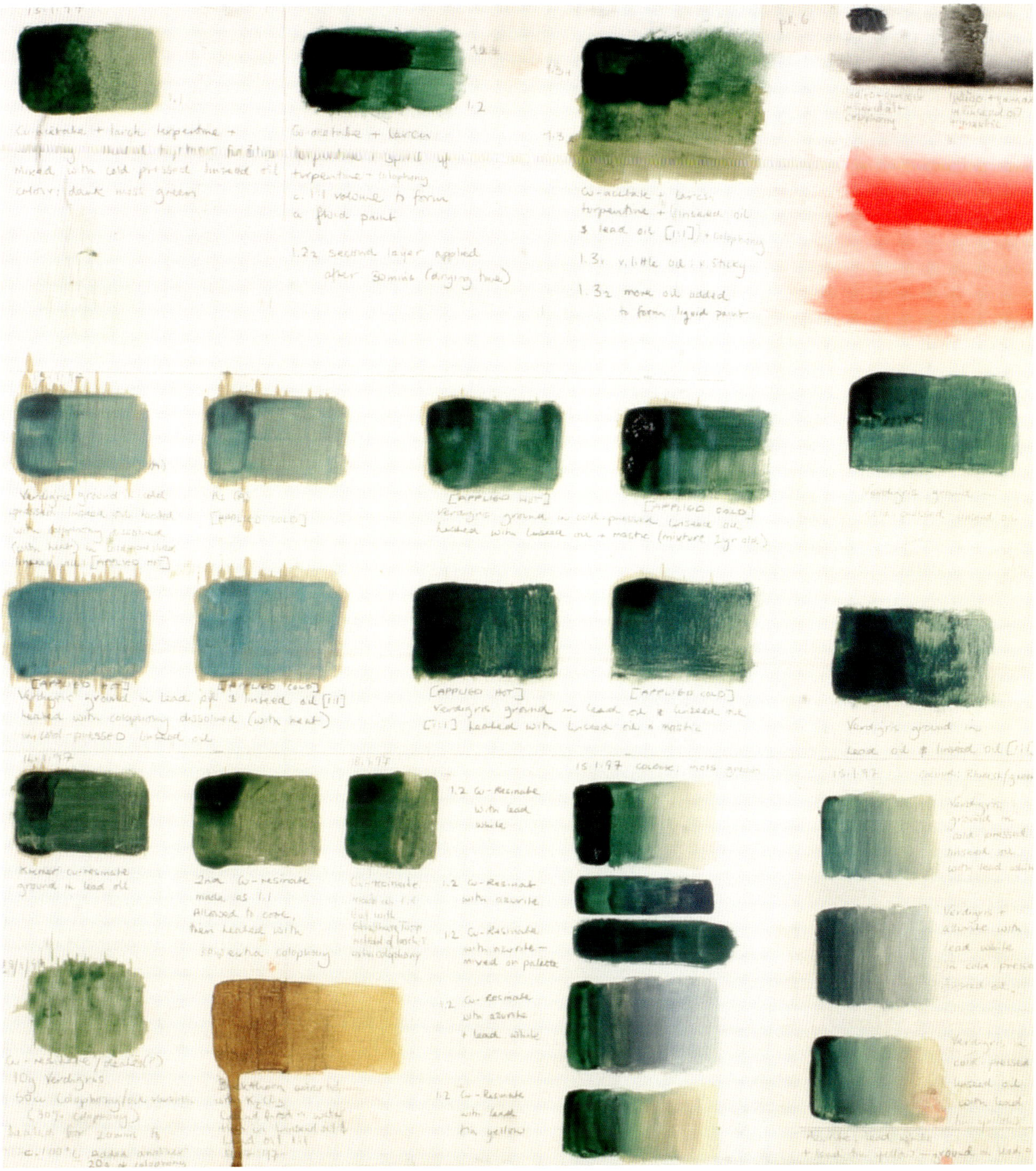

Figure 20 *Panel showing trials with copper greens.*

Notes

1. Reynolds was renowned for scraping down Venetian paintings to discover the layers beneath. This knowledge was quoted by the artist Julius Caesar Ibbetson in his publication in 1803 'of An Accidence,or Gamut, of Painting in Oil and Water Colours', 40. See Bomford and Leonard 2004.
2. 'The teaching of historical painting techniques and reconstructions at the Academy of Fine Arts in Dresden has had a long tradition ever since the formation of the degree programme for the training of conservators in 1974. Today the course extends over the first three years of the study. It first comprises the introduction of historical and modern pigments as well as binding media and their combination. Thereupon, painting techniques of historical periods are executed consecutively, starting with the early Italian technique of the fourteenth century and early Northern technique of the fifteenth century, followed by the seventeenth-century Flemish technique. The course is completed with the execution of a full reconstruction of a painting of choice at the Old Masters Picture Gallery, Dresden. The teaching of historical painting techniques provides emerging conservators with profound knowledge about artists' materials and how they were employed. It is in the school's firm conviction that this awareness is the basic requirement for a pertinent and successful interpretation and treatment of artworks.' Personal communication with ex-student, Esther Rapoport.
3. Ruhemann (1968: 32) wrote about copying paintings in the Prado: 'I soon discovered how hopeless it was to attempt merely to imitate the surface of the painting and to try to match each

tone directly, in one solid layer, with modern pigments. It gradually dawned on me that the old masters built up their works from within, while the average modern artist – from about the early nineteenth century onwards – rendered in one solid layer only the surface impression of what he saw.'

4. Von Aderkas, E. 2010. 'X-ray Fluorescence Spectrometry of Easel Painting Layers', unpublished third-year project, Hamilton Kerr Institute.

References

Armenini, G.B. 1977. *On the True Precepts of the Art of Painting*, E.J. Olszewski (tr. and ed.). New York: Burt Franklin & Co.

Bomford, D. and Leonard, M. (eds) 2004. *Readings in Conservation*. Los Angeles: Getty Conservation Institute.

Brunello, F. 1982. *Il libro dell'arte:commentato e annotato da Francesco Brunello con una introduzione di Liciso Magagnato*. Vicenza: Neri Pozza Editore.

Cennini, Cennino, 1960. *The Craftsman's Handbook, 'Il libro dell'arte'*, D.V. Thompson (tr.). New York: Dover Publications.

Federspiel, B. 1995. 'Questions about medieval gesso ground'. In *Historical Painting Techniques, Materials and Studio Practice*, A. Wallert, E. Hermens and M. Peek (eds) 58–64. Marina del Rey, CA: Getty Conservation Institute.

Ruhemann, H. 1968. *The Cleaning of Paintings: Problems and Potentialities*. London: Faber and Faber.

Saunders, D., Spring, M. and Higgitt, C. 2002. 'Colour changes in red lead containing paint films'. In *Preprints of ICOM-CC13th Triennial Meeting*, R. Vontobel (ed.) vol. 1, 455–63. London: James & James.

van de Wetering, E. 1986. *Studies in the Workshop Practice of the Early Rembrandt*. Amsterdam: Universität Amsterdam.

van Eikema Hommes, M.H. 2005. 'Interpreting historical sources on painting materials and techniques: the myth of 'copper resinate' and the reconstruction of indigo oil paints'. In *Art of the Past: Sources and Reconstructions*, M. Clarke, J. Townsend and A. Stijnman (eds) 16–24. London: Archetype Publications.

Woudhuysen-Keller, R. 1995. 'Aspects of painting technique in the use of verdigris and copper resinate'. In *Historical Painting Techniques, Materials and Studio Practice*, A. Wallert, E. Hermens and M. Peek (eds) 65–9. Marina del Rey, CA: Getty Conservation Institute.

Woudhuysen-Keller, R. 2008. 'Reconstruction of tempera painting techniques: some examples, including *gesso sottile*'. In *Art Technology: Sources and Methods*, S. Kroustallis, J.H. Townsend, E. Cenalmor Bruquetas, A. Stijnman and A. San Andres Moya (eds) 166–73. London: Archetype Publications.

HOUSEWIFE CHEMISTRY

Spike Bucklow

In typical self-deprecating style, Renate Woudhuysen-Keller refers to her research as 'housewife chemistry'. However, whenever demonstrating the production of lake pigments to students – after the crushed beetles, alum and lye have stopped fizzing – she invariably writes the theoretical chemical reaction on the nearest available piece of paper,[1] even if that paper is often a coffee filter. Such housewife chemistry is an important thread that runs through Renate's doctoral thesis (Woudhuysen-Keller 2001).

As the phrase suggests, housewife chemistry operates in the overlap between two disciplines – housewifery and chemistry – although, historically, the disciplines were not always quite so distinct. Up to the seventeenth century, the distinction between the mundane and the marvellous or between superstitious practice and scientific method was very fluid. A blend of both was found in popular books of facts, *Fachliteratur* (Eamon 1982), and commonplace or household books (Clemens 1933). John Partridge's *Treasurie of Commodious Conceits and Hidden Secrets*, which saw 16 editions between 1584 and 1629, contained a mix of medical, cosmetic, cooking, dyeing, ink-making and stain-removing recipes (Eamon 1994: 250–59). Consequently, housewives were recognised as a potential source of wisdom and technical knowledge and, in 1686–87 for example, John Aubrey wrote that 'old wives-fables ... ought not to be quite rejected; there may be some truth and usefulness to be elicited out of them' (Eamon 1994: 260). This should come as no surprise since running the household has long been seen as analogous to running the state and works 'dealing with these [domestic] worldly concerns took their place alongside works of theology and moral philosophy as subjects of learned discourse' (Romano 1996: 3).

Today, by contrast, the overlap between housewifery and chemistry – as disciplines on an equal footing – has effectively vanished. Of course, housewives (who can be male or female) still use chemistry, but the relationship between housewifery and chemistry has changed radically. A housewife's work can be divided into two main categories – tasks that involve creation and tasks that involve maintenance. Maintenance jobs, such as cleaning, use chemicals, and creative jobs, such as cooking, also use chemicals.[2] But in both cases, the chemicals are now often provided preprepared, in laundry formulations or in microwave-ready meals, for example. And whilst some housewives still cook, much cookery has

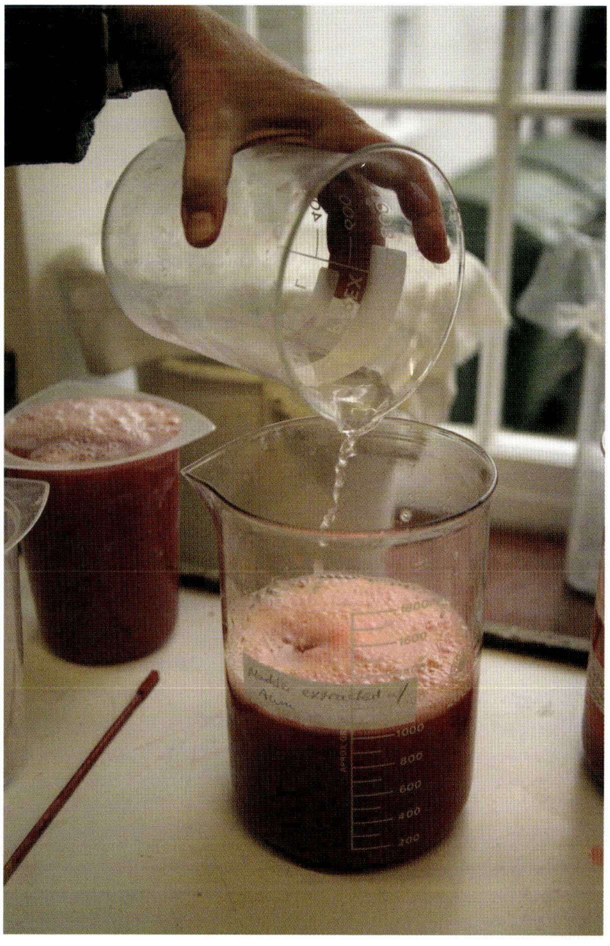

Figure 1 *Adding potash to madder in alum.*

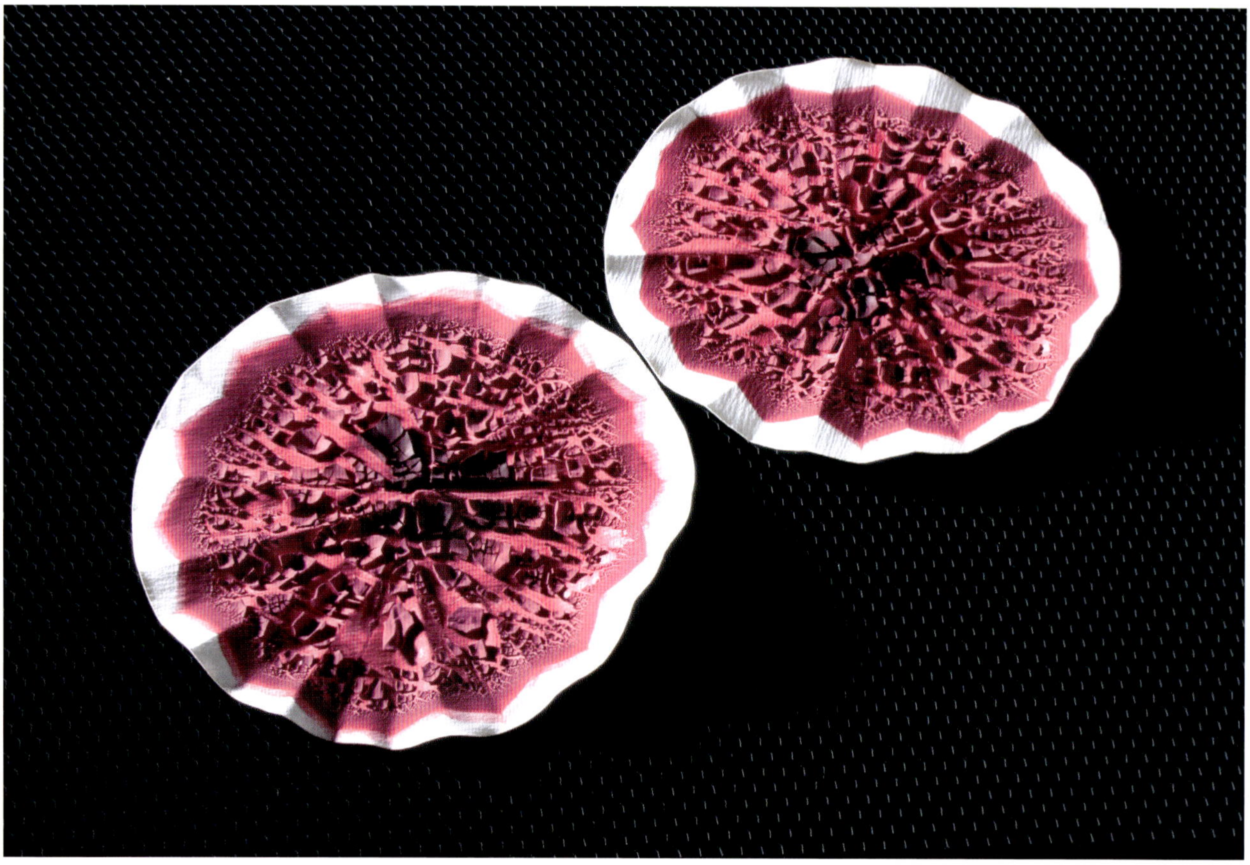

Figure 2 *Lake pigment drying on filter papers.*

been deskilled, yet also simultaneously transformed into a TV spectator sport (Sutton 2006). Today, chemistry is actively harnessed by producers and housewifery is largely undertaken by passive consumers.

The phrase, 'housewife chemistry', concisely embodies tensions due to the relative status of the two sexes and what C.P. Snow called the 'two cultures'.[3] Housewife chemistry is central to Renate Woudhuysen-Keller's approach to conservation and these cultural tensions are evident in her research. They were also evident in her introduction to the profession, which she learned about in a book entitled *350 Professions for Young Girls*. The book included restoration so, encouraged by her mother in 1967, Renate applied to the Doerner Institute, Munich. She was told that they only trained young men.[4]

Conflicting cultures

Tensions between C.P. Snow's two cultures are evident in the scientific analysis of artists' materials and methods, in part because of different approaches to visual phenomena in the humanities and in science. This cultural difference has been studied in the context of positron emission tomography (PET) functional brain-mapping, for example, since, in the words of a medical physicist, 'everybody gets excited about imaging' but 'it's a double-edged sword, because it's nice to get into the media but it also sometimes tends to be denigrated by other scientists in other scientific domains as glitz and showboating rather than serious science' (Beaulieu 2002: 75–6).

The sciences have a hierarchy of types of evidence and visual images have low status. The scientists who create PET active brain scans insist that they are 'not pictures, they're statistical maps' (Beaulieu 2002: 59). But clinicians want to interpret pictures, not juggle statistics. One professional group is interested in measurements whilst the other is interested in representations and the cultural difference between laboratories and hospitals makes working in the overlap problematic (Beaulieu 2002: 65). In the analysis of artists' materials and methods, the danger is that paintings simply provide a pretty or prestigious and accessible application area for science. The analysis of paintings might help to extend instruments' functionality and it certainly raises science's profile in the media, but providing insight into artists' processes and their products is much more difficult. At the same time, it must be acknowledged that the application of science to art has helped conservators establish their activity as an independent discipline (Clavir 1998).

Renate Woudhuysen-Keller's programme of research is important precisely because it operates at the boundaries of disciplines that are now seen as radically distinct. For example, chemistry is taught formally in schools and universities and is practised collectively within a recognised career structure whereas housewifery is acquired informally and experientially and is practised in relative solitude with little or no social or financial recognition. Yet the difference – between chemistry as a codified and quantifiable discipline on the one hand, and housewifery as casual and qualitative drudgery, on the other – may not always be quite so distinct.

Upon closer inspection, a generally unacknowledged overlap between housewifery and chemistry emerges. A recent study of postgraduate students in the laboratory (actually biochemists and geologists, not chemists) documented the process of socialisation that accompanies the inevitable changes in the way science is perceived by early-career scientists (Delamont and Atkinson 2002). Central to this change is the recognition that scientific experiments often, or even frequently, do not work. This discovery comes as a shock to young researchers, since 'undergraduate laboratory experiments have been chosen and stage-managed by lecturers so that they do, routinely, produce "correct" results' (Delamont and Atkinson 2002: 87). Part of the problem for doctoral students is that 'practical science is no longer experienced as stable and predictably manageable' (Delamont and Atkinson 2002: 90). Students' anxiety is exacerbated because their review of the literature does not prepare them for the harsh realities of bench chemistry since 'scientific work that is in the public domain of journal papers appears to have "worked" independently of personal agency, chance, trial-and-error and other contingencies' (Delamont and Atkinson 2002: 92). Postgraduate students are helped through this uncomfortable period in their training by postdoctoral researchers and supervisors who support them with practical maxims such as 'what has not yet worked may well work eventually' and 'what has worked once will work again' (Delamont and Atkinson 2002: 104). If successful, at the end of the process, they publish their own research in the conventional style, with all the messy bits edited out.[5]

All established scientists have undergone this process of professional enculturation and those with a teaching capacity assist in the induction of others. They recognise the awkward practical details within their own research groups but are hesitant to acknowledge them to a wider audience. For example, a survey on the unpredictability of chemistry experiments undertaken through a respected professional journal elicited numerous personal responses but no on-the-record statements. The phenomenon is so common in laboratories that it 'was jokingly blamed on the phases of the moon' (Ashley Smith 2000a). The unrepeatable nature of much practical science has since been alluded to in the conservation literature (Ashley Smith 2000b), and the issue has been examined in detail by statisticians (Ioannidis 2005). It has even led to fundamental questions about the scientific method, based upon how results are influenced by individual and collective human nature as well as more obvious factors such as commercial interests. This is 'a very sensitive issue for [all] scientists' (Lehrer 2010: 54–5), not just for chemists, and a very

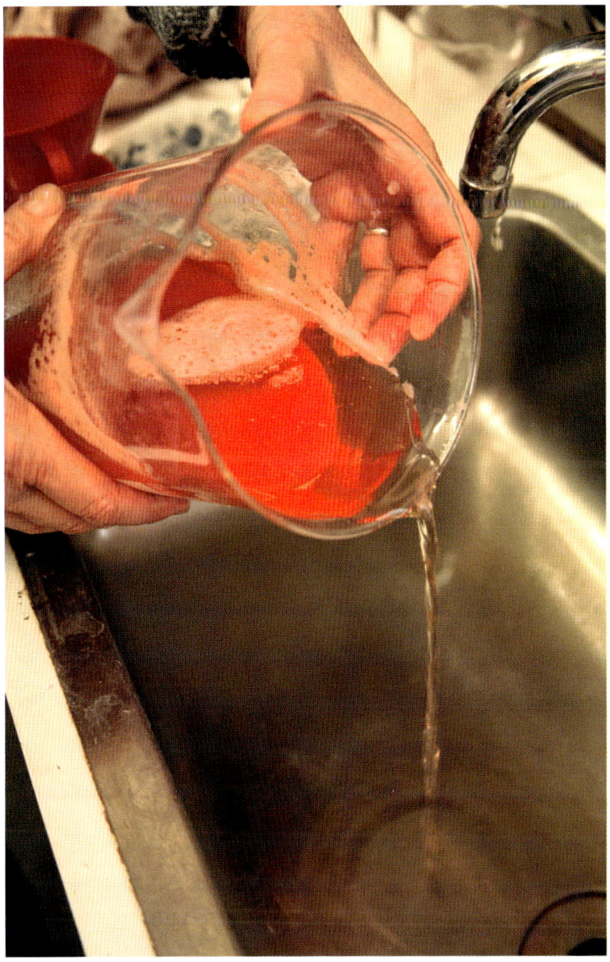

Figure 3 *Decanting potassium sulphate solution.*

deep-rooted one since, out of 432 claims about the connection between particular genes and diseases, only one claim could be consistently replicated (Lehrer 2010: 56).

In other words, even if it is not widely recognised, parts of the scientific community have recently acknowledged that there is an aspect of chemistry which is just like cooking. Practical vicissitudes are experienced in the scientist's laboratory, in the kitchen and also in the artist's studio. And, although they are judged by very different criteria, the end products of those activities – chemicals, meals or paintings– are not always repeatable.

The process by which vicissitudes are accommodated in an individual's practice is the acquisition of craft, whether the craft of a chemist, a PET-interpreting clinician, a cook or a painter. Studying the craft of artists draws upon two main sources – the works of art considered as physical objects,[6] and the treatises written by painters describing their methods and materials.[7] In his study of crafts, the sociologist, Richard Sennett, looked at the ways in which instructions were written in cooking recipes. These are worth reviewing as we are generally more familiar with the preparation of food and the criteria for judging the results than we are with preparing and judging painters' materials or methods. Cooking recipes can therefore throw light upon artists' recipes.

Cooking recipes

Sennett compared four late twentieth-century recipes that described how to recreate a French early nineteenth-century stuffed chicken dish (the original recipe was not considered). One was presented in terms of a list of specific procedural commands, such as 'force the flesh loose from the breastbone' (Olney 1985: 206; Sennett 2008: 183). Another was presented in terms of the cook's tactile experience, suggesting that 'cutting a sinew is like cutting a piece of string' (Child and Beck 1970: 2, 362; Sennett 2008: 185). A third provided a pastoral narrative that accounted for the state of the aged bird's flesh, for example (David 1970: 402; Sennett 2008: 187). The fourth was not published but was written by Sennett's own Persian émigré cookery teacher and it was structured in metaphor. Whereas the published recipes were up to four pages long, *Madame Benshaw's Recipe for Poulet à la d'Albufera* was very short. In its entirety, it reads:

> Your dead child. Prepare him for new life. Fill him with the earth. Be careful! He should not over-eat. Put on his golden clothes. You bathe him. Warm him but be careful! A child dies from too much sun. Put on his jewels. This is my recipe. (Sennett 2008: 189–91)

The first recipe – with its specific procedural commands – was an example of writing as denotation. It is similar in style to the instructions found in computing manuals or, if not exclusively graphic, on loose-leaf sheets accompanying self-assembly flat-pack furniture. The limitations of denotation are associated with the level of experience that is assumed to be shared between the person describing the process and the person attempting to interpret the description. The other three recipes all acknowledge differences in writers' and readers' experiences and engage the imagination to try to bridge the gap. One identified with the cook and focused on the sensual feedback that the practitioner – expert or novice – received during the process. The next identified with the context in which the process was undertaken, encouraging the novice to empathise with the expert's circumstances. And the last identified with the food, likening the process to the performance of a ritual, thus giving the novice clues about the expert's attitude toward the task.

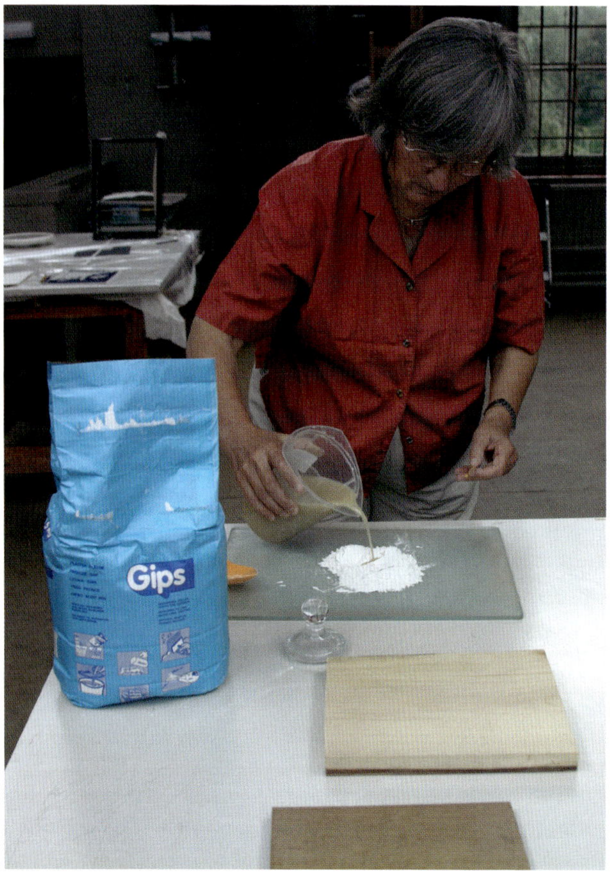

Figure 4 *Renate adding animal glue to gypsum.*

The first recipe unrealistically assumed a 'level playing field' whilst the second recognised different levels of skill or experience. The last two recipes used narrative and metaphor to encourage the novice to reframe the problem in novel terms, in order to release them from the obstacles that may accompany their habitual approaches to problem-solving (Sennet 2008: 238).

The four cooked chicken recipes are illuminating because, whilst the material (chicken) might be familiar to the authors of cookery books and their readers, the method (early nineteenth-century French cooking) was not familiar to either. The authors and readers were separated from the original process by a cultural gap of over 150 years as well as by a language barrier. This required the authors to devise strategies to overcome the cultural gap and it required readers to respond to those strategically different ways of representing the same process. The recipes are all ways of reframing a problem in an attempt to facilitate the finding of a solution.

When giving instructions, there is not a clear-cut choice between expository and literary descriptions since the idea of a strict boundary between the literal and the metaphorical has been challenged robustly (Sacks 1981). Yet most early twenty first-century Western readers probably consider the first type of recipe to be more 'objective' than the three recipes that made appeals to the imagination. It is, after all, the style in which most technical instructions are given. But this apparent objectivity, such as the instruction to 'cook at 130 degrees Centigrade', rests upon frames of reference that tend to be quite limited both in time and in space.

For example, the recipe's nineteenth-century originator may not have understood such an instruction since, although the Centigrade scale was invented in 1742, its early use was predominantly experimental and industrial, so its adoption in 1812 in chef Carême's kitchen is unlikely. The quantification of heat was contentious and early nineteenth-century brewers who used their elbows, rather than thermometers, to test temperature were described as 'blind and unconscious agent[s] in the performance of a chemical work' (Wigney 1835: 64; Sibum 1995: 91).

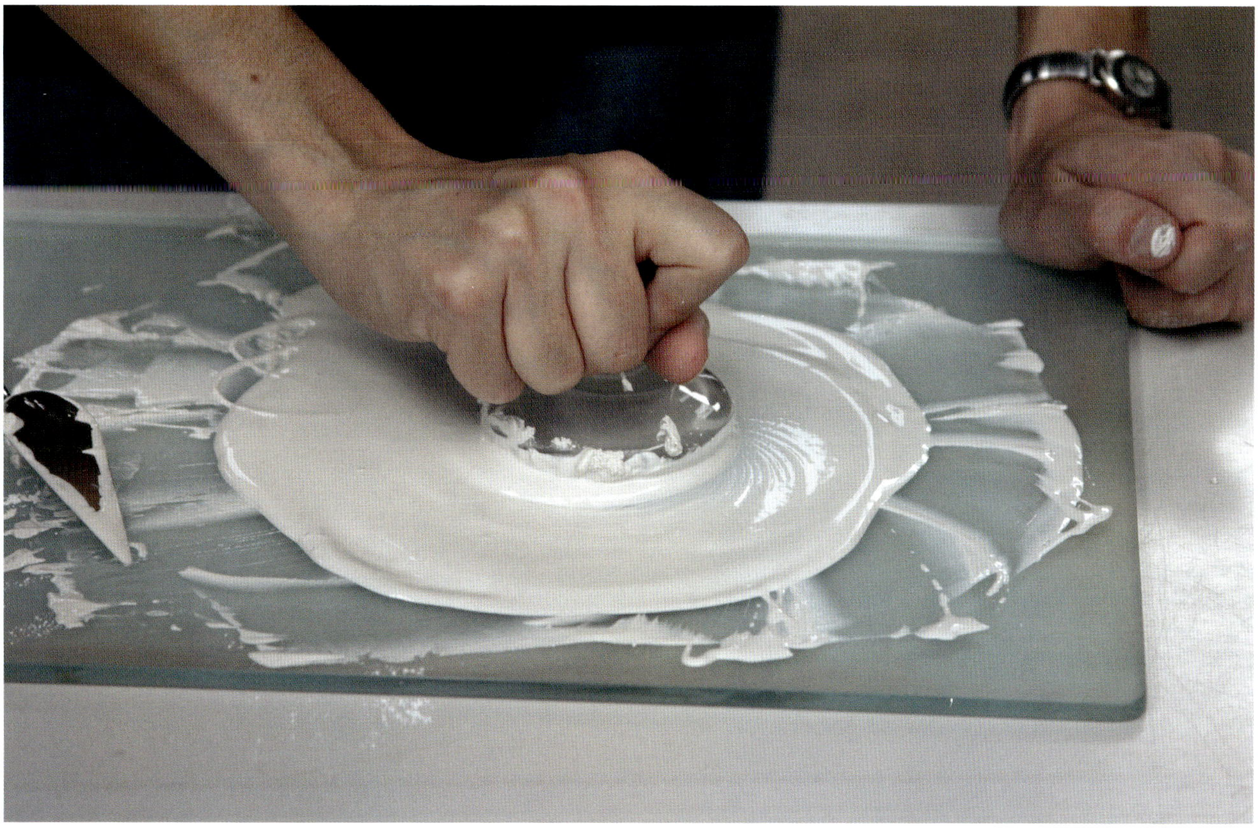

Figure 5 *Grinding gypsum in animal glue.*

And artists' recipes that predate the eighteenth century obviously could not specify exact temperatures so, for example, when copper was used to stain glass, a 'very gentle fire' (Merrifield 1967, 2: 526) turned the glass red whilst heating till 'thoroughly red hot' (Merrifield 1967, 1: 204) turned it green.

The interpretation of a very simple instruction in a late twentieth-century cookbook – 'cook at 130 degrees Centigrade' – also requires the modern reader's familiarity with technical terms. Confusion could arise because the Centigrade scale is now officially known as the Celsius scale. The name of the scale was changed from Centigrade to Celsius at an international conference in 1948 but the new name's uptake varied and the American cookbook was evidently not in the terminological vanguard. In fact, reference to a temperature in terms of either Centigrade or Celsius in an American cookbook is unexpected. In domestic contexts in the United States of America, a completely different system of measuring temperature is usually used. This system is based on the Fahrenheit scale, which dates from 1724. So, in order to follow the instruction, the late twentieth-century American reader must have known that 130 degrees Centigrade was the same as 130 degrees Celsius. They must also have known how to convert between the Centigrade or Celsius and Fahrenheit scales.[8] In time, the instruction may become even more difficult to follow as both the Fahrenheit and Centigrade or Celsius temperature scales may be succeeded by Rankine, Kelvin or others yet to be determined (Chang 2004).

Even in cultures where the Centigrade or Celsius scale is operative, the apparently simple cooking instruction still poses potential problems for the reader. Gas ovens refer to temperatures with a nominal 'mark' and further instruction is required in order to convert 130°C (or about 270°F) into 'just under gas mark 1' (which corresponds to 140°C or 275°F) (Smith 1998). A recipe book may or may not provide a table of conversions between Celsius and Fahrenheit or a table of conversions for ovens calibrated with 'marks', so other manuals may be required. And in cultures that do not routinely use mass-produced and pre-calibrated ovens, following the apparently objective instruction would also require access to an additional and separate piece of equipment – a thermometer.

So the 'level playing field' of background knowledge assumed by the first recipe's author is actually quite limited. When the first recipe's culturally determined assumptions are acknowledged explicitly, the last recipe's apparently subjective 'Put on his golden clothes' might actually claim to be more objective. The last recipe does at least refer directly to the object in question, a roast chicken, rather than to accessory equipment. The novice's ability to understand the reference to 'golden clothes' is not contingent upon having access to industrially produced white goods (which break down and require complex infrastructures), conventional metrics (which are repeatedly revised), conversion tables (which get lost), or measuring devices (which suffer the same disadvantages as consumer goods but are, in addition, initially more scarce). It is

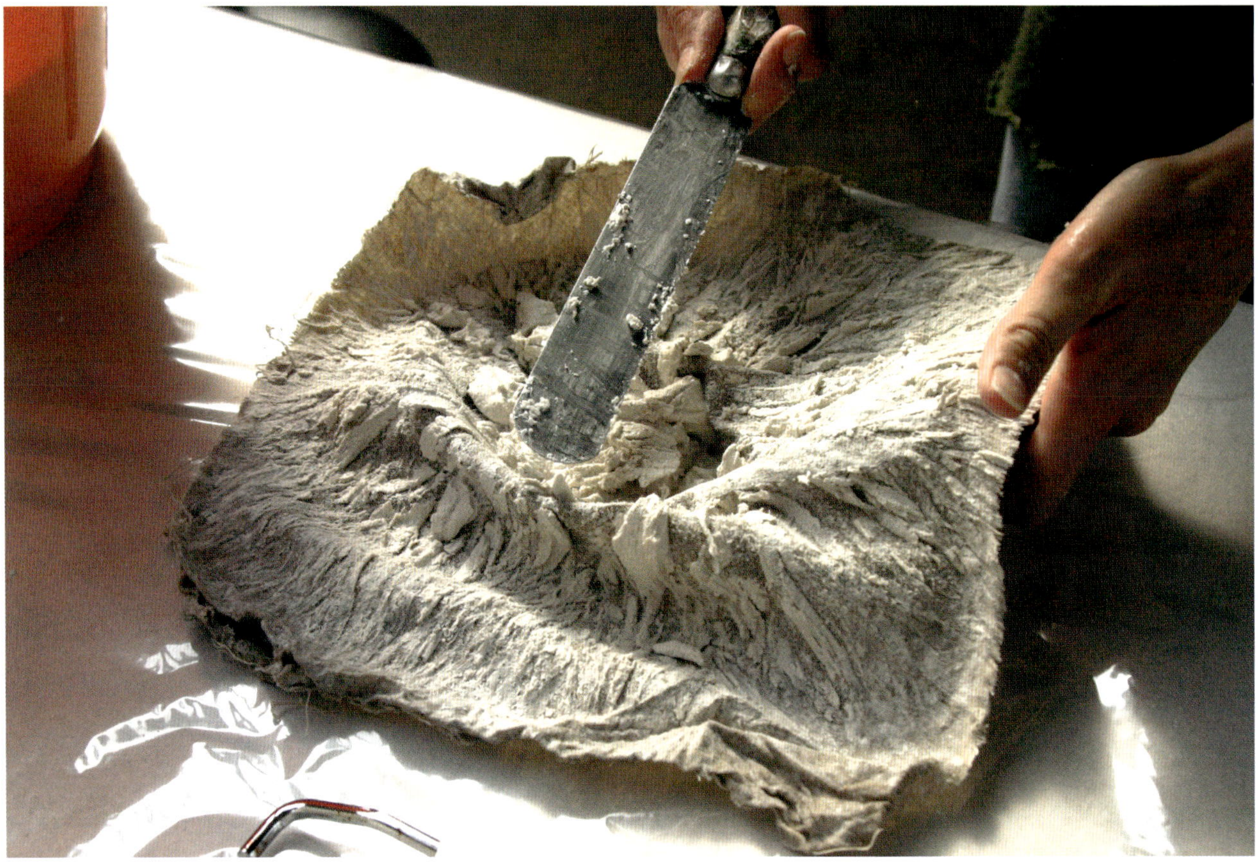

Figure 6 *Preparing gesso cakes.*

inevitable that serviceable white goods and their required infrastructures, the agreed standardised measures, translation manuals and monitoring equipment will all become scarcer over time. For example, a recent experimental reconstruction of Joule's early nineteenth-century work on heat was unable to use his – thoroughly documented – thermometer since the original has been destroyed, a replica could not be made and the embodied skills to use it no longer exist.[9] It follows that the recipe that referred to '130 degrees Centigrade' will become increasingly difficult to follow over time. On the other hand, technological changes outside the kitchen will not significantly affect interpretation of the recipe that referred to the chicken's 'golden clothes'.

All descriptions have shelf-lives and, paradoxically, the more precisely specified they are the less durable they become. The factors that are currently recognised as objective actually depend upon external frames of reference that are culturally contingent. Subjective sympathy and imagination, on the other hand, are experiential and may therefore be more broadly shared. And whilst Joule's precision thermometer has been lost, we still have elbows.[10] It follows that, in procedural instruction, vagueness and reference to embodied qualities might be a virtue. After all, 'cutting a sinew is [not exactly] like cutting a piece of string'. But it is close enough to give the idea.

Housewife chemistry is like cooking but it is not cooking. In cooking it is said that 'the proof of the pudding is in the eating' whereas in the reconstruction of artists' materials, 'the proof of the pigment / paint / passage / painting is in the looking' and not – bearing in mind the conflict between hospital clinicians and laboratory scientists – in the measuring.[11] (Although in fact, tasting was also a part of quality control for artists' ingredients such as gum arabic (Clarke 2011: 118), or for assessing preparations such as azurite (Clarke 2011: 105), and it even determined chemical nomenclature – lead acetate was known as 'sugar of lead' because of its sweet taste.) However, in the absence of access to a living craft tradition, the individual's guidance depends upon the interpretation of written instructions. If this is true of simple cooking instructions, which vary widely in style and content, then it is also true of the similarly varied instructions left by artists in their manuals. And the older they are, the harder they are to interpret.

Artists' recipes

Some artists' ingredients were straight from the kitchen and would have been very familiar to cooks. For example, arrowroot was used as a thickener for soups (Mrs Beeton 1907: 154), and it was also used in nineteenth-century paint recipes.[12] Artists' manuals also contain hints about issues of gender and status in the workshop similar to those found in the kitchen. For example, Cennino described the

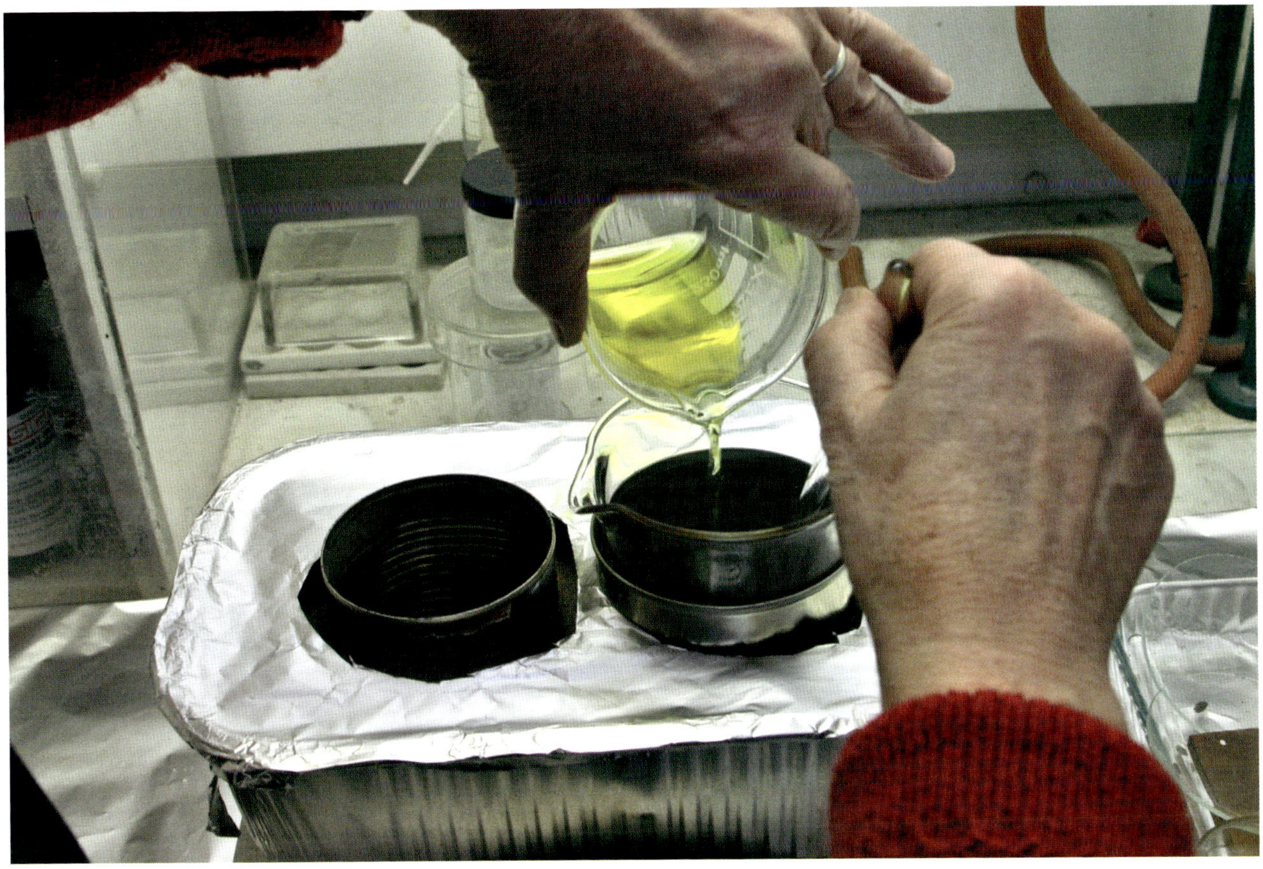

Figure 7 *Making amber varnish in a sand bath.*

purification of lapis lazuli to make ultramarine 'an occupation for pretty girls rather than men' and, without any explanation, warned 'Just beware of old women' (Cennini 1960: 39).

The reality of pigment production may have differed from the rhetoric since the finest ultramarine purchased in 1508 by Michelangelo for the Sistine Chapel was probably made by (male) Jesuits (Gage 1993: 137) and Cennino recommended (male) friars as a source of vermilion recipes (Cennini 1960: 24), so it is likely that different social constraints were associated with different materials. Cennino also described how to make verdigris, which he said was 'manufactured by alchemy', but did not specify the alchemist's gender (Cennini 1960: 33). From the twelfth century onwards, verdigris was manufactured in and around Montpellier and by the eighteenth century Montpellier verdigris was exported across Europe (Benhamou 1984: 172). Only one part of the process involved men, bonded workers who crushed the verdigris – all aspects of the craft and trade were controlled by women.[13] Earthenware pots, 'seed' copper strips, process details and trade positions were handed from mother to daughter and it was said that these women 'seemed to glow with health, from the octogenarians who had spent sixty years in the trade to the newborns who accompanied their mothers to the job' (Benhamou 1984: 177). All Montpellier verdigris trade was controlled by eight female brokers. In the late eighteenth century the average female wage was 60% that of equivalent work by a male. However, one of the verdigris brokers earned 12 times the wage of an average craftsman and more than double Diderot's income as he was assembling his Encyclopaedia (Benhamou 1984: 180).

Economically significant quantities of verdigris are no longer made by women in the south of France nor is the best ultramarine now made by Jesuits in Florence.[14] What remain of historic practices are surviving examples of the end products, paintings, and a small number of treatises that describe the processes. Unlike the authors of the four roast chicken recipes, the authors of historic artists' manuals were not attempting to describe processes that might have been practised 150 years earlier in a foreign country. Some authors, such as Johannes Alcherius (a lawyer) and Théodore Turquet de Mayerne (a doctor) described practices that they had observed as interested parties. But other authors, such as the craftsmen Theophilus and Cennino, described their own practice which they would have known intimately, although they nonetheless left many gaps in their written accounts. Yet the lack of specificity in many, if not most, historic artists' manuals need not necessarily be interpreted as the author's inability to specify. Like Madame Benshaw, Richard Sennett's Persian émigré cookery teacher – or, for completely different reasons, like the scientist who reports his work with no reference to personal struggle – the artist may have simply chosen not to specify some aspects of the process.

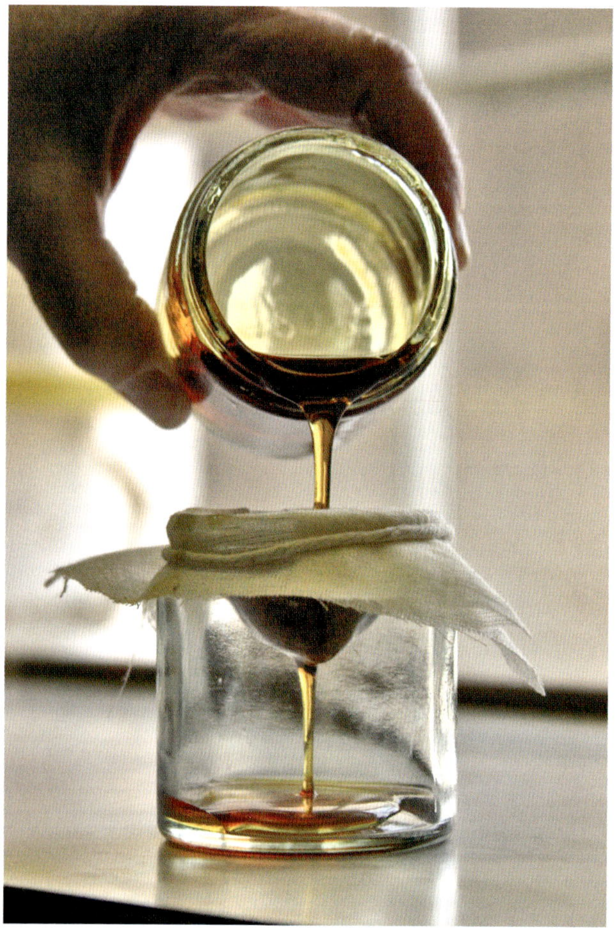

Figure 8 *Filtering amber varnish through muslin.*

Which particular aspects of artists' processes were documented, and how they were documented, depended upon the motivation of the author or compiler of the manual and their level of practical experience or reasons for writing. The result is that recipes appear to be very selective. For example, more written descriptions of the process for preparing ultramarine exist than the process for preparing azurite, yet it is probable that, in practice, more azurite was used than ultramarine. The reasons for the written bias may originate outside the workshop, since ultramarine was more expensive and prestigious than azurite. But reasons for the bias may also have existed inside the workshop, since ultramarine's preparation was easily specifiable (it involved numerous identifiable ingredients) whilst azurite's was relatively un-specifiable (it involved complex bodily actions) (Bucklow and Woudhuysen-Keller forthcoming).

Artists were not alone in this bias against documenting manual dexterity and embodied skills. At its very outset, the modern scientific programme also chose to focus on techniques that could be characterised with materials, dismissing tasks 'which consist principally in the subtle motion of the hands or instruments [as] less use' (Bacon 1605: 257–8; Houghton 1941: 38). The influence of this centuries-old materialist approach to studying craft can still be seen in conference proceedings and academic papers that report the application of modern science to the study of artists' techniques. Other historians, on the other hand, have long recognised that craft techniques 'were only the visible tip of a submerged mass of relationships' (Mathias 1975: 110) so that crafts could operate effectively only within the 'gestural collectives' or 'communities of skill' that were specifically located both historically and geographically (Sibum 1995).

In other words, artists' techniques were dependent upon social factors outside the workshop that cannot be reconstructed. But to the extent that they can, factors within the workshop have to be considered if artists' techniques are to be reconstructed with any success. And when attempting to reconstruct factors within the workshop it is important to acknowledge that even that which is documented is not certain. For example, artists' materials were not standardised. Whether natural or synthetic in origin, materials were prepared in relatively small batches that could show significant chemical variation both between and within batches (Cennini 1960: 34). Yet artists were less interested in their materials' chemical identity than in their physical properties and variations in physical properties could be adjusted by changes in craft practice or by the addition of compensating ingredients.[15] Artists were, of course, used to accommodating variation because physical properties, such as drying times, varied with the weather and seasons as well as from batch to batch.

Consequently, although modern science can characterise some artists' materials with precision, the value of that information is limited by modern science's disengagement from artists' methods. It follows that reconstructions of artists' techniques (a combination of their materials and their less well characterised methods) cannot aim for precision. In that respect, reconstructions of historic artists' techniques constitute approximate 'diagnostic adventures' rather than exact deductive tests (Hacking 1975: 35–7), and thereby inevitably retain an aspect of the original 'craft mysteries'.

Reconstructions

Reconstructions play a central part in training conservators at the Hamilton Kerr Institute (HKI), just as copying historically played a central part in training artists in studios.[16] The primary role of these reconstructions is to give the student a tangible experience of the painting process. This is deemed desirable because there is a qualitative difference between the formal study of paintings and engagement in the process of painting. For example, pigments and media can be identified and the sequence of work can be determined with some confidence by analysis, but the working properties of single materials, composites and laminate are much more complex.

So, a microscopic cross-section through paint can identify a layer of bole (red clay in glue) or a layer of gold, and

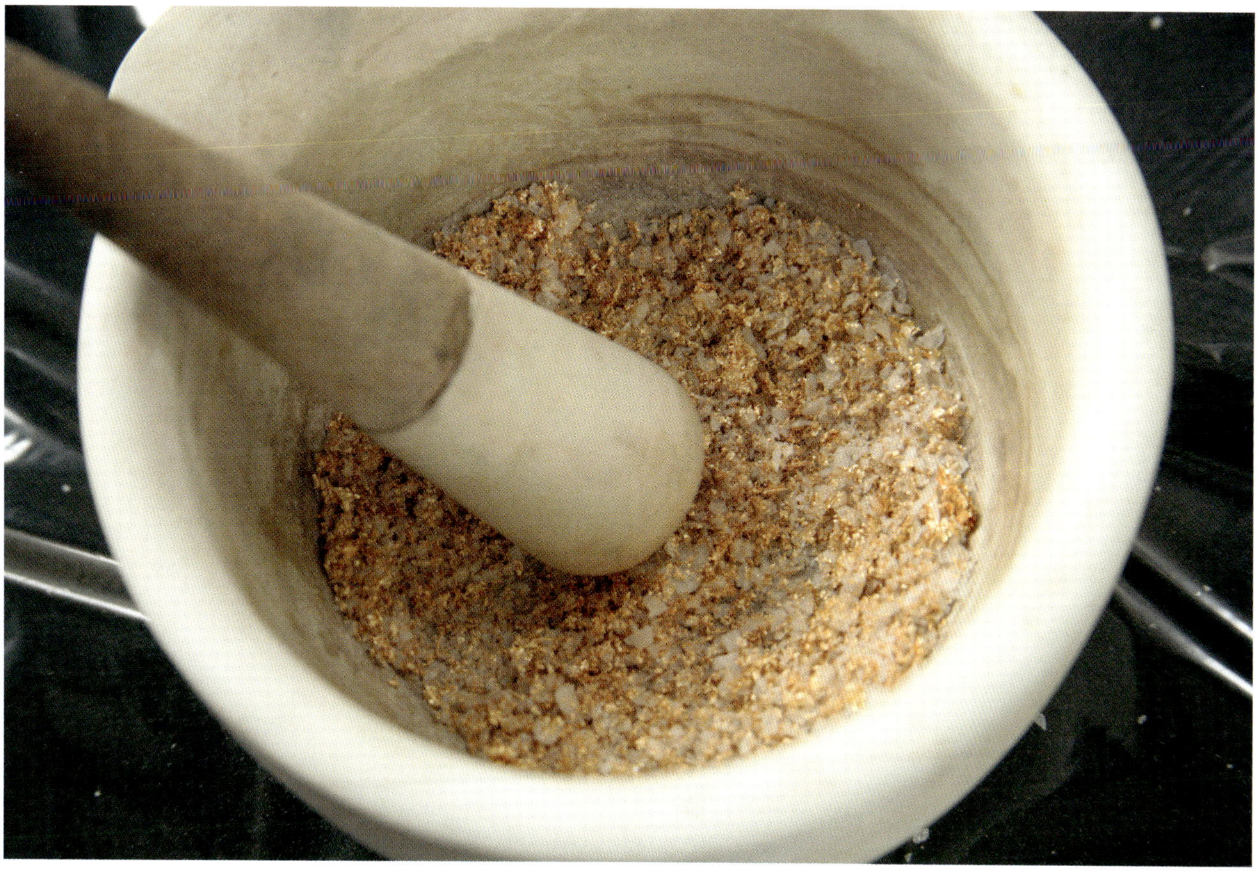

Figure 9 *Making shell gold from gold leaf and salt.*

each layer can be measured. The typical thickness of gold leaf is around one quarter of a micron, or 250 nanometres (Bomford *et al.* 1996: 22). Such a fact might be of interest to a historian of science because medieval artists were able to work within one or two orders of magnitude of what is now called nano-technology, equipped with nothing more than a hammer, anvil and earth-impregnated animal skins (Theophilus 1979: 29–30). Yet nanometres and microns are very far from our everyday experience so the quantification of gilding remains an abstract concept. The experience of gilding, on the other hand, is visceral. If the leaf is touched with a finger it can adhere so strongly that it is destroyed by any attempt to remove it; also, breathing at the wrong time can cause the sheet of gold to float through the air and fall in a crumpled mass.

Of course, quantitative analyses of cross-sections through gilding have their value (Bucklow 2009b: 344), but I would suggest that the student's visceral experience of gilding is a more effective way of imparting a working understanding of gilded panel paintings. At the HKI, it is hoped to extend this aspect of reconstructions as tools for studying the working properties of materials by collaborating with contemporary artists.[17]

A secondary value of reconstructions is their ability to illustrate processes, where they are left incomplete, and, where completed, to illustrate the approximate original appearance of paintings that have changed over time. This last function can also be fulfilled by digital reconstructions.[18] Such illustrations cannot be definitive, yet they impart information in a readily accessible manner and can be reinforced by information that is less immediately accessible in artists' treatises. For example, seventeenth-century painters extended their range of green pigments with mixtures of blue and yellow. They did not paint blue leaves in flower pieces, but used mixtures of permanent blues and fugitive yellows, which have since faded to radically shift the colour balance in their work.

No claims are made that the HKI's reconstructions are historically accurate. Such claims have been made elsewhere within the conservation profession and technical art history but an informed debate about historical authenticity has not taken place, as it has in other disciplines (Butt 2002). Indeed, it might be fair to say that 'historical accuracy' is to technical art history what 'reversibility' is to conservation, and reversibility has been called a 'Holy Grail' and a 'utopian myth' (Muñoz Viñas 2002: 25). No one, for example, would claim that a modern setting of a Shakespeare play is historically accurate, even if performed on the stage of London's Globe Theatre (a modern reconstruction of a seventeenth-century theatre, built in the shadow of a re-purposed mid-twentieth-century power station). However, even a Shakespeare production seen in a modern cinema can provide a flavour of the original and offer insight. Likewise, the reconstructions outlined in this volume offer flavours and insights when interpreted with knowledge of their limitations.

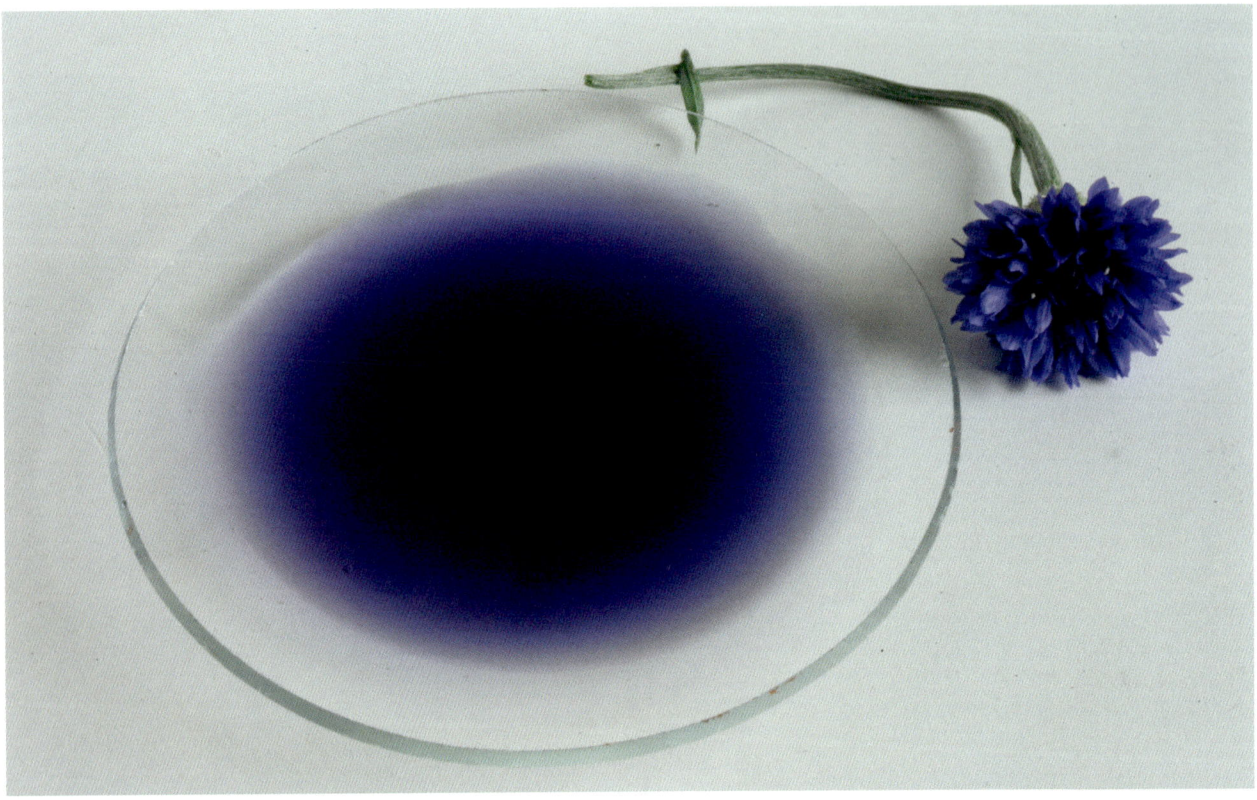

Figure 10 *Cornflower blue extract.*

The supposed historical accuracy of a reconstructed pigment, paint or painting is a reflection, in the conservation profession, of science's focus on replicability or repeatability – something that has been called an 'obsession' that 'distracts from the real problem which is faulty [experimental] design' (Lehrer 2010: 56). Experimental designs for reconstructing pigments, paints and paintings differ, as do the expectations of repeatability. The conditions under which pigments are reconstructed may be theoretically repeatable (such as laboratory experiments) whereas the conditions under which paintings are painted are not at all repeatable. And theoretically, the replicability of simple paint reconstructions would be somewhere between the two. Yet in reality, even the reconstruction of historic pigments is far less replicable than modern laboratory experiments, which are themselves less than perfectly replicable as we have seen.

Reconstructions are, in part, informed by the technical examination of paintings. But here again their precision is limited because the scientific analysis of works of art has not yet addressed the issue of replicability. Indeed, a survey of those paintings that have been analysed shows that much laboratory-based instrumental activity could be seen as 'glitz and showboating rather than serious science' because of its heavy bias on big-name artists.[19] On the other hand, housewife chemistry – such as the reconstruction of pigments, paints and paintings – has the potential to go a significant way towards addressing issues of repeatability and significance, precisely because it engages directly with the craft uncertainties associated with tacit knowledge, undocumented and embodied skills.

It has been said that 'for many current scientific fields, claimed research findings may often be simply [little more than] accurate measures of the prevailing bias' (Ioannidis 2005: 1). Given this assessment of the current 'scientific' method, the differences between the laboratory-based instrumental analysis of paintings and the studio-based practical reconstructions of paintings could be reassessed. And indeed, analogous questions have been raised comparing laboratory-based and clinic-based activities in medicine (Vandenbroucke 2004). It is therefore to be hoped that the fruits of housewife chemistry – even if imprecise – may be given more credence in future.

In addition to the pigment and paint reconstructions alluded to in this paper, paintings have been reconstructed over a period of 30 or more years. Some have been on television,[20] one is in a museum next to the fragmented original (Heard and Bucklow 2009), but the majority are still in the HKI.[21] Each reconstruction offered unique experiences for the individuals involved and also provides a general understanding for students who follow, as well as a potential research resource. Whilst the reconstructions outlined in this volume may not be 'historically accurate', rigorous efforts have been made to ensure that they are – to borrow a phrase from the discipline of music – 'historically informed'. The following guidelines have informed all reconstructions of artists' materials and methods at the HKI:

- Reconstructions try to emulate processes rather than products.

- Ingredients are as close as to the originals as can be determined.[22]
- Tools are as close as possible to those that were originally available.[23]
- The success or failure of the task is judged by hand and eye.[24]
- There is always more than one solution to a problem.
- If it does not work now, then it was not what the artist did.
- If it does work now, then it may be related to what the artist did.
- If it is quick and simple, then it may be closer to what the artist did.

Of course, this final guideline must also acknowledge that a 'quick and simple' solution may be slow and hard to obtain and that a complex problem can be solved incrementally as a series of smaller problems, each of which may have 'quick and simple' solutions. (See, for example, the white-ribbed tulip in the painting by Jan van Os.[25])

The tacit subsuming of multiple simple problems into complex un-specifiable tasks is one reason why the skills involved in housewifery, or indeed any other craft activity, are today increasingly unrecognised. Contemporary 'tick-box' and 'bean-counting' culture puts a premium on accountability and those tasks that cannot be fully specified tend to be overlooked.[26] The cookery (as opposed to cleaning) side of Renate Woudhuysen-Keller's 'housewife chemistry' explores how a painter's vision was materialised, investigating the gap between what artists wrote and what can be observed in their paintings.

Such housewife chemistry can reopen the door to the sensuous data that was effectively banished by post-Lavoisier-style science (Perrin 1981). One of its values is to bring back into focus the historic artist's extraordinary, but largely unsung, craft skills. The insights obtained by exploring such high-level human skills are a source of inspiration for many students of art and, given the neglect of craft and its indispensable role in many activities, those insights have relevance beyond the museum and gallery.

Acknowledgements

I would like to thank the following for recommending reading: Jonathan Ashley Smith (for Lehrer), Sachiko Kusukawa (for Lynch), Nick Marston (for Butt) and Adèle Wright (for Romano). I would also like to thank Lucy Wrapson for suggesting the topic and, most of all, Renate Woudhuysen-Keller for teaching me about artists' techniques. I also gratefully acknowledge the support of the Monument Trust.

Notes

1. The crushed insect extract, a mixture of anthraquinone derivatives, is absorbed into the substrate generated thus: $2AlK(SO_4)_2 + 3K_2CO_3 + 3H_2O \rightarrow 2Al(OH)_3\downarrow + 4K_2SO_4 + 3CO_2\uparrow$.
2. Many chemicals have found their way from the modern domestic and cosmetic contexts into the conservation studio; see Bucklow forthcoming.
3. C.P. Snow, British scientist and novelist, gave a highly influential Rede lecture on 7 May 1959 at Senate House in Cambridge (UK), lamenting the split between the sciences and humanities, see Snow 1959.
4. Renate Woudhuysen-Keller discussed this when interviewed for the FAIC Oral History Project which is housed at Winterthur Museum, Library, and Archives, USA.
5. It is not just awkward facts about practical difficulties that are elided from the literature as it is also rare for the effect of an individual's personal qualities to be acknowledged formally in professional literature; see Grevenstein-Kruse and van der Wetering, in this vol.
6. See, for example, Kimbriel and Noh, in this vol.
7. See, for example, Lara Broecke ('Reconstructing the preparation layers of a late fifteenth-century panel painting from Seville') and Alison Stock ('Preparing a copper panel for painting; a late sixteenth-century reconstruction'), in this vol.
8. Conversion factors are: °C = (°F – 32) × 5/9 and °F = (°C × 9/5) + 32.
9. Joule read the instrument to 1/200 of a degree Fahrenheit; see Sibum 1995: 76, 105.
10. Mothers still know to test a baby's bathwater with their elbow; Mary Kempski, pers. comm., December 2011.
11. Artists are interested in the appearance of paint layers, not their thickness. The two are connected, but attention is given to the former, not the latter. Similarly, pianists are interested in sounds and 'attend through' their fingers. The reconstruction of a score is therefore judged in terms of musical effect rather than muscular performance; see Polanyi (1967: 18).
12. Winsor & Newton. www.hki.fitzmuseum.cam.ac.uk/archives/wn/detail1.php?urc=10P022L01.
13. The female domination of these aspects of working copper are cosmologically appropriate since copper was a 'feminine' metal, associated with the planet Venus which was, in turn, personified by the goddess of love; see Bucklow 2009a: 118–26.
14. As an aside, Winsor & Newton's artists' paint brushes are made by women in the port of Felixstowe. The townswomens' manual dexterity had previously been employed in mending fishing nets. Ian Garrett, pers. comm., October 2011.
15. These ingredients could be transitory (diluents) or in minute quantities (surfactants) and therefore difficult to detect reliably. Also, very small variations within individual ingredients (particle sizes) can have very large consequences.
16. See Chui and Phenix, in this vol.
17. With Sigrid Holmwood (dyestuffs) and with Onya McCausland (earths), for example.
18. See Titmus, in this vol.
19. This charge could also be levelled at technical art history because of its use of technical images (see Beaulieu 2002). Just as models in mass media are airbrushed, so scientific imagery is also heavily processed (Lynch 1985). Mainstream science has recognised the need to regulate illustrative materials (Editorial 2006) but conservation science and technical art history have yet to follow.
20. See Miller and Patrick, in this vol.
21. See Kempski, in this vol.
22. Except where the reconstruction fulfils a limited didactic role; see Miller and Patrick, in this vol.
23. Historic tools were not reconstructed, but modern hand (not power) tools are used.
24. For example, reconstructions have yet to be systematically examined by paint cross-section.
25. See Bucklow ('Reconstruction of a fruit and flower piece by Jan van Os'), in this vol.
26. This tendency has its roots in the eighteenth century. See, for example, the 1737 retraining of Gobelins' dyers, which was structured in a manner that was further developed in the military; see Foucault 1979: 156–9.

References

Ashley Smith, J. 2000a. 'Letter to the editor', *Chemistry in Britain* 36(7): 22–3.

Ashley Smith, J. 2000b. 'Developing professional uncertainty'. In *Tradition and Innovation*, A. Roy and P. Smith (eds) 14–17. London: IIC.

Bacon, F. 1605. *Of the Proficience and Advancement of Learning, Divine and Human*. Oxford: Leon Lichfield.

Beaulieu, A. 2002. 'Images are not the (only) truth; brain mapping, visual knowledge and iconoclasm', *Science Technology and Human Values* 27(1): 53–86.

Beeton, I. 1907. *Mrs Beeton's Book of Household Management*. London: Ward, Lock and Co.

Benhamou, R. 1984. 'Verdigris and the entrepreneuse', *Technology and Culture* 25(2): 171–81.

Bomford, D., Dunkerton, J., Gordon. D., Roy, A. and Kirby, J. 1996. *Art in the Making: Italian Painting before 1400*. London: National Gallery Publications.

Bucklow, S. 2009a. *The Alchemy of Paint*. London: Marion Boyars.

Bucklow, S. 2009b. 'Materials, wages and painting at Westminster'. In *The Westminster Retable: History, Technique, Conservation*, P. Binski and A. Massing (eds) 341–53. Turnhout: Harvey Miller Publishers.

Bucklow, S. forthcoming. 'The cultural context of cleaning science'. In *Going Beneath the Surface*, L. Humphreys (ed.).

Bucklow, S. and Woudhuysen-Keller, R. forthcoming. 'Processes and pigment recipes; azurite', *The Hamilton Kerr Institute Bulletin* 4.

Butt, J. 2002. *Playing with History: The Historical Approach to Musical Performance*. Cambridge: Cambridge University Press.

Cennini, Cennino 1960. *The Craftsman's Handbook, 'Il libro dell'arte'*, D.V. Thompson (tr.). New York: Dover Publications.

Chang, H. 2004. *Inventing Temperature: Measurement and Scientific Progress*. Oxford: Oxford University Press.

Child, J. and Beck, S. 1970. *Mastering the Art of French Cooking*. New York: Knopf.

Clarke, M. 2011. *Medieval Painters' Materials and Techniques: The Montpellier* Liber diversarum arcium. London: Archetype Publications.

Clavir, M. 1998. 'The social and historical construction of professional value in conservation', *Studies in Conservation* 43(1): 1–8.

Clemens, J.R. 1933. 'Fifteenth century English recipes for the making of pigments', *Art and Archaeology* 34: 206–10.

David, E. 1970. *French Provincial Cooking*. London: Penguin.

Delamont, S. and Atkinson, P. 2002. 'Doctoring uncertainty; mastering craft knowledge', *Social Studies of Science* 31(1): 87–107.

Eamon, W. 1982. *Studies on Medieval Fachliterature*. Brussels: Scripta, Medieval and Renaissance Texts and Studies.

Eamon, W. 1994. *Science and the Secrets of Nature*. Princeton, NJ: Princeton University Press.

Editorial 2006. 'Not picture-perfect', *Nature* 439: 891–2.

Foucault, M. 1979. *Discipline and Punishment: The Birth of the Prison*. Harmondsworth: Peregrine.

Gage, J. 1993. *Colour and Culture*. London: Thames and Hudson.

Hacking, I. 1975. *The Emergence of Probability*. Cambridge: Cambridge University Press.

Heard, C. and Bucklow, S. 2009. 'Reconstruction of the Westminster Retable'. In *The Westminster Retable: History, Technique, Conservation*, P. Binski and A. Massing (eds) 392–400. Turnhout: Harvey Miller Publishers.

Houghton, W.E. 1941. 'The history of trades: its relation to seventeenth century thought as seen in Bacon, Evelyn and Boyle', *Journal of the History of Ideas* 2(1): 33–60.

Ioannidis, J.P.A. 2005. 'Why most published research findings are false', *Public Library of Science, Medicine* 2(8) e124. www.plosmedicine.org/article/info:doi/10.1371/journal.pmed.0020124.

Lehrer, J. 2010. 'The truth wears off', *The New Yorker* 13 December 2010: 52–7.

Lynch, M. 1985. 'Discipline and the material form of images: an analysis of scientific visibility', *Social Studies of Science* 15(1): 37–66.

Mathias, P. 1975. 'Skills and the diffusion of innovations from Britain in the eighteenth century', *Transactions of the Royal Historical Society* 25: 93–113.

Merrifield, M.P. 1967. *Original Treatises on the Arts of Painting*, 2 vols. New York: Dover Publications.

Muñoz Viñas, S. 2002 'Contemporary theory of conservation', *Reviews in Conservation* 3: 25–34.

Olney, R. 1985. *The French Menu Cookbook*. Boston: Godine.

Perrin, C.E. 1981. 'The triumph of the Antiphlogistians'. In *The Analytic Spirit: Essays in the History of Science in honour of Henry Guerlac*, H. Woolf (ed.) 40–63. Ithaca, NY: Cornell University Press.

Polanyi, M. 1967. *The Tacit Dimension*. London: Routledge and Kegan Paul.

Romano, D. 1996. *Housecraft and Statecraft: Domestic Service in Renaissance Venice*, 1400–1600. Baltimore, MD: Johns Hopkins University Press.

Sacks, S. 1981. *On Metaphor*. Chicago: University of Chicago Press.

Sennett, R. 2008. *The Craftsman*. London: Allen Lane.

Sibum, H.O. 1995. 'Reworking the mechanical value of heat', *Studies in the History and Philosophy of Science* 26(1): 73–106.

Smith, D. 1998. 'Conversion tables'. In *Delia's How to Cook, Book 1*. London: BBC Worldwide.

Snow, C.P. (1959) *The Two Cultures and the Scientific Revolution*. Cambridge: Cambridge University Press.

Sutton, D. 2006. 'Cooking skill, the senses and memory: the fate of practical knowledge'. In *Sensible Objects: Colonialism, Museums and Material Culture*, E. Edwards, C. Gosden and R.B. Phillips (eds) 87–118. Oxford: Berg.

Theophilus 1979. *On Divers Arts: The Foremost Treatise on Painting, Glassmaking and Metalwork*, J.G. Hawthorne and C.S. Smith (tr.). New York: Dover Publications.

Vandenbroucke, J.P. 2004. 'When are observational studies as credible as randomised trials?' *The Lancet* 363: 1728–31.

Wigney, G.A. 1835. *Theoretical and Practical Treatise on Malting and Brewing*. Brighton: Philips and Co.

Woudhuysen-Keller, R. 2001. *Das Farbbuechlin Codex 431 aus dem Kloster Engelberg. Ein Rezeptbuch über Farben zum Färben, Screiben und Malen aus dem späten 16. Jahrhundert*. PhD dissertation, University of Zürich.

TOWARDS A NEW ENGLISH CENNINO

Lara Broecke

Introduction

The idea to make a new translation of Cennino Cennini's *Il libro dell'arte*, the well-known Italian treatise on artists' techniques, thought to have been written *c.*1400, grew out of a project to reconstruct an early Italian painted crucifix as a commission for the Catholic Chaplaincy in Cambridge (Fig. 1).[1] In the course of this work, Cennino's treatise was frequently consulted in Thompson's translation (Cennini 1960). In order to clarify some points, the English translation was compared with the Italian edition by the Milanesi (Cennini 1859); this brought to light discrepancies between the two texts, prompting the realisation that more than one interpretation of the original manuscripts might be possible, and that this might not always be signalled in Thompson's translation. In order to ascertain the extent of the weaknesses in Thompson's translation it was necessary to compare it to the original manuscripts.[2] On doing so, a large number of problems, varying in their nature and magnitude, were uncovered. Thompson himself was aware of some of these, stating in his unpublished papers of the 1970s:

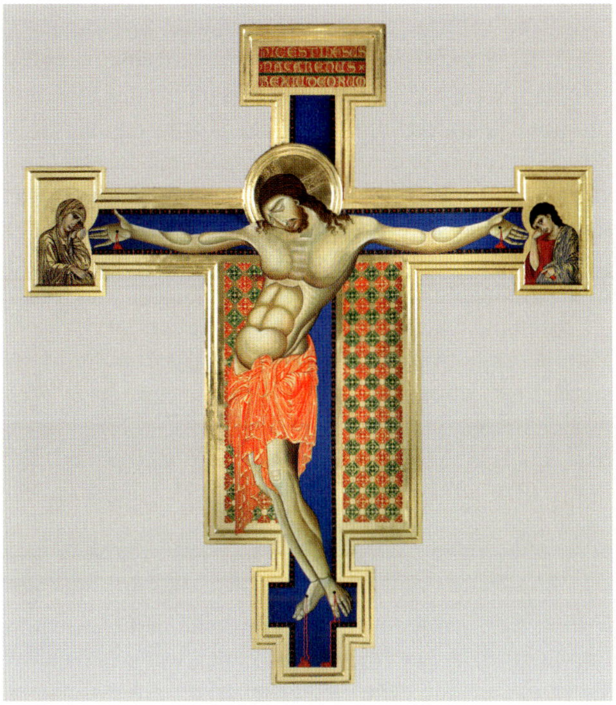

Figure 1 *A reconstruction of an early Italian-style crucifix.*

> My translation of Cennino's *Libro dell'Arte* was made nearly fifty years ago and shows its age though for want of a better it is still read. The workshop English of 1930 is no longer current. That I cannot correct. But over the years since The Craftsman's Handbook first appeared I have become aware of faults which need to be corrected. (Clarke 2007)

The most pressing of these, in Thompson's opinion, was the translation of the word *pastello* in chapters 60 and 62 of the treatise (on the preparation of azurite and ultramarine) as 'plastic' (Cennini 1960: 35, 37–8):

> Not only has the word 'plastic' taken on a multitude of meanings then undreamt of and all inappropriate; but the key to the right translation lay unnoticed in the text. When all the ingredients have been put together, Cennino says clearly 'Poi … fanne un pastello, tutto incorporato insieme.' That is, the *pastello* is something not to be compounded but to be made out of a mixture already compounded, in this case that can be nothing but a 'cake'. And 'cake' is a legitimate translation of *pastello*. (Clarke 2007)

Outdated English, however, was not the only problem to be uncovered in Thompson's translation. There were straightforward mistakes of translation and omission of individual words, there were instances of erroneous interpretation of the Italian grammar, ambiguities or alternative readings not signalled in the translation or notes, unnecessary 'corrections' to the Italian to make it read better or to disguise mistakes made by Cennino himself and there was one intentional omission towards the end of chapter 70 for reasons, seemingly, of propriety. Most of these problems were relatively insignificant in themselves but together, over the whole treatise, they amounted to a misrepresentation of the original Italian.

This accusation of misrepresentation is not made here in a spirit of shaming or ridiculing Thompson, whose translation was a vast improvement on its predecessors, is widely read, and has served its purpose admirably since its first publication in 1933. However, as Thompson himself put it in reference to Lady Herringham's 1899 translation of Cennino (Herringham 1930), 'I venture to criticize it … not in dispraise of her translation, for it has shown its merit, but rather to justify a new one' (Cennini 1960: x). Thompson wrote this a mere 34 years after the publication of Lady Herringham's translation; 79 years after the publication of Thompson's translation critical investigation has, once again, justified a new version.

The manuscripts

The first task for the translator of any medieval literature must be to decide which source should be translated. Most medieval literature exists in more than one manuscript; the readings in these manuscripts will vary, as copyists over the years will have made errors and emendations which are then repeated and augmented in each subsequent copy. If two different copyists have copied the same manuscript then two different heritages of errors and emendations will exist concurrently; in fact, for many manuscripts there are more than two. Some of the manuscripts will not have survived to the present day and the provenance of those which do survive may be difficult to establish.

In the case of medieval artists' manuals, which usually take the form of collections of 'recipes', the problems are compounded by the fact that an 'original' manuscript may, in addition to original material, also contain material that is drawn from already existing manuals; subsequent copyists may then have removed or added material to suit their purposes. Hawthorne and Smith note, for example, of Theophilus, 'Most of the manuscripts were copied as component parts of compilations of information from several different sources and many contain interpolations from other works … with nothing to indicate the different origin of this material' (Theophilus 1979: xviii); Clarke describes the Montpellier *Liber diversarum arcium* (LDA) as consisting of many original recipes, probably written around 1300, but also a number of earlier Northern European recipes, all supplemented with Italian recipes added by fourteenth-century copyists (Clarke 2011: 1).

A key question for the translator then is: of what does the 'authentic text' consist? Does it include compiled material as well as original material? If some manuscripts include particular material which others omit, how should that material be handled? Which of several similar manuscripts should be selected as the basis for the translation, and is it permissible to combine manuscripts in order to create a more comprehensive source?

Fortunately, in the case of Cennino, the position is not as complicated as with some other texts. The content all appears to be original and, although four manuscripts exist, two are considerably later copies made directly from the earliest manuscript. The earliest extant manuscript (part of Codice Mediceo Laurenziano P.78.23), usually known as L, has been held by the Biblioteca Mediceo-Laurenziana in Florence since at least 1575. The date 1437, given at the end of the manuscript, is supported both by the style of script and the watermark on the paper (Cennini 2006: 33–5). The vocabulary of the manuscript contains many words of northern Italian, Venetian and Paduan dialect, probably reflecting Cennino's biography, which saw him in Padua between at least 1398 and 1401, with a Paduan wife (Cennini 2006: 13, 20).

Manuscript R, in the library of the Palazzo Medici-Riccardi (Codice Riccardiano 2190), can be dated by its script to the late sixteenth or early seventeenth century. In this manuscript the dialect words have been 'tuscanised' and where there are obvious errors of transcription they are different from those found in L, showing that R is independent of L.

Manuscripts P (Codice Palatino 818 in the Biblioteca Nazionale Centrale di Firenze) and V (Codice Vaticano Ottoboniano 2974 in the Biblioteca Vaticana) are clear copies of L, preserving its dialect words, omissions and errors and introducing errors of their own.

In view of its early date and 'authentic' vocabulary, L would seem the obvious choice as the basis for a translation. However, a page from L has been lost and the text presumably contained in this page is attested only in R. For this reason, it is logical, while using L as the principal basis for a translation, to supplement it with the missing section from R. It is also useful to consult R for possible clarification where it is difficult to either read or understand L.

The importance to the translator or editor of choosing a sound basis from which to work is paramount. Many earlier translations and editions of Cennino have been found to contain errors caused by their reliance on an unsound source and have therefore been superseded. The first Italian edition of Cennino, made by Tambroni in 1821, was based on manuscript V. This meant that the material from L's missing page was not presented and also that errors in transcription made by the copyist of V were retransmitted by Tambroni. The first translation into English, by Mrs Merrifield in 1844, was based on the Tambroni edition. The second translation into English, by Lady Herringham in 1899, was based on the Milanesi edition of 1859 which, although made from manuscripts L and R and an improvement on Tambroni, included errors of transcription and interpretation.

Thompson's translation, first published in 1933 and reissued in 1960, was based on his own careful edition of the Italian, using photographs of manuscripts L and R (Cennini 1932). It therefore represented a significant improvement on its predecessors. In addition to a translation which was more faithful to the earlier manuscripts, Thompson also offered useful notes based on his extensive knowledge of early writings on artists' materials and techniques and his practical experience of tempera painting. Almost every page of the book attests to the latter and it is evident that Thompson was sincere when he wrote in its preface, 'the real business of translation is a "laboratory" matter, involving a knowledge of each rule in practice' (Cennini 1960: xiii).

A major difficulty in the translation of technical treatises is that the necessary practical and intellectual skills and experience are rarely combined in one person. Linguistic ability must be coupled with historical knowledge of the society in which the original treatise was written, practical experience of the processes described (which will ensure knowledge of correct equivalent technical terms and without which it is almost impossible to interpret some of the more convoluted explanations that the translator may encounter) and a good acquaintance with comparable texts; in the case of art technological sources some knowledge of chemistry and physics will also be desirable, as will facility of expression in any translator. In Thompson these diverse attributes came together and it is unsurprising that he has gone unchallenged for almost 80 years. Only by engaging in extensive consultation, enlisting the assistance of a wide variety of experts, can a new translator hope to succeed.

'Mistakes' and discrepancies

Having once fixed on a source text to use as the basis for the translation, the translator must decide how to deal with apparent 'mistakes' in this text and with discrepancies between it and the other extant texts. 'Mistakes' in the text may take many forms and each will require a different approach. In some cases, by comparing texts it may be possible to deduce that a mistake existed in the original (non-extant) manuscript. For example, if a mistake recurs in two or more independent manuscripts it is likely to derive from an earlier text from which both manuscripts descend. In the case of Cennino, since L is close in date to the conjectured date at which the treatise was originally written, mistakes that are common to both L and R are likely to have been present in Cennino's own manuscript. Frezzato notes several editorial-type problems in Cennino which are common to both L and R, such as the never-to-be-fulfilled promise, in chapter 31, to explain the use of gum arabic later in the treatise and the announcement of the end of the fourth part of the book at the beginning of chapter 103 and then again at the beginning of chapter 112. He says of these anomalies: 'The examples cited reveal a jumbled state of affairs for which the copyists cannot easily be held responsible; more likely, it is due to the fact that the work was never brought to completion'[3] (Cennini 2006: 23).

In this case there is nothing to be done; the translator cannot insert into the treatise an explanation of how to use gum arabic, and choosing at which of the two points to end the fourth section of the book would constitute a major, arbitrary intervention. The translator must then accept that the original is flawed and present it as such.

The same approach can be applied to single word mistakes in the original text. For example, in chapter 83 of his treatise, describing the painting of blue drapery on walls, Cennino advises that the drapery should first be laid in with a dark brown colour in fresco; both L and R then read, 'Then, in fresco, take azurite … add a little glue to it … In addition, add an egg yolk to this blue.'[4] The fact that binders are being added to the blue pigment shows that it is not being used in *fresco*, but in *secco*; Cennino has clearly made a slip here and written *frescho* where he meant *secco*. It would be tempting to correct this mistake in the translation, perhaps with a footnote to indicate the correction. However, if the idea of the translation is to present Cennino's 'original' text as nearly as possible to the reader then this is as much a falsification as adding a section on the use of gum arabic would be; to translate *secco* where Cennino wrote *frescho* would be to translate his presumed intention and not his actual text. In this case the translator should surely write 'fresco' with a footnote to explain why 'secco' was probably intended.

There are cases, however, where it may be permissible for the translator to 'correct' the original text. One such case occurs in chapter 93 of Cennino's treatise, where L reads, 'Ritorna arritrarre overo macinare di cholore in cholore' (L: 18v)[5] ('Go back to pulling in or pounding one pigment at a time') and R reads similarly, although the spelling is not always the same. *Ritrarre* ('pulling in') makes little sense here, and elsewhere in the treatise the verb *macinare* ('to pound') follows *tritare* or *triare* ('to grind') in a verbal pattern typical of Cennino, where he offers two words of very similar meaning as alternatives.[6] In view of the similarity between *ritrarre* ('to pull in') and *ritriarre* ('to regrind') it seems very likely that Cennino made a simple typographical error. The linking of *triare* with *macinare* would already have been familiar to the reader by this stage in the treatise, therefore the omission of the letter may not have been noticed at all. If there were a convenient English word, just one letter different to 'grinding' and with the meaning 'pulling in', it could perhaps be used here to mirror the mistake in the Italian. However, no such word exists and to translate *ritrarre* as 'pulling in' would give the English-speaking reader the impression of a far more disturbing mistake than actually existed in the original text. It seems more faithful to the original in this case to 'correct' Cennino's mistake in the translation, adding a footnote to explain that this has been done.

Where there is a discrepancy between two manuscripts, this may signal a copyist's error in one or both of the manuscripts. Such errors may result from simple slips or from misunderstandings due to a lack of knowledge of the subject matter. Clarke notes that 'when a practical text was copied by a practising craftsman, the likelihood of an error that results in meaninglessness is naturally very much reduced' (Clarke 2011: 63). However, the likelihood of an intentional adjustment to the text is very much increased, and this is another cause of discrepancies between manuscripts. Neven, discussing a change to recipe ingredients from one manuscript to another, comments that:

> On the one hand, this may be due to palaeographical problems that resulted in a word being misunderstood and thus being replaced by another well-known one; on the other, it may also correspond to a deliberate technical improvement by the author of the recipe. (Neven 2010: 68)

She proposes reconstruction as a useful tool for resolving cases of this kind. However, it is not clear that if one ingredient works better than the other in practice it must therefore be the ingredient intended by the original author of the recipe; as she herself says, the original recipe may have been altered intentionally precisely because it did not work, so that the 'correct' ingredient in practical terms may not be the 'correct' ingredient in terms of reconstruction of the source text.

Some simple slips by the copyist are easy to spot. For example, in chapter 79 of Cennino's treatise, when describing how to paint a shot drapery with lac, L reads 'campegialo di laccha biancha e gialla di carnazion o vuoi di giallorino' (L: 16v) ('lay it in with white and yellow lac, with flesh colour or, if you prefer, with giallorino') while R has 'campeggialo di lacca bianchegialo d'incarnatione, o vuoi di giallorino' (R: 39) ('lay it in with lac, lighten it with flesh colour or, if you prefer, with giallorino'). The reading in L makes no sense as there is no such thing as 'white lac'; moreover, in both the preceding and the succeeding chapters *biancheggialo* ('lighten it') is found in L in very similar contexts to chapter 79 as presented in R. This is a clear case of a copyist losing concentration and not realising the absurdity of what he is writing through lack of knowledge of the subject matter. In this case, the translator can substitute the reading in R for that in L as it is a more likely representation of what would have appeared in Cennino's original text.

There are cases where the mistake is more difficult to spot. In chapters 186 to 188[7] Cennino gives instructions for casting life-size human figures, figurines and medallions in metal or gesso. For the material from which the mould should be made, both L and R repeatedly cite *cera* ('wax') in chapters 186 and 187. It is, however, patently impossible to cast metal or gesso in a wax mould, since the molten metal or hot gesso would melt the mould. Frezzato sensibly suggests reading *crea* (a Venetian form of *creta*, 'clay') for *cera* (Cennini 2006: 233, n. 223; 226–7, n. 140) and *crea* is in fact found in one position in R, in chapter 187, while *terra* ('earth') appears in R in chapter 188. The mistake, which occurs repeatedly, pertains to both manuscripts, therefore it might seem that, as in the case of *frescho* for *secco* (above), the mistake is Cennino's and should be retained in the translation as significant evidence that Cennino is describing processes of which he has no experience. However, while Cennino may not have had direct experience of casting figures, he certainly had experience of working with wax, as many other recipes throughout the treatise feature wax, and he clearly knew that wax becomes liquid on heating. While a passing reference to wax moulds for hot materials might plausibly be put down to a lapse in concentration on Cennino's part, the sustained descriptions in these chapters make it hard to believe that Cennino would not have noticed the problem. It seems far more likely that the copyists, unfamiliar with the processes and materials described and also with the Venetian dialect term *crea* ('clay') both mistakenly 'corrected' the (correct) original to the erroneous but more familiar *cera* ('wax'). The appearance of *crea* ('clay') and *terra* ('earth') in R in chapters 187 and 188 supports this hypothesis. In this case then, the translator may wish to correct the copyists' mistakes in order to render more closely Cennino's original text.

One important thing to bear in mind is that, where there is an awkward or grammatically incorrect reading in one manuscript and a straightforward reading in another, the straightforward one cannot be assumed to be more authentic. In a number of cases the reading of Cennino's treatise in L is clumsy or unexpected while that in R is smooth and predictable. Throughout the treatise, however, Cennino's grammar is somewhat muddled and his use of language unusual, while the tuscanisation of words in R shows that the copyist of R engaged in conscious editing; it therefore seems more likely that the 'sanitised' readings in R stem from well-meaning copyists 'tidying up' Cennino's text rather than that the jarring readings in L derive from copyists' slips. To take one example, towards the end of chapter 134, on gilding, Cennino suggests picking up scraps of gold for faulting with the handle of a brush (Fig. 2). L reads 'bangniando co labri un poco di copo l'asticciuola del pennello' (L: 22r) ('wetting the brush handle with your lips a little cupped') while R reads 'bagniando co labri un poco da capo dell'asticiuola, del peneletto' (R: 58) ('wetting the end of the brush handle a little with your lips'). R has the smoother and more expected reading but there is no reason why the idiosyncratic reading in L should be considered erroneous. As L is closer in date and, most likely, vocabulary (see above) to Cennino's original text than R, the translator should give it preference, while adding

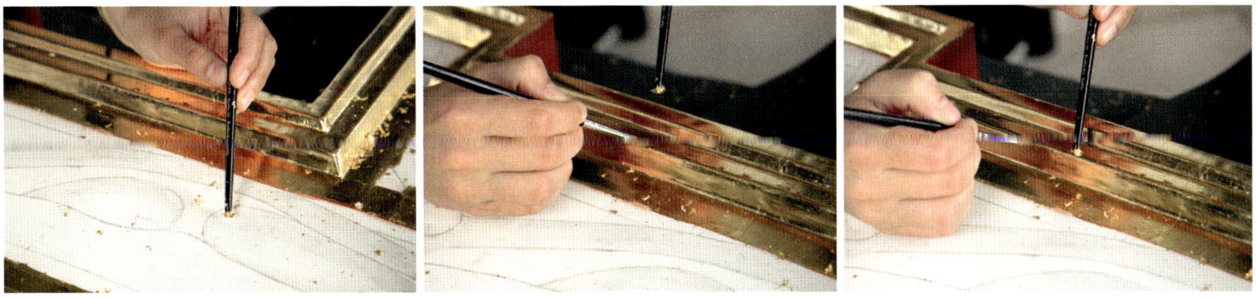

Figure 2 *The process of picking up tiny pieces of gold for faulting using the dampened end of the brush.*

a footnote to alert the reader to the alternative reading in R. Not to allow the reading in L is to risk obliterating the singular character of Cennino's text by mistaking, as perhaps the copyist of R has done in this case, his idiosyncrasies for errors.

Methodology and style

Another problem for the translator, touched upon in the preceding discussion, is how to recognise and render the style of the original. Identifying the style of the text is problematic because elements of style may have been excised or adjusted by copyists, who may then have imposed their own style on the text. In the case of texts constituting collations of recipes, the copying from various sources may mean that there is no uniform style. Clarke recognises this, remarking: 'since the LDA is a composite text, where possible the translation aims to preserve the style of each individual component, to aid in distinguishing phases of compilation' (Clarke 2011: 93).

The collation process may also serve to eliminate personal touches; Clarke (2011: 49) notes that the compiler of the LDA takes out parts of the recipes that are 'impractical, verbose or cover unrelated techniques'. Cennino's text, too, has been subjected to 'normalisation' by the copyists. Frezzato observes that, 'The Venetian dialect terms contained in the manuscripts are what remains after a campaign of tuscanisation waged by the copyists: it is not, therefore, easy to establish how many were originally present'.[8] For the translator this poses a problem: if the original text was entirely in Venetian dialect then there would be no need to signal this in the style of the translation – it would simply be a question of translating from Venetian dialect into modern English. On the other hand, if the original text was in, for example, Tuscan Italian with a sprinkling of Venetian dialect terms (the impression given by the manuscripts), it might be desirable in the translation to try to convey the difference between the dialect terms and the rest of the text. In the case of Cennino, since the nature of the original text is unknown, it seems most sensible to translate it without approaching the dialect terms differently from the rest of the text to avoid giving the reader an impression of disjuncture that the original text may not have had.

There can also be difficulty in separating the author's personal style from the style of the period and place in which the treatise was written. This can only be done by someone familiar with a wide range of literature from the same period and place. It is helpful to try to separate these because it is generally desirable to convey elements of the author's personal style in the translation, while style due to period and place is less desirable; the idea of a translation is usually to render language from another time and place into the modern target language, rather than into something approximating the target language from a similar period to the source text.

Turner writes of translation: 'The work of the translator may be compared to that of the musical arranger who rewrites a piece for a different instrument or group of instruments' (Turner 2006: 168). Having decided on the essence of the text to be translated then, the translator must decide what mode of translation to employ; that is, which instruments to write for. The choice will, of course, depend on the type of literature in question; poetry will require a very different approach to a technical treatise. The approach selected will also depend heavily on the intended readership.

Contemporary readers of technical treatises generally see them as historical documents, and therefore the contemporary approach to translation is often 'archaeological', adhering as closely to the source text as possible. Nadolny champions this methodology, stating that:

> Both translating literally and for meaning are approaches that have certain advantages, but it is important to consider the context. Literal rendition is most preferable, but if it proves unworkable, it is essential that the translator indicates any change to a more interpretive mode. (Nadolny 2008: 7)

One pitfall of this approach is that it can result in awkward English where the original was not awkward, so that the translation is true to the letter but not to the spirit of the original. Clarke warns that 'The apparently consistent clarity in the best known of published mediaeval craft treatises is spurious, and is largely the result of over-interpretation and over-smoothed translations that are more in the nature of paraphrases' (Clarke 2011: 62). The translator must, of course, beware of conveying clarity where there is none, but he must equally beware of the converse.

Thompson's approach to translation was perhaps typical of a period when interest in applying the techniques described in medieval treatises to produce original works of art meant that the treatises were likely to be used as working manuals. His stated aim when translating Cennino was 'to give first place wherever possible to the convenience of the practicing [sic] student and painter' (Cennini 1960: xiii). It is for this reason that he gives obsolete measurements in feet and inches and uses then-current workshop terminology: 'every effort has been made … to translate [Cennino's materials and methods] into the resources of modern commerce and the idiom of modern craftsmen. Thus *minio* is translated as "red lead"' (Cennini 1960: xiii). He was evidently willing to accept what he considered slight mistranslations in his efforts to privilege the needs of the modern craftsperson as he comments, when criticising translations of Theophilus, 'Both [Dodwell and Hawthorne-Smith] translate *minium* as "red lead", although "minium" has a long history of use in English. Though *minium* was certainly a red lead, it was probably not the color which bears that name nowadays' (Thompson 1967: 317).

Thompson's approach also meant rendering the text more 'readable' so that it would be more convenient for the modern craftsperson to use, making him perhaps guilty of the 'over-smoothing' described by Clarke. In the preface to his translation of Cennino, Thompson admits, 'I have tried to keep something of the flavor of his writing, but have felt as free to recast an awkward sentence as to spell correctly the words with which I translate the misspelled words of my original' (Cennini 1960: xvii). There is not quite an equivalence, however, between misspelling and awkward sentence structure; spelling was fluid in the medieval period and, in addition, a genuine misspelling would be the result of a simple slip on the part of Cennino or one of the copyists and would, in most cases, easily be passed over by the medieval Italian reader (see the discussion of *ritrarre* for *ritriarre* above). An awkward sentence structure, on the other hand, cannot result from a simple slip, and would affect the ease of reading for the medieval reader. If the aim of the translator is to convey the experience of a medieval person reading Cennino's original text, therefore, the translator should retain awkward sentence structure. This was not Thompson's aim, however, and he therefore considered 'over-smoothing' admissible in order to facilitate comprehension for the modern craftsperson.

Mrs Merrifield, in the prefaces to her translations of both Cennino and the Le Begue manuscripts, feels obliged to defend her decision not to excise any of the text. In the Le Begue preface she writes:

> Among the various recipes, many of which may be traced to a very early period, it will not occasion surprise that some should be found which partake of the barbarism of the times when they were written. Absurd, and perhaps useless, as a few of these may be considered, except as forming part of the History of Art, it has been thought advisable to publish the whole of the MSS. in order to satisfy the reader that nothing important has been omitted. (Merrifield 1849: vi)

In the preface to Cennino's treatise we find:

> As the work is strictly practical, and, with one exception, entirely free from the metaphysical disquisitions with which the early Italian works on painting so much abound; and as the book itself is a rather curious specimen, even in its English dress, of the style and manners of the time in which it was written, it has been thought advisable to publish the whole of it. (Merrifield 1844: vi)

The idea that parts of the source text might be omitted on the grounds that they are 'not relevant' seems shocking to the contemporary historian, but this is simply an extension of the copying, compiling and editing process to which most manuscripts have been subjected over the centuries; Clarke notes that, when taking recipes from earlier sources, 'the LDA retains … only that which is of interest to a painter' (Clarke 2011: 45). It is only relatively recently that it has been deemed unacceptable to excise parts of a source text on grounds of irrelevance and, in the case of Cennino, even in the 1930s Thompson saw fit to excise a certain passage in chapter 70 (on the ideal proportions of a man's body).

Mrs Merrifield's translation was motivated by a commission to gather information on fresco technique in order to facilitate the redecoration of the Houses of Parliament (Burns 2011: 4–5). Her translation therefore, like Thompson's but with more urgency, had to fulfil the function of a strictly practical teaching manual to meet the requirements of a royal commission; hence her need to defend the inclusion of 'irrelevant' material.

The aim in the new translation of Cennino is, as far as possible, to convey to the modern English-speaking reader the experience of a fifteenth-century reader studying Cennino's original text. This means that, while obvious spelling mistakes are not to be rendered in English, awkward sentence structure is. Elements of style that seem to be Cennino's own are to be retained while those that stem from the time and place in which the treatise was written are not, on the grounds that these would have been 'invisible' to a contemporary reader. The English is to stick as closely as practicable to the Italian but not slavishly so, in order that the fluency of Cennino's language should not be lost in the attempt to force modern English into a medieval Italian idiom.

Specific difficulties

Having wrestled with the broader questions associated with translation, the translator must then engage with

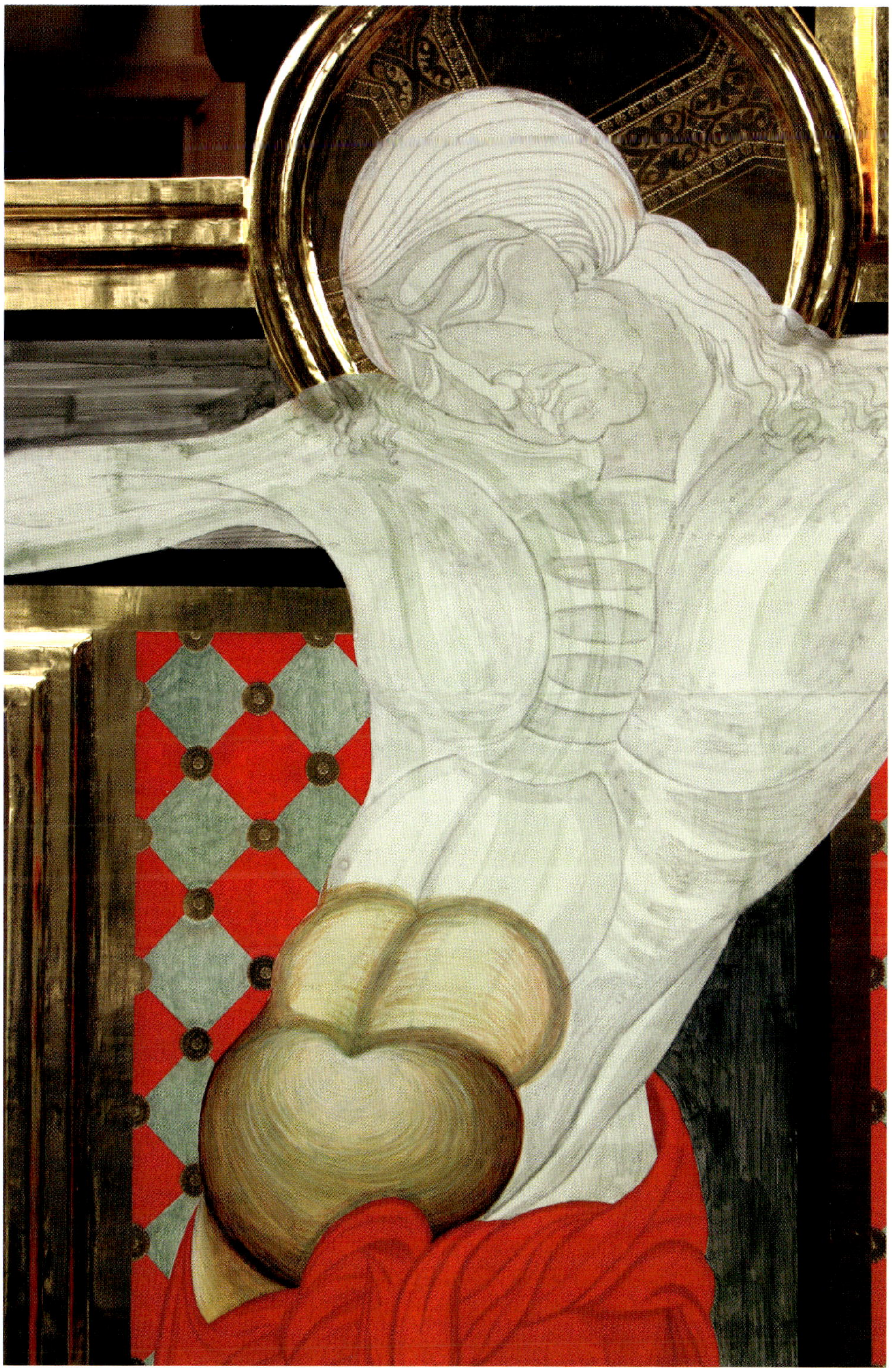

Figure 3 Verdaccio *layer on the figure of Christ forming the basis for the flesh painting.*

numerous specific difficulties in the course of rendering the source text into the target language. One major cause of difficulties is multivalency; one language does not map exactly onto another and there will frequently be occasions when a single word in one language needs to be translated by a variety of words, depending on context, in the other, and vice versa.

In translating treatises on painting, one area fraught with difficulty is colour terminology. To begin with, the word *color* in Latin or *colore* in Italian stands for both the English words 'pigment' and 'colour'. Clarke notes this problem in both the LDA and the *Secretum philosophorum* (Clarke 2011: 209) and it is no less a problem in Cennino's treatise. It is generally desirable, in translating, to be consistent in matching words in the original language with those in the target language, as only in this way can the reader of the translation get any impression of the frequency of use of certain terms and also the conscious or subconscious cross-referencing in which the author of the original text may have engaged. Presumably for this rea-

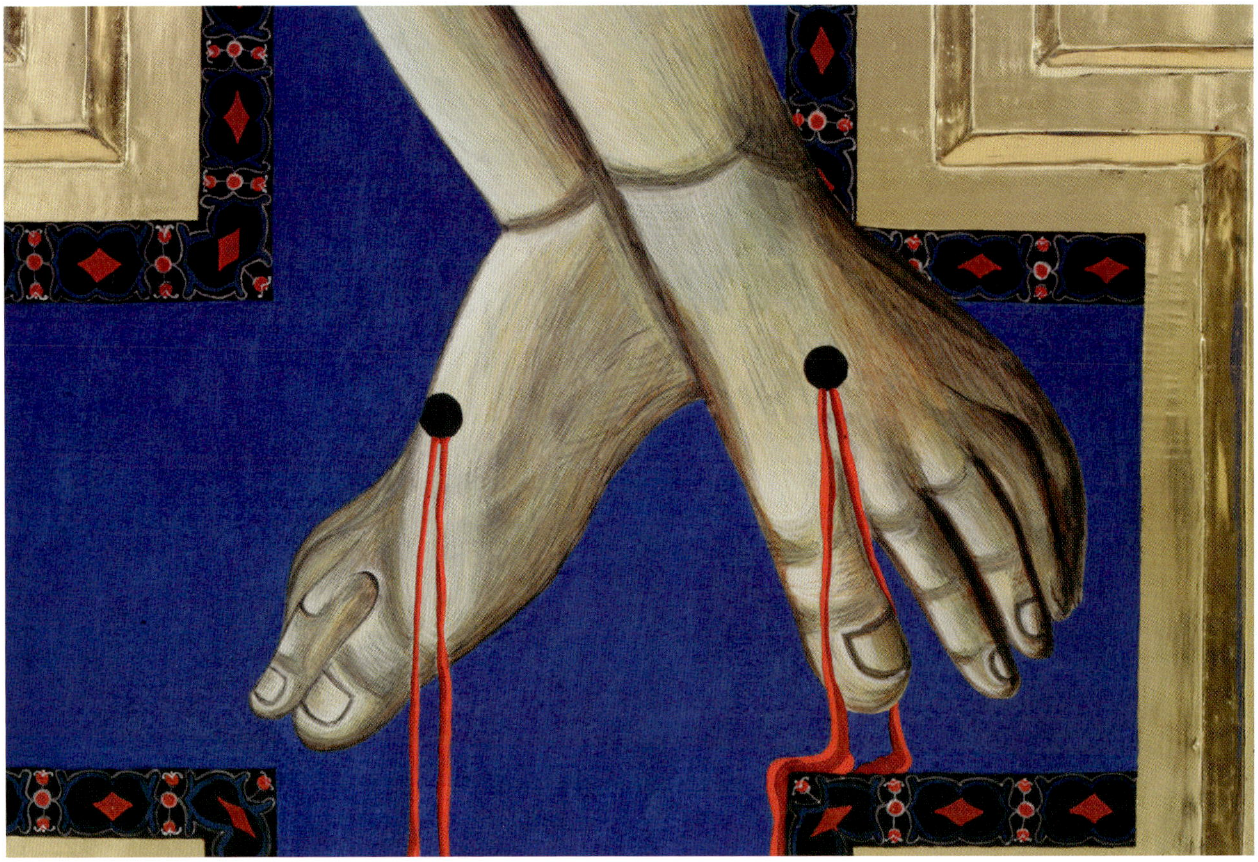

Figure 4 *A* sanguignio *outline can be seen around Christ's feet.*

son, Thompson chooses to translate *colore* consistently as 'color' throughout his translation of Cennino. The result is easily intelligible to the English-speaking reader, but it is not natural; a clear example occurs in chapter 47, on orpiment, where Thompson is constrained to write, 'Sparrowhawks are physicked with this color against a certain illness which affects them' (Cennini 1960: 29). A case can be made here for abandoning consistency in favour of retaining the fluency of the original Italian, using 'pigment' in this particular sentence and elsewhere, as appropriate, but 'colour' in other contexts. This can even mean using two different translations of the same Italian word in a single sentence; for example, in chapter 46, on *giallorino*, we find 'beautiful greenery and grass colours are made with this pigment', where 'colours' and 'pigment' both translate *color(e)*.

Where the terms for specific colours are concerned, the difficulty is often that the range of hues encompassed by a colour term in one language, in one period, will not be the same as that encompassed by the closest colour term in the target language of the translation. One example from Cennino is the use of *rosso*, usually considered to map almost exactly onto modern English 'red'. In chapter 83 of his treatise, instructing on the painting of a blue mantle using azurite, Cennino writes that, if the blue is rather light in tone the egg yolk used to bind it should come from farm eggs 'che sono ben rossi' (L: 17r) ('which are thoroughly 'red'). Egg yolks may have a range of colours from light yellow to deep orange, but they are never red. The incongruence of *rossi* to the English reader in this context draws attention to the Italian for 'yolk', *rossume*; the egg yolk is named for its colour, and that colour is *rosso*. Elsewhere in the treatise *rosso* describes, for example, vermilion, which is unequivocally 'red'. Clearly, the medieval Italian term *rosso* encompassed a wider range of hues than contemporary English 'red' does, describing both red and deep orange. When *rosso* is used for vermilion it has to be translated as 'red', but in the description of egg yolks 'che sono ben rossi' the translation 'ruddy' might be more appropriate, retaining a link to 'red' while encompassing a wider range of colour. Once again, consistency has to be abandoned in order to avoid translating natural Italian into absurd English.

Another problem to confront the translator is the occurrence of terms or usages of terms only attested in the source text. Mrs Merrifield writes, 'In such cases the Translator has endeavoured, by maturely considering the context, and by consulting other eminent works on the same subject, to express what is conceived to be the meaning of the Author' (Merrifield 1844: xxii). Of course if, after following Mrs Merrifield's method, the meaning still cannot be determined, a blank must be left in the translation or it must be made very clear that any translation of the term is tentative. Fortunately, this kind of problem does not occur frequently in Cennino. One example is *puzza*, near the beginning of chapter 134. Cennino is suggesting that, before gilding on panel, a gesso hook should be run over the bole to check for any 'puzza e nocciolo o granellino' (L: 21v) ('*puzza* and lump or piece of grit'). The *Lessicografia della Crusca* (Accademia della Crusca 2000–2004) defines *puzza* as 'pus',[9] but this clearly does not fit in the context. Frezzato suggests that *puzza* has been written for *pagliuzza* ('piece of fluff') or similar, influenced by the proximity of *pezza* ('rag') in the subsequent sentence (Cennini 2006: 227, n. 144). However, it is also possible that Cennino is here using *puzza* by extension for the blister in which the pus is found; blisters or bubbles occur frequently in bole and 'blister' sits better alongside 'lump' and 'grit' than 'piece of fluff'. If this is indeed what Cennino is doing it is impossible to know whether he was coining this extension here or whether it was a common or at least not unusual usage of the word *puzza* in medieval Italian. The translator must judge the relative strengths of the arguments for each translation and make a decision on which to use, while noting the uncertainty of the translation in a footnote.

Other terms that cause difficulties for the translator are those that simply have no equivalent in English. These must be translated by several explanatory words, losing the fluency of the original language, or left in the original language with an explanatory footnote. Happily, in Cennino, the Italian technical terms have very often been adopted into English. For instance, the term *verdaccio* occurs repeatedly throughout Cennino's treatise; there is no one word in English that conveniently describes a green underlayer for painted flesh, and to use a clumsy translation such as 'green underlayer' throughout the treatise would become very tiresome for the reader and create an impression of clumsiness where there is none in the Italian (Fig. 3). Fortunately, however, *verdaccio* has long been subsumed into the language of art historical discourse in English for precisely these reasons and it is, therefore, permissible simply to use the original Italian word in the English translation. More problematic is the comparable *sanguignio* which Cennino tells us, in his chapter on painting dead bodies, is the proper term for the mixture of black and dark sinoper used to outline passages of flesh (Fig. 4). This term has not entered the English language although no neat translation exists. It nevertheless seems most sensible to leave the term in the original language, since the context makes it very clear what it means.

The new translation

The challenges facing the translator of any technical treatise are manifold, ranging from identification of a source text, through questions of methodology and style to specific problems relating to particular words. Perhaps the greatest challenge to the translator in the case of Cennino, however, is in summoning the courage openly to criticise Thompson's translation. Any re-translation, however reluctantly, constitutes a criticism of the preceding translation and, where the previous translator is a figure of Thompson's stature, questioning his authority can feel like hubris; strong argumentation must be marshalled in order to persuade the reader of the need for re-translation. While this can, at times, be frustrating it provides excellent discipline, as every point of contention must be considered to exhaustion. Also sobering is the knowledge that the new translation will be treated equally critically by a contemporary and future readership with an ever-growing knowledge of technical art history and of the problems of interpretation associated with the manuscripts on the subject.

No translation can be perfect and none can match the ideals of every interested reader. Perhaps the best that can be hoped for is that the new Cennino in English will be linguistically rigorous, open in admitting its own shortcomings as well as those of the original manuscript and its copyists, and that it will bring the reader a little closer than previous translations have done to the experience of the medieval Italian reader engaging with Cennino's own manuscript.

Notes

1. Undertaken at the Hamilton Kerr Institute, Cambridge University, 2006–8.
2. The manuscripts were consulted using high quality black and white digital photographs of the original manuscripts provided by the Italian libraries concerned.
3. Author's translation of: 'Gli esempi a cui si è fatto riferimento mostrano una situazione di disordine che non può essere facilmente imputata ai copisti dei manoscritti, ma più probabilmente al fatto che l'opera non è mai giunta a compimento'.
4. Author's translation from manuscript L: 'poi in fresco tolli azurro della mangnia ... mettivi dentro un poco di colla ... anchor metti nel detto azurro un rossume du uovo' (L: 17r).
5. The numeration used for manuscript L is that found in the upper right of the pages, with 'r' standing for recto and 'v' for verso.
6. In chapter 4: 'tritare over macinare' (L: 2r); in chapter 35: 'triato over macinato' (L: 43r); in chapter 37 'non bisogna triarlo ne macinarlo' (L: 43v).
7. The Milanesi numbering, given in the footnotes to Thompson's translation (Cennino 1960: 129–30).
8. Author's translation of: 'I venetismi contenuti nei manoscritti sono quanto resta di un'operazione di toscannizzazione condotta dai copisti: non è perciò facile stabilire quanti fossero quelli presenti in origine'.
9. 'Umor corrotto, che si genera nelle bolle, o piaghe' ('Rotten bodily fluid, which is generated in blisters or ulcers').

References

Accademia della Crusca 2000–2004. *Lessicografia della Crusca*. http://193.205.158.203/index.jsp (accessed 16 November 2011).

Burns, T. 2011. 'Cennino Cennini's *Il libro dell'arte*: a historiographical review', *Studies in Conservation* 56(1): 1–13.

Cennini, Cennino 1859. *Il libro dell'arte, o trattato della pittura di Cennino Cennini da Colle di Valdelsa; di nuovo publicato, con molte correzioni e coll'aggiunta di più capitoli tratti dai Codici Fiorentini, per cura di Gaetano e Carlo Milanesi*, G. Milanesi and C. Milanesi (eds). Florence: Felice Le Monnier.

Cennini da Colle di Val d'Elsa, Cennino d'Andrea 1932. *Il libro dell'arte: Text*. D.V. Thompson Jr. (ed.). New Haven, CT: Yale University Press.

Cennini, Cennino 1960. *The Craftsman's Handbook, 'Il libro dell'arte'*, D.V. Thompson (tr.). New York: Dover Publications.

Cennini, Cennino 2006. *Il libro dell'arte*, F. Frezzato (ed.). Vicenza: Neri Pozza Editore.

Clarke, M. 2007. '*Pentimenti*: D.V. Thompson's corrections to his translation of Cennini' (unpublished draft, quoted by kind permission of the author).

Clarke, M. 2011. *Medieval Painters' Materials and Techniques: The Montpellier* Liber diversarum arcium. London: Archetype Publications.

Herringham, C.J. 1930. *The Book of the Art of Cennino Cennini: A Contemporary Practical Treatise on Quattrocento Painting. Translated from the Italian, with Notes on Mediaeval Art Methods by Christiana J. Herringham.* London: George Allen & Unwin Ltd.

Merrifield, M.P. 1844. *A Treatise on Painting Written by Cennino Cennini in the Year 1437; and First Published in Italian in 1821, With an Introduction and Notes, by Signor Tambroni: Containing Practical Directions for Painting in Fresco, Secco, Oil and Distemper, With the Art of Gilding and Illuminating Manuscripts Adopted by the Old Italian Masters.* London: Edward Lumley.

Merrifield, M.P. 1849. *Original Treatises, dating from the XIIth to XVIIIth Centuries, on the Arts of Painting, in Oil, Miniature, Mosaic, and on Glass; of Gilding, Dyeing, and the Preparation of Colours and Artificial Gems; Preceded by a General Introduction; with Translations, Prefaces and Notes* (2 vols), vol. 1. London: John Murray.

Nadolny, J. 2008. 'European documentary sources before *c*.1550 relating to painting grounds applied to wooden supports: translation and terminology'. In *Preparation for Painting: The Artist's Choice and its Consequences*, J.H. Townsend, T. Doherty, G. Heydenreich and J. Ridge (eds) 1–13. London: Archetype Publications.

Neven, S. 2009. 'Comparative analysis of painting recipes: a new contribution to the study of the texts of the Strasbourg family'. In *Sources and Serendipity: Testimonies of Artists' Practice*, E. Hermens and J.H. Townsend (eds) 65–71. London: Archetype Publications.

Tambroni, G. 1821. *Di Cennino Cennini: trattato della pittura*. Rome: Paolo Salviucci.

Theophilus 1979. *On Divers Arts: The Foremost Treatise on Painting, Glassmaking and Metalwork*, J.G. Hawthorne and C.S. Smith (tr.). New York: Dover Publications.

Thompson, D.V. 1967. 'Theophilus Presbyter: words and meaning in technical translation', *Speculum* 42(2): 313–39.

Turner, A. 2006. 'Translation and criticism: the stylistic mirror', *The Yearbook of English Studies* 36(1) 'Translation': 168–76.

Manuscripts

L: C. Cennini, 1437. Biblioteca Mediceo-Laurenziana, Florence, Codice Mediceo Laurenziano P.78.23.

P: C. Cennini, eighteenth century. Biblioteca Nazionale Centrale di Firenze, Florence, Codice Palatino 818.

R: C. Cennini, late sixteenth/early seventeenth century. Biblioteca Medici-Riccardi, Florence, Codice Riccardiano 2190.

V: C. Cennini, *c*.1737. Biblioteca Vaticana, Rome, Codice Ottoboniano Vaticano 2974.

RECONSTRUCTING THE EXCEPTIONAL: THE DECORATION OF THE WINGFIELD ORGAN

Madeleine Katkov

A piece of rotting timber, discovered by chance in the graveyard shed at St Andrew's church, Wingfield, Suffolk, was the trigger for a unique project. Closer inspection showed that it was the remains of the soundboard of an early sixteenth-century organ. Although it is likely that most English medieval churches would have had at least one organ, none has survived the Reformation intact (Easton and Bicknell 1995).[1] This otherwise complete lack of physical evidence made the find particularly significant. It was even more fortunate because it is the soundboard that can provide most information about the finished instrument, giving the number, size and layout of the pipes. There was sufficient evidence for a reconstruction to be attempted, and the Early English Organ Project was set up to manage it in the 1990s (Gwynn 1996).[2]

The primary purpose of the reconstruction was for musical research, and the question of the physical appearance of the organ was raised relatively late (Fig. 1). Painted decoration was felt to be the most likely finish (Fig. 2). The soundboard was dated to the 1530s (Gwynn 1996) by which time polychromy had become an essential part of the decorative ensemble in churches, and had, in East Anglia, reached a peak of sophistication and refinement in the English context. The use of polychromy was so ubiquitous that it was assumed that organs would have been included. I was asked to decorate the reconstructed case and pipes using historically appropriate materials and techniques, to a scheme devised by Timothy Easton.

The woodwork of the organ case had been copied from panelling, dated through dendrochronology to the 1530s, at Otley Hall, Suffolk (Gwynn 1996). This presented something of an anomaly: the proportions of this domestic panelling were classical, with rectangular panels and flat framework. Classical proportions, already the height of fashion in secular settings at this date, occur in churches elsewhere in the country. In contrast, it is a marked feature of East Anglian church furnishings that relatively little trace of Renaissance influence can be found. It began to be adopted at about this date in some chantry chapels[3] and tombs but liturgical furnishings, such as screens, tend to retain the tall thin panels, vertical thrust and richly moulded frames of the Gothic style. A defining feature of the associated polychromy is the interplay of shapes and colours. The deeply moulded carving is designed to exploit the aesthetic properties of the paint. This effect would be lost with the existing organ case, so the authenticity of the final appearance would inevitably be compromised.

The commission was a practical one, without a research brief, and carried out under commercial restraints. However the scope of the project – far greater than many trials of historic techniques – provided ample opportunity for experimentation and observation. In spite of its limitations, the many intriguing practical issues that arose can offer a valuable contribution towards scholarship in the field (Katkov 2004). This paper focuses on three aspects of the reconstruction: considerations about the choice of colour and patterns; the practical handling and preparation of the historic materials on a larger scale than often attempted; and insights into the organisation of large-scale projects and site-work practice of the peripatetic medieval craftsmen.

The rules of polychromy

The requirements of reconstruction necessitated a new approach and a different line of enquiry from my previous professional encounters with East Anglian polychromy as a conservator. Polychromy is characterised by a strict code of colour and pattern usage, governed by religious, heraldic and aesthetic constraints, which determined the choice of pigments, motifs and elaboration. In order to produce a design that would look authentic, it was necessary to

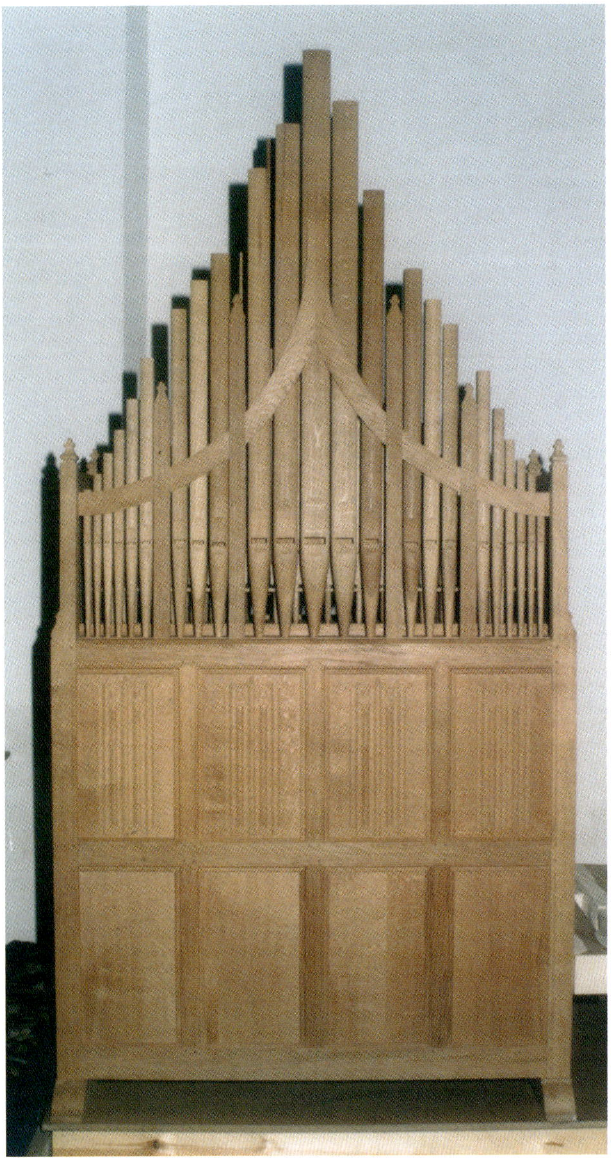

Figure 1 *The reconstructed Wingfield organ before painting. (Photograph: Madeleine Katkov.)*

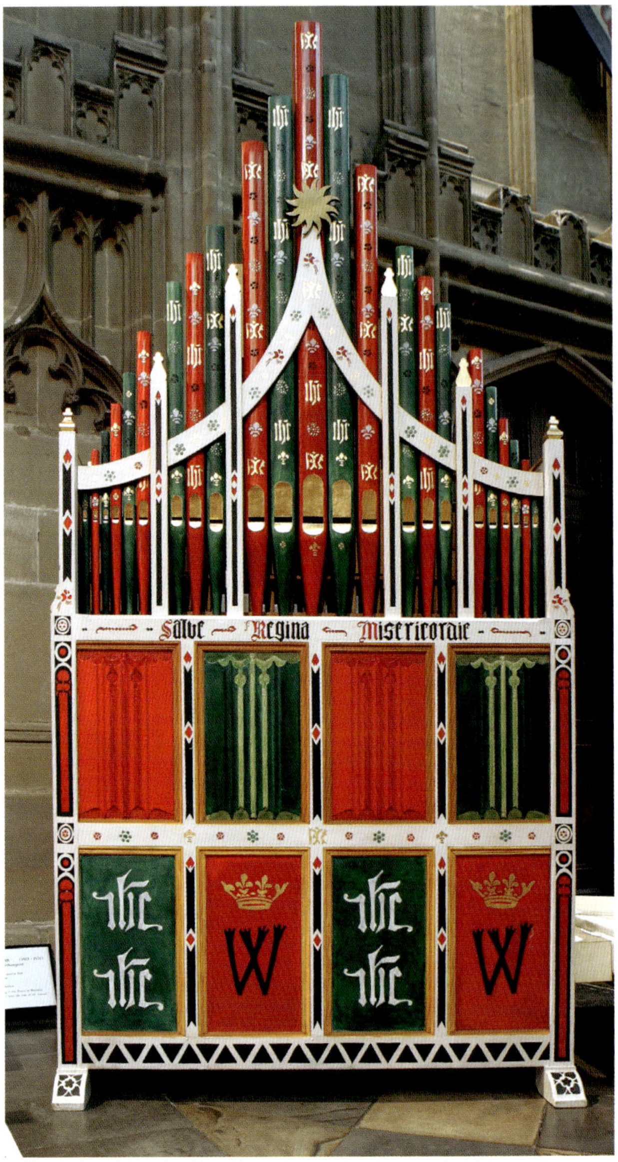

Figure 2 *The reconstructed Wingfield organ after painting. (Photograph: Madeleine Katkov.)*

understand how the medieval craftsman made decisions about which colours and patterns to use. The lack of a prototype for the reconstruction of the decoration meant that elements of surviving schemes on other furnishings would have to be translated for use on the organ. It was essential to have a grasp of the fundamentals so that this could be done appropriately. Fortunately there is no lack of examples of polychromy in East Anglia; the many furnishings – principally screens – provided a rich and diverse field of study (Baker 2011).

While the purpose of figure panels on screens is clear (that is, providing representations of the saints for devotion), the polychromed architectural elements also played a part liturgically. The overall arrangement served to indicate and emphasise the focal points of worship and to mark liminal points, where structures border onto a more sacred space beyond. A hierarchy of complexity existed, the design growing in elaboration, the pigments becoming richer and the motifs more detailed, converging on the main liturgical furnishing such as the rood or high altar, and points of transition such as the screen, ceilure or reredos. These arrangements are directional: they work when viewed from the nave and are aimed at the congregation, playing an indispensable role in the theatre of medieval worship. The polychromy on architectural structures, which is often much greater in surface area than on panels and with more costly decoration, is much more than a mere decorative surround – it serves to sanctify the paraphernalia of worship and to enhance the mystery of the liturgy.

That was one devotional aspect of polychromy, but there were others. Often motifs with symbolic connotations were incorporated into the patterns and stencils, providing prompts for prayer: sacred monograms and Marian references abounded; the language of flowers was used, for example lilies, pomegranates, carnations; endless

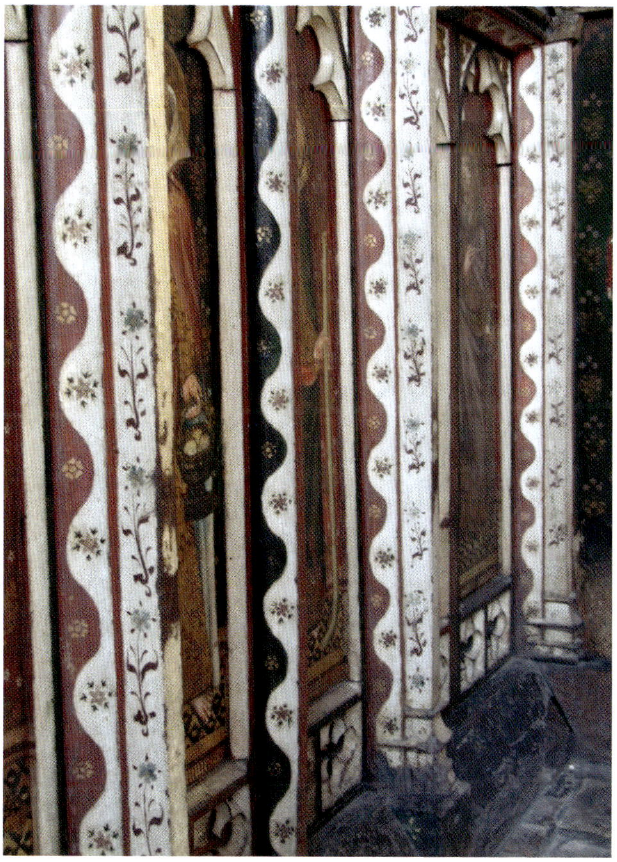

Figure 3 *Wave pattern on the screen at Worstead, Norfolk. (Photograph: Madeleine Katkov.)*

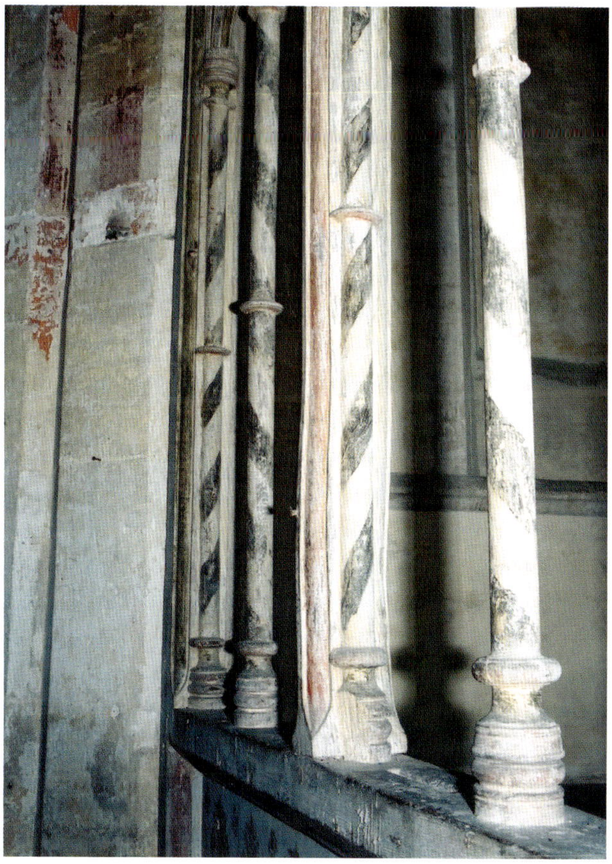

Figure 4 *Barber's pole decoration on the screen at Thompson church, Norfolk. (Photograph: Madeleine Katkov.)*

carved vine trails were richly coloured. Colour also helped to create the illusion of sacred space close at hand, the blue and gold of roofs, ceilures, canopies and coving evoking the heavens. The act of beautifying a church was in itself a form of devotion. Donors would pay for decorative schemes as an act of piety and a form of chantry provision (Baker 2011: 91). The alchemy involved in the preparation of the materials, the mystery surrounding the transformation of rock and metal into dazzling, gleaming surfaces, made painting a particularly satisfactory and appropriate form of devotion (Bucklow 2009).

Even in more secular settings colours had strong symbolic connotations. Medieval philosophy described the world according to an interconnected system of complementary opposites. Thus the celestial spheres related to the bodily humours which determined the four temperaments. These in turn were linked with the elements fire, water, air and earth. All manner of things were divided and classified in this way, not least colours. So, for example, red made from iron or mercury corresponded to Mars or choler or fire, whose complementary opposite would be a copper green related to Venus (Bucklow 2009). The outcome of this interpretation of the world can be seen in the constant occurrence of alternating red and green in medieval polychromy schemes.

It was clear that the choice and combination of colours, and the type and elaboration of designs, was subject to a highly sophisticated and complex system of belief and understanding. The surviving schemes that constitute our evidence would have been imbued by the devout layman with layers of meaning that are largely lost to us, and that are just beginning to be addressed. Much progress has been made in this field since the organ reconstruction was painted a decade ago (Bucklow 2009). It was necessary to avoid contravening its strictures when recreating a scheme as anomalies that would have confounded a medieval worshipper are likely to have an unauthentic ring even now.

The symbolic conventions in no way compromised aesthetic considerations. The purpose of the carving was to maximise the effect of the colours. Matt and dark colours were used in recesses as a foil for brighter, glossier ones on extremities, taking full advantage of the effects of shadow and light. Incongruous colours were used adjacent to each other for vibrancy. An overall harmony was achieved with a good understanding of colour values: red and green, being more or less equal in tone, balance when alternated, but do not contrast sufficiently when superimposed; they work side by side, but not one on top of the other. Black, white, gold and silver offer the strongest contrasts, standing forward from the rest of the palette, and are commonly used for applied motifs.

Some designs are associated with particular mouldings, and in this case it is the purpose of the pattern to

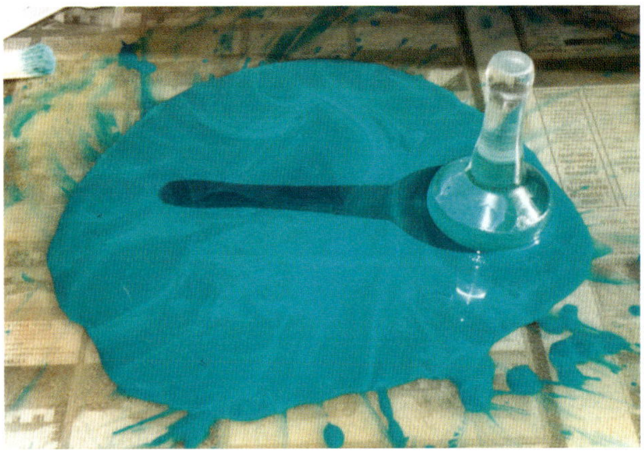

Figure 5 *Consistency of paint for backgrounds. (Photograph: Madeleine Katkov.)*

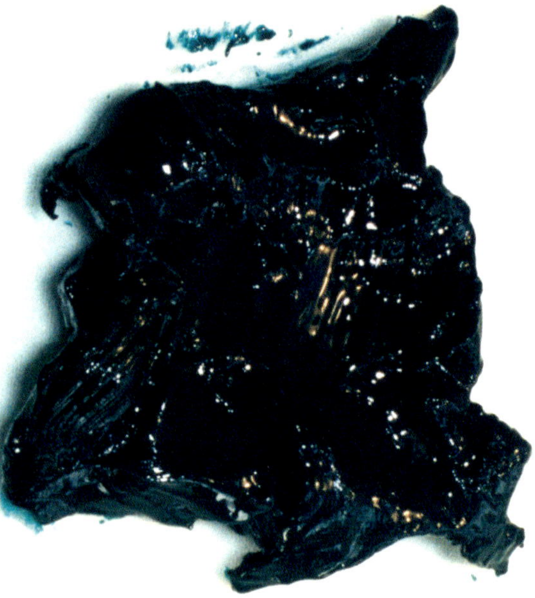

Figure 6 *Consistency of paint for stencils. (Photograph: Madeleine Katkov.)*

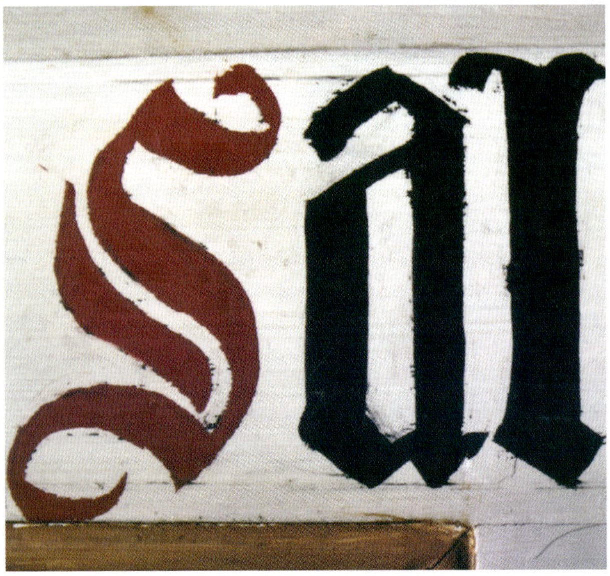

Figure 7 *Inscription, reconstructed Wingfield organ. (Photograph: Madeleine Katkov.)*

maximise the contours of that particular carved profile. When a wave pattern is put onto an S moulding there is a playful interaction of the two- and three-dimensional shapes (Fig. 3). The contrasting colours of a barber's pole can look like a coil of ribbon in freefall (Fig. 4). These patterns are seldom found on other shapes of moulding. An acute understanding of colour values and relationships is evidenced everywhere in these schemes. This highly sophisticated ability to juggle shapes and colours for maximum dramatic effect is the distinguishing feature of late medieval East Anglian polychromy.

When applying these criteria to the decoration of the organ, we assumed it would come relatively low down in the scale of elaboration, certainly considerably lower than the altar, screen or ceilure, possibly equal to, or below, the pulpit, font and roof. A modest scheme therefore seemed appropriate. The colour combinations and decorative motifs were taken directly from East Anglian screens. The discussion as to where the organ was sited also had a bearing on the type of decoration chosen; its original location within the church was far from certain (Gwynn 1996). Some musical experts thought it was mainly for use in the Lady Chapel, but would occasionally have stood in front of the nave screen, so for ground level furnishings a red-and-green-based scheme would have been an obvious choice. However, the beam over the parclose screen in Wingfield church is reinforced to increase its load-bearing properties, and the organ would have fitted neatly on top of it, in which case a blue-and-white based decoration might have been more suitable.

Materials, methods and handling properties

Once a suitable design had been agreed, the question of paint application arose. The primary concern was that the texture, luminosity and finish of the paint should be as authentic as possible. The aim was to reproduce the exact quality and appearance of an early sixteenth-century scheme otherwise there was no justification for going to the trouble of using original materials. The preparation, mixing, applying and general handling of these materials was not straightforward, but as so often, it was in addressing the problems that most was learnt about the task in hand.

The pigments used were lead white, vermilion, red lead, verdigris, carbon black, yellow ochre and lead-tin yellow. Historic pigments produced using authentic, traditional methods were obtained from Kremer, Keith Edwards and Cornelissen. Pigments tend to generate a great deal of fascination and there is a considerable body of knowledge on the subject. The method of handling the medium to achieve the desired effect, however, was a much more problematic variable, and proved to be elusive. Jo Kirby, then of the National Gallery, mentored the project and advised that these pigments would have been mixed in raw linseed oil and stand oil. She also said that there are

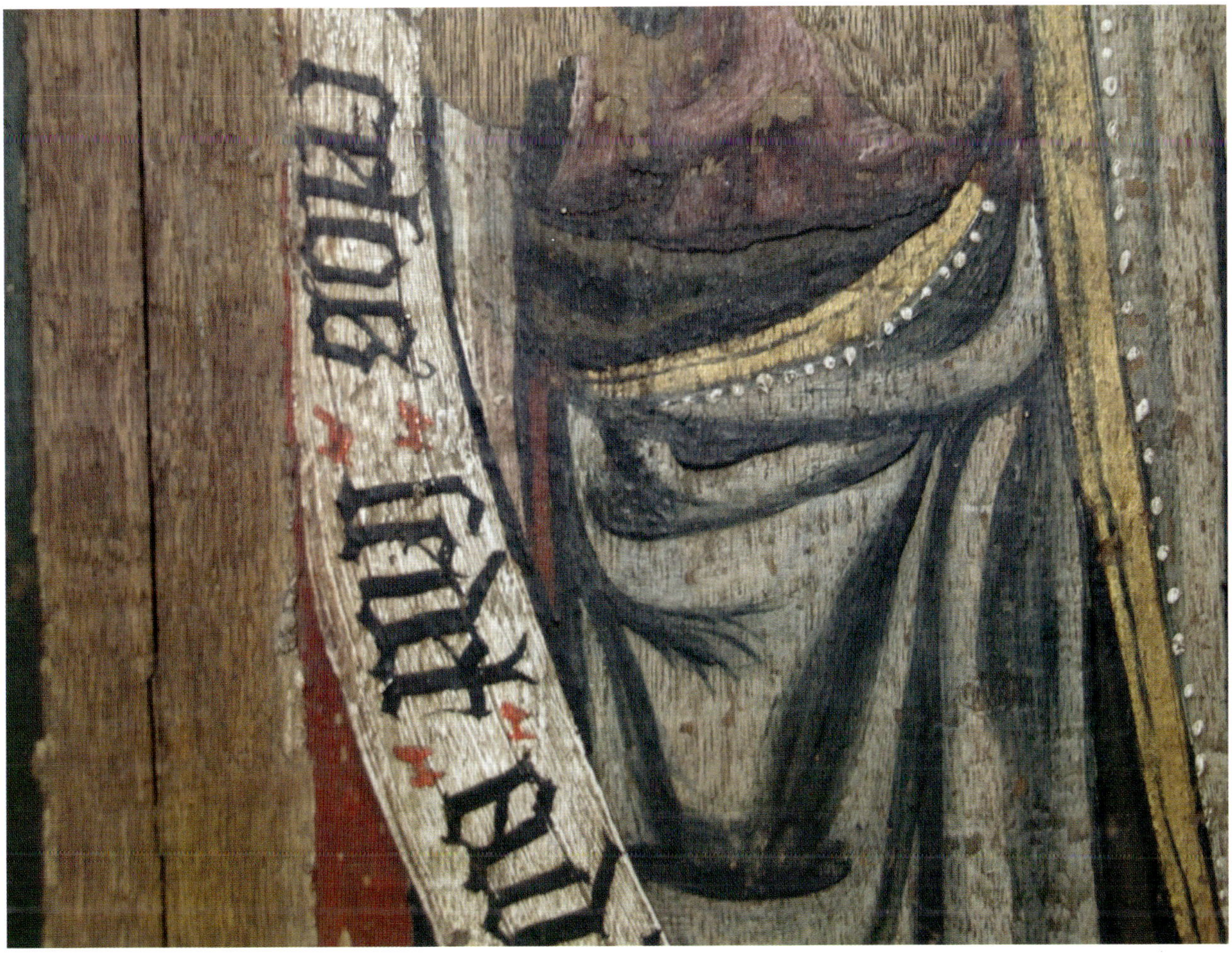

Figure 8 *Inscription from the screen at Ringland church, Norfolk. (Photograph: Madeleine Katkov.)*

barely any references to turpentine at this date, and it is thought that thinners were not used. These strictures were followed wherever possible in the preparation of mixes for the organ.

Sample test panels prepared in the two or three months prior to starting the project were of little help because of the slow drying time. The paint altered markedly over the first six months, and visibly even a year later, so that the final appearance of the mixtures could not be ascertained in a shorter period. The proportion of pigment to medium, and of raw linseed oil to stand oil, and the length of time needed for grinding, could not be verified beforehand and remained a matter of trial and error.

The addition of stand oil to the mix affects its consistency while fresh, and its luminosity when dry. In the short term it means that the grinding process takes considerably longer and makes the mix less easy to brush out thinly and smoothly. However it is not certain whether these furnishings were always originally varnished; if so, they were often only partially varnished, so the high gloss in many instances must have been achieved with a measure of stand oil. The long-term effect of adding this medium was not appreciated in the relatively short time available for trials, and none was added to the background red and green of the organ. These colours had a very high sheen for the first couple of years while they were drying, but now look uncharacteristically matt. Stand oil must have been regularly and liberally used historically, but a differentiation between types of oil is not generally referred to in recipes.

Although the figure panels in medieval churches are much studied, it was necessary to focus on their somewhat neglected decorative surrounds, which differ technically in marked ways. On figurative panels all the painted features, such as flesh tones, garments and background, tend to be painted directly onto the preparation layer and lie on the same plane. On the frames there is a uniform background colour, with the decorative motifs (usually in thick *impasto*) sitting on top. The challenge in the preparation of colours for panel paintings lies in achieving a similar consistency when the properties of each pigment are varied and handle so differently when mixed in oil. For frameworks the opposite is true: different thicknesses, appropriate for the function, are developed for each mix. So background colours that needed to be brushed out evenly and thinly over large areas were best used relatively fluid (Fig. 5), while at the other end of the spectrum the *impasto* for stencils was extremely dense (Fig. 6).

Some aspects of the skills of the medieval craftsman in paint handling remained elusive. There were particular

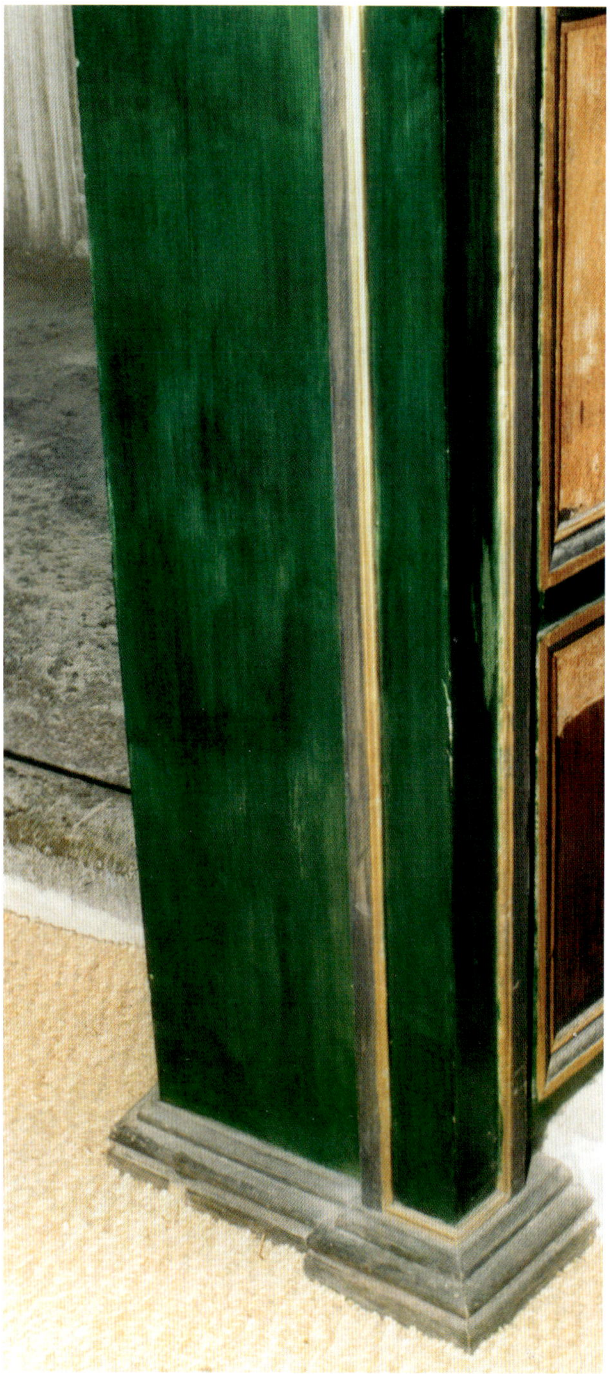

Figure 9 *Verdigris panel at Bolsover Castle, English Heritage. (Photograph: Madeleine Katkov.)*

problems with the use of black, green and stencils. It proved difficult to reproduce the characteristics of medieval script, where the paint is typically of very dense consistency but has wispy serifs, clearly applied in single, flowing strokes. On the organ, in order to achieve the control and precision needed for the lettering, it was necessary to thin the black paint with a little turpentine. Because oil paint dries from the outside in, it forms a distinctive smooth and glossy skin, and this effect is largely lost when the mix is thinned; neither can thinned paint lie in such high relief on the surface. It also has a tendency to retract from incised guidelines and needs several strokes (Figs 7 and 8). It is not clear how the combination of thick *impasto* and fluidity was achieved by the medieval craftsman.

Verdigris has always had a notorious reputation for being tricky to handle and both Leonardo da Vinci and Cennino Cennini complained about it (Woudhuysen-Keller 1995: 65). Our problem was the uneven distribution of pigment in the mix resulting in a very patchy appearance in terms of light and dark shades. This effect is apparent in every modern use of this pigment encountered, including English Heritage reconstructions and National Gallery test panels (Fig. 9). Our surface was pitted with pigment granules, especially noticeable when gilded stencils were superimposed (Fig. 10). Where historic verdigris survives in good condition it can appear as smooth and even as stained glass.

The handling of stencils proved another process that was difficult to master. It was necessary to exert pressure evenly around the central opening, especially on carved surfaces, in order to achieve a crisp outline with no seepage under the edges. The hand holding the stencil then got in the way of the brush. This would have been less of an issue if the paint had been stippled, but it is extremely unusual to find medieval stencils stippled; they are generally in thick *impasto*, with visible brushstrokes ending in a lip against the side of the stencil (Fig. 11). Considerable time was spent carefully cleaning the back of the stencil after each use. The whole process turned out to be rather awkward and slow, while for the medieval craftsman stencilling was presumably an efficient and speedy way to cover large areas in pattern (Fig. 12). The organ stencils were cut from a traditional material, a wax-impregnated card, but maybe some other material, parchment perhaps, might hold more tightly to the surface.

Gradually some tricks of handling became apparent. The mix for motifs was best applied fresh while the paint was most fluid and malleable and could reach into the points of the stencils. For backgrounds, however, it was easiest to use it after a few days, when it was just beginning to go tacky and would adhere better. The phenomenon of paint retracting can sometimes be observed in historic settings (Figs 13 and 14). This occurred on the organ when fresh thin paint was applied to a dry ground and can be avoided by accurate timing between layers and pre-preparing the paint.

A feel for the most appropriate tools and equipment gradually developed. Predictably, bristle brushes were best for brushing out background colours and fine hair more suitable for detailed work. There was also a difference in the containers used: for broad brushwork a small crock or tub allowed a larger quantity of paint to be stirred frequently, whereas for fine work the shallow ridges of a cockleshell were perfect for adjusting the amount of paint on the brush. The chalk ground was lightly smoothed with the straight metal blade of a French polisher's scraper, stems of the plant mare's tail or scouring-rush (*Equisetum*) having proved somewhat arduous and ineffective.

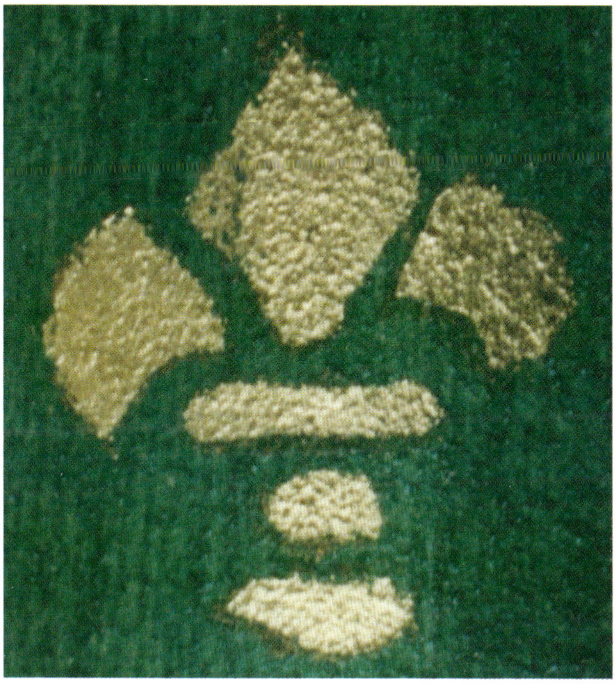

Figure 10 *Gold stencil on verdigris, Wingfield organ. (Photograph: Madeleine Katkov.)*

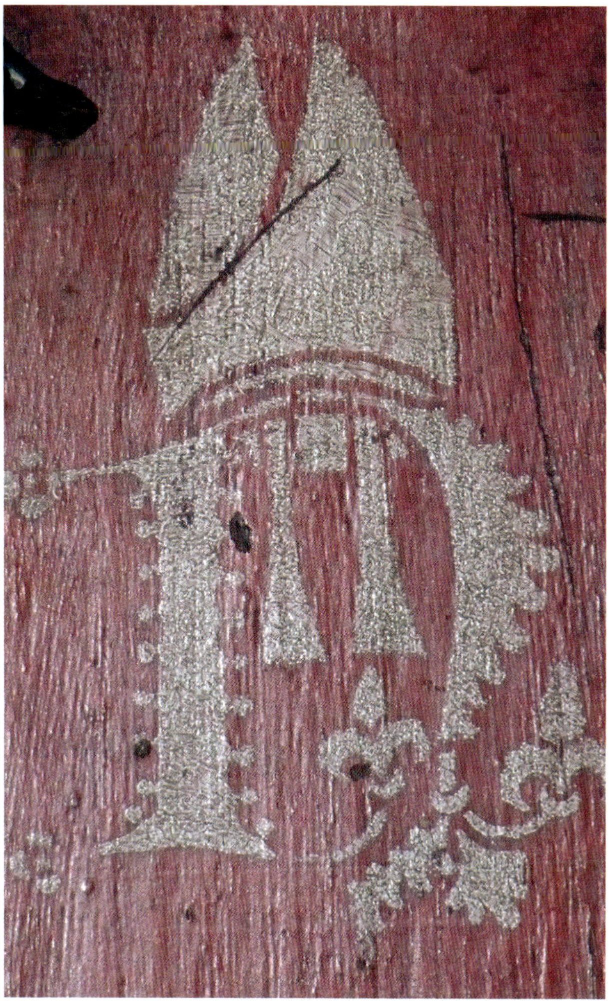

Figure 11 *Stencil from parclose screen, Castle Acre church, Norfolk. (Photograph: Madeleine Katkov.)*

Workshop logistics

The temperamental nature of these materials can inspire only admiration at the masterful way they were handled under the conditions of their use in the sixteenth century. The logistics of transport, supplies and labour must have been considerable on larger projects, many of which were undertaken *in situ* (Baker 2011). Some screen-painting workshops operated over a wide distance: the so-called Ranworth workshop, for example, which was probably based in Norwich, operated from Hunstanton on the north Norfolk coast to Southwold in Suffolk, a radius of some 50 miles, more than a day's ride.[4] The craftsmen must have stayed away from base for long periods. The quantity of materials that needed transporting was significant – not only pots, paints and brushes, slabs and mullers, pestles and mortars, but materials for preparatory drawing and making stencils, paper, parchment, measuring sticks, plumb lines, compasses, carpentry tools and so on. One imagines cartloads rather than saddlebags.

Drying times would need to be carefully planned to limit time lost in waiting. On the carved elements the angles between mouldings provide a stop for the brush, ensuring that the colours do not run into each other. The painter could run a colour brush up and down one facet with a swift sure stroke. The background colours were thus relatively quick to apply. There was then a wait of two weeks, or at least 10 days, until they were touch dry and could be covered with decorative motifs.

Another aspect that needed careful timing was grinding. This does not refer to the crushing of pigments into powder – these could often be bought ready to use from grocers or apothecaries[5] – but rather the dispersion of the pigment in a

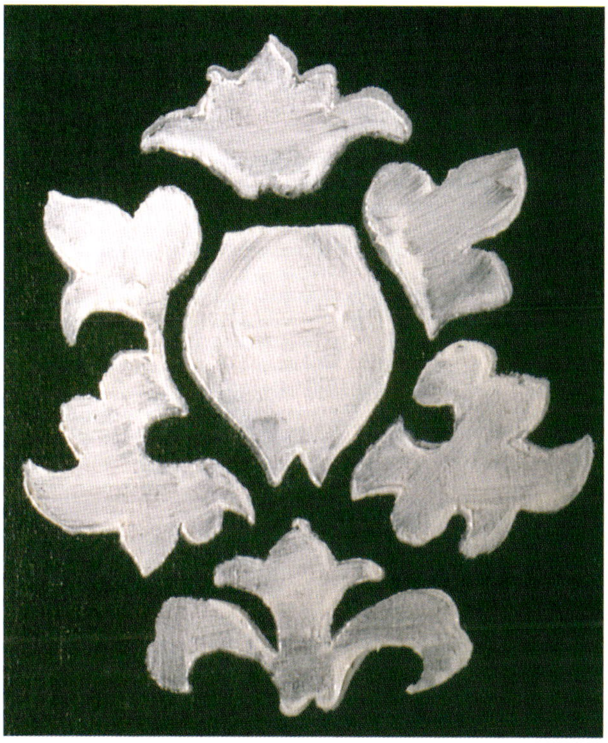

Figure 12 *Stencil from the Wingfield organ. (Photograph: Madeleine Katkov.)*

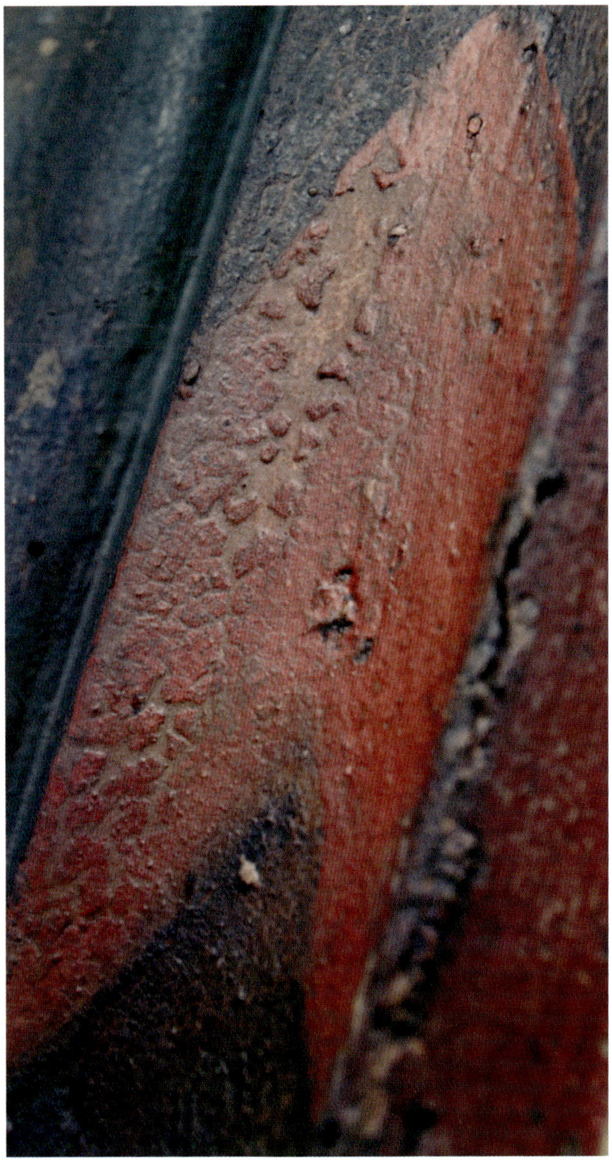

Figure 13 *Retracting paint on the Audley chapel screen, Hereford Cathedral. (Photograph: Madeleine Katkov.)*

medium. The purpose is to separate every grain and coat it with the medium to form a coherent film and distribute the particles evenly. There is no scientific way of determining when the process is complete, but as with the change that takes place in bread-making when the dough is sufficiently kneaded, the consistency alters, and in this case the muller eventually slips more evenly over the mix.

The most striking thing about grinding was how long it takes. The size of the batch was defined by the quantity of pigment and medium that would fit comfortably onto the slab, the ideal size of a slab being big enough for the arm to describe a circle while exerting even pressure, approximately 2 ft square ($60cm^2$). At a rough estimate each batch produced enough paint to cover barely 5 sq ft ($150cm^2$) of organ. It took about three hours to prepare and less than half an hour to apply. Doubtless the practised late-medieval painters were much more efficient than this, but it serves to illustrate at least that the preparation must have taken considerably longer than the application.

Given these time constraints, it is interesting to speculate on how a peripatetic master might have arranged his team. Additional help for mechanical tasks on larger projects would surely have been sought, but for which tasks and who would have been employed? Extra grinding boys must have been essential for vast areas such as roofs. Apprentices would, of course, have been used, but maybe also some local labour. In the accounts for the decoration of the banqueting hall at Greenwich in 1527 grinding boys were listed separately from the artists, suggesting that local unspecialised labour was sometimes hired in for this sort of work (Foister 2001).

Another part of the process for which unspecialised labour might have been used was the chalk ground. On church furnishings this tends to vary greatly in thickness and consistency, and local materials are used. In Devon, for example, the preparatory layers are red, like the soil of that county (Plummer and Hulbert 1990). When experts from the Hamilton Kerr Institute examined the retable at Thornham Parva, Suffolk, they were able to show that the chalk used for the ground probably came from an outcrop some seven miles from where it was painted (Massing 2003). This localisation, rather than standardisation, might well indicate the involvement of casual labour.

There is documentary evidence of craftsmen with related skills working on furnishings, but traditionally the master craftsman always prepared the most precious colours and painted the most important parts of the figures (Baker 2011). While the logistics of organisation on each job would have depended on the circumstances, the organ reconstruction highlighted the complex range of processes and skills that had to be coordinated.

Conclusion

The organ would have played its part in the transformation of the church interior into a space where the worshipper could be given a glimpse of heaven on earth. The vocabulary of polychromy dictated not only the choice and arrangement of colours and patterns, but also precisely the pigments and techniques to be used. Although research into historic paint techniques has been ongoing for some time, we still cannot get close enough to the medieval artist's intimate familiarity with the properties of his materials, or his versatility, ingenuity and competence in handling them. The skills and knowledge handed down over generations provided a tacit understanding which is not easy to recapture today. Even the more modest schemes required a level of technical mastery that is admirable, considering the conditions under which they were produced. This project of decorating the organ was exploratory, and ultimately may have been more useful, through the technical challenges that arose, as a learning experience than as an exercise in accurate reconstruction.

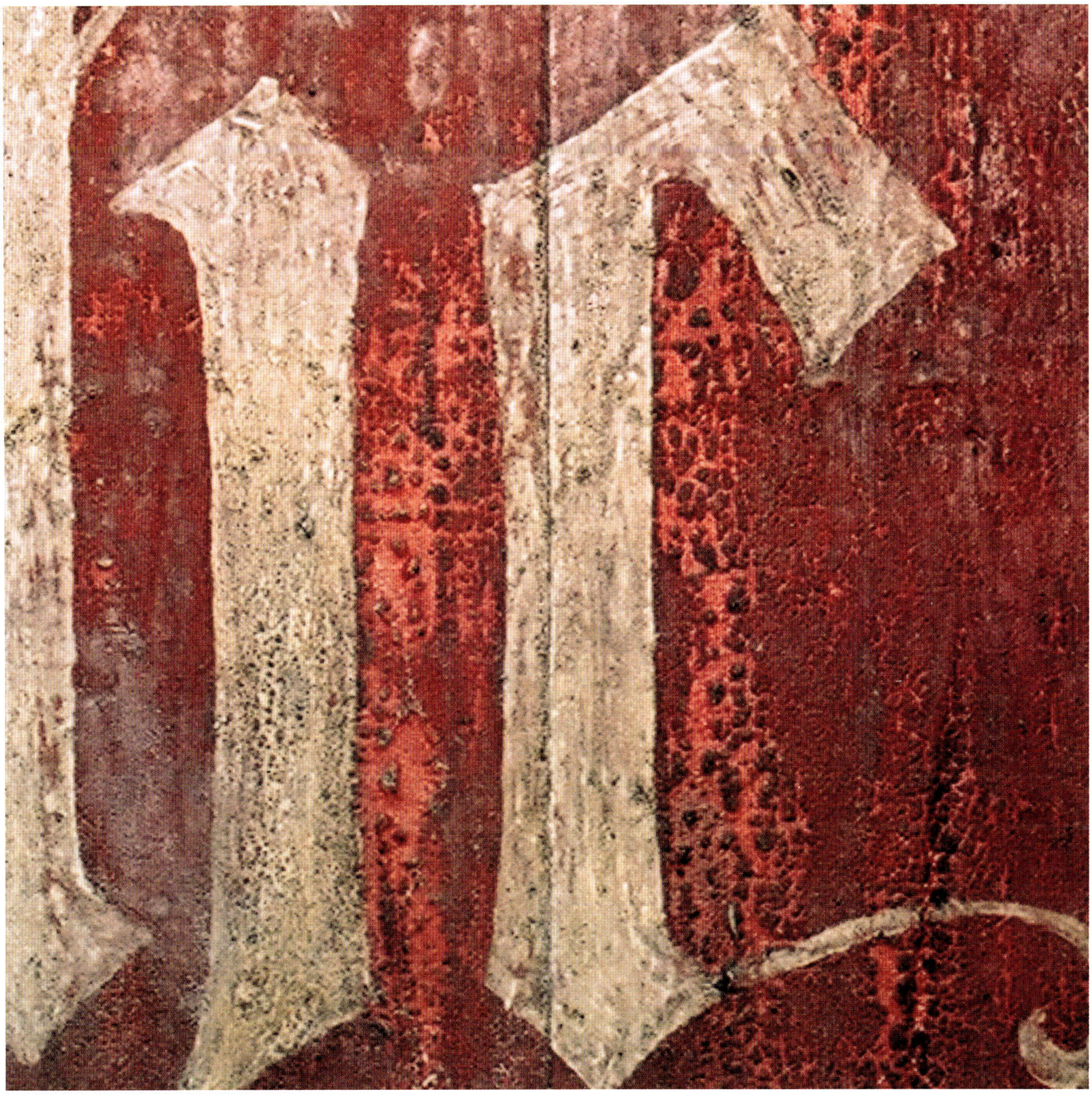

Figure 14 *Retracting paint on the screen at Mattishall Burgh church, Norfolk. (Photograph: Madeleine Katkov.)*

Material suppliers

- L. Cornelissen & Son, Artists' Colourmen, 105 Great Russell St, London WC1B 3RY
- Keith Edwards, 10 Kinglake Place, Nottingham NG2 1NT
- Kremer Pigmente GmbH & Co. KG, Hauptstr. 41–47, DE 88317 Aichstetten

Notes

1. A soundboard from another Suffolk church organ was found in Wetheringsett, Suffolk, in 1977.
2. For further information about the project see: www.rco.org.uk/eeop.php and www.goetzegwynn.co.uk/tudor.shtml.
3. For example in Thomas Spring's chantry screen at Lavenham, for which see Tracy and Harrison 2011.
4. I am grateful to Pauline Plummer for this observation.
5. I thank Andrea Kirkham for this observation.

References

Baker, A. 2011. *English Panel Painting 1400–1558: A Survey of Panel Paintings on East Anglian Rood Screens*. London: Archetype Publications.

Bucklow, S. 2009. *The Alchemy of Paint*. London: Marion Boyars.

Easton, T. and Bicknell, S. 1995. 'Two Pre-Reformation organ soundboards: towards an understanding of the form of early organs and their position within some Suffolk churches', *Proceedings of the Suffolk Institute of Archaeology and History* 38(3): 268–95.

Foister, S. 2001. 'Holbein's paintings on canvas: the Greenwich festivities of 1527'. In *Hans Holbein: Paintings, Prints and Reception*, Studies in the History of Art 60, M. Roskill and J.O. Hand (eds) 108–23. Washington, DC, New Haven, CT and London: National Gallery of Art.

Gwynn, D. 1996. 'Two English pre-Reformation organ soundboards', *The Organ Yearbook* 26: 1–27.

Katkov, M. 2004. 'The Wingfield Organ: Painted Decoration. A Report on the Research and Execution'. Unpublished report.

Massing, A. (ed.) 2003. *The Thornham Parva Retable: Technique, Conservation and Context of an English Medieval Painting*. London and Turnhout: Harvey Miller Publishers.

Plummer, P. and Hulbert, A. 1990. 'English polychromed church screens and the problems of their conservation in situ'. In *Cleaning, Retouching and Coatings: Technology and Practice for Easel Paintings and Polychrome Sculpture*, J. Mills and P. Smith (eds) 47–51. London: IIC.

Tracy, C. and Harrison, H. 2011. 'Thomas Spring's Chantry and Parclose at Lavenham, Suffolk', *Journal of the British Archaeological Association* 164(1): 221-259.

Woudhuysen-Keller, R. 1995. 'Aspects of painting technique in the use of verdigris and copper resinate'. In *Historical Painting Techniques, Materials, and Studio Practice*, A. Wallert, E. Hermens and M. Peek (eds) 65–9. Marina del Rey, CA: Getty Conservation Institute.

ASPECTS OF PAINTING TECHNIQUE IN THE *MADONNA AND CHILD WITH ST ANNE* ATTRIBUTED TO GIAN GIACOMO CAPROTTI, CALLED SALAI

Sue Ann Chui and Alan Phenix

The *Madonna and Child with St Anne* attributed to Gian Giacomo Caprotti, called Salai, an associate of Leonardo da Vinci, was brought from the Hammer Museum at the University of California Los Angeles (UCLA) to the Paintings Conservation Department at the J. Paul Getty Museum for study and treatment in preparation for an exhibition at the Musée du Louvre.[1] Dated to 1508–1513, the Hammer painting is a version, on the same scale, of the same subject painted by Leonardo now at the Louvre, and was almost certainly created in the master's studio. The *Madonna and Child with St Anne* has come down to us in remarkable condition from both a structural and aesthetic point of view. The panel has been virtually unaltered since it was constructed, and the paint surface remains very much intact with relatively few discrete losses. This paper describes aspects of the painting technique for which analysis of cross-sections greatly enhanced our understanding. Some of the interesting findings include a methodical approach to the paint build-up with the occurrence of intermediate varnish layers, and evidence of the use of both a textile and the hand to manipulate blue and red glazes.

The *Madonna and Child with St Anne*, 1508–1513 from UCLA has often been referred to as a copy of Leonardo da Vinci's painting of the same subject in the Musée du Louvre, Paris, but it is in fact more aptly described as a 'version' of Leonardo's painting, with elaborations to the background and changes in the figures' clothing (Fig. 1). In a wooded landscape, perched on a rocky edge with blue mountains in the distance, the Virgin sits on St Anne's lap as she bends down to hold the Christ Child who grasps a lamb by the ears. There are no exact contemporary copies of the Leonardo painting, only versions of it. One list includes 27 versions; among them, the UCLA version is considered the most important and closest to Leonardo's work (Musée du Louvre 1952: 43–4; Delieuvin 2011).[2] However, close copies of the UCLA St Anne do exist, such as the *St Anne with Virgin, Child and Lamb* of similar dimensions in the Museo d'Arte Antica del Castello Sforzesco, Milan (Delieuvin 2011).[3]

Leonardo recorded in his writings that a certain Giacomo came to live with him 'on St. Mary Magdalen's day, 1490, aged 10 (Leonardo da Vinci 1989: 266). In the early twentieth century Giacomo was identified as Gian Giacomo Caprotti di Oreno, called Salai or Salaino (Shell and Sironi 1991: 95). According to Vasari, Salai was both 'graceful and handsome, with beautiful curly hair', and 'certain works in Milan which are said to be by Salai were retouched' by his master (Vasari 1991: 563; Fairbrother and Ishikawa 1997: 35).[4] Salai overlapped in the studio with Giovanni Antonio Boltraffio and Marco d'Oggiono, two of Leonardo's better known associates. He was not only a painter, but also acted as Leonardo's representative, meeting with agents of patrons, and with other artists.[5] He remained in the service of his master until Leonardo's death in 1519 in France. Salai himself died in 1524.

Today, there are few extant paintings attributed to Salai. The UCLA painting was first attributed to Salai in the late eighteenth century (Shell and Sironi 1991: 104). In addition to the *Madonna and Child with St Anne*, a *Head of Christ* appeared on the market in 2007 that is apparently the only signed and dated work by the artist.[6] Most recently, a copy of the *Mona Lisa* at the Museo del Prado, Madrid, has been ascribed to Salai (Mottin 2011b).[7]

The earliest mention of the UCLA *Madonna and Child with St Anne* places it in the sacristy of the church of San Celso in Milan in the seventeenth century, where it was first considered to be a work of Leonardo da Vinci; it remained there until 1826. It then passed into the collection of Prince Eugene Beauharnis, Viceroy of Italy,

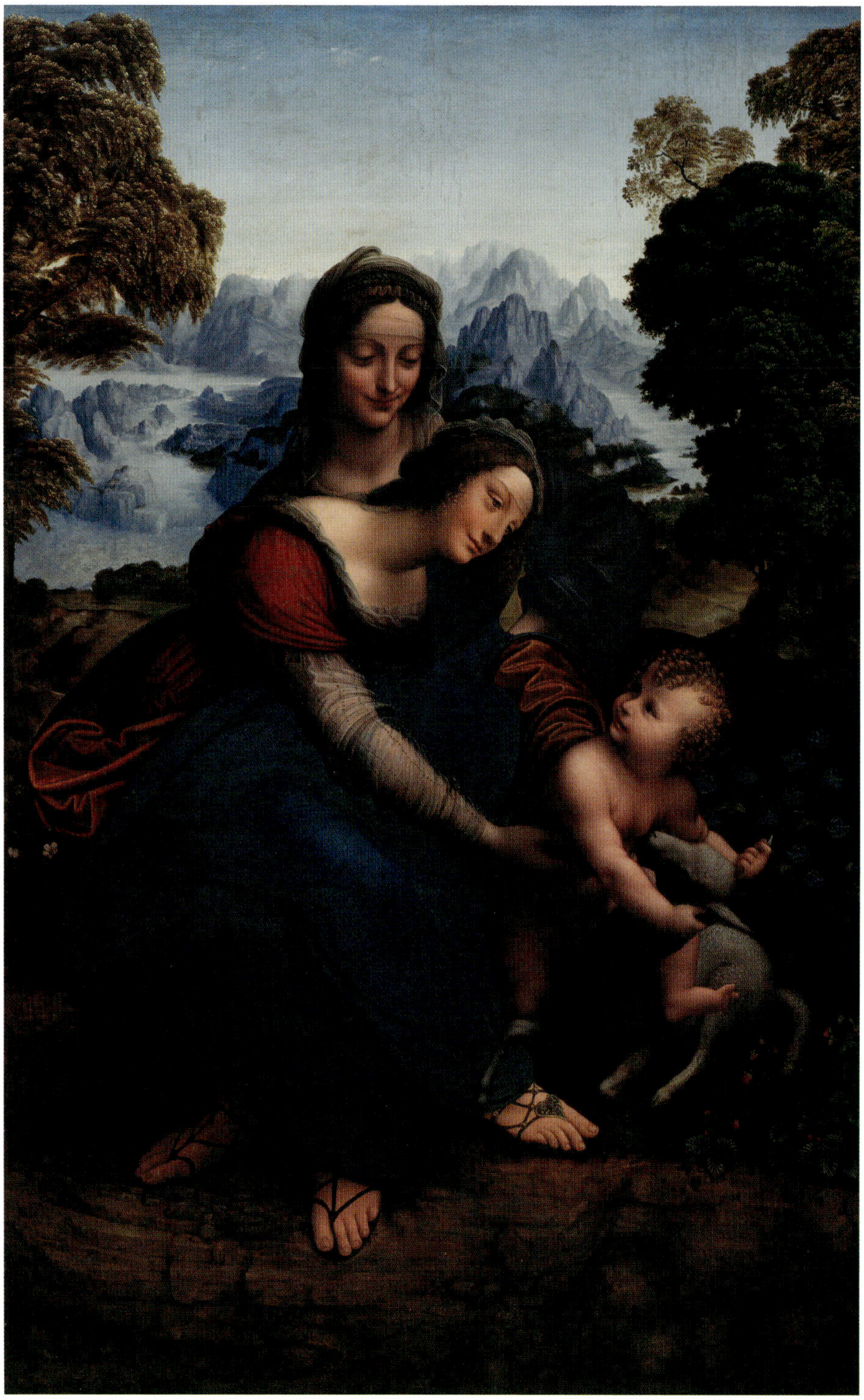

Figure 1 *Workshop of Leonardo da Vinci, Gian Giacomo Caprotti, called Salai,* Madonna and Child with St Anne, *1508–1513, oil on panel, 177.8 × 114.3 cm (70 × 40 in.). Collection University of California, Los Angeles. Hammer Museum. Willitts J. Hole Collection. Before conservation. (Photograph courtesy of the J. Paul Getty Museum, Los Angeles.)*

followed by Prince Leuchtenberg of St Petersburg. After the Russian Revolution, a Swedish syndicate acquired the painting and it was brought to New York by Dr Gregor Paulsson of Stockholm University. Shortly thereafter it must have been acquired by Willets J. Hole, who in turn bequeathed the painting to UCLA in 1938 (Valentiner 1949: 25; Goldblatt 1961: 108–13; Shell and Sironi 1991: 104; Delieuvin 2012: 166).[8]

Support

One of the most remarkable features of the painting by Salai from a conservation point of view is that the wooden support is remarkably close to original condition. It has not been thinned and has undergone only a few conservative repairs. Because the support of the Leonardo *St Anne* has miraculously survived without major alterations as well,

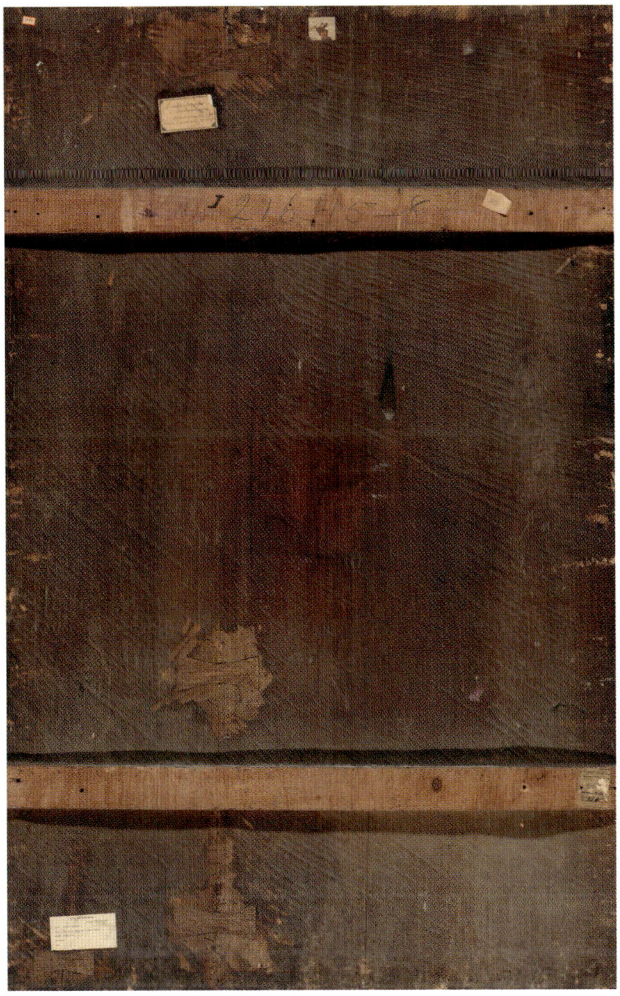

Figure 2 *Gian Giacomo Caprotti, called Salai,* Madonna and Child with St Anne, *reverse. (Photograph courtesy of the J. Paul Getty Museum, Los Angeles.)*

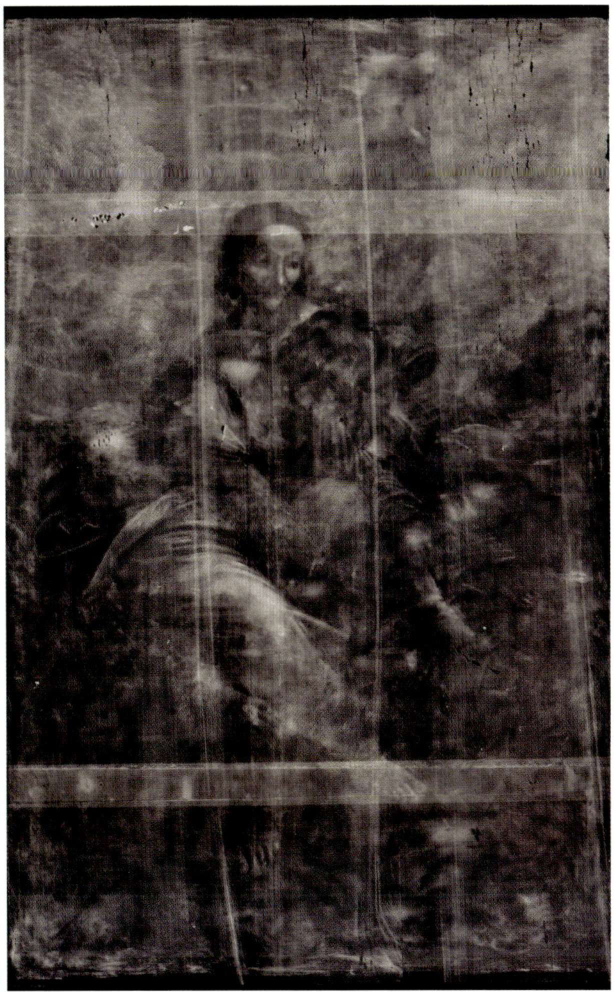

Figure 3 *X-radiograph of Gian Giacomo Caprotti, called Salai,* Madonna and Child with St Anne. *(Photograph courtesy of the J. Paul Getty Museum, Los Angeles.)*

intriguing technical comparisons can be made between the two paintings.

The panel support is composed of three butt-joined vertical boards, estimated to be poplar, with two cross battens dovetailed into the structure (Fig. 2). Two wide boards flank a narrower board, all tangentially cut as can be gleaned from the end-grain and X-radiograph. In the X-radiograph, the outer boards – but possibly all three – look as if they were cut from the same tree because of the similarity of the dense grain pattern (Fig. 3). Overall, the panel is 115.3 cm wide, approximately the same width as Leonardo's *St Anne* (without the additions) and a version from a French private collection, but the UCLA painting is 178.5 cm high, taller than both of these versions by around 10 cm.[9]

The X-radiograph also revealed the presence of four dowels in each join symmetrically placed across from each other. The placement of the dowels is similar to that found in the Leonardo painting, though the panel consists of four boards rather than three as in the Hammer painting (Martin *et al.* 2005: 28). The dowels, which are 8.5–10 cm long, have tapered ends and are shorter than the tapered dowel holes (Fig. 4).

The width and thickness of the individual boards indicate an economical use of wood in the construction of the panel. The boards each taper slightly across their widths, preserving the natural taper of the tree trunk. Little wood is wasted by not squaring each board before assembly of the panel. The outer boards are widest at the bottom, while the middle board is widest at the top. The thickness of the panel differs slightly from side to side varying from 2.0 to 2.8 cm, which is thin for an Italian painting on poplar, but is comparable with the thicknesses of the other two versions. This preservation of variation in thickness also demonstrates how the panel maker maximised the amount of wood available.

The two cross battens appear to be original, but in the past they have been thinned with a saw to about half of their original thicknesses.[10] The cross battens are estimated to be a coniferous wood, cut sub-radially. Both battens taper from right to left. The top batten protrudes on the right side by 1 cm showing shrinkage across the width of the panel.

There are long, diagonal, parallel, slightly furrowed tool marks, 0.5–1.4 cm wide, on the reverse that go across the joins and span the width of the panel. These marks

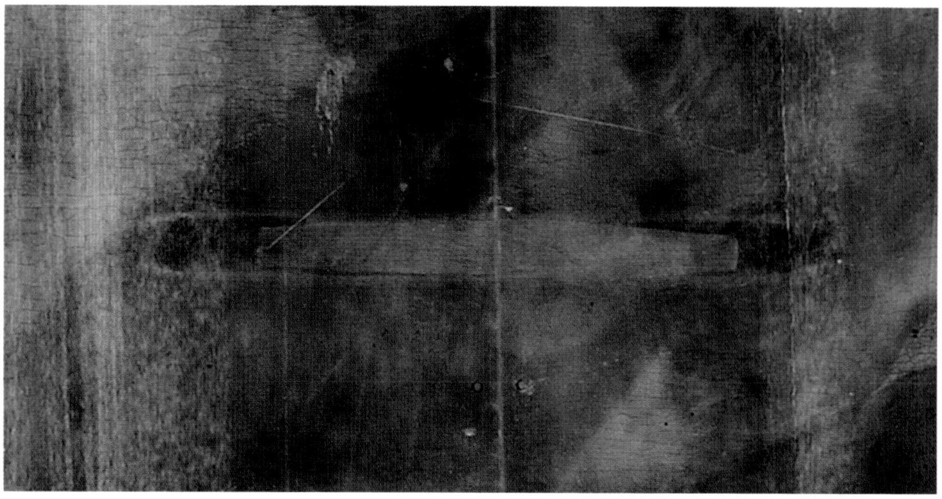

Figure 4 *Detail of a dowel in the X-radiograph. (Photograph courtesy of the J. Paul Getty Museum, Los Angeles.)*

were probably made using a narrow plane with a curved blade and sole.[11] They appear very similar to the marks on the reverse of Leonardo's *St Anne*. The similarities in the panel construction, from the dowel placement to the thickness and tool marks, all suggest that the two panels were made in the same workshop. One could even argue that the UCLA panel is of higher quality because it has fewer joins than the Louvre panel, and the three, individual planks are free of knots, unlike the boards in the Leonardo painting and the version from a French private collection.[12]

Preparation and underdrawing

There are bare wood margins at the top and bottom of the painting about 1.0–1.5 cm wide. There are no wood margins on the sides and they do not appear to have been trimmed. The blue sky paint spills over the gesso burr in several spots at the top and onto the wood margin as evidence of a temporary frame used during the application of the preparation that was removed or shifted during the painting phase.

The ground appears to be a conventional calcium sulphate gesso bound with animal glue (Mazurek 2011).[13] After the gesso ground is a second preparatory layer of *imprimatura*, essentially comprising lead white, that seemingly covers the entire panel surface. In the upper central region of the panel, two applications of similar material have been applied. Rather surprisingly, the panel already had cracks in it when the preparation was applied as these were filled in and appear opaque in the X-radiograph.

Infrared examination with an Osiris camera[14] revealed underdrawing in both liquid and dry media in some parts of the painting, mostly in the heads and feet of the figures (Fig. 5). Some of the underdrawing also shows subtle changes in the composition. In the face of St Anne, lines in the nose (which was originally smaller) and in the lips were applied in a liquid medium with a fine brush, but lines in her brows appear to have been executed with a dry medium such as charcoal. The contours of the top of her head and shoulder are made with broad dry marks. A broad liquid stroke delineates the back of the Christ Child's neck which was originally less wide. The veil on top of the Madonna's head had a smoother contour like that in the Leonardo Virgin, indicated by a simple brushed line also in a dry medium. The mountains to the left of St Anne's head were laid out with a few sketchy, dry strokes.

Dry lines in the Virgin's foot show that the big toe was slightly longer, and the toe next to it was originally drawn higher. Dry lines also appear in St Anne's left foot showing that the longest toe was closer to the big toe. It is interesting to note that in this painting, the one by Leonardo and the one in a French private collection, underdrawing is visible only in the foot of the Virgin and St Anne's left foot, but not in her right foot.

No underdrawing was found in the Virgin's face or in the rest of the painting, and no *spolvero* dots were detected, as were observed in the Leonardo *St Anne* (Mottin 2011a), but one must keep in mind that red or brown pigments and iron gall ink, which might have been used in the laying out of the composition either from a cartoon or done freehand, would not be detected with infrared reflectography (IRR). The scale of the figures in the Hammer painting is comparable with the two previously mentioned paintings, and some of the composition corresponds precisely among them, but there is no definitive answer as to how the design was transferred.[15]

The similarities in scale between the paintings were established through a tracing made of the version from the French private collection which, when overlaid on the Leonardo painting, shows that the figures coincide.[16] The same tracing placed over the UCLA painting shows that the figures correspond quite closely with slight variations of usually 1–2 cm; it does not exactly correspond with the French paintings. Where the tracing corresponds almost precisely is around the heads of St

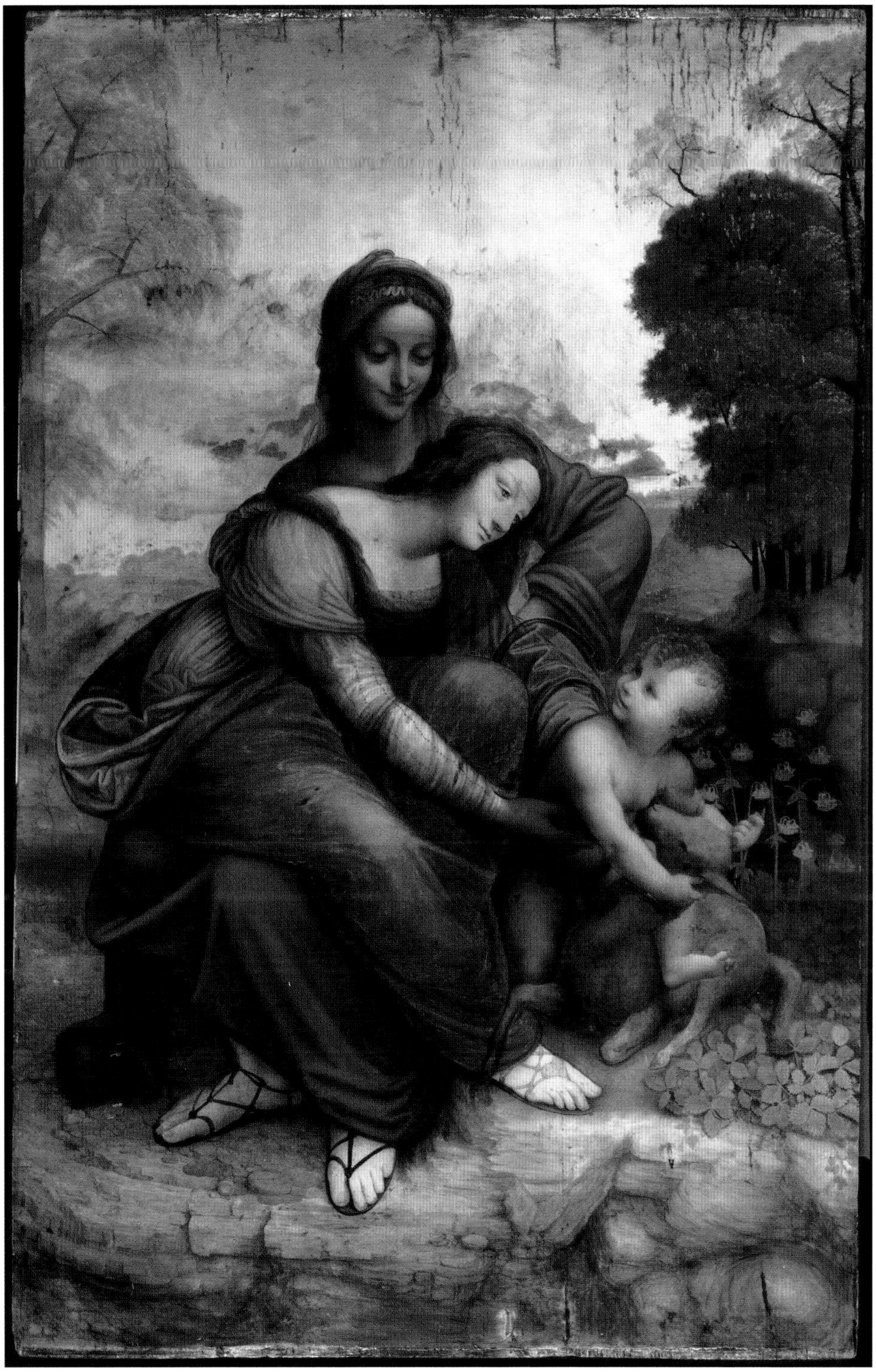

Figure 5 *Infrared reflectogram of Gian Giacomo Caprotti, called Salai,* Madonna and Child with St Anne. *(Photograph courtesy of the J. Paul Getty Museum, Los Angeles.)*

Anne and the Madonna. The largest variations are: St Anne's left foot, which is 2 cm longer than the French version; the lamb's tail, which is shorter by 3.5 cm and ends in a straight, flat tip in contrast to the French tip which curves up slightly to the right; the lamb's front leg which is bent at a more acute angle and is higher than the French one by 1 cm.

The head of St Anne is very close but slightly thinner than in the French paintings. The right sleeve of the Madonna is less puffy, and her right arm is a little wider by as much as 1 cm. Her foot is about the same size as the French one, but the blue drapery is slightly more extended. The Virgin's neckline is a little higher. St Anne's right foot is the same size, but also has a little more drapery covering it. The Christ Child's head is slightly wider, the lamb's head is higher and its hind leg and bent leg are higher up and shorter. The most variation seems to be around the Child and lamb.

Figure 6 *Figure on reverse seen under UV fluorescence. (Photograph courtesy of the J. Paul Getty Museum, Los Angeles.)*

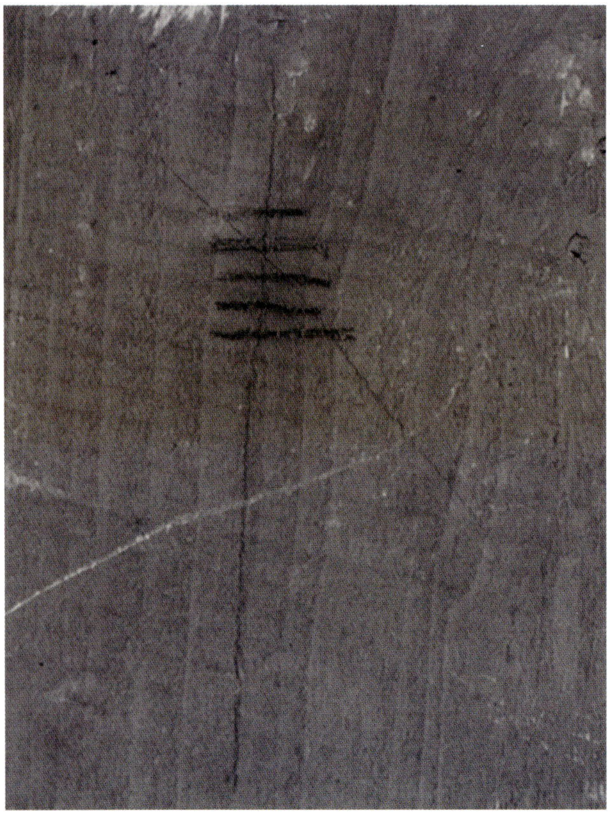

Figure 7 *Diagram on reverse, infrared reflectogram. (Photograph courtesy of the J. Paul Getty Museum, Los Angeles.)*

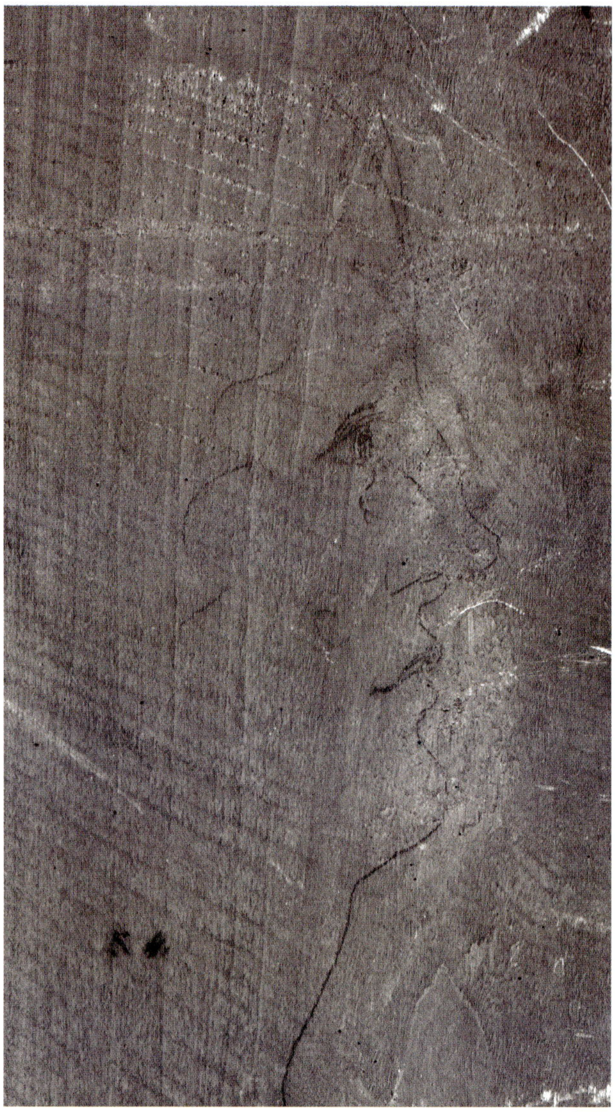

Figure 8 *Drawing of person in profile on reverse, infrared reflectogram. (Photograph courtesy of the J. Paul Getty Museum, Los Angeles.)*

Besides the underdrawing, a series of different marks in the X-radiograph – appearing to be short, filled incision lines, dark incision lines, X-ray opaque lines and dark passages where material seems to have been wiped away – give some clues to the artist's method of laying out the composition at different stages during the painting's execution. The marks seem to relate to the composition as they are mostly located in and around the figures. The reason for their presence might be that they were the result of a traced cartoon, registration marks for key points of the composition such as the intersection of the shoulder and neck, or aids in the positioning of single-element cartoons that were combined in the painting.[17]

On the reverse of the painting, drawings were found under examination with ultraviolet light (UV) and IRR. A figure holding what might be a baby could be seen under UV (Fig. 6). More easily discernible with IRR were crossed lines with a series of parallel lines intersecting the angles, perhaps a perspective diagram, and a man in profile (Figs 7 and 8).

Painting technique and *pentimenti*

The UCLA painting is a highly finished version of the Leonardo *St Anne*, which some consider to be incomplete. Dated by scholars later than the Leonardo painting, Leonardo's intentions for the latter have been said to be found in the UCLA painting (Delieuvin 2011). Moreover, the high finish can still be admired because the paint surface and fine details are so well preserved.

The artist used pigments typical of the time: lead white, vermilion, lead-tin yellow, yellow and red iron oxide earths, natural ultramarine (lapis lazuli), and an arsenic sulphide pigment probably orpiment. Other pigments indicated by microscopical and chemical analysis[18] include azurite, a transparent copper green, at least one organic red lake on an alum-derived substrate, and some form of carbon black. The extensive use of ultramarine in this painting is noteworthy. Indeed, the alternative mineral blue pigment, azurite, seems to have been used in a relatively restricted way; it appears mixed mostly with white in the underpainting layers of the distant mountainous background. Despite the slight greenish appearance of the Madonna's blue robe, azurite has not been used in the painting of that drapery; ultramarine is the blue pigment present, with some red lake also included. Another distinctive feature of the painting technique is the extensive use of one or more shades of red lake pigment. In some instances, as in the Madonna's inner red robe, the lake appears remarkably well preserved, with little perceptible fading.

Examination of paint cross-sections demonstrated that many passages of the painting had surprisingly complex stratigraphies. Mostly, the samples reflected a methodical build-up of the paint layers. A striking feature of some of the samples is the marked difference in colour between paints at different levels in the layer structure. It is not entirely clear if, and in which cases, these variations within a sample are the artist's intentional sequence of painting the particular passage concerned or are alterations in colour scheme or composition (that is, *pentimenti*); the samples may reveal unusual modelling techniques for the draperies and/or a change of conception about the drapery colours and forms. One instance of this phenomenon occurs in the Madonna's blue mantle (Fig. 9). The first paint applications on the white *imprimatura* are transparent crimson red – effectively glazes – which, rather curiously, are then painted over with one or more layers of dark grey paint that in turn provide a foundation for the final application of royal blue paint composed essentially of ultramarine and a little red lake. The dark grey underpainting might be interpreted as an intentional foundation, for optical purposes, of the blue drapery, a practice known in fourteenth- and fifteenth-century Italian painting; whether the initial crimson red layers similarly represent intentional underpainting for the blue, or are associated with a different initial conception for the Madonna's robe, is not certain. There are several aspects of this unusual sequence of paint layers that are intriguing: a transparent glaze as the first paint application, rather than relatively opaque body colour, is rather strange and seems counter to painting practice at the time; the grey layer(s) in the Madonna's mantle would essentially obliterate the red lake layer, so what would be the function of the crimson red? Interestingly, a red lake layer has also been found under the blue drapery of the Virgin by Leonardo (Mottin 2011b).[19] Red lake under blue (without intervening grey paint) has also been noted in paintings by Raphael where it clearly serves as intentional underpainting, not connected with a *pentimento* (Ritano and Seccaroni 2008: 98–9). Whether the same intention is at work here, in the Salai, remains open to conjecture.[20]

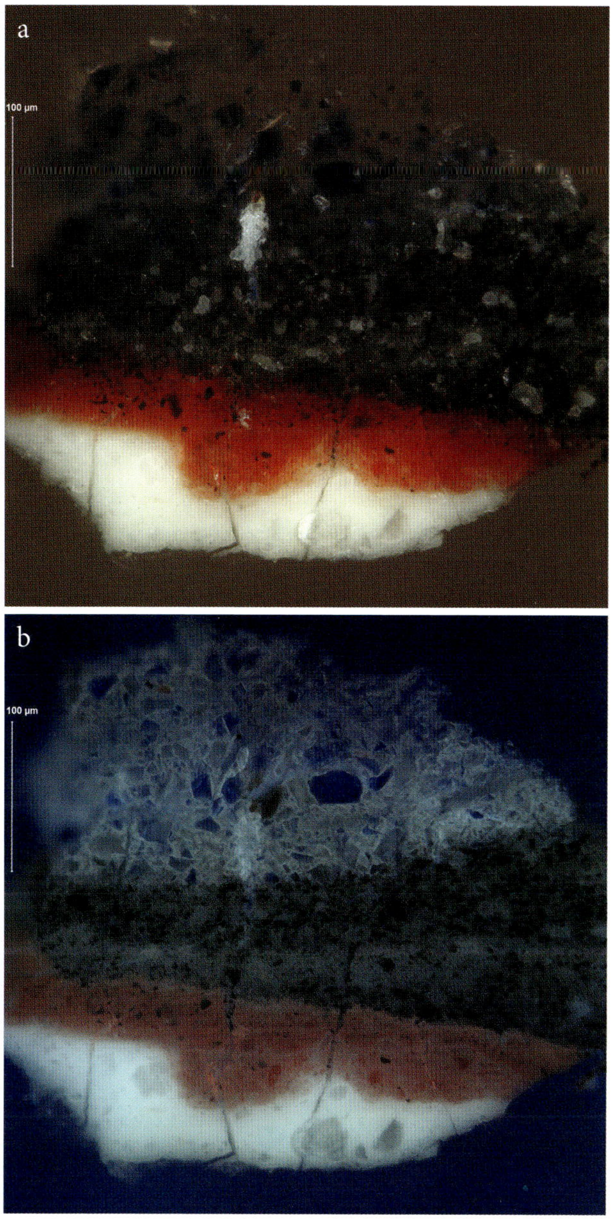

Figure 9 *(a) Cross-section from the Madonna's blue robe, crossed polarising filters, 30× objective power. The uppermost blue paint, composed of ultramarine with some red lake, is underpainted with a series of dark grey layers and, below that, two layers of transparent crimson. (b) UV fluorescence of (a), 30× objective power. (Photographs by Alan Phenix © 2012 J. Paul Getty Trust.)*

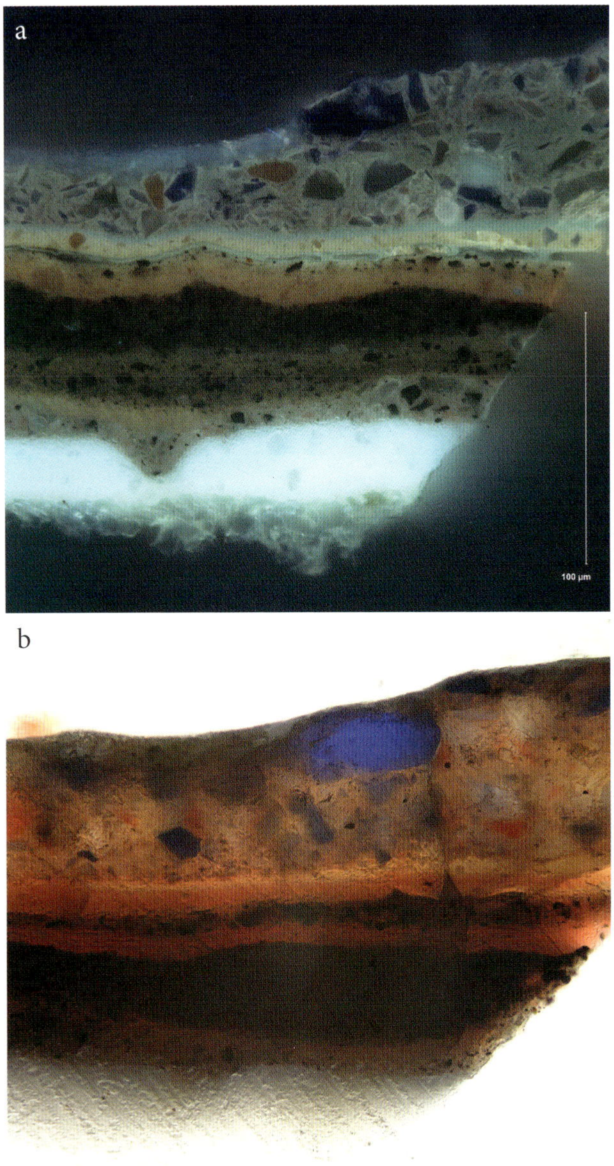

Figure 10 *(a) Sample from St Anne's purple sleeve, prepared as a conventional cross-section, viewed under incident UV fluorescence conditions, 50× objective power. The sample shows the complex stratigraphy of this passage of painting: ground and* imprimatura *superimposed by a series of dark reddish brown paints and red glaze; an intermediate varnish followed by a further red glaze; a second intermediate varnish and the final, uppermost layer of purple that renders the drapery. (b) Same sample as in (a), converted to thin-section, viewed in transmitted light, 50× objective power. The colours of the glaze layers are clearly evident, as are the intermediate varnishes. The uppermost purple paint is composed of ultramarine, red lake and a little black. The ground and* imprimatura *layers are not visible here. (Photographs by Alan Phenix © 2012 J. Paul Getty Trust.)*

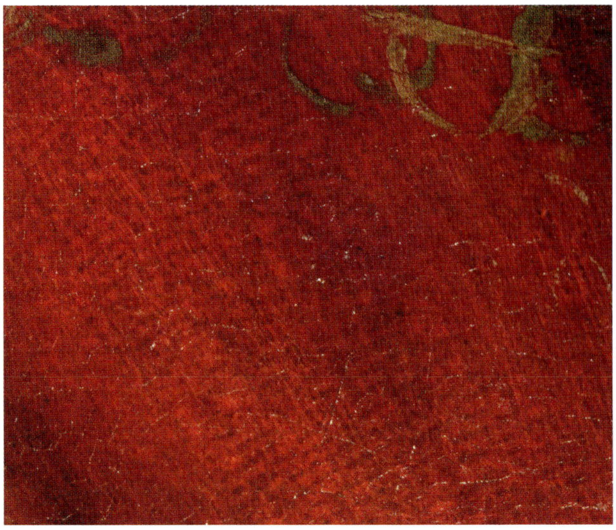

Figure 11 *Photomicrograph detail of fingerprints in red glaze on the Madonna's shoulder, 7.1× objective power. (Photograph courtesy of the J. Paul Getty Museum, Los Angeles.)*

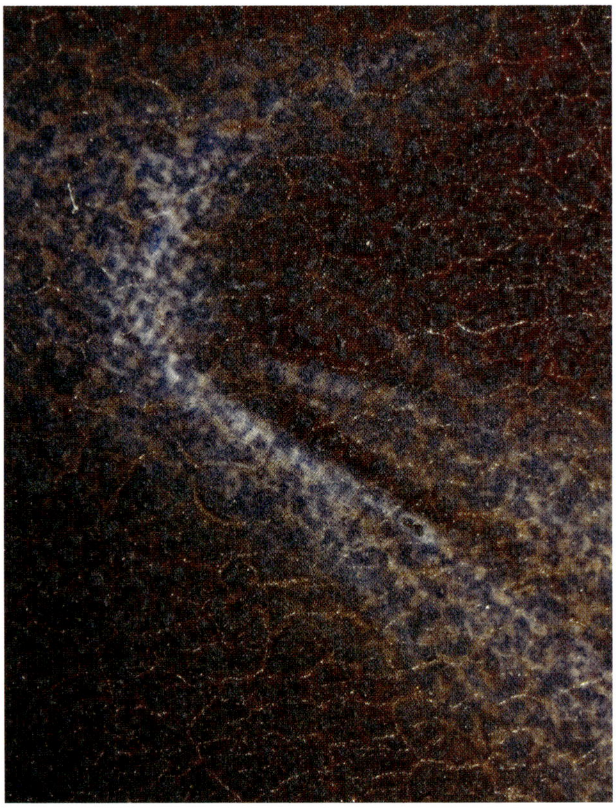

Figure 12 *Photomicrograph detail of textile imprint in blue glaze on St Anne's sleeve, 7.1× objective power. (Photograph courtesy of the J. Paul Getty Museum, Los Angeles.)*

Another notable instance of the phenomenon of complex stratigraphy with strong internal variation in paint colour appeared in samples that were obtained from different locations in the purple clothing of St Anne (see one example in Fig. 10). The deep purplish hue of this drapery is rendered by one or more layers of paint composed of ultramarine and red lake; in all the samples, beneath the uppermost purple paint, lies a near-consistent sequence of dark red and red-brown paints of varying transparency that in itself appears to represent a quite fully modelled drapery in that colour range. In each sample, between the lower strata of red and red-brown paints and the upper one(s) of purple, there is something of a discontinuity, represented by a thin glaze of pure red lake and unpigmented organic material, probably intermediate varnish. In two of the three samples from this drapery, the transitional red

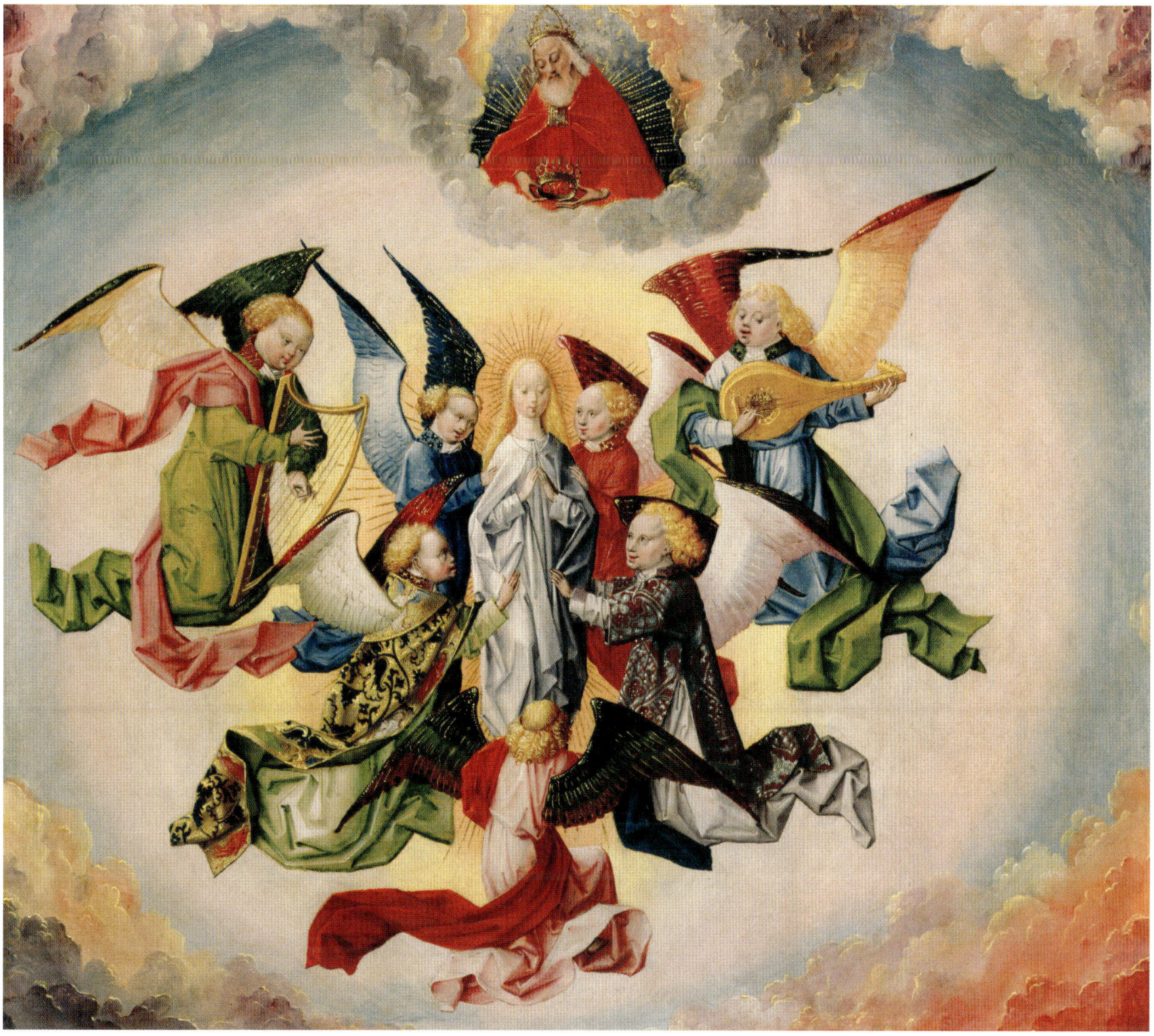

Figure 13 *Master of the Saint Bartholomew Altarpiece,* The Meeting of the Three Kings with David and Isaiah: Verso: Assumption of the Virgin. *Netherlandish, before 1480, oil and gold leaf on panel, 62.9 × 71.8 cm (24¾ × 28¼₆ in.) (96.PB.16). (Photograph courtesy of the J. Paul Getty Museum, Los Angeles.)*

lake glaze is actually sandwiched between two layers of intermediate varnish, as evident in Figure 10a. As in the previous case of the Madonna's blue mantle, this unusual stratigraphy invites the question of whether it represents a deliberate continuous sequence of paint applications for the rendering of this drapery, or whether the internal hue variation indicates a change of colour scheme during the course of painting. In the case of St Anne's robe, the weight of evidence might lean more towards the latter conclusion: that is, that St Anne's drapery was changed from modulated dark red and red-brown to purple during the course of the painting's execution. The evidence supporting this hypothesis includes the strong internal boundary in the stratigraphies of all cross-section samples from St Anne's robe indicated by the intermediate varnish layers that are contiguous with the last red glaze, and the occurrence of the same essential sequence of red and red-brown paints as the lower strata in a sample from the now mostly obscured flap of St Anne's robe, lower left, that was painted over to become part of the rocky seat on which the figures are sitting. It may not be entirely coincidental that a well worked-up modelled drapery in shades of red to red-brown is seemingly embodied in the lower strata under the purple of St Anne's robe of the Salai painting, and that the same figure's drapery (or at least the lower part of it) is in the same general colour range in the Louvre Leonardo version of the composition.

The highly finished nature of the painting technique is reflected in the large areas of extant glazes present in the Madonna's red sleeve and blue drapery, and St Anne's purple sleeve where traces of fingerprints and the imprint of a textile were left behind. Many papillary lines were left in the Madonna's red sleeve on her proper right shoulder from the use of fingers in the final application of red lake glaze (Fig. 11). Before this, the sleeve had already been worked up to a very finished state with red lake on top of a mixture of lead white and red lake, and was then varnished. Traces of fingerprints can be seen in the shadows

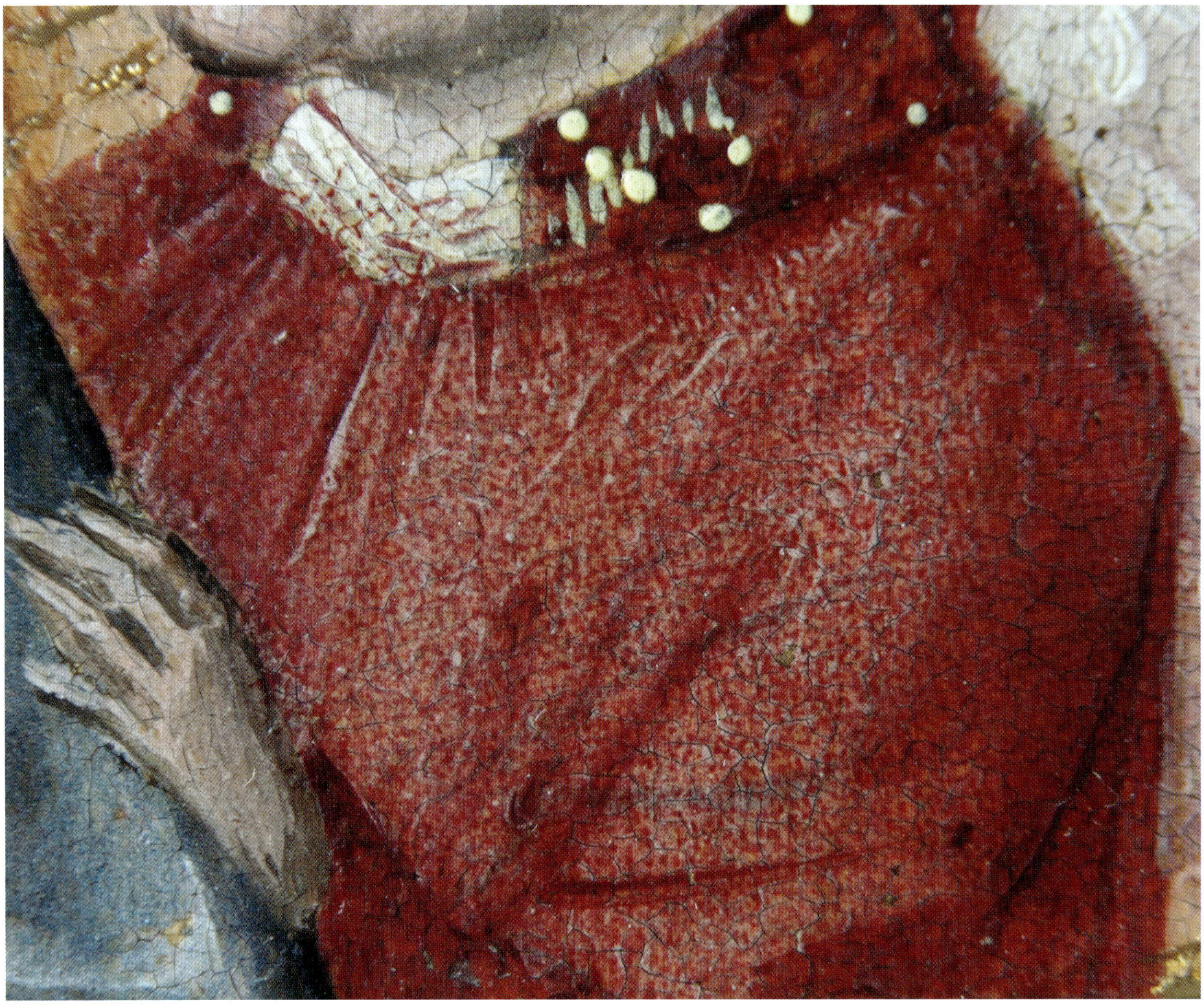

Figure 14 *Master of the Saint Bartholomew Altarpiece,* The Meeting of the Three Kings with David and Isaiah: Verso: Assumption of the Virgin. *Detail of textile imprint in red glaze of the angel's garment. (Photograph courtesy of the J. Paul Getty Museum, Los Angeles.)*

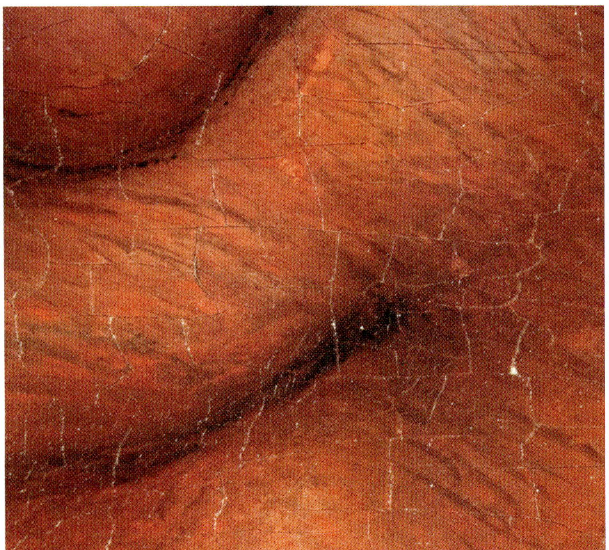

Figure 15 *Photomicrograph detail of paint strokes around St Anne's nose and lips, 7.1× objective power. (Photograph courtesy of the J. Paul Getty Museum, Los Angeles.)*

of St Anne's face around her left cheek and chin. Prints from fingers or the palm are found in the Madonna's blue mantle over her legs, and are especially noticeable in the highlighted area of her thigh. The technique of using the hand to uniformly distribute a glaze layer is described in Armenini's sixteenth-century treatise *On the True Precepts of the Art of Painting*. Specifically, for a green 'veil' he instructs to pat it with 'the palm of the hand' to even out its application; the same procedure is recommended for lake and smalt (Armenini 1997: 194; 1988: 145; Woudhuysen-Keller 1995: 66). A row of fingerprints is also found in the trees on the left, but they are located in a lower paint layer.

In St Anne's sleeve, instead of papillary lines, a distinctive grid-like pattern of tiny dots appears in the blue glaze – evidence that a piece of textile was used to even out its application (Fig. 12). Armenini also states that a 'little cotton wool covered with linen' can be tamped on top of the glaze to obtain the same results as with the hand (Armenini 1997: 194; 1988: 145; Wouduysen-Keller 1995: 66). Another example of the use of a textile with glaze is found in the *Assumption of the Virgin*, the verso of a late fifteenth-century double-sided panel by the Master of the

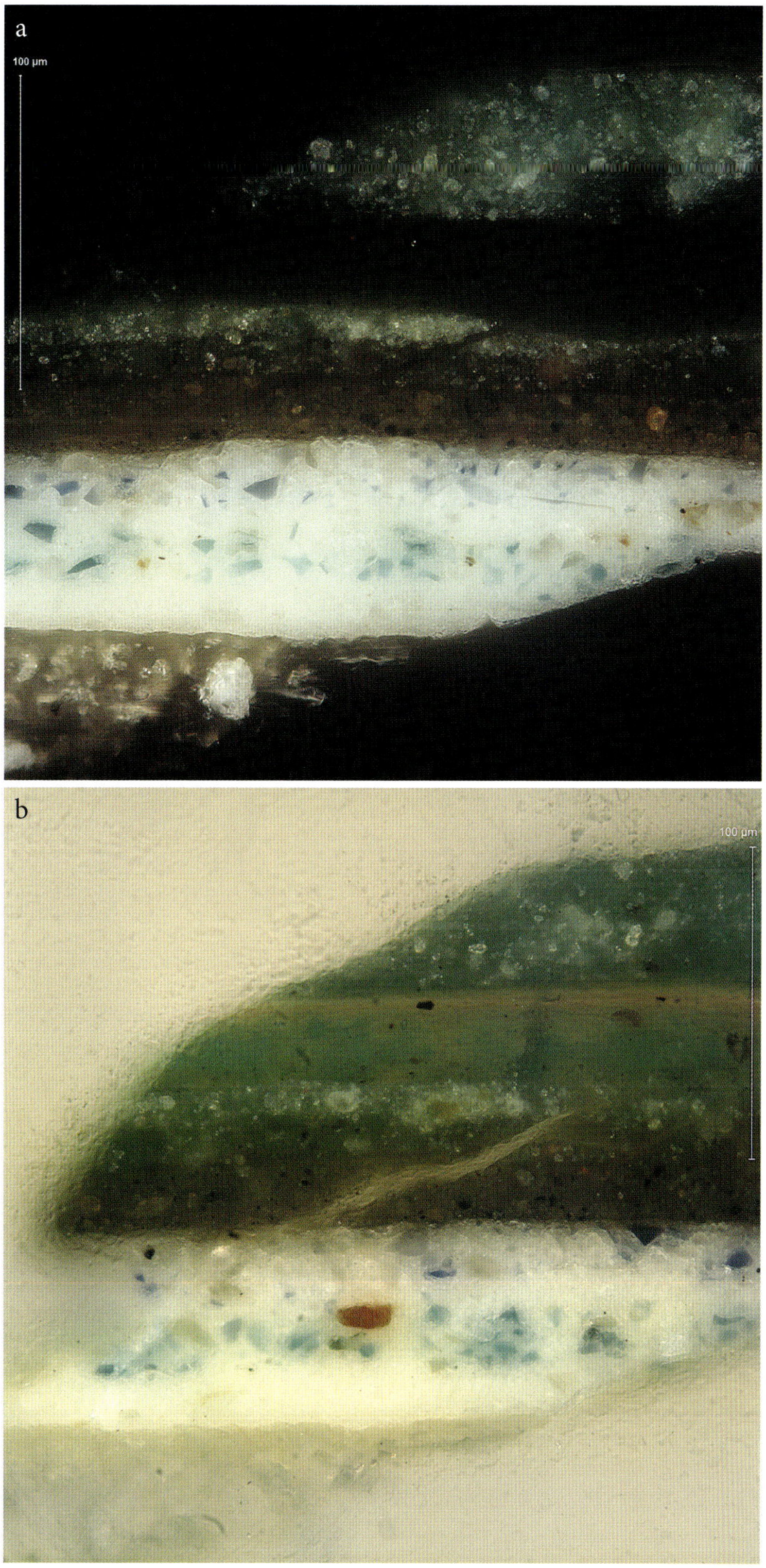

Figure 16 *(a) Sample from the trees upper right, prepared as conventional cross-section, viewed under incident light; crossed polarising filters; 50× objective power. This sample shows the complex layer structure of the trees on the right side of the painting. The ground and white* imprimatura *are superimposed first by a series of pale blue paints associated with the painting of the mountainous landscape: the lower pale blue layer contains azurite, the upper one ultramarine. There follows a brownish underpaint for the trees which is overlaid by a thin layer of intermediate varnish and then a series of dull green paints of varying opacity/transparency that is topped by a very transparent brownish green glaze. A second intermediate varnish precedes final layers of transparent and semi-opaque blue-green. (b) Same sample as in (a), converted to thin-section, viewed in partial transmitted light. Same scale; 50× objective power. The colours of the glaze layers and the intermediate varnishes are now more clearly evident. (Photographs by Alan Phenix © 2012 J. Paul Getty Trust.)*

St Bartholomew Altarpiece (J. Paul Getty Museum). The imprint of a textile is found in the red dress of the angel to the immediate right of the Virgin (Figs 13 and 14).

The flesh tones, principally in and around the faces, are constructed with many fine, parallel brushstrokes, reminiscent of tempera painting (Fig. 15). These are the only areas in the painting where this type of brushstroke is found. The rest of the painting is executed more loosely and analysis strongly indicates walnut oil as the binding medium (Mazurek 2011).[21] Drying cracks typically found in oil paint are present in the Virgin's thick blue mantle.

A reserve left for St Anne's head was noted in the IRR. The trees, however, were painted over the sky, which was already completed. In the IRR the trees on the left are lighter than those on the right side indicating they were painted differently. This observation is corroborated by cross-sections that also show that the trees are quite different in execution: the trees on the left are executed much more directly – in just two or three layers – than those on the right which have a surprisingly complicated build-up of opaque paints, glazes and intermediate varnish (Fig. 16). In the vegetation of the lower background there may also be two different hands in evidence when comparing the flowers to the left of the Madonna with those to the right of the lamb. On the left, the grasses and pink flowers are thinly and quickly painted with delicate, thin highlights, in contrast to the columbine and strawberries on the right which have much more body and are executed less deftly.

The foregoing discussion alludes to one of the most striking outcomes from examination of cross-section samples from the painting: the finding in many of them of an intermediate varnish layer, and sometimes more than one such coating. Indeed, the use of intermediate varnish seems a distinctive feature of this artist's painting practice. It can be observed that the varnish layer sometimes lies between distinct early and later phases of the painting connected to apparent changes in specific parts of the composition, but more commonly it occurs close to the later stages of painting, in which cases it may represent applications of artists' 'retouching varnish', prior to the final subtle adjustments and additions of detail.

Besides the *pentimenti* described above, more changes were detected in the paint layers with both IRR and X-radiography, and often reflect Leonardo's composition in the Musée du Louvre, which had been elaborated upon in the UCLA picture. In the IRR, St Anne's sleeve was originally slimmer and had a protruding cuff; the rock under her clearly had a flap of fabric hanging over it that folded laterally on the ground; the Madonna's blue mantle over her proper left sleeve in its first conception was simply draped and continued down to her wrist without the undulating folds of the orange lining. The latter two *pentimenti* are also observable in paint cross-sections. The red paint in the rock represents the drapery that was initially planned. In the Madonna's sleeve a deep crimson layer followed by an ultramarine blue under the now visible orange-brown of the exposed lining are interpreted as representing an earlier state (purplish blue or blue-grey) for that section of drapery (Fig. 10). All of these earlier compositional intentions are found in Leonardo's painting.

Other *pentimenti* detected in the IRR include: different plants in the right middle background where blue columbine flowers have replaced groups of three small leaves growing from a central stem; the Child's head and neck which were narrower, and his proper left shoulder that may have been slightly higher. In the X-radiograph there was something else immediately next to the Child's proper left shoulder, and the Madonna's neckline was perhaps more closed than it appears now.

Conclusion

The exceptional preservation of the panel support and paint film of the UCLA *Madonna and Child with St Anne* has allowed much information about the materials and technique of the painting to be extracted. Comparison with Leonardo's version of the same composition demonstrates similarities in the panel construction which strongly suggest that the supports were made in the same workshop. Though the paintings are of the same scale, we do not fully understand how the composition was transferred from the master to his assistant as the underdrawings visible through IRR are incomplete in both paintings and stylistically different from each other. Differences in the handling of the paint in the two paintings are obviously visible on the surface where Leonardo has quickly, loosely and thinly applied his paints in contrast to the more rigid, thicker layers of paint laid down by Salai. A comparison of the X-radiographs also shows a difference in the application of the paint as the figures in the Leonardo *St Anne* are hardly distinguishable, while in the UCLA painting the features of the composition are more radio-opaque and defined.

The complexity of the painting technique found in Salai's *Madonna and Child with St Anne* was revealed by cross-section analysis. This is in contrast to a simpler build-up of paint by Leonardo in his *St Anne*. Some similarities exist such as the presence of red lake as a base layer, but there are no reported intermediate varnish layers in Leonardo's version. The use of red lake as an underpaint in Italian painting needs further investigation as it is a rare occurrence in Italian painting, but is used in both the Salai and Leonardo *St Anne* paintings. The *pentimenti* present in the UCLA *Madonna and Child with St Anne* – most dramatically, the opening of the sleeve to reveal the orange lining, and the transformation of the drapery flap into a rock – indicate that Leonardo's composition was still evolving during its execution. The exhibition at the Musée du Louvre will certainly further enrich our understanding of Leonardo da Vinci's *St Anne* composition and its relationship to the different versions.

Postscript

Since the time the manuscript was submitted, the attribution of the *Madonna and Child with St Anne* has changed from Andrea Salai to the Workshop of Leonardo da Vinci. This new attribution does not preclude Salai as the author, but allows the possibility that others, such as Francesco Melzi and the Master himself, had a hand in the painting (Delieuvin 2012: 166).

Acknowledgements

We sincerely thank the following for their collaboration: Vincent Delieuvin, Musée du Louvre; Bruno Mottin, Centre de recherche et de restauration des musées de France (C2RMF); Cindy Burlingham, Hammer Museum; Joy Mazurek, Getty Conservation Institute; Yvonne Szafran, Laura Rivers, Gene Karraker, J. Paul Getty Museum; Tiarna Doherty, Smithsonian American Art Museum; Ciro Castelli, Andrea Santacesaria, Opificio delle Pietre Dure; George Bisacca, Metropolitan Museum of Art.

Notes

1. The exhibition (March–June 2012) focused on the newly restored *St Anne* by Leonardo da Vinci, and brought together over 100 works related to the painting including the UCLA *Madonna and Child with St Anne*.
2. 'La plus fameuse est celle peinte par Salai ou Melzi sous les yeux de Léonard et retouché par celui-ci' (Musée du Louvre 1952: 43).
3. The painting is oil on canvas, measuring 164 × 114 cm, which is more than 10 cm shorter than the UCLA *Madonna and Child with St Anne* (Fiorio 1997: 320–21).
4. 'Vaghissimo di grazie e di bellezza, avendo begli capelli ricci e inanellati ... certi lavori, che in Milano si dicono essere di Salaì, furono ritocchi da Lionardo.'
5. Salai is mentioned as a contact for Leonardo in a letter by an agent of Isabella d'Este, Fra Pietro da Novellara (Leonardo da Vinci 1989: 273); and Salai was sent by another agent of Isabella, Alvise Ciocha, to consult with Perugino who was working on a project for her (Beltrami 1919: 96–7).
6. Gian Giacomo Caprotti, called Salai, *Head of Christ*, signed and dated lower right *I RACCHIE[S]0T/ × FE×SALAI/ ×1511× [DN]*, oil on panel, 21⅝ × 14¾ in. (55 × 37.5 cm). Sotheby's Old Master Paintings (N08282) New York 01/25/07–01/26/07, Lot 34.
7. This attribution is partially based on comparison with the infrared reflectogram of the UCLA *Madonna and Child with St Anne*.
8. Carlo Borromeo was also named as a previous owner by Francesco Antonio Albuzzi in the eighteenth century, but this is now believed to be a misunderstanding caused by confusion with another painting attributed to Raphael which did belong to Borromeo that was hanging next to the *Madonna and Child with Saint Anne* (Shell and Sironi 1991: 104; Delieuvin 2012: 166).
9. The Louvre panel appears to have been cut down at the bottom because the dowels seen in the X-radiograph at the bottom were much closer to the bottom edge than at the top. In the UCLA painting, the dowels nearest the top and bottom edges are placed at about the same distance away from the edges.
10. They probably originally looked like the cross battens on Leonardo's *St Anne, Virgin and Christ Child* in the Louvre which have large marks described as from a chisel and mallet (Marette 1961: figs 56 and 59).
11. These rather narrow tool marks could be characteristic of a Lombard workshop as these are not typical of Florentine panel construction; Bissaca 2011. Similar tool marks might be found on the reverse of paintings by Ambrogio Bergognone (*c*.1460–1523) in the church of the Tempio Civico della Beata Incoronata, Lodi; Castelli 2011.
12. The presence or absence of knots was observed in the X-radiographs. Bruno Mottin and Vincent Delieuvin graciously allowed me to view images of the Leonardo and French private collection X-radiographs.
13. A fragment of ground from one sample was analysed using standard protocols for proteins by gas chromatography-mass spectroscopy involving ethyl chloroformate derivatisation of the constituent amino acids. The ground layer in this sample was found to contain 2% protein, the amino acid profile of which matched animal glue with a correlation coefficient of 0.99; see Schilling and Khanjian 1996.
14. The Osiris camera made by Opus Instruments, UK has an indium gallium arsenide (InGaAs) sensor and an operational wavelength range of 0.9–1.7 μm.
15. None of the cross-section samples from the painting showed evidence for applied drawing on either the ground or the *imprimitura*.
16. Bruno Mottin, C2RMF, made the tracing and kindly lent it to me.
17. For a discussion on single element cartoons, see Syson and Billinge 2005, esp. 458–60.
18. Primarily by environmental scanning electron microscopy with energy dispersive X-ray analysis (ESEM-EDX).
19. For a discussion of cross-sections examined from the *St Anne* by Leonardo da Vinci, see Martin *et al.* 2005: 28–30. See Figures 4 and 5 for the red lake layer under the Virgin's blue mantle.
20. Rather than pure red lake, pink underpainting composed of varying amounts of red lake and lead white can be found for blues in Italian painting as is the case in the *Madonna and Child* attributed to Giovanni Antonio Boltraffio, Leonardo's close associate, in the Szépmüvészeti Múzeum, Budapest; in Giotto's *Crucifix* in Santa Maria Novella; and in paintings by Fra' Bartolomeo and Raphael. See Phenix 2009; Bracco and Ciappi 2002; Buzzegoli *et al.* 1996; Rioux 1990.
21. Seven samples from the painting were analysed by gas chromatography-mass spectroscopy for identification of the organic binding media. These analyses were carried out by Joy Mazurek of the Getty Conservation Institute. The samples were analysed using established protocols for identification of oils, waxes, and resins, which involved preliminary derivatisation (methylation/transesterification) using the reagent Meth-Prep II (methanolic [*m*-trifluoromethyl phenyl] trimethylammonium hydroxide). Oils were identified on the basis peak area ratios for indicative fatty acid methyl esters, using the procedure of Mills from the National Gallery, London. Azelate: palmitate (A:P) ratios indicated the presence in all samples of drying oil; in all these instances palmitate: stearate ratios were in the range 2.2–3.2, which suggests walnut oil. All the paint samples analysed were found to contain dehydroabietic acid, from pine resin, in very small amounts as compared with the amount of drying oil present.

References

Armenini, G.B. 1977. *On the True Precepts of the Art of Painting*, E.J. Olszewski (ed. and tr.). New York: B. Franklin.

Armenini, G.B. 1988. *De' very precetti della pittura*, M. Gorreri (ed.). Turin: Giulio Einaudi editore s.p.a.

Beltrami, L. 1919. *Documenti e memorie riguardanti la vita e le opere di Leonardo da Vinci*. Milan: Fratelli Treves.

Bisacca, G. 2011. Personal communication. Metropolitan Museum of Art, New York.

Bracco. P. and Ciappi, O. 2002. 'Technique of execution, state of conservation and restoration of the Crucifix in relation to other works by Giotto: the painted surface'. In *Giotto: The Crucifix in Santa Maria Novella*, M. Ciatti and M. Seidel (eds) 273–359. Florence: EDIFIR Edizioni.

Buzzegoli, E., Castelli, C., Giovannini, C., Kunzelman, D., Parri, M., Petrone, P., Ramat, A, Santacesaria, A. and Saritani, O. 1996. 'La tecnica di Fra' Bartolomeo: Studi e ricerche'. In *Fra' Bartolomeo: l'età di Savonarola e la scuola di San Marco*, S. Padovani (ed.) 293–318. Venice: Marsilio Editori s.p.a and Regione Toscana-Giunta regionale.

Castelli, C. 2011. Personal communication. Opificio delle Pietre Dure, Florence.

Delieuvin, V. 2011. Personal communication, Musée du Louvre, Paris.

Delieuvin, V (ed.). 2012. *La Sainte Anne: l'ultime chef-d'oeuvre de Léonard de Vinci*. Paris and Milan: Musée du Louvre and Officina Libraria.

Fairbrother, T. and Ishikawa, C. 1997. *Leonardo Lives: The Codex Leicester and Leonardo da Vinci's Legacy of Art and Science*. Seattle and London: Seattle Art Museum in association with University of Washington Press.

Fiorio, M. T. (ed.) 1997. *Museo d'Arte Antica del Castello Sforzesco. Pinacoteca. Tomo primo.* Milan: Electa.

Goldblatt, M. 1961. *Leonardo da Vinci*. New York: The Citadel Press.

Leonardo da Vinci. 1989. *Leonardo on Painting: An Anthology of Writings by Leonardo da Vinci with a Selection of Documents Relating to his Career as an Artist*, M. Kemp (ed.), M. Kemp and M. Walker (tr.). New Haven, CT: Yale University Press.

Marette, J. 1961. *Connaissance des primitifs par l'étude du bois: du XIIe au XVIe siècle*. Paris: Éditions A. & J. Picard & Cie.

Martin, E., Scailliérez, C., Le Chanu, P., Rioux, J-P. and Volle, N. 2005. '*La Vierge, l'Enfant Jésus et sainte Anne* de Léonard de Vinci: creation et transmission d'un chef-d'oeuvre', *Technè* 21: 26–34.

Mazurek, J. 2011. Organic Analysis Laboratory, 21 September. Los Angeles: Getty Conservation Institute.

Mottin, B. 2011a. 'Leonardo da Vinci's *The Virgin and Child with Saint Anne* (Musée du Louvre, Paris): new infrared reflectography'. In *Studying Old Master Paintings: Technology and Practice*, M. Spring, H. Howard, J. Kirby and A. Roy (eds) 65–71. London: Archetype Publications in association with the National Gallery.

Mottin, B. 2011b. Personal communication. Centre de recherche et de restauration des musées de France (C2RMF), Paris.

Musée du Louvre 1952. *Hommage à Léonard de Vinci. Exposition en l'honneur du cinquième centenaire de sa naissance*. Paris: Éditions des musées nationaux.

Phenix, A. 2009. 'Scientific report, L.2008.26, *Madonna and Child*, Giovanni Antonio Boltraffio'. Getty Conservation Institute, Los Angeles, CA.

Rioux, J.P. 1990. 'Appendice: La *Grande Sainte Famille* de François 1er: remarques sur la technique picturale'. In *The Princeton Raphael Symposium: Science in the Service of Art*, J. Shearman and M.B. Hall (eds) 54–5. Princeton, NJ: Princeton University Press.

Ritano, P. and Seccaroni, C. 2008. 'Attorno all'imprimitura'. In *Raffaello: la rivelazione del colore*, M. Ciatti, C. Frosinini, A. Natali and P. Riitano (eds) 95–103. Florence: EDIFIR Edizioni.

Schilling, M.R. and Khanjian, H. P. 1996. 'Gas chromatographic analysis of amino acids in ethyl chloroformate derivatives, Part 3. Identification of proteinaceous binding media by the interpretation of amino acid composition data'. In *Preprints of ICOM-CC 11th Triennial Meeting*, J. Bridgland (ed.) 211–19. London: James & James.

Shell, J. and Sironi, G. 1991. 'Salaì and Leonardo's legacy', *The Burlington Magazine* 133(1055): 95–108.

Syson, L. and Billinge, R. 2005. 'Leonardo da Vinci's use of underdrawing in the *Virgin of the Rocks* in the National Gallery and *St Jerome* in the Vatican', *The Burlington Magazine* 147 (1228): 450–63.

Valentiner, W.R. 1949. *Leonardo da Vinci Loan Exhibition, June 3 to July 1, 1949.* Los Angeles County Museum of Art.

Vasari, G. 1991. *Le vite dei più eccellenti pittori, scultori e architetti*. Rome: Newton Compton (reprint).

Woudhuysen-Keller, R. 1995. 'Aspects of painting technique in the use of verdigris and copper resinate'. In *Historical Painting Techniques, Materials, and Studio Practice*, A. Wallert, E. Hermens and M. Peek (eds) 65–9. Marina del Rey, CA: Getty Conservation Institute.

RECONSTRUCTING INTERMEDIATE LAYERS IN EARLY NETHERLANDISH PAINTINGS

Abbie Vandivere

A 'work in progress' in the background of *St Luke Drawing the Virgin* attributed to the circle of Hugo van der Goes shows us part of a painting that is usually hidden from view (Fig. 1).[1] St Luke appears to be making a preparatory sketch for a painting that he will later execute on a panel that sits on an easel behind him. The panel in the background is surrounded by a white frame, but the area that is going to be painted is not white: it is flesh-coloured.[2] Perhaps the flesh colour on the panel is an intermediate layer: a paint layer of a single tone (usually semi-transparent) that was applied over the surface of the ground?[3]

This paper explores the function and appearance of intermediate layers in fifteenth- and sixteenth-century Netherlandish paintings. Possible reasons for applying an intermediate layer include: isolating the ground, fixing the underdrawing, leaving the underdrawing partially visible and acting as a base tone. This study combines literature and source research, results from technical examinations, and reconstructions made with historically appropriate materials.

Terminology and the *primuersel*

The term 'intermediate layer' will be used in this paper to refer to a (semi-) translucent layer of a single tone, which is composed of a binding medium (usually oil) and, in some cases, pigments.[4] It is applied over the entire surface of the ground, usually after the underdrawing but before the rest of the paint layers. Other terms describe layers that perform similar functions. In historical treatises on Italian painting, *imprimatura* was used by Vasari (1550) and Armenini (1587). De Mayerne (1620) used the French *imprimeure*. Modern words include priming and preparatory layers. These terms are not necessarily synonymous as each defines a slightly different type of layer with a different purpose.[5] One seventeenth-century term refers specifically to a flesh-coloured intermediate layer: *primuersel*.[6] It was used by Karel van Mander, the poet and painter who wrote the *Schilder-boeck* (1604). In *Foundations of the Noble and*

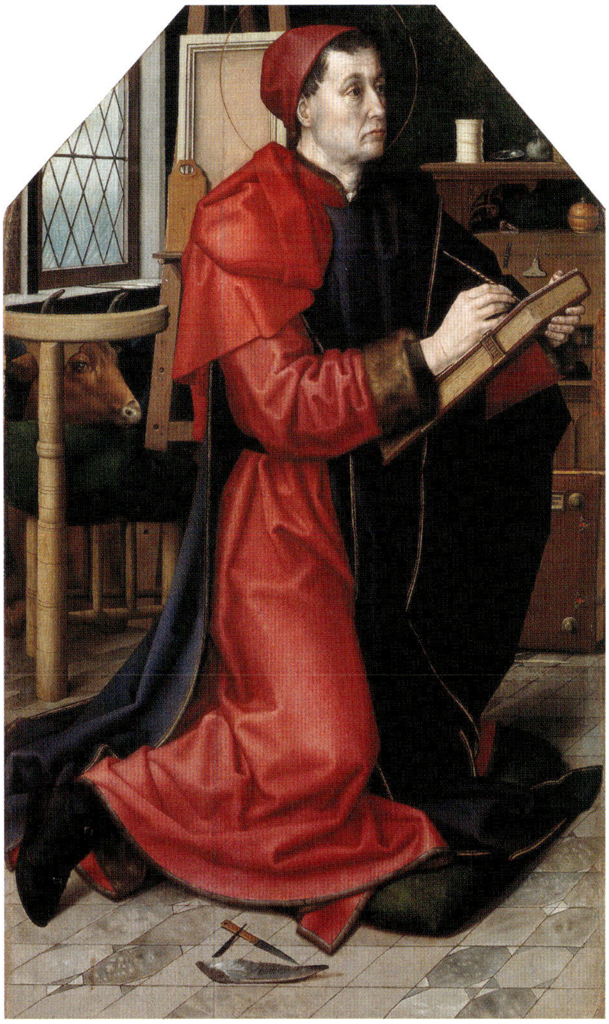

Figure 1 *Circle of Hugo van der Goes,* St Luke Drawing the Virgin, *c.1480, Museu Nacional de Arte Antiga, Lisbon. (Photograph: José Pessoa, Divisão de Documentação Fotográfica – Instututo dos Museus e da conservação, I.P.)*

Table 1 *A selection of fifteenth- and sixteenth-century Haarlem School panel paintings with intermediate layers from the collections of the Frans Hals Museum (FHM), Haarlem and the Rijksmuseum, Amsterdam.*

Artist / Painting / Date / Collection	Underdrawing	Type of IL / Thickness of IL / No. of samples	Pigments in IL	Binding medium of IL / Method of analysis	Similarity to van Mander's *primuersel*?
Geertgen tot Sint Jans, *Holy Kinship*, *c.*1490 (Rijksmuseum)	Liquid UD (finely ground black chalk) applied with brush before the IL	White layer, 2–4 μm, found in 4 of 14 samples	Lead white	?	× flesh-coloured ? oil medium √ applied after UD ? translucent √ left to dry ? base tone
Geertgen tot Sint Jans, *Adoration of the Magi*, *c.*1490 (Rijksmuseum)	Dry UD (black chalk) in the landscape. Wet UD applied with a brush for contours in the foreground. Both applied before the IL	White layer with prominent diagonal brushstrokes, *c.*8 μm, found in 8 of 9 samples	Lead white	?	× flesh-coloured ? oil medium √ applied after UD ? translucent √ left to dry ? base tone
Jan Cornelisz. Vermeyen, *Holy Family*, *c.*1530 (FHM, on long-term loan from the Rijksdienst voor het Cultureel Erfgoed)	Contours applied on top of the IL (liquid UD with lamp or bone black). Some hatching with a dry material in top left corner	Opaque peach-coloured, 5–20 μm, found in 8 of 9 samples	Lead white, organic red, vermilion, (charcoal?) black, possibly chalk	?	√ flesh-coloured ? oil medium × applied after UD × translucent √ left to dry √ base tone
Jan van Scorel, *Jerusalem Pilgrims*, *c.*1528 (FHM)	Dry material (probably black chalk) applied on top of IL	White, 12–48 μm, found in 12 of 12 samples	Lead white	Oil / unspecified	× flesh-coloured √ oil medium × applied after UD ? translucent √ left to dry ? base tone
Jan van Scorel, *Mary Magdalene* *c.*1530 (Rijksmuseum)	Dry material (probably black chalk) applied on top of IL. Lines skip across the surface of the IL	White layer with visible brushstrokes	Presumably lead white	?	× flesh-coloured ? oil medium × applied after UD ? translucent √ left to dry ? base tone
Maarten van Heemskerck, *Draper's Altar*, 1546–47 (FHM)	A first phase of UD not detectable with IRR then dry material (black chalk?) lines hatched on top of IL in some areas	Streaky white layer with visible brushstrokes, 5–15 μm, found in 10 of 24 samples	Lead white	Oil / Staining with Sudan Black B, counterstain with amido black AB2	× flesh-coloured √ oil medium ? applied after UD ? translucent √ left to dry ? base tone
Maarten van Heemskerck, *St Luke Painting the Virgin*, 1532 (FHM)	None revealed with IRR. Some dry lines (possibly black chalk) in the representation of a painting on the easel	Fairly dark grey, 6–24 μm, found in 3 of 5 samples	Lead white, many black particles, possibly red-brown particles	?	× flesh-coloured ? oil medium ? applied after UD ? translucent √ left to dry √ base tone (for background)
Maarten van Heemskerck, *Ecce Homo*, 1559/60 (FHM)	Black liquid UD in the middle panel (master?) / dry black chalk on the wings (assistant?)	Light grey (central panel is slightly darker than the wings), 0–15 μm, found in 21 of 28 samples	Outside of wings: lead white, fine black (charcoal), organic red, a little chalk	Possibly proteinaceous / Staining with amido black AB2 and fuchsin S	× flesh-coloured × oil medium ? applied after UD ? translucent √ left to dry ? base tone
Karel van Mander, *Adoration of the Shepherds*, 1598 (FHM, on long-term loan from the RCE)	No UD detectable with IRR	13–30 μm, found in 3 of 4 samples	Lead white, vermilion, azurite, black	?	√ flesh-coloured ? oil medium ? applied after UD ? translucent √ left to dry √ base tone

Notes: IL = intermediate layer; UD = underdrawing; IRR = infrared reflectography

Free Art of Painting – the didactic poem that precedes the *Schilder-boeck* – van Mander describes painting techniques used by his fifteenth- and early sixteenth-century Netherlandish predecessors. In the margin of folio 47v he noted 'they drew their subject on the ground and applied an oily layer over it,' then he elaborates:

> Some took some charcoal black finely ground with water, then drew and shaded together their subject very skillfully, each part as it should. They then applied on top a fine, thin *primuersel* through which you could see everything and behold: the *primuersel* was flesh coloured. When this was dry they saw their subject almost half finished before their eyes, after which they set up everything and finished in one layer.[7]

Several qualities of the *primuersel* can be inferred from this quotation. Van Mander defined it as: a flesh-coloured layer bound in oil applied after the underdrawing that was translucent enough to allow the underdrawing to remain visible, which was left to dry before the artist worked up the rest of the painting, and which simplified the painting process by acting as a base tone. Van Mander suggested that applying a *primuersel* was a relatively common practice; however, it has seldom been identified on actual Netherlandish paintings from the fifteenth and sixteenth centuries. Examples can be linked to artists active in Haarlem, northern Netherlands, and their paintings form the basis for this investigation. Van Mander lived in Haarlem while writing the *Schilder-boeck*, in which he recounts the lives of several of the artists discussed in this paper.

Case studies and reconstructions

Table 1 gives an overview of some of the artists and paintings that were used as case studies as part of this investigation into intermediate layers and the *primuersel*. A technical examination of all of these works was undertaken using a stereomicroscope and documented with digital photography.[8] Intermediate layers are not usually visible at the surface because they are covered with layers of paint, therefore paint samples taken during previous conservation treatments were re-examined.[9] Based on the information collected from the technical examination and published sources, reconstructions were made using historically appropriate materials. The aim of the reconstructions was to determine whether the intermediate layers conformed to van Mander's definition of the *primuersel*, and whether they fulfilled the assumed functions of an intermediate layer. Both illusionistic and non-illusionistic (schematic) reconstructions were made to explore the interaction between the intermediate layer and the underdrawing and paint layers. The reconstructions were aged naturally for two to three months before being sampled. The samples were mounted as cross-sections and examined under a stereomicroscope in normal and ultraviolet (UV) light. A list of materials and the processes that were used to make the reconstructions can be found in Table 2 (p. 72).

Four types of intermediate layers were reconstructed: unpigmented 'isolation' layers, white, grey and flesh-coloured layers. This range of colours was based on the types of intermediate layers that were encountered in the technical examination of fifteenth- and sixteenth-century paintings. Some Flemish painters, including Dirk Bouts, Petrus Christus, Hans Memling and Jan Gossaert, applied lead white intermediate layers (Campbell *et al.* 1997: 23). In the northern Netherlands, so did the early Haarlem painter Geertgen tot Sint Jans (Wallert *et al.* 2001; Faries 2007–08). Although less common than white or flesh-coloured intermediate layers, grey layers were used by Netherlandish artists in both the north and south (Campbell *et al.* 1997: 23–4), including Dirk Bouts, Hieronymous Bosch and Maarten van Heemskerck. Flesh-coloured layers were used by both Flemish artists (Campbell *et al.* 1997: 24) – Rogier van der Weyden, Jan van Eyck, Gerard David and Jan Gossaert– and Northern artists such as Maarten van Heemskerck (van Asperen de Boer 1987) and Jan Cornelisz. Vermeyen (Bagley-Young 2008).

Functions of an intermediate layer

Several reasons why artists might have chosen to apply intermediate layers have been suggested in art historical and technical literature. They fall into four categories: isolating the ground, fixing the underdrawing, leaving the underdrawing (partially) visible, and acting as a base tone. Each of these assumed functions will be addressed with reference to van Mander's definition of the *primuersel*.

Isolation: does it prevent oil medium from the paint layers from being absorbed into the ground?

It is difficult to judge whether early Netherlandish painters typically applied a layer of oil on top of the ground and/or underdrawing before beginning to paint. In cross-sections, a thin film of oil at the interface between the ground and the paint layers is an indication that the artist might have applied an unpigmented intermediate layer. More often, the oil would have been partially absorbed by the ground. In cross-sections, this is sometimes visible as a translucent or yellowish band at the top of the ground, or a band with a different fluorescence in UV light. In the reconstructions made as part of this study, oil was often absorbed into the upper part of the ground. In cross-sections, the transparent band often stopped at the interface between the two upper strata: the horizontal lines between the thin layers of the ground (Vandivere 2011: 3; Figs 2 and 3). Also, the oil was absorbed into the tiny air bubbles that inevitably formed even though the ground was smoothed and sanded.

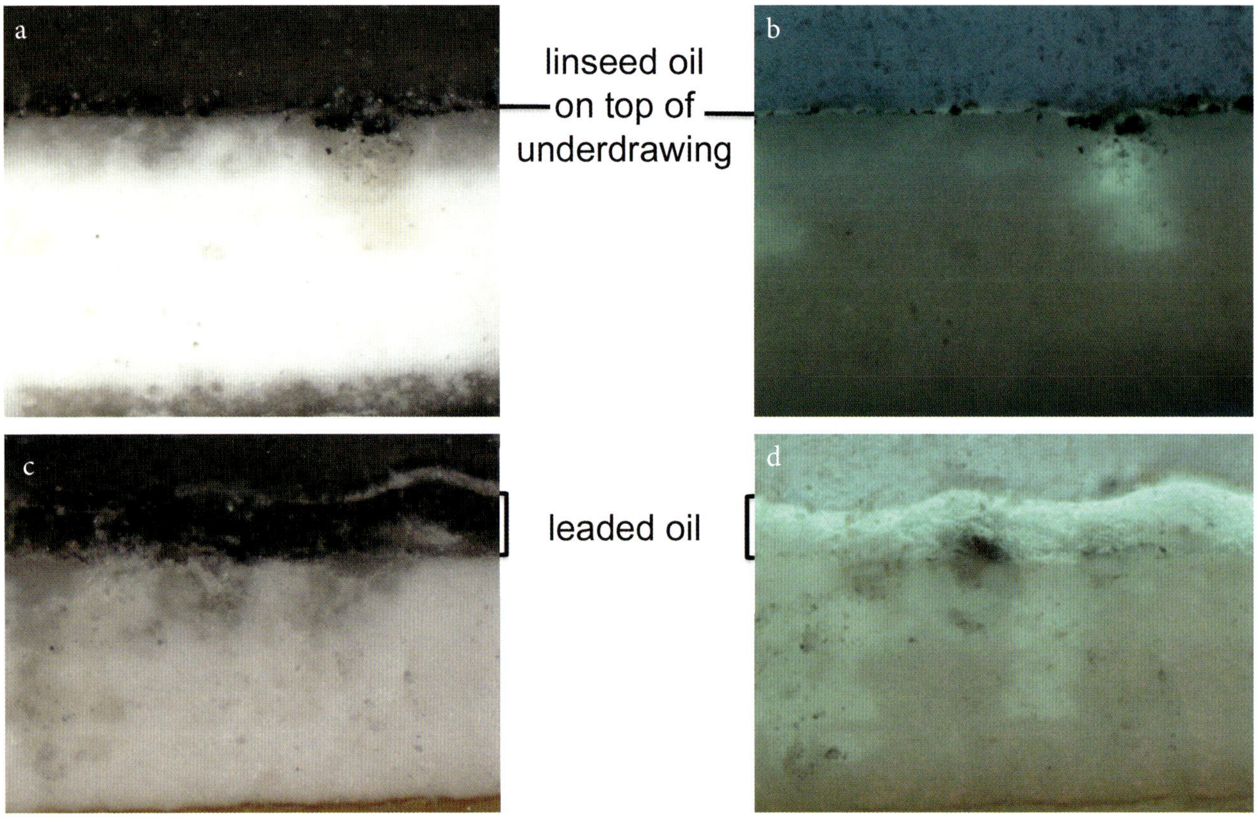

Figure 2 *Cross-sections from schematic reconstructions (magnified 200×). (a) Intermediate layer of cold-pressed linseed oil applied on top of underdrawing (charcoal black with water); (b) same as (a) in UV light. (c) Intermediate layer of leaded oil applied directly on top of the ground; (d) same as (c), in UV light. (Photographs: Abbie Vandivere.)*

An unpigmented intermediate layer is often referred to as an 'isolation layer' because it forms a barrier between the ground and the paint.[10] It prevents the ground from absorbing the binding medium, which may result in a matt or uneven surface. The layer itself is partially absorbed into the ground preventing more oil from being leached from the paint. An intermediate layer that contains oil and pigments performs the same function. Reconstructions showed that a tidemark of oil often appeared around brushstrokes when paint was applied directly to the ground; however, if an intermediate layer was applied first, the paint could be brushed smoothly over the surface and no tidemark appeared. Samples from the reconstructions suggest that cold-pressed linseed oil formed an adequate isolation layer; it was itself (at least partly) absorbed into the upper part of the ground and once it dried, it prevented more oil from being absorbed from the paint. Leaded oil was even more effective: it formed a thicker rubbery film at the surface, and less of the intermediate layer was absorbed into the ground (Fig. 2).[11]

One consequence of applying an oil-based isolation layer is that it affected the colour of the ground. Reconstructions of unpigmented isolation layers show that even a thin layer of linseed oil would tint the ground a light beige colour. This seems to argue against the theory that the Flemish Primitives achieved luminous colours because the white ground reflected through overlying glaze layers.[12] Perhaps this is the reason why some artists applied a white intermediate layer.

Analysis has shown that some artists used oily, aqueous, resinous or emulsion-based media in their intermediate layers.[13] It is often difficult to analyse the medium of intermediate layers because they are thin (generally less than 10 µm), and are usually positioned at an interface between an aqueous layer (the ground, composed of chalk and animal glue) and an oil layer (paint).[14] In the case of glue-based isolation layers, this is exacerbated because they might contain the same glue as the ground itself. It is unclear how widespread the practice of applying glue intermediate layers was in early Netherlandish paintings. So far, no fifteenth- or early sixteenth-century Northern sources for glue-based intermediate layers have been found. In reconstructions, a dilute (10%) layer of rabbit-skin glue was very effective because it dried quickly and remained colourless, leaving the reflective white surface of the ground unaffected. However, when pigments were added to the glue layer, it was difficult to achieve an even colour because the layer dried quickly.

Fixing: does it prevent the underdrawing from smudging when paint layers are brushed on top?

Another function of an unpigmented intermediate layer was to fix the underdrawing and prevent it from smudging

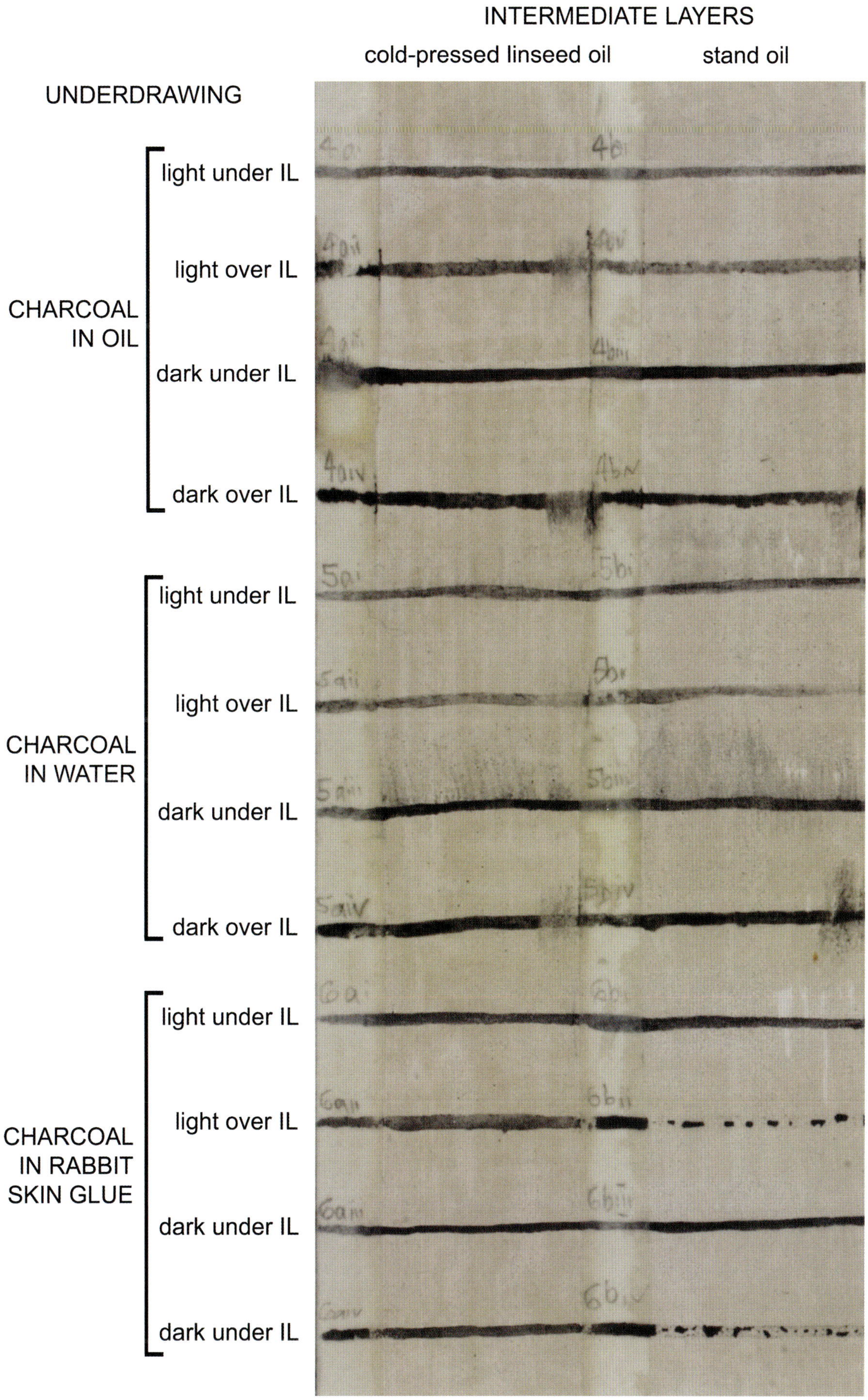

Figure 3 *Detail of schematic reconstruction. (Photograph: Abbie Vandivere.)*

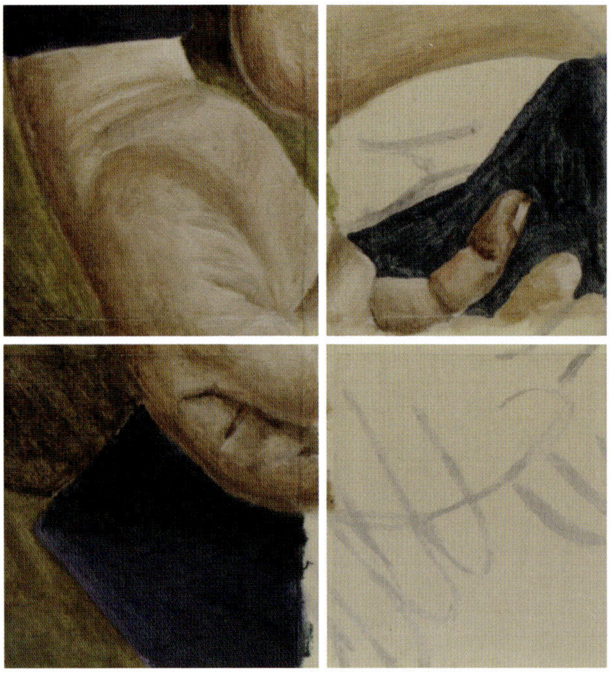

Figure 4 *Illusionistic reconstruction of a detail of Rogier van der Weyden,* Descent from the Cross. *The lower right quadrant shows the underdrawing visible through the intermediate layer. The upper right quadrant shows the initial paint layers. The left half shows a further stage of completion. (Photograph: Abbie Vandivere.)*

or being picked up by the brush during painting. Schematic reconstructions were made to test this assumed function (Fig. 3). Both dry and wet underdrawing materials were tested (Table 2). Light and dark lines were applied, both under and over different types of unpigmented intermediate layers.

In the aforementioned quotation on the *primuersel*, Karel van Mander mentioned that the artist started by making an underdrawing using 'charcoal black finely ground with water.' No binding medium was specified, so reconstructions were made using a brush to apply an underdrawing without any binding medium – just water.[15] Surprisingly, this worked provided that not too much pigment was used. When an intermediate layer was applied on top, some pigment was picked up on the brush but the line remained legible. Once the intermediate layer had dried, no more loose underdrawing material remained on the surface therefore it would not be picked up in subsequent paint layers.

Van Mander specified that the *primuersel* was applied thinly *on top of* the underdrawing. In the reconstructions, the intermediate layer did indeed fix most types of underdrawing and stop it from being picked up in subsequent paint layers. The application of an intermediate layer would only smudge the underdrawing if the lines were not sufficiently dry or there was too much pigment on the surface (that is, in the dark lines). There were no problems applying 'like over like'; there was not significantly more smudging if an oil layer was applied on top of an oil-based underdrawing or a layer of rabbit-skin glue was applied over an aqueous underdrawing.[16] However, some negative interactions between underdrawing material and intermediate layer were observed.[17] For instance, an underdrawing bound in oil medium often created a brownish tidemark on the ground around the line – when an intermediate layer was applied on top, this remained visible as a bright 'halo' (Fig. 3). Some lines became fainter when the intermediate layer was applied, particularly the dry lines applied with a charcoal stick. This could be a desirable quality if an artist used charcoal to lay in an initial sketch, but then did not want it to remain visible during subsequent phases of painting.[18]

In another passage from the didactic poem, van Mander mentions how his late sixteenth-century contemporaries applied a *primuersel* that differed slightly from that used by his predecessors. According to van Mander, the later painters often applied their underdrawing *on top of* the intermediate layer: 'On top of the *primuersel*, they purely and clearly draw what they had in mind using a thinly-tempered fluid paint, or use a pencil to draw neatly.'[19] Analysis suggests that this configuration was uncommon in the fifteenth and early sixteenth century. A few examples from the 1530s, in paintings by Jan van Scorel and Jan Cornelisz. Vermeyen (discussed later in this paper), may be intermediaries between the technique of van Mander's predecessors and his contemporaries. Applying an underdrawing on top of an intermediate layer was tested in the schematic reconstructions (Fig. 3). For the most part, it produced legible lines, but they were more irregular and slightly darker than the lines beneath the intermediate layers. Some negative interactions occurred when the underdrawing was applied on top of the intermediate layer. It was difficult to apply a dry underdrawing material such as black chalk on top of a layer of oil because it scratched into the oil layer without leaving a mark. Also, some aqueous media beaded up when applied on top of an oily layer.[20] In this configuration, the *primuersel* did not prevent the underdrawing from smudging when the paint was applied on top; it simply acted as an isolation layer.[21]

Visibility: is it a translucent layer 'through which you can see everything' and use the lines of underdrawing as a guide?

Van Mander's quotation states that the *primuersel* was (semi-) transparent: it is a pigmented intermediate layer 'through which you could see everything', thereby leaving the underdrawing visible. Intermediate layers in actual paintings are usually thin – often less than 10 μm thick – so even though they may contain opaque pigments, they still remain rather transparent. This would allow the artist to use the lines of underdrawing as a guide for applying the paint. It has also been suggested that applying a flesh-coloured layer helped to even out underdrawing lines of different intensity, making them a more uniform grey colour (van Asperen de Boer *et al.* 1992: 17). Schematic reconstructions were made using different types of underdrawing applied beneath coloured intermediate layers.

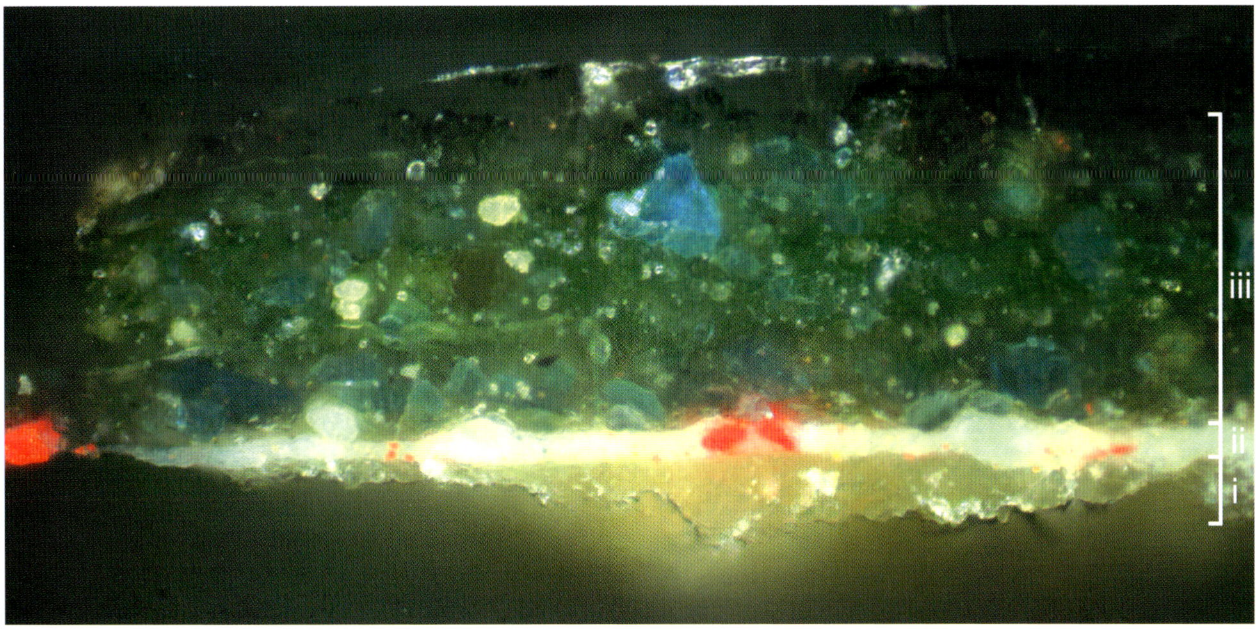

Figure 5 *Cross-section (magnified 500×) sampled from the green curtain in Jan Cornelisz. Vermeyen,* Holy Family, *c.1530: (i) ground layer; (ii) intermediate layer; (iii) green paint layers. (Image courtesy of Frans Hals Museum, Haarlem.)*

They showed that most lines remained visible beneath a layer of similar thickness and composition to the flesh-coloured intermediate layers found in actual paintings.[22] Also, the lines became a more muted, greyish colour, and the lines of different intensities achieved a more uniform tone. Some negative effects – such as the aforementioned 'halo' surrounding the underdrawing bound in oil – were less obvious through a pigmented intermediate layer than an unpigmented isolation layer.

Rogier van der Weyden used flesh-coloured intermediate layers in many of his paintings. Reconstructions of the *Seven Sacraments* (1445–50, Koninklijk Museum voor Schone Kunsten, Antwerp) suggested that the type and thickness of intermediate layer that he applied would be translucent enough to allow the underdrawing to show through at an initial phase of painting, but that the drawing could be minimised as more paint layers were applied.[23] This may also have been true for the *Descent from the Cross* (*c.*1440, Museo Nacional del Prado, Madrid). Samples show that the intermediate layer contains lead white, chalk, carbon black and earth pigments in an oil medium.[24] The intermediate layer is thin (6–10 μm) in relation to the paint layers. Because of this relatively thick paint application, the intermediate layer has little visual effect at the painting's surface. An illusionistic reconstruction of the Virgin's hand gave similar results to the *Seven Sacraments* reconstructions (Fig. 4). The underdrawing was visible when the intermediate layer was applied, and it gave lines of differing intensities a more even, greyish tone.[25] The drawing remained visible when the first thin layers of paint were applied. This was somewhat distracting in the area where there is a *pentimento*: an infrared reflectogram shows that her fingers were originally drawn extended (Garrido *et al.* 1983: 45). This change is not ultimately visible through the paint layers in the *Descent from the Cross.* As more paint layers were applied to the reconstruction to mimic the thickness and intensity of the original painting, the underdrawing gradually faded. Also, the influence of the flesh-coloured intermediate layer was barely visible at the surface. Although it was initially a useful base tone for the flesh tones, it disappeared as more layers were applied.

Base tone: does it make the 'subject almost half finished' and simplify the painting process so that it could be 'finished in one layer,' especially in the areas of flesh?

Flesh-coloured intermediate layers typically contain a mixture of pigments: lead white, black, and red – usually vermilion, but sometimes organic red or an iron oxide (earth) pigment. This combination results in a greyish pink colour. If this were used as the base tone for painting flesh, it suggests that the artists may have been conscious to give the layer both the warm and cool tones found in real skin.[26]

Van Mander wrote: 'When [the *primuersel*] was dry they saw their subject almost half finished before their eyes, after which they set up everything and finished in one layer.' Examination of actual paintings showed that some artists exploited the colour of the intermediate layer to simplify the process of painting skin. Jan Cornelisz. Vermeyen, who trained in Haarlem, applied a pinkish intermediate layer to both parts of the diptych of the *Holy Family* (*c.*1530, Rijksdienst voor het Cultureel Erfgoed, on loan to the Frans Hals Museum, Haarlem) and *Cardinal Erard de la Marck* (*c.*1530, Rijksmuseum, Amsterdam).[27] The layer is between 5 and 20 μm thick and contains particles of lead white, red lake, vermilion

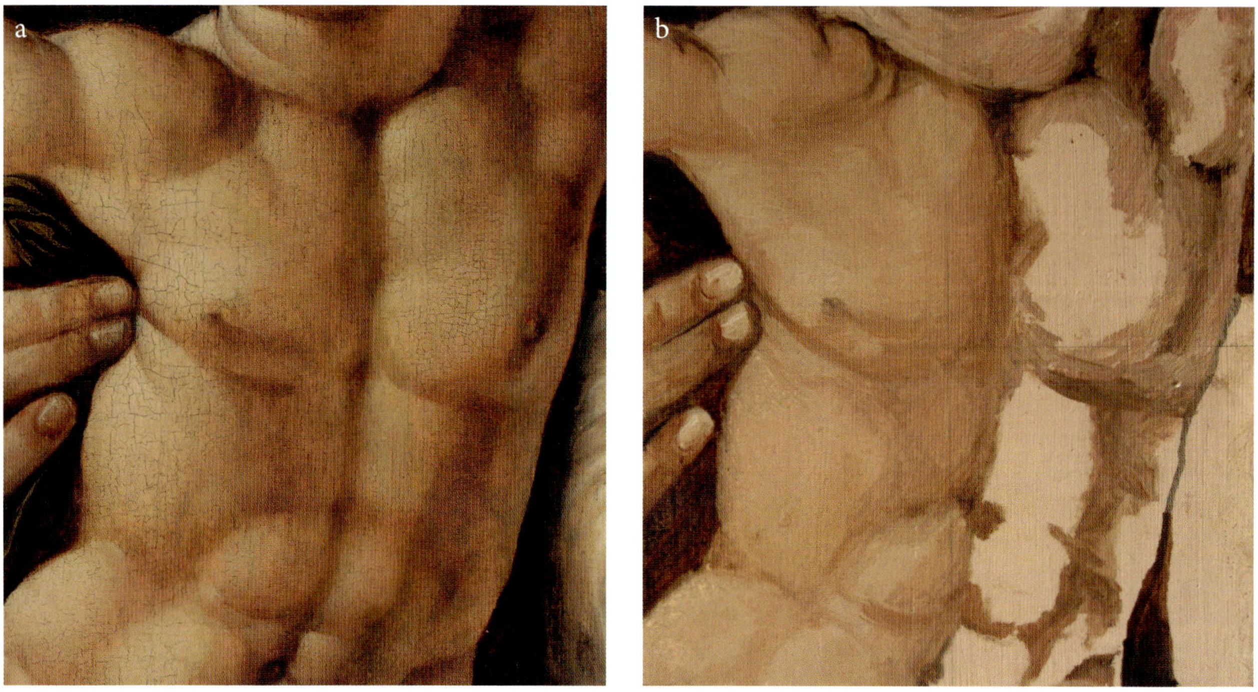

Figure 6 *(a) Detail of Christ's chest from Jan Vermeyen,* Holy Family. *(Image courtesy of Frans Hals Museum, Haarlem.) (b) Illusionistic reconstruction. The left side shows the completed reconstruction, the right side shows the reconstruction before the paint layers were blended. (Photograph: Abbie Vandivere.)*

and charcoal black (Fig. 5). Remarkably, he applied underdrawing *on top of* this intermediate layer, perhaps because the relatively opaque layer might have made it difficult to follow if it were underneath. The pinkish intermediate layer has an important optical function. It is visible through thin or translucent paint in several areas of the *Holy Family*: it gives a warm glow to the heavens and shines through from beneath diaphanous clothing. In the flesh tones, the intermediate layer was left exposed (or barely covered) to create the mid-tones (Fig. 6a). A cross-section from a mid-tone in Christ's chest shows that the intermediate layer is visible at the surface of the sample: Vermeyen created the mid-tones in the flesh by leaving the intermediate layer exposed. On top of the intermediate layer – which served as a mid-tone – he applied shadows and highlights in a single layer, then blended everything together.

In an illusionistic reconstruction of Christ's chest, I tried to approximate the way that Vermeyen applied the paint (Fig. 6b). The flesh-coloured layer played a major role in acting as a base tone and simplifying the painting process. The final blended effect is similar to the actual painting and could be achieved very quickly. This efficient and direct technique seems to perfectly illustrate van Mander's statement that a flesh-coloured *primuersel* would make the subject 'almost half-finished ... after which [the artist] set up everything and finished in one layer'. He referred to this type of paint application as 'ten eersten opghedaen'.[28] Miedema translates this phrase as 'finished in one session,' where the paint was mixed on the palette and applied directly in a single layer.[29]

Other artists who applied flesh-coloured intermediate layers did not exploit the optical effect of the layer as much as Vermeyen. As previously mentioned, the paint layers are thicker in Rogier van der Weyden's *Descent from the Cross*. The intermediate layer has little effect on the overall tone of the picture because there are few areas where it is visible at the surface. In terms of conforming to van Mander's definition of the *primuersel*, the *Descent from the Cross* meets most (but not all) of the criteria. Although it could be described as a base tone, it does not appear to have simplified the painting process or taken advantage of the 'ten eersten opghedaen' method. However, in his later portraits, Rogier van der Weyden progressively made more and more use of coloured intermediate layers by using them to model the upper surface of the flesh tones (Metzger and Palmer 2008).

In search of van Mander's *primuersel*

Besides the aforementioned quotations (fol. 47r and 47v–48r), van Mander mentions the *primuersel* again in the *Schilder-boeck*. In his description of the life of Hieronymous Bosch, he specifically mentions Bosch as an artist who used the *primuersel* effectively: 'Like some other old Masters, he used to draw his subjects onto the white of the panel, laying over that a translucent flesh-coloured *primuersel*, and also allowed the ground to contribute to the effect' (Miedema 1994–95: fol. 216v). A few paintings by Hieronymous Bosch have flesh-coloured intermediate layers.[30] From visual inspection and technical literature, it appears that the *Pedlar* (*c.*1490–1505, Museum Boijmans

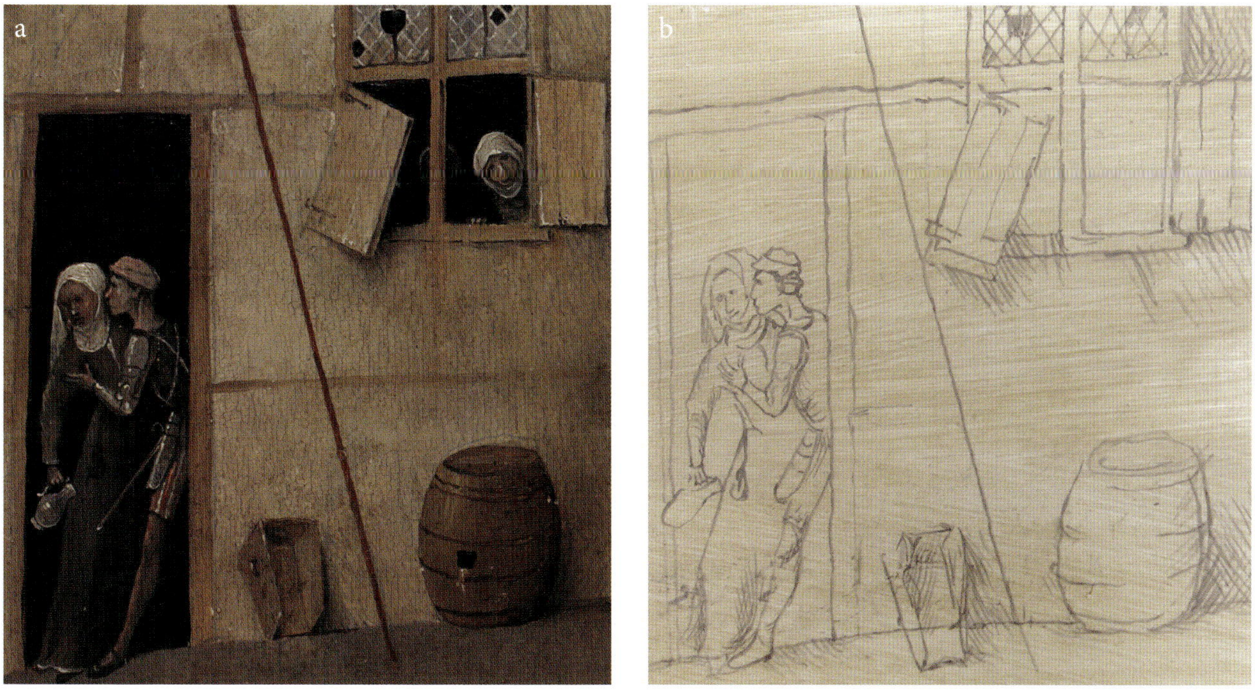

Figure 7 *(a) Detail of Hieronymous Bosch,* Pedlar, c. *1490–1505, Museum Boijmans van Beuningen, Rotterdam. (b) Illusionistic reconstruction made by Charlotte Caspers. (Photographs: Abbie Vandivere)*

van Beuningen, Rotterdam) has an intermediate layer that conforms to the qualities of the *primuersel* that were laid out by van Mander. There seems to be a translucent greyish flesh-coloured layer that was applied after the underdrawing.[31] We do not know whether it was bound in an oil medium, but presumably the intermediate layer was left to dry before the paint layers were applied. It seems to serve as a mid-tone for the overall beige tonality of the composition. In the building to the left, the paint layers are thin and semi-translucent, exploiting the colour of an underlying layer (Fig. 7a).[32] A reconstruction of this area made by Charlotte Caspers shows how such a layer might have appeared when it was applied over the underdrawing (Fig. 7b).[33]

The relation between the *primuersel* and the intermediate layers found in other paintings was complicated. The paintings used as case studies do not always conform to the specific qualities van Mander described (see Table 1, last column). Van Mander specified that the *primuersel* was a layer bound in oil that was applied after the underdrawing and was translucent enough to allow the underdrawing to remain visible. It was left to dry before the artist worked up the rest of the painting, and simplified the painting process by acting as a base tone. Some actual paintings fit a few of the specific qualities, but not all of them. Some intermediate layers were probably bound in oil, but there are several examples in aqueous media such as glue or egg, and many more where the medium cannot be identified. The intermediate layer was not always applied *after* the underdrawing. For example, in Vermeyen's *Holy Family*, the underdrawing was on top of the layer, and the layer itself was rather opaque. His contemporary, Jan van Scorel, almost always applied his underdrawing on top of the intermediate layer (Faries 2011). Furthermore, he did not always allow the layer to dry before working up the rest of the painting. In the *Lamentation of Christ with a Donor* (*c.*1530–35, Centraal Museum, Utrecht), the dry black chalk underdrawing scratched into the lead white intermediate layer. Reconstructions showed that indentations of comparable depth and appearance could be achieved when the underdrawing was applied 8–24 hours after the intermediate layer. Van Mander mentioned that the *primuersel* was dry before the rest of the painting was worked up. Reconstructions show that unpigmented layers (even those made with leaded oil) could take several weeks to dry completely, but incorporating certain pigments accelerated the drying. Also, the idea that an intermediate layer simplified the painting process by acting as a base tone seems

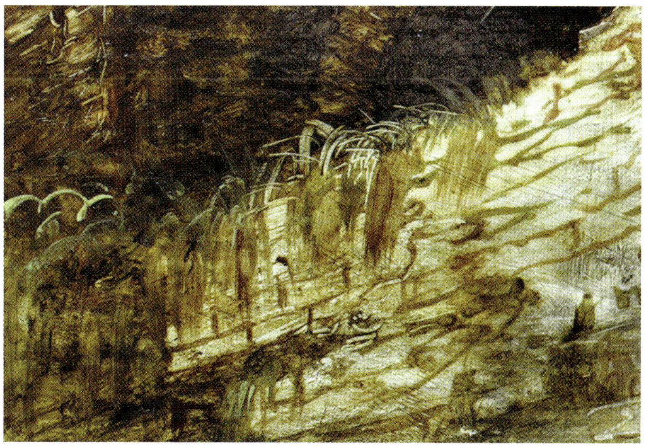

Figure 8 *Detail of Karel van Mander,* Adoration of the Kings, *1598, Rijksdienst voor het Cultureel Erfgoed, on loan to the Frans Hals Museum, Haarlem. (Photograph: Jessica Roeders.)*

Table 2 *Materials and methodology for the reconstructions described in this paper.*

Layer	Materials / Supplier	Proportions / Method of preparation and application / Thickness*	Paintings reconstructed as case studies
Panel	*European oak panels*, ± 24 × 52 × 0.12 cm: Amsterdamsche Fijnhouthandel, www.fijnhout.nl *Rabbit-skin glue*: Kremer Pigmente GmBH & Co. KG, http://kremer-pigmente.de/en	Sized wood with two coats of rabbit-skin glue in demineralised water (5% w/v on recto, 10% w/v on verso)	All
Ground	*Champagne chalk*: Kremer Pigmente *Rabbit-skin glue*: Kremer Pigmente	10% RSG in demineralised water warmed to ±50°C. Added sifted chalk until it was saturated, then mixed. Applied to panel with a brush in 7 layers. Upper layers scraped with a metal scraper. Last layer sanded with 320 grit sandpaper. Surface wiped with dry *chamoix*. Each layer was ±30 μm thick, and the total thickness was ± 210 μm (measured from cross-section)	All
Dry UD	*Black chalk*: *schwarze kreide*, Kremer Pigmente *Black chalk*: *pietra nera*, Zecchi Colori. www.zecchi.it *Charcoal stick*: H and 2B, Zecchi Colori	For the Geertgen tot Sint Jans case study, black chalk was applied directly to the ground. For the Jan van Scorel reconstruction, black chalk was applied on top of the lead white layer after 4.5, 8, 24 and 30 hours	Schematic reconstructions Geertgen tot Sint Jans, *Adoration of the Magi* Jan van Scorel, *Lamentation of Christ with a Donor*
Wet UD	**Pigments** *Charcoal powder*: *houtskoolpoeder* made from beech branches: Verfmolen de Kat, www.verfmolendekat.com *Bone black and lamp black*: Kremer Pigmente **Binding media** *Cold-pressed linseed oil extra (for dry pigments)*: Zecchi Colori *Rabbit-skin glue (10% in water)*: Kremer Pigmente *Gum arabic*: unknown source and concentration *Egg white*: biological egg	Dry pigment was combined with binding medium until a suitable consistency was achieved. The UD was applied with a fine sable brush. For the schematic reconstructions, charcoal was chosen because it came in a very fine powder that worked well with all of the binding media. Several intensities of UD were tested (different ratios of pigment to binding medium). For the illusionistic reconstructions, the infrared reflectograms of the paintings were used as a reference	Schematic reconstructions Geertgen tot Sint Jans, *Adoration of the Magi* (charcoal in gum arabic) Rogier van der Weyden, *Descent from the Cross* (charcoal in gum arabic) Jan Vermeyen, *Holy Family* (bone and lamp black were tried in aqueous and oil media, applied on top of the IL)

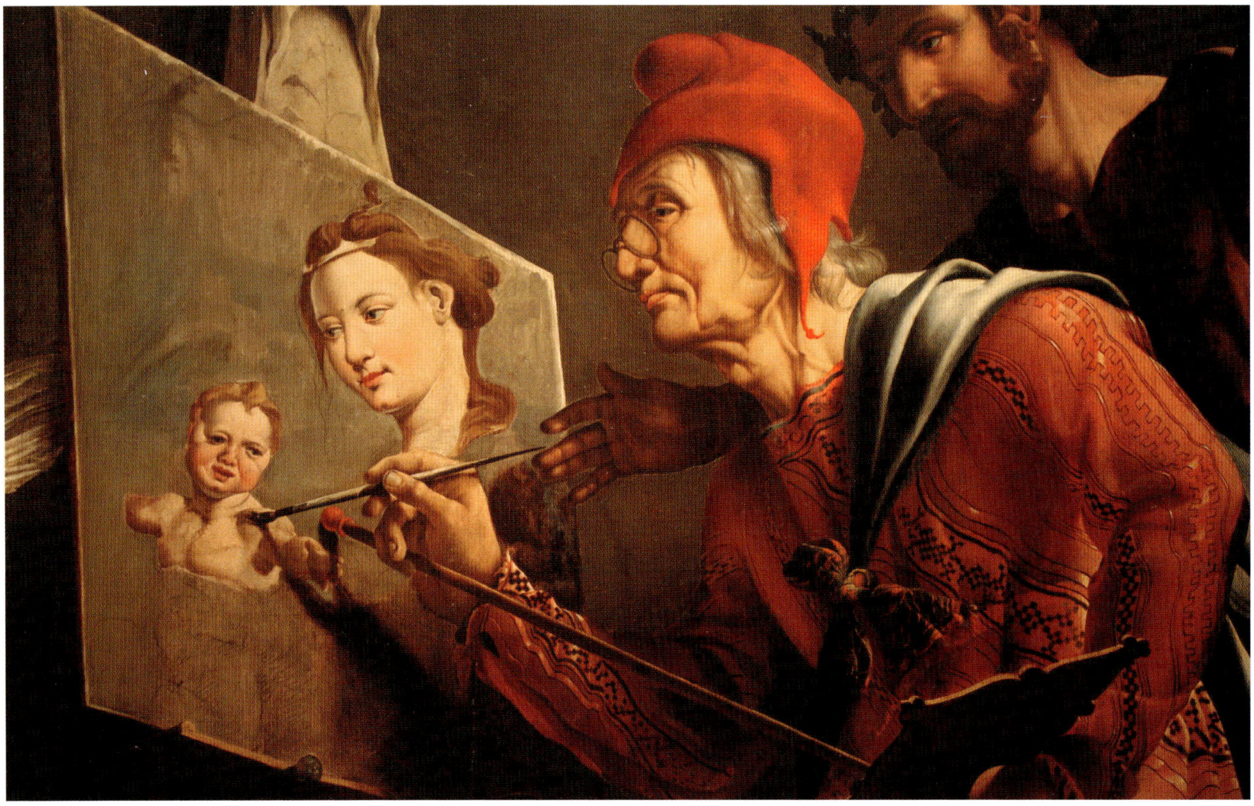

Figure 9 *Detail of Maarten van Heemskerck,* St Luke Painting the Virgin, *1532, Frans Hals Museum, Haarlem. (Photograph: Abbie Vandivere, courtesy of Frans Hals Museum, Haarlem.)*

Table 2 *Materials and methodology for the reconstructions described in this paper* cont'd

Layer	Materials / Supplier	Proportions / Method of preparation and application / Thickness*	Paintings reconstructed as case studies
IL	*Unpigmented 'isolation layer', cold-pressed linseed oil*: Zecchi Colori	Applied thinly with a 1–1.5 in. brush	Schematic reconstructions
	Stand oil: Zecchi Colori		
	Sun-thickened oil: Zecchi Colori		
	Rabbit-skin glue (10% in water): Kremer Pigmente		
	Leaded oil, made from cold-pressed linseed oil from Zecchi Colori + *lead(II)oxide* from Kremer Pigmente	6:1 ratio of linseed oil to lead(II) oxide. Oil warmed to 110°C, stirred, and left to cool. Applied thinly on top of the ground with a brush. For the schematic reconstructions, used by itself, and tested mixed with chalk (champagne chalk, Kremer Pigmente)	Schematic reconstructions Tried as binding medium (mixed with pigments) for: Rogier van der Weyden, *Descent from the Cross*
	White IL *Pigment: stack-process lead white*: Rublev colours, Natural Pigments www.naturalpigments.com *Binding medium: cold-pressed linseed oil*: Zecchi Colori	The pigment and oil (ratio ±5 g pigment to 1 ml oil) were ground together on a glass slab with a muller to achieve a workable paint. For the Geertgen tot Sint Jans case studies, attempted to achieve thicknesses of 8 μm (brushing out as thinly as possible) and 50 μm (thick enough to just obliterate the UD)	Schematic reconstructions Geertgen tot Sint Jans, *Adoration of the Magi* Jan van Scorel, *Lamentation of Christ with a Donor*
	Flesh-coloured IL *Pigments: lead white* from Natural Pigments; *charcoal* from Verfmolen de Kat; *other pigments (iron oxide, vine black, vermilion, red lake, champagne chalk)* from Kremer Pigmente *Binding medium: cold-pressed linseed oil* from Zecchi Colori, or *leaded oil* (see recipe above)	Varying amounts of pigment and oil were ground together on a glass slab with a muller in order to achieve a workable paint and a colour that matched the layer on the painting. The thicknesses achieved were: Jan Vermeyen and Rogier van der Weyden: 15–20 μm	Schematic reconstructions Jan Vermeyen, *Holy Family* Rogier van der Weyden, *Descent from the Cross* (tried both binding media)
Paint layers	*Pigments*: same as above *Binding medium: cold-pressed linseed oil*: Zecchi Colori	Varying amounts of pigment and oil were ground together on a glass slab with a muller in order to achieve a workable paint. The thicknesses were not measured	Jan Vermeyen, *Holy Family* Rogier van der Weyden, *Descent from the Cross*

Notes: * Unless otherwise mentioned, the thickness of the wet layers was measured using a film thickness gauge: BYK, www.byk.com/instruments/products/physical-properties_filmthickness_wetfilmthickness_1_en_US.php , PG-3507: 5–150 μm. UD = underdrawing; IL = intermediate layer

to be a relatively late development that accompanied the direct, efficient 'ten eersten opghedaen' technique.

The *primuersel* seems to have been more commonly used by painters who trained in and around Haarlem, which is where van Mander lived when he wrote the *Schilder-boeck*. Perhaps one of his reasons for writing about the lineage of the *primuersel* was to promote the superiority of the techniques of his region, rather like other writers of technical treatises such as Giorgio Vasari and Cennino Cennini. Perhaps he wanted to establish a lineage for the coloured grounds that became commonplace in Haarlem at the end of the sixteenth century.[34] Specifically, it was a way of justifying his own technique. His painting of the *Adoration of the Kings* (1598, Rijksdienst voor het Cultureel Erfgoed, on loan to the Frans Hals Museum, Haarlem) features a *primuersel*-like layer that has a significant visual effect in the architecture. To create bricks and foliage, he scratched into the wet paint layers to expose the intermediate layer (Fig. 8).

St Luke and the *primuersel*

Returning to the Lisbon *St Luke Drawing the Virgin* mentioned at the start: does the panel in the background depict a *primuersel* (Fig. 1)? There appears to be a flesh-coloured layer of a single tone that was applied over the whole surface of the ground. It does not seem to have been applied on top of an underdrawing since there is no underdrawing visible. The artist may have illustrated a technique that he saw in the workshop; unfortunately, few examinations of other paintings by Hugo van der Goes have so far been undertaken, so it is difficult to determine whether artists from his circle applied flesh-coloured intermediate layers. It seems that a *primuersel*-based technique was not used in the Lisbon *St Luke*; cross-sections showed that the paint layers were applied directly on top of the ground layer, or perhaps on top of an unpigmented isolation layer.[35]

There is another painting of St Luke in which an intermediate layer is prominently depicted. In Maarten van

Heemskerck's *St Luke Painting the Virgin* (1532, Frans Hals Museum, Haarlem), the saint has a half-finished painting on the easel in front of him (Fig. 9). The white ground on his panel appears to be covered by a grey intermediate layer with dry black underdrawing on top. The technique St Luke is employing differs slightly from that of van Heemskerck himself; however, van Heemskerck did apply a dark grey intermediate layer across the whole painting (van Asperen de Boer 1987: 105). The grey layer does not substantively contribute to the final effect in the skin tones, which are rather opaquely painted. Perhaps his attempt to use a dark grey underlayer was an experimental method based on Italian influences.[36]

It is intriguing that in both of these depictions of St Luke the overall technique of the painting seems to differ from the panels depicted within them.[37]

Conclusion

Reconstructions made in this study were instrumental in addressing the questions about the assumed functions of intermediate layers. The layers were effective in preventing some (if not all) of the oil medium from paint layers being absorbed into the ground. The intermediate layers fixed the underdrawing when required and prevented it from being picked up in paint layers. In almost all cases, underdrawing beneath an intermediate layer remained visible, provided the layer was not too thick. The grey and flesh-coloured intermediate layers expedited the painting process by acting as a base tone. This was most successful in the flesh tones of paintings by Vermeyen and van Heemskerck, which seemed to exploit the direct 'ten eersten opghedaen' method.

Case studies of actual paintings also clarified the relationship between intermediate layers and the *primuersel*. An artist's choice to apply coloured intermediate layers may have been an impetus for, or response to, the overall simplification of layer structure and more economical technique that came about as the sixteenth century progressed (Faries 2006). Especially in the cases of van Scorel, van Heemskerck and Vermeyen, it may also have developed in response to Italian influences.

Van Mander gives only one impression about the *primeursel*, but there is a more diverse situation borne out in reality. His references to the *primuersel* in the *Schilder-boeck* seem to be connected to his agenda of promoting Haarlem's painting pedigree, or indeed justifying his own painting technique. The Haarlem painters were rather innovative in their adoption of coloured intermediate layers. Their techniques are probable precursors to the introduction of coloured grounds in the Netherlands, which occurred around 1575 (Hendriks 2006: 80). Over time, coloured grounds superseded the use of lightly tinted intermediate layers; the change in technique was apparently related to the transition from the use of panel to canvas as a painting support (Miedema and Meijer 1979). Hopefully this investigation of the *primuersel* will better illuminate this transitional period and the visual effect it had on Netherlandish painting.

Acknowledgements

This research was undertaken as part of the project 'The Impact of Oil: A History of Oil Painting in the Low Countries and its Consequences for the Visual Arts, 1350–1550' (www.impactofoil.org), funded by the Nederlandse Organisatie voor Wetenschappelijk Onderzoek (NWO) and directed by Prof. Dr. Jeroen Stumpel and Prof. Dr. Jan Piet Filedt Kok.

I would like to thank: Liesbeth Abraham, J.R.J. van Asperen de Boer, Charlotte Caspers, Eric Domela-Nieuwenhuis, Esther van Duijn, Caroline van der Elst, Lauren Fly, Ella Hendriks, Jan Piet Filedt Kok, Mireille te Marvelde, Cathy Metzger, Hessel Miedema, Marie Postec, Jessica Roeders, Jana Sanyova, Astrid Smeets, Ron Spronk, Maartje Stols-Witlox, Anna Tummers and Arie Wallert.

Notes

1. I would like to thank Charlotte Caspers for bringing this example to my attention. The technique and restoration of this painting is discussed by Beaumont *et al.* 1981.
2. In early Netherlandish paintings with a fixed frame, it was typical to apply the ground layer to both the painting and the frame at the same time; see Wadum 1998: 160.
3. It is not meant to represent bare wood because it looks very different from the wooden easel and the palette in front of it.
4. The term was introduced by van Asperen de Boer *et al.* 1986: 108.
5. For a discussion of terminology, see Wadum 1995.
6. In the Dutch language, the suffix '-sel' often turns a verb into a noun (e.g. *kooksel*, *druksel* or *brouwsel*); from this it follows that the *primuersel* is a noun that describes the result of the act of priming. In late sixteenth- and early seventeenth-century texts, the suffix '-sel' usually means 'deriving from' and implies a change in state. Perhaps the *primuersel* suggests the first thing that changes the state of the painting, similar to the word *beginsel* ('beginning', 'origin', or 'basis'); see: www.etymologiebank.nl. This etymology was suggested by Mark Clarke, a specialist in historical sources.
7. Van Mander 1604, fols 47v, 48r. The English translation of this section is from Stols-Witlox (2012: 167). An annotated Dutch version is Miedema 1973.
8. Unless stated otherwise, I conducted the technical examinations and took the detail photographs. Digital photographs were taken using a Canon EOS 40D camera and a Canon EFS 60mm macro lens. The paintings were photographed in the museum environment therefore the lighting circumstances varied per situation. During research on location, a portable microscope (Zeiss OpMi-1 86372) was used in most cases to examine the paint surface. If samples are not specifically mentioned, the observations are based on my examination.
9. Unless stated otherwise, the samples from Rijksmuseum paintings were taken and analysed by Arie Wallert and me. The paint cross-sections were examined with a Leica DMLM microscope (magnifications 50×, 100×, 200×, 500× and 1000×). Images in direct incident light (bright field), and ultraviolet light (filter cube BL/VIO C105) were recorded with a digital Leica DFC 420 C camera. Samples from the Frans Hals Museum were taken by conservators and analysed by me using the same equipment mentioned above. I would like to thank the Frans Hals Museum and the Rijksmuseum for allowing access to their samples.
10. Coremans and Philippot (1953: 17) refer to it using the French term *couche d'impermébilisation* (isolating coating). They contrast this with a *couche d'impression*, which may also contain pigment.
11. This result confirms the findings of Thielen and Brinkman (Brinkman 1993), who tried to replicate the intermediate layer in Jan van Eyck's *Ghent Altarpiece* (1432, St Bavo Cathedral, Ghent)

and found that leaded oil gave the best results for effectively isolating the ground and approximating the appearance of the layer in cross-section (Brinkman 1993: 211).

12. On the other hand, this discoloration could also have been a desirable quality: to tone the bright white ground slightly.
13. Proteinaceous layers were found in paintings at the National Gallery, London, including works by van Heemskerck, Bouts, the workshop of Memling and Campin (Campbell *et al.* 1997: 23; Dunkerton 1988: 28).
14. Ferreira *et al.* 2008 describe a method by which the composition of intermediate layers was analysed using microscopy, Fourier transform infrared spectroscopy (FTIR), secondary ion mass spectrometry (SIMS) and scanning electron microscopy with energy dispersive X-ray analysis (SEM-EDX).
15. It is unclear whether he literally meant that the underdrawing should have no binding medium; perhaps 'charcoal black finely ground with water' refers to the material the artist should use to grind the pigment. Alternatively, he may have meant an aqueous medium such as glue or gum.
16. This challenges the statement made by Périer-D'Ieteren (1985: 20): if an oil-based intermediate layer of lead white were applied on top of a drawing in charcoal or black chalk that was not bound in an aqueous medium, then the layer would erase the drawing and sully the preparation. I would like to thank Charlotte Caspers and Émilie Froment for their assistance in translating and interpreting this section.
17. The interaction between underdrawing and intermediate layers was researched by Astrid Smeets in reconstructions made for the project 'Infrared Reflectography: Evaluative Studies', organised by the Universiteit van Groningen, 2005 (unpublished). I would like to thank Astrid Smeets for her help, particularly during the preparatory phase of this research.
18. For an example of a charcoal grid that was (deliberately or unintentionally) dusted off before the paint was applied, see Dunkerton *et al.* 1988: 26.
19. van Mander 1604: fol. 47r (my translation).
20. The most obvious examples of beading up were charcoal in rabbit-skin glue and charcoal in gum arabic applied on top of a layer of stand oil or a layer of sun-thickened oil. It is unclear why this created such a negative effect, especially as there was no beading up when the same underdrawing was applied on top of cold-pressed linseed oil.
21. In the reconstructions, a finger was used to smudge the underdrawing on the right side of each test. In almost all cases, the underdrawing did not smudge once both the intermediate layer and the drawing were dry. Only two combinations smudged easily: charcoal in water (no binding medium) in combination with any oily intermediate layer, and charcoal bound in linseed oil in combination with any oily intermediate layer (until both layers had dried for several weeks/months).
22. Schematic reconstructions of flesh-coloured intermediate layers were based on Rogier van der Weyden's *Descent from the Cross* and Jan Vermeyen's *Holy Family*.
23. Reconstructions were made by Marie Postec and La Cambre students; see Postec 2012: 149–50.
24. For more information about the sample and the composition of the intermediate layer, see van Asperen de Boer 1996: 21–5 and Keune 2005: 24. The medium of the intermediate layer is likely to be a leaded oil based on the micro secondary ion mass spectrometry (SIMS) analysis performed in Ferreira *et al.* 2008 Beneath the intermediate layer, there are a few particles of underdrawing visible in the cross-section. A recent examination suggests that Rogier van der Weyden may also have made changes or corrections to the underdrawing on top of the intermediate layer (Mozo 2009).
25. van Asperen de Boer *et al.* (1992: 143) presumed that Rogier van der Weyden exploited this effect.
26. This could also explain why some artists applied grey intermediate layers.
27. See Bagley-Young 2008. The initial research into these paintings was carried out by Ron Spronk and Cathy Metzger for Hand *et al.* 2006: 236–9.
28. Van Mander uses variations on this phrase several times in the *Schilder-boeck*, including fols 48r and 210v.
29. Miedema 1994–95. The phrase 'ten eersten opghedaen' has also been translated as 'in one go' (Miedema 1994–95: commentary on fol. 216v: 16–19) and 'setting … things down at the first' (Filedt Kok 1972–73: 136). In his commentary about fol. 201v: 10–11, Miedema contrasts 'ten eersten opghedaen' with the laborious method used by the earlier Netherlandish painters, which involved the application of successive transparent layers. After describing the *primuersel*, van Mander mentions Jan van Eyck as an artist who applied his paint directly, and implies that he is among the modern predecessors who employed the *primuersel* (fol. 48r). The *Ghent Altarpiece* (1432, St Bavo Cathedral, Ghent) is so far the only painting by van Eyck found to have a layer resembling the *primuersel*. It is medium-rich (most likely a leaded oil), probably containing chalk and lightly pigmented with red and black particles (for more information see Brinkman 1993: 211 and Coremans and Philippot 1953: 17, 75). However, cross-sections and technical examinations suggest that the meticulous layering that van Eyck used to paint certain colours does not entirely conform to the 'ten eersten opghedaen' technique; see Coremans and Philippot 1953: 75–6.
30. Paintings by Bosch from the collection of El Prado, Madrid, have been examined; see Garrido and Van Schoute 2001: 42. *The Seven Deadly Sins Tabletop* and the *Temptation of St Anthony the Hermit* have pinkish intermediate layers. Many of Bosch's other paintings have white or grey intermediate layers. Bosch's use of the *primuersel* is discussed in greater detail in Vandivere (forthcoming).
31. The distribution of this layer is unclear. Under the microscope in 'open' areas of the composition, there appeared to be black particles and possibly red particles applied in a thin layer over the ground. The underdrawing is easily visible through the thin paint layers and has a greyish tone. Presumably this effect has become more pronounced as the transparency of pigments in oil has increased over time; however, the paint layers are so thin that they may have always been somewhat visible; see Filedt Kok 1972–73: 140.
32. The flesh of the main figure was executed with pink paint on top of this layer, but perhaps the tone of the intermediate layer helped to simplify this process.
33. Caspers tried out several combinations of materials for the intermediate layer. In this case, the build-up is: ground (made of chalk and animal glue); an underdrawing (ivory black in gum arabic) applied with a brush; an intermediate layer containing lead white, red ochre, yellow ochre, azurite and lamp black bound in linseed oil; see Caspers 2010.
34. In the early seventeenth century, grey and reddish ground layers were used by the Haarlem mannerists (Hendriks 2006: 80).
35. Beaumont *et al.* 1981: 71–8. The ground is composed of chalk and animal glue, impregnated at the top with oil.
36. This painting immediately preceded his journey to Italy, but he had already begun to explore Italian techniques. Heemskerck used grey intermediate layers again later in his career (Table 1).
37. Within van Heemskerck's painting, the small panel shows a technique that aligns more with that of Jan van Scorel; it gives the illusion of a dry underdrawing applied on top of a white or greyish intermediate layer. Both painters worked in the same studio around 1527. *St Luke Drawing the Virgin* from the circle of Hugo van der Goes may be a copy after a lost composition; perhaps this original composition used a technique that was more similar to the panel depicted in the background.

References

Bagley-Young, A. 2008. 'Jan Cornelisz. Vermeyen's *Cardinal Erard de la Marck* and *The Holy Family*: a diptych reunited?', *The Burlington Magazine* 150(1259): 76–82.

Beaumont, M.A., Reis-Santos, L., Pawels, H., Baudoin, F., Viana, M.F., and Picciochi Alves, L.M. 1981. *S. Lucas retratando a Virgem: pintura*. Lisbon: Museu Nacional de Arte Antiga.

Brinkman, P. 1993. *Het geheim van Van Eyck: aantekeningen bij de uitvinding van het olieverven*. Zwolle: Waanders.

Campbell, L., Foister, S. and Roy, A. 1997. 'Methods and materials of Northern European painting in the National Gallery, 1400–1550', *National Gallery Technical Bulletin* 18: 6–55.

Caspers, C.C. 2010. 'A historical reconstruction of the *Pedlar* by Jheronimus Bosch'. In *Second International Jheronimus Bosch Conference: The Sources of Bosch*, J. Bradley, E. De Bruyn and A.M. Koldeweij (eds) 56–71. 's-Hertogenbosch: Waanders.

Coremans, P. and Philippot, P. 1953. *L'Agneau Mystique au Laboratoire: Examen et Traitement, Les Primitifs Flamands: III. Contributions a l'etude des Primitifs Flamands*. Antwerp: De Sikkel.

Dunkerton, J., Burnstock, A. and Smith, A. 1988. 'Two wings of an altarpiece by Maarten van Heemskerck', *National Gallery Technical Bulletin* 12(1): 16–35.

Faries, M. 2006. 'Making and marketing: studies of the painting process'. In *Making and Marketing: Studies of the Painting Process in Fifteenth- and Sixteenth-century Netherlandish Workshops*, M. Faries (ed.) 1–14. London and Turnhout: Brepols.

Faries, M. 2007–08. 'Geertgen tot Sint Jans: continuing studies of the painting process', *Simiolus* 33(1/2): 22–32.

Faries, M. 2011. 'Jan van Scorel's drawing and painting technique'. In *Catalogue of Paintings: 1363–1600: Centraal Museum, Utrecht*, L.M. Helmus and M. Faries (eds) 23–32. Utrecht: Centraal Museum.

Ferreira, E., Morrison, R. and Boon, J. 2008. 'Imaging chemical characterisation of preparatory layers in fifteenth and sixteenth-century Northern European panel paintings'. In *Preparation for Painting: The Artist's Choice and its Consequences*, J.H. Townsend, T. Doherty, G. Heydenreich and J. Ridge (eds) 50–58. London: Archetype Publications.

Filedt Kok, J. P. 1972–73. 'Underdrawing and drawing in the work of Hieronymous Bosch: a provisional survey in connection with the paintings by him in Rotterdam', *Simiolus: Netherlands Quarterly for the History of Art* 6(3/4): 133–62.

Garrido, C. and Van Schoute, R. 2001. *Bosch at the Museo del Prado: Technical Study*. Madrid: Museo del Prado, Aldeasa.

Garrido, J.M.C, Pérez, M.C.G, van Asperen de Boer, J.R.J. and Van Schoute, R. 1983. 'Algunas cuestiones técnicas del *Descendimiento de la Cruz* de Rogier van der Weyden', *Boletin del Museo del Prado* 4(10): 39–50.

Hand, J.O., Metzger, C. and Spronk, R. 2006. *Prayers and Portraits: Unfolding the Netherlandish Diptych*, National Gallery of Art, Washington, DC. New Haven, CT and London: Yale University Press.

Hendriks, E. 2006. 'The use of the ground colour'. In *Painting in Haarlem 1500–1850: The Collection of the Frans Hals Museum*, N. Kohler (ed.) 79–81. Ghent: Ludion.

Keune, K. 2005. *Binding Medium, Pigments and Metal Soaps Characterised and Localised in Paint Cross-sections*. PhD dissertation, MolArt project, University of Amsterdam.

Metzger, C.A. and Palmer, M.R. 2008. 'The creative process in Rogier van der Weyden's portraits'. In *Invention: Northern Renaissance Studies in Honor of Molly Faries*, J. Chapuis (ed.) 64–85. Turnhout: Brepols.

Miedema, H. 1973. *Karel van Mander: De grondt der edel vry schilderconst*. Utrecht: Haentjes Dekker & Gumbert.

Miedema, H. 1994–95. *Lives of the Illustrious Netherlandish and German Painters, from the First Edition of the Schilder-boeck (1603–1604)*. Doornspijk: Davaco.

Miedema, H. and Meijer, B. 1979. 'The introduction of coloured ground in painting and its influence on stylistic development, with particular respect to sixteenth-century Netherlandish art', *Storia dell'arte* 35: 79–98.

Mozo, A.G. 2009. 'New IRR of the *Descent from the Cross* (Prado)'. Paper presented at the *Rogier van der Weyden in Context Colloquium, Leuven, 22–24 October 2009*.

Périer-D'Ieteren, C. 1985. *Colyn de Coter et la technique picturale des peintres flamands du XVe siècle*. Brussels: Lefebvre & Gillet.

Postec, M. 2012. 'Technical reconstructions based on *The Seven Sacraments* by Rogier van der Weyden: an experimental approach'. In *Rogier van der Weyden in Context*, L. Campbell, J. van der Stock, C. Reynolds and L. Watteeuw (eds) 147–57. Leuven: Peeters.

Stols-Witlox, M.J.N. 2012. 'Grounds for easel painting, 1400–1900'. In *The Conservation of Easel Paintings*, J.H. Stoner and R. Rushfield (eds) 161–88. Oxford: Routledge.

van Asperen de Boer, J.R.J. 1987. 'A technical study of some paintings by Maarten van Heemskerck'. In *Color and Technique in Renaissance Painting: Italy and the North*, M.B. Hall (ed.) 105–14. Locust Valley, NY: J J Augustin.

van Asperen de Boer, J.R.J. 1996. 'On the painting technique of the Master of Flémalle panels at Frankfurt'. In *Robert Campin: New Directions in Scholarship*, S. Foister and S. Nash (eds) 21–5. London and Turnhout: Brepols.

van Asperen de Boer, J.R.J., Faries, M. and Filedt Kok, J.P. 1986. 'Painting technique and workshop practice in northern Netherlandish art of the sixteenth century'. In *Kunst voor de Beeldenstorm*, J.P. Filedt Kok, W. Halsema-Kubes and W.T. Kloek (eds) 106–16. Amsterdam: Rijksmuseum.

van Asperen de Boer, J.R.J., Dijkstra, J. and van Schoute, R. 1992. 'Underdrawing in paintings of the Rogier van der Weyden and Master of Flémalle groups', *Nederlands Kunsthistorisch Jaarboek* 41: 1–58.

van Mander, K. 1604. *Het schilder-boeck*. Digitale bibliotheek voor de Nederlandse letteren, www.dbnl.org/tekst/mand001schi01_01/.

Vandivere, A. 2011. 'In search of van Mander's *primuersel*: intermediate layers in early Netherlandish paintings'. In *Preprints of the ICOM-CC 16th Triennial Conference, Lisbon, 19–23 September 2011*, 1–10.

Vandivere, A. (forthcoming 2013) '"A translucent flesh-coloured *primuersel*": intermediate layers and visible underdrawing in Bosch's paintings'. In *From the Ground Up: Surface and Sub-surface Effects in 15th- and 16th-Century Netherlandish Paintings*, PhD dissertation, University of Amsterdam.

Wadum, J. 1995. '*Primuersel* of *imprimatura*?' *kM* 15: 39–40.

Wadum, J. 1998. 'Historical overview of panel-making techniques in the northern countries'. In *The Structural Conservation of Panel Paintings. Proceedings of a Symposium at the J. Paul Getty Museum, Los Angeles, 24–28 April 1995*, 149–77.

Wallert, A., Tauber, G. and Murphy, L. 2001. *The Holy Kinship: A Medieval Masterpiece*. Amsterdam: Rijksmuseum.

SEBASTIANO DEL PIOMBO'S *ADORATION OF THE SHEPHERDS*: ON THE PURSUIT OF COLOURISTIC SPLENDOUR IN A 'LOST' PAINTING

Christine S. Kimbriel and Youjin Noh

In the early nineteenth century, Lord Fitzwilliam bought a panel painting attributed to Giorgione showing the adoration of the shepherds.[1] In 1816, it was part of the large bequest of paintings left to the University of Cambridge forming the core of the Fitzwilliam Museum collection. The attribution of the painting changed several times during the nineteenth century and finally settled on Sebastiano del Piombo in the early twentieth. Throughout its life the painting has undergone two transfers, the first from its original panel substrate to canvas, a treatment that had detrimental results. In its heavily damaged state the painting has for many years languished in the store of the Hamilton Kerr Institute (HKI) awaiting a decision for or against restoration (Fig. 1).[2]

For the recent Sebastiano del Piombo exhibition in the Gemäldegallerie in Berlin, the brief catalogue entry for the (not exhibited) *Adoration of the Shepherds* ended on a sad note: 'however much it may be painful to say this, the

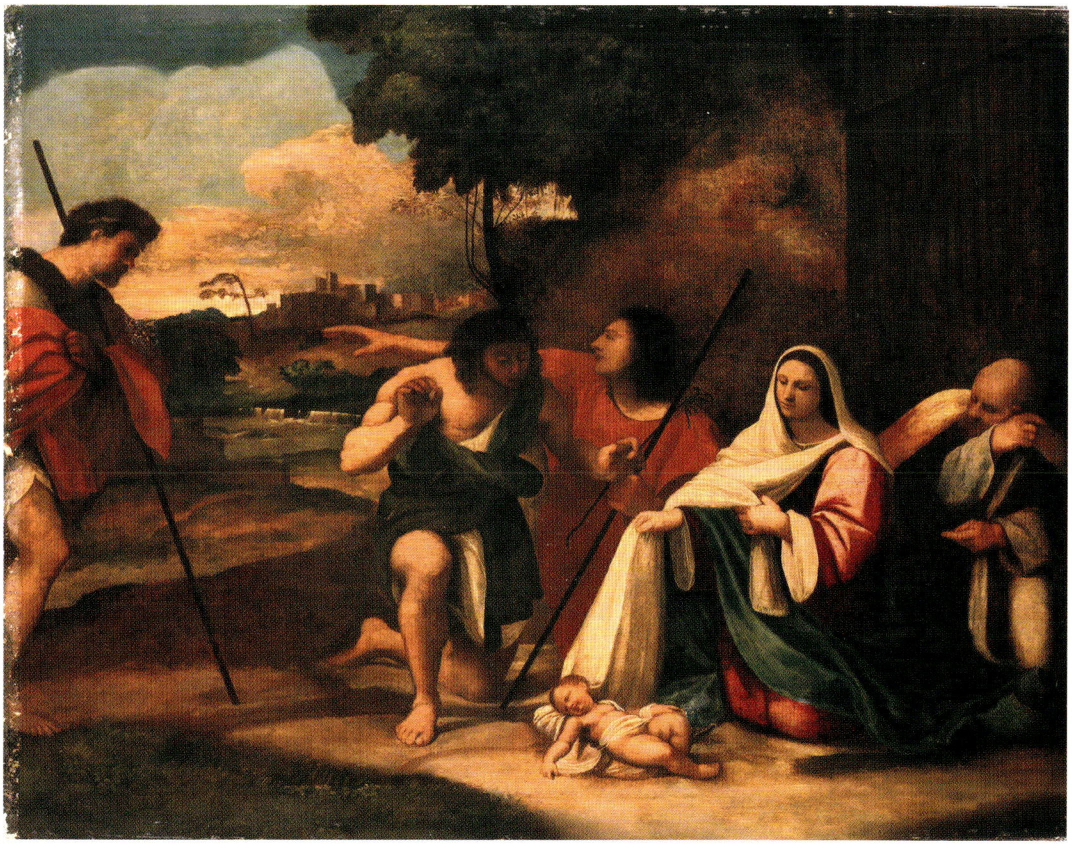

Figure 1 *Sebastiano del Piombo,* The Adoration of the Shepherds, c.*1512, oil on panel (transferred to canvas), 163 × 126 cm, The Fitzwilliam Museum, Cambridge. Before cleaning.*

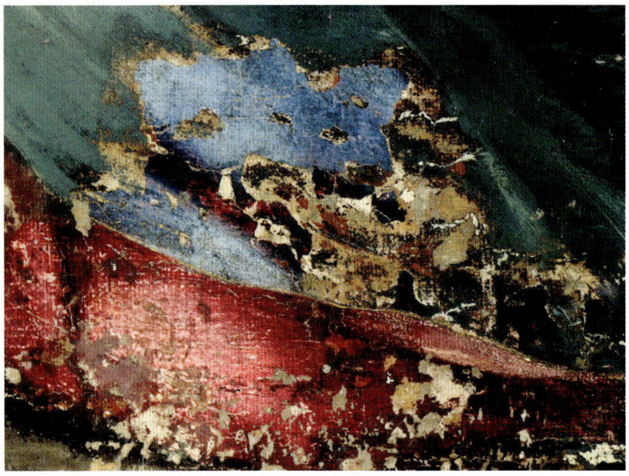

Figure 2 *Sebastiano del Piombo,* The Adoration of the Shepherds, *detail (20 × 14.9 cm) showing the Virgin's blue drapery during overpaint removal.*

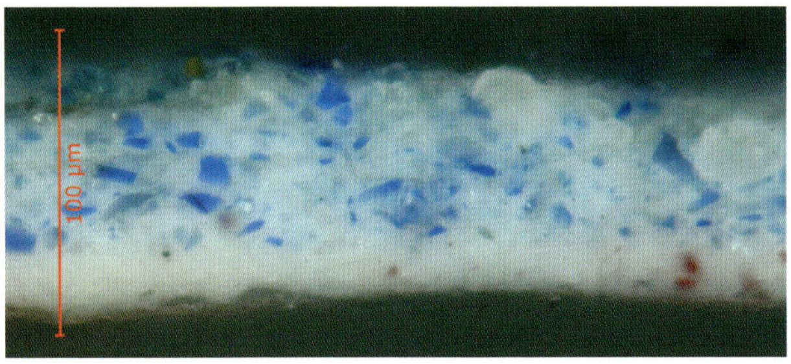

Figure 3 *Cross-section micrograph from the sky (mid-tone) showing pink* imprimatura, *followed by two paint layers with ultramarine blue and lead white. Overpaint, containing azurite, is present towards the left.*

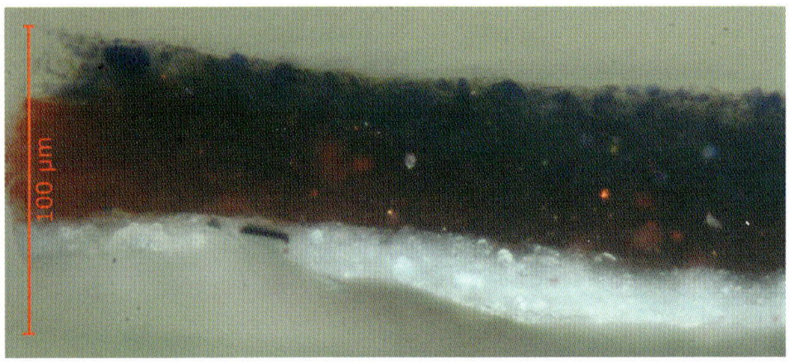

Figure 4 *Cross-section micrograph from the Virgin's blue drapery (shadow) showing white* imprimatura, *thick red glaze and ultramarine blue paint layer.*

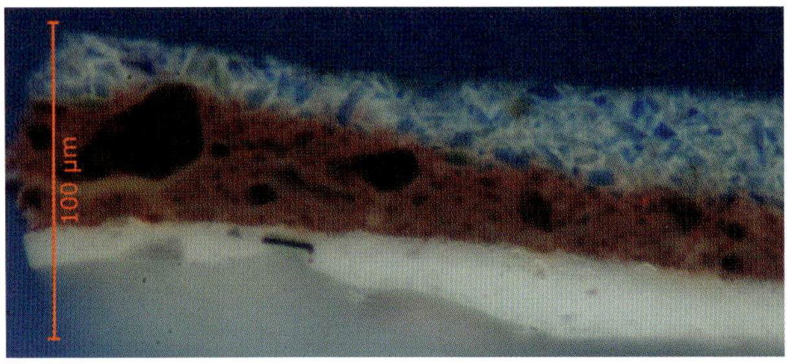

Figure 5 *As with Figure 4. UV illumination shows double application of red lake underlayer.*

painting must at present be considered lost' (Lucco 2008: 128). In spite of the severely compromised state of the painting however, the value of Sebastiano's 'lost' *Adoration* was recognised by the curators of the Fitzwilliam Museum, as well as by Renate Woudhuysen-Keller who, when offered the opportunity to undertake the demanding task of cleaning and restoring it, accepted the challenge. A full reintegration of losses with imitative retouching was envisioned, which would allow Sebastiano's compromised painting to take its place once more among the admired surviving works of a great Renaissance painter. Furthermore, the existence of an early copy of the work in the stores of the Musée du Louvre would provide an invaluable source of information for the reintegration of losses.[3]

The cleaning of the *Adoration of the Shepherds* is now complete and in spite of the many losses, the original colour palette of this intimate religious scene can once again be appreciated for the first time in centuries. Paradoxically, its damaged condition in some ways facilitates a closer study of the painting technique. The various degrees of loss and abrasion provide 'windows' through which the layering technique can be observed. As the surface of the painting has already been ruptured throughout, targeted sampling for technical analysis has likewise been possible.

Of particular interest to Renate were the surviving passages of the Virgin's brilliantly blue garment uncovered during cleaning (Fig. 2). A large passage of flowing folds in this garment has, however, been lost in the eighteenth-century transfer. To achieve an in-depth understanding of the original execution of this striking paint passage, and to aid in the reinstatement of it in retouching, a reconstruction using historically accurate methods and materials has been undertaken in which the extant original sections have been imitated as closely as possible. The reconstruction is informed by close visual observation as well as by the evidence provided by technical analysis. In its own right it therefore forms a study in historical painting techniques very much in the spirit of Renate's own research and teaching.

The first section of this article presents the results of the technical analyses undertaken on sample material from the surviving blue paint passages (the Virgin's drapery, Joseph's tunic and the sky) followed by a brief introduction of the use of red underlayers for blue paint passages in Italian painting leading up to the work of Sebastiano. A third section looks at other occurrences of red undermodelling and blue paint layers in Sebastiano's own oeuvre. Drawing on the preceding analyses, the context in which the *Adoration of the Shepherds* might have been executed is considered and the final section is concerned with key aspects and findings from the reconstruction process.

Technical investigation

The technical examination of the blue paint passages focused on cross-section analysis. Three samples were taken from the sky, four from Joseph's tunic and four from the Virgin's drapery. In each area a highlight, a mid-tone and a shadow area were chosen. After red lake was found under the blue paint layers in the Virgin's drapery, three

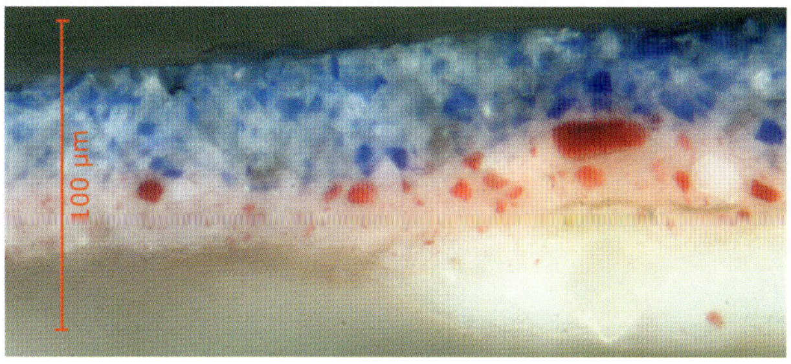

Figure 6 *Cross-section micrograph from the Virgin's blue drapery (mid-tone) showing white* imprimatura, *pink undermodelling and an ultramarine blue paint layer with lead white.*

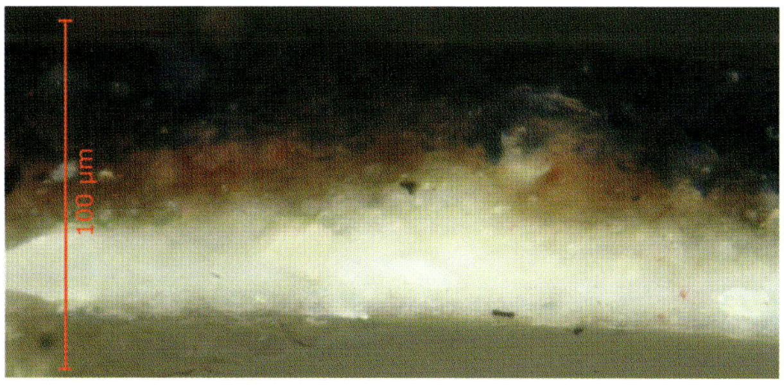

Figure 7 *Cross-section micrograph from Joseph's blue garment (shadow) showing fragmentary gesso ground, white priming, brownish red undermodelling and ultramarine blue paint layer.*

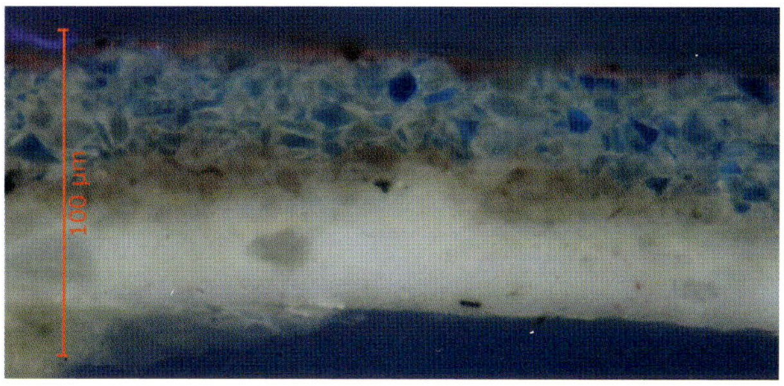

Figure 8 *As with Figure 7. UV illumination shows thin red lake layer applied over ultramarine blue paint.*

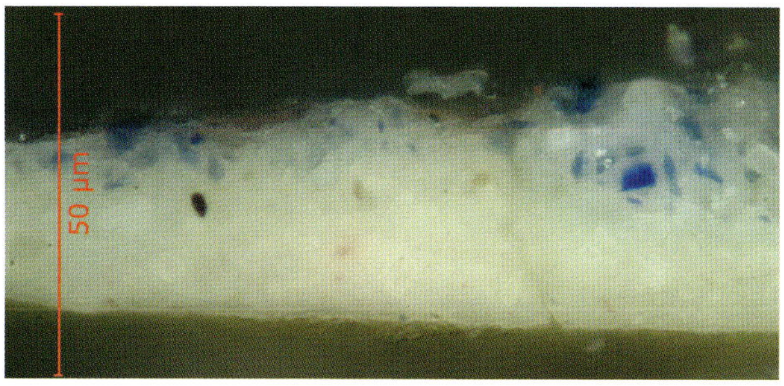

Figure 9 *Cross-section micrograph from Joseph's blue garment (highlight). Remnants of gesso ground, pale pink* imprimatura *followed by an ultramarine blue paint layer with lead white.*

more samples were taken from her red dress to allow for comparison. Dispersions in some cases supplemented the cross-sections when polarised light microscopy (PLM) analysis was considered necessary to elucidate aspects that neither reflected light microscopy nor scanning electron microscopy with energy dispersive X-ray analysis (SEM-EDX) of the cross-sections could answer. With the exception of amido black 10B staining tests for protein executed on some of the cross-section samples, binding medium analysis was not pursued in this investigation. The appearance of the surviving original paint passages and the layer build-up found in the sample material strongly suggested the predominant use of a drying oil.[4]

In the sky, all samples show an *imprimatura* layer containing lead white[5] with a small admixture of a crimson red lake. The pinkish *imprimatura* is visible throughout in the sky due to abrasion. Towards the horizon, where clouds catch the light of the sun, it may have been used as a partially visible underpaint for the modelling of the clouds.[6] In the paler passages of the sky, two to three thin paint layers of similar appearance consisting of ultramarine blue mixed with lead white are present (Fig. 3). Towards the horizon lead white is omitted from the paint layer, but a minor admixture of red lake has been added to the ultramarine.[7]

The cross-sections from the Virgin's blue drapery show the use of the same three pigments found in the sky. The presence of a lead white *imprimatura* with few or no red lake particles confirms the transition of the *imprimatura* to white in the lower part of the painting. A highly finished undermodelling executed entirely in red lake with a variable admixture of lead white is present throughout (compare Figs 4–6). The high content of aluminium in the layer suggests an alum substrate, and the lack of orange fluorescence under ultraviolet (UV) illumination points to an insect dye, most likely kermes, as opposed to madder.[8] In the deep shadows, little or no lead white appears to be present in either the red lake layer or in the ultramarine blue paint layer on top, and the red lake undermodelling is applied in at least two separate layers to intensify the depth of the colour, as is common practice with glaze layers. It is however remarkable to see such a large quantity of a very expensive colourant used in an underlayer. For the brilliant blue highlights and mid-tones, a slightly paler mixture of ultramarine blue and lead white is followed by a thin application of pure ultramarine.

In Joseph's tunic the crimson red lake undermodelling of the Virgin is replaced by an equally highly finished modelling in a brownish red lake (Figs 7 and 8). SEM-EDX analysis of this layer shows a negligible presence of aluminium and a high content of calcium. Although the colour of this brownish layer could easily be interpreted visually as a translucent brown earth pigment, no iron was found to be present. Recipes for the production of redwood lakes such as brazilwood have commonly been found to specify a chalk-based substrate (Kirby *et al.* 2005), and although these lakes are known to fade rapidly, their use in an underlayer would have afforded some protection. It is, however, difficult to say with certainty that it has not undergone some changes over time; a variation in tone to a more crimson hue in areas where abrasion has left it exposed could indeed suggest a colour change. Equally, the colour difference may indicate that more than one type of lake was used.[9] In any case,

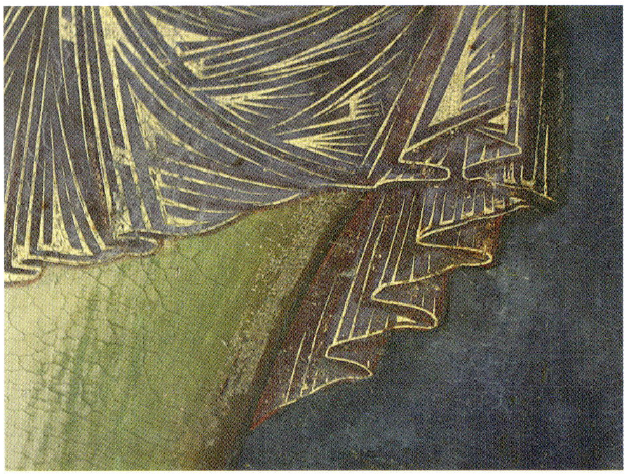

Figure 10 *Master of the Franciscan Crucifixes,* Crucifix, *about 1254. Detail showing ultramarine blue with copious mordant gilding on a sumptuous red lake-containing underpaint. (Pinacoteca Nazionale di Bologna.)*

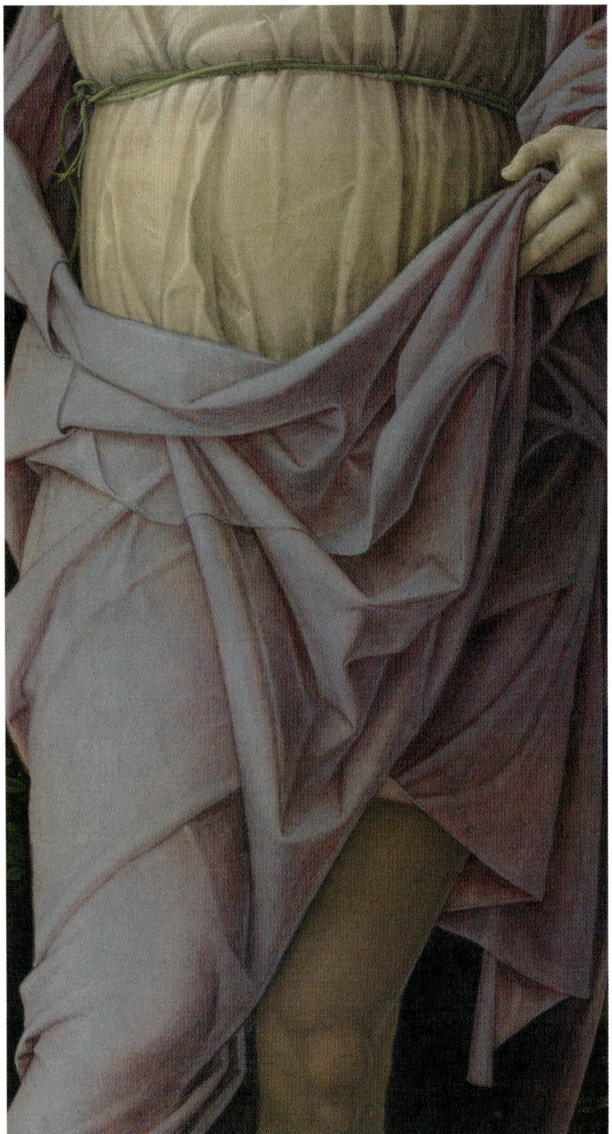

Figure 11 *Andrea Mantegna,* The Virgin and Child with the Magdalen and St John the Baptist, *about 1490–1505, tempera on canvas. Detail of St John the Baptist. (© The National Gallery, London.)*

there can be little doubt that a difference in hue from the bright crimson in the Virgin's underlayer was intentional from the outset. The highlight on Joseph's tunic (Fig. 9), painted with ultramarine in lead white, shows no trace of the red undermodelling, but a colourless particle with a noticeable bubble formation analysed with SEM-EDX was found to be potassium-rich glass. Although glass was not otherwise identified with certainty in the sample material examined, it is possible that Sebastiano added minor proportions of glass to increase translucency or improve drying properties in some paint passages.[10] The wear to Joseph's tunic has resulted in an almost complete loss of a final red glaze similar in hue to that in the undermodelling for the Virgin's drapery and red dress. The remnants of this glaze are now only visible in the cross-section samples, where traces of it are present in all four samples – not only from the dark passages where it would have served to deepen the shadows of the garment with a purplish tinge, but in the highlight sample as well, suggesting that a thin red glaze was applied throughout.

From the technical evidence provided by the sample material, some characteristics of the painter's approach to the execution of the blue paint passages have become evident. First, Sebastiano followed a carefully predetermined plan for the build-up of his paint layers. All samples display a clear layer structure without hints of *pentimenti*. Secondly, each layer was allowed time to dry prior to the application of the next (for the thick red glazes of the undermodelling this may have required considerable patience), and the surviving paint passages show no signs of drying-related problems. Thirdly, Sebastiano chose to limit himself to only four pigments, two of which – kermes lake and ultramarine – were among the most expensive available. As a result of these decisions for material simplicity, these paint passages seem almost to embody an ideal of purity both in execution and appearance. It is surely no coincidence that they are employed for the depiction of the Virgin in particular.

The specific batch of ultramarine, which appears to be the same across all blue paint passages examined, does however have unusual characteristics that are worth noting. From examination of the cross-sections it is clear that the particles are all of similar size and shape, though a considerable proportion of them appear pale grey or colourless. A suspicion that these could be mainly calcite impurities from insufficient processing of the lapis lazuli, or an admixture of glass or smalt, was not confirmed by analysis. Instead, the particle morphology is suggestive of associated minerals that can occur with veins of lazurite, such as afghanite and haüyne. Although these minerals are blue in mass, they are colourless when ground to the particle size present in the sample material, but like lazurite, they are members of the sodalite group and are known to occur with veins of lazurite in some Afghan deposits.[11]

Sebastiano's use of this batch of ultramarine raises interesting questions: would the colourless particles have increased the translucency of the pigment and was this property recognised by, and desirable to, Sebastiano? Or, on the contrary, was this considered to be a lower grade of the precious ultramarine blue, perhaps purchased at a reduced cost? The deliberateness of the layering technique employed by the artist, as well as the liberal use of expensive red lake for the underlayers, points to the former possibility. As will be argued below, Sebastiano intended to show off his skill at rendering exquisite Venetian colours, and he is unlikely to have been short of funds during the execution of this painting. It is therefore improbable that the cost of ultramarine blue of a quality that was to his liking would have been a limiting factor.

Blue on red: tradition and innovation

The radiant ultramarine blue with its red underlayer in the Virgin's drapery (Fig. 2) is not in its conception a unique occurrence in Italian art. The superimposition of blues and reds has a long tradition in the tempera technique that can be appreciated in surviving examples of thirteenth-century religious works (Fig. 10).[12]

Mantegna, who developed the egg-tempera technique to perfection in the fifteenth century, could with only one or two exceedingly thin paint layers achieve a full range from pink to purple to blue hues in his depiction of intricate *cangiante* garments. With this painting technique, the thinness of his paint applications allowed the white of the preparatory layer (either the bare gesso or an *imprimatura*) to lend luminosity to the semi-transparent paint layers on top in spite of the matt finish resulting from the use of the egg medium (Fig. 11).[13]

Mantegna was the son-in-law of Jacopo Bellini whose own son, Giovanni Bellini, became the most influential painter of the early Venetian Renaissance.[14] Although there is no evidence that Mantegna ever lived and worked in Venice for any length of time, the influence on Giovanni (hereafter referred to as 'Bellini') of his brother-in-law can be seen in some of his early works in egg tempera. However he would soon adopt the oil medium to an increasing extent and is considered to have mastered this medium fully by the time he executed his Pesaro altarpiece begun in 1471 (Dunkerton 2003: 207). Bellini's success meant that he was able to run a workshop of unprecedented size. He is thought to have welcomed apprentices, taking an almost paternal interest in his young protégés (Humfrey 2006: 42), a notion that to a great extent rests on the fact that Vasari, in his *Lives of the Artists*, claimed that the majority of the great Venetian artists of the next generation, including Giorgione, Lorenzo Lotto, Sebastiano and Titian, were all at one point apprenticed to Bellini.[15]

Bellini's transition from tempera to oil was a gradual one, with the technical examination of many of his paintings showing evidence of egg tempera, *tempera grassa* and oil within the same paintings (Dunkerton 2003). It is clear from his surviving early works that Bellini – like Mantegna – fully mastered the tempera medium and that the technical aspects of the tempera technique, such as the carefully pre-planned underdrawing and hatching of the shadows, the thin build-up of layers and the repetitive narrow brushstrokes, were retained to a great extent in many of his later oil paintings and perhaps never fully abandoned. In his *Virgin of the Trees* in the Galleria dell'Accademia (Venice), an autograph work of 1487, what appears to be a pale pink underpaint (whether modelled or not is unclear due to the good condition of the paint layer on top) is just visible in the highlights. Here, it is allowed to shine through the intensely blue paint of the Virgin's drapery resulting in a subtle *cangiante* effect. A similar example is the version of the *Virgin and Child between Two Saints* in the Museu Nacional del Prado (Madrid) (Fig. 12), a Bellini workshop production of about 1490. The delicate purple of the Virgin's dress can be seen upon close inspection to have a thin red under-modelling followed by a translucent application of blue mixed with white. Although the medium in both cases has been found to be oil, the paint application is that of the tempera technique with thin, meticulous and repetitive strokes of the brush.

According to Vasari, Sebastiano learned the first principles of the art of painting from Bellini. He soon, however, came under the influence of Giorgione, who introduced into Venice 'the newer manner, with its superior harmony and increased vividness of colouring' (Vasari 1851: 59). Vasari also claimed that Sebastiano acquired Giorgione's 'manner' to a considerable degree. The historical accuracy of Vasari's accounts has been discussed at length elsewhere and is not the subject of this paper,[16] but this latter suggestion is somewhat confirmed by the complicated and intermingled attribution history of works

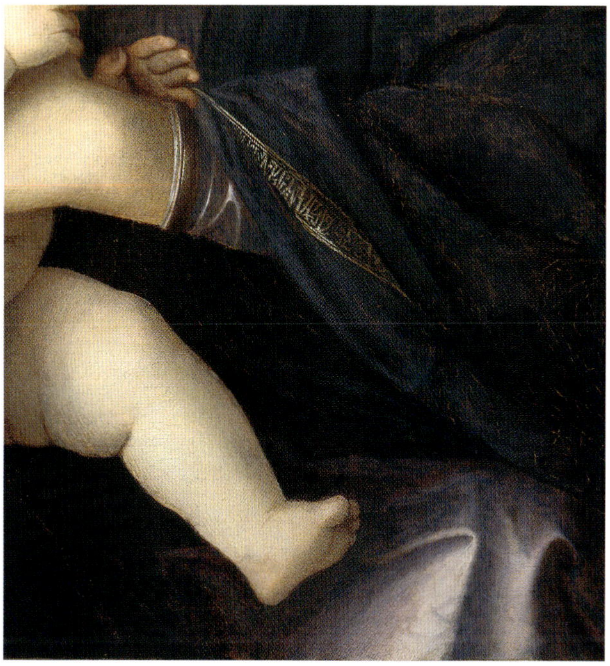

Figure 12 *Workshop of Giovanno Bellini,* The Virgin and Child between Two Saints, *about 1490, oil on panel. Detail of the Virgin's garments. (© Museo Nacional del Prado, Madrid.)*

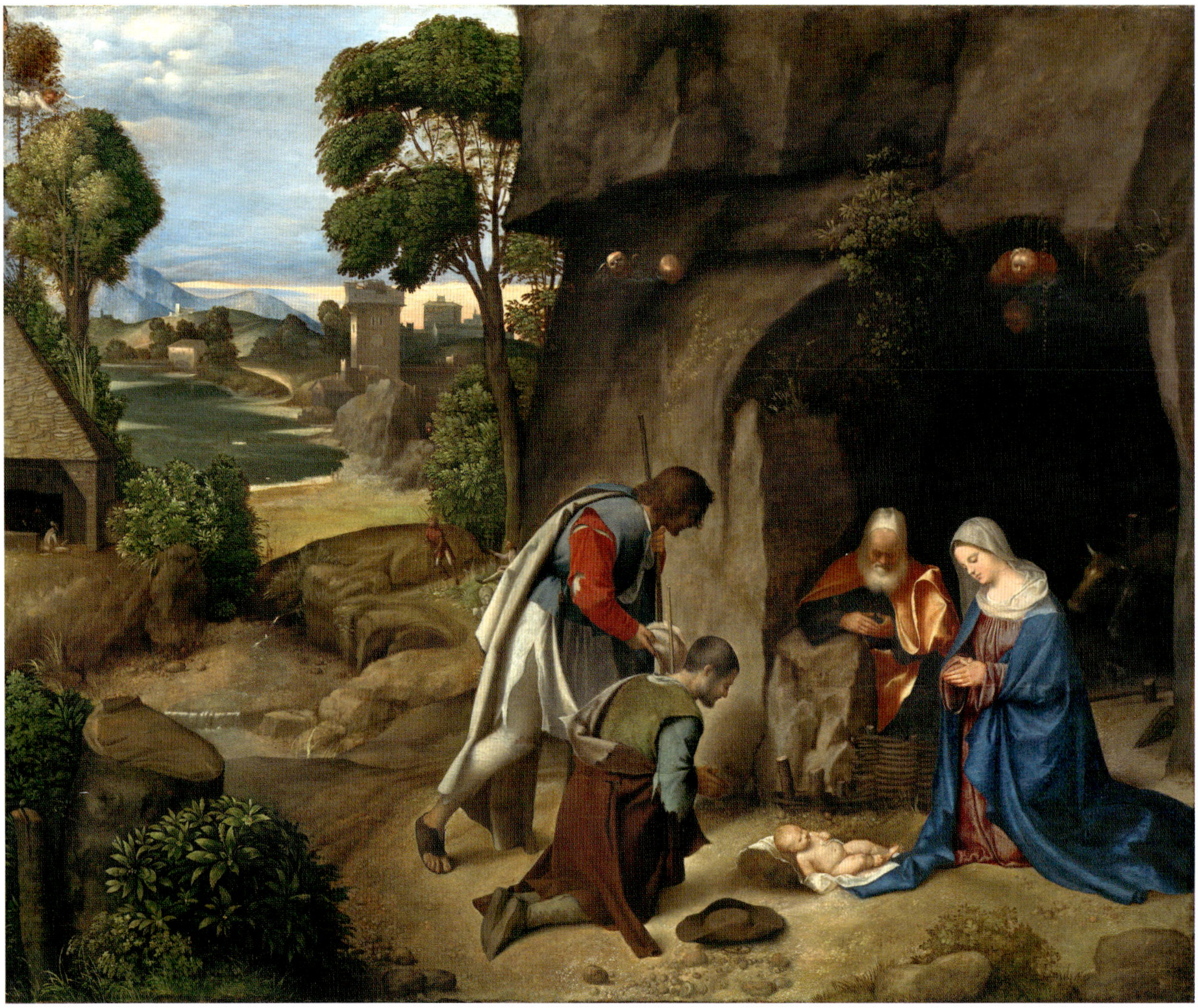

Figure 13 *Giorgione,* The Adoration of the Shepherds *(the Allendale Nativity), 1505–10, oil on panel, 90.8 × 110.5 cm. (© The National Gallery of Washington.)*

by Giorgione and Sebastiano (as well as by Titian). The brevity of Giorgione's oeuvre, the extent to which the chronology of his surviving works lacks factual evidence and the uncertainty about the nature of his relationship with Sebastiano all pose challenges to the comparison between the output of these two artists in the first decade of the sixteenth century. However Giorgione's two versions of his *Adoration of the Shepherds* – the Allendale Nativity in Washington, DC (Fig. 13) and the unfinished version in Vienna[17] – offer compelling similarities that confirm the influence that Giorgione, seven years

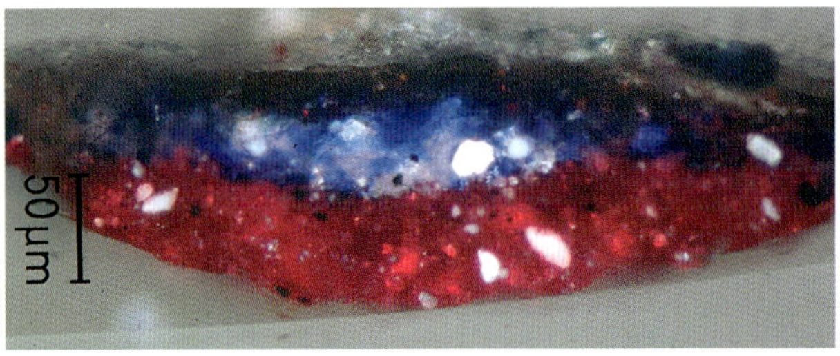

Figure 14 *Giorgione,* The Adoration of the Shepherds *(the Allendale Nativity). Cross-section from the Virgin's blue robe. (© The National Gallery of Washington.)*

his senior, seems to have had on the young Sebastiano. Giorgione's intimate, asymmetrical composition with its new emphasis on the lyrical landscape is considered a novelty in the long tradition for the depiction of this subject matter (Lucco 2006) and Sebastiano's composition strongly echoes it while at the same time introducing characteristic differences. As spectators, we are brought closer to the miraculous scene through the way in which the figures are considerably larger than in the Giorgione compositions and inhabit the entire foreground of the painting. A feeling of immediacy is furthermore introduced by the sense of movement in the composition, not least with the third shepherd having only partly entered the scene from the left. The landscape also figures prominently in all three versions, one of the better-preserved details of which is the body of water in the Sebastiano. In Giorgione's Allendale Nativity, this element is reduced to a much less monumental feature. It is, however, the colouristic similarities between the three paintings and the techniques with which they were achieved that are the subject of our current inquiry, and a striking comparison can be made between the cross-sections from the

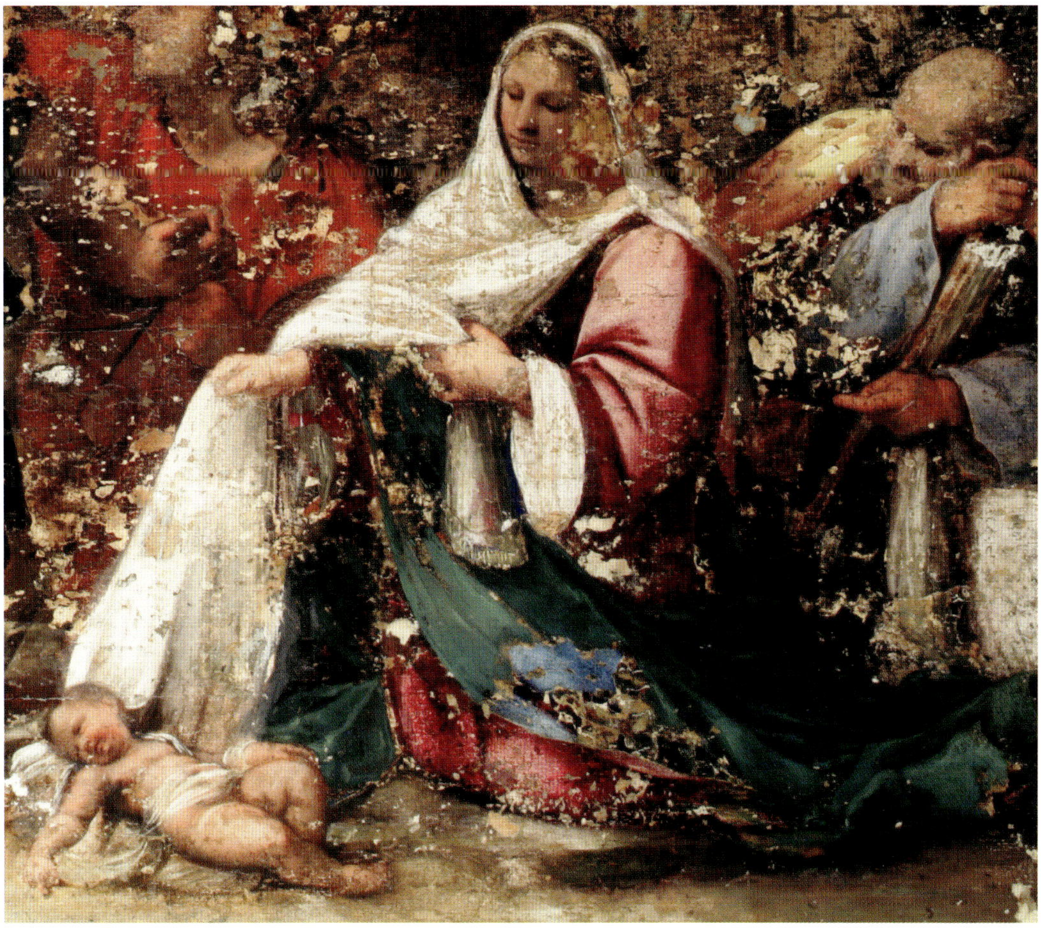

Figure 15 *Sebastiano del Piombo,* The Adoration of the Shepherds. *Detail of the Holy Family during cleaning.*

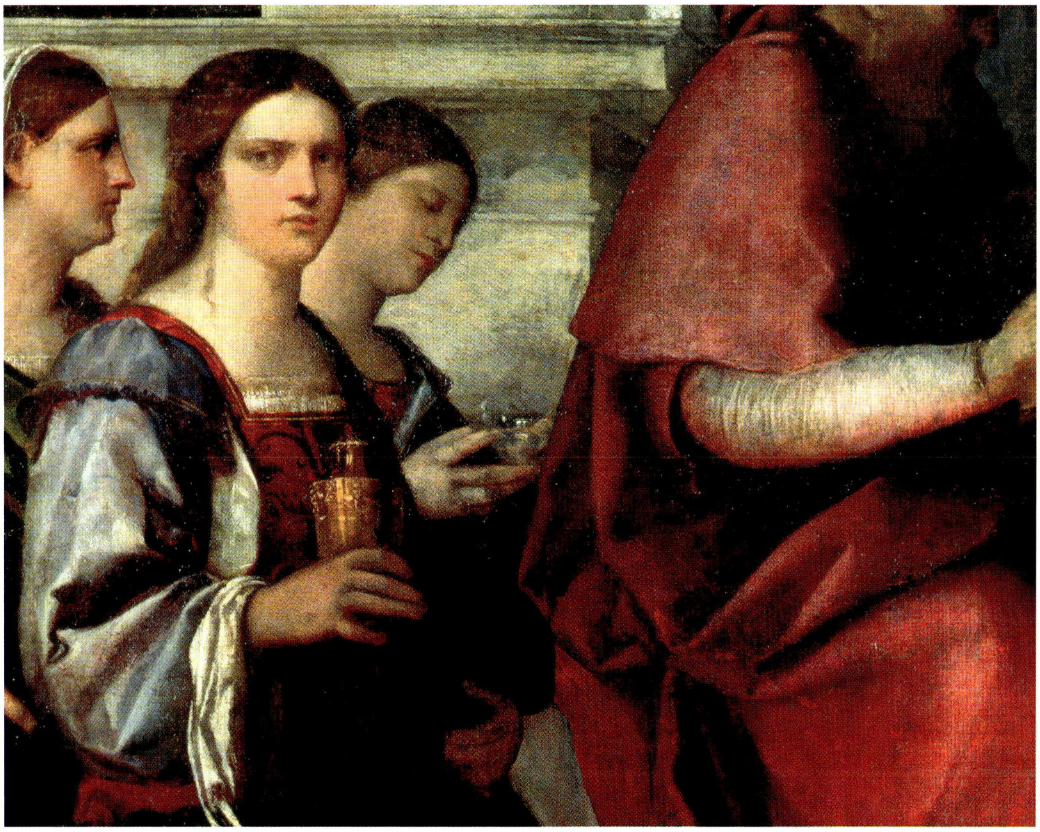

Figure 16 *Sebastiano del Piombo,* St John Chrysostom Altarpiece, *1508–10, oil on canvas, San Giovanni Grisostomo, Venice. Detail. (© Cameraphoto Arte Veneziana/The Bridgeman Art Library.)*

Virgin's drapery in Sebastiano's *Adoration* and those from the Virgin of the Allendale Nativity (Fig. 14). Giorgione, like Sebastiano, applied a thick red glaze under the ultramarine blue paint.[18] He also applied a red glaze under the blue of Joseph's tunic,[19] which is visually evident especially in the Vienna version. For the deep shadows of the Virgin's robe, Giorgione, unlike Sebastiano, added a thin purple glaze. As evidenced by the cross-sections and reconstructions however, Sebastiano did apply a thin red glaze over the blue of Joseph's tunic, the visual result of which is discussed below.

In spite of these similarities it would be conjecture to claim that here is a direct example of Sebastiano taking in Giorgione's new manner of 'superior harmony' and 'colouristic vividness', to use Vasari's wording. And some of the compositional and conceptual differences briefly introduced above likewise point to the execution of Sebastiano's *Adoration of the Shepherds* falling somewhat later than Giorgione's two paintings of the same subject matter. However, it is not unthinkable, in view of the striking juxtaposition in all three paintings of blue, red and yellow in the group of the Holy Family and the methods used to achieve them, that Sebastiano was indeed referring to a colour vocabulary and method of execution used by Giorgione (Fig. 15).

Blue on red in Sebastiano's early works

Just as the particular execution of the blue paint layers in Sebastiano's *Adoration of the Shepherds* does not constitute a unique occurrence on the scene of Italian art of the period, neither is it exclusive to this painting within his own oeuvre. However, few examples of red or pink underlayers are evident in his surviving Venetian works. Technical examination of the Galleria dell'Accademia *Sacra Conversazione*, considered to be one of Sebastiano's earliest works (Hirst 1981), has shown that although the blue pigment used throughout the painting was ultramarine, the Virgin's blue robe was achieved with a mixed paint layer of lead white and lapis, followed by a pure lapis glaze (Casoli *et al.* 2010). The blues of the unfinished *Judgement of Solomon* at Kingston Lacy likewise appear to be executed using only ultramarine blue pigment, but again, although a complicated layer structure is present as a result of extensive compositional revision, no underlayers containing red lake were found under blue paint passages (Laing 1988). One occurrence in Sebastiano's Venetian paintings can however be found in the *St John Chrysostom Altarpiece* (*c.*1508–10, San Giovanni Grisostomo, Venice) (Fig. 16), where sample material from the sleeve of Mary Magdalene clearly shows an underlayer of lead white and red lake followed by a paint layer of lead white and lapis lazuli (Fig. 17).[20] In this work, the bordeaux colour of the saint's garb was achieved not with superimposed layers of red and blue, but with a mixed paint of red lake, smalt and lapis over a pale purple underlayer (Casoli *et al.* 2010).[21]

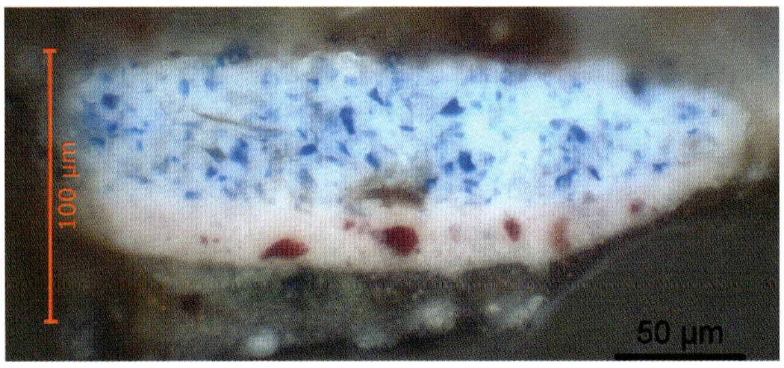

Figure 17 *Sebastiano del Piombo,* St John Chrysostom Altarpiece. *Cross-section from the blue sleeve of Mary Magdalene showing the grey priming as well as the pink underlayer for the ultramarine and lead white paint layer. (© Polo Museale Veneziano, Archivo Fotografico.)*

Sebastiano del Piombo left Venice for Rome in the summer of 1511, invited by one of the wealthiest men of his time, Sienese banker Agostino Chigi. Sebastiano appears to have commenced a scheme of fresco decorations for his suburban Villa Farnesina immediately upon arrival (Carratù 2008). In Rome, he soon became associated with Michelangelo, who provided him with drawings for his works on several occasions, one of which is the *Pietà* in Viterbo (Italy), in which two radiant blues of the Virgin's tunic and drapery respectively are emphasised against a backdrop of a night landscape and sky. While the drapery is underpainted with grey, the paler tunic has a warm glow due to the presence of a pink underlayer of lead white and red lake. Both paint passages are executed in ultramarine blue with admixtures of lead white (Marocchini 2004).

In a recent study of the *Raising of Lazarus*, executed 1517–19 – undoubtedly one of Sebastiano's masterpieces and painted in direct competition with Raphael's *Transfiguration* – the materials and build-ups of the blue and mauve paint passages were examined in detail (Dunkerton and Howard 2009). The central figure of Christ is, like the Virgin in the *Adoration of the Shepherds*, clad in a crimson red garment (Fig. 18). It is painted as though lit by a heavenly light so strong as to render parts of it almost white, and a brilliant blue drapery falls around the figure. With the intensity of the pure hues of the blue and the red, Christ stands out from the surrounding crowd of people painted in garments of either more dull, mixed or broken colours. In both the *Adoration* and the *Lazarus*, the elevated status of the Virgin and of Christ respectively is communicated to a great extent through this masterly use of colour juxtapositions. The shadows of Christ's exquisite blue drapery in the *Raising of Lazarus* were achieved by using a lapis lazuli pigment of an extremely pure grade consisting of intense blue particles only. For mid-tones and highlights lead white was added. A pink underlayer with red lake is present under this blue, but is not modelled. In its execution, Christ's blue drapery is closer to the blue paint layers in the *Adoration* than are any of the other blue and mauve paint passages in this large painting. In Martha's mauve garment a red undermodelling

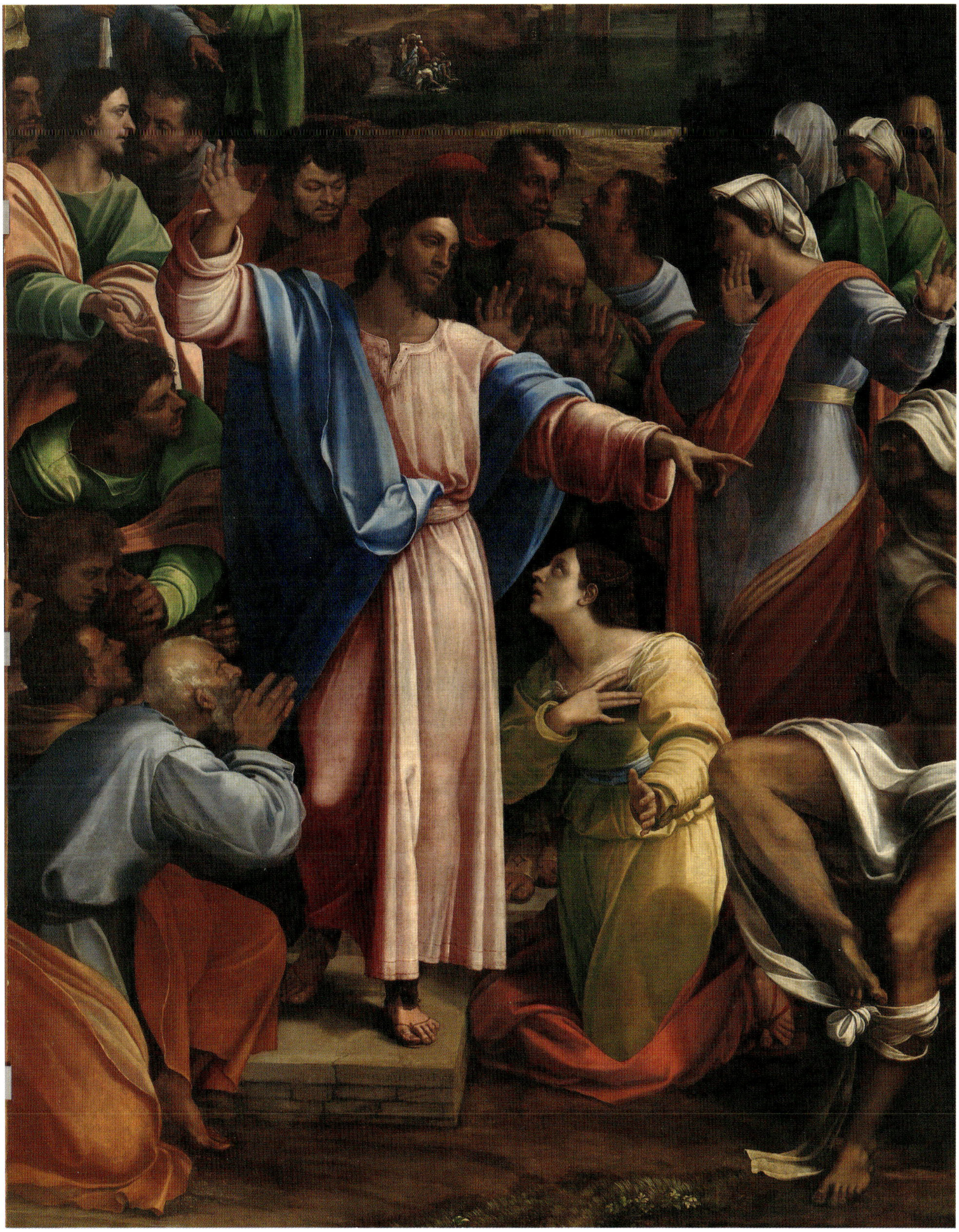

Figure 18 *Sebastiano del Piombo,* The Raising of Lazarus, *1517–19, oil on panel (transferred to canvas). (© The National Gallery, London. Detail.)*

is present, however it consists of red earth mixed with ultramarine, and the paint layer on top is a mixture of ultramarine, lead white and red lake. For the kneeling St Peter, whose appearance is reminiscent of Joseph in the *Adoration*, the dusty blue of his tunic (originally of a warmer hue, as would have been the case in the Joseph figure with its now lost red glaze), is achieved by superimposing a layer of lead white with very little ultramarine and (now faded) red lake on an underlayer of azurite and lead white. Azurite is likewise present in

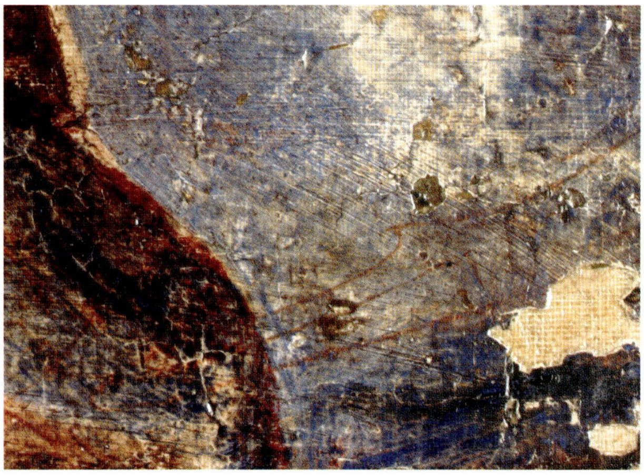

Figure 19 *Sebastiano del Piombo,* The Adoration of the Shepherds. *Detail (6 × 4.5 cm) of Joseph's sleeve where sketchy underpainting in thin red paint is visible through an abraded paint passage.*

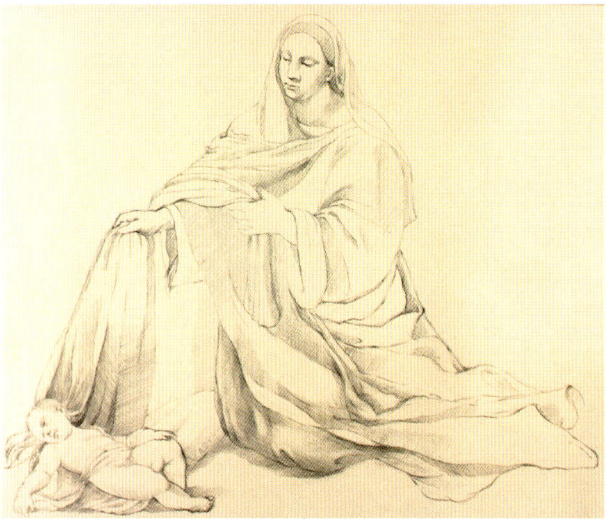

Figure 20 *Cartoon created for the reconstruction.*

the sky, where it is used in an underlayer with lead white and red lake. Lapis, red lake and lead white make up the pigment mixture in the paint layer on top, while azurite dominates the sky towards the horizon. Here it has contributed to the deterioration of the medium resulting in considerable darkening.

The Adoration of the Shepherds in context

The *Adoration of the Shepherds* is thought to have been painted in the period immediately surrounding Sebastiano's move to Rome (Lucco 2008: 128). How does his execution of blue paint passages in this painting compare with other works of his early career? As discussed above, the first example of a pink underlayer amongst his surviving Venetian works occurs in the *St John Chrysostom Altarpiece*, one of the late Venetian works possibly painted less than a year before Sebastiano left the city. The next example given, painted between 1513 and 1516, is the Viterbo *Pietà*, which likewise has been shown to have a localised, pink underlayer for one of the blue paint passages. In this painting, as in the *Adoration* and possibly in the *Raising of Lazarus* as well, an *imprimatura* is present, which changes tone or colour at an approximately horizontal line halfway down the painting. While the change in the *Adoration* is from pink to white from top to bottom, the *Pietà* goes from near white to grey (Marocchini 2004), and the *Lazarus* possibly from darker grey to paler grey (Dunkerton and Howard 2009). Sebastiano used grey *imprimature* increasingly in his Roman works, but the priming in his portrait of *Salome* in the National Gallery (London), possibly one of his last works painted in Venice, also has a pale grey priming (Dunkerton and Spring 1998: 122), as does the *St John Chrysostom Altarpiece* (Casoli *et al.* 2010).

While the published technical examinations of the *Chrysostom* and *Pietà* altarpieces did not reveal whether the red underlayers are modelled, the examination of the *Raising of Lazarus* showed that while modelling of the red underlayer was undertaken for some blue passages (such as the Martha figure), it was not for others (Christ's blue drapery). In the *Lazarus*, executed well after Sebastiano's establishment in Rome however, and here looking narrowly at the blue and purple paint passages, his palette has expanded to include several other pigments and his layering technique has become more diverse. With this grand painting of 1517–19, Sebastiano is not only participating, but competing on the stage of the foremost painters in Rome at the time – Raphael in particular. With his *Adoration of the Shepherds*, however, although a Roman influence is hard to dismiss,[22] his colours remain Venetian, and they are painstakingly and exquisitely executed. Vasari described how Sebastiano painted the frescoes in the Villa Farnesina in the Venetian manner, and further that he executed works in oil of which 'much account was made in Rome' for the way in which 'he had obtained from Giorgione a certain mode of colouring which was tolerably soft' (Vasari 1851: 60). On this basis, it does appear extremely plausible that the *Adoration* was executed soon after Sebastiano's arrival in Rome during the period in which he enjoyed the financial support and patronage of Agostino Chigi, and that it was indeed meant to display his skill at Venetian splendour of colour.[23]

The reconstruction

The present investigation into the execution of Sebastiano's *Adoration of the Shepherds* focuses narrowly on the red lake and blue paint passages, and preparatory aspects of the reconstruction will therefore not be discussed in detail here. Due to the damaged state of the painting, some elements of the original execution cannot be fully ascertained, such as the nature of the original wooden substrate, ground layers and underdrawing. These aspects of the reconstruction have been approached by using materials and methods likely to have been employed by Sebastiano, either because they were common in the period, or were

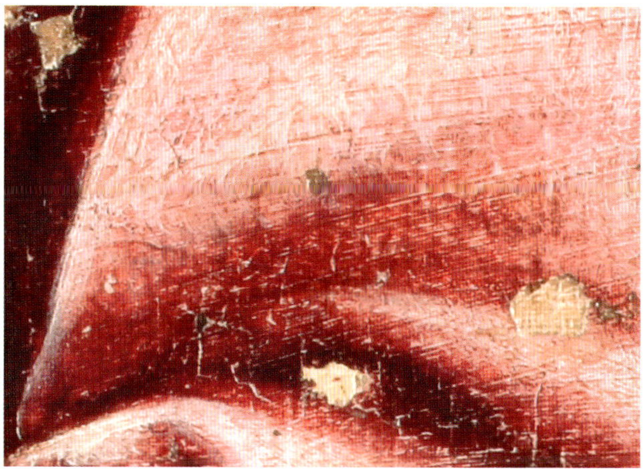

Figure 21 *Sebastiano del Piombo,* The Adoration of the Shepherds. *Detail (6 × 4.3 cm) of the Virgin's sleeve showing the transition between highlights, mid-tone and shadow. The brushy texture of the* imprimatura *is visible throughout.*

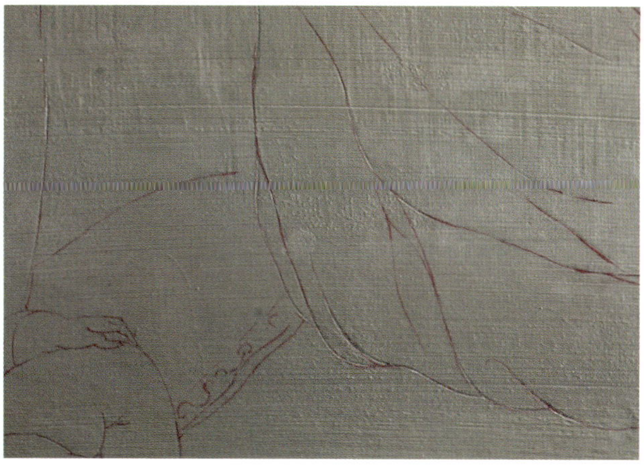

Figure 22 *Detail of the reconstruction taken in raking light showing the incised lines of the design, transferred onto the gesso, showing through the brushy* imprimatura. *The lines have been reinforced with red lake.*

employed in other works by the artist. For the reconstruction of the Virgin's red garment and blue drapery, a poplar panel (59 × 74 cm) was constructed, knot holes were filled and the panel was sized with several applications of rabbit-skin glue, followed by several coatings of *gesso sottile*.[24]

Compositional design and underdrawing

Although infrared photography of the *Adoration of the Shepherds* did not show evidence of a carbon-based underdrawing it cannot be ruled out that such an underdrawing was lost, along with most of the original gesso, during the transfer process. However, examination of other works by the artist show little evidence of carbon-based underdrawings, and the argument has been made that Sebastiano – at least during his Venetian period – took a freer approach to underdrawing than his contemporaries.[25] Incisions, however, outline several figurative elements in the *Adoration*, including Joseph's stick, the Virgin's drapery, and even a previous position of the leg of the far left shepherd. This shows that at least some of the figurative elements were transferred onto the panel after the application of the *imprimatura* using life-size cartoons.[26] Incision lines were likewise found along the outlines of the figures in the Viterbo *Pietà*, painted between 1513 and 1516 (Marrochini 2004: 91). In this altarpiece very thin lines of carbon-based underdrawing (but without any hatching) were revealed to be present by infrared reflectography (Bellucci and Frosinini 2004). In the *Adoration*, further development of the design was undertaken in a reddish brown paint, traces of which can be seen in many places on the figures. Its

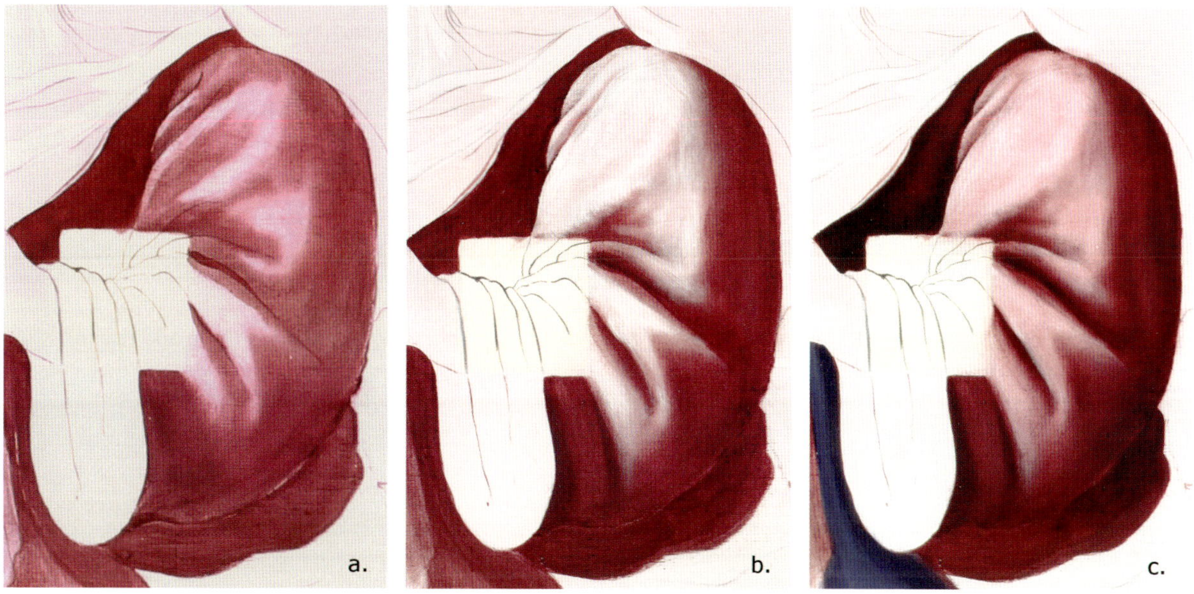

Figure 23 *Reconstruction of the Virgin's red garment: (a) first application of red glaze; (b) three applications of red glaze and one application of lead white in the highlights; (c) final red glaze applied over the white highlights.*

character, where visible due to either wear or because it was intentionally used as a visible outline, seems to suggest that modifications occurred throughout the painting process rather than in a single campaign prior to the application of colour. One example of sketchy, painted lines that were not subsequently followed in the painting phase can be seen through a worn paint passage in Joseph's sleeve (Fig. 19).

Sebastiano's method of developing the details in his composition during the painting process (instead of neatly and consistently following a preconceived design) along with the considerable loss of original paint passages, constituted challenges for the reconstruction process. One cannot adopt the spontaneity and improvisation which to a great extent characterise Sebastiano's original method of execution. The reconstruction of the missing sections of the drapery was therefore undertaken based on tracings of the remaining original details supplemented by filling in the losses with the evidence given by the Louvre copy, as well as by the overpaint previously removed (Fig. 20). The draperies in other paintings by Sebastiano were studied to gain a better understanding of common traits characterising Sebastiano's depiction of folds and falls of copious fabric.[27] The drawn design for the reconstruction was transferred to the panel by overlaying and incising the lines through the drawing with a charcoal-covered interleaf in between to make the lines more visible.[28]

Imprimatura *and reinforcement of the design*

Sebastiano's *imprimatura* was generally applied with broad, horizontal strokes which, upon drying, have retained their brushy texture throughout (Fig. 21).[29] For the reconstruction, an *imprimatura* layer consisting of lead white, which for the upper part of the panel was mixed with a small proportion of red lake, was applied with a bristle brush. Both underdrawing and incision lines remained visible through the *imprimatura* and were reinforced with red lake in oil once the *imprimatura* had dried (Fig. 22), imitating the thin red lines visible on the original painting. These lines were particularly visible within the Virgin's white veil, but could also be seen along outlines of her red lake garment, where their sympathetic colour allows them to integrate visually with the paint layers.

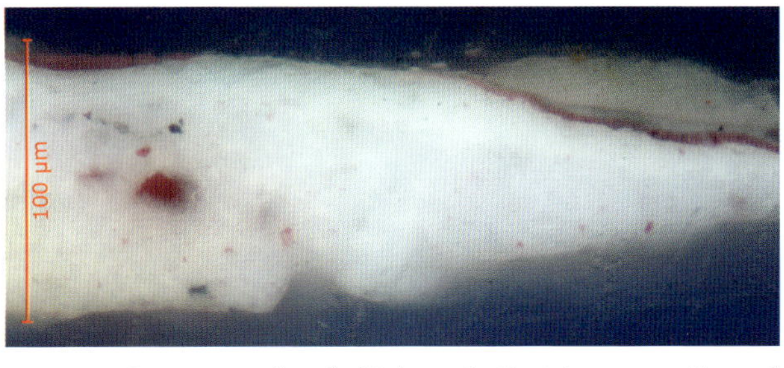

Figure 24 *Cross-section from highlight in the Virgin's garment. The pink* imprimatura *is followed by a pure white paint layer over which sits the remnants of a red glaze. The remaining layers are secondary.*

Red, pink and white: painting and glazing

Although binding medium analysis was not carried out on sample material from the *Adoration,* both linseed and nut oil has been identified in other works by Sebastiano (Casoli *et al.* 2010; Dunkerton and Howard 2009). Lead oil (linseed oil heated with lead acetate added to improve its drying properties) was therefore employed for the reconstruction. No dilution with turpentine was undertaken, as it was found to desaturate the glazes and leave a matt finish very unlike Sebastiano's.

Cochineal lake prepared from the dried scale insects and precipitated onto alum was used for the red paint passages in the reconstruction.[30] To achieve an even, saturated finish it was necessary to apply it in several layers. A filbert sable brush was used for the initial application; a second, dry brush was then employed to spread and thin it (Fig. 23). Each layer increased the warmth of the purplish red, which initially seemed somewhat cooler than the red hue of Sebastiano's original. A small amount of carbon black was found to have been mixed into the paint of the darkest shadows of the red garment in order to increase their depth.

When attempts were made to prepare a mid-tone of red lake mixed with lead white on the palette, the result was a somewhat dull pink with a grey tinge that bore little resemblance to the mid-tones of the Virgin's garment. The lead white initially used was a commercially prepared lead white, and tests were therefore made using stack method lead white prepared at the HKI instead, to ascertain whether blending without a resulting greyness could be achieved. The lead white made with this traditional method did not however make an appreciable difference.[31] On further examination of the paint surface under magnification it became clear that minimal mixing of white and red had taken place for the execution of the Virgin's red garment. Instead, the transition between the white highlights and the pure glaze was achieved with single, swift flicks of a bristle brush loaded with lead white onto the dry red glaze, which prevented the greyness of pre-blending the two colours on the palette.[32] It was, however, paramount to put a thin oiling-out layer onto the red glaze prior to painting over the white highlight. A small sable brush was then used to thin the white across the red glaze. This created a turbid medium effect extremely close to that present on the *Adoration* at the point of transition between the bright, buttery highlight and the translucent glaze (Fig. 21). However, microscopy and cross-sections show that a final red glaze layer (now mostly lost but still present in the troughs of the paint throughout the paler passages) had originally been painted over highlights and mid-tones (Fig. 24). The result of this loss is a more extreme transition between highlights and shadows than originally intended, as well as turbid medium effects where thin scumbles of lead white had been applied over the red lake to indicate subtly a fold in the fabric. Reintroducing this glaze on the reconstruction brings greater harmony to

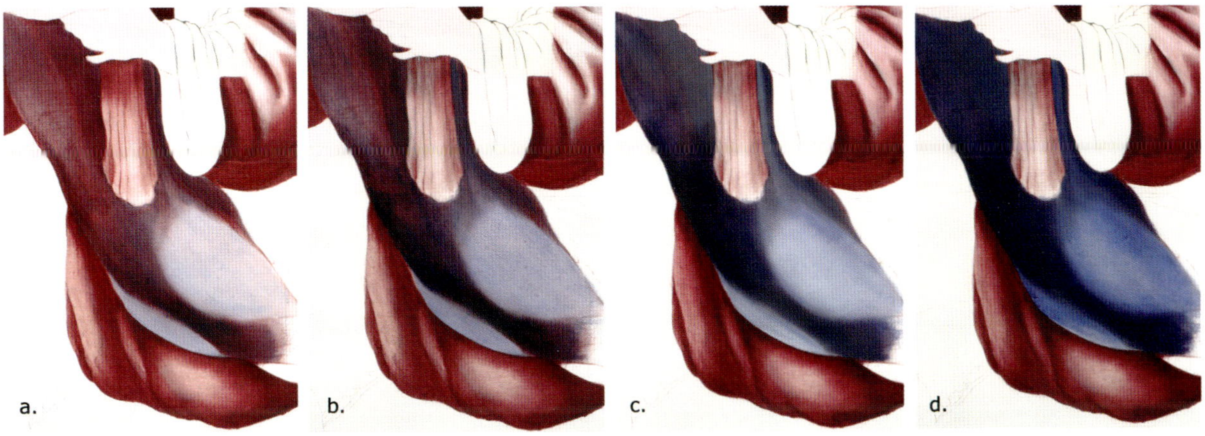

Figure 25 *Reconstruction of the Virgin's blue drapery: (a) first application of ultramarine and lead white over the red undermodelling; (b) second application of ultramarine blue and lead white; (c) third application of ultramarine blue and lead white; (d) final ultramarine blue glaze.*

the red of the Virgin's garment, emphasising the enamel-like quality of this paint passage as a whole. It also covers the turbid medium effect achieved in the reconstruction, the final appearance being warmer and offering a more balanced counterweight to the bright blue of the Virgin's drapery (Fig. 23c).

Having gained a better understanding of the behaviour of red lake and lead white in the Virgin's garment, the undermodelling for the blue drapery was executed. The cross-sections from this paint passage indicate that Sebastiano applied at least two layers of pure red lake under the dark passages of the blue drapery, but that he mixed red lake and lead white for the undermodelling under paler passages of the drapery. As it was found during the reconstruction of the Virgin's red garment that mixing, rather than superimposing, lead white and red lake gives a less attractive, greyer hue, it is interesting that Sebastiano chose to mix red lake and lead white for the undermodelling, rather than simply glazing with red lake over the white *imprimatura*, and leaving highlight passages unpainted. However, when applying the ultramarine blue paint layers on top, it became clear that the visual result of the blue over pure red lake as opposed to over a mixed pink is radically different, and it must be assumed that Sebastiano anticipated this as he was painting his underlayer. For the reconstruction, two applications of pure red lake or pink respectively were applied for the undermodelling of the blue drapery.

The problem of the ultramarine blue

The biggest challenge of the reconstruction process was to find a natural ultramarine pigment that would allow us to imitate the radiant blue of the Virgin's blue drapery satisfactorily. Renate Woudhuysen-Keller, in previous reconstructions, had noted the tendency of commercially available natural ultramarine to become more greenish blue in oil, or grey when mixed also with lead white, thereby killing the pure hue of the blue in a fashion quite unlike ultramarine blue passages in many original paintings. A recent workshop held at the Institute by lapis expert David Margulies, involving the grinding and washing of different grades of lapis stone, meant that ground lapis material not previously commercially processed was available to be tested alongside Afghan and Chilean natural ultramarine pigment from Kremer Pigmente GmbH & Co. KG. However, neither the Kremer pigments nor Margulies's ground lapis, when painted out in oil with or without lead white, possessed the clarity of hue that characterises the Virgin's drapery in Sebastiano's original. As the colour of ultramarine is less affected by particle size than is azurite (another important mineral blue), we suspected impurities in the material to be the cause of the 'impure' colour. We therefore proceeded to undertake extensive PLM analysis, comparing the various commercial products with our own ground lapis supplied by Margulies, alongside pigment samples from the *Adoration*. We found that compared with the dispersions from the original painting's blue paint passages, a considerable amount of anisotropic, colourless material – most likely calcite – of a very small particle size was consistently present in all of the dispersions. This material furthermore tended to agglomerate around the larger lazurite particles in the Margulies samples, rendering them colourless and light-scattering under magnification. It was possible to achieve a considerable improvement of the pigment by submitting it to several further washings, carefully pouring off the water before the paler material had the chance to settle. The rinsing process rendered a selection of grades that in dispersion showed a reduced content of tiny, anisotropic particles. When applying this material ground in oil to a primed surface it no longer had the slightly greenish tinge that the oily saturation of the calcite material gave, and it furthermore lent itself to mixing with lead white without turning grey.[33] However, none of the pigments available for the

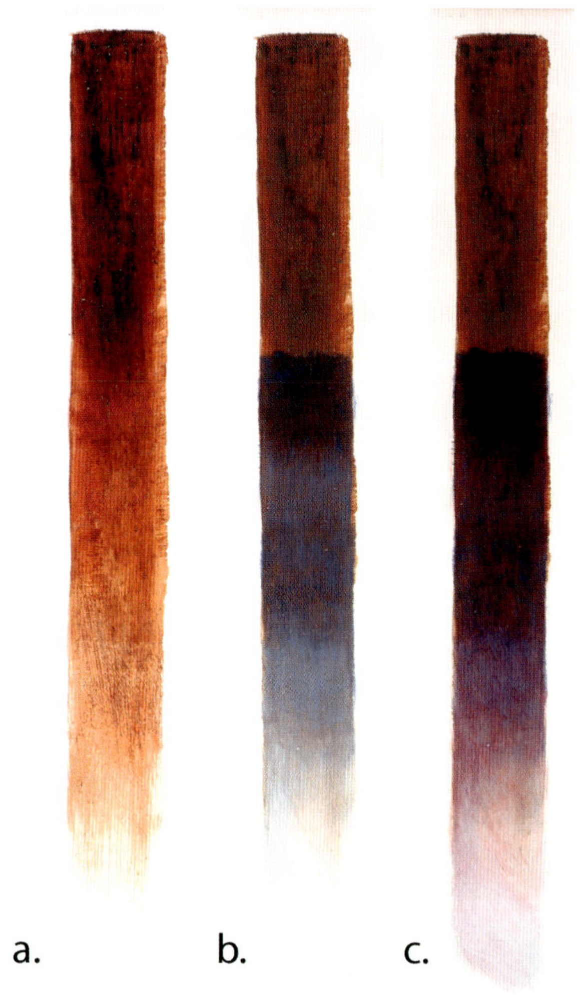

Figure 26 *Reconstruction of the colour scheme of Joseph's blue tunic: (a) redwood lake on pinkish white* imprimatura*; (b) ultramarine blue mixed with lead white; (c) thin glaze of cochineal lake over blue paint layer.*

reconstruction contained the pale or colourless particles suspected to be various sodalite minerals present in the batch of ultramarine employed by Sebastiano. Although adding ground glass was considered as a substitute for the translucent mineral particles, it was felt that evaluating the results of the reconstruction without adding a potentially inappropriate substitute to the ultramarine would give clearer results.

As mixing the better grades of the washed ultramarine blue with lead white did not result in greyness, creating transitions between highlights and mid-tones was less challenging than with the red lake. The shadows were painted using the best, washed Afghan ultramarine from Kremer without any addition of lead white. The first thin application was extremely transparent, giving the passage a deep purple colour (Fig. 25a). The highlights were painted with a small admixture of the Margulies pigment in stack method lead white. For the mid-tones, Kremer Afghan ultramarine with only a tiny amount of lead white was used, and minimal blending was undertaken where it merged with the highlights.[34] When applying the second and third layers of pure ultramarine in the shadows, the paint layer started to cover the undermodelling layer and turned rather opaque (Fig. 25 b and c). These areas of shadow on the Virgin's drapery in the *Adoration* still appear saturated, dark and somewhat translucent, but this finish could not be achieved on the reconstruction. The possible use of a resinous medium in the original could be the reason for the greater saturation,[35] but perhaps a more plausible reason lies with the different composition of the blue pigment. The material used for the reconstruction lacks the high proportion of translucent particles that is likely to have increased the translucency of Sebastiano's pure blue paint passages.

A final important point relates to the surprising variety of hues that could be achieved depending on the configuration of lighter or darker undermodelling in red, and the ultramarine applied on top (with or without admixtures of lead white). Although the sample material from the *Adoration* consistently showed a selection of blue, grey and colourless particles of similar size and morphology, localised variations in hue of the blue paint passages on the Virgin's drapery initially suggested to us the possibility that Sebastiano used different batches of ultramarine. This thesis cannot be ruled out based purely on the limited sample material but it did become evident when attempting to reconstruct these paint passages, that pure ultramarine applied over a darker underlayer made it appear slightly greenish, while applying it over a paler passage of the undermodelling gave it a reddish tinge. Differences in the hues of the Kremer and the Margulies ultramarine likewise were clearly detectable. This delicate balance between the blue, the red and the white made the reconstruction process extremely challenging and it must be concluded that considerable understanding and experience would have been necessary to predict the visual effect of these combinations.

Joseph's blue tunic

In response to the findings from the cross-section analysis, showing that a final red glaze similar to the one found on the Virgin's red garment had been all but completely lost from Joseph's tunic (Fig. 8), a small reconstruction focusing narrowly on the original colour range of this paint passage was carried out alongside that of the Virgin. Despite significant colouristic similarities between Giorgione's depictions of *The Adoration of the Shepherds* and Sebastiano's painting, there is a noticeable divergence in the central group of the Holy Family: where Joseph in Giorgione's depictions wears a dark, purplish tunic, the tunic of the Joseph in Sebastiano's painting – in its current condition – is predominantly bright blue. In this worn condition, its colour competes with the blue of the Virgin's drapery. To approach the original colours of this paint passage, a brownish redwood lake glaze layer was first applied over a white *imprimatura*, followed by an application of pure ultramarine blue over the darkest section of this undermodelling. For the paler passages and highlights lead white was added, and a final, extremely thin glaze of cochineal lake was applied on top. The result was a vibrant, deep purple that appears surprisingly close to Giorgione's Joseph (Fig. 26). It can be concluded, therefore, that Sebastiano in his own depiction of Joseph did not deviate nearly as far from Giorgione's colour scheme as its current appearance would imply. Rather the reconstruction suggests that he did in fact give Joseph's tunic a much more subdued colour in comparison to that of the Virgin's drapery.

Conclusion

Our attempts at reconstructing one of the most important paint passages in the *Adoration of the Shepherds* have demonstrated above all the enormous skill and know-how with which Sebastiano manipulated his materials to achieve exquisite results. He must have been keenly aware of the visual impact of the layering and mixing of only a small handful of pigments with greatly varying covering power and behaviour in oil. In spite of the damage the painting has suffered, the surviving paint passages still show how subtle variations were achieved with very few materials. Sebastiano exploited the properties of these materials to perfection, and seemingly with great ease. The appreciation gained during the project for the conscious and premeditated manipulation of the ultramarine blue in particular makes it likely that Sebastiano was acutely aware of the properties of this specific, idiosyncratic batch of ultramarine with its high content of transparent particles, and that he used it to achieve clear, gem-like colours that still, in spite of the damage, captivate and intrigue. When we tried to take shortcuts, such as pre-mixing colours and using partially purified pigments, the result in every instance was unsatisfactory. This confirms what had already been suggested by the sample material: that Sebastiano executed the blue paint passages with great care and preplanning, and that no corners were cut in the process. The losses incurred by the painting have in this instance paradoxically afforded us the opportunity to increase our understanding of, and appreciation for, the working methods of a highly accomplished, Italian Renaissance painter. That so much inherent splendour is still to be found in this work suggests that perhaps Sebastiano del Piombo's *Adoration of the Shepherds* should not be considered 'lost' after all.

Acknowledgements

A great many people deserve our sincere thanks for generously taking the time to share useful information with us, to undertake analysis and for allowing us to republish relevant images alongside our own: Barbara Berrie, Jacques Castaing, Joanna Dunn, Nicholas Eastaugh, Maria Dolores Gayo García, Martina Griesser, Paul Joannides, David Margulies, Elke Oberthaler, Héléne Rousselière, David Scrase, Claudio Seccaroni, Stefano Volpin and Philippe Walter. We are also grateful to our HKI colleagues, Spike Bucklow and Helen Glanville in particular for extensive help and support, and to Rupert Featherstone for allowing us the time to pursue Sebastiano's painting technique through technical analysis, reconstructions, and art historical research.

Notes

1. Records show that the painting was in the collection of Philippe, Duc d'Orleans, Regent of France, by 1727. It still had its original panel substrate at this date, but had been transferred to canvas prior to 1863. Michael Levey has suggested that the transfer was undertaken by Haquin in the 1770s, when the *Raising of Lazarus*, now in the National Gallery, London, was likewise transferred. It was bought by Lord Fitzwilliam on 14 February 1800. The second transfer to a new canvas took place in 1929–30 (personal communication, David Scrase, Fitzwilliam Museum, Cambridge). For the attribution to Giorgione, see Buchanan (1824: 126).
2. The painting was brought to the HKI in 1977 where initial examination, followed at a later stage by X-radiography and cleaning tests, revealed the extent of damage present underneath the overpaint.
3. This copy has been lent to the Fitzwilliam Museum and is currently at the HKI.
4. The amido black 10B stain positively stained the remnants of a yellow-white, porous ground layer present in a few of the samples. While contamination from the later conservation treatments cannot be completely ruled out, it is very likely that the consistent stain indicates the presence of an animal glue used as a binder for the gesso ground. SEM-EDX analysis furthermore confirmed the predominant presence of calcium and sulphur as expected for a gypsum ground.
5. The lead white-containing *imprimatura* and paint layers have been found to consistently contain a few very large particles or aggregates that appear more translucent and grey than the surrounding white matrix. SEM-EDX analysis confirmed that they are lead-based, however it is possible that they are particles of neutral lead carbonate (cerussite) (Dunkerton 2003: 221) present within the whiter, basic form of lead carbonate (hydrocerussite). Recent research has shown that different grades of Venetian lead white were available. In Giovanni Bellini's *Feast of the Gods*, painted in 1514, the *imprimatura* contains greatly varied particle sizes and consists of a mixture of cerussite and hydrocerussite while the paint layer above contains only hydrocerussite and the particles are small and homogenous (Berrie and Matthew 2011: 298–9).
6. The *imprimatura* is not pink throughout but appears to transition into white at an undulating line of transition halfway down the painting. In retouching losses in the sky (in this case using egg tempera as the binding medium, followed by MS2A glazes), it was noted that the correct blue tone was much easier to achieve over a pink underlayer than over pure white. For that reason, the pink *imprimatura* with its costly content of red lake must be assumed to have been a well-considered application underneath the sky in its entirety, as it clearly affects the final colour of the paint layers on top, in spite of their high lead white content.
7. SEM-EDX analysis showed a raised content of silicon and potassium in the blue paint layer, which could suggest an admixture of glass, although only a single glass particle was otherwise identified in a highlight in Joseph's tunic. Glass could have been added to increase the speed of drying, or perhaps to increase translucency of the deep blue paint layer.
8. Kermes and cochineal dyestuff (in this case New World cochineal is unlikely, as Sebastiano painted his *Adoration* only about 20 years after Columbus's first discovery of the West Indies) have been found to contain considerable amounts of phosphorus from the scale insect. The phosphorus content drops considerably, however, if the dye is extracted from dyed cloth (Kirby *et al.* 2005: 73). SEM-EDX analysis showed a consistent but low content of phosphorus

of about 3% in the crimson red glazes in the Virgin's drapery. The analysis furthermore showed varying but considerable amounts of sulphur (up to 20%), which may be remnants of undissolved protein stemming from cloth in the dye extraction process.

9. A mixture of brazilwood and kermes lake was found in an underlayer in Raphael's *Ansidei Madonna*, National Gallery, London, painted 1505, where fading of the brazilwood to a yellow hue has resulted in a dark, brownish-purple colour somewhat similar to that in Joseph's tunic (Roy *et al.* 2004: 22).
10. Powdered glass is not an uncommon occurrence in early sixteenth-century Italian painting. Perugino and Raphael both appear to have used it extensively, consistently in red lake layers where it probably served as a siccative, but also in other paint layers and even in the latter's *imprimature* (Spring 2003). Giorgione added a siliceous material, most likely glass, to his red lake underpaint for the Virgin's blue robe in the Allendale Nativity, National Gallery of Art, Washington, DC (Berrie 2006); see Fig. 14. Likewise Giovanni Bellini, to whom, according to Vasari, Sebastiano apprenticed himself early on (Vasari 1851: 59), started adding blue glass (smalt) to his ultramarine blue paint layers in his later oil paintings (Dunkerton 2003: 208; Tranquilli 2001: 60, 82). However in Sebastiano's *Adoration*, the glass particle identified in the ultramarine blue paint layer of the sky is colourless, and although it was found to be rich in potassium, the lack of cobalt likewise argues against smalt. Furthermore, no clear indication of the addition of glass to the red lake layers was confirmed. In a later painting by Sebastiano, the *Raising of Lazarus*, 1517–19, powdered glass was identified in the red lake glazes (Dunkerton and Howard 2009).
11. Known deposits include Sar-e Sang and Robat, both in the Koksha Valley, Badakhshan province. We are grateful to Nicholas Eastaugh of Art Access Research, London, for undertaking the PLM and UV/visible/near-IR microspectrophotometric analysis on sample material from Joseph's blue tunic.
12. That Sebastiano's immediate predecessors and contemporaries found inspiration for the superimposition of blues on reds in works of art of the thirteenth and early fourteenth century, including from the *morellone* in fresco painting, has likewise been suggested by Riitano and Seccaroni (2008) in relation to Raphael's and Fra' Bartolomeo's Florentine works.
13. For cross-section micrograph examples showing the build-up of thin blue and red glaze paint layers of about 15–20 μm thickness in Mantegna's *The Man of Sorrows with Two Angels*, Statens Museum for Kunst, Copenhagen, see Roy 2009: 90–91. For close-ups showing his use of the white preparatory layer as a mid-tone see Filtenborg 2009: 97.
14. Giovanni Bellini's importance was well recognised in his own lifetime. During Dürer's stay in Venice from 1505 to 1507, in his correspondence with his friend and business liaison Pirckheimer, Dürer refers to Bellini as the greatest artist in Venice (Schütz 2004: 105).
15. For a more in-depth account of the interrelationships between these artists in the first three decades of the sixteenth century see Humfrey (2006).
16. See for example Kallab (1908) or Rubin (1995), the latter in which Vasari's intentions as a historian are evaluated at length.
17. The relationship between the Allendale Nativity and the Vienna version, traditionally thought to be that of original and later copy, has most recently been examined by Anderson (2004: 173), who suggests a contemporaneous and autograph execution based on technical evidence (infrared photography and X-radiography). There is considerable divergence in the proposed date of execution for these works, ranging from as early as 1500 (Lucco 2006) to 1510: http://www.nga.gov/fcgi-bin/timage_f?object=432&image=1403&c=gg16 (website of the National Gallery of Art, Washington).
18. Due to the limited sample material from the Allendale Nativity and an otherwise well-preserved paint surface it is not clear whether or not the red glaze present under the ultramarine blue is modelled.
19. Personal communication with Elke Oberthaler (Kunsthistorisches Museum, Vienna) and Joanna Dunn (National Gallery of Art, Washington, DC).
20. Although no comparative analysis has been undertaken, the appearance of the ultramarine blue used for Mary Magdalene's sleeve bears strong similarities to that found in the *Adoration of the Shepherds*. In cross-section, the particle size and shape is comparable, and a similar proportion of pale and colourless particles appears to be present.
21. The *St John Chrysostom Altarpiece* is generally considered to be one of Sebastiano's later Venetian works and its colours, it has been suggested, bear some resemblance to those of Dürer's *Feast of the Rose Garland*, completed 1506, in the nearby church of San Bartolomeo di Rialto (Lucco 2008: 108). Interestingly, the technique used by Dürer to achieve the bordeaux red shadows in Maximilian I's voluminous, deep red garment in this altarpiece consists of the application of an underlayer of lead white with a small addition of red lake, ultramarine blue and smalt followed by a red glaze (Třeštík and Šefců 2006: 278) – a similar approach and pigment choice to Sebastiano's in St Chrysostom's purplish red garb. In turn, Dürer took inspiration for his *Feast of the Rose Garlands*, painted to convince critics that he was as capable a painter as he was a draughtsman, from Bellini's *St Zaccaria Altarpiece* (1505), not least in his colouring of Maximilian's red garment which imitates that of St Jerome in Bellini's work (Luber 2005: 89, 114).
22. A probable connection between the *Adoration of the Shepherds* and a sheet containing sketches attributed to Sebastiano in the Biblioteca Ambrosiana, Milan (F 290 inf. n.22) has been suggested by both Hirst 1981 and Joannides and Barbieri 2008. The main drawing on the verso is a careful study of the Roman copy of *Hercules Chiaramonti*, now in the Giardino della Pigna in the Vatican, which Sebastiano presumably made soon after his arrival in Rome. The other sketches relate to his painting of the *Death of Adonis*, *c.*1511–12, but a sketch of a reclining body and a torso of a satyr (?) may relate to the Christ Child and middle shepherd respectively in the *Adoration of the Shepherds*. It was further pointed out by Joannides (personal communication) that the Virgin's gesture of lifting the veil occurred in Raphael's *Madonna of Loreto*, probably to be dated *c.*1510 and which, in any case, antedates Sebastiano's arrival in Rome. This painting, usually thought to have been commissioned by Pope Julius II, but according to Joannides more likely commissioned by Agostino Chigi, hung in Santa Maria del Popolo in Rome, where Sebastiano would undoubtedly have seen it.
23. The cleaning of the painting also revealed the traces of intricate gilded borders of the draperies of the Virgin, Joseph and two of the shepherds, another feature that would have emphasised the precious appearance of the colourful garments.
24. The application of *gesso sottile* usually follows upon the application of the *gesso grosso*, however *gesso grosso* can be omitted (Cennini 1933: 73). For a detailed account of historical panel preparation methods and their reconstruction, see Woudhuysen-Keller (2008).
25. See Seccaroni (2009: 130). An exception is the *Judgement of Solomon*, in which carbon-based underdrawing on the gesso ground and *spolvero* technique was found. It is possible that more advanced infrared examination methods could reveal carbon-based underdrawing to be more consistently present in Sebastiano's works.
26. The strong similarities in the folds of the Virgin's sleeve to those in *The Sacred Conversation* (*c.*1506, The Metropolitan Museum of Art, New York) might support the claim that Sebastiano used and reused designs and cartoons.
27. Perhaps not surprising, the study of Sebastiano's drapery designs shows an emphasis on the elegant effect and movement that the draperies introduced to the compositions, rather than on depicting a convincingly natural behaviour of functional garments.
28. This was done onto the gesso ground, rather than onto the *imprimatura*. The lines were reinforced with iron gall ink prior to the application of the *imprimatura*, to ensure that they remained visible. It should be noted that this approach, for the reasons outlined

in the text, deviates from the evidence found on the painting, however it allowed us to transfer our design with relative ease without the need for further development of the design freehand.

29. The direction of the brushstrokes changes and becomes irregular in the severely damaged tree and building above the Holy Family and shepherds.
30. Although it is more likely that Sebastiano used kermes lake for the *Adoration*, the kermes insect is not available for purchase today.
31. The stack method lead white was analysed with X-ray diffraction (XRD) and was found to be almost pure hydrocerussite (basic lead carbonate) with a small presence of the rare plumbonacrite. The occurrence of plumbonacrite during the production of stack method lead white is pH dependent, and as it is unstable it may in time turn into hydrocerussite. We are grateful to J. Castaing, H. Rousselière and P. Walter of the Centre national de la recherche scientifique (CNRS), Paris, for undertaking the analysis. As discussed in note 5, examination of lead white paint layers in a small selection of Renaissance paintings has shown that cerussite, a less desirable, greyish form of lead carbonate is often present (Berrie and Matthew 2011). It is conceivable that a considerable cerussite content can lower the covering power of lead white, thereby lessening the grey quality in mixes with red lake. Cross-section examination has shown that it may be present in the *Adoration*, although further analysis would have to be undertaken to confirm this.
32. As the highlights of this paint passage in Sebastiano's painting exhibit very pronounced brushstrokes suggesting a buttery texture of the paint, the lead white was prepared a few days prior to painting, which allowed the paint to commence drying, giving a more paste-like consistency.
33. In spite of the noticeable improvement to the colour, we were unable to satisfactorily remove the agglomerating material around the blue particles in the Margulies ground lapis. It is highly likely that the method of extracting different grades of ultramarine described in Cennini (1933: 36–9) achieves a purification that washing and massaging the ground lapis in water cannot, but the preliminary investigations undertaken for this project did not include testing other methods of refinement apart from the simple process of washing. We hope therefore to pursue a more detailed discussion of our findings, and to continue our investigation into the factors that influence the colour and purity of the ultramarine in future research.
34. Sebastiano frequently employed a chiaroscuro technique with great effect in his rendering of fabrics, having relatively sharp transitions between highlights and shadows with very limited use of mid-tones; this has been noted by Casoli *et al.* 2010: 120.
35. One would expect the condition of the original paint layer to be considerably worse than is the case had, for example, a pine resin been used, as resins tend to be damaged more readily than oil by unsympathetic cleaning campaigns. Furthermore, the current appearance of the shadow areas does not indicate a different medium to other paint passages.

References

Anderson, J. 2004. 'Giorgione da Castelfranco: *The Adoration of the Shepherds*'. In *Giorgione: Myth and Enigma*, S. Ferino-Pagden and G. Nepi Scirè (eds) 173. Milan: Skira editore.

Bellucci, R. and Frosinini, C. 2004. 'La *Pietà* di Sebastiano del Piombo: da una cartone di Michelangelo? Tra indagini tecniche e letterarie'. In *Notturno Sublime: Sebastiano e Michelangelo nella Pietà de Viterbo*, C. Barbieri (ed.) 97–105. Rome: Viviani Arte.

Berrie, B. 2006. 'Analytical Report WA665 1939.1.289 BHB'. January 22. Unpublished technical report. National Gallery of Art, Washington DC.

Berrie, B. and Matthew, L. 2011. 'Lead white from Venice: a whiter shade of pale?' In *Studying Old Master Paintings: Technology and Practice*, M. Spring (ed.) 295–301. London: Archetype Publications.

Buchanan, W. 1824. *Memoirs of Painting, with a Chronological History of the Importation of Pictures by the Great Masters into England since the French Revolution*, vol. 1. London: R. Ackermann.

Carratù, T. 2008. 'Sebastiano del Piombo: frescoes in the Farnesina'. In *Sebastiano del Piombo 1485–1547*, G. Scandiani (ed.) 130–33. Milan: Federico Motta.

Casoli, A., Fiorin, E., Lazzarini, L. *et al.* 2010. 'Sebastiano del Piombo a Venezia: materiali e technica pittorica di alcune sue opere'. In *Sebastiano del Piombo e la Cappella Borgherini nel contesto della pittura rinascimentale, Kermes Quaderni*, S.A. Esteban, B. Marocchini and C. Seccaroni (eds) 117–22. Florence: Nardini.

Cennini, C. 1933. *The Craftsman's Handbook: The Italian 'Il libro dell'arte', Cennino d'Andrea Cennini*, D.V. Thompson (tr.). New York: Dover Publications, Inc.

Dunkerton, J. 2003. 'Bellini's technique'. In *The Cambridge Companion to Giovanni Bellini*, P. Humfrey (ed.) 195–225. Cambridge: Cambridge University Press.

Dunkerton, J. and Howard, H. 2009. 'Sebastiano del Piombo's *Raising of Lazarus*: a history of change', *National Gallery Technical Bulletin* 30: 26–51.

Dunkerton, J. and Spring, M. 1998. 'The development of painting on coloured surfaces in sixteenth-century Italy'. In *Painting Techniques: History, Materials and Studio Practice*, A. Roy and P. Smith (eds) 120–30. London: International Institute for Conservation of Historic & Artistic Works.

Filtenborg, T. 2009. 'Mantegna's *Man of Sorrows with Two Angels*: examination and restoration'. In *La technique pictorale d'Andrea Mantegna, Techne Hors-série*, M. Menu and É. Ravaud (eds) 93–8. Paris: Réunion Musées Nationaux.

Hirst, M. 1981. *Sebastiano del Piombo*. Oxford: Clarendon Press.

Humfrey, P. 2006. 'Masters and pupils, colleagues and rivals'. In *Bellini, Giorgione, Titian, and the Renaissance of Venetian Painting*, D.A. Brown and S. Ferino-Pagden (eds) 38–53. New Haven, CT: Yale University Press.

Joannides, P. and Barbieri, C. 2008, 'Sebastiano del Piombo. Recto: *Studies for Venus and a Sleeping Figure*. Verso: *Copy after a Reclining Hercules and other sketches*'. In *Sebastiano del Piombo 1485–1547*, G. Scandiani (ed.) 256–7. Milan: Federico Motta.

Kallab, W. 1908. *Vasaristudien: Von Wolfgang Kallab, mit einem Lebensbilde des Verfassers, aus dessen Nachlasse hrsg. von Julius v. Schlosser*, J.v. Schlosser (ed.). Vienna: W. Grasser & Kie.

Kirby, J., Spring, M. and Higgitt, C. 2005. 'The technology of red lake pigment manufacture: study of the dyestuff substrate', *National Gallery Technical Bulletin* 26: 71–87.

Laing, K. 1988. '*The Judgement of Solomon*', *The Hamilton Kerr Institute Bulletin* 1: 23–9.

Luber, K.C. 2005. *Albrecht Dürer and the Venetian Renaissance*. Cambridge: Cambridge University Press.

Lucco, M. 2006. 'Giorgione: *Adoration of the Shepherds* ('Allendale Nativity')'. In *Bellini, Giorgione, Titian, and the Renaissance of Venetian Painting*, D.A. Brown and S. Ferino-Pagden (eds) 116–18. New Haven, CT: Yale University Press.

Lucco, M. 2008. 'Sebastiano del Piombo: *Saint Chrysostom and Saints*' and 'Sebastiano del Piombo: *The Adoration of the Shepherds*'. In *Sebastiano del Piombo 1485–1547*, G. Scandiani (ed.) 106–9 and 128–9. Milan: Federico Motta.

Marocchini, B. 2004. 'La *Pietà* di Viterbo: la tecnica di esecuzione'. In *Notturno Sublime: Sebastiano e Michelangelo nella Pietà de Viterbo*, C. Barbieri (ed.) 89–95. Rome: Viviani Arte.

Riitano, P. and Seccaroni, C. 2008. 'Attorno all'imprimitura'. In *Raffaello: la rivelazione del colore. Il restauro della Madonna del Cardellino della Galleria degli Uffizi*, M. Ciatti, C. Frosinini, A. Natali *et al.* (eds) 159–67. Florence: Edifir.

Roy, A. 2009. 'The place of the Copenhagen *Man of Sorrows with Two Angels* in Mantegna's technical oeuvre'. In *La technique pictorale d'Andrea Mantegna, Techne Hors-série*, M. Menu and É. Ravaud (eds) 88–92. Paris: Réunion Musées Nationaux.

Roy, A., Spring, M. and Plazzotta, C. 2004. 'Raphael's early work in the National Gallery: paintings before Rome', *National Gallery Technical Bulletin* 25: 4–35.

Rubin, P.L. 1995. *Giorgio Vasari: Art and History*. New Haven, CT: Yale University Press.

Schütz, K. 2004. 'Dürer in Venice: a few comments on the relationship between German and Venetian painting around 1505'. In *Giorgione: Myth and Enigma*, S. Ferino-Pagden and G. Nepi Scirè (eds) 105–10. Milan: Skira editore.

Seccaroni, C. 2009. 'Bilancio statistico e riflessioni sulla tecnica pittorica di Sebastiano del Piombo'. In *Sebastiano del Piombo e la Cappella Borgherini nel contesto della pittura rinascimentale, Kermes Quaderni*, S.A. Esteban, B. Marocchini and C. Seccaroni (eds) 126–36. Florence: Nardini.

Spring. M. 2003. 'Perugino's painting materials: analysis and context within sixteenth-century easel painting'. In *The Painting Technique of Pietro Vannucci, called Il Perugino. Proceedings of the LabS TECH Workshop*, B.G. Brunetti, C. Seccaroni and A. Sgamellotti (eds) 21–8. Rome: Nardini Editore.

Tranquilli, G. 2001. 'Madonna degli alberetti' and 'Pietà (Pietà Donà dalle Rose)'. In *Il colore ritrovato: Bellini a Venezia*, R. Goffen and G. Nepi Scirè (eds) 60–61, 82–3. Milan: Electa.

Třeštík, J. and Šefců, R. 2006. 'Restorers' investigations: painting technique'. In *Albrect Dürer: The Feast of the Rose Garlands 1506–2006*, O. Kotkovà (ed.) 255–79. Prague: Národní galerie v Praze.

Vasari, G. 1851. *Lives of the Most Eminent Painters, Sculptors and Architects*, vol. IV, Mrs J. Foster (tr.). London: Henry G. Bohn.

Woudhuysen-Keller, R. 2008. 'Reconstruction of tempera painting techniques: some examples, including *gesso sottile*'. In *Art Technology: Sources and Methods*, S. Kroustallis, J.H. Townsend, E. Cenalmor Bruquetas, A. Stijnman and A. San Andres Moya (eds) 166–73. London: Archetype Publications.

RECONSTRUCTING TOWARDS A BETTER UNDERSTANDING: A STUDY OF MISSING UNDERDRAWINGS IN VAN MIEREVELT'S PORTRAITS

Charlotte Caspers, Johanneke Verhave and Margreet Wolters[1]

Introduction

This paper describes how reconstructions have been used to gain a better understanding of the painting techniques and working processes of the portrait painter Michiel van Mierevelt (1566–1641). During research (2007–2011)[2] into Van Mierevelt's large oeuvre, a number of questions arose about the underdrawing stage of his paintings, the main one being the 'missing underdrawing' in paintings that without doubt must have had some sort of layout on their preparation layers.[3] Did Van Mierevelt use a material that is invisible with infrared reflectography? During our research we concluded that things might be more complicated.

After a short introduction to Michiel van Mierevelt and his workshop we focus on the methods of underdrawing found in his portraits and the related questions. The second half of the paper discusses the reconstructions: why we chose certain materials and techniques, how they appear when studied with infrared reflectography (IRR) and visual light (VIS), and what this might tell us about Van Mierevelt's practices.

The study was carried out with general painting practice of the seventeenth century in the Netherlands in mind and we hope that our work can help others studying underdrawings of this period.

The Van Mierevelt portrait studio

The master painter Michiel van Mierevelt had a thriving portrait studio in his hometown of Delft.[4] After a period of training with the Utrecht history painter Anthonie Blocklandt (1533/34–1583), Van Mierevelt was registered in the Delft St Luke Guild around 1583–85 and soon focused his production fully on the painting of portraits. The earliest dated portraits known are from 1592, but his career and reputation gathered momentum with the commission of a portrait of the Stadholder Maurits in 1607 (Fig. 1). Van Mierevelt would reproduce this painting,

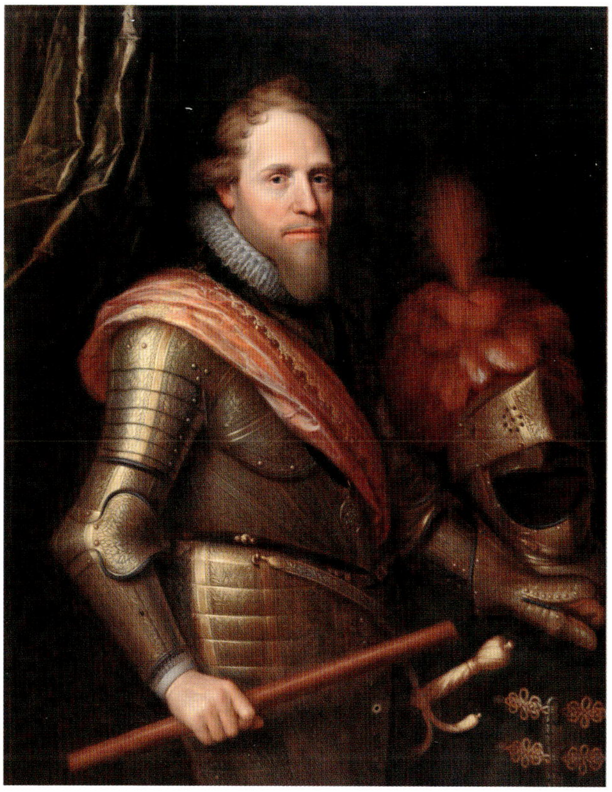

Figure 1 *Michiel van Mierevelt,* Portrait of Maurits, *1607, oil on panel, 111.2 × 84 cm, PDS68b. (Photograph courtesy of Tom Haartsma, Museum het Prinsenhof, Delft.)*

a

b

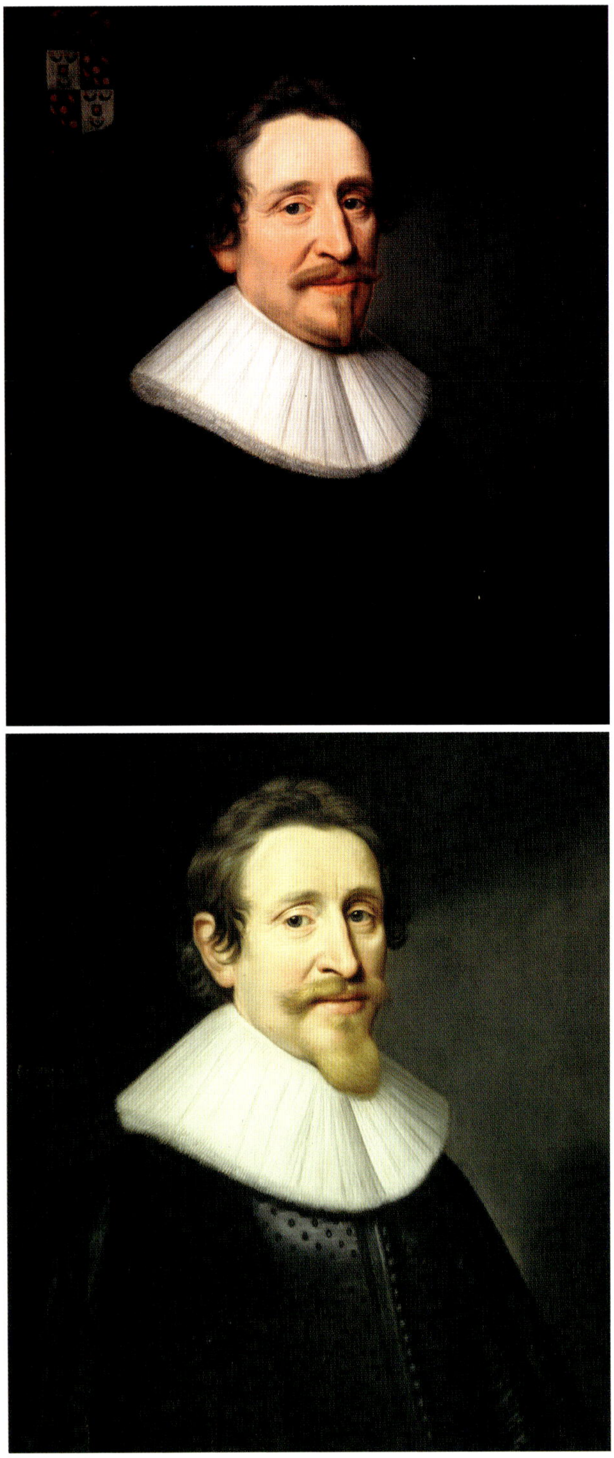

Figure 2 *Two types of the portrait of Hugo de Groot: (a) painted in 1631 (PDS71); (b) painted in 1635 (PDS72). (Photographs courtesy of Tom Haartsma, Museum het Prinsenhof, Delft.)*

and other portraits of the Dutch court and elite, dozens or maybe even hundreds of times. Thus his oeuvre is quantitatively impressive, with up to 1000 remaining portraits, but is not characterised by variation; about half of the total production consists of copies.

Within the recent inventory of Van Mierevelt's oeuvre a short list of the most popular portraits was drawn up giving the following as the top three (in terms of number of known copies made): Stadholder Maurits (42),

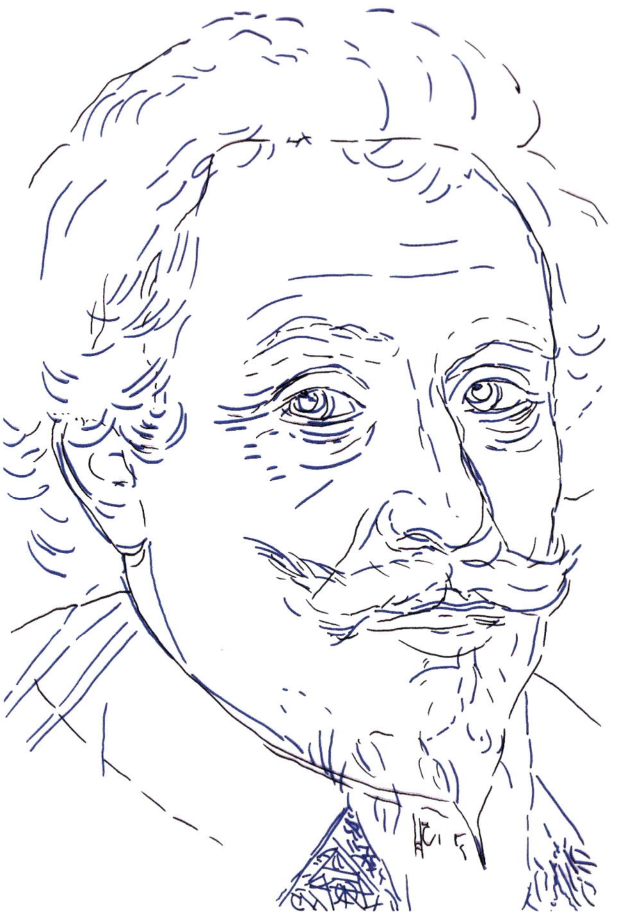

Figure 3 *Superimposed tracings of the portrait of Ernst Casimir (blue lines, PDS68f) and Dirk van der Dussen (black lines, B65-17) illustrate Van Mierevelt's use of a standard model for faces. (Photograph: Johanneke Verhave for the research project 'Van Mierevelt's factory'.)*

Stadholder Frederik Henrik (36) and Pensionary Johan van Oldebarnevelt (18).[5] Comparisons within these series of copies show that the faces have exactly the same measurements even though the portraits evolve with the age of the sitter and changes in style of clothing and hair (Fig. 2).[6]

Further comparison between different portraits has shown that the faces of sitters are remarkably similar in composition and size (Fig. 3), implying the use of a standard format for a man's and a woman's face, which would be adjusted to the specific features of the sitter (Jansen *et al.* 2011: 96–8). Both the copying of the portraits and the use of a standard format would imply the use of underdrawing; the minute exactness in the copies, especially in the faces, suggests they are very unlikely to have been painted freehand.[7]

The use of underdrawing in the Van Mierevelt studio

In a group of the earliest portraits of Stadholder Maurits (1607–1609) pronounced and detailed underdrawing was observed in the faces. Sharp, relatively wide and dark lines are clearly distinguishable in visible light in at least four portraits (Fig. 4).[8] Later portraits of Maurits (from

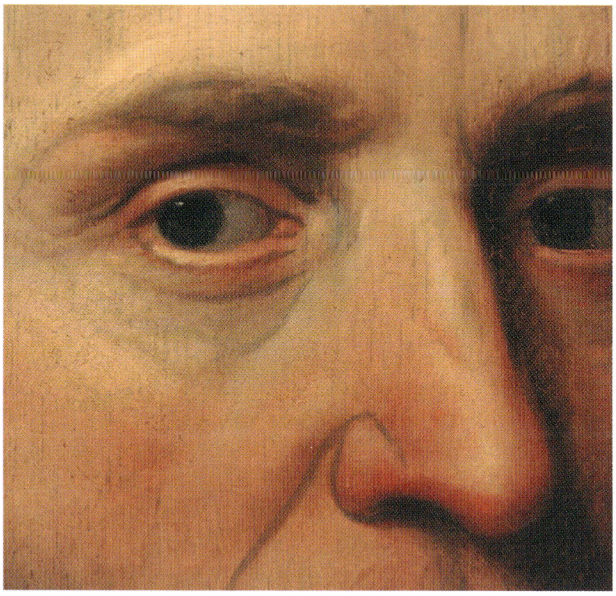

Figure 4 *Lines of underdrawing in the face of an early portrait of Maurits, detail of the 1607 version in the State Collection (EK BS 1.13-02). (Photograph: Johanneke Verhave for the research project 'Van Mierevelt's factory'.)*

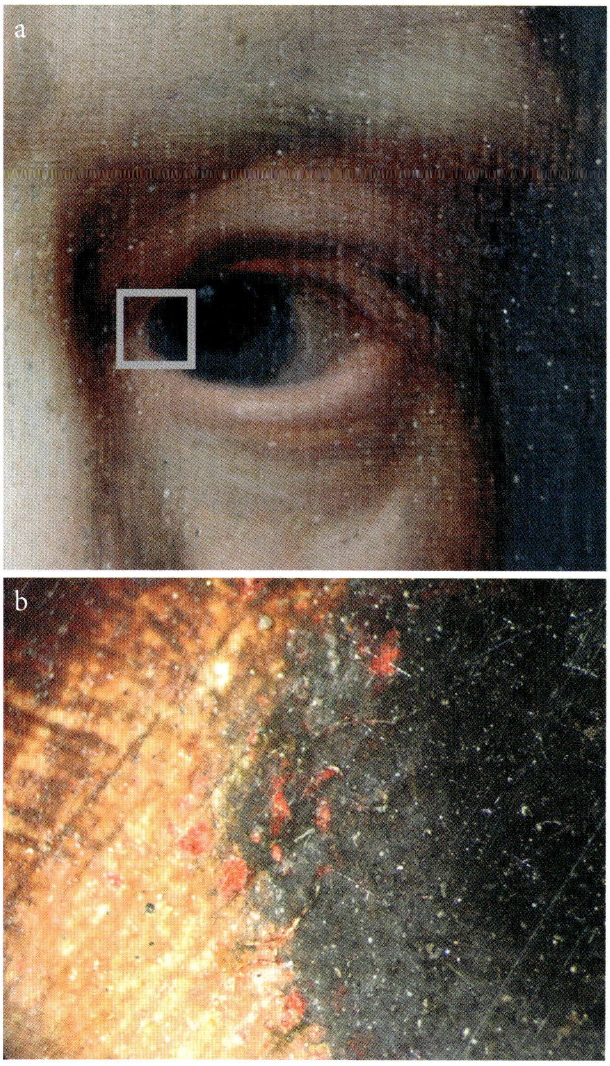

Figure 5 *Evidence of the use of red paint as underdrawing material in the left eye in the portrait of François Spiering (PDS147): (a) site of (b) photomicrograph, illustrating that it is not easy to identify the presence of this underdrawing. (Photograph: Johanneke Verhave for the research project 'Van Mierevelt's factory'.)*

1613 onwards) do not reveal this type of underdrawing. Except for some very sparse black lines in some faces, no dark underdrawing was found in Van Mierevelt's other portraits. These occasional lines were situated in the folds of the skin, around the eyes and nose. Study with a microscope could often not clarify whether these lines belonged to an underdrawing or had been applied in the painting stage to deepen the areas of shadow.

While initially looking for black underdrawing, we found red preparatory lines in some portraits. Sometimes these lines were present along contours of faces and collars, but they were most often encountered under the pupils and along the arches of the eyes (Fig. 5). The lines are quite robust (*c*.2–3 mm wide) with a lot of body. Red lines found in the portrait of Edward Cecil (National Portrait Gallery, NPG 4514) were particularly exceptional; the lines are located along all the features of the face and are wide and spotty in character.

The red underdrawing line along the contour of the head in the portrait of François Spiering (Museum het Prinsenhof, PDS147) was sampled and found to consist of red lake with the addition of a substantial amount of chalk, a little yellow earth and vermilion (Fig. 6).[9] The sample shows the red lake on top of both the *imprimatura* layer and a local whitish underpaint for the face.[10]

Along the contours, the red lines do not have a visual function at the paint surface, but the red tone sometimes seems to have been used in the final appearance of the eyes, thus functioning as an underdrawing as well as a warm contour line for the upper eyelid. With this double function in mind more lines might be identified as part of the underdrawing; for example, brown contour lines found around noses. That Van Mierevelt occasionally used different paint mixtures to indicate shapes in

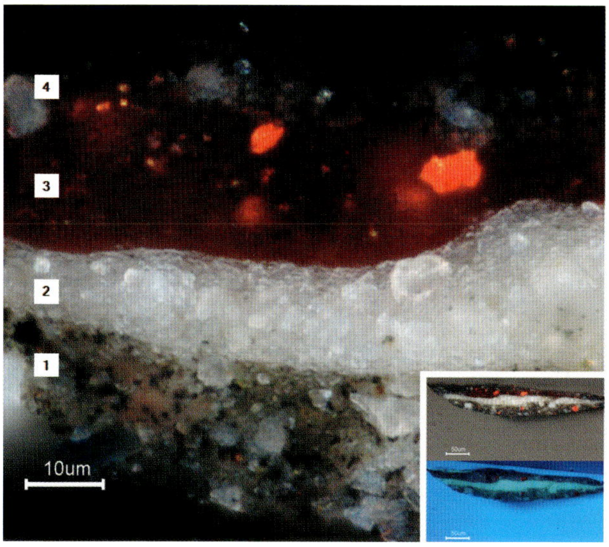

Figure 6 *Cross-section from the contour of François Spiering's head. Layer 3 corresponds to the red underdrawing. The paint has been found to contain mostly red lake and chalk, with the addition of some vermilion and yellow ochre. (Photograph courtesy of Katrien Keune and Annelies van Loon, montage by Johanneke Verhave.)*

the preparatory stage is evidenced by the portrait of Stadholder Frederik Hendrik (Museum Het Prinsenhof, PDS68b) where the armour has been boldly indicated with several brushstrokes in a thick white paint.[11]

IRR research on the Van Mierevelt portraits

In the early Maurits portraits the black lines found on the surfaces of the paintings could be made more visible with IRR. In addition it became clear that the extensive underdrawing was transferred via pounced cartoon. Small dots were found in two portraits in exactly the same position, indicating the use of one and the same pounced cartoon. Both the material used for the pouncing and the liquid paint used to connect the dots appear very clearly on the IRR images and so are assumed to be carbon-based. All the facial features are indicated with the underdrawn lines, and short hatchings mark shadow areas (Fig. 7). The hatchings seem to be added freehand, as their direction varies in the different versions of the portrait of Maurits.

However the IRR research resulted in very few findings in other portraits. In some portraits 'suspicious' dark lines underneath the eyes were enhanced. The red contour lines

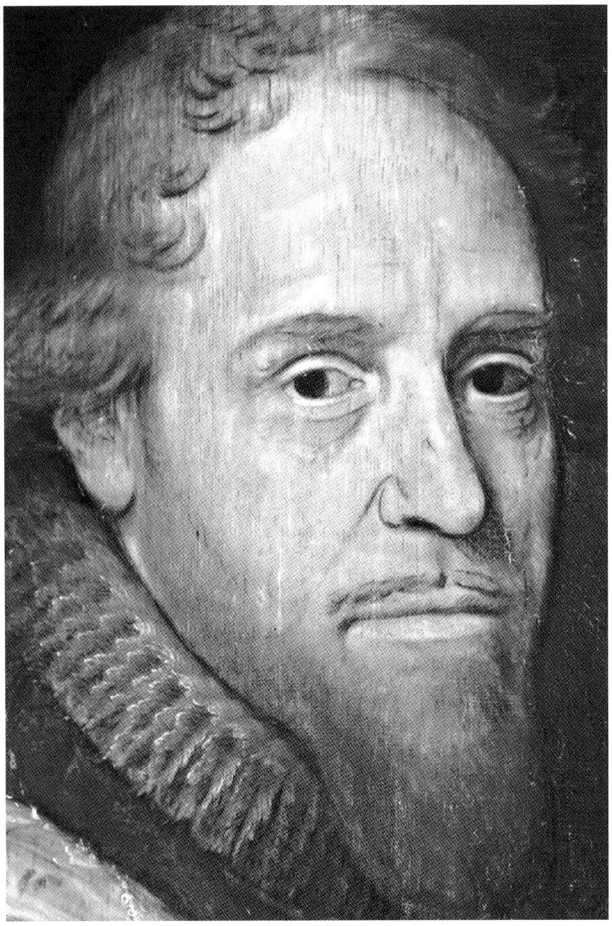

Figure 7 *IRR detail of the face of Maurits (PDS68b), which reveals an elaborate underdrawing in fluid dark lines. Dots referring to the use of a pounced cartoon are most obvious in the curly hair, in the eyebrows and in the lines under Maurits's right eye. (Photograph courtesy of Margreet Wolters, Rijksbureau voor Kunsthistorische Documentatie (RKD).)*

are unsurprisingly very difficult to distinguish on the IRR image, even when they are not covered with subsequent paint layers; at best they show as a grey mid-tone.

In conclusion, the study of the portraits from Van Mierevelt's studio has revealed the use of different underdrawing techniques: a pounced cartoon fixed with liquid black paint; sparsely used dark lines; preparatory contour lines in red; a single instance of underdrawing in white paint. However, these findings are rare – after examination with IRR most paintings do not reveal the use of underdrawing at all.

Introduction to underdrawing in paintings of the Dutch Golden Age

It is generally assumed that underdrawing is much less common in seventeenth-century Netherlandish paintings than in paintings of previous centuries.[12] However, changes in painting practice, such as the use of coloured priming, make it more difficult to find underdrawings. When a painter chose to use an unorthodox 'drawing' material, such as different oil paints, the study of underdrawing becomes more complicated. The publication of IRR research on the seventeenth-century Bredius collection shows, however, that underdrawing is found in more cases than would be expected.[13] Where research with IRR reaches its limitations regarding the different materials used for the underdrawing, unfinished paintings and drawings can give additional information. Red and white chalk, for example, are rather common materials but easily missed when studying paintings with IRR.[14] Studying paint surfaces with the aid of a microscope proved an essential and accessible method in assessing seventeenth-century underdrawing practice, such as the monochrome brown sketch found in the paintings of Vermeer or the red lake underdrawings in the work of Van Mierevelt discussed above (Gifford 1998: 185–90).

The methods used for the transfer of drawings in the case of copies are not often discussed with reference to seventeenth-century Dutch paintings, though a few examples show that different techniques were applied. The use of pounced cartoons seems very rare, while the use of transferring with white chalk is beautifully illustrated by a surviving drawing by Adriaen van der Werff.[15] Copying paintings with the help of a grid is found in the seventeenth century, but mostly related to the practice of scaling up paintings, as commonly found in the *modelli* made for tapestries and large-scale altarpieces in the studio of Peter Paul Rubens (Lammertse and Vergara 2003: 26–31). His pupil Anthony van Dyck has been found to have painted red lines along the contours of his finished portraits to make a counterproof for a new version (Bauer 2007). So far the use of red lake paint as an underdrawing material has been found mostly in portraits.[16] It is possible that de Mayerne is referring to its use when he writes that it is best to fix underdrawing lines with a 'common lake'.[17]

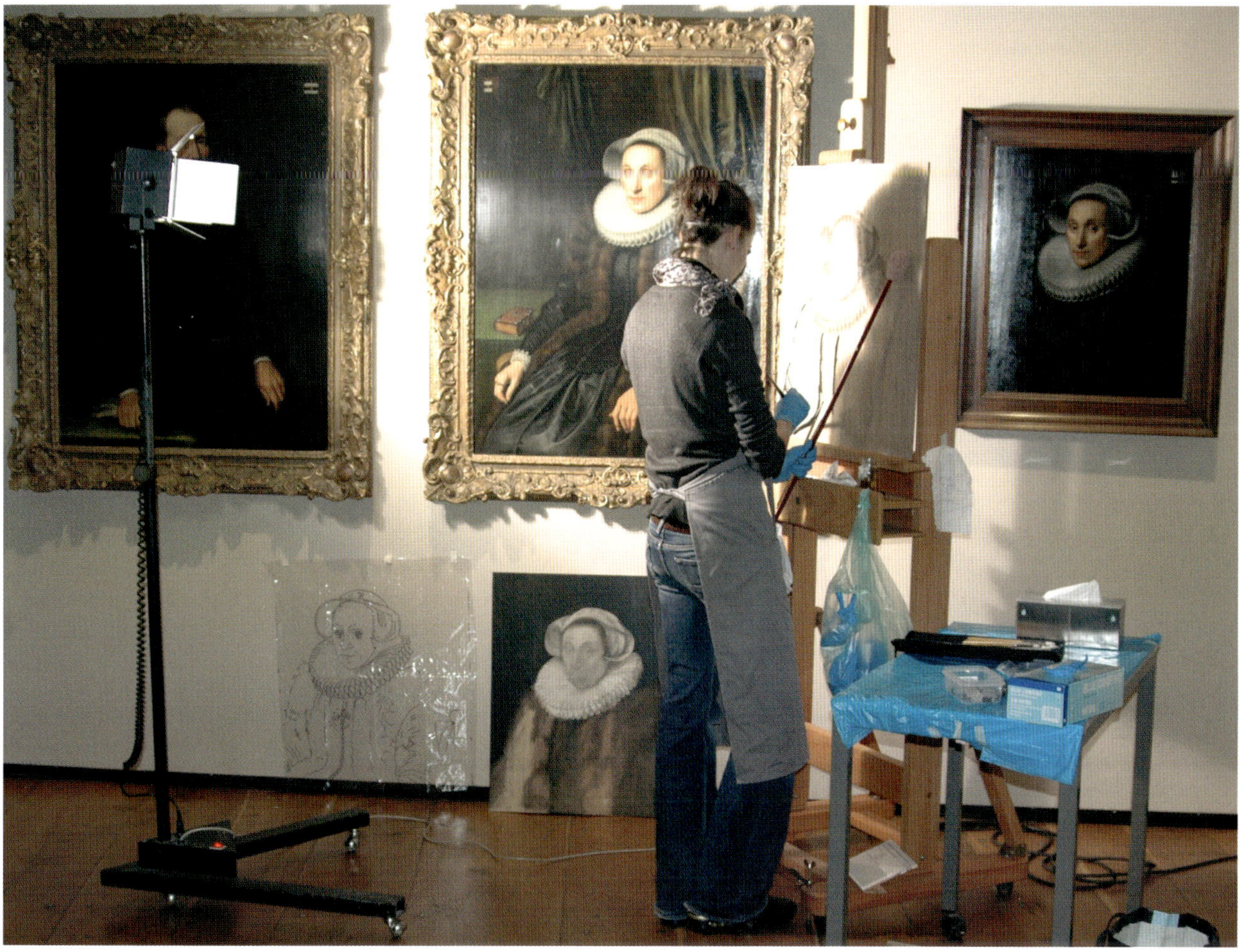

Figure 8 *Charlotte Caspers working on the reconstructions of Van Mierevelt's portrait of Sara Bosschaerts in the gallery. (Photograph: Charlotte Caspers, Johanneke Verhave and Margreet Wolters.)*

Research questions and method

The research results described above raised the following questions concerning the underdrawing stage of Van Mierevelt's paintings:

- Why is so little underdrawing found? Should we be looking for underdrawing material that does not show in IRR?
- Which method of transfer could Van Mierevelt have used, besides the early findings of pouncing?
- Did he change something in his technique through which the traces of the pounced drawing became invisible? Or did he stop using it? And if so why might he have discontinued the use of this pounced underdrawing?
- How easy is it to apply an underdrawing with red lake paint and is there a (painterly) benefit in the addition of chalk?
- Though known to be hard to detect using infrared, can the red lake paint be made evident in some form in IRR when one knows that it is present? And can this be used as a reference in situations where its use is not confirmed?
- Is such an underdrawing in paint meant to be seen in the final paint surface?

Two different types of reconstructions were made in the attempt to answer these questions: (1) painterly reconstructions of the portrait of Sara Bosschaert (1619) (Figs 15–17) and (2) tests of various underdrawing materials and transfer methods.[18] The first type of reconstruction had as its main purpose the study of Van Mierevelt's painting technique. These reconstructions were made as part of the research project 'Van Mierevelt's factory' and were executed next to the original painting in the exhibition (Fig. 8). The second type of reconstruction was executed specifically for this paper to explore a selection of underdrawing materials and techniques, which could have been used by Van Mierevelt's studio (Fig. 9), and is discussed in depth in the following section.

The underdrawing reconstructions

Because we wanted to gain insight into how Van Mierevelt could have transferred the outlines of a face, we chose to reconstruct an image (Maurits's right eye) instead of

Table I *Overview of underdrawing tests.*

	Loose pigment				Paint: where the box is shaded the paint was applied on top of each of the loose pigments listed to the left				
Material ⇒ Transfer method ⇓	Lamp black	Burnt umber	Red lake (madder)	White chalk	Lamp black in gum	Lamp black in oil	Burnt umber in oil	Red lake (madder) in oil	Red lake (madder) + white chalk in oil
Tracing: unfixed	×	×	×	×					
fixed	×	×	×	×	×				
fixed	×	×	×	×			×		
fixed	×	×	×	×				×	
Pouncing	×	×	×	×					
Template						×	×	×	×
Counterproof						×	×	×	×

straight lines. The reconstructions were executed on radially cut oak panels, covered with a thin chalk and glue ground, superimposed with a warm and medium-rich *imprimatura* layer.[19] This preparation of the panels was based on the analyses of the ground layers in Van Mierevelt's portraits in general, including the use of a very thin chalk and glue layer that barely filled the wood grain; the specific combination of pigments in the reconstructions imitates the *imprimatura* of the portrait of Stadholder Maurits (Fig. 1). The *imprimatura* paint was left to dry for about one week before the different reconstructions of underdrawing were applied directly on this layer.

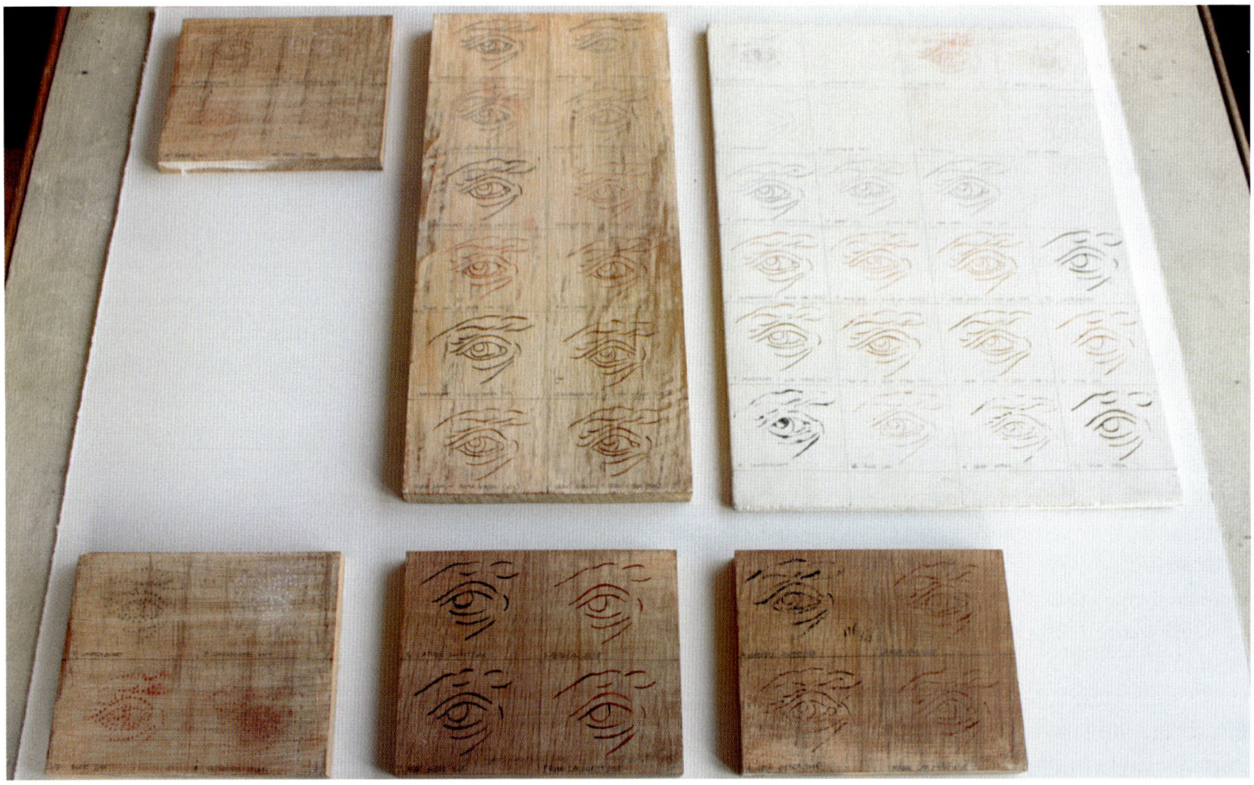

Figure 9 *Overview of the 28 reconstructions on panels primed with a thin chalk-glue ground and oil-based* imprimatura *and their references on the panel primed with a thick, white chalk-glue ground (before the application of two layers of flesh paint). (Photograph: Charlotte Caspers, Johanneke Verhave and Margreet Wolters.)*

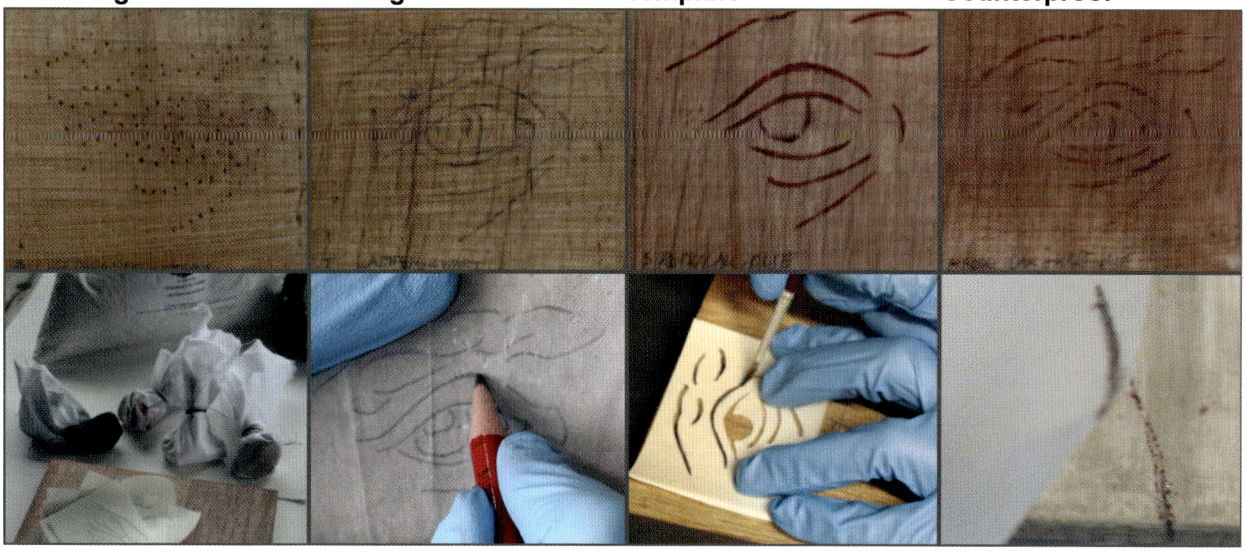

Pouncing: 'Underdrawing applied by pouncing loose pigment through the holes of a pounced cartoon'

Above: The dotted image of a pouncing.
Below: Bags with loose pigment used to pounce the pigment through the holes of the pounced cartoon.

Tracing: 'Underdrawing applied by tracing the lines of a drawing which back is covered with loose pigment.'

Above: The thin lines of a tracing.
Below: Tracing the drawing and thus pressing the pigment from its backside on the prepared support.

Template: 'Underdrawing applied by painting in the lines of a template'.

Above: The mechanic lines resulting from the use of a template.
Below: Application of oil paint with a brush using a template.

Counterproof: 'Underdrawing applied by rubbing wet oil paint from a sheet of paper on the prepared support.'

Above: The broken and textured lines resulting from the use of a counterproof.
Below: Lifting the paper and the line of wet oil-paint that remains on the imprimatura layer. (Photo Laura Kolkena)

Figure 10 *The four transfer methods. (Photograph: Charlotte Caspers, Johanneke Verhave and Margreet Wolters, montage by Pim Smits.)*

The transfer methods of pouncing, tracing, template and counterproof were selected since they can efficiently reproduce copies,[20] and are further explained and illustrated in Figure 10. In the pounced underdrawing we used the same distance between the dots as measured in the Maurits portrait. The tracings were carried out with loose pigment (unfixed) and also with loose pigment subsequently fixed with a painted line (with various pigments bound in gum arabic or oil). The selected materials were chosen because they were either found in some of Van Mierevelt's paintings (carbon black and red lake), or because they could have been used in the seventeenth century and are expected to be difficult to trace after paint application (burnt umber and white chalk).[21] The various combinations of transfer methods totalled 28 tests, as listed in Table 1. These 28 tests were also applied on a white, thickly applied chalk and glue ground with no *imprimatura* to evaluate the influence of contrast between underdrawing and the layer(s) beneath on the traceability with IRR.

Within the frame of this paper it is impossible to discuss all tests and results in detail. Some general observations are presented with a more extensive focus on the insights related to the research subject. The reconstructions discussed in the next sections are (unless mentioned otherwise) those on the warm *imprimatura*, rather than those on the white ground.

Findings from the underdrawing reconstructions: transfer methods

The underdrawing of Maurits's eye could effectively be reproduced with all four transfer methods. In terms of time and effort in relation to the end result, the unfixed tracing proved to be the most efficient method and the pouncing the least. The loose pigment particles of the unfixed tracing were surprisingly well bound by the oil of the relatively fresh *imprimatura* layer, resulting in clear thin lines, which held when they were painted over with the flesh colours (Fig. 11). The fixed tracings required one extra step of application: redrawing the traced lines with paint. However, this method does not take much extra time and has the advantage over the unfixed tracing that the initial lines are more protected and that the underdrawing can contribute to the painted surface if desired.[22] The pouncing resulted in an unclear matrix of dots (Fig. 10). Connecting these dots to a workable underdrawing was only possible using the principal drawing as a guide.[23] Use of both a template and a counterproof worked better than expected (Figs 10 and 15).[24] The underdrawn lines of both techniques 'stand up' and can be distinguished easily with raking light. However, the lines made with the template were mechanical and lacking in subtlety. The counterproof executed in madder lake oil paint, with or without the addition of chalk, resulted in lines that have a

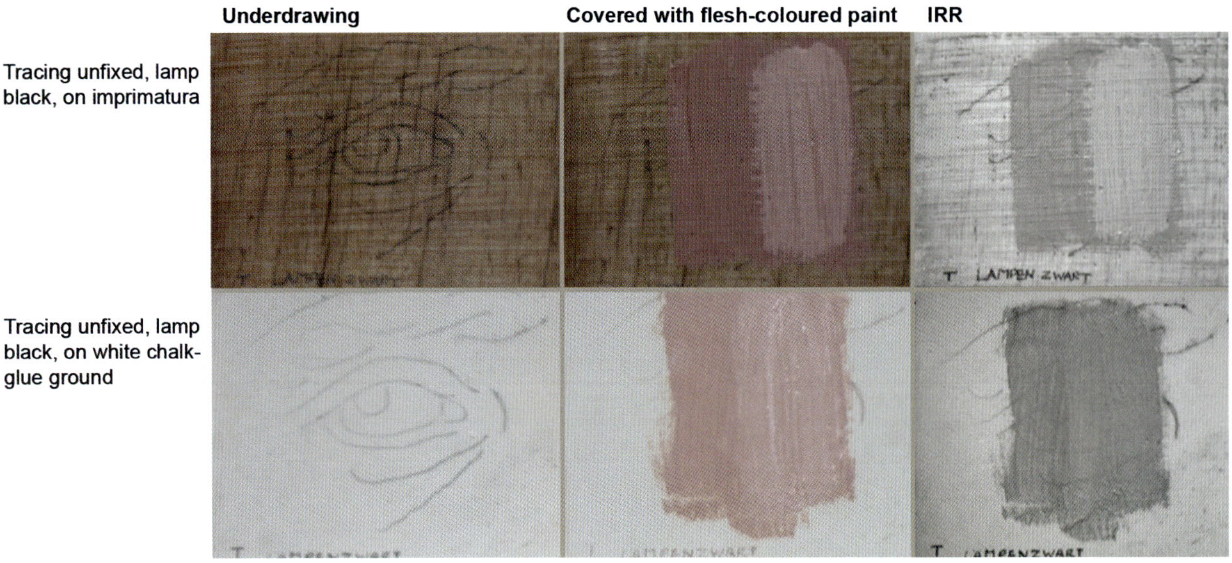

Figure 11 *Underdrawing of unfixed tracing with lamp black: comparison between VIS and IRR. The VIS images before and after application of the flesh-coloured oil paint were photographed in different light circumstances. The colours of the images in the second column have been manipulated in Photoshop for these assemblies. (Photograph: Charlotte Caspers, Johanneke Verhave and Margreet Wolters, montage by Pim Smits.)*

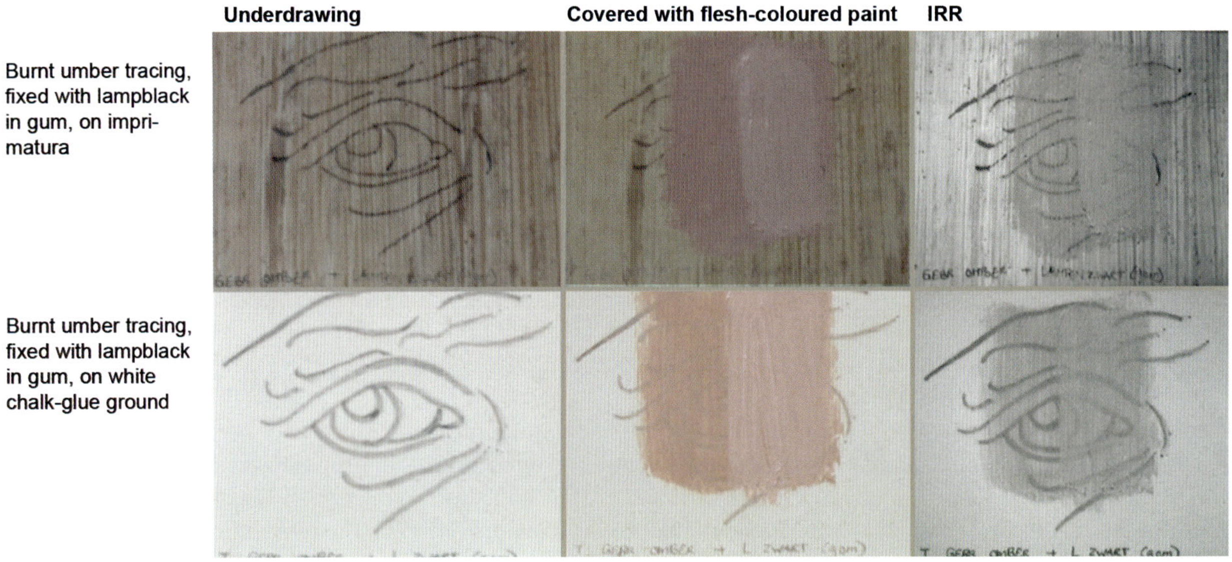

Figure 12 *Underdrawing of burnt umber tracing fixed with lamp black in gum arabic: comparison between VIS and IRR. The VIS images before and after application of the flesh-coloured oil paint were photographed in different light circumstances. The colours of the images in the second column have been manipulated in Photoshop for these assemblies. (Photograph: Charlotte Caspers, Johanneke Verhave and Margreet Wolters, montage by Pim Smits.)*

surface texture comparable with the underdrawing found in the portrait of Edward Cecil mentioned earlier (Figs 10 and 15); the lines are quite wide and spotty. This could indicate that Van Mierevelt used a counterproof in this specific portrait.

Findings from the underdrawing reconstructions: pigments and paints

All four pigments (lamp black, burnt umber, madder lake, white chalk) could be sufficiently distinguished to function as underdrawing when used as loose pigment (pouncing and unfixed tracing). The white chalk, however, became more transparent shortly after application due to interaction with the oil of the *imprimatura*.

The relief of the brushstrokes of the *imprimatura* layer gave the lines traced with lamp black a broken structure, and the appearance of thin black chalk lines (Fig. 11).[25] The other pigments did not give such lines when traced. When the tracings were fixed, both the underlying pigments and the ground layers influenced the appearance of the lines in the underdrawing. For example, a tracing with white chalk on the *imprimatura* subsequently fixed with lamp black in gum resulted in wide lines and the lamp black paint was hard to control during application. In comparison, tracing with burnt umber fixed with the same black paint gave thin broken lines (Fig. 12).

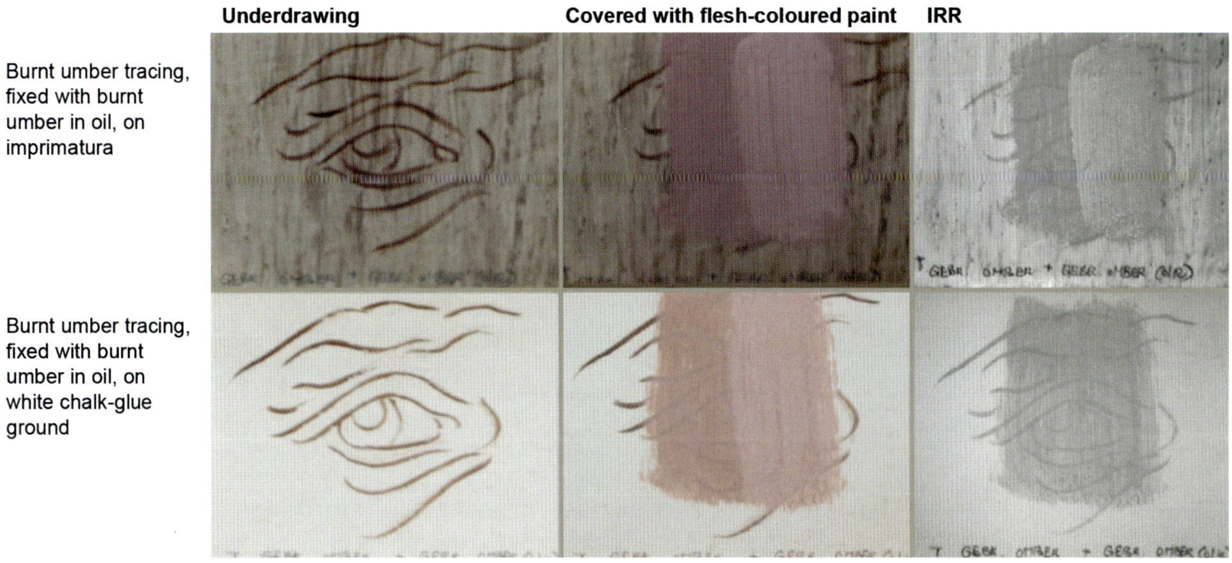

Figure 13 *Underdrawing of burnt umber tracing fixed with burnt umber in oil: comparison between VIS and IRR. The VIS images before and after application of the flesh-coloured oil paint were photographed in different light circumstances. The colours of the images in the second column have been manipulated in Photoshop for these assemblies. (Photograph: Charlotte Caspers, Johanneke Verhave and Margreet Wolters, montage by Pim Smits.)*

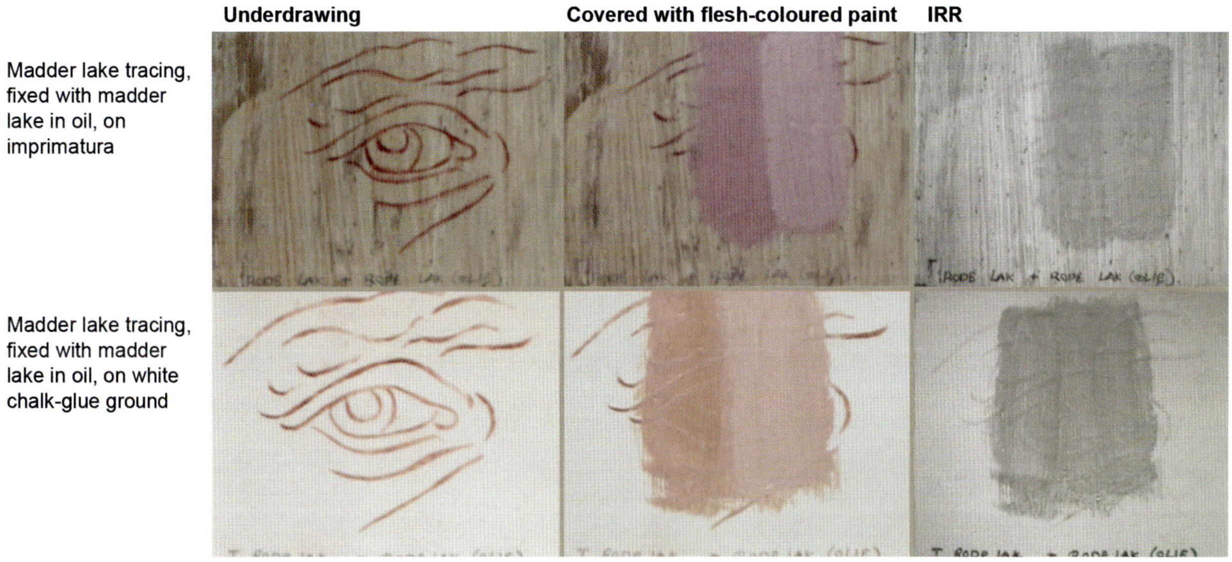

Figure 14 *Underdrawing of madder lake tracing fixed with madder lake in oil: comparison between VIS and IRR. The VIS images before and after application of the flesh-coloured oil paint were photographed in different light circumstances. The colours of the image in the second column have been manipulated in Photoshop for these assemblies. (Photograph: Charlotte Caspers, Johanneke Verhave and Margreet Wolters, montage by Pim Smits.)*

The same burnt umber tracing on the chalk and glue ground, again fixed with lamp black in gum, resulted in wider lines (Fig. 12). All tracings fixed with oil paint gave fluid lines, which clearly have the appearance of having been applied with a brush (Fig. 13). As already mentioned above, both counterproof and template resulted in lines with noticeable relief. The lines of the counterproof method have a rough surface (Figs 10 and 15), whereas the lines painted with the help of the template have a smooth and closed surface. The various oil paints all behaved in a more or less similar way; there was no apparent difference in the handling properties or the visual results of the pure madder lake paint or the madder lake with the addition of chalk.

Findings from the underdrawing reconstructions: paint application over the underdrawing

The flesh-coloured paint on top of the various underdrawings was applied by the same person and care was taken to apply the paint in a uniform manner, giving constant pressure. During painting the pigment dots of the pounced cartoon were wiped out, giving a smudgy surface, especially when lamp black (as a loose pigment) had been used. All unfixed lines made using a tracing disappeared under the first paint layer. The traced lines fixed with paint were much more visible through the paint layers and remained so through the second paint layer. Lines fixed with the lamp black and burnt umber oil paint could be distinguished

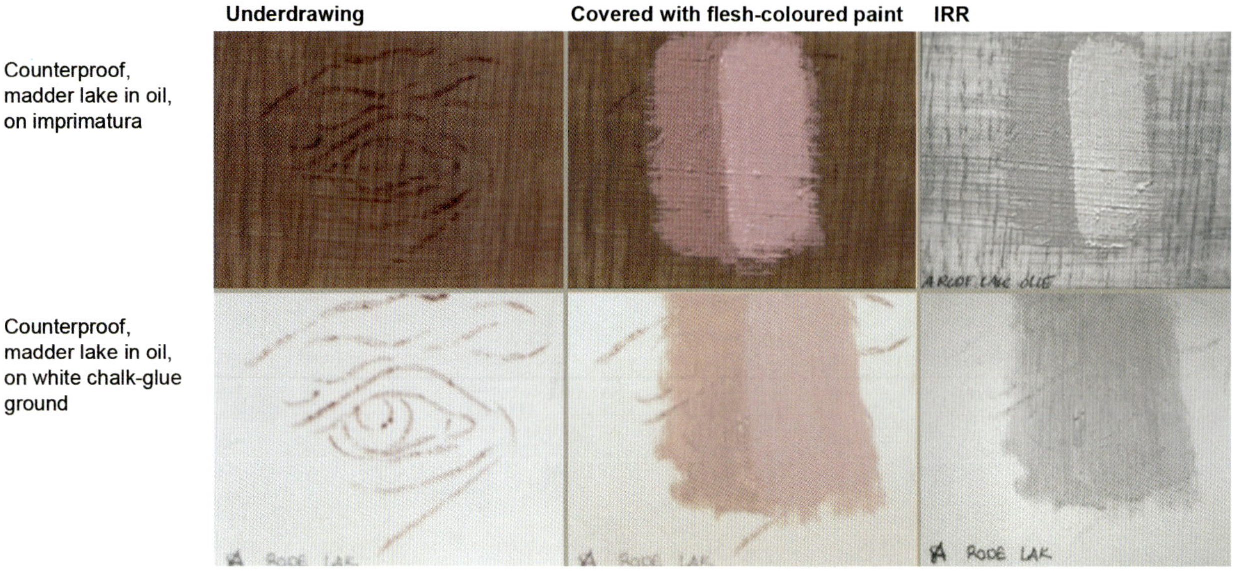

Figure 15 *Underdrawing using a counterproof with madder lake oil paint: comparison between VIS and IRR. The VIS images before and after application of the flesh-coloured oil paint were photographed in different light circumstances. The colours of the image in the second column have been manipulated in Photoshop for these assemblies. (Photograph: Charlotte Caspers, Johanneke Verhave and Margreet Wolters, montage by Pim Smits.)*

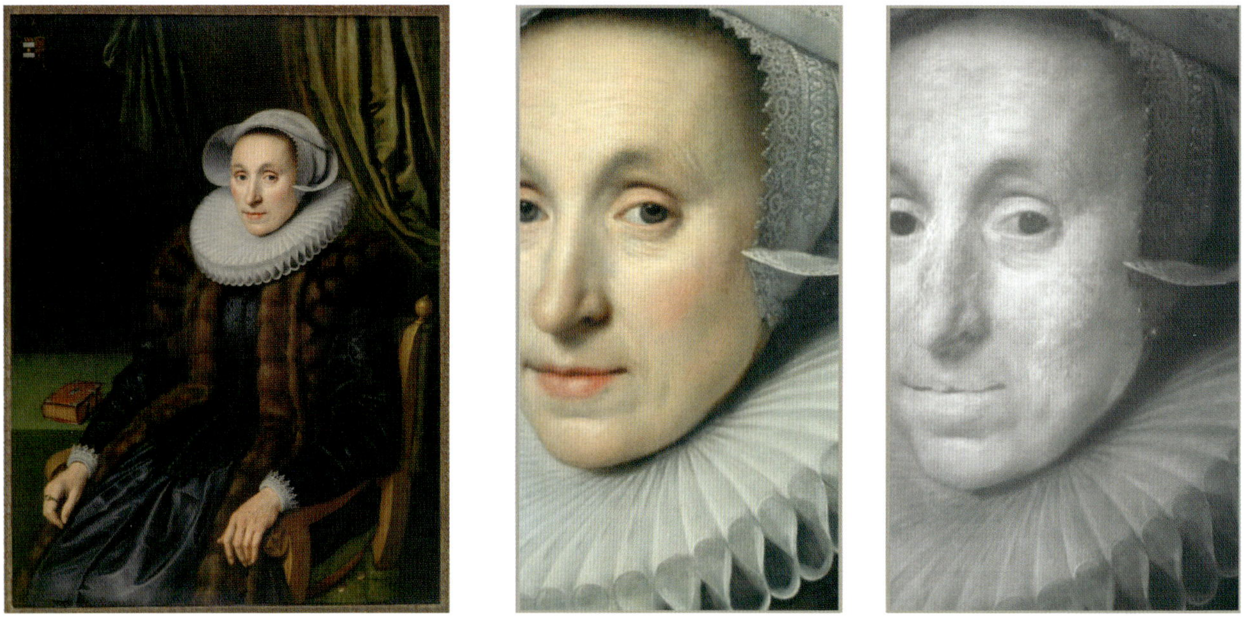

Figure 16 Left: *Michiel van Mierevelt,* Portrait of Sara Bosschaert, *1619 (B1-19). (Photograph courtesy of Tom Haartsma, Museum het Prinsenhof, Delft.)* Middle: *Detail of face.* Right: *IRR of detail of face. (Photographs: Charlotte Caspers, Johanneke Verhave and Margreet Wolters (IRR).)*

best and it is interesting to note that these paints had an influence on the flesh-coloured paint on top: after one day of drying the paint was more matt on top of the lines. The lines produced with the counterproof and the template did not remain as visible as the fixed lines, but were more distinguishable in raking light.

Evaluating the reconstructions with IRR

The number of underdrawings on the toned *imprimatura* layer that could be detected by IRR was unexpected. The umber and madder lake paints could be observed when covered by a single paint layer, but when covered by the second layer of paint they became fairly invisible (Figs 13 and 14). On the white chalk and glue ground, the same paints could, on the contrary, still be discerned with IRR under a second paint layer (Figs 13 and 14).[26] Almost all lines containing lamp black were visible under the second paint layer (Fig. 12) (except for the unfixed lamp black tracing). The lines produced by counterproof and template could be discerned on both underlayers but this was due more to light reflection caused by their *impasto* than by a difference in contrast (Fig. 15). The pouncing and unfixed tracings could hardly be distinguished with IRR when covered by paint – only the lamp black tracing was visible under the first paint layer.

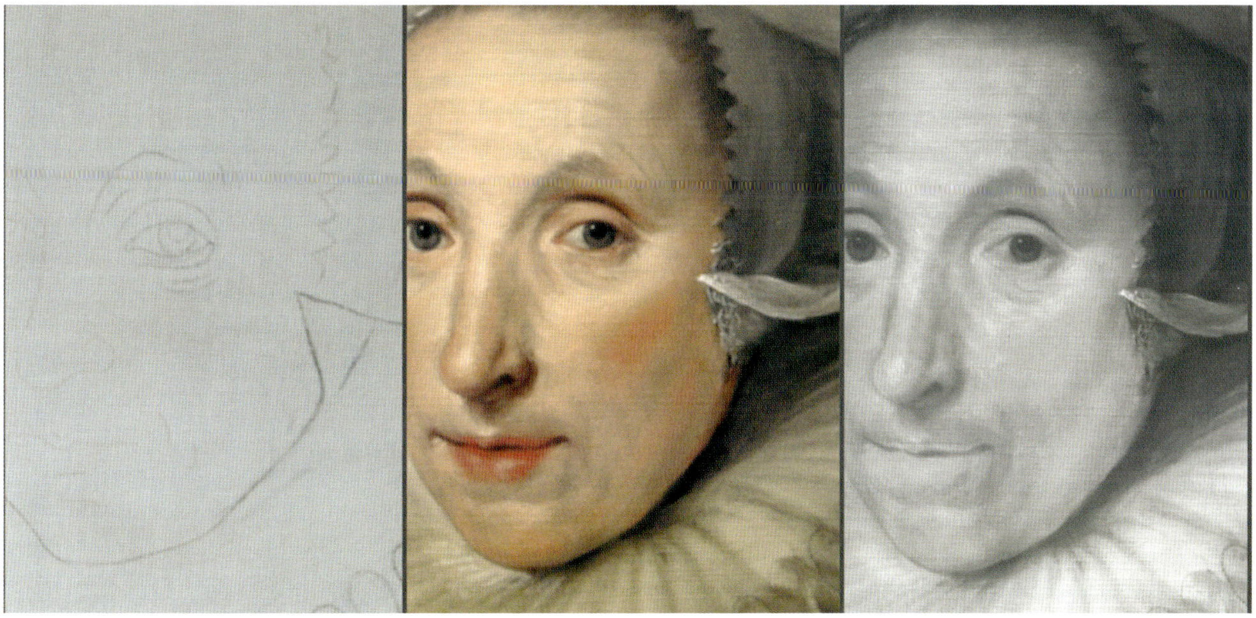

Figure 17 *Detail of reconstruction A, portrait of Sara Bosschaert with lead white underpainting.* Left: *Underdrawing (tracing of burnt umber partly fixed with lamp black in gum arabic) on lead white layer.* Middle: *Paint layers (dead colour phase) at moment of IRR.* Right: *IRR of reconstruction. (Photographs: Charlotte Caspers, Johanneke Verhave and Margreet Wolters (IRR).)*

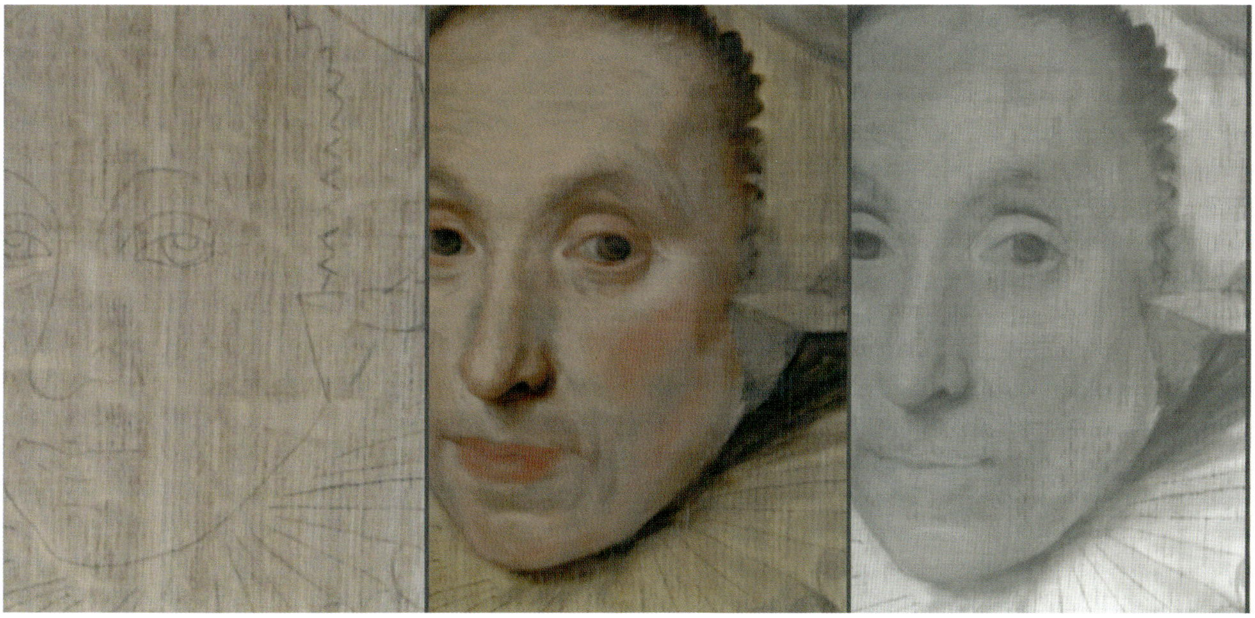

Figure 18 *Detail of reconstruction B, portrait of Sara Bosschaert without lead white underpainting.* Left: *Underdrawing (tracing of burnt umber fixed with lamp black in gum arabic) on warm imprimatura layer.* Middle: *Paint layers (dead colour phase) at moment of IRR.* Right: *IRR of reconstruction. (Photographs: Charlotte Caspers, Johanneke Verhave and Margreet Wolters (IRR).)*

Now the question remains of whether the lines that were revealed using IRR would also be found and recognised as underdrawing in the more complex structure of a painting. The two reconstructions of the portrait of Sara Bosschaert offered an opportunity to study this.

The portrait of Sara Bosschaert was reconstructed twice (Fig. 16). Reconstruction A is painted on a lead white underpaint (oil) on top of an oil-bound *imprimatura* (Fig. 17).[27] In reconstruction B the portrait is painted directly on top of the *imprimatura* (Fig. 18).[28] Except for some suspicious lines under Sara's nose, no underdrawing was found in the original portrait with either VIS or IRR. The two reconstructions were underdrawn with a burnt umber tracing, fixed with lamp black bound in gum arabic.[29] In reconstruction A, part of the burnt umber tracing was left 'unfixed'. When the faces in the reconstructions were studied with IRR, hardly any underdrawing was found in either portrait.[30] Some suggestive lines appeared, but it was impossible to make a clear distinction between the underdrawing lines and comparable lines in the painted stage.

This seems remarkable since the carbon black underdrawing of reconstruction A was applied on a white paint layer and the carbon black underdrawing lines of reconstruction B were only covered by sparse and thinly applied paint. The fact that we cannot reveal the underdrawing in these reconstructions seems to be the result of Van Mierevelt's working method and painting technique. As discussed before, Van Mierevelt followed his portrait standard very precisely and it is very probable that the dark lines of upper paint in the shadow areas coincide with the lines of the underdrawing, whereas the paint in lighter areas has more hiding power since the paint is applied more thickly and in many layers. This coinciding of lines in a low contrast area of shadow makes visual identification of a line almost impossible.[31] Though the making and interpreting of reconstructions is to a certain extent subjective, we believe we have illustrated that Van Mierevelt's portraits may be underdrawn – even with carbon black – though no underdrawing is detected; the reconstructions show that it can in fact be difficult to find a carbon-based underdrawing that is known to exist.

Conclusion

Through the reconstructions accompanying the Van Mierevelt research we gained more insight into the appearance and working properties of seventeenth-century underdrawing materials. More materials applied to the toned underground of our *imprimatura* subsequently covered by paint could be detected with IRR than was expected (burnt umber and madder lake paints and all paints containing lamp black). It is also possible that IRR can give more information about the first layout of a painting when it is combined with reference material such as reconstructions.[32] The reconstruction tests also showed that one should be careful with the visual interpretation of underdrawing materials: for example, lines of lamp black bound in gum and applied with a brush over the brushstrokes of the *imprimatura* looked rather like black chalk lines (Fig. 12).

We found that all transfer methods used function well to transfer a standard format. The unfixed tracing was the most efficient method for copying (on a fresh oil-bound preparation layer) and the pounced cartoon the least. The possibility of more efficient transfer methods might have led Van Mierevelt to abandon the use of the pounced cartoon, but this remains speculative.

Madder lake could be used without problems as an underdrawing material in all transfer methods. The madder lake oil paint tended to need a little more drying time than other paints, but this was unlikely to have been a problem in a large production studio such as Van Mierevelt's. The red lake applied with the counterproof method resulted in marks comparable to lines seen in one particular portrait by Van Mierevelt. As expected, the madder lake underdrawings do not appear in IRR when applied on an *imprimatura* and covered by more than one paint layer. A microscope still seems to be the best and most accessible tool to search for this type of underdrawing. The warm character of the lines does sometimes seem to support areas of shadow, such as the eyelids in a portrait, but at the current time it cannot be concluded that this was done deliberately.[33]

By studying the painterly reconstructions of the portrait of Sara Bosschaert we concluded that an underdrawing can be present in a painting without being found, even when the drawing is applied with a material that would be expected to be detected with IRR. Factors such as the thickness of underdrawn lines and the number of paint layers on top seem to have considerable influence, especially on a toned underlayer. In the case of Van Mierevelt, his precise manner of painting seems to contribute to the problem of a 'missing underdrawing'.

Notes

1. Renate Woudhuysen-Keller taught Charlotte Caspers and Johanneke Verhave during their training as paintings conservators at the Stichting Restauratie Atelier Limburg (SRAL) Maastricht. Charlotte Caspers has been especially interested in researching painting technique by means of reconstructions and has learned and taught alongside Renate on several occasions. Margreet Wolters followed the Amsterdam Maastricht Summer University (AMSU) summer course in 1997.
2. The research project 'Van Mierevelt's factory' was hosted by the Museum het Prinsenhof in Delft from 2007 to 2011, with the financial support of the Mondriaan Foundation. The project combined art historical, archival and material technical research into Van Mierevelt's extensive oeuvre, concluding with the exhibition *The Portrait Factory of Michiel van Mierevelt* (23 September 2011–4 March 2012), Museum het Prinsenhof, Delft, and the accompanying catalogue: Jansen *et al.* 2011.
3. The research of the actual paintings has been executed alongside the above described research project funded by the Mondriaan Stichting. As a result of this paper we have set up a spin-off research project focusing on Van Mierevelt's underdrawing.
4. Art historical and archival research into the painter, his studio and his oeuvre has been carried out by Anita Jansen, curator at Museum het Prinsenhof and project leader of the research project 'Van Mierevelt's factory'. For the present brief summary we have used her research results as described in chapters 2 and 3 in Jansen *et al.* 2011.
5. The numbers are based on a core group of portraits that we recognise as executed by Van Mierevelt and his studio. The actual production of these portraits must have been much higher; Jansen *et al.* 2011: 51.
6. To compare the portraits tracings were made on thick Melinex sheets.
7. Likewise the portrait of Archbishop William Warham by Hans Holbein the Younger has been found to have been copied several times, also in the seventeenth century, using an extensive underdrawing. See the research results on the National Portrait Gallery (London) website: *Tudor and Jacobean Portraits Database*, www.npg.org.uk/collections/search/portraitConservation/mw06595/William-Warham?
8. This is now more visible than in the seventeenth century due to the greater transparency of the paint layers.
9. Analysis has been carried out with scanning electron microscopy with energy dispersive X-ray spectroscopy (SEM-EDX); the type of red lake used has not been identified; Van Loon and Keune 2010.
10. The chalk glue ground, situated only in the deeper parts of the structure of the wooden support, is not included in this sample. The red line has the same thickness as the preparatory layers, and appears twice as thick as the subsequent grey paint layer of the background.

11. The painting has recently been restored by Annetje Boersma (Rotterdam). During the treatment she found these white brushstrokes especially in the arms of Frederik. They are used to indicate both contours and highlights in the armour. The lines were subsequently covered with paint, giving them more the function of an underdrawing.
12. Two publications are devoted to the different techniques of underdrawing employed in painting: Kirsch and Siejek 2004 and Bomford (2002). The first publication refers to seventeenth-century underdrawing albeit briefly. The following examples of (technical) literature give an idea about the use of underdrawing in seventeenth-century paintings. Early seventeenth-century artists often continued working in the technique of the sixteenth century, using a white ground with a carbon-containing (usually water-based) underdrawing, whereas later painters preferred the use of grey or brownish pigments in oil for their sketches; these observations are drawn from the study of seventeenth-century still life painters: see Wallert 1999. Seventeenth-century landscape artists such as Jan van Goyen and Alexander Keirincx have been found to use a black underdrawing: see Sluijter-Seijffert and Wolters 2009. Portrait painters such as Johannes Verspronk and Gerrit Dou have been documented as using an underdrawing: see Hendriks 1998: 242–5, figs 2, 4 6, 8, 12; Wadum 2000: 170, 184. Carel Fabritius seems to have used a carbon-containing underdrawing in the special case of a painting for a 'perspective box' (National Gallery, London, NG 3714) whereas it has not been found in his other paintings: Duparc 2004: 26–7. The use of underdrawing in other perspectives is much more common, as found in church interiors by Pieter Saenredam and others: Giltaij 2000.
13. Buijsen 2001. This publication also demonstrates that IRR research can contribute to a better understanding of the painting technique; if not in underdrawing then in the study of the paint build-up.
14. An interesting example is the small unfinished oil painting on paper by Adriaan van der Venne (Rijksmuseum Amsterdam, SK-A-1776). An abandoned drawing in red chalk is visible under a drawing with white chalk lines. IRR study and documentation by Edwin Buijsen has shown that the chalk lines are visible on the IRR image where they are not covered with paint; see Bikker *et al.* 2007: 384–5.
15. The drawing is part of the Bredius collection and was used for the painting in the Boijmans van Beuningen; see Buijsen 2001: 44–6.
16. Very recently four portraits attributed to Thomas de Keijser (Amsterdam Museum) have been found to have an underdrawing in red paint. The lines were found in the same areas as in Van Mierevelt's portraits: along contours and in the eyes. Preliminary X-ray fluorescence (XRF) analysis of one such line revealed the presence of a red lake, some vermilion and some earth pigment. We are very grateful to Indra Kneepkens, Emily Froment (University of Amsterdam) and Arie Wallert (Rijksmuseum Amsterdam) for sharing these observations with us.
17. 'D'autres tirent leurs traitz avec de la laque commune et ceste cy est la meilleure maniere de toutes les autres cy dessus': Berger 1901: 278–9.
18. Most materials for the reconstructions were ordered from Kremer Pigmente. They are sufficiently close to seventeenth-century materials for the purpose of this study, but are not as historically accurate as described by Carlyle and Witlox (2005).
19. In the reconstructions this layer consists of: chalk, red earth, red lead and burnt umber bound in lead oil. These pigments were identified in Jansen *et al.* 2011: 93 and Verhave 2007: 27. The lead oil was prepared according to a recipe from Renate Woudhuysen-Keller: cold-pressed linseed oil (Kremer) mixed with lead(II) oxide (6:1 mass ratio) and heated for about 20 minutes until 110°C is reached. The lead oil is afterwards diluted with cold-pressed linseed oil (1:1 volume ratio) (personal communication).
20. Templates and the use of a counterproof are less common methods of transferring underdrawings than pounced cartoons and tracing. They are, however, successful methods for 1:1 reproduction. The use of a counterproof in combination with red lake is reported to have been used by Van Dyck to copy his own paintings (Bauer 2007: 99–101). The use of a copying grid as a method of transfer has not been tested in this research, though we did encounter one painting during the Van Mierevelt research project that seems to have been modelled for copying with the use of a grid of horizontal lines. The minute similarities in Van Mierevelt's faces throughout the oeuvre contradict the use of a grid, at least for the faces.
21. Burnt umber was chosen because it was expected to match the (warm) areas of shadow around eyes and noses in the portraits. It was assumed that umber would be difficult to trace with IRR.
22. This advantage applies mostly to tracing on a chalk and glue ground; fixing the tracing on the oily *imprimatura* layer was hardly necessary.
23. The pouncing was not fixed for this specific series of reconstructions as a result of practical restrictions. One reconstruction of pouncing with lamp black, fixed with a lamp black in gum tracing had been made by Charlotte Caspers for the exhibition, making extra reconstructions superfluous.
24. During paint application it is important not to move the counterproof or template otherwise the paint will smear the surface. The tests executed for this research were of a small format – a larger format such as Van Mierevelt's portraits might be problematical. During a reconstruction course at the University of Amsterdam the counterproof method was tried out on a larger scale, which seemed to work well.
25. At the symposium organised for Molly Faries's retirement in 2005, Astrid Smeets presented comparable findings of fluid underdrawing materials appearing different in IRR, relating these to her study of underdrawings in Brueghel's studio.
26. Only the madder lake counterproof was hard to distinguish.
27. Such a layer was found in several Van Mierevelt portraits as a local underpaint for the faces, as in the aforementioned portrait of Maurits (Verhave 2011: 95).
28. Comparable to the *imprimatura* layer used in the tests discussed above.
29. These materials were chosen since no traces of the red lake could be observed by microscope.
30. We chose to focus on the face of Sara Bosschaert for this study. Other areas (such as the collar) were not yet covered with paint at the time of the IRR study, which leads to a clearly visible 'underdrawing' in IRR (Figs 17 and 18).
31. It has to be mentioned that the carbon black underdrawing on a white paint layer in the Maurits portrait could be easily distinguished with IRR and that the thickness of underdrawing lines is also an important factor.
32. The paint applied on top of the underdrawing tests was painted out evenly, whereas the reality of a painting is much more complex due to differences in layer thickness and contrast.
33. We would like to thank the following for their generous assistance: Anita Jansen, Laura Kolkena, Mark Boers, Theo van Galen, Herman den Otter, Paul Versteeg, Pim Smits and Leif Stubbe-Teglbjaerg.

References

Bauer, L. 2007, 'Van Dyck: replicas and tracings', *The Burlington Magazine* 149: 99–101.

Berger, E. 1901. *Beitrage zur Entwickelings-geschichte der Maltechnik. Quellen fur Maltechnik wahrend der Renaissance und Folgezeit (XVI.–XVIII. Jahrhundert) in Italiern, Spanien, den Niederlanden, Deutschland, Frankreich und England nebst dem De Mayerne Manuskript.* Munich: G.D.W. Callwey.

Bikker, J., Bruijnen, Y. and Wuestman, G. 2007. *Dutch Paintings of the Seventeenth Century in the Rijksmuseum Amsterdam. Vol. 1 Artists born between 1570–1600.* Amsterdam: Rijksmuseum.

Bomford, D. (ed.) 2002. *Art in the Making: Underdrawings in Renaissance Paintings.* London: National Gallery Publications.

Buijsen, E. 2001. *Onder de Huid van Oude Meesters, zeventiende-eeuwse schilderijen onderzocht met infraroodreflectografie*. Den Haag: Museum Bredius en Stichting RKD.

Carlyle, L. and Witlox, M. 2005. 'Historically accurate reconstructions of artist's oil painting materials'. In *Art of the Past: Sources and Reconstructions*, M. Clarke, J.H. Townsend and A. Stijnman (eds) 53–9. London: Archetype Publications.

Duparc, F.J. (ed.) 2004. *Carel Fabritius 1622–1654*, Mauritshuis, Den Haag, exh. cat. Zwolle: Waanders.

Gifford, M. 1998. 'Painting light: recent observations on Vermeer's technique'. In *Vermeer Studies*, I. Gaskell and M. Jonker (eds) 185–99. Washington, DC: National Gallery of Art and New Haven, CT: Yale University Press.

Giltaij, J. 2000. 'Scientific examination of the underdrawing of seventeenth-century architectural painters'. In *The Paintings of Pieter Jansz. Saenredam (1597–1665): Conservation and Technique*, J.R.J. van Asperen de Boer and L.M. Helmus (eds) 32–55. Utrecht: Centraal Museum.

Hendriks, E. 1998. 'Johannes Cornelisz. Verspronck: the technique of a seventeenth-century Haarlem portraitist'. In *Looking Through Paintings: The Study of Painting Techniques and Materials in Support of Art Historical Research*, E. Hermens (ed.) 227–67. Baarn: de Prom and London: Archetype Publications.

Jansen, A., Ekkart, R. and Verhave, J. 2011. *De Portretfabriek van Michiel van Mierevelt*, Museum het Prinsenhof, Delft, exh. cat. Zwolle: Waanders.

Kirsch, K. and Siejek, A. 2004. 'Die Unterzeichnung auf dem Malgrund – Graphische Mittel und Übertragungsverfahren im 15.-17. Jahrhundert', *Kölner Beiträge zur Restaurierung und Konservierung von Kunst- und Kulturgut* 11.

Lammertse, F. and Vergara, A. 2003. *Peter Paul Rubens, Het Leven van Achilles*. Rotterdam: Museum Boijmans van Beuningen and Madrid: Museo del Prado.

Sluijter-Seijffert, N. and Wolters, M. 2009. 'Samenwerking tussen Alexander Keirincx en Cornelis van Poelenburg belicht', *Oud Holland* 122(1): 14–42.

van Loon, A. and Keune, K. 2010. *De Fabriek van Mierevelt. Chemische Analyse van de Verflagen* (unpublished technical report).

Verhave, J. 2007. *De Maiesteyt sijns aensichts' Michiel van Mierevelt schildert prins Maurits*, unpublished thesis, SRAL.

Wadum, J. 2000. 'Rembrandt under the skin: the Mauritshuis portrait of Rembrandt with Gorget in retrospect', *Oud Holland* 114(2): 164–87.

Wallert, A. (ed.) 1999. *Still Lifes: Techniques and Style. The Examination of Paintings from the Rijksmuseum*, exh. cat. Rijksmuseum, Amsterdam. Zwolle: Waanders.

DOES THE DE MAYERNE MANUSCRIPT REFLECT CONTEMPORARY STUDIO PRACTICE?

Alison Stock

Introduction

The de Mayerne manuscript was compiled between 1620 and 1646 and, although the author was a physician, it is deemed a reliable source on painting methods and materials as it records information obtained from at least 69 artists working at the English court.[1] It was decided to test the text's authority by comparing some of the content concerning painting techniques and materials with physical evidence available in paintings by artists whom de Mayerne knew and wrote about. Five paintings that had been treated and examined by staff and interns at the Hamilton Kerr Institute (HKI) were selected and their conservation reports and technical analyses studied. The findings from the reports were compared with extracts from Fels' English translation of the manuscript to test whether de Mayerne's notes were consistent with evidence found in the paintings themselves (Fels 2001).

Théodore Turquet de Mayerne (1573–1655)

Théodore Turquet de Mayerne was born near Geneva and became a physician at the English court in the seventeenth century. He had a keen interest in painting but was known primarily, before the nineteenth century, for his contributions to science.[2] He talked regularly to artists about their practice, noting down his discussions, forming an eclectic, erratic diary of ideas, recipes, hints and tips that has become known as the de Mayerne manuscript.

The manuscript records technical information under headings such as 'common colours for oil painting' and 'making canvas, calico, taffeta watertight' (Fels 2001: 149, f. 6; 164, f. 19). De Mayerne seems to write mainly for his own indulgence, but sometimes it seems as if his intent was to produce a manual. For example, one section entitled 'short treatise on the way to learn painting and to be able to mix paints' includes a sketch of how to arrange colours on the palette.[3] This is followed by the incongruous medical advice for 'the bite of a mad dog' (Fels 2001: 247, f. 135), which reminds the reader that the author was not an artist, but a physician. His interest in the arts was forgotten for 200 years until the revival of traditional artistic techniques in the middle of the nineteenth century; the first English translation appeared as late as 2001.[4]

Comparisons between physical evidence and the manuscript

This study involved examining the following aspects of painting technique in the manuscript: the ground preparation, underdrawing, and the application of paint layers.[5] These techniques are then identified in the technical literature relating to five contemporary portraits with particular reference to the painting of flesh colours and draperies.[6] The same process was then undertaken for painting materials including pigments, media, driers and extenders.

Three major contemporary court painters were selected from artists who de Mayerne had consulted and written about in the manuscript: van Somer, Mytens and Van Dyck.[7] Correspondingly, reports from the following paintings were studied:

- Van Somer, *Portrait of Elizabeth, Countess of Kent*, 1620, The Fitzwilliam Museum, hereafter referred to as van Somer's *Countess of Kent* (Fig. 1).
- Van Somer, *Portrait of Elizabeth, Queen of Bohemia*, 1621, Parham Park, hereafter referred to as van Somer's *Queen of Bohemia* (Fig. 2).

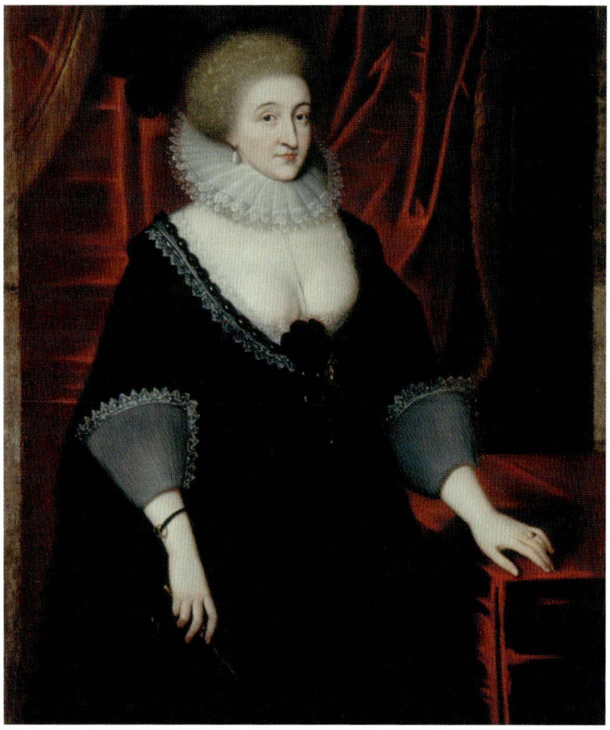

Figure 1 *Van Somer,* Portrait of Elizabeth, Countess of Kent, *1620, The Fitzwilliam Museum, Cambridge.*

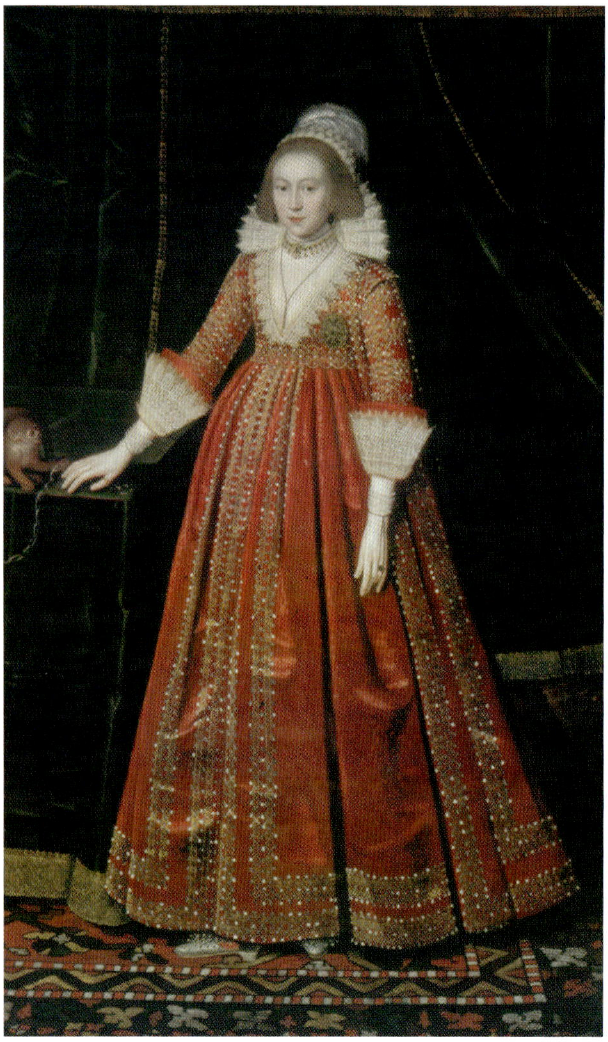

Figure 2 *Van Somer,* Portrait of Elizabeth, Queen of Bohemia, *1621, Parham Park.*

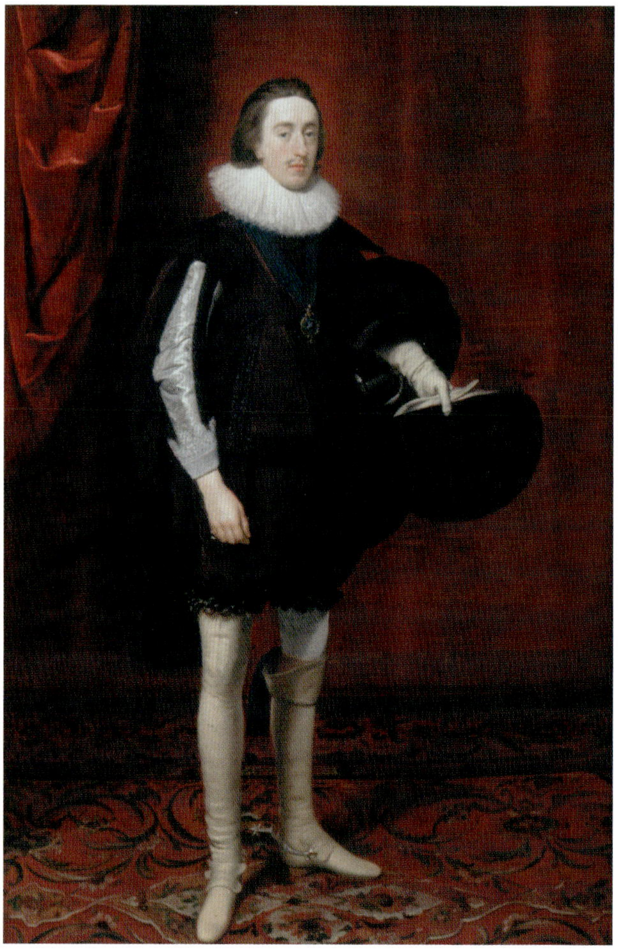

Figure 3 *Mytens,* Charles I, as Prince of Wales, *1621, Parham Park.*

- Mytens, *Charles I, as Prince of Wales*, 1621, Parham Park, hereafter referred to as Mytens' *Prince of Wales* (Fig. 3).
- Mytens, *Charles I*, 1628, Royal Collection, hereafter referred to as Mytens' *Charles I* (Fig. 4).
- Van Dyck, *Archbishop Laud*, 1635, The Fitzwilliam Museum, hereafter referred to as van Dyck's *Archbishop Laud* (Fig. 5).

Ground

De Mayerne claims that 'the undercoat is of the greatest importance' and that on 'undercoating, according to whether it is good or bad, the beauty of and liveliness of the colours depend' (Fels 2001: 155, f. 10; 229, f. 98). Therefore, his main concern was with the aesthetic of the ground rather than the technical function: 'ochre has the goodness to accept all sorts of colours like white, blue, lake without spoiling them, as umber does', and 'never use red lead for undercoating, because it fades and spoils all the other colours' (Fels 2001: 172, f. 11; 227, f. 96). He often specifies a recipe – most commonly lead white and black in oil.[8] It is almost as if in some cases he has carried out his own experiments. For example:

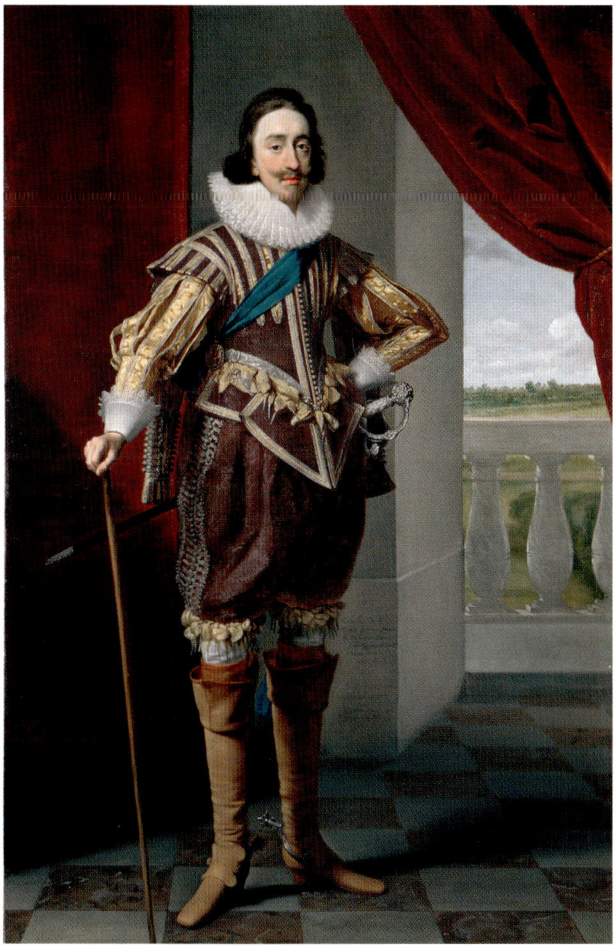

Figure 4 *Mytens,* Charles I, *1628, Royal Collection. (Supplied by Royal Collection Trust /© HM Queen Elizabeth II 2012)*

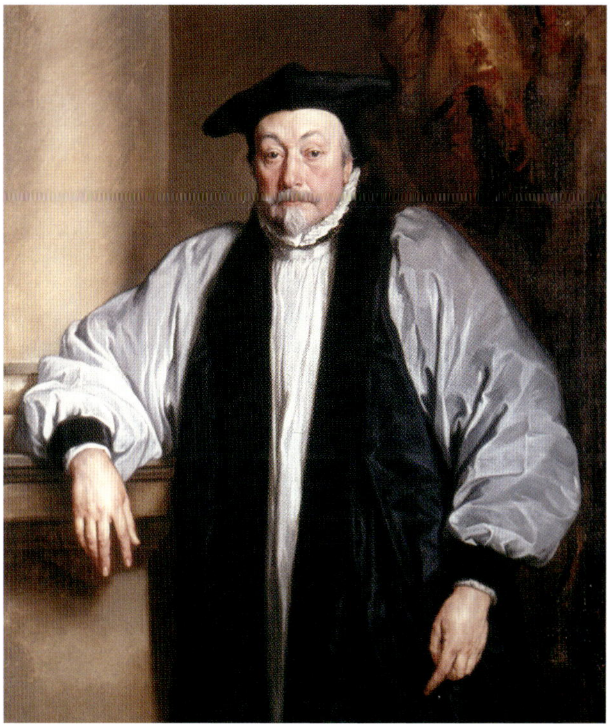

Figure 5 *Van Dyck,* Archbishop Laud, *1635, The Fitzwilliam Museum, Cambridge.*

> Prepare bolus 2lb, umber 2oz, ground together with oil, and apply. Dry in 2 or 3 days. Finally ceruse, 1 lb, umber 1oz let dry. No red lead ([marginal note:] no good. Cracks. The canvas should be rubbed down with pumice when everything is dry). (Fels 2001: 221, f. 89)

De Mayerne often writes about a double ground; the very first entry in the manuscript on the subject of grounds is derived from a London 'under coater' named Wallon, which translates as 'man from the East', perhaps indicating a foreign source. Wallon suggests to 'lightly undercoat' with brown red or dark English red, and when dry smooth with a pumice stone and follow with a 'second and last layer with white lead … burnt charcoal and a little umber earth, so that it dries quicker' (Fels 2001: 148, f. 5). This double ground has become synonymous with seventeenth-century technique, and is exactly what is found in Mytens' *Charles I*, with a lower ground of red earth, lead white and bone black and upper ground of lead white and black (Sauerberg 1999: 4) (Fig. 6). Similarly, Van Dyck's *Archbishop Laud* has a pinkish lower ground layer composed of lead white, red earth and a black pigment, and a white upper ground of lead

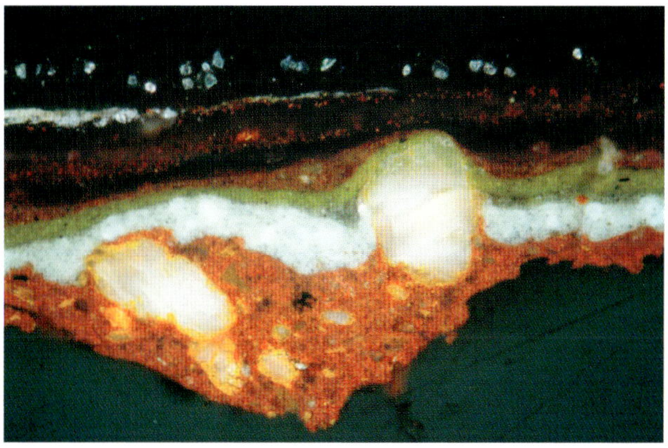

Figure 6 *Mytens,* Charles I*: cross-section from drapery showing double ground with strong red lower layer of red earth, bone black and lead white and upper layer of lead white and black. On top of the ground are two layers of dead colouring (grey followed by green), followed by a layer of red opaque paint with a red glaze on top (the following layers are overpaint).*

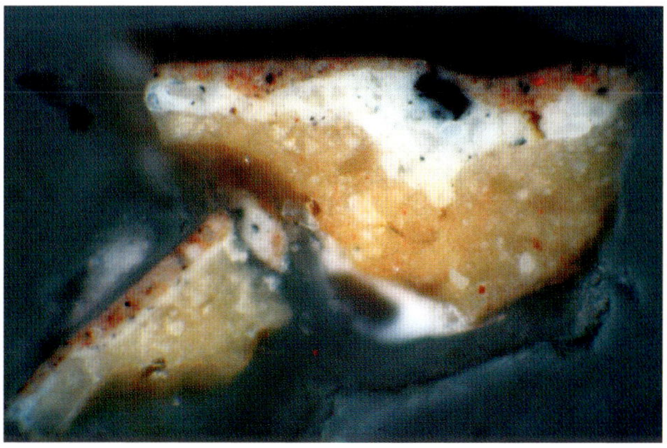

Figure 7 *Van Dyck,* Archbishop Laud*: cross-section from the left thumb showing the double ground that has a paler orange lower layer and white upper layer. The flesh colour is painted directly on top.*

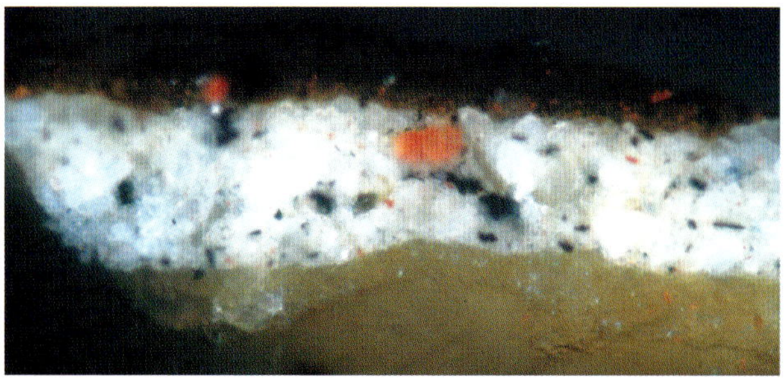

Figure 8 *Van Somer,* Countess of Kent*: cross-section from the background showing pale grey single ground comprising lead white, chalk and vine black tempered with the addition of finely ground earth colours.*

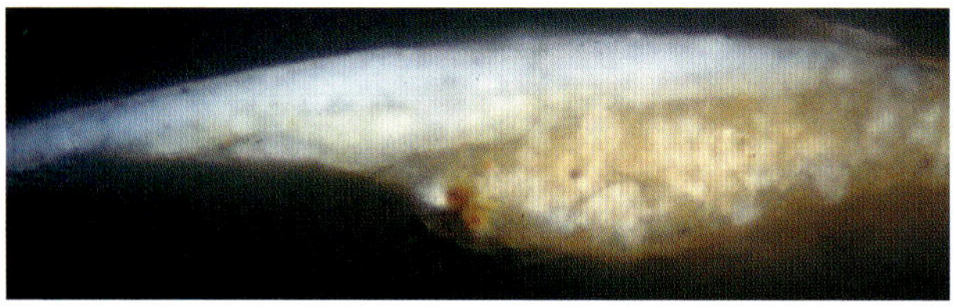

Figure 9 *Van Somer,* Queen of Bohemia*: cross-section from the white lace of the cuff showing pale yellow/brown single ground comprising lead white, chalk, black and iron earth pigments.*

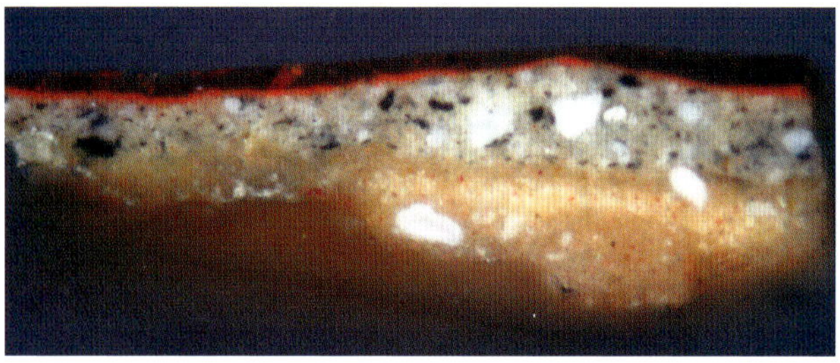

Figure 10 *Mytens,* Prince of Wales*: cross-section from the carpet (red area) showing the double ground with pale yellow lower layer (chalk, lead white, vine black, red lead, earth colours) and pale grey upper layer (lead white, vine black, red lead and earth colours). On top is the red underlayer for the carpet.*

white and carbon black with a small amount of red and brown ochre (Keller and Groen 1981: 1) (Fig. 7). Kirby suggests that painters' canvases of this time were bought ready primed (Kirby 1999: 28), and the fact that three paintings in this study have the same ground, painted in London at a similar time, could confirm this, especially as they are consistent with the description of an 'under coater's' work by de Mayerne.

The grounds of the other two paintings differ slightly. Van Somer's two portraits have single pale grounds, possibly because they were painted slightly earlier and the double ground may not yet have become fashionable at this time (Figs 8 and 9). Mytens' *Prince of Wales* has a double ground, but the lower layer is a warm off-white rather than a strong red (Fig. 10). The ground in Mytens' *Charles I* was found to be chalk-rich, suggesting 'a cheap way of reducing absorbency of the canvas' (Stonor *et al.* 2002: 8). This functional aspect of the ground was not mentioned by de Mayerne.

Underdrawing

The information about underdrawing in the manuscript is limited. An entry entitled 'of the design of pictures and their first sketching out', describes how:

> first sketching is done with chalk crayon or yellow ochre or willow charcoal or another soft material that can easily be removed ... it is nevertheless necessary to wipe the picture clean before painting, so that the mentioned chalk does not come into contact with the paints and dirty them. (Fels 2001: 230, f. 100)

This method of drawing cannot be identified using current examination techniques, and the only painting in this study that did not present any evidence of underdrawing was Van Somer's *Countess of Kent*. The fact that this painting has a grey ground may have encouraged the artist to use white chalk.

De Mayerne mentions alternative techniques: 'others draw with a brush and black oil paint ... others with common writing ink ... others finally trace their strokes with common lake and this is better than any method cited above'. Mytens' *Prince of Wales* confirms the use of a brush to apply the drawing where some underdrawing is visible with the naked eye. This is thick, black and fluid, suggesting the application of oil paint with a long brush. Similarly, Mytens' *Charles I* also has some underdrawing visible with the naked eye (Sauerberg 1999: 4). Van Dyck's *Archbishop Laud* may demonstrate the use of lake for underdrawing, where various shades of reddish brown to dark brown preparatory brushstrokes were seen outlining the features of the face and hand.

Paint layers

'Dead-colouring' is important to de Mayerne, as he claims that it should be 'just as good as the second coat, otherwise, everything will be spoiled' (Fels 2001: 227, f. 96). The paintings in this study all demonstrate areas of local dead colouring. Van Somer's *Queen of Bohemia* has a grey underlayer for the head, and Mytens' *Prince of Wales* has a red underlayer for the carpet (Figs 11 and 12). Mytens appears to have paid particular attention to the underlayer for his blues: for example, the blue sash in the *Prince of Wales* has a red lake underlayer, presumably to give the blue a purplish hue (Stonor *et al.* 2002: 10) (Fig. 13). In contrast, his *Charles I* uses a grey underlayer for the blue – a variation in technique that may suggest he chose underlayers carefully according to how they would affect the final appearance.

De Mayerne's interest in dead colouring is also evident from a conversation with a London painter, Anna Carlisle, from whom he learnt:

> in Italy the painters lightly paint over the first layer of painting, called 'the dead-colours', as soon as it is dry

> with varnish, in order to prevent the paints from discolouring. They let this varnish layer dry and paint on it. (Fels 259, f. 150)

The conservation reports examined in this study do not indicate that any intermediate varnish layers were used by these artists. Perhaps this practice did not reach the northern painters working in England, or this particular source was not reliable.

De Mayerne describes how to work with different colours; for example, when working with red:

> First the 'dead-colours' must be applied, that is put on the first layer of cinnabar and lake, and then allow it to dry. One should glaze with fine lake and over that deepen with lake and, in the deepest places, with ivory black. (Fels 2001: 222, f. 90)

Mytens' *Charles I* shows a similar type of layer structure in a cross-section taken from the red curtain. In this case grey has been used as an underlayer, followed by green, then opaque red followed with lake glazes (Fig. 6). In cross-section each layer has a distinct interface with the next, indicating that the artist has allowed each layer to dry, as de Mayerne recommends. It is interesting to note that the green layer is not made from green pigments, but from yellow lake and bone black. When de Mayerne lists green as a pigment in his list of pigments he notes that 'all sorts of green can be produced from various mixtures of Dutch pink, yellow ochre, ash blue, white lead, and earth black' (Fels 2001: 147, f. 4).

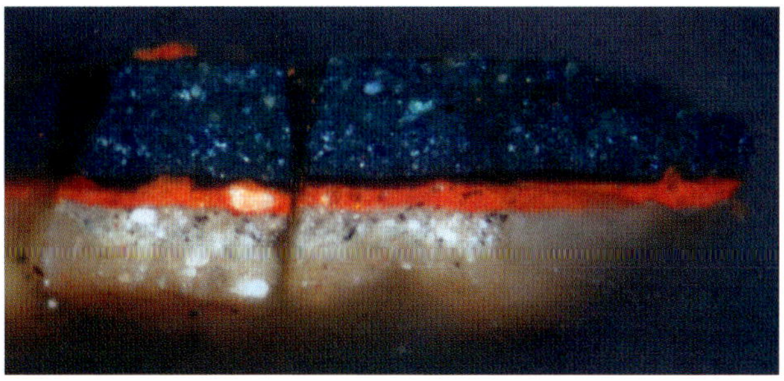

Figure 11 *Mytens,* Prince of Wales: *cross-section from the carpet (green area) showing green laid over the red underlayers.*

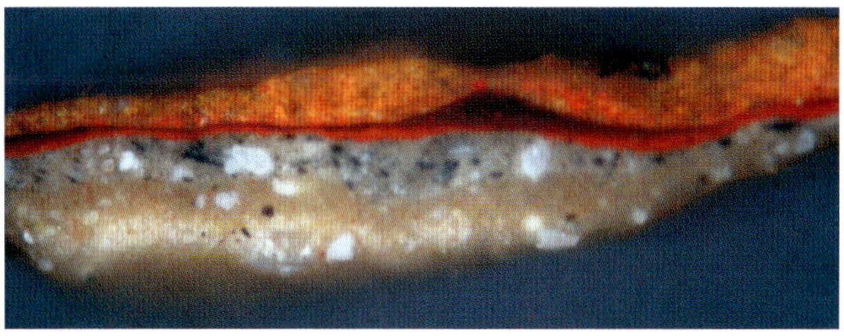

Figure 12 *Mytens,* Prince of Wales: *cross-section from the carpet (orange area) showing orange laid over the red underlayers.*

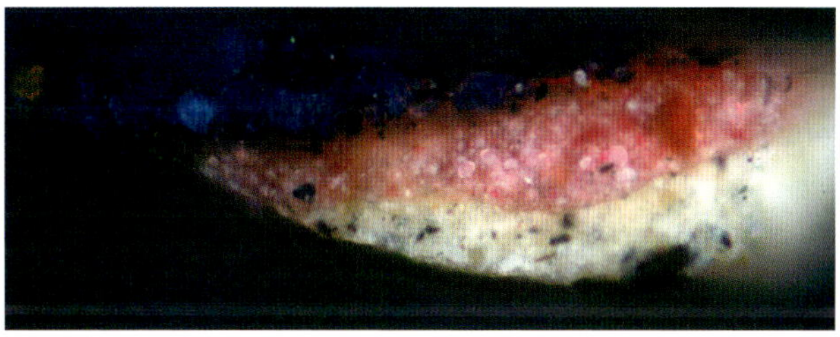

Figure 13 *Mytens,* Prince of Wales: *cross-section from the blue sash showing the red lake underlayer under the blue ribbon.*

Pigments

De Mayerne's interest in painting materials is evident in his discussions on the development of fast-drying oils, the production of the best colours and how to make them permanent, and how to produce the best varnishes.[9] The first entry in the manuscript concerns pigments: 'in painting with oil the painter needs only a few paints and from the mixing of these few the rest emerge' (Fels 2001: 147, f. 4). Van Somer's *Countess of Kent* is consistent with this as the conservation record describes a simple palette containing just 11 pigments.[10]

De Mayerne makes two lists of pigments. The list at the start of the manuscript names 18 pigments: white lead, coal black, lamp black, red lake, vermilion, brown red, yellow ochre, Dutch pink, massicot, umber (natural and burnt), ash blue, smalt, ultramarine, verditer, Cologne earth, minium, verdigris and indigo (Fels 2001: 147, f. 6). Later in the manuscript, the list extends to 33, adding to those above: ceruse, Lyons lake, common lake, Chinese lake, rosette, rust ochre, turquoise, green azure, blue azure, indigo, bister, ivory black, willow black, soot black and tournesol. This proves that while an artist may have selected a limited palette, the choice of pigments was extensive.

The de Mayerne manuscript describes using lamp black and ivory black in black drapery, silk, or satin (Fels 2001: 219, f. 88). Bone black was found in the black chasuble of Van Dyck's *Archbishop Laud.* Ivory black was found in dispersions taken from the grey trimming of the dress of Van Somer's *Queen of Bohemia* noting that the 'particles were markedly brown, indicating an incomplete charring of the bone' (Brett 2002: 9). A discussion with Mytens reveals how 'burnt stag horn ground with water on stone becomes brown as an earth or ochre. If you mix the same with oil on the palette there is a beautiful black like jet' (Fels 2001: 224, f. 93). A cross-section from the black costume in Van Somer's *Countess of Kent* showed the presence of carbon black.

De Mayerne describes how to make purple 'with smalt and lake for the darkest parts; so that it dries, a little drying oil prepared with lead monoxide is added' (Fels 2001: 152, f. 8). A purple of this composition is found in Mytens' *Charles I* (Fig. 14) with smalt that is now discoloured. However, in Mytens' *Prince of Wales*, the purple costume has been economically set down with a single layer of almost black purple made from red lake, lead white and carbon black (Fig. 15).[11] Perhaps artists were unwilling to

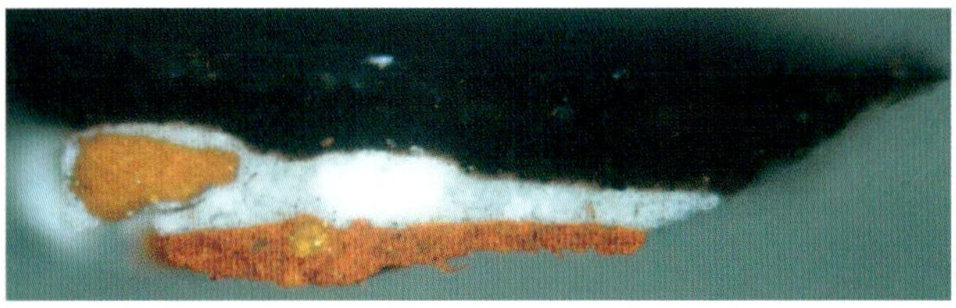

Figure 14 *Mytens,* Prince of Wales*: cross-section from the purple trouser leg showing how smalt was used to make purple (now discoloured).*

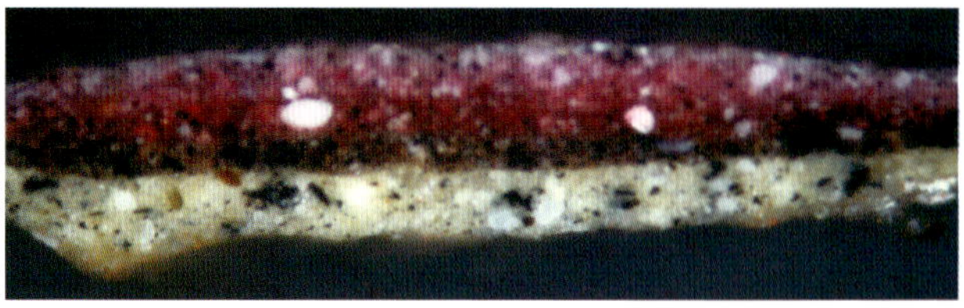

Figure 15 *Mytens,* Prince of Wales*: cross-section from a highlight of the purple robe showing that blue pigment has not been used to achieve purple.*

admit to de Mayerne that they sometimes omitted blue when mixing purple, as it is not commented on in the manuscript.

Paint media

De Mayerne offers vast amounts of advice regarding media, such as the best oil to use, different methods of preparation, and suggestions for siccatives. De Mayerne records a discussion with Van Dyck stating that 'linseed oil is the best of all; it is superior to nut oil, which is much greasier, and poppy seed oil which becomes so and thickens easily' (Fels 2001: 260, f. 152). On heat bodying, Mytens says, 'the more the oil is heated the better it is refined and much more suited for mixing with paints' (Fels 2001: 161, f. 16). Medium analysis was not carried out on any of the portraits examined in this study.

However, the conservation report from Mytens' *Prince of Wales* suggests that the majority of the paint passages are linseed oil, but the blue sash has a different texture which may indicate the use of a different medium (Stonor *et al.* 2002: 10). De Mayerne recorded a discussion on blues and greens with Van Dyck who often applied these colours 'with gum water, and after they were dry spread varnish over them', adding that 'the secret is to make the colours stick to the oily undercoat by rubbing in garlic or onion juice' (Fels 2001: 260, f. 153). This technique may have been used in this portrait by Mytens, which would explain the unusual texture.

Driers and extenders

De Mayerne records the drying times of different oils and paints: 'linseed oil simmered with vitriol calcinated dries punctually in 2 to 3 hours' and 'umber dries in 2 hours in the summer, lead white in 2 to 3 days' (Fels 2001: 165, f. 20; 222, f. 91). He mentions pigments with drying difficulties:

> The difficulty of drying pertains to lake and all sorts of black. Lake dries with zinc vitriol. Ivory black with verdigris. Soot black with umber earth. [Marginal note] Zinc vitriol and verdigris should only be mixed with the paints as needed and not when ground. (Fels 2001:88, f. 88)

The conservation record from Van Somer's *Countess of Kent* specifically identified verdigris as a drier (Stonor *et al.* 2003: 12). Verdigris was also found in Mytens' *Prince of Wales* and, because there are no green passages in this painting, it was probably included as a drier.

A sample from the brown underlayer of the curtain in Van Dyck's *Archbishop Laud* contains brown and yellow ochre, umber, a little bone black, some chalk and some lead white. The umber may have been included as a drier for this dead colour. In addition, the presence of potassium, sodium and cobalt from a similar area in the curtain suggests the addition of glass as a drier. A pigment dispersion from an area of the costume containing red lakes in Van Somer's *Queen of Bohemia* showed isotropic shards of ground glass, presumably added as a drier. De Mayerne mentions the use of glass in a recipe for the preparation of a desiccating linseed and poppy seed oil:

> Add a little umber, enough to make the oil rise two fingers above the umber, simmer until the oil thickens to a syrup and turns brown, and use it that way. Lead monoxide serves the same purpose as lacquer, but Venetian glass is best ... [Poppy seed oil] does not dry easily itself, but it is ground with Venetian glass. (Fels 2001: 215, f. 84; 165, f. 20)

Another additive identified in paint passages in the portraits, but not discussed in the manuscript is chalk.[12] This was detected in Van Somer's *Countess of Kent* and *Queen of Bohemia* used in the glazes 'to give body to paint' and 'to make greater impasto possible' (Brett 2002: 9). Chalk was also found in cross-sections in both Mytens' *Charles I* and *Prince of Wales,* and Van Dyck's *Archbishop Laud.*

Conclusion

It has been demonstrated that the entries concerning painting materials and techniques from the de Mayerne manuscript examined in this study have all appeared somewhere in the technical evidence from just five contemporaneous paintings. The painting demonstrating the most de Mayerne characteristics was Mytens' *Charles I*; the double ground with bright red lower layer examined in cross-section is just as the manuscript describes, and there is evidence of underdrawing also mentioned in the manuscript. The paint layers are consistent with the layering described by de Mayerne, from the dead layer (in this case grey) in the red curtain, followed by an opaque red layer modelled with glazes, and even the admixture used for purple is consistent with de Mayerne. However, as with all written sources on painting technique, no definitive authority on painting technique and materials from one particular period exists. Deviations from the manuscript were also discovered, such as a double ground used with a pale lower layer, and the alternative admixture for purple. The presence of chalk as an extender was widespread and yet not discussed in the manuscript.

Although limited, this study has shown that the parallels drawn between the paintings and the text reveal the de Mayerne manuscript to be a reliable source. It is further acknowledgement of how technical analyses of paintings can be combined with contemporary sources in order to advance our understanding of artists' materials and techniques in context.

Acknowledgements

Thanks are due to Renate Woudhuysen-Keller, Spike Bucklow and Ian McClure for their support and advice during writing this study as a student. I am also grateful to the authors of the comprehensive conservation reports that were used: Simon Bobak, Helen Brett, Karen Groen, Ann Massing, Ian McClure, Kate Stonor, Anna Sanden, Marie Louise Sauerberg and Renate Woudhuysen-Keller. Without their attention to detail and technical analyses this study would not have been possible.

Notes

1. These include painters, engravers, miniaturists, apothecaries, goldsmiths and furniture makers. He also referred to printed sources such as artists' and manufacturers' manuals, and works by other physicians and botanists. His sources were mostly Dutch, Flemish or French Huguenot immigrants to London. See Fels 2001: 333–8; Trevor-Roper 1993: 264–93; Talley 1981.
2. He initially practised medicine in Paris with the *premier médecin* to Henry IV. He was offered the post of *premier médecin* by Henry IV in 1609, but de Mayerne accepted an offer from James I of England instead. After his death in 1655 de Mayerne's papers were handed down through a succession of physicians and in 1753 his medical works were published.
3. While his main focus is painting technique, entries also exist on illuminating, engraving, etching, gilding, paper production and even the odd stray medical note.
4. A note about the manuscript was published by Charles Eastlake in his *Materials for the History of Oil Painting*, later republished as the *Methods and Materials of Painting of the Great Schools and Masters* (Eastlake 1960: 546–8). The first transcription appeared in 1902 by the German painter Ernst Berger, reproducing the disorderly format of the original. The Dutch scholar J.A. van de Graaf published his thesis on the de Mayerne manuscript in 1958 and, in an attempt to make the treatise more coherent, added an appendix on oil painting and arranged the stages of production into support, priming, pigments, oil and varnish. The 2001 translation is by Donald Fels Jr.
5. This choice relates to procedures that were mentioned both in the manuscript and technical analyses of the paintings.
6. All were painted within the dates the manuscript was compiled. De Mayerne also gives a large amount of advice on painting landscapes, but the technical evidence available at the HKI favoured portraiture.
7. Van Somer arrived in London from Antwerp in 1616. He and de Mayerne were connected through the court and they were also neighbours on St Martin's Lane. On Van Somer's death 1621, Mytens succeeded as court portrait painter to James I, and Charles I appointed him 'picture-drawer' in 1625. His royal patronage continued until 1634. Van Dyck arrived from Antwerp in 1623 and became the next court painter, after Charles noticed his portrait of Lanier (Master of the King's Music and responsible for acquisitions to the Royal Collection). De Mayerne was friends with Lanier, and through him relations were facilitated between Van Dyck and de Mayerne.
8. De Mayerne is more preoccupied with the colours used in the ground rather than binding medium, and most entries describe the pigments 'ground in oil'; Fels 2001: 155, 217, 221, ff. 11, 87, 221. It should also be mentioned here that de Mayerne describes a different method for preparing panels using chalk (ff. 11, 90).
9. Entries also exist on illuminating, engraving, etching, gilding, paper production and even the odd stray medical note.
10. Lead white, chalk, carbon black, vermilion, red lead, red earth, red lake (madder), yellow earth, umber, verdigris, lead tin yellow; Stonor *et al.* 2003: 12.
11. Stonor *et al.* 2002: 9. This pigment mixture has also been detected in Rubens' *Samson and Delilah* and Van Dyck's *Woman and Child* in the National Gallery, London, noted as quite rare; Plesters 1983: 45.
12. Ceruse is mentioned as a pigment in the de Mayerne manuscript that Berger translates as 'common white lead which receives the addition of chalk'; Fels 2001: 293.

References

Brett, H. 2002. 'Attributed to Paul van Somer called *Elizabeth, Queen of Bohemia* from Parham Park, Sussex, 1621'. Unpublished technical report, HKI 2088 (Hamilton Kerr Institute).

Eastlake, C. L. 1960 *Methods and Materials of Painting of the Great Schools and Masters*, vol. 1. New York: Dover Publications Inc. [1st edn 1847].

Fels, D. Jr. 2001. *Lost Secrets of Flemish Painting: Including the First Complete English Translation of the De Mayerne Manuscript. British Museum. B. M. MS. Sloane 2052.* Hillsville, VA: Alchemist.

Keller, R. and Groen, K. 1981. 'Van Dyck's *Archbishop Laud*, from the Fitzwilliam Museum, Cambridge, 1635'. Unpublished technical report, HKI 568 (Hamilton Kerr Institute).

Kirby, J. 1999. 'The painter's trade in the seventeenth century: theory and practice', *National Gallery Technical Bulletin* 20: 5–49.

Plesters, J, 1983. '*Samson and Delilah*: Rubens and the art and craft of painting on panel', *National Gallery Technical Bulletin* 7: 30–49.

Sauerberg, M.L. 1999. 'Daniel Mytens' *Charles I* from the Royal Collection, 1628'. Unpublished technical report, HKI 1945 (Hamilton Kerr Institute).

Stonor, K., McClure, I. and Massing, A. 2002. 'Daniel Mytens' *Charles I, as Prince of Wales* from Parham Park, Sussex, 1621'. Unpublished technical report, HKI 2087 (Hamilton Kerr Institute).

Stonor, K., Sanden, A., Bobak, S. and McClure, I. 2003. 'Paul van Somer's *Elizabeth Countess of Kent* from the Fitzwilliam Museum, Cambridge, 1621'. Unpublished technical report, HKI 2130 (Hamilton Kerr Institute).

Talley, M.K. 1981. *Portrait Painting in England: Studies in the Technical Literature before 1700.* London: Paul Mellon Centre for Studies in British Art.

Trevor-Roper, H. 1993. 'Mayerne and his manuscript'. In *Art and Patronage in the Caroline Courts*, D. Howarth (ed.) 264–93. Cambridge: Cambridge University Press.

FURTHER OBSERVATIONS ON COROT'S LATE PAINTING TECHNIQUE

Kate Stonor, Sarah Herring and Hayley Tomlinson

Introduction

In 1999, as part of the important publication *Barbizon: Malerei der Natur-Natur der Malerei*, Renate Woudhuysen-Keller published a technical study of two late paintings by Corot that she had treated at the Hamilton Kerr Institute (Woudhuysen-Keller 1999). The collection of paintings by Corot in the National Gallery, London, is currently being studied as part of the forthcoming catalogue of nineteenth-century paintings;[1] recent research has provided comparative information to complement Woudhuysen-Keller's study. This paper discusses the technical examination of three contemporary paintings by Corot in the National Gallery collection: NG 2625 *The Leaning Tree Trunk* (1860–65) (Fig. 1); NG 2626 *The Wood Gatherer* (1865–70) (Fig. 2) and NG 2630 *Cows in a Marshy Landscape* (*c.*1873) (Fig. 3). Through examination of the artist's materials and techniques it is possible to gain a better understanding of Corot's working method and the aesthetic results he hoped to achieve, helping to broaden our understanding not only of the artist but of nineteenth-century painting practices in general and the influence of commercially available artists' materials.

Corot's late style is markedly different from that of his early career. From the 1850s it became softer and subtler, using a restricted range of colours, emphasising instead tonal harmonies. His brushwork also changed; he often painted extremely thinly, leaving the underpaint and, at times, the ground visible. His late works are characterised by innumerable small touches of paint, particularly in the foliage, creating a shimmering effect. Throughout his life he followed a particular order of painting: 'a good method to follow: on your white canvas, begin with the strongest tone. Follow in order as far as the lightest tone. It is not logical to begin with the sky.'[2] However, in his late works his habitual reworking of the foliage and sky often results in areas of multiple paint layers and 'final' adjustments.

Corot also increasingly produced repetitions of compositions. In some cases these were reduced copies commissioned by collectors and dealers; in many others they were an amalgamation of locations and scenery, based on sketches made on the spot, memories, or other studio compositions, in which the initial scene could become increasingly diluted.

NG 2625 The Leaning Tree Trunk *(Robaut 1905: 1121)*

The right side of this picture is dominated by a dense mass of foliage and the gnarled trunk of a tree. Two single trunks stand out in the foreground, the one on the left reaching right across the picture. *The Leaning Tree Trunk* is very closely related to *The Bent Tree (Morning) (Ville d'Avray, Bouleau Pond)* (1860–65) (Robaut 1905: 1122, National Gallery of Victoria, Melbourne, Felton Bequest 338-2). The basic composition is shared by a large number of other paintings, of which one of the earliest in the series is *Ville d'Avray. Lake with the Leaning Tree Trunk* (1860–65) (Robaut 1905: 1497, Musée des Beaux-Arts, Reims, 907.19.66). The motif for the leaning branches Corot took from a drawing made in 1826 during his first trip to Italy, *Clump of Trees at Civita Castellana* (National Gallery of Art, Washington, DC, 1990.47.1) (Fig. 4). The Reims painting follows the disposition of the trees in the drawing almost exactly but by the time Corot painted NG 2625 and the Melbourne picture the single tree trunks have broken away to stand in front as two decorative and more stylised elements.[3] The general profusion of branches has also been eliminated in favour of a sparser scene.

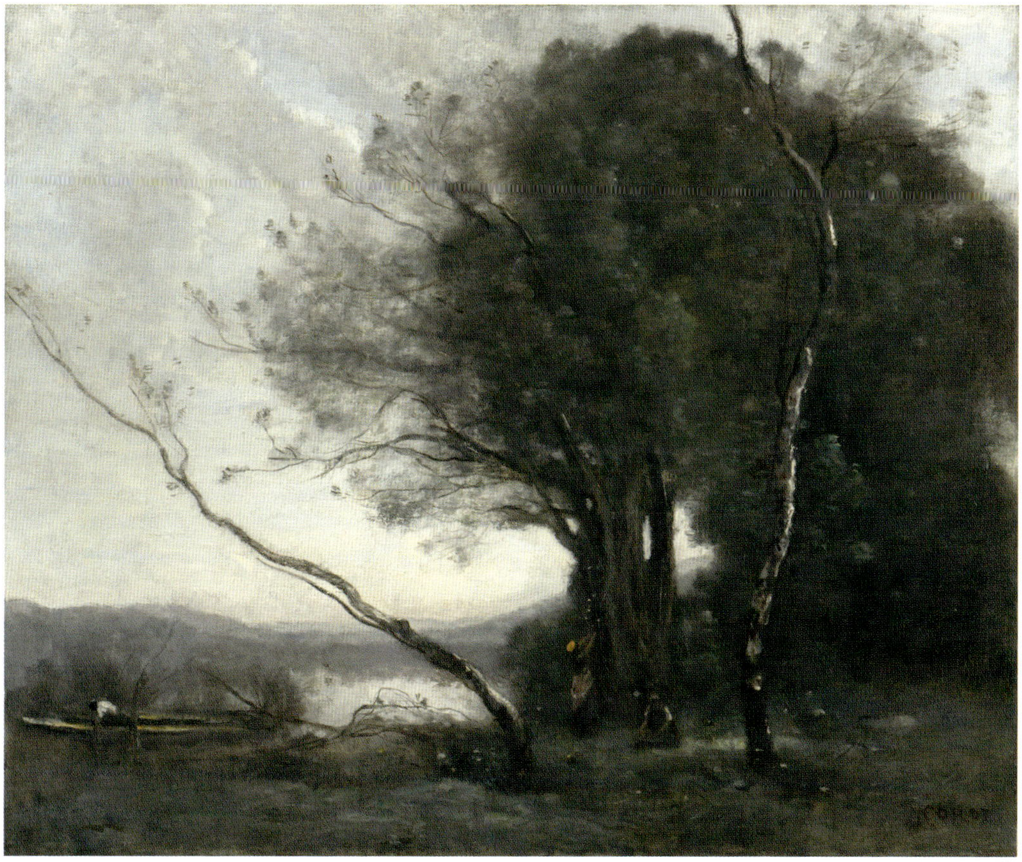

Figure 1 *Jean-Baptiste-Camille Corot,* The Leaning Tree Trunk, *about 1860–65, oil on canvas, lined, 49.7 × 60.7 cm (NG 2625). (© The National Gallery, London.)*

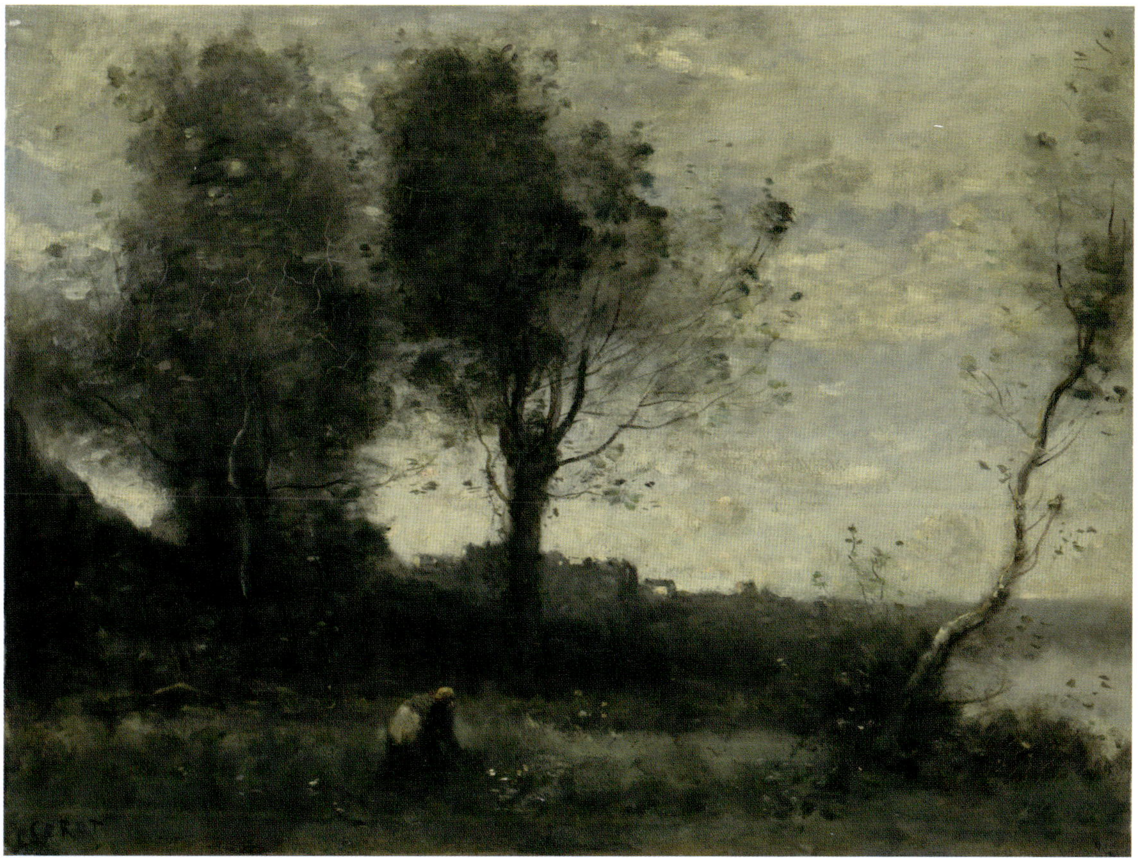

Figure 2 *Jean-Baptiste-Camille Corot,* The Wood Gatherer, *perhaps 1865–70, oil on canvas, lined, 45.7 × 64.1 cm (NG 2626). (© The National Gallery, London.)*

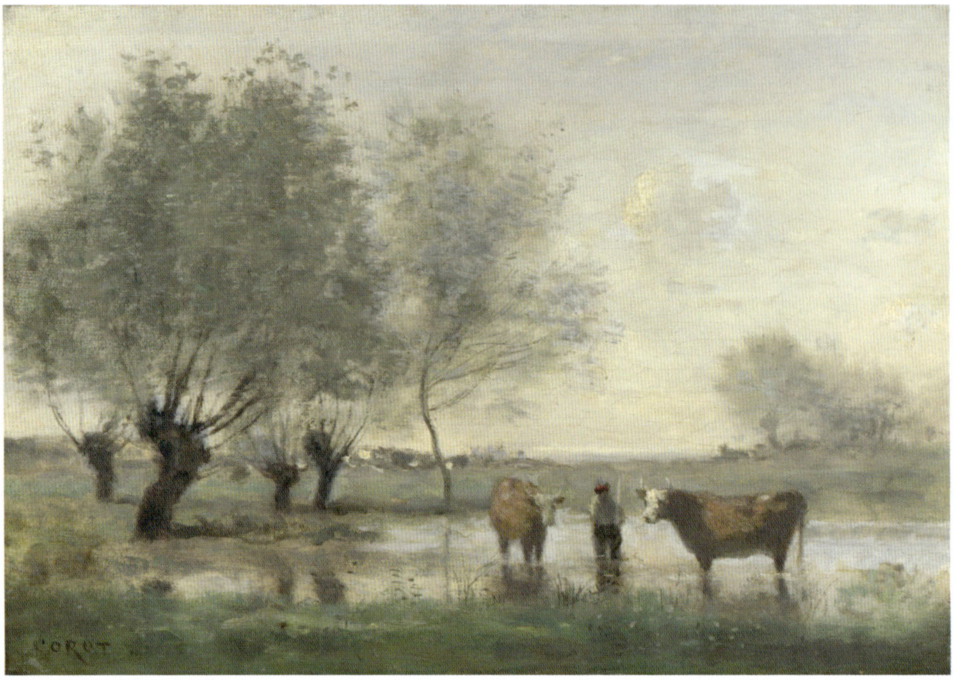

Figure 3 *Jean-Baptiste-Camille Corot,* Cows in a Marshy Landscape, *c.1873, oil on canvas, 24.1 × 34.9 cm (NG 2630). (© The National Gallery, London.)*

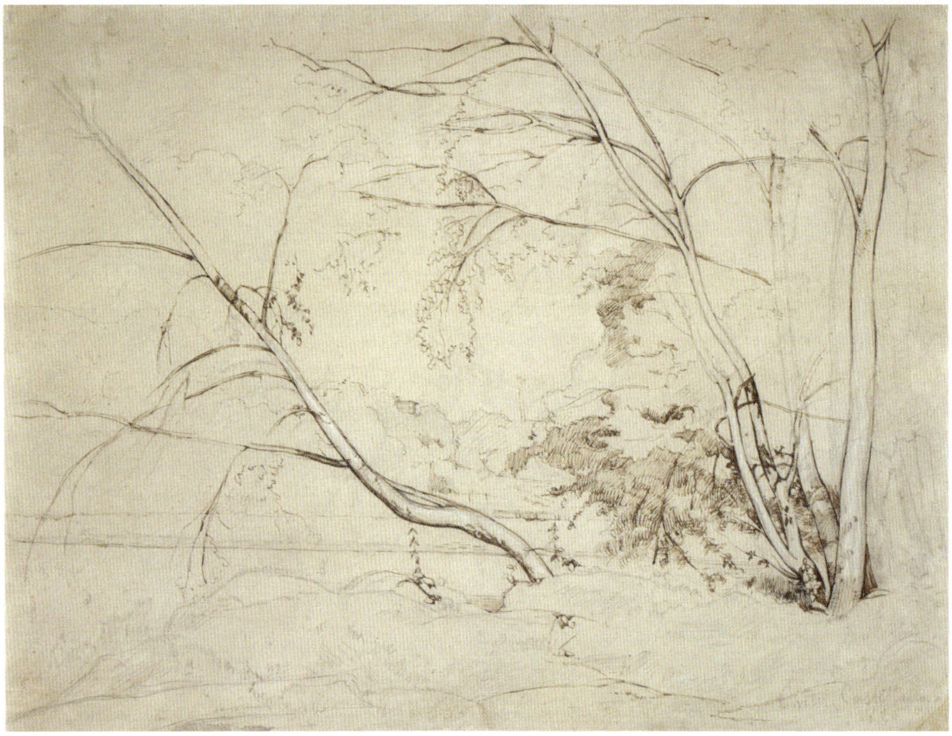

Figure 4 *Jean-Baptiste-Camille Corot,* Clump of Trees at Civita Castellana, *1826, pen and brown ink and graphite with white heightening on brown wove paper, 26.5 × 35.2 cm. (© National Gallery of Art, Washington DC (1990.47.1). Gift of Walter H. and Leonore Annenberg, in Honour of the 50th Anniversary of the National Gallery of Art.)*

NG 2626 The Wood Gatherer *(not in Robaut)*

In the foreground a figure, possibly a woman, stoops to gather wood. Two large trees behind her partly obscure a sunlit hilltop town, while to the right a single twisted trunk leans out over a misty lake. These features are common in Corot's late studio landscapes, and ultimately derive from scenery painted during his three visits to Italy in 1825–28, 1834 and 1843. In some versions the buildings are strongly individualised, as in *Paturage bordé de Saules (Vachère au Grand Bonnet)*, *c.*1855–65 (Robaut 1905: 1135, Cartwright Hall Art Gallery, Bradford), where the town in the distance is still quite highly developed and Italianate in feeling; a distinctive domed roof, towards the lake, is perhaps based on Bernini's church of St Thomas in Castel Gandolfo. In *The Wood Gatherer* they are more generic, but nevertheless given a touch of southern sun with strong touches of cream and rose-coloured paint.

NG 2630 Cows in a Marshy Landscape *(Robaut 1905: 1978)*

This silvery-grey landscape under an even light is typical of Corot's late work, as is the touch of red on the man's hat, often added by Corot as a bright and colourful accent in compositions otherwise built up of tonal values. Beyond the grassy plain, there is a suggestion of a village; a series of short strokes includes some touches of bright white and cream that indicate buildings caught by the sunlight. In the right background there are further buildings, this time in shadow. Although these structures are not specific enough to identify a location, the general composition can be compared with *Gisors, Paturages Marécageux* (private collection, Robaut 1905: 2157), painted in the open air in October 1873. NG 2630 shares features such as the water-logged landscape, cows, cowherd and, in the left foreground, the striking feature of the prominent willow with its distinctive twisted trunk. This painting could possibly be described as a pared-down version of the *Gisors* view, painted at a later date in the studio.

All three of the paintings under discussion are on canvas supports, executed in an oil medium. *The Leaning Tree Trunk* and *The Wood Gatherer* are both in excellent condition, though the latter has a considerably yellowed varnish.[4] The condition of *Cows in a Marshy Landscape* is not as good. Although thinly painted, it appears to be significantly abraded, particularly in the trees. The status of the chalky-looking white paint in the trees, water and parts of the sky is not entirely clear. Although not impossible that it represents late, rather clumsy artist's reworking, it could be strengthening overpaint applied by another hand.[5] The painting also has a slightly yellowed and ingrained varnish.

Supports and grounds

Like many of his Barbizon contemporaries, Corot appears to have used commercially prepared canvases. However, he showed no apparent loyalty to any one supplier as numerous canvas stamps have been found on his works. Of the paintings in this study the only unlined canvas, *Cows in A Marshy Landscape* (*c.*1873) was found to have a stamp from Cadart et Luquet at 79 Rue de Richelieu, Paris (Fig. 5). On stylistic grounds, the painting is dated later than the period (1863–67) in which Cadart et Luquet occupied this address, and it seems likely that the canvas sat in Corot's studio for some time before he painted it.[6] This seems a reasonable assumption given that the artist occupied the same studio for a great number of years and was financially

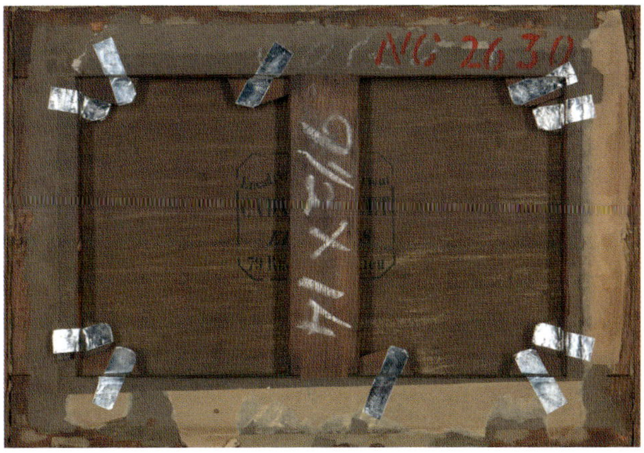

Figure 5 *Corot,* Cows in a Marshy Landscape *(NG 2630): reverse showing canvas stamp. (© The National Gallery, London.)*

independent. A canvas stamp from Jérome Ottoz, 22 rue Labruyère, Paris, has been observed on the reverse of another National Gallery Corot painting dated to 1871.[7] Other artists' suppliers linked to Corot include Maison Belot,[8] Colcomb-Bourgeois, for whom he was said to have been a 'valued customer' (Constantin 2001: 49), and Ange Ottoz. Woudhuysen-Keller's study identified an Ange Ottoz stamp, dating from 1857 to 1860, on the reverse of *Danse des Nymphes* (1860–65) (Woudhuysen-Keller 1999: 195), again possibly indicating an elapse of time between the purchase and painting of the canvas. In addition to artists' suppliers, stamps for Beugniet (Constantin 2001: 51), a dealer and restorer, Tempelaere, also dealers, and Detrimont have been found on works by Corot.[9]

The three National Gallery paintings are all small works on canvas and relate to standard sizes that could be bought ready-stretched from an artists' supplier. With reference to canvas sizes given in the catalogue of the Bourgeois Aîné company (one of the largest producers of artists' materials in Paris), *The Leaning Tree Trunk* measures 497 × 607 mm and closely matches portrait (*figure*) format No. 12; *Cows in a Marshy Landscape* is 244 × 353 mm and corresponds to a landscape (*paysage*) format No. 5; *The Wood Gatherer* at 480 × 651 mm relates to a landscape No. 15.[10] Though Corot clearly preferred a small and more intimate format for his paintings, no obvious pattern was observed regarding his choice of supports, even when taking into account the entire collection of works by Corot at the National Gallery.

The canvases had a thread count ranging from relatively coarse for *The Wood Gatherer* (12 × 12 threads per cm^2) through the fine plain weave of *The Leaning Tree Trunk* (23.5 × 23 per cm^2) to the very fine plain twill fabric of *Cows in a Marshy Landscape* (26 × 39 threads per cm^2).[11] The fine canvas used on *The Leaning Tree Trunk* is close to that used on *Danse des Nymphes*, which was purchased from Ange Ottoz and had a thread count of 22 × 22cm^2, whilst *Cows in a Marshy Landscape* is even finer with a count more equivalent to the very fine and densely woven canvas of *Les Evaux*, which measured 34 × 28 threads per cm^2 (Woudhuysen-Keller 1999: 194, 192). Certainly,

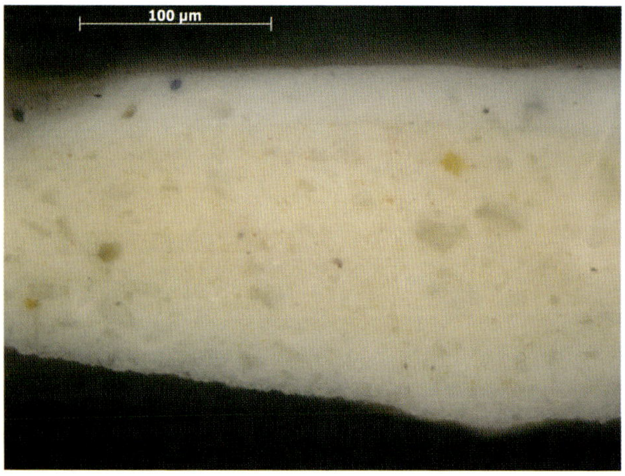

Figure 6 *Corot,* Cows in a Marshy Landscape *(NG 2630): cross-section from the cobalt blue containing sky showing the thick commercial priming layer composed of lead white, barium sulphate, calcium carbonate and yellow ochre. (© The National Gallery, London.)*

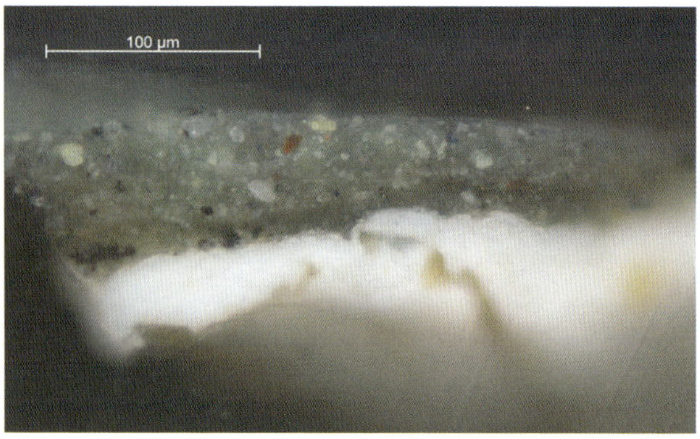

Figure 7 *Corot,* The Leaning Tree Trunk *(NG 2625): cross-section from the mid-green foreground showing the thin off-white ground composed predominantly of lead white with a thin overlying ébauche layer. The green paint is composed of a complex mixture of lead white, Naples yellow, yellow lake, French ultramarine, red earth, bone black, cobalt blue, cadmium yellow and vermilion possibly with a little Prussian blue. (© The National Gallery, London.)*

as observed by Woudhuysen-Keller, Corot appears to select fine canvases[12] and the difference in fabric across the three National Gallery paintings may account, in part, for the different primings subsequently employed.

The very fine canvas, *Cows in a Marshy Landscape*, has a single layer of off-white priming composed of lead white with silicates, barium sulphate and calcium carbonate extenders and a little yellow ochre (Fig. 6).[13] The priming extends onto the tacking margins and, together with the canvas stamp, strongly suggests a commercial application. By contrast, the thinly applied white priming on the fine canvas, *The Leaning Tree Trunk*, appears to have been applied by the artist. Cusping is evident in the X-radiograph and the priming does not extend onto the tacking edges, which have been partially preserved even though the painting has been lined. This 'artist's priming' is much simpler in its composition and consists of almost 'pure' lead white with a little yellow ochre and a trace of aluminium silicates, possibly associated with the ochre (Fig. 7).

The coarser canvas of *The Wood Gatherer* is much more complicated as it has a triple priming layer (Fig. 8). The first two layers are broadly similar in composition and appear to be a commercial 'double ground' as, although the tacking edges were removed when the painting was lined, there is nothing to suggest that the format has been reduced and no cusping is present in the X-radiograph. Like *Cows in a Marshy Landscape*, these layers are composed of lead white with barium sulphate and a little yellow earth. The lower layer also contains a considerable amount of calcium carbonate, while the upper layer does not appear to contain calcium carbonate but has a slightly higher proportion of barium sulphate and a little silica. Double grounds are commonly found on nineteenth-century paintings, where a layer pigmented with cheaper pigments – such as calcium carbonate and barium sulphate – is used to fill canvas weave followed by a lead-white dense layer that creates a smooth, opaque white surface for painting. Colour merchants' catalogues of the period commonly sold ready-made canvases either *à grain*, with a single application of ground leaving a rough/grainy texture, or *lisse* which denoted a double application and produced a smoother surface (Callen 2000: 37). Over the 'double ground' on *The Wood Gatherer*, an additional thin white priming composed of lead white with only a little barium sulphate, trace of earth and black has been applied. Again, the absence of a high proportion of extenders, as seen in *The Leaning Tree Trunk*, suggests an artist's application for this layer. So, perhaps due to the coarser canvas weave of *The Wood Gatherer*, Corot decided that an additional priming layer was necessary to give a smoother surface on which to paint. Consequently, the thick multilayered ground is rather rigid and inflexible and has undoubtedly contributed to the development of age craquelure.[14]

Almost all the paintings by Corot in the National Gallery collection are painted on a white or off-white ground. This appears to reflect the general taste of Barbizon artists in the works studied for the forthcoming catalogue, where white or off-white primings are by far the majority with only a few supports primed with grey, brown, beige or peach coloured grounds. As shown by this small sample, the use of barium sulphate in ground layers on French nineteenth-century paintings is common. A general survey of paintings from this period in the National Gallery collection shows that grounds from the first half of the century tend to be composed of lead white mixed with calcium carbonate but that mixtures of lead white and barium sulphate begin to appear in the 1840s. Barium sulphate in grounds is taken up more particularly after the mid-century until it seems common during the 1870s, overtaking calcium carbonate as an additive.[15] However, calcium carbonate can sometimes be found mixed with barium sulphate, as is the case with *Cows in a Marshy Landscape* and *The Wood Gatherer*, and other extenders (such as silicates) have also been identified. Adding barium sulphate was said to make the priming smoother

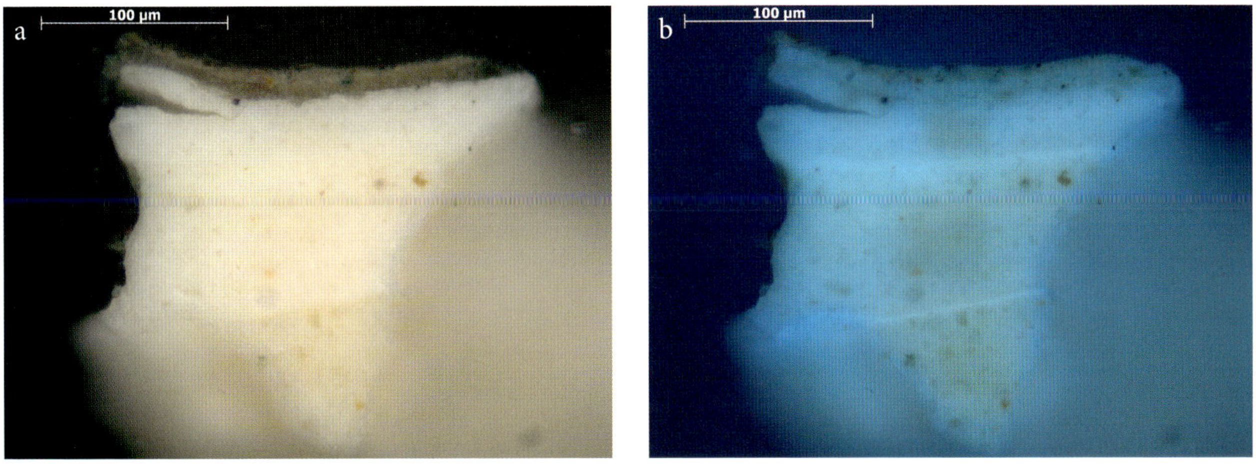

Figure 8 *Corot,* The Wood Gatherer *(NG 2626): cross-section from the brown-green foreground showing the complex 'triple' ground in both (a) normal and (b) ultraviolet light. (© The National Gallery, London.)*

and brighter, giving a slightly more matt and absorbent surface to work on (Rioux and Pomarède 1998: 122) and may reflect a change in taste as well as the availability of new materials over time. It is also interesting to note that there was no obvious consistency between the primings of canvases bearing the same canvas stamp but this is not unexpected given that a variety of primings was available on the ready-made canvases offered by colour merchants.[16]

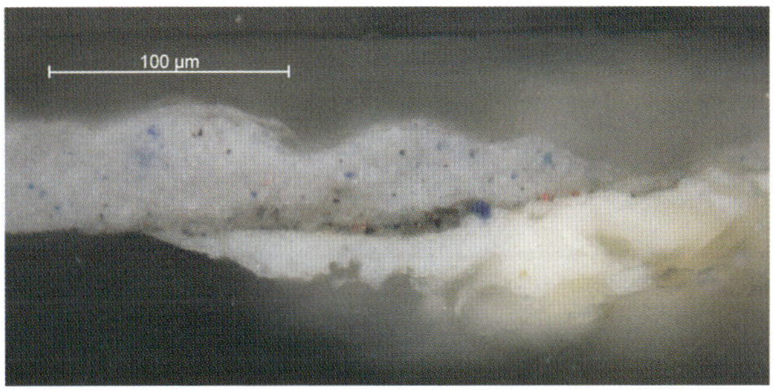

Figure 9 *Corot,* The Wood Gatherer *(NG 2625): cross-section taken from the grey-mauve distant hills showing the* ébauche *layer going over the off-white ground. The pale blue paint is composed of lead white with French ultramarine, fine and intensely coloured cobalt blue and a particle of greenish cerulean blue, bone black and a little vermilion. A particularly intensely coloured cobalt blue particle can be seen incorporated into the grey* ébauche *layer. This gave a peak for nickel when analysed by SEM-EDX. (© The National Gallery, London.)*

Technique

All three paintings were examined using infrared photography or reflectography but no evidence of any underdrawing was detected.[17] Woudhuysen-Keller similarly reports on the apparent absence of preliminary drawing on *Danse des nymphes* (1860–65) (Woudhuysen-Keller 1999: 195). According to Robaut's account, Corot did most of his underdrawing in white chalk, only turning to pencil for the finer details (Roquebert 1998: 82–3). Certainly, underdrawing in white chalk would not be detected by infrared, but it seems an unlikely material to employ over white priming. Traces of carbon-based underdrawing have been identified on two of the paintings previously examined at the National Gallery, both of which date from much earlier in the artist's career: NG 3285 *The Roman Campagna, with the Claudian Aqueduct* (*c.*1826) and NG 6439 *Peasants under the Trees at Dawn* (*c.*1840–45) (Herring 2009: 88 and 95 respectively); also in other works from the 1830s (Roquebert 1998: 84) indicating, perhaps, that Corot changed his methods in later life. However, he undoubtedly did plan his compositions and, in line with academic practice, usually began with a monochrome *ébauche* (initial painted lay-in) in which the principal forms would be set down.[18] A thin black/brown layer is visible over the priming in three of the cross-sections taken from *The Leaning Tree Trunk*, indicating the use of a wash-like laying-in paint in the landscape, composed of bone or ivory black and earth pigments (Figs 7 and 9).[19] Since there is no such layer under the sky, it supports the presence of an *ébauche* rather than a wholescale toning layer applied to adjust the colour of the priming. In *Cows in a Marshy Landscape*, the most thinly

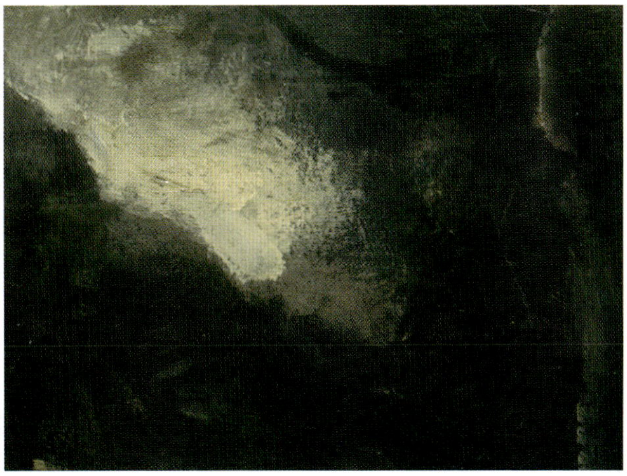

Figure 10 *Corot,* The Wood Gatherer *(NG 2626): detail showing exposed area of mushroom-coloured paint used for the* ébauche *visible to the left of the tree. (© The National Gallery, London.)*

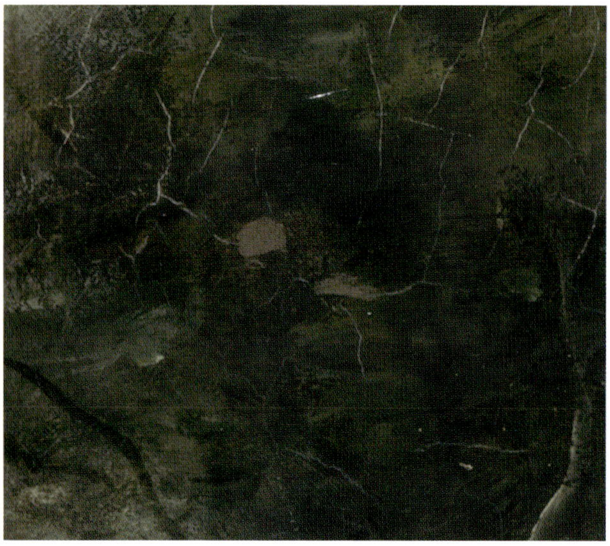

Figure 11 *Corot,* The Wood Gatherer *(NG 2626): detail showing mushroom-coloured paint used as a final highlight in the tree at the left. (© The National Gallery, London.)*

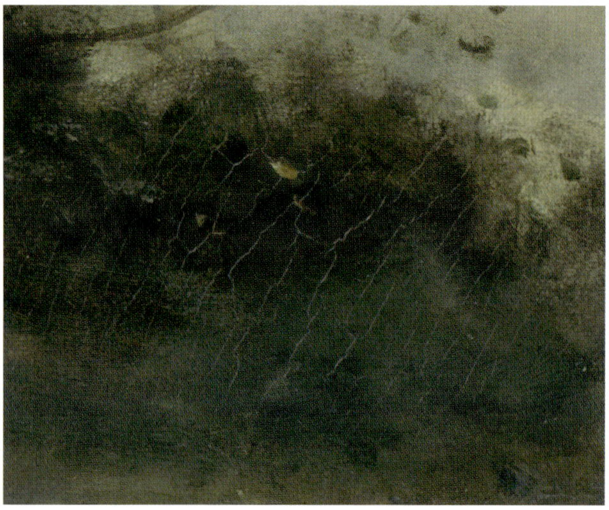

Figure 12 *Corot,* The Wood Gatherer *(NG 2626): detail showing 'scrubby' paint application. (© The National Gallery, London.)*

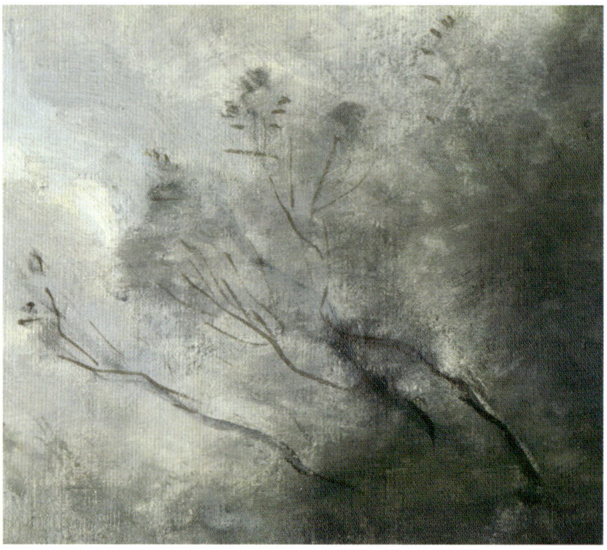

Figure 13 *Corot,* The Leaning Tree Trunk *(NG 2625): detail showing the boundary between tree and sky. (© The National Gallery, London.)*

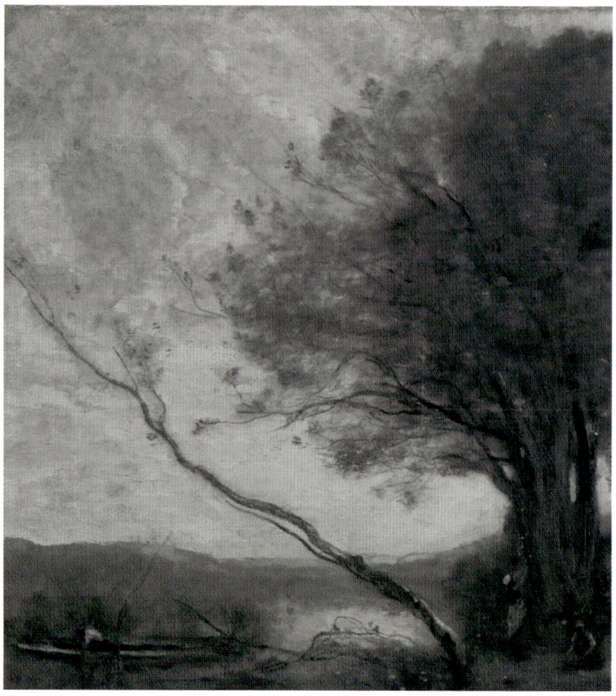

Figure 14 *Corot,* The Leaning Tree Trunk *(NG 2625): detail from infrared photograph. (© The National Gallery, London.)*

painted of the three works, there is a minimal *ébauche*: a very thin and muted grey/green under the trees and grass. In *The Wood Gatherer* there is evidence of a beige and mushroom-coloured underpaint beneath the landscape, left visible to the left of the tree (Fig. 10). Although Corot seems to have followed academic practice in the use of an *ébauche*, he was not linear or rigorous in his working methods. In particular, it is interesting to note how the warm mushroom colour used first for the *ébauche* is later employed on top of the tree, at the highlight stage (Fig. 11). Corot himself acknowledged this feature of his painting practice: 'I'm never in a hurry to arrive at the detail … I keep going back without cease, without being stopped by anything and without a system'.[20]

The succeeding paint layers are relatively thin and this is particularly true of *Cows in a Marshy Landscape* where the priming shows through in many places. Paint tends to be applied either in long, smooth strokes or in a dry, somewhat 'scrubby' fashion (Fig. 12). It is only the uppermost layers and highlights which are applied in the short 'stabby' touches that give the shimmering effect so often associated with Corot.[21] The pigment mixtures used for these paint layers are rather complicated and, unsurprisingly, the resultant colours somewhat muted. As mentioned above, both the thin application of paint and preference for muted tones are typical of Corot's style in the 1860s and 1870s, as is the artist's use of small dashes of pure, bright cadmium orange (or bright red in the case of *Cows in a Marshy Landscape*) to effect a contrast.

Although there was an undeniable change in Corot's brushwork and use of colour from his early to late career, the order in which he built up his compositions remained remarkably consistent. He always painted his trees first

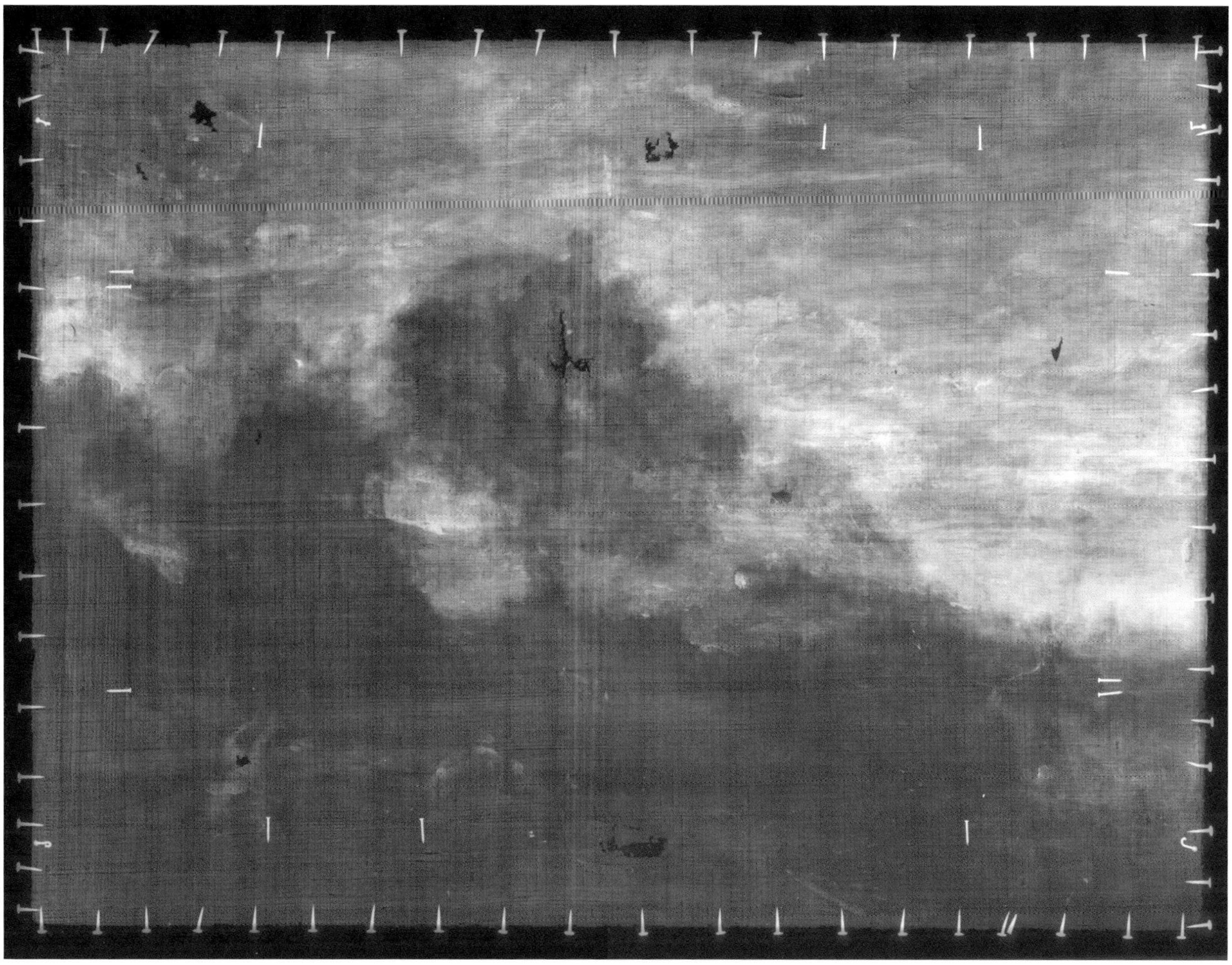

Figure 15 *Corot,* The Wood Gatherer *(NG 2626): X-radiograph mosaic, digitally image processed to lessen the influence of the stretcher bar. (© The National Gallery, London.)*

and the sky last, bringing the sky closely around the edge of the trees before adding extra branches and foliage on top, thus blurring the boundary (Fig. 13). However, as touched on previously, despite Corot's evident planning of his compositions, the artist did not work in a rigid fashion, and compositions were often not finalised until late in the painting process. Evidence of reworkings is found throughout his career, probably carried out later in the studio rather than in front of the motif (Roy 1999: 333). Herring describes the important modification to the design of the National Gallery's NG 3237 *Avignon from the West* (*c*.1836), and the numerous revisions made to NG 6439 *Peasants under the Trees at Dawn* (*c*.1840–45) (Herring 2009: 91–4, 95–6). Roquebert describes important *pentimenti* in several paintings from Corot's mid-to-late career (Roquebert 1998: 86–7). Likewise, Woudhuysen-Keller identified significant compositional changes to *Les Evaux* (1855–65) (Woudhuysen-Keller 1999: 193). In the case of *The Leaning Tree Trunk*, it is clear from the infrared photograph (Fig. 14) that Corot painted out branches of the central tree at a late stage to make the arrangement sparer.[22] The reworkings of *The Wood Gatherer*, however, are the most marked and have had significant implications

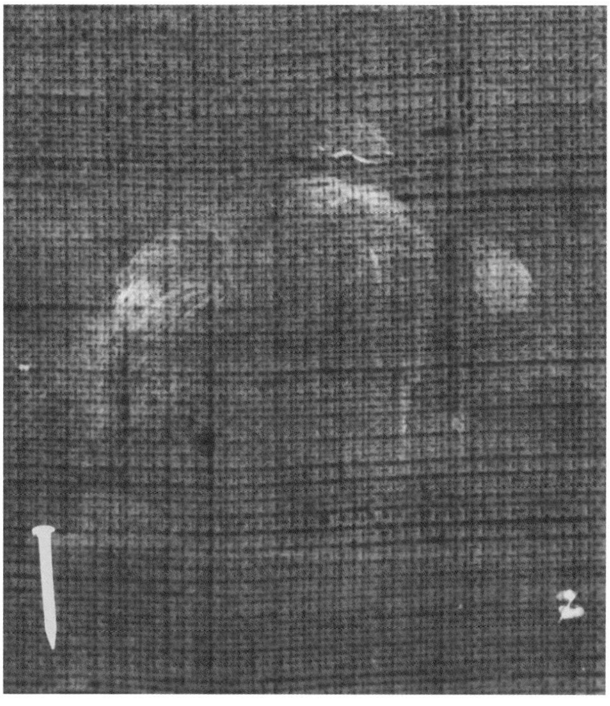

Figure 16 *Corot,* The Wood Gatherer *(NG 2626): X-radiograph detail showing two earlier positions of the bent figure's head. (© The National Gallery, London.)*

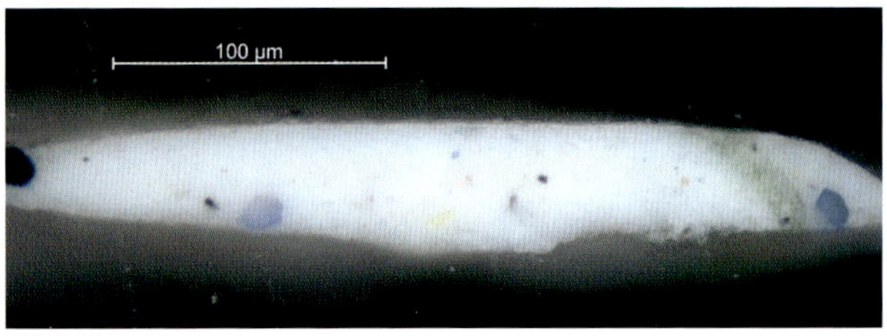

Figure 17 *Corot,* Cows in a Marshy Landscape *(NG 2630): sample taken from the water showing large, pale cobalt blue particles in a lead white matrix. (© The National Gallery, London.)*

for the painting's appearance. Although the X-radiograph reveals reserves left for the trees, the trees were originally intended to be much smaller, particularly that on the left (Fig. 15). Cross-sections reveal four or five layers of differently coloured paint on top of the priming (Fig. 19). Unsurprisingly, this has led to the formation of prominent drying craquelure, most obviously in the left-hand tree.[23] The figure of the wood gatherer has also undergone significant alterations: two additional positions for the bent figure's head are visible in the X-radiograph (Fig. 16).

There has been some debate as to whether Corot used glazes, a debate possibly complicated by the vulnerability of glazing layers to harsh cleaning procedures in the past. A glaze layer has been reported on *Concert champêtre*, begun in 1844 (Chantilly, Musée Condé) (de Wallens 2001: 685–6), and another tentatively identified on the National Gallery's NG 3816 *Monsieur Pivot on Horseback* (*c.*1853) (Herring 2009: 97). No glazes were identified on the paintings examined by Woudhuysen-Keller or on the three paintings that form the subject of the present study. Rather, Corot seems to employ quite medium-rich, translucent paint layers to create similar optical effects (Fig. 7).

Binding medium

Almost all of the paint passages analysed on works by Corot at the National Gallery were found to contain heat-bodied drying oils, whether linseed, walnut, poppy or a combination.[24] Small quantities of natural resins were also found to have been added to paints in a significant proportion of the samples and this could not always be explained by varnish contamination.[25] Heat bodying would have improved the drying properties of the paint, enabling a smooth glossy surface with fewer visible brushstrokes; the addition of a little resin would have improved the working properties and increased the transparency and gloss of the paint. The binding medium of a green paint sample taken from *The Leaning Tree Trunk* was identified as heat-bodied walnut oil, with small traces of pine resin and possible traces of dammar resin and it is interesting to note that pine resin quite often appears added to the greens in works by Corot. He may have simply added a little varnish to his tube paint but oil-resin mediums, such as *huile copal* and Haarlem siccative,[26] were also readily available from colour merchants and may have been used. Indeed, samples from the green foreground paint and the white sky of *Cows in a Marshy Landscape* both contained agathic acid in addition to heat-bodied linseed oil. This did not appear to be connected to a varnish layer and suggests the presence of some copal resin within the paint medium. These findings, indicating the inclusion of resinous media, seem to be supported by the examination of an 1855 palette in the Lucas collection at the Baltimore Museum of Art, where analysis of paints and a 'medium droplet' by gas chromatography-mass spectrometry (GC-MS) identified linseed oil with pine resin or colophony (Klein 1999: 182).

Palette

Corot's palette has been discussed elsewhere, with authors such as Burmester and Denk (1999), Roy (1999) and Herring (2009) noting the artist's early use of newly invented pigments such as emerald green, cobalt blue and, perhaps most notably, viridian.[27] The National Gallery's collection shows Corot's clear preference for the expensive cobalt blue when painting skies, something also observed by Woudhuysen-Keller, as well as his consistent use of the new cadmium orange and yellow pigments and French ultramarine.[28] Also, a little cerulean blue (cobalt stannate with associated magnesium) was identified mixed with lead white, cobalt blue, French ultramarine, a little bone black and vermilion in the distant hills of *The Wood Gatherer* (Fig. 9). Again, given that the pigment is thought to have been introduced in 1860 (Bomford *et al.* 1990: 211) and the painting is dated to about 1865–70 this is an early occurrence. Interestingly, two types of cobalt blue seem to have been employed on all three paintings. One is pale in colour with very high aluminium content (Fig. 17), the other is more intensely coloured with a lower proportion of aluminium relative to cobalt and a consistent trace of nickel (Fig. 9). Contemporary colour merchants' catalogues, such as Lefranc, appear only to list one type of cobalt blue but later documents, such as the Bourgeois catalogue, list both *bleu de cobalt* and *bleu de cobalt ordinaire* (1888: 82), whilst in 1885 Lechertier Barbe offer a *bleu de cobalt de Dresde* (1885: 56) indicating the possible availability of different grades or types of cobalt blue.

Corot shows a clear and consistent preference for bone black[29] and lead white.[30] *The Wood Gatherer* is one of the few paintings where a little charcoal black has been observed alongside ivory black in the sky. Zinc white has been identified on a number of paintings, including *The Wood Gatherer* and *The Leaning Tree Trunk*, but it is usually found in small amounts in association with Naples yellow, lead antimony oxide, and could be a manufacturer's addition to a ready-made tube mixture.

More traditional pigments are also employed by Corot: vermilion, red, yellow and orange ochres, brown earth, Prussian blue and red and yellow lake. The strongly

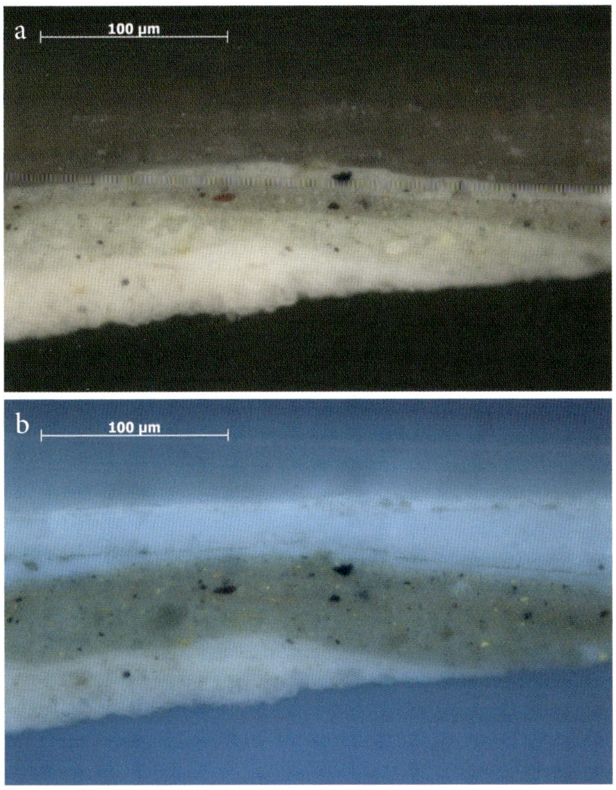

Figure 18 *Corot,* Cows in a Marshy Landscape *(NG 2630): cross-section taken from the green foreground shown in (a) normal and (b) ultraviolet light. The yellow lake pigment is barely visible in normal light but has two distinct fluorescences in ultraviolet light, where larger, rounded, warm yellow and more needle-like, bright yellow particles are visible in the green paint layers. Both particle types produced similar results with SEM-EDX analysis giving peaks for magnesium and calcium indicating Indian yellow. The lowest, pale green paint layer contains barium sulphate. (© The National Gallery, London.)*

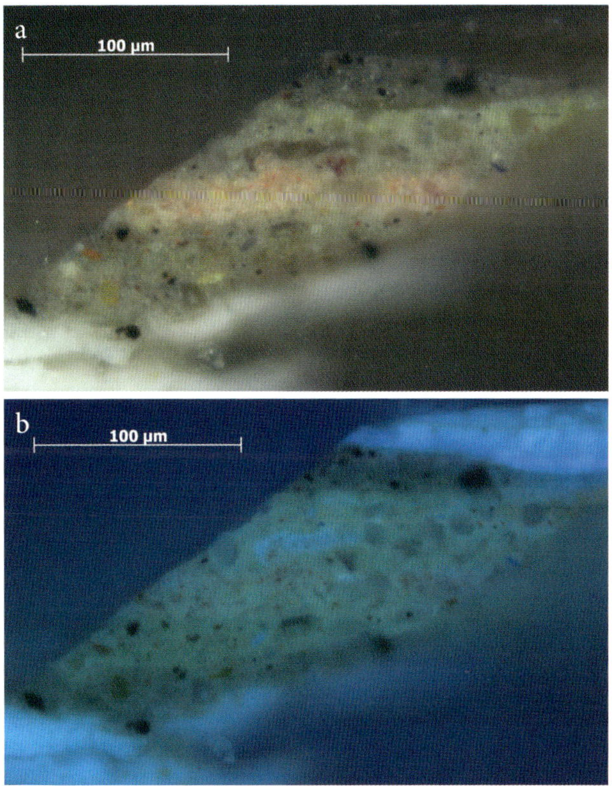

Figure 19 *Corot,* The Wood Gatherer *(NG 2626): cross-section taken from the edge of a large aperture drying crack in a grey-green tree shown in (a) normal and (b) ultraviolet light. The rounded, transparent starch particles present in the uppermost green layer can be seen more clearly in ultraviolet. Barium sulphate and silicates were also identified in the pinkish orange layer. The yellow, orpiment particle can be seen in the lowest paint layer at the right and is visually distinct from the pale Naples yellow particle at the left. (© The National Gallery, London.)*

coloured greens, such as viridian and emerald green, are usually tempered with other colours such as earths and lakes. In 1873 it was reported of Corot that:

> He doesn't use green or viridian … he prefers to mix his own [greens using] sienna earth and burnt sienna with cobalt or yellow ochre with Prussian or mineral blue, cadmium yellow with yellow lake and all the shades without premeditation or a formula worked out in advance.[31]

This certainly appears to be true of the samples taken from the three paintings examined for this study where greens are produced from exceedingly complex pigment mixtures, although emerald green was identified in some samples. As Woudhuysen-Keller has noted, Prussian blue is often found in conjunction with yellow pigments as a component of complex green mixtures. Although Woudhuysen-Keller found Prussian blue mixed with chrome yellow, in the paintings examined for this study it was more commonly found in mixtures with Naples yellow and yellow lake. It is notable that on his first trip to Italy (1825–28), Corot wrote to the colour merchant Colcomb-Bourgeois requesting good quality antimony yellow and Mars yellow (Constantin 2001: 52), perhaps showing a preference for the less 'acid' shades of yellow. He also states in a letter dated 1849:

> In my opinion cadmium and antimony (Naples yellow) are known to be good stable colours. I always have them. I am also happy with yellow lake. I am passionate for this colour, only I think that it is best for glazing. *Laque Robert*[32] is the most stable.[33]

Two types of yellow lake were identified in samples: one on an aluminium substrate and another with a distinct fluorescence in ultraviolet light suggesting Indian yellow (Fig. 18). Indian yellow has been identified on a number of Corot's paintings in the National Gallery and commonly two types of particle are visible with distinct appearances in UV light. Scanning electron microscopy with energy dispersive X-ray (SEM-EDX) analysis shows that they both contain calcium and magnesium, elements present in the salts of the xanthone compound euxanthic acid, which gives the pigment its colour (Eastaugh *et al.* 2004: 193), but often the warm coloured particles seem to contain relatively more calcium and the brighter particles relatively more magnesium. Indian yellow is listed in colour merchants' catalogues for the period as 'jaune indien', costing three times the price of Naples yellow.[34]

Interestingly, a Lefranc catalogue dated to 1858 lists four different grades of Indian yellow, suggesting some variation in the manufacturing process.[35]

Notably, a single particle of orpiment was identified in a sample taken from *The Wood Gatherer* (Fig. 19a).[36] This is unusual for this date when so many new yellows were available, but Harley states that good supplies of the mineral were imported from China during the early nineteenth century and the synthetic form, usually referred to as 'King's yellow', was readily available in the eighteenth century (Harley 2001: 94). The 1855 Lefranc catalogue lists English colours from Newman and Ackermann, including King's yellow (*Jaune du roi*), but these are probably intended for watercolour since they are sold by the *tablette*. The sampled pigment appears more consistent with a synthetic orpiment than the mineral form, but is anomalous as the only instance where it has been identified on a painting by Corot at the National Gallery.[37] It has, however, been tentatively identified in a brown paint on a palette attributed to Corot.[38]

Overall, Corot's paints were quite complex with single paint layers containing numerous different pigments; for example, three different blues could be found in a single paint passage[39] (Fig. 9) and up to nine differently coloured pigments in his muted greens (Fig. 7). In addition to these pigments several paint extenders were observed. Barium sulphate was identified in mixed greens, pinks (Fig. 19), pale blues and yellows, demonstrating its common addition to tube paints as well as grounds. This was something observed also by Woudhuysen-Keller, who identified barium sulphate mixed with lead white, French ultramarine and cobalt blue in the sky of *Les Evaux* (Woudhuysen-Keller 1999: 193). Small additions of calcium carbonate were identified in a warm yellow paint passage on *The Wood Gatherer* and silicates were also observed,[40] but barium sulphate was found more extensively. Starch grains were also present as an adulterant in the mixed green paint layers of *The Wood Gatherer* (Fig. 19b) – something that has been seen elsewhere on Corot paintings and is occasionally associated with Prussian blue paints.[41]

Conclusion

Comparison of the National Gallery's research with Woudhuysen-Keller's study has reinforced many consistencies in Corot's materials and techniques: his interest in new pigments, his preference for fine canvas supports, his frequent reworking of compositions and consistent order of painting. It has also highlighted the change of brushwork and preference for more muted colours based on complex pigment mixtures seen in his late career. In addition to the developments identified in Corot's work, broader trends in nineteenth-century France have been emphasised, such as artists' greater reliance on ready-made materials – for example, tube paints and primed canvases – and the increased use of barium sulphate in ground preparations and as a paint extender.

Acknowledgements

We would like to acknowledge Ashok Roy, David Bomford, John Leighton and Raymond White who worked on these paintings in the early phase of the cataloguing programme and, more recently, Rachel Grout, Catherine Higgitt, Christopher Riopelle and Anne Robbins. We are extremely grateful to Rachel Morrison who undertook medium analysis of the paintings examined for this study and helped to interpret previous results. We would also like to thank Rachel Billinge who kindly undertook infrared reflectography on some of the works and Larry Keith who offered his advice and support.

Notes

1. This paper represents research carried out for Volume I of the *Catalogue of Nineteenth-Century Paintings* which is due to be published in 2014.
2. Corot, Carnet 17, *c.*1855–60, Robaut 1905: 3054. Quoted in Roquebert 1998: 91.
3. For a full description of the relationship between the different versions and illustrations see the catalogue entry by Sarah Herring, published online, www.nationalgallery.org.uk.
4. *The Leaning Tree Trunk* was cleaned and restored at the National Gallery in 1980, the only one of the paintings to have been treated there since their arrival as part of the Salting bequest in 1910.
5. The 'chalky' white paint is applied over the varnish. It is thin and translucent and contains a high proportion of zinc white. This contrasts with Corot's usual preference for lead white, observed by Klein; see Klein 1999: 187.
6. Robaut describes his first visit to Corot's studio where he observed hundreds of pictures at different stages of painting stacked up against the walls. Quoted in Roquebert 1998: 76–7.
7. This stamp, dated between 1862 and 1870, was found on NG 2628 Corot's *A Wagon in the Plains* and also on NG 6416 *Seascape with Figures on a Cliff* by a follower of Corot.
8. A Maison Belot canvas stamp has been found on the back of a Corot painting; see Labreuche 2011: 233. Belot is listed in the Paris *Annuaire et Almanach du Commerce* until 1934 and it is interesting to note that Ange Ottoz was Belot's apprentice; see Constantin 2001: 51. See also Labreuche 2004.
9. A 'Detrimont' stamp from the period after 1868 when the business occupied the 27 Lafitte address was identified on NG 2135 Corot's *The Marsh at Arleux* (1871). 'Detrimont' is listed in the 1871–72 *Annuaire et Almanach du Commerce* under 'Tableaux (March. de)' but is not listed under 'couleurs', suggesting that they are dealers rather than suppliers of artists' materials. Roquebert, however, describes them as artists' suppliers and it could be that they fulfilled both functions; Roquebert 1998: 81.
10. Canvas sizes taken from the 'Toiles Pour Peinture A L'Huile Tendues Sur Chassis' table in the 1888 Bourgeois Aîné catalogue.
11. Callen states that twill, or *coutil*, fabrics were in use throughout the nineteenth century, with plain twill being the most common; Callen 2000: 32.
12. Roquebert (1998: 81) notes that Corot used increasingly fine canvases after about 1840 and particularly after 1865. Artists' suppliers sold canvases in a range of weave counts and qualities from coarse, cheap fabrics intended for studies referred to as *pochades* or *études* through *toile ordinaire* and *demi-fine* to *fine*. Other variants were also available such as *toile extra-fine* etc.; see Callen 2000: 31. It is difficult to know exactly which category these canvases fall into as weave counts can vary but it is likely that *The Wood Gatherer* is a *toile ordinaire*, *The Leaning Tree Trunk* is a *toile fine* and *Cows in a Marshy Landscape* an *extra-fine* or *très-fine*.
13. All pigments were identified using SEM-EDX.
14. This is rather different to the type of preparation Corot is said to have favoured since, according to Burty (cited in Roquebert 1998: 81), he preferred canvases that were 'souples et non couvertes de préparations quie les rendent parfois cassantes'.

15. This trend was also reflected in the study undertaken by C2RMF (formerly LRMF) in 1997; Rioux and Pomarède 1998.
16. As mentioned above NG 2628 and NG 6416 both have 'Jérome Ottoz' stamps. The former has a warm off-white/ biscuit-coloured ground composed of lead white and calcium carbonate with orange earth and a trace of aluminium silicates; the latter has an almost pure white ground containing lead white and barium sulphate with small additions of calcium carbonate and aluminium silicates.
17. Infrared reflectography was carried out using the OSIRIS digital infrared scanning camera with an indium gallium arsenide (InGaAs) sensor. Some paintings had been previously documented with infrared photography.
18. In fact, after Corot's death, mention is made of 'paintings at the *ébauche* stage or in the process of execution' in the inventory of his studio. Translated from 'tableaux ébauchés ou en cours d'exécution' in Roquebert 1998: 77–8.
19. The *ébauche* of *The Leaning Tree Trunk* is quite similar in appearance to the brown glaze-like underlayers or *sauce* recommended by academic practitioners; see Roy 1999: 332.
20. Translated from the French: 'Je ne suis jamais pressé d'arriver au detail … Je reviens sans cesse, sans être arête par rien et sans système.' In Robaut, quoting lines from a conversation between Corot and his friend Poitot; see Roquebert 1998: 84.
21. Woudhuysen-Keller suggests the presence of a very thin oiling-out layer before the application of the final highlights on *Les Evaux* and *Danse des nymphes*, which would have saturated the painting and enabled the artist to better judge the effect of the highlights (Woudhuysen-Keller 1999: 194–5). No corresponding layer was found on the three paintings examined for this study. An unpigmented layer has been identified in three samples from NG 3816 *Monsieur Pivot on Horseback* (*c*.1853). However, this was applied prior to a complete repainting of the canvas with a new composition (Herring 2009: 96–102).
22. The infrared photograph shows that the initial composition was closer to the earlier Reims painting, *Ville d'Avray: Lake with the Leaning Tree Trunk*, and may help to establish a chronology for these compositions.
23. The phenomenon of 'wrinkling paint and gaping traction craquelure' was also observed on the *St Sebastian* in Walters Art Gallery, Baltimore (USA) and was cited as a common occurrence on paintings reworked by Corot between 1851 and 1874; Klein 1999: 178. The white paint visible through the open aperture cracks in *The Wood Gatherer* is a generalised, lower layer very different to the localised lead white underpaint that Woudhuysen-Keller identified on *Les Evaux*; Woudhuysen-Keller 1999: 193.
24. Medium analysis was undertaken by Raymond White and Catherine Higgitt using GC-MS, often complemented with Fourier transform infrared spectroscopy (FTIR).
25. See Herring (2009: 87) including table by Ashok Roy and Rachel Morrison (110–11) for a discussion and full results. See also White *et al.* 1998: 90–91.
26. Probably a copal-type varnish heated and mixed with oil and a diluent such as turpentine; Reissner 2008: 10.
27. Viridian was identified on NG 3285 *The Roman Campagna, with a Claudian Aqueduct* dated to about 1826. This is the earliest recorded use of viridian; see Herring 2009: 90.
28. Pigment identification was carried out using SEM-EDX.
29. The term bone black has been used but analysis often indicated the presence of a small amount of magnesium alongside larger peaks for calcium and phosphorus in SEM-EDX suggesting ivory black.
30. The Corot palette found in the studio in Arras and preserved by Dutilleux (*c*.1855–58) was analysed by Benoit and found to contain two whites – a pure lead white and a lead white mixed with barium sulphate; Roquebert 1998: 89.
31. Broadly translated from the French: 'il n'emploie aucun vert ni émeraude; … il aime mieux les composer à sa manière, terre Sienne et brûlée avec cobalt ou ocre jaune avec du bleu de Prusse ou minéral, du jaune cadmium avec laque ocre et tous les tons y passent et sans premeditation ni formule arrêtée d'avance', Robaut 4° Y B3 949 II: 15. In Roquebert 1998: 90.
32. Eight different types of this are listed in the 1858 Lefranc catalogue; it is probably a red lake based on madder rather than a yellow lake (Jo Kirby-Atkinson, pers. comm.).
33. Broadly translated from the French: 'À mon avis le cadmium et l'antimoine sont des couleurs reputes bonnes et solides. J'en ai toujours. J'en suis content pour la laque jaune. Je suis passionné pour cette couleur, seulement je pense qu'elle est plus favourable au glacis. La laque Robert passé pour plus solide.' Letter from Corot to Constant Dutilleux, 14 January 1849 (Paris Bibliothèque Nationale de France, Cabinet des Estamps, Corot. Lettres à C. Dutilleux et à A. Robaut. Autographes, YB3 946 rés.) In de Wallens 2001: 685.
34. Prices come from Lefranc 1863 green catalogue (18); 1855 brown catalogue (15).
35. 'Jaune indien en nature, lavé surfin, lavé no. 1, lavé no. 2'. Lefranc yellow catalogue, 1858 (3).
36. SEM-EDX also gave minor peaks for antimony and aluminium as well as large peaks for arsenic and sulphur.
37. A single particle of orpiment was also identified in a blue layer from NG 4182 *Landscape*, Imitator of Courbet.
38. Corot's unused palette from the Lucas collection, Baltimore Museum of Art; Klein 1999: 183.
39. This might suggest a tube mixture since homogenous mixtures of cobalt blue and synthetic ultramarine have been found on other paintings by Corot; Roquebert 1998: 89.
40. Silicates were identified in earth-containing paints and may be associated with the pigment rather than a deliberate addition to the paint by the manufacturer.
41. Starch was found in a Prussian blue containing paint on NG 2135 Corot's *The Marsh at Arleux*.

References

Bomford, D., Kirby, J., Leighton, J. and Roy, A. 1990. *Art in the Making: Impressionism*. London: National Gallery and New Haven, CT: Yale University Press.

Burmester, A. and Denk, C. 1999. 'Blue, yellow and green on the Barbizon palette', *Zeitshrift für Kunsttechnologie und Konservierung* 13(1): 79–87.

Callen, A. 2000. *The Art of Impressionism: Painting Technique and the Making of Modernity*. New Haven, CT and London: Yale University Press.

Constantin, S. 2001. 'The Barbizon painters: a guide to their suppliers', *Studies in Conservation* 46(1): 49–67.

de Wallens, G. 2001. 'Corot as a copyist at the Louvre, and new evidence on his technique', *The Burlington Magazine* 153: 685–6.

Eastaugh, N., Walsh, V., Chaplin, T. *et al.* 2004. *Pigment Compendium: A Dictionary of Historical Pigments*. Amsterdam: Elsevier Butterworth-Heinemann.

Harley, R. 2001. *Artists' Pigments*. London: Archetype Publications.

Herring, S. 2009. 'Six paintings by Corot: methods, materials and sources', *National Gallery Technical Bulletin* 30: 86–111.

Klein, E. 1999. 'An investigation into the painting technique of the two versions of Corot's *St Sebastian Succoured by Holy Women*'. In *Barbizon: Malerei der Natur – Natur der Malerei*, A. Burmester, M.F. Zimmermann and C.H. Heilmann (eds) 178–91. Munich: Klinkhardt & Biermann.

Labreuche, P. 2004. 'Les fournisseurs parisiens des toiles et chassis des années 1800 à 1880: une étude à partir de peintures conserves au museée Condé', *Le Musée Condé* 61: 35–56.

Labreuche, P. 2011. *Paris, capitale de la toile à peindre XVIIIe–XIXe siècle* (L'art et l'essais 9). Paris: CTHS Editions.

Reissner, E. 2008. 'Ways of making: practice and innovation in Cézanne's paintings in the National Gallery', *National Gallery Technical Bulletin* 29: 4–30.

Rioux, J-P. and Pomarède, V. 1998. 'Les préparations au blanc de plomb en France au XIXe siècle: Jean-Baptiste Corot *Portrait de Claire Sennegon*', *Techne* 7: 121–4.

Robaut, A. 1905. *L'oeuvre de Corot. Catalogue raisonné et illustré, précédé de l'histoire de Corot et de ses œuvres par E. Moreau-Nélaton, ornée de dessins et croquis originaux du maître* (4 vols). Paris: Floury.

Roquebert, A. 1998. 'Quelques observations sur la technique de Corot'. In *Corot, un artiste et son temps. (Actes des colloques organisés au Musée du Louvre par le Service Culturel les 1er et 2 mars 1996 à Paris et par l'Académie de France à Rome, Villa Médicis, le 9 mars 1996 à Rome)* 73–97. Paris: Klincksieck.

Roy, A. 1999. 'Barbizon painters: tradition and innovation in artists' materials'. In *Barbizon: Malerei der Natur – Natur der Malerei*, A. Burmester, M.F. Zimmermann and C.H. Heilmann (eds) 330–42. Munich: Klinkhardt & Biermann.

White, R., Pilc, J. and Kirby, J. 1998. 'Analyses of paint media', *National Gallery Technical Bulletin* 19: 74–95.

Woudhuysen-Keller, R. 1999. 'Observations concerning Corot's late painting technique'. In *Barbizon: Malerei der Natur – Natur der Malerei*, A. Burmester, M.F. Zimmermann and C.H. Heilmann (eds) 192–200. Munich: Klinkhardt & Biermann.

SHOCKING A MOCK-UP: RECREATING THE DAMAGES AND HISTORICAL TREATMENTS FOUND IN EDVARD MUNCH'S MONUMENTAL AULA PAINTINGS TO TEST MATERIALS AND PROCEDURE FOR MAROUFLAGING A MAROUFLAGE

Karen Mengshoel, Mirjam Liu and Tine Frøysaker

Introduction

In 1916, Edvard Munch (1863–1944) produced his largest monumental, public paintings for the Festival Hall (the Aula) of Oslo University (UiO). The 11 works consist of 18 pieces of twill and tabby weave canvases, a white, water-sensitive ground (often left bare) followed by both lean and saturated oil colours with no varnish (Frøysaker 2007: 248–9). The paintings are located at the same level along three of the Aula walls and cover a total of *c.*220m^2. All formats have a height of *c.*4.5 m, but the widths vary from *c.*1.6 to 11.5 m.

From their completion to the present, the paintings have endured eight invasive campaigns/interventions. On three different occasions, the paintings were taken down from their niches by restorers and conservators: during 1925–26, in 1940 and in 2009. During the 1925–26 intervention the stretchers were replaced and a white, glue-bound priming layer was applied to the reverse of the paintings. In 1940, the paintings were cut down in haste, rolled and taken out of the Aula for safe-keeping during World War II (WWII), incurring a complete loss of their tacking edges in the process. After the war, the lack of canvas edges was compensated for through their first (semi-rigid) marouflage onto 4–6 mm thick sheets of Masonite, supported from the back by a wooden framework. The recent structural campaign by the Munch Aula Paintings Project (MAP)[1] entailed removal of the framework from 1945–46 and a second (rigid) marouflage onto honeycomb panels (Frøysaker *et al.* 2011a).

Prior to the reinstallation of the paintings in the Aula during the spring of 2011, and in preparation for the recent marouflage, several tests were performed including the making of a half-scale mock-up[2] of the planned laminate structure. Suggestions from other authors include trying out a 'dummy lining' to visualise all steps and modifications of materials and procedures (Mehra 1984: 32), or putting a dry-fit arrangement of the painting onto its new reverse-side sandwich layers before applying any vacuum, pressure or heat (Berger 2000: 93). Since no relevant literature on a double marouflage was found, empirical tests on a mock-up were even more important. The practical reconstructions were executed in a temporary studio in Oslo over the course of a couple of months between the surface cleaning treatment (2009) and structural conservation (2010) of the 11 large-scale canvases.

The main objective of the mock-up was to test the suitability of new materials and procedures for the second marouflage; however, it was also intended to imitate the paintings' canvas, glue size and ground, and their past treatment history.[3] In addition, the mock-up would provide the conservators with valuable experience for the pending structural treatment. Due to time constraints and the number of materials involved, two categories were established: first, the reconstructions of Munch's original materials, and the materials of the previous restorers, which would be representative and contemporary (though historical accuracy was of lesser importance, should this prove to be too demanding or time-consuming); secondly, the recipes, materials and procedures, which needed to be identical to those intended for the original paintings in order to verify their suitability for the treatment.

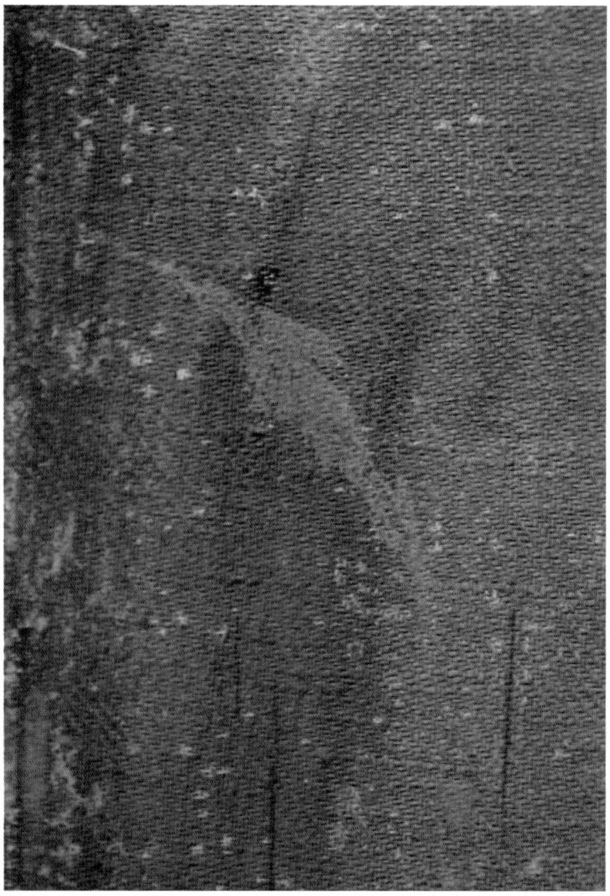

Figure 1 *The verso preparation, which has penetrated the canvas, is visible on the painting's surface as white spots. Residues of glue paste from the 1946 marouflage is visible as light brown splashes. (Photograph: Karen Mengshoel 2009.)*

Original materials and materials for the mock-up

Canvas

Although they are likely to all be linen canvases (Frøysaker 2008: 5), the original supports in the Aula paintings differ widely. They are of two different weave patterns, and the thread counts vary from *c.*7 × 7 threads per cm^2 in *History* to *c.*13.5 × 16.5 in one of the pieces in *Spirits in the Flood of Light*. The formats comprise one, two or three pieces of canvas.[4] The joins between these canvases were hand sewn.

These differences in the canvas characteristics made it necessary to generalise when selecting the canvas for the mock-up. The chosen textile was a commonly found tabby weave linen canvas, with a thread count of 14 × 15 per cm^2 from Kunstnernes Eget Materialutsalg AL (KEM).[5] This was the only canvas available that was not preprepared with a ground by the manufacturer, but was visually quite similar to the majority of the paintings' canvases.

Glue size

The paintings have a non-original water-soluble verso preparation (from 1925–26), which may have disrupted a possible glue size in the canvas. As a result of this secondary layer and the 1945–46 marouflage materials, access to the back of the original canvas was not possible. Microscopy (10–500×) of cross-sections using visible and ultraviolet light did not give a conclusive indication as to whether or not an original sizing layer was present. However, traditionally, most easel paintings of this period have glue sizing of some sort. It was assumed that a sizing layer was present, even if it was not visible and/or had merged with the verso priming. Rabbit-skin glue was the only animal glue readily available hence the canvas on the mock-up was sized with a solution of this glue (see Table 1).

Ground

As with the canvases, the grounds vary on the Aula paintings. Based on visual observations, some grounds are slightly transparent and somewhat greyish in colour while some are opaque white. Some grounds also are clearly applied by hand with visible brushstrokes while others appear to have no traces of the application tool. Finally, some grounds are very thinly applied and others quite thickly. Initially, non-destructive analyses (energy dispersive X-ray fluorescence (EDXRF)) indicated that all grounds contain chalk, zinc and lead (Frøysaker and Liu 2009: 49), but these readings may also include the reverse side preparation (Frøysaker *et al.* 2011b: 54, 62). Nine paintings have water-soluble and absorbent grounds while the remaining three have non-absorbent grounds that show only a slight degree of water sensitivity. Water solubility of the grounds indicates that the first nine are based on glue while the remaining three may have some addition of oil, which would decrease water solubility. Although Fourier transform infrared spectroscopy (FTIR) analyses are not conclusive, they support this suggestion.

The ground in the mock-up was a recipe described by Doerner (1984: 13–14), modified to improve its working properties, as well as roughly match the original ground's visual appearance (see Table 1).

Secondary materials

Reverse side preparation

In 1926, a preparation layer was applied to the paintings' reverse side (Frøysaker 2008: 7). The reason for this could be that the paintings were already severely soiled by 1925. Past restorers may have assumed that dirt was penetrating from the brick wall through to the front, and in turn applied an isolation layer in an attempt to stop this soiling.[6] FTIR analysis results were not conclusive. The analyses indicated the presence of two different binders, protein and oil, in addition to chalk, lead white and probably zinc white. The preparation is water-soluble, therefore most likely contains more animal glue than oil.

Table 1 *Materials.*

Material	Source	Original recipe	MAP adjustments
Glue size	Kaland 1974	70 g bone glue in 1L water Heated to 50°C	Bone glue was substituted with rabbit-skin glue because of availability and the amount was reduced to 50g/L
Ground layer	Doerner 1984	Same as glue size Added zinc white and chalk 1:1 to a workable consistency	More water added for a ground more similar to the ground on the original paintings
Reverse-side preparation	Doerner 1984	Same as glue size Added zinc white and chalk 1:1 to a workable consistency	More chalk and water added
Rye flour paste for marouflage	Kaland 1974	150 g rabbit-skin glue in 3L water Heated to 50°C Added rye flour to a workable consistency Venetian turpentine	Exclusion of Venice turpentine, as this was functioning as a plasticiser
Rye flour paste for adhering wooden framework to Masonite	Kaland 1974	Same as rye flour paste for marouflage	

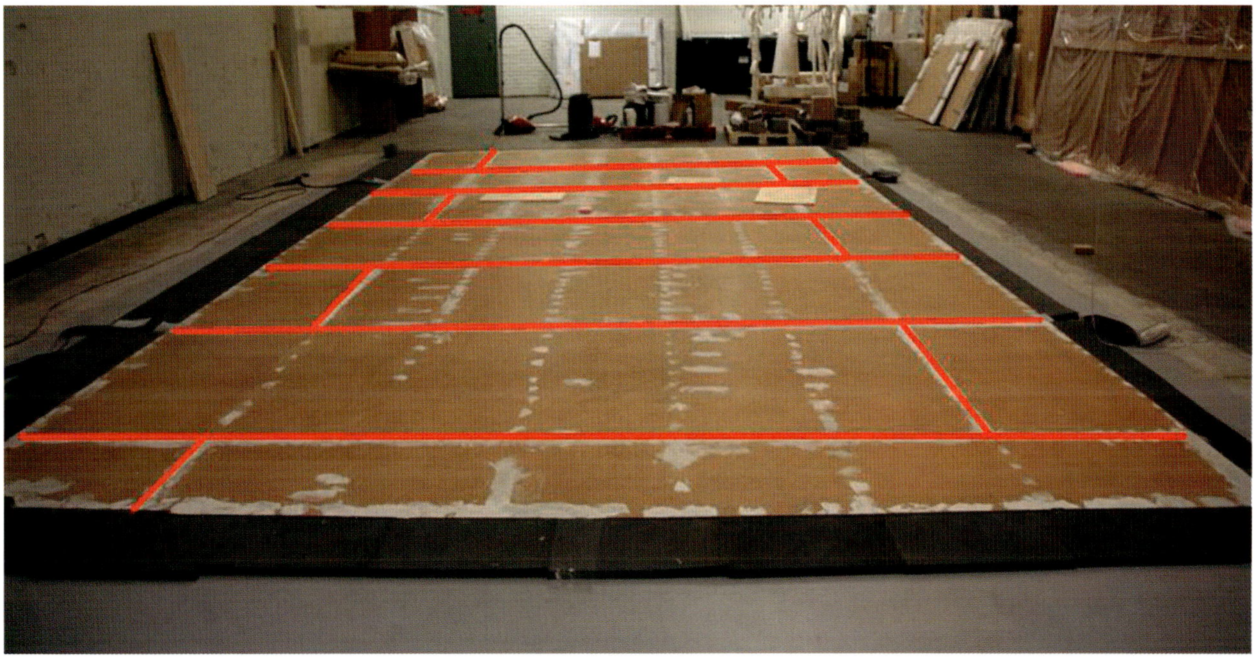

Figure 2 *Marouflage in a 'brickwork' pattern of Masonite sheets. (Photograph: Karen Mengshoel 2010.)*

In some areas, this preparation has been pushed through the open weave of the canvas (Fig. 1) and formed beads on front of the paintings. In some of these beads pinholes are visible. This further supports the assumption of a water-containing glue, such as animal glue. Microscopy of cross-sections (10–500×) shows that, in some cases, this preparation has penetrated the weave and merged with the original ground.

The most important qualities for this layer in the mock-up were its function as an isolating layer and its ability to absorb moisture. Due to time constraints and health and safety concerns, only animal glue, chalk and zinc white were used, excluding lead white and oil. To mimic the verso preparation of 1925–26, the conservators simply modified the ground solutions by adding more water and chalk.

The first marouflage

After WWII, the paintings were brought back to the university Aula and marouflaged with rye flour paste onto sheets of Masonite.[7] It is possible that the recipe used in the marouflage of the Aula paintings is based on a recipe for lining on a rigid support by Bjørn Kaland (1974: 43), who was a member of Dørje-Haug's team. The post-war Masonite was held in place from the back by a wooden framework, attached by glue paste and nails. These Masonite sheets were supplied in a 3.66 × 1.22 m format. The sheets were put together in a 'brickwork' pattern (Fig. 2). The timber was of two sizes: 9.1 × 2.7 cm and 6.9 × 2.3 cm.

A combination of new Norway spruce timber and modern Masonite was chosen to recreate the first marouflage.

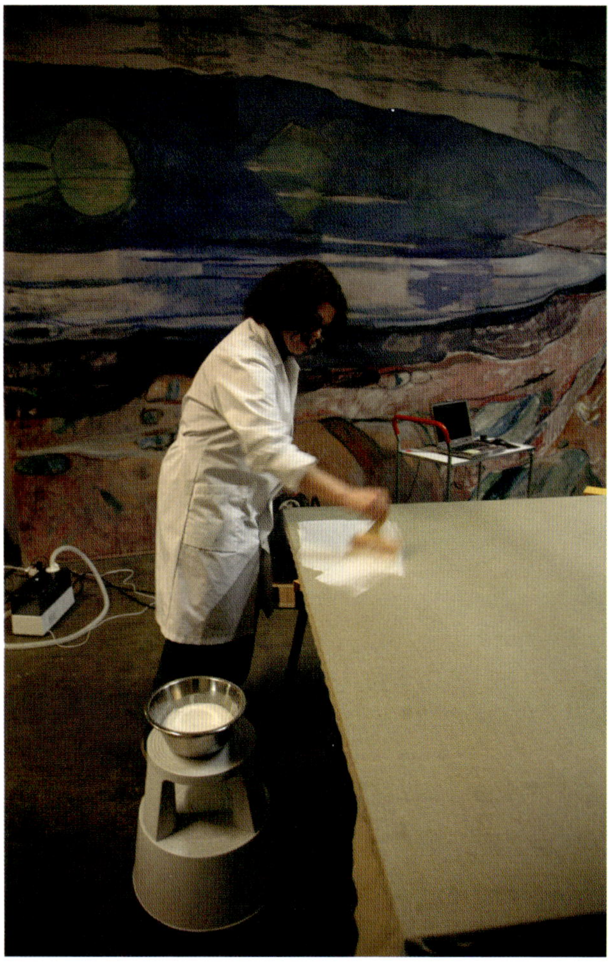

Figure 3 *The canvas was mounted on a wooden stretcher, glue size was applied, and finally two layers of ground. (Photograph: Mirjam Liu 2009.)*

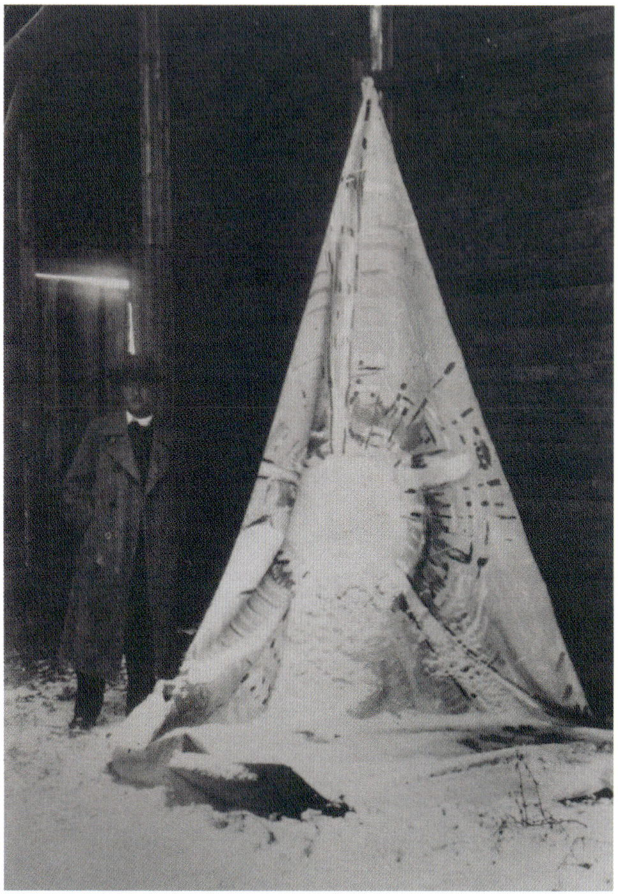

Figure 5 *A painted sketch for* The Sun *(MM B 2394 (F)) stored outdoors at Munch's studio. Note there is no evidence that the finished Aula paintings were stored outdoors. (Photograph: A.F. Johansen (?) 1911.)*

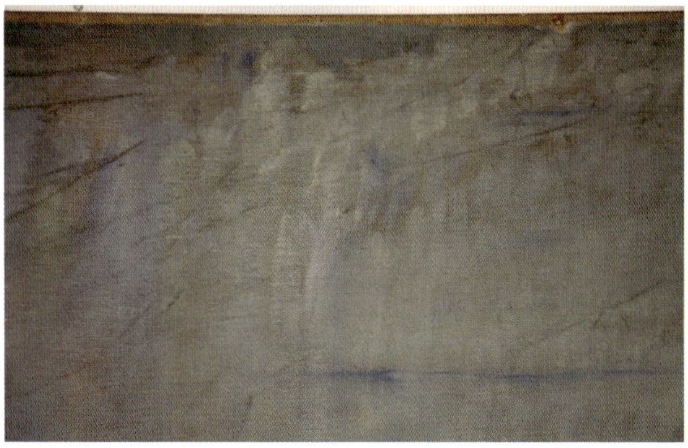

Figure 4 *Diagonal damages in the upper half of* History. *(Photograph: Mirjam Liu 2011.)*

Today these materials are readily available, and their content and construction has not changed significantly (although modern Masonite may contain fire-retardant materials). Kaland's recipe for rye flour glue paste was modified by excluding Venice turpentine. The solvent would have been used as a plasticiser, and for the purpose of the mock-up this was unnecessary, since one of the goals was to achieve a new glue paste that was similar to the aged, hard and brittle one. Bone glue was not available and was substituted with rabbit-skin glue – this was not ideal but unavoidable. Since rabbit-skin glue is stronger than bone glue, the ratio of glue to water was reduced to compensate.

Constructing the mock-up and performing tests on the mock-up canvas

The mock-up was constructed so that the majority of all the different processes, from stretching the canvas to attaching the new marouflage, were performed. In addition, the viability of the new marouflage material and method was tested. To mimic the behaviour of the original paintings, the mock canvas was stretched unwashed on a wooden stretcher measuring 200 × 170 cm with one cross bar in each direction.[8] Glue size and two layers of ground were then applied by brush with appropriate drying time between applications (Fig. 3). To recreate the treatment in 1926, a preparation layer was applied to the verso while the stretcher was still attached.[9]

Distinctive diagonal damages can be observed on the upper half of *History* (Fig. 4), the origin of which has puzzled the MAP conservators. Several possible scenarios have been posed as reasons for these damages assuming that they were caused during the many installations and deinstallations of the painting in question, either in the Aula or in the artist's studio – Munch himself did numerous trial hangings both *in situ* and in his studios, as evidenced by the many diverging pinholes along the edges. It was suggested that the damages may have occurred as a result of the heavy painted canvas hanging from only a few nails (Fig. 5) during mounting and dismounting. Another suggestion was that the hasty deinstallation during WWII may have caused the damages, either due to the method of removal or because the painting fell to the floor (either from the upper edge or one of the upper corners). Lastly, it was proposed that Munch might have painted it upside down in order to gain better access to the top half, and that the painting had fallen to the floor from this position.

As mentioned, the Aula paintings were cut from their stretchers in 1940. Not much is known about what happened in these hectic days during the war, but it is clear that it was done in haste, and without extensive planning and proper tools. The conservators cut the mock-up canvas from its stretcher quickly to mimic the urgency that must have affected the 1940 dismounting. The scenario that the painting might have fallen to the floor at some point was also investigated. Tests were performed by dropping the unmounted mock-up canvas from a stepladder (approximately 4 m high) from one of the corners and from the middle of one of the edges (Fig. 6).

The mock-up was significantly smaller than the original canvases and therefore much lighter. The manner in which a painted canvas folds and bends when dropped to the floor is of course influenced not only by the stiffness of the canvas, but also by its weight. Hence, additional 'drop tests' were performed with Kraft paper and unprepared polyester sailcloth.[10] The purpose was to visualise the manner in which materials of different stiffness fall, and to look for similarities to the phenomenon observed in the Aula paintings. Kraft paper and sailcloth were mounted on a wooden stretcher and dropped at different stages during demounting. The folds and creases that occurred from the remaining nails were studied and documented (Fig. 7).

After cutting the canvas from the stretcher, it was 'mistreated' in different ways to imitate damages that might have occurred during handling of the original paintings. The mock-up canvas was rolled first with the front facing inwards, then facing outwards to see if the ground cracked or lost adhesion. The roll was then rammed vertically into the floor (Fig. 8). This action might reflect improper handling of the canvas rolls or imitate long-term vertical storage. Furthermore, the mock-up roll was also bent to imitate a possible rough handling while the canvas was in transport and storage (Fig. 9). The goal of this 'crash test' was to see if these actions would create damages similar to those observed in *Men Reaching towards the Light* (Fig. 10).

To recreate the 1946 marouflage, a timber framework with Masonite was constructed in the manner observed on the Aula paintings. The glue paste was then applied to the Masonite with a spatula. Correspondence states that the paintings were rolled onto a 1 m diameter cylinder with the front facing inwards.[11] It is not known if all the paintings were rolled onto these rollers, but it is assumed that the smallest paintings may not have been on rollers due to their narrow widths (*c.*1.6 m). From this core, the paintings were then unrolled onto the Masonite. The mock-up was marouflaged by heat and pressure applied by an electric iron through Kraft paper (Fig. 11).[12] A surprisingly large amount of pressure and heat was necessary to achieve adherence between canvas and Masonite. The mock-up was then left to dry under pressure.

Testing the materials and procedure of the second marouflage

The ageing 1946 marouflage had substantial structural problems that also affected the aesthetic properties of the paintings. The wooden framework in particular had caused damage and needed replacing.[13] Moreover the wooden structure had functioned as a cold bridge producing a recurring rectangular pattern from dirt accumulations on the paintings' surfaces. In 2008, it was decided to replace the framework and add a new marouflage.

During 2010, the wooden framework from 1946 was replaced with honeycomb panels. These materials are

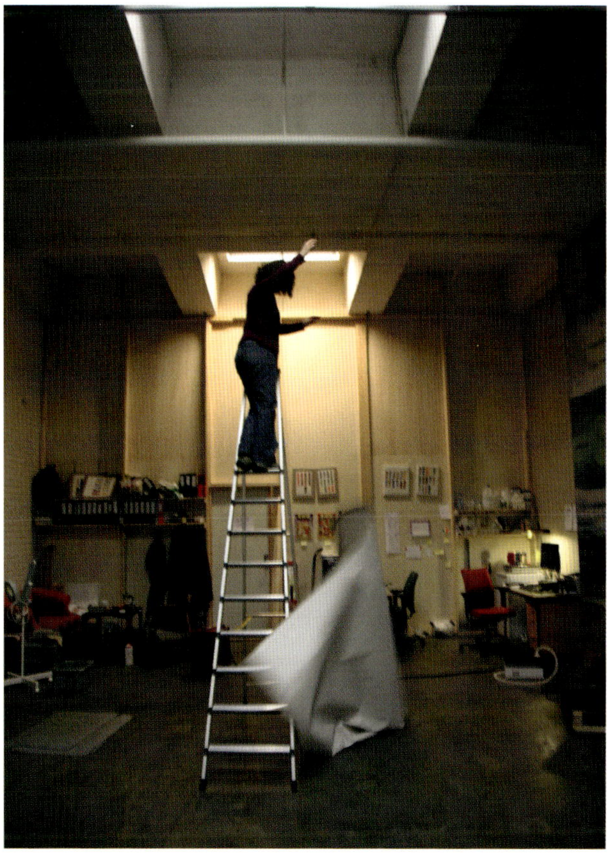

Figure 6 *The mock canvas was dropped to the floor from a stepladder. (Photograph: Mirjam Liu 2009.)*

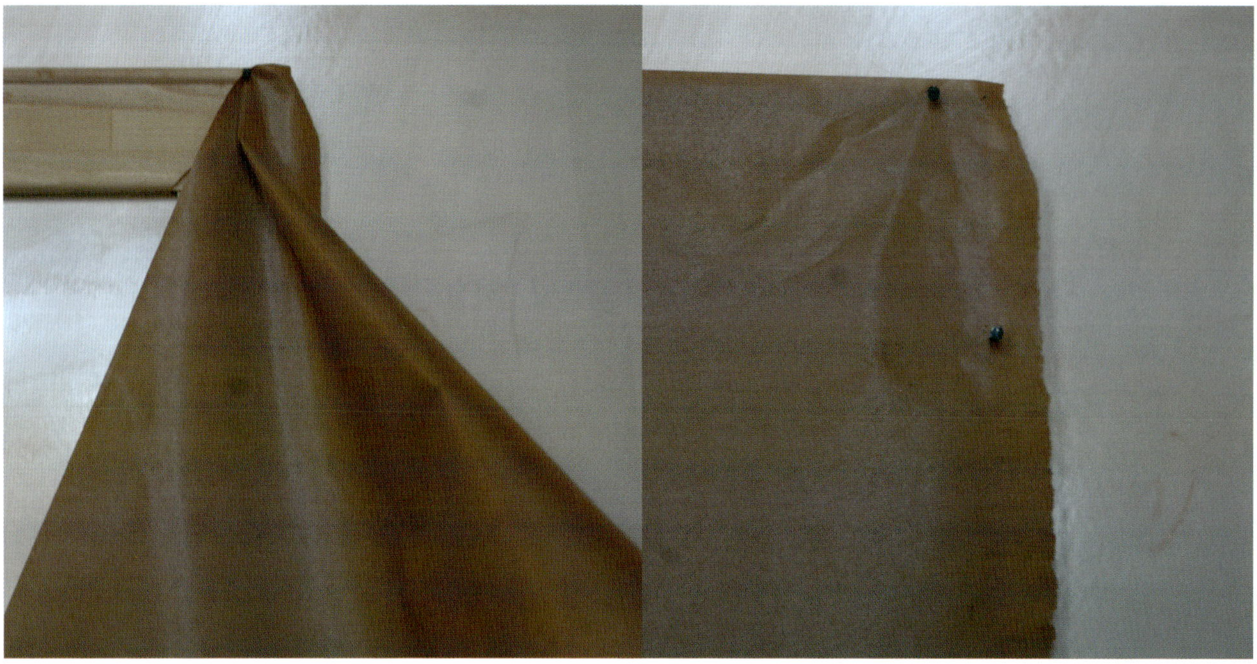

Figure 7 *Folds and creases in drop tests on Kraft paper. (Photograph: Karen Mengshoel 2011.)*

thermally and dimensionally inert and homogenous, and should increase the stability of the original paintings. The conservators developed a list of specifications for the new materials.[14]

Replacement of the timber framework with a new marouflage was considered a complicated and delicate process.[15] It was essential to test the planned process to confirm the suitability of the materials and treatment. To our knowledge, a double marouflage has never been performed on this scale, hence the mock-up was necessary to test materials and gain practical experience. Acting as a test piece was in fact the main purpose of the mock-up.

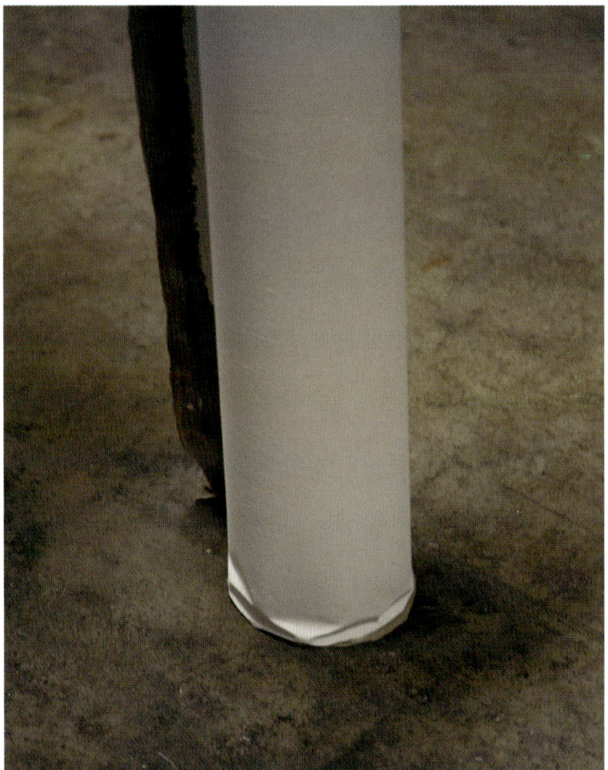

Figure 8 *The canvas roll was rammed vertically into the floor. (Photograph: Mirjam Liu 2009.)*

To imitate the removal of the framework, the mock-up was turned face down onto sheets of foam on the studio floor.[16] The new marouflage would be performed on the same surface, not on a working table, due to the sheer size of the paintings. The timber framework was then cut into smaller pieces (Fig. 12) and dislodged by a single tap with a hammer. A concern before the treatment was that the glue for the second marouflage would travel through the gap between the Masonite sheets and bond to the 1926 preparation layer and the back of the canvas. The gaps were sealed with a commercial filler (Lettsparkel LS 104), but this material was so brittle that the slightest movement caused it to crack.

Different strategies and materials were tested to check degrees of penetration: a piece of canvas in rye flour glue paste placed over the cracked filler; cracked filler; masking tape; sports tape; open gap (0.5 mm) and piece of canvas in rye flour paste. Gaps between Masonite sheets as well as holes and undulations were then filled with the same filler and sanded to obtain a surface that was both perfectly even and gave tooth to the glue layer before bonding. The edges of the Masonite sheets were masked with silicone tape to ensure that no glue overflowed the edges and bonded to the front. The new two-component adhesive was mixed and spread onto the Masonite with a dental spatula and the honeycomb panels carefully positioned onto the mock-up. Then the test marouflage was left to dry overnight under pressure. The vulnerable edges

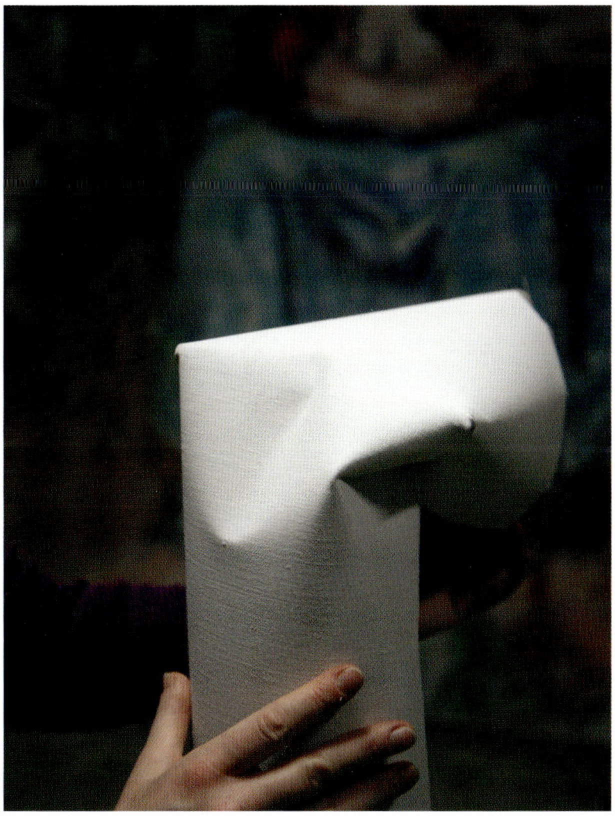

Figure 9 *The canvas roll was bent. (Photograph: Mirjam Liu 2009.)*

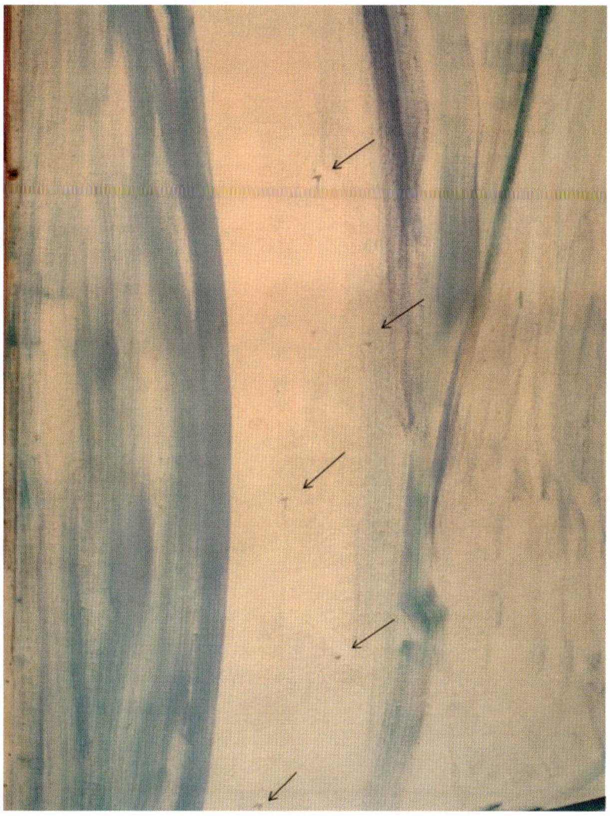

Figure 10 *Damages in* Men Reaching towards the Light. *(Photograph: Karen Mengshoel 2009.)*

of the honeycomb panels were also sealed with aluminium cappings to ease handling and to protect the edges from damage.[17] Finally, after setting, the mock-up was cut into pieces (Fig. 13) to investigate the structure of the double marouflage and to observe the effectiveness of the different filling materials in the gaps between the Masonite sheets.

Varying temperatures on the paintings' surfaces had led to uneven distribution of surface dirt in the past. A special doorway (5.6 × 0.55 m) was installed in the north wall to accommodate the movement of the larger paintings in and out of the Aula (Mengshoel *et al.* 2012). The wall with the new door was obviously a weak spot, since the door was placed directly behind *The Sun*, and uneven soiling of the painted surface might occur. The honeycomb panel's properties as insulating layer between the painting and the brick wall was tested through temperature measurements. The mock-up was placed across the section of the wall known to have the largest differences in temperature (Fig. 14). The bare wall's surface temperatures varied from 6.5 to 12°C across the measuring area.[18] When the mock-up piece was in place, in the same position as the painting would be,[19] its canvas surface temperatures varied from 11 to 12°C.[20] This result implies that the reinstalled paintings will be at lower risk of accumulating airborne pollution with the new honeycomb mounting as opposed to the older 1946 framework that acted as a cold bridge to the outer wall.

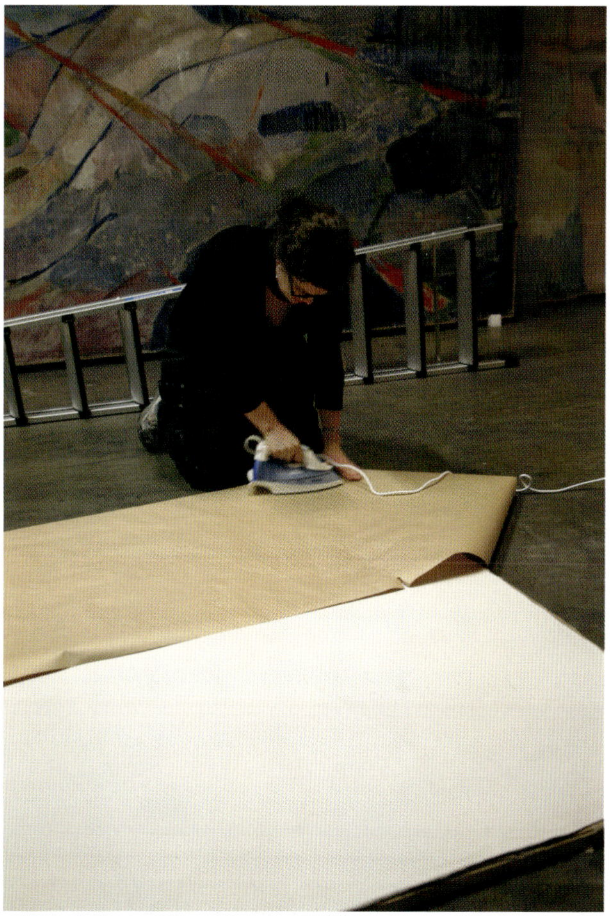

Figure 11 *Heat and pressure applied through Kraft paper. (Photograph: Mirjam Liu 2009.)*

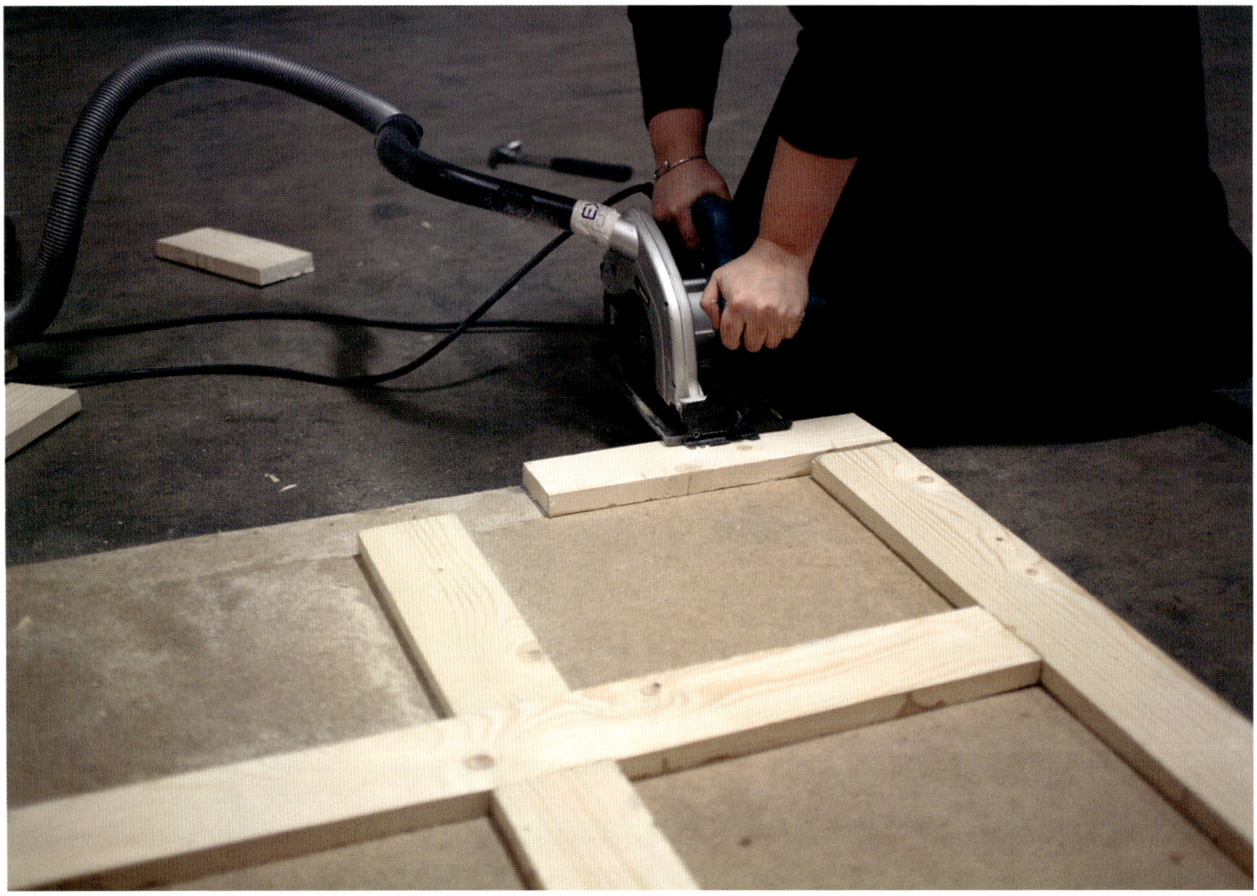

Figure 12 *The timber framework was cut into smaller pieces and dislodged by a single tap with a hammer. This procedure was practised on the mock-up before the treatment of the original paintings. (Photograph: Karen Mengshoel 2010.)*

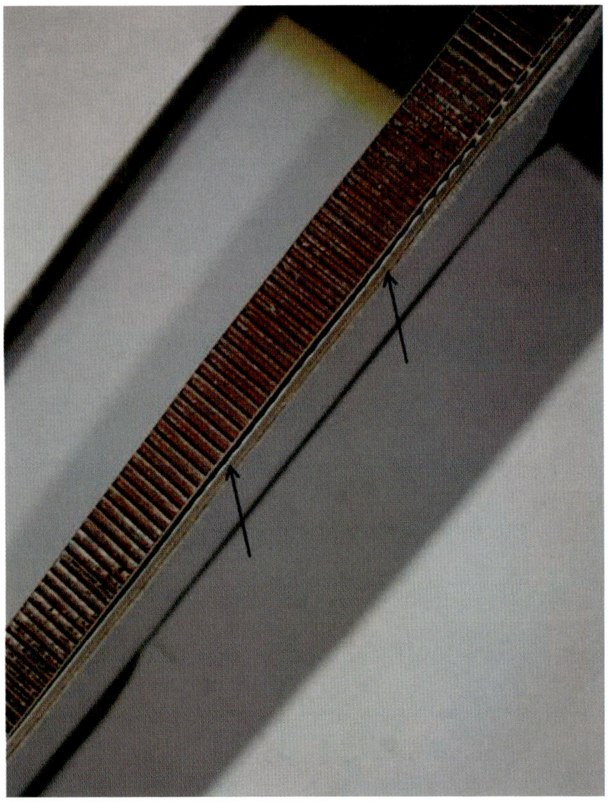

Figure 13 *The mock-up of the double marouflage was cut into pieces. (Photograph: Karen Mengshoel 2010.)*

Results and discussion

As previously mentioned, the main purpose of the mock-up sandwich was to determine the suitability of the new marouflage's materials and method. Nevertheless, the tests performed on the canvas itself, as well as the reconstruction of the first marouflage, provided valuable information.

The diagonal lines observed along the upper edge of *History*, close to the top left corner (Fig. 4), were similar to those recreated in both Kraft paper and sailcloth by dropping the left corner of the canvas while the right corner was still attached to the stretcher (Figs 7 and 15). Despite no archival evidence of the painting being dropped, the conservators consider this scenario to be plausible, since handling a painting this size, unmounted, must have been a heavy and difficult process, and accidents may very well have occurred without being reported; when, or how many times this may have happened is not possible to determine.

Dropping the canvas from a height, both from an upper corner and from the middle of the upper edge, created distinctive damages in the mock-up's ground layer in the bottom half (Fig. 16). These damages also form diagonal lines. The lines in *History* are found along the upper edge; if caused by a fall, this would imply that the painting must have been hung upside down. Turning the painting upside

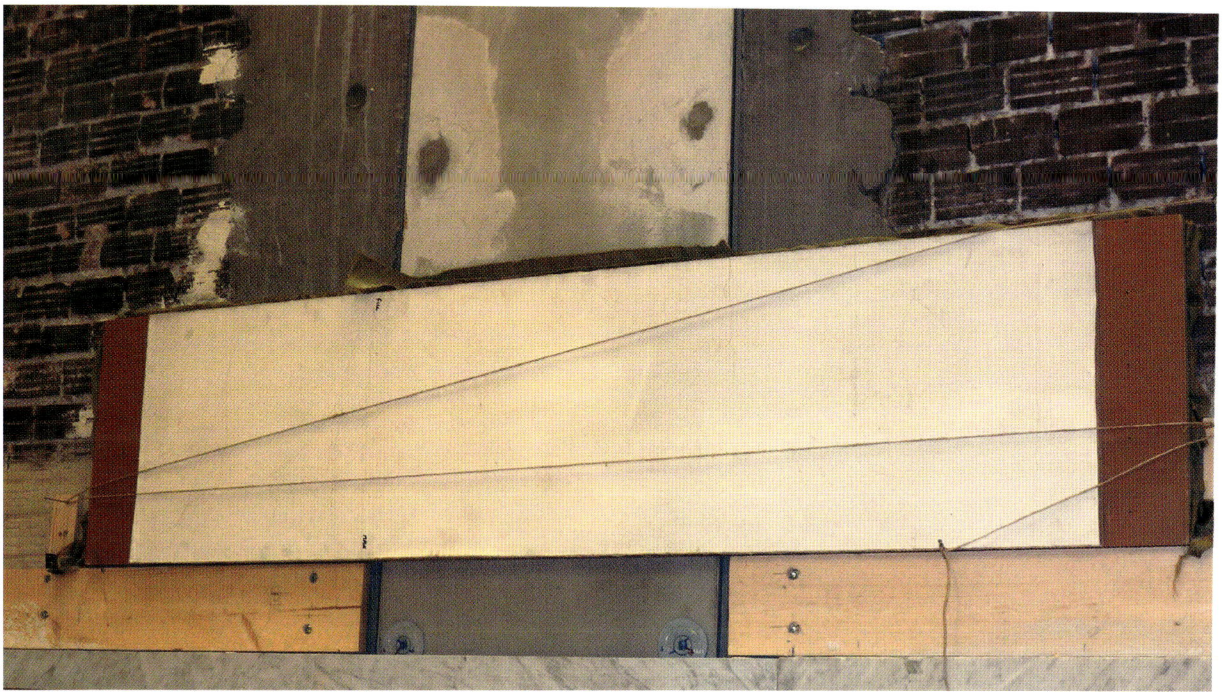

Figure 14 *A section of the mock-up was placed in front of a 'weak spot' on the wall to measure the material's thermal insulation capacity. (Photograph: Jens Treider, January 2011.)*

down could have been a way of seeing the composition in a new way during the painting process, or, perhaps, of gaining access to the higher sections. No archival evidence supports the notion that Munch worked on the paintings upside down.

The rolling and shocking of the test canvas after it was cut off its stretcher showed two different types of damage. The action of rolling the canvas did not in itself display any visible damages to the canvas or its ground layer. The reason for this is probably the young age of the ground. However, ramming the roll into the floor, to simulate long-term vertical storing of the canvas rolls and improper handling, showed compression of the canvas leading to characteristic folds (Figs 8 and 16). This type of damage is not found on any of the Aula paintings hence it is not likely that these paintings have been subjected to this type of handling and/or storage.[21] Rolling (with the ground layer facing out), and subsequently bending the roll, also resulted in distinctive damages in the mock-up's ground layer. These damages occurred as regular loss of ground at the point where the canvas had the most severe bend. The damages in the mock-up are very similar when compared with *Men Reaching towards the Light* (Figs 10 and 16) and the conclusion was that this painting may very well have been subjected to this type of handling.

By reconstructing the first marouflage, new knowledge was gained about how the paintings were treated in 1945–46 as well as on several phenomena observed on the paintings. During the reconstruction it became very clear that considerable expertise must have been involved when the paintings were marouflaged onto Masonite. It was obvious that the MAP conservators were not as experienced as their predecessors in this particular treatment. As a result the reconstruction was not as structurally sound, the gaps between the wood fibre sheets were larger and more nails than necessary were used to attach the Masonite to the framework. The conservators were surprised at how much glue, pressure and heat was required to achieve a satisfactory bond between the marouflage support and canvas. The sheer size of the paintings must have made them difficult to manoeuvre and align onto the Masonite, and it would have necessitated walking or crawling on, or building a bridge over, the paintings' painted side during the lining process. In addition, the large size of the paintings, as well as the application of heat through Kraft paper, must have made it difficult to keep an overview of the process and ensure a satisfactory bond throughout the whole structure.

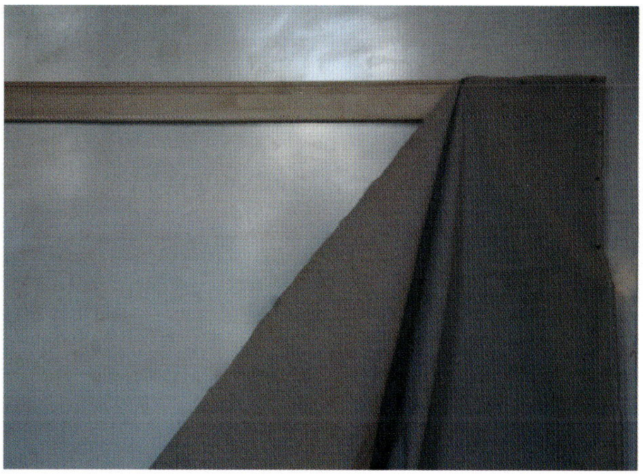

Figure 15 *Drop test on sailcloth partly mounted on wooden stretcher. (Photograph: Karen Mengshoel 2011.)*

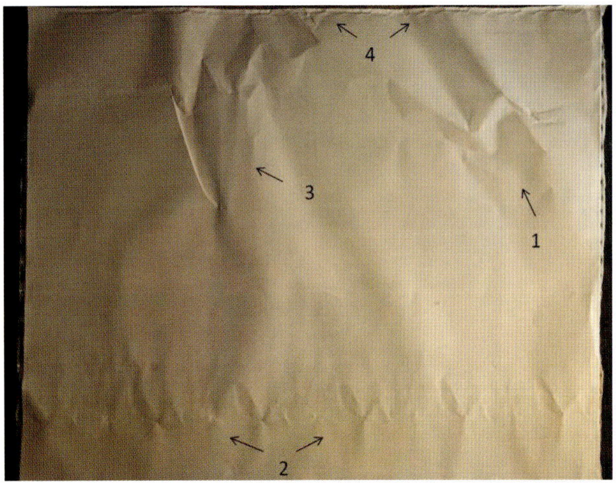

Figure 16 *Distinctive pattern in mock canvas after drop tests. (1) Creases after impact when dropped from opposite corner; (2) damages after bending of the canvas roll; (3) creases after impact when dropped from the upper edge; (4) pattern in canvas after the canvas roll was rammed into the floor. (Photograph: Karen Mengshoel 2009.)*

Even on the 'small' mock-up, these issues were a challenge. This in turn made it more difficult to achieve good attachment between canvas and Masonite. Furthermore, randomly located air pockets were observed between the Masonite and canvas. This phenomenon is also observed on the paintings themselves (Frøysaker *et al.* 2011a: 266), and it was thought that they were either a result of delamination due to ageing of the glue paste or that they had simply been present since the first marouflage. The presence of areas of blind cleavage on the mock-up suggests that many of the same voids below the paintings were present at the time of the 1945–46 marouflage. However, it is not possible to establish if these local delaminations have become larger due to ageing of the glue paste.

The conservators observed that some glue paste was present on the front of the mock-up. Such residues are also found on the surface of the Munch paintings (Fig. 1). It was thought that these residues were a result of carelessness in 1945–46, but after reconstructing the mock-up it was understood that some of this superfluous and misplaced material is very difficult to avoid. Neat application of glue paste, even on a smaller scale, can be difficult, as the glue paste is runny and easily becomes messy. In addition, there is a time constraint to the process: the glue must not dry out before aligning the canvas on the Masonite sheets. This indicates that splashes of glue paste on the painted surfaces were caused by the general handling properties and working time of the glue paste rather than inattentiveness of the past restorers.

Testing of the new marouflage procedure and materials was considered successful. The method of removal of the mock-up's 'old' marouflage woodwork was viable and provided a valuable opportunity to gain experience before performing the procedure on the reverse side of the original paintings. After cutting the mock-up into several pieces across the Masonite joint, it was clear that all of the gap filling materials could be used. In fact, the adhesive did not penetrate through the gaps even in places without any filling materials. It was decided to use commercial fillers on Masonite joints on the original paintings as a precaution. This filling material was chosen because it was readily available in large quantities, had good working properties, and did not give bulk in the marouflage sandwich. This was important since the new marouflage glue layer did not compensate for unevenness of more than 1 mm.

However, cutting up the mock-up showed a severe disbond between the Masonite and the honeycomb panel (Fig. 13). This was not caused by the procedure itself, but rather by the fact that the working floor was very uneven. These blind cleavages covered large areas of the mock-up and would represent a severe threat to the paintings' stability after mounting *in situ*, should the same phenomenon occur in the Aula paintings.

Without a solution to this problem, the planned structural treatment of the paintings could not be performed satisfactorily. In discussion with the manufacturer (AIM Composites), two different strategies of solving this problem were considered: increasing pressure from the back of the honeycomb or levelling the floor. Increasing pressure was deemed unsuitable due to the fact that the honeycomb panels were so stiff that the pressure needed to obtain a satisfactory bond would be too great for the paintings. In addition, applying this amount of pressure would be impossible to execute with the equipment available. Hence, the studio floor was levelled as evenly as possible to reduce the risk and number of voids.[22] The new marouflage significantly improved the stiffness of the whole structure and therefore increased the stability of the mock-up. Thermal testing of the insulating capacity of the mock-up showed that the new marouflage material greatly improved the structure's insulating ability as well as giving the mock-up's canvas surface a more even temperature. Aluminum capping along the second marouflage provided an aesthetically pleasing finish in addition to drastically improving the mounting procedure and protecting the structure's edges.

Conclusion

The construction of the mock-up vastly improved the understanding of the damages on, and the past treatments of, the Aula paintings. As a result, the conservators can now give more informed explanations of the different phenomena present in the paintings, and provide future conservators with a better starting point for conservation treatments. The recipes were divided into two categories: pre-2008 and post-2008. Despite historical inaccuracies in the former category, the recipes served the purpose of the mock-up.

The shock testing of the mock-up canvas improved the general understanding of damage mechanisms during mounting and storage, although only some of them were comparable with those found in the original Aula

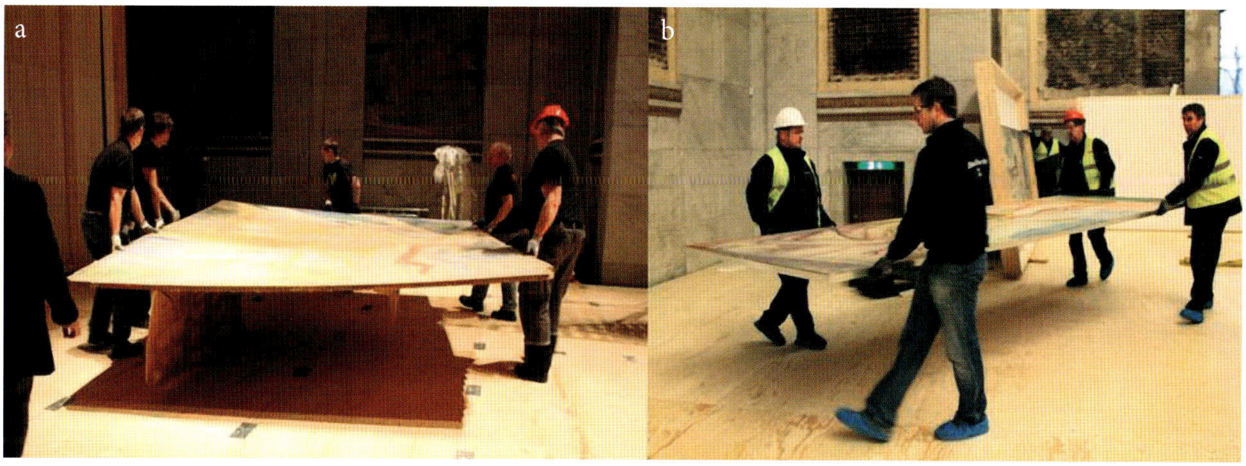

Figure 17 *Installation of the Aula paintings: (a) the semi-rigid post-war marouflage; (b) the present and rigid double marouflage. (Photograph: Karen Mengshoel 2009, 2011.)*

paintings. Furthermore, the reconstruction of the paintings' first marouflage gave us a renewed respect for the past restorers and their considerable expertise.

Constructing a full stratigraphic test piece provided an opportunity to examine and evaluate the materials, practice and procedures for the second marouflage. This opportunity was essential since the success or failure of the trial marouflage would be decisive for the execution of the planned treatment. The mock-up verified the viability of the procedure and the materials, but it also revealed some crucial shortcomings such as voids in the marouflage due to the unevenness of the studio floor.

Marouflaging the marouflaged Aula paintings proved to be a successful intervention. The paintings are now structurally sound and safely installed (Fig. 17) in their niches with functional and aesthetically suitable mountings.

Finally, the mock-up was further cut up into several small and handy pieces. They serve as samples of the double marouflage with easily visible stratigraphy demonstrable for educational purposes. These samples also include the picture frame fastened with Velcro and lined with a woollen felt tape (Fig. 18). Moreover, the larger mock-up pieces will still be used for testing in an ongoing MA project[23] examining the numerous incidents of tide lines and water stains in Munch's Aula paintings from past water leakages through the Aula roof.

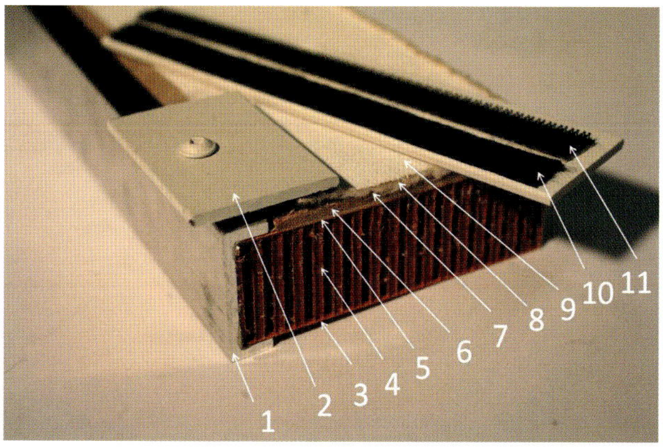

Figure 18 *The mock-up is used to demonstrate the stratigraphy for educational purposes: (1) aluminium capping; (2) decorative frame; (3) glass fibre skin; (4) honeycomb core; (5) glue layer (two-component modified epoxy); (6) Masonite; (7) rye flour paste (not visible in the photo); (8) canvas;, (9) ground layer; (10) woollen felt tape; (11) Velcro tape. (Photograph: Karen Mengshoel 2011.)*

Acknowledgements

We are grateful to Renate for her many teaching hours at Conservation Studies, IAKH, UiO, for sharing her knowledge and enthusiasm on practical reconstructions and for her valuable comments on the Munch Aula Paintings Project. We also thank Katrine Strandskogen Scharffenberg, Hans-Petter Aamodt, Petter Halvorsen, Jens Treider, Jamie Barnes and Shaun Maika for taking part in the making of the current reconstructions and tests, Hanne Moltubakk Kempton for FTIR analysis, Technical Department UiO for funding and Joel Taylor for editing.

Materials and suppliers

- AIM Composites Ltd. (www.aimcomposites.com/):
  - Honeycomb panels Flitelam GN2
  - Aerok 2100 produced by Forgeway and distributed by AIM Composites Ltd.
  - Aerok 9170: A: 1050601 and B: 1030502 (hardening agent). Epoxy resin by AIM Composites Ltd.
  - Araldite AY 103/HY 991, produced by Hunstman Advanced Materials and distributed by AIM Composites Ltd.
  - Silicone tape
- Kunstnernes eget materialutsalg (KEM) (www.kem.no/)
  - Stretcher 200 × 170 cm
  - Rabbit-skin glue (63025 Hasenleim, Würfel aus Hasenfellen, Kremer pigmente)
  - Linen canvas 14 × 15 threads/cm^2
  - Chalk
  - Zinc white
- Maxbo (www.maxbo.no/)
  - Filling material (Lettsparkel LS 104 Nordsjö) produced by Nordsjö, distributed by Maxbo

Notes

1. More information can be found online at: www.hf.uio.no/iakh/english/research/projects/aula-project/index.html.

2. Half-scale meaning the same width as the smallest painting and half its height (*c*.1.7 × 2 m).
3. Munch's applications of oil colours were not copied on the mock-up.
4. Remarkably, the two largest formats were made up of single canvases.
5. KEM is the leading artist supply store in Oslo.
6. The preparation probably contains zinc and this might also have been intended as a slight antiseptic.
7. The marouflage was performed by a team of restorers led by Ole Dørje-Haug, the chief restorer at the National Gallery in Oslo. Archival research produced receipts from acquisition of Masonite and Venice turpentine, and later reports show that the glue paste was made from animal glue and rye flour.
8. Conservators would normally wash canvases before use to remove any residues of industrial materials from the production process. Artists would probably not do so.
9. At the time, the conservators assumed that this was the right sequence of events, but later it was pointed out that it most likely happened with the stretcher removed, since the original stretchers were replaced the same year. This discrepancy, however, was of minor importance.
10. Lascaux polyester sailcloth. P110 215 g/m^2.
11. Letter from Bjørn Kaland, Bergen, to Svein Wiik, 17 December 1973, UiO Historical Museum (KHM) archive.
12. Applying heat through Kraft paper during the marouflage was based on remains of Kraft paper found on the surface of *Women Reaching towards the Sun*. Many *pastose* areas show signs of being heated and flattened, and Kraft paper was melted into the paint surface during treatment.
13. The wooden framework had created many severe problems; the concave and convex warping of the paintings, acute flaking paint and visible cracks running through the paint and ground layers down through the canvas support. The nails used for fixing the framework to the Masonite boards were putting pressure on the verso of the canvases and could, with time, penetrate through.
14. The materials should be non-toxic, chemically inert, non-hygroscopic, have sufficiently long setting time to allow for working, no thermal dimensional change, no off-gassing and good ageing properties. The honeycomb panels consist of aramid impregnated paper core between glass fibre skins (AIM 2011 spec sheet), and the marouflage glue was a two-component modified epoxy, Aerok 2100.
15. For a more detailed discussion of the 2010 marouflage, see Frøysaker *et al.* 2011a.
16. Cyclododecane was tested on the mock-up as facing material for the original paintings.
17. These cappings would also function as a stable support for the mounting screws that would secure Munch's paintings in their niches in the wall, as well as fastening points for the decorative frames. A sample of this capping was also mounted on the mock panel to test functional and aesthetical suitability.
18. The measurements were performed by architect Jens Treider when the outdoor temperature was −8°C and indoors *c*.15°C.
19. Including a 22–30 mm wide gap of air between the brick wall and the honeycomb.
20. In January 2012, multiple *in-situ* infrared photographs of the double marouflage paintings gave no larger differences than 1°C in surface temperature, and only in a few, limited areas.
21. They are however observed on some of the painted sketches of the Aula paintings that have been stored on different rollers since Munch's collection was bequeathed to the City of Oslo in 1944. An example can be observed on sketch MMB 3467 for *History* (Tveit 2011: 122–3).
22. In discussion with AIM Composite Ltd. it was agreed that 10% disbond was acceptable and would not affect the stability of the new marouflage and the paintings significantly. A larger percentage would require filling additional glue through the verso of the new marouflage. This was possible due to the fact that the honeycomb panels were constructed with small holes at regular intervals.
23. Working title: 'Tide lines on Munch's Aula Paintings' by Katrine Strandskogen Scharffenberg.

References

Berger, G.A. 2000. *Conservation of Paintings: Research and Innovations*. London: Archetype Publications.

Doerner, M. 1984. *The Materials of the Artist and their Use in Paintings, with Notes on the Techniques of the Old Masters*, E. Neuhaus (tr.). London: Harcourt, Inc.

Frøysaker, T. 2007. 'The paintings of Edvard Munch in the Assembly Hall of Oslo University: their treatment history and the Aula project', *Restauro* 4: 246–57.

Frøysaker, T. 2008. 'Bevaring av Edvard Munchs Aula-malerier før og nå', *Kunst og Kultur* 91(1): 2–17.

Frøysaker, T. and Liu, M. 2009. 'Four (of eleven) unvarnished oil paintings on canvas by Edvard Munch in the Aula of Oslo University: preliminary notes on their materials, techniques and original appearances', *Restauro* 1: 44–61.

Frøysaker, T., Liu, M. and Ford, T. 2011a. 'Backing Munch: past and recent attachment of Edvard Munch's monumental Aula paintings to rigid supports', *Zeitschrift für Kunsttechnologie und Konservierung* 2: 257–71.

Frøysaker, T., Miliani, C. and Liu, M. 2011b. 'Non-invasive evaluation of cleaning tests performed on "Chemistry" (1909–1916): a large unvarnished oil painting on canvas by Edvard Munch', *Restauro* 4: 53–63.

Kaland, B. 1974. *Klisterdubleringer og klisteroppskrifter. Dublering av lerretsmalerier. Rapport fra konserveringsseminar 6–10 mai 1974 i Nasjonalgalleriet. Oslo 1974.*

Mehra, V.R. 1984. 'Cold lining and its scope: some case histories'. In *Preprints of the ICOM-CC 7th Triennial Meeting*, D. de Froment (ed.) 31–4. Paris: International Council of Museums in association with the J. Paul Getty Trust.

Mengshoel, K., Liu, M., Moltubakk Kempton, H. and Frøysaker, T. 2012. 'Moving monumental Munch: from listed building to temporary studio – and back'. In *Moving Collections: Processes and Consequences*, I.A. Tank Bronken, S. Braovac, T.M. Olstad and A.A. Ørnhøi (eds) 65–72. London: Archetype Publications.

Tveit, E.S. 2011. *Edvard Munchs monumentale aulaskisser: Porøs maling, fleksibilitet og opprulling*. MA dissertation, Conservation Studies, IAKH, University of Oslo.

RECONSTRUCTING RED LAKES IN TRADITIONAL PAINT SYSTEMS

Daniela Leonard

The fading of light-sensitive organic red lake pigments is of particular interest to conservators because it has a direct effect on the painted surfaces of works of art. The nature of such degradation means that the act of viewing an object may also cause damage, resulting in irreversible changes to aspects of the artist's original intention (Burnstock 1988; Burnstock *et al.* 2005; Johnston-Feller and Bailie 1982; Saunders and Kirby 2001, 2004).

In 2009, a third-year student project was begun at the Hamilton Kerr Institute (HKI) to investigate red lakes used in layers and in mixtures with a variety of inorganic pigments, the final results of which will be discussed in a separate publication. The goal of this project was to evaluate both the immediate visual effect of artists' choices of materials and technique, and the subsequent effects of light ageing. To this end, several sets of paint samples were made and aged, either naturally or artificially, for a total of 14 months. The experimental design of this project highlights the problems that are faced when testing the internal mechanisms of complex objects. It is not possible to make an exact duplicate of a unique work of art so how can one recreate and age a paint passage, for example, in a manner that will provide useful insight into the degradation of the original? A purely scientific approach requires maximum control over as many variables as possible, which may provide clear results, but tends to offer very specific information that is far removed from the original object. This project was designed to balance modern scientific methods with artistic reconstructions in order to provide broader results that will be more relevant to real paintings. This paper first lays out the project development and ends with a discussion of the experiences gained in the physical qualities of oil paint, which resulted from making reconstructions in a manner determined by this particular cross-disciplinary approach.

Historically, red lake pigments were among the most highly valued artist pigments, not only for their visual qualities, but also because of the labour required for their production. All derive from plant or insect sources gathered by hand, some of which were shipped great distances to be sold in European markets. These materials were used primarily to dye cloth, but once the colour is extracted from the raw dyestuff it can also be used to dye an inert substrate, such as chalk or aluminium hydroxide, to form a red pigment. Particularly when mixed in an oil medium, the refractive index of the substrates traditionally used for lake colours results in transparent red glazes, for which these pigments were highly prized. Red lakes were also often used in opaque mixtures with inorganic pigments; for example, with lead white to make shades of pink or with a variety of blue pigments to make shades of purple (Saunders and Kirby 1994: 79).

For modern conservators, a major obstacle to gaining information about the past use of organic pigments has been the difficulty of identifying them in works of art. The presence of inorganic components such as calcium or aluminium may be confirmed through the use of scanning electron microscopy with energy dispersive X-ray (SEM-EDX) analysis, but determining the identity of the organic component is more complicated.[1] The greatest limitation of the techniques currently in use is the size of the sample required due to the relatively low pigment concentrations of red lake glazes (Kirby and White 1996: 56–7). In practice, this means that it is often difficult to identify which red lake has been used in a painting, ultimately hampering attempts to more accurately understand the alterations that have occurred.

The characteristics of any extractable dye material are variable and depend on many factors, such as the location of the plant or animal, the conditions in which they lived, and the point within their life cycle that they were collected. The colour of the pigment derived from any given batch of dyestuff can also be affected by the recipe used, the temperature and pH of the dyeing vat, and the thoroughness

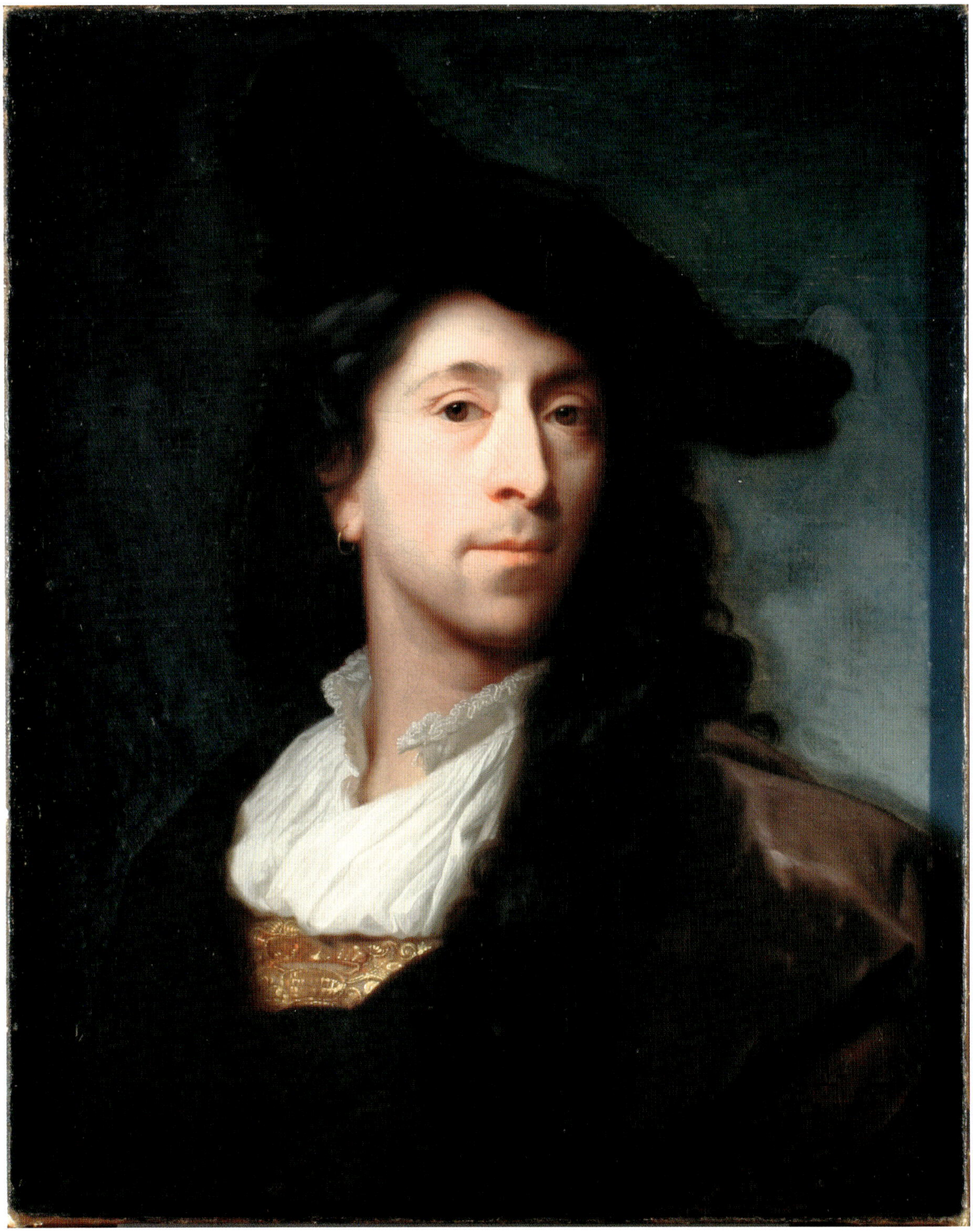

Figure 1 *Godfried Schalcken (1643–1706),* Self Portrait, *The Fitzwilliam Museum, Cambridge (368).*

of washing and filtering (Kirby *et al.* 2005: 80). Finally, the visual appearance of the paint itself will be determined by particle size, the selected medium, the concentration of pigment and the artist's technique, including admixed pigments and layer structures. The stability of the resulting paint passage will be influenced by all of these factors, along with the environmental conditions in which the painting is maintained. Although the molecular structures of the different colorants are known and studies on the fading of organic paints have determined some general behavioural trends, the relationship between the organic component, the inorganic substrate and the chosen medium is complex, and the mechanisms operating within the paint layer have yet to be more accurately defined.[2]

Two previous studies guided the development of this project. The first was undertaken by Ruth Johnston-Feller, who demonstrated that algorithms used to guide the mixture of colours in the paint industry could also match a

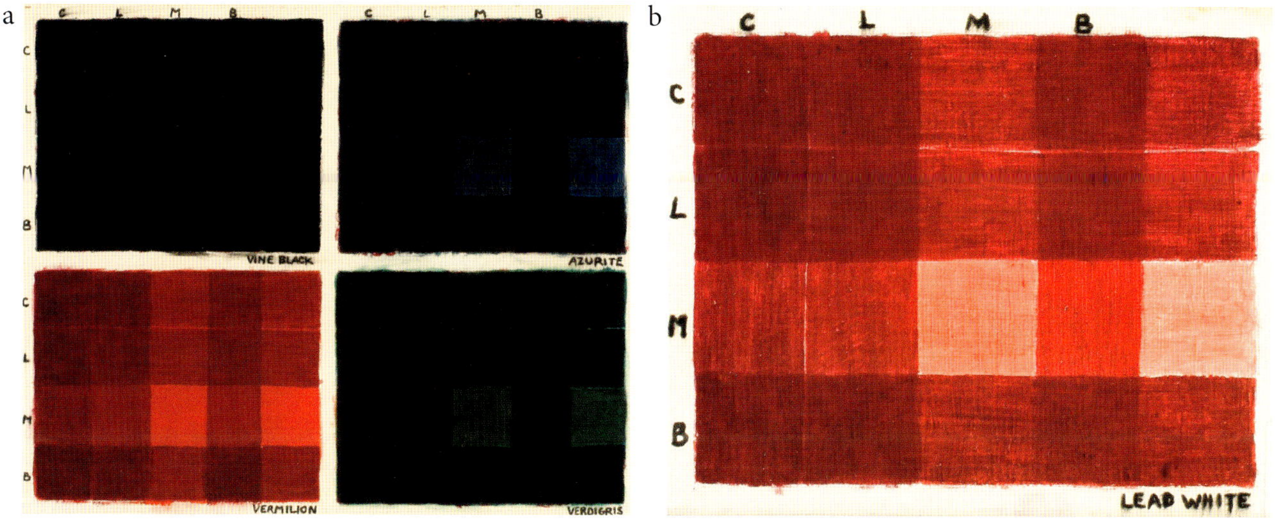

Figure 2 *Layer samples of cochineal, lac lake, madder and brazilwood (C, L, M, B respectively) painted in layers on top of (a) vine black, azurite, vermilion and verdigris (from left to right), and (b) lead white.*

faded mixture of alizarin crimson and titanium white, thus determining the concentration of the colorant that remains (Johnston-Feller *et al.* 1984). Through the use of these colour-matching computations, and mathematical modelling with Kubelka-Munk's equations, she was able to show that fading follows first-order kinetic behaviour (Johnston-Feller *et al.* 1984: 115). In other words, the rate of pigment loss is not constant, but continuously changes in proportion to the concentration that remains. Importantly, she was also able to show that visual alterations do not directly correlate with physical damage (Johnston-Feller *et al.* 1984: 125–6). It is easier for us to detect change in mid-tones than in deep glazes, meaning that mixtures containing approximately equal ratios of red and white will appear to fade at a faster rate.

The second study was a series of experiments undertaken by David Saunders and Jo Kirby who focused on traditional materials, measuring only visual colour changes (Saunders and Kirby 1994). Saunders and Kirby compared a variety of red and yellow lake pigments, testing their relative stability to light, as well as the effects of different methods of extraction, substrates and media. They also evaluated the visual changes of red lake and lead white mixtures, and their results corroborate those of Johnston-Feller, as well as the observed loss of mid-tones in real paintings (Saunders and Kirby 1994: 90–91).

It was determined that this project would expand on the results of the work undertaken by Saunders and Kirby by testing the behaviour of traditional red lake pigments in combination with colours other than lead white in order to gain insight into lakes' relationships with pigments commonly used in paintings. Only examples of admixtures and layer structures identified in paintings treated at the HKI were selected in order to keep the project closely tied to artistic practice.

The first step was to select examples of both layer structures and admixtures from the *c.*5,000 images in the HKI cross-section database. In order to have a manageable scientific experiment with meaningful results, it was necessary to simplify the constituents found in the cross-sections, thus reducing the number of variables and allowing for direct comparison between test samples. Therefore, rather than attempt to make exact reconstructions, it was decided to reduce underlayers and mixtures to a single inorganic pigment based on the overall colour of the original paint passage. The red lakes chosen were cochineal, lac lake, madder and brazilwood. These lakes were selected based on traditional use and current availability, as well as use in past studies. The four red lakes would be tested both in layers applied over, and in mixtures with: vine black, azurite, vermilion, verdigris and lead white. Further to this, and in order to compare the effects of blue pigments of varying quality, ultramarine and smalt would be tested in mixtures with the red lakes.[3] It was decided to also carry out a case study of a seventeenth-century painting in the Fitzwilliam Museum: Gottfried Schalcken's *Self Portrait* (Fig. 1) (Massing and Groen 1988). In this case, a full reconstruction of the underlayers used for the figure's red shawl was attempted using information gained through analysis of the cross-section with SEM-EDX and through colour measurements of passages on the painting.

The experiment included three sets of samples: one to be artificially aged in a light box at the HKI; one to be hung under normal gallery conditions at the Fitzwilliam Museum, Cambridge; and one to be kept in the dark as a control. Colour measurements would be taken with a Minolta CR-221 colorimeter at the start, and at various intervals during the 14 months of the project in order to maintain a quantifiable record of the colour changes that occurred.

Pine wood panels were sized with rabbit-skin glue and covered with a chalk ground applied with a brush. The

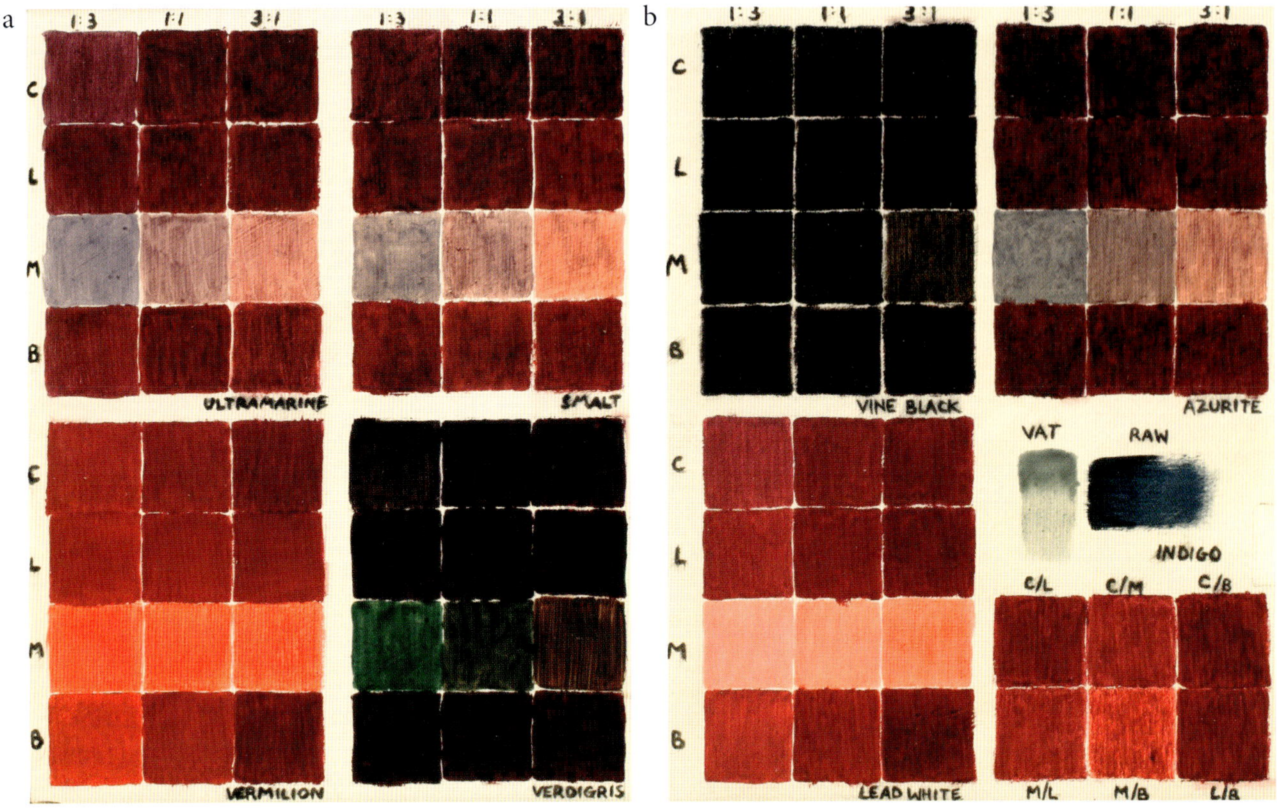

Figure 3 *Mixture samples of cochineal, lac lake, madder and brazilwood (C, L, M, B respectively) painted in mixtures at ratios of 1:3, 1:1 and 3:1 with (a) ultramarine, smalt, vermilion and verdigris (from left to right), and (b) vine black, azurite, lead white and mixtures of each lake in ratios of 1:1 (from left to right).*

chalk surface was primed with lead white, which served as an isolation layer for subsequent oil paint layers. Linseed oil was selected as the medium for all of the sample paints, based on its common use.[4]

It was common practice for artists to paint lakes in multiple layers (Kirby *et al.* 2005: 82). Overlapping layers could be achieved by crossing horizontal and vertical stripes of the four red lakes over each chosen inorganic underlayer. In this way, an example of each red lake overlaid on each of the others was achieved, in addition to the four squares of single red lake layers, resulting in a total of 20 squares for every inorganic underlayer tested (Fig. 2).

The set of admixtures would have ideally included five or six different ratios of red lake to inorganic pigment, as had been done by Saunders and Kirby; however, due to time constraints the number was reduced to three ratios for each lake, resulting in 12 squares for every inorganic pigment tested. As it was also common practice for artists to mix different lakes with each other, a set of samples was prepared of each of the lakes mixed in ratios of 1:1 (Fig. 3) (Kirby and White 1996: 67).

Analysis of Godfried Schalcken's *Self Portrait* revealed that the ground layer consists of an earth, lead white and chalk in ratios of approximately 2:3:6, and that the dead colouring underneath the red lake glaze consists of an earth, bone black, red lead and chalk in ratios of approximately 1:1:2:2. It must be acknowledged that such information extrapolated from small samples provides only an approximate idea of the material structure of the original paint passages, and cannot be used to judge the accuracy of colours selected for a reconstruction. In this case, the ground layer was exposed along the tacking edges and a colorimeter was used to match a raw umber for the earth pigment identified in the samples. A red ochre was chosen for the reconstruction of the dead colouring layer based only on the visual analysis of small losses on the painting.

The chosen red lake pigments were made at the HKI following sixteenth-century recipes translated by Renate Woudhuysen-Keller (Appendix 1). The general procedure is similar for all lakes. The colour was extracted from the raw dyestuff and then absorbed onto a substrate.[5] Chalk can be used for this purpose, but for all of the lakes included in this project aluminium hydroxide crystals were precipitated through the combination of alum and potash in solution.[6] The dyed crystals constitute the lake pigment. Once the particles have settled, the potassium sulphate solution that remains is poured off. The pigments are then washed repeatedly with clean water, filtered, and allowed to dry. The resulting caked pigment can be ground in water to regulate the particle size and improve the handling properties of the paints (Fig. 4).

A mistake made when preparing the madder lake served as a reminder of the effects of the preparation stage on the visual quality, and presumably the stability, of these pigments. The recipe for madder instructs that the roots be soaked overnight, the resulting brown liquid poured off, and the roots washed several times before extraction.

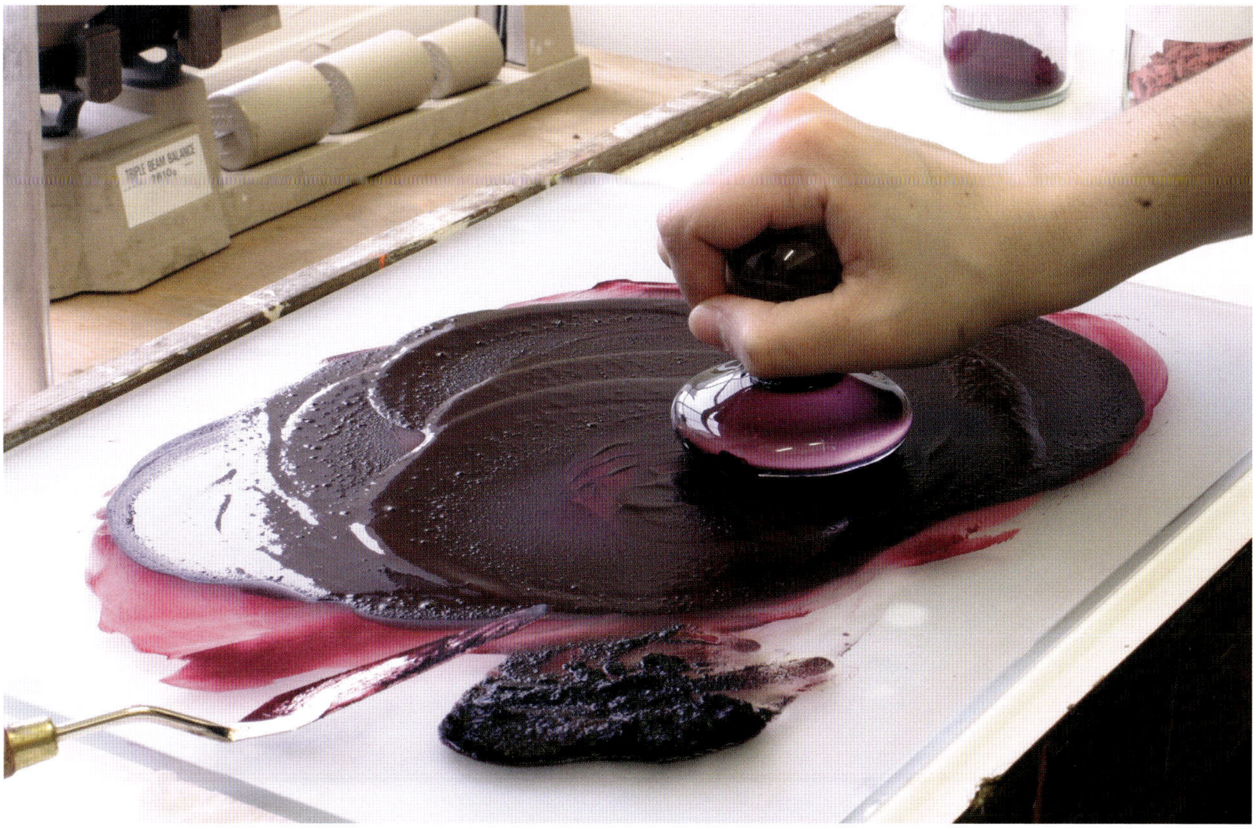

Figure 4 *Grinding cochineal in water to regulate pigment size.*

Instead, the roots were soaked only for several hours before washing, and were not washed more than once. The pigment that resulted contained a brown colour that should have been removed before extraction with alum. A second extraction was made from the same roots and a pink pigment was obtained; however, the tinting strength of the dye was noticeably reduced. Other characteristics of the pigment, such as oil absorption, were also found to have altered.[7] Just as the inorganic pigments used for this project are modern variants of traditional materials, the lakes made at the HKI were, by necessity, approximations of historically produced paints. It is important to note that artists may not have controlled the manufacturing of their lakes, as the pigments could be purchased as a commercial product.

The lead white applied to the sample sets as a priming layer did not provide a pure white colour and had a tendency to form *impasto*, which meant that, as on a typical painting, the surface on which the samples were painted was not entirely even. Variations in colour further caused by the uneven application of paint layers with a brush were addressed by taking multiple colour readings of the sample squares in order to determine an average for each.

The base colours for the layer samples were painted and allowed to dry completely. Vermilion dried in several days without the use of a siccative, but azurite and verdigris required two coats to provide even base colours and two weeks to dry properly. It was decided to add lead-tin yellow to the verdigris underlayer and red lead to the vine black underlayer in order to speed drying. These pigments had been found in the selected cross-sections, and an exception on the decision to use single pigments was made for this practical reason. Walnut oil was chosen instead of linseed oil in the lead white and azurite underlayers, because of its traditional use for white and blue pigments. However, this dramatically slowed the drying time of these layers to the point that the red lakes could not be applied for two weeks. Considering this significant increase in drying time, it seems unlikely that walnut oil would have been used for underlayers.

As the concentration of organic lake pigment has been found to affect the rate of fading, it was necessary to control the pigment volume concentration of the paints to maintain consistency across the samples. This was achieved by measuring the weight of pigment and counting the drops of oil. It was noted that the lakes exhibited slightly different oil-absorption rates, which may have been due in part to variations in the substrate resulting from the extraction process (Kirby *et al.* 2005: 80). After some experimentation for the layer samples, it was decided that 8–10 drops of linseed oil and a single dab of mastic (added to improve flow properties) would be used for every 0.1 g of lake pigment. Another concern was the thickness of the layer, as fading has been found to occur only to a depth of approximately 20 μm (Feller *et al.* 1986: 65). Layer thickness could not be precisely controlled with a brush, but an effort was made to cover equal areas with equal amounts of red lake and to paint the layers as evenly as possible.

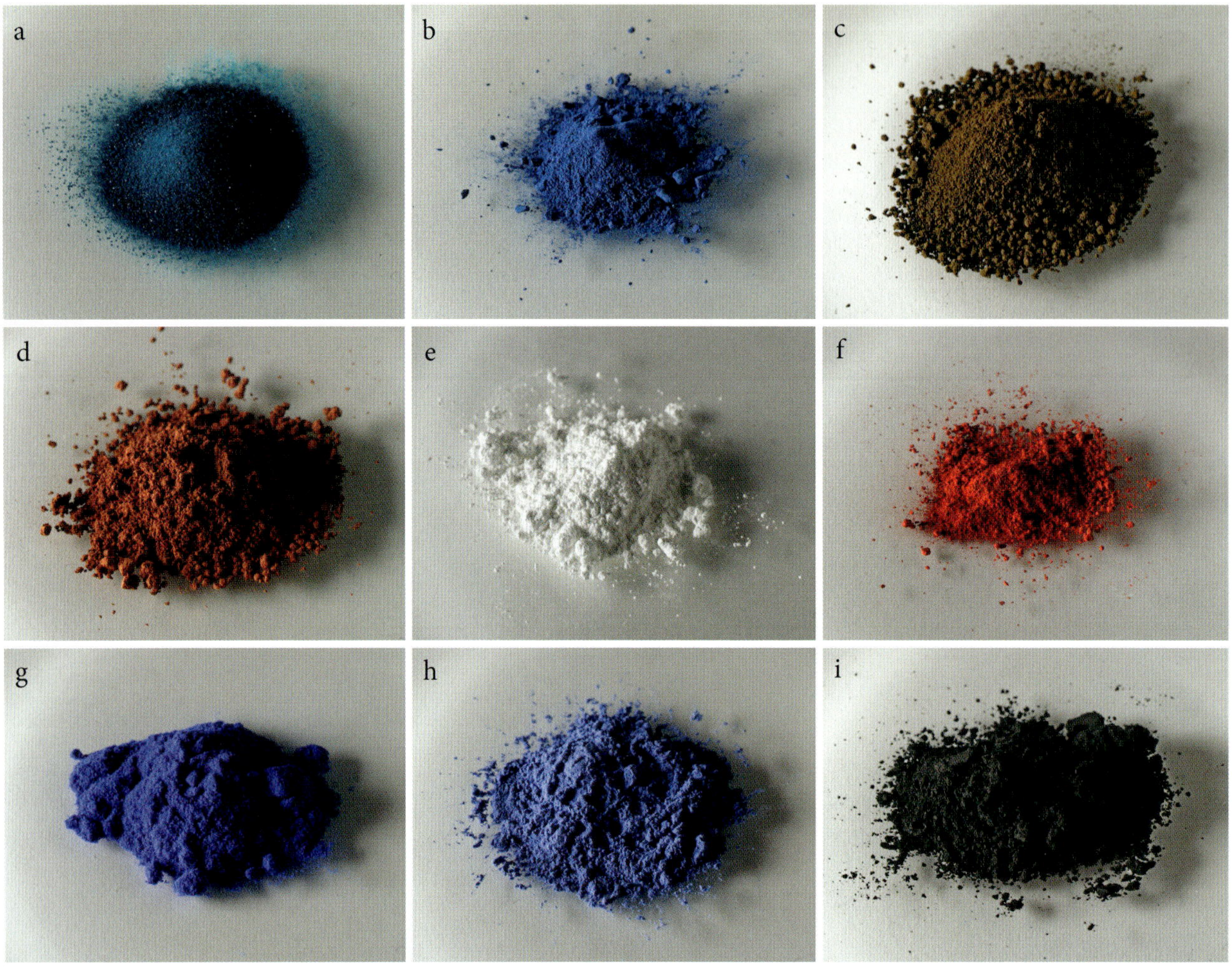

Figure 5 *Equal weights (1 g) of the inorganic pigments used in this project of (a) verdigris; (b) azurite; (c) raw umber; (d) red ochre; (e) lead white; (f) vermilion; (g) smalt; (h) ultramarine and (i) vine black.*

The total concentration of pigment was also maintained across all of the admixtures tested to enable a direct comparison between paints with widely different physical properties. Beginning with verdigris, it was determined that a total of 0.2 g of pigment in 10 drops of linseed oil was sufficient to paint three squares (one for each of the control, artificial ageing and natural ageing samples) without excess paint. The total pigment weight of 0.2 g could then be easily broken down into three ratios: 0.15 g:0.05 g, 0.10 g:0.10 g and 0.05 g:0.15 g (or 3:1, 1:1 and 1:3) organic to inorganic pigment. This solution proved to be problematic because some inorganic pigments (e.g. vermilion) are more dense than others (e.g. carbon black), meaning that equal weights of different pigments result in different amounts of paint, even when the volume of oil remains constant. In retrospect, a better solution might have been to maintain the same concentrations of red lake pigment (i.e. 0.05 g/0.10 g/0.15 g in 10 drops of oil) and allow the ratio of inorganic pigment to change according to the oil absorption of each.

Once all of the samples were painted, it was noted that many colours sank and became matt while others remained glossy. The reflection of a diffuse white light from the surface would affect the colour measurements therefore it was decided that the samples should be varnished for a better assessment of any fading that occurred. In order to monitor any difference in colour that might arise from alterations in the varnish layer, small sections of the white borders were left bare to serve as a standard against the varnished areas. Dammar resin was chosen for its good saturation properties. The varnish was brushed onto the surface of the samples in a single layer.

Painting the samples for this project provided a direct experience of the pigments tested and, as would be expected, each pigment demonstrated the typical characteristics that have determined past use. The challenge was to find a simple means of describing the experience so that the paints could be easily compared. In an attempt to present a simple means of assessing the qualities of the inorganic pigments tested, a table was made of the following characteristics, as noted before the addition of red lakes: texture of the dry pigment; texture in oil; handling properties; visual qualities (Appendix 2).

Overall, the texture of the dry pigments was found to range from the dusty powder of vine black to the hard grains of verdigris (Fig. 5). Azurite resembled fine sand

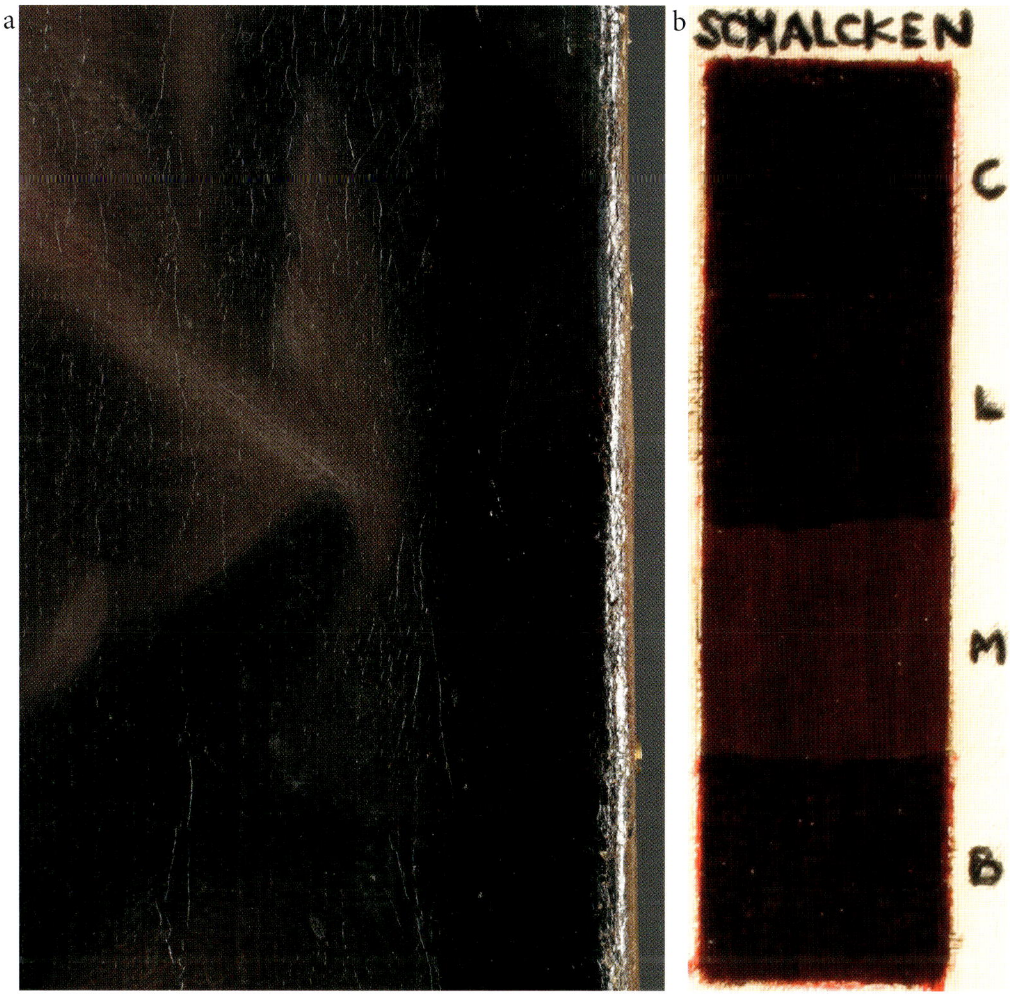

Figure 6 *(a) Detail of Godfried Schalcken's* Self Portrait: *the figure's cloak on the lower right side; (b) Schalcken sample with cochineal, lac lake, madder and brazilwood (C, L, M, B respectively) in single layers over reconstructed underlayers.*

while ultramarine was more powdery. Smalt had an interesting texture, as the particles tended to cling to each other while stacking to form a fluffy mass. Lead white, vermilion and the ochre pigments used in the Schalcken reconstruction were all heavier powders that clumped together like damp earth. The lakes were difficult to assess because their textures were affected by being ground in water, which caused them to form hard flakes, like fine dried clay.

The effects of texture on the visual qualities of the oil paints were most noticeable between the three blue pigments tested in mixtures. Azurite is extremely difficult to paint because of its grainy texture. Although the addition of red lake pigments improved its handling, the pigment particles tended to clump together, creating a patchy effect. Smalt could be manipulated into somewhat smoother layers, but also clumped and did not combine easily with the lakes, tending to separate as the paint was applied. Ultramarine was by far the easiest blue pigment to use, and could be applied more evenly than azurite or smalt. Verdigris, in contrast to the blues, has even harder grains when dry, but can be ground more thoroughly in oil without losing its colour, forming a heavy glaze that pulls at the brush like honey. The other pigments tested, including the red lakes themselves and the mixtures prepared for the Schalcken reconstruction, also exhibited good handling properties when compared with the blue pigments.

The constraints set by the experimental design of the project played a role in the interpretation of the handling of the paints in oil, as a skewed impression resulted from the range of oil absorption rates exhibited by the different pigments. This was not an issue for verdigris and the blue pigments, which all required similar amounts of oil as that chosen for the mixture samples. In the case of the other inorganic pigments tested, the underlayers painted for the layer samples provided a better opportunity for proper comparison. For example, vine black and vermilion both became smooth, easily extendable paints when prepared for optimum handling properties, but were complete opposites when mixed with equal amounts of oil. The vine black created a large amount of stiff paint, whereas the vermilion produced a small amount of runny paint. Lead white as an underlayer formed thick, sticky impasto, but as a mixture also became thin and runny.

The tinting strengths of the different pigments influenced the visual properties of the prepared paints, and this in combination with the three ratios selected for the mixture samples affected the comparison between the layers and mixtures. The red lakes (except for madder) had a medium tinting strength among the pigments tested, and both lead white and the blue pigments allowed the lakes to play a greater visual role. When freshly painted over lead white, cochineal and lac lake were a similar purplish red hue, whereas brazilwood was a warmer red. Madder appeared light pink, but had it been prepared correctly it would have been a strong, raspberry red colour. The mixture samples appear similar, but mixing with white creates a turbid effect that does not occur when the lakes are applied in layers. The lakes layered over azurite resulted in very dark purple colours, whereas the mixtures using the three blue pigments exhibited much more of the lakes' influence in the selected ratios, resulting in brighter reddish purples, particularly with ultramarine.

The visual difference between layers and mixtures of red lakes in combination with verdigris, vermilion and vine black was much less pronounced than with the blue pigments. Verdigris is not strongly tinting, yet formed very dark reds or muddy greens that were close to black, in large part because the majority of the visible spectrum is absorbed by combining red and green. Vermilion has a high tinting strength in normal conditions, but only a small amount was included in each mixture, reducing its influence. Vine black also has a relatively strong tinting strength and completely overpowered the lake pigments, creating saturated maroon to deep black colours in both layers and mixtures. The Schalcken reconstructions resulted in dark, red to purple-red colours that were comparable with passages on the real painting preserved along the edges by the frame rebate (Fig. 6).

The variety of characteristics presented by the traditional materials used in this project was well understood by artists, and limitations such as the grainy texture and weak tinting strength of azurite created challenges that were overcome through adaptations of technique. The composition and layer structure of any given paint passage was determined not only by the desired visual effect, but also by the physical nature of the materials that were available. The act of reconstructing a painting can help gain insight into the artist's intentions, as it allows for a better understanding of the full creation process than can be achieved through scientific testing of materials in isolation. There is no denying the value of information that has been gained through the scientific study of painting materials, but as the experience of undertaking this project has shown, reconstructions used in conjunction with analysis provide additional information that cannot be gained through scientific means alone. It has been recognised that the natural degradation of artists' materials affects our viewing experience, and can influence our interpretation of a work. It is hoped that by increasing our knowledge of the degradation process, we can understand the alterations that have taken place and ultimately improve the care of works of art so that further change can be delayed while access is maintained.

Appendix 1: Preparation of lake pigments

Cochineal

20 g dried cochineal beetles
20 g potash in 1L hot water
40 g alum in 1L warm water

The dye was extracted by soaking the beetles in a warm potash solution for over an hour. The beetles were then filtered out and the pigment precipitated with alum. The pigment was washed, filtered, ground in water and allowed to dry.

Madder

500 g madder roots
150 g alum in 1L hot water
150 g potash in 1L hot water

The roots should be soaked overnight in warm water and then washed several times (in the first extraction the roots were washed only once after several hours). The washed roots were then soaked for nine days at approximately 40°C. A hot alum solution was added and the roots were soaked overnight. The roots were then filtered out and the dye precipitated with potash. The pigment was washed and filtered, but found to be a muddy pink colour. Another extraction was then made by soaking the filtered roots with alum for five more days. The roots were filtered again and the dye precipitated once more with potash. The pigment was then washed, filtered, ground in water and allowed to dry.

Brazilwood

100 g brazilwood shavings
75 g alum in 1.5L hot water
50 g potash in 1L hot water
A pinch of chalk

The plant fibres were heated for six hours. The dye was then extracted with alum and allowed to soak overnight. The shavings were filtered out and the pigment precipitated with enough potash to form a neutral solution (pH 7). The pigment was then washed, filtered, ground with water and allowed to dry.

Lac lake

The lake was prepared in 2002. The pigment was extracted with alum and precipitated with potash.

Appendix 2: Table of inorganic pigments

Pigment	Texture when dry	Texture in oil	Handling properties	Visual qualities
Azurite	Grains like fine sand	Wet sand	Difficult to spread; particles have a tendency to clump	Bright, semi-transparent blue colour; low tinting strength
Lead white	Clumps and sticks like a clay	Thick, creamy paste	Easy to paint; can be spread thinly, but tendency towards *impasto*	Off-white; low tinting strength
Raw umber	Clumps like sandy clay	Wet, gritty clay	Very easy to spread; not smooth, pulls at the brush	Greenish brown colour; high tinting strength; has a tendency to sink
Red ochre	Clumps like sandy clay	Wet, smooth clay	Easy to paint; slightly smoother than raw umber	Muddy red colour; high tinting strength
Smalt	Sticky powder, clumps and fluffs	Wet smooth sand	Difficult to spread, but doesn't clump as much as azurite	Similar to ultramarine initially, but loses brilliance when dry; low tinting strength
Ultramarine	Light, soft sand or powder	Smooth paste	Paints out more smoothly than smalt and azurite; combines better with other pigments in mixtures	Bright, semi-transparent blue colour; low tinting strength
Verdigris	Gritty like fine, hard sand	Thick honey	Requires a great deal of grinding, but then easily spread	Semi-transparent green glaze; low tinting strength; appears pale at first, but darkens once dry
Vermilion	Heavy powder, clumps	Thin, smooth paste	Extremely easy to paint; requires low media content	Bright red colour; high tinting strength
Vine black	Very light, dusty powder	Thin, smooth paste	Extremely easy to paint; requires high media content	Deep black colour; high tinting strength

Notes

1. For a discussion of the tools available for the analysis of organic pigments see Kirby and White 1996: 57–9.
2. It has been noted that particle size influences stability, as larger particles are often found to retain their colour in cross-sections where smaller particles have faded. It has been suggested that the surface area to volume ratio may be a determining factor; see van Eikema Hommes 2004: 153.
3. It was determined that any visual differences between ultramarine, smalt and azurite used in layers would most likely be too minimal for inclusion in this project.
4. The linseed oil used contained lead siccatives (prepared by Renate Woudhuysen-Keller at the HKI).
5. All of the lakes produced for this project were extracted directly from raw materials. No attempt was made to extract colour indirectly from dyed cloth. See Saunders and Kirby 1994: 83.
6. The empirical formula for the reaction that takes place is: $2AlK(SO_4)_2 + 3K_2CO_3 + 3H_2O \rightarrow 2Al(OH)_3 + 4K_2SO_4 + 3CO_2$.
7. This accident presented an extreme case, but Dr George Kremer of Kremer Pigmente GmbH & Co. KG suggests that impurities from lake production due to inadequate washing are a significant factor in the subsequent stability of the resulting paint film (pers. comm., 2011).

References

Burnstock, A. 1988. 'The fading of the Virgin's robe in Lorenzo Monaco's *Coronation of the Virgin*', *National Gallery Technical Bulletin* 12: 58–65.

Burnstock, A., Lanfear, I., van den Berg, K.J., Carlyle, L., Clarke, M., Hendriks, E. and Kirby, J. 2005. 'Comparison of the fading and surface deterioration of red lake pigments in six paintings by Vincent van Gogh with artificially aged paint reconstructions'. In *Preprints of the ICOM-CC 14th Triennial Meeting*, I. Verger (ed.) 459–66. London: Earthscan Ltd.

Feller, R.L., Johnston-Feller, R. and Bailie, C. 1986. 'Determination of the specific rate constant for the loss of a yellow intermediate during the fading of alizarin lake', *Journal of the American Institute of Conservation* 25(2): 65–72.

Johnston-Feller, R. and Bailie, C. W. 1982. 'An analysis of the optics of paint glazes: fading'. In *Science and Technology in the Service of Conservation*, N.S. Brommelle and G. Thomson (eds) 180–84. London: IIC.

Johnston-Feller, R., Feller, R.L., Bailie, C. and Curran, M. 1984. 'The kinetics of fading: opaque paint films pigmented with alizarin lake and titanium dioxide', *Journal of the American Institute of Conservation* 23: 114–29.

Kirby, J. and White, R. 1996. 'The identification of red lake pigment dyestuffs and a discussion of their use', *National Gallery Technical Bulletin* 17: 56–80.

Kirby, J., Spring, M. and Higgitt, C. 2005. 'The technology of red lake pigment manufacture: study of the dyestuff substrate', *National Gallery Technical Bulletin* 26: 71–87.

Massing, A. and Groen, K. 1988. 'A self-portrait by Godfried Schalcken', *The Hamilton Kerr Institute Bulletin* 1: 105–8.

Saunders, D. and Kirby, J. 1994. 'Light-induced colour changes in red and yellow lake pigments', *National Gallery Technical Bulletin* 15: 79–97.

Saunders, D. and Kirby, J. 2001. 'A comparison of light-accelerated ageing regimes in some galleries and museums', *The Conservator* 25: 95–104.

Saunders, D. and Kirby, J. 2004. 'The effect of relative humidity on artists' pigments', *National Gallery Technical Bulletin* 25: 62–72.

van Eikema Hommes, M. 2004. *Changing Pictures: Discoloration in 15th–17th-century Oil Paintings*. London: Archetype Publications.

'... AND NOW YOU SEE IT!': THE USE OF DIGITAL RECONSTRUCTIONS IN PAINTING CONSERVATION

Chris Titmus

Arguably one of the biggest advances in conservation in the last 30 years is the changing use of photography, or imaging as we now call it. To attempt many of the reconstructions that we currently undertake would have been impractical and costly during the era of film photography. The pace of change in the last 20 years, since the advent of widely available digital photography, has been remarkable; the quality of the equipment and software now used is virtually unrecognisable from their earliest versions, with capabilities well beyond many people's imaginations. Here is a brief resume of digital reconstructions that have been undertaken at the Hamilton Kerr Institute (HKI) in the last few years, to illustrate the utility of this ever-changing technology.

The Westminster Retable, Westminster Abbey, London

Conservators have appreciated the advantages of recording their work using photographs, virtually from the inception of the photograph itself. Many early examples exist and are still used for reference today, for example in assessing the changing condition of a painting or the effect of subsequent restorations. During the 1998–2005 treatment of the Westminster Retable, we were fortunate to have access to photographs from the Westminster Abbey archive, taken by Sir Emery Walker in 1897, along with others by an unknown photographer taken in 1964, documenting changes that had occurred during the intervening years. Other campaigns of photographic documentation occurred in 1936 and 1971 (Binski and Massing 2009). Sir Emery Walker's images, however, only illustrate specific areas: no overall shot, if taken, has survived. As part of the conservation treatment, it was considered important to be able to compare the early photographs with the then-current condition of the painting, and that having an image of the whole retable in a single shot would prove very useful. This required using all the individual detail shots and combining them into a complete piece (Figs 1 and 2).

If taken at face value, it might seem a straightforward task simply to stick all the photographs together, but it proved rather more complex. The Westminster Retable is three dimensional, with numerous architectural features that might cast shadows. To add to the complexity, the

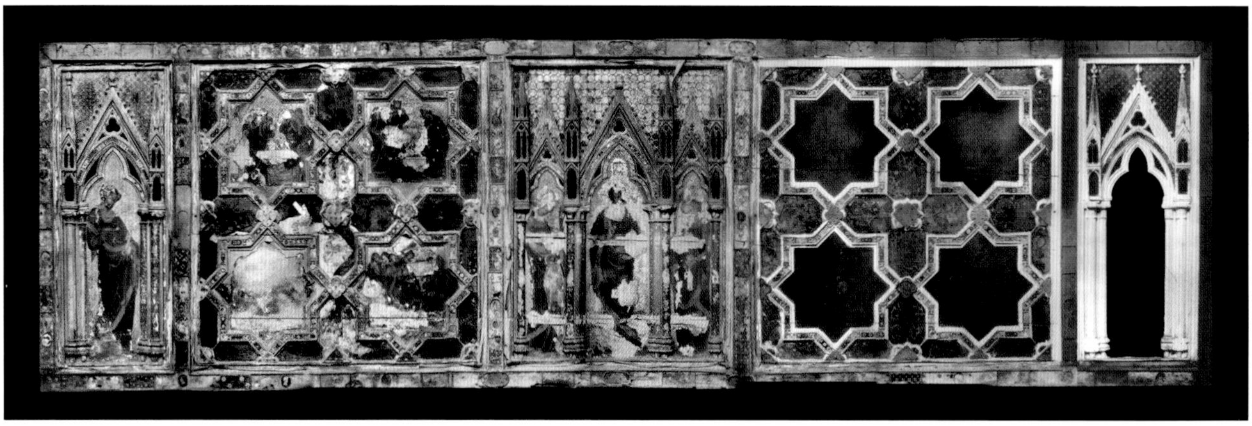

Figure 1 *Composite image from photographs taken by Sir Emery Walker, 1897, of the Westminster Retable. (Image courtesy of the Dean and Chapter, Westminster Abbey.)*

1897 photographic details were all taken from slightly different angles giving small changes in perspective; there are also slight differences in magnification. This combination of small variations – hardly evident when viewed individually – made the shots problematic to assemble. When attempting to blend them into a unified image, a number of anomalies soon appeared; the photographs were not taken with the intention of being a matched set that could be joined together as one.

The process was started by digitising and patching the images together as a rough set in the correct positions, using 'layers' in Adobe Photoshop, to ensure that we had a complete image with no missing segments. Each layer was then examined in turn to adjust the perspective and select which areas gave the best match to the adjoining part. Whilst the final image has to appear to the viewer as though it is a picture taken from a single viewpoint, and every care is taken to maintain accuracy of the component images, it should never be considered suitable for acquiring accurate measurements or positional data; for that purpose photogrammetry of the Westminster Retable was undertaken by Stuart Robson of University College London (Binski and Massing 2009: 427–31). The final result is a reasonable match when compared with an image taken in a single shot, and served as an aid to the conservators in assessing the changes undergone by the painting since 1897.

The Thornham Parva Retable, St Mary's, Thornham Parva, Suffolk

The conservation of another medieval retable, in Thornham Parva, was carried out by a team from the HKI between 1996 and 2003 (Massing 2003). This retable is thought to have been originally made for Thetford Priory in Norfolk, and supporting research suggests that a medieval frontal now in the Musée de Cluny, Paris, was part of the same altar ensemble (Norton *et al.* 1987). The aim of this reconstruction was to try to recreate an impression of how the two would have looked together *in situ* as they were originally intended. Whilst the retable was then freshly restored, the frontal still had a coating of discoloured varnish. More problematic still, a section had also been removed some centuries ago and subsequently vanished or been destroyed, leaving the frontal with only four scenes rather than the original five (Fig. 3). The first stage was therefore to reconstruct the missing section of the frontal using the existing end-section as a starting point. The timber frame and background were copied and swapped to form the basis for the replacement. The background area was carefully retouched digitally to remove the image leaving the pattern clear for the replacement scene. Research carried out by Paul Binski identified the scene that would most likely have been in the missing section: the *Annunciation*. Fortunately, a comparable image from the same period was located on the Peterborough Psalter in the Bibliothèque Royale de Belgique, albeit a manuscript illumination and on a very different scale (Fig. 4). Having placed the figures onto the frontal, the robes were re-coloured to match the overall appearance of the other figures, providing an impression of how the original might have looked (Figs 5 and 6).

For the setting of the altarpiece reconstruction, a local village church, St Mary Magdalene in Ickleton, Cambridgeshire, was identified as reasonably representative of the period. As with many medieval churches it contains features added during the Victorian era (Fig. 7). It was also suggested that we should set the image in St Mary's church, Thornham Parva, where the retable is currently sited. The final outcome is a blend of both these possible locations. There was considerable debate over how much the church interior should be manipulated to get the right balance: to make it appear like a medieval priory as opposed to a modern parish church.

The interior of Ickleton church was chosen to form the basic setting. A digital photograph of this was retouched to reduce the Victorian content whilst leaving some of the wooden panelling and red carpets to retain a more current feel. Ickleton's altar was replaced with that from St Mary's, Thornham Parva, along with its candlesticks. As both the retable and the frontal had been photographed in photographic studios for different purposes, it was important to set them into the scene with care to match the lighting of the church setting. The relative position of each piece was calculated to retain its size and perspective relative to the setting, considering also the scaling

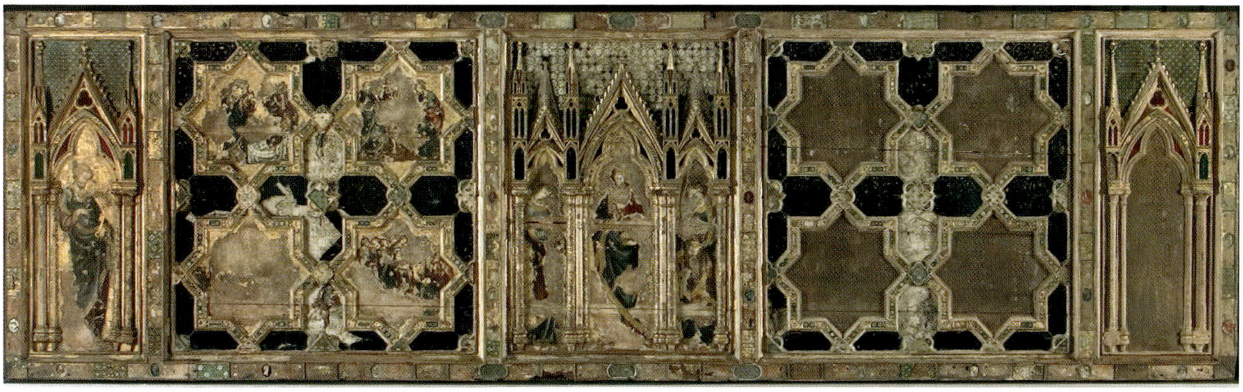

Figure 2 *After treatment image of the Westminster Retable taken in a single shot. (Photograph courtesy of the Dean and Chapter, Westminster Abbey.)*

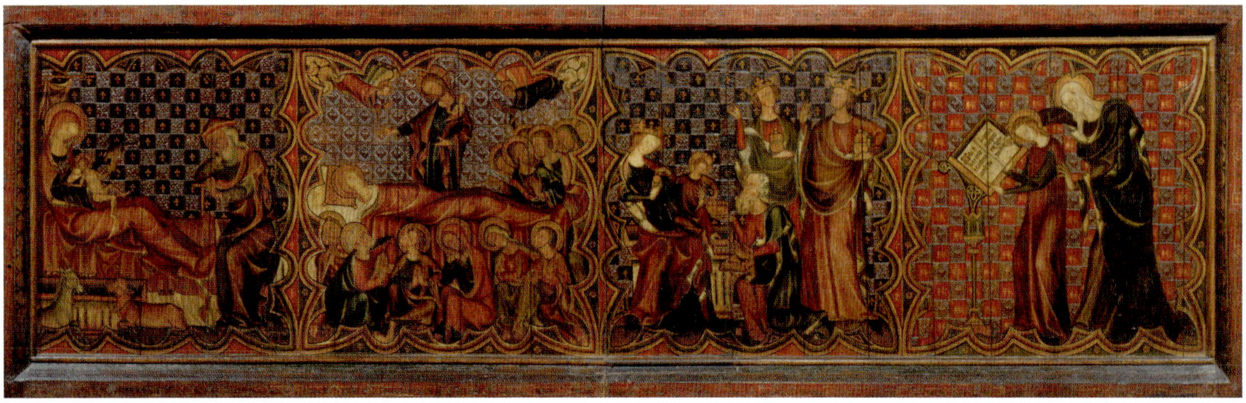

Figure 3 *Original frontal,* Scènes de la vie de la Vierge. *(Photograph courtesy of Musée de Cluny, Paris, © RMN/Jean-Gilles Berizzi.)*

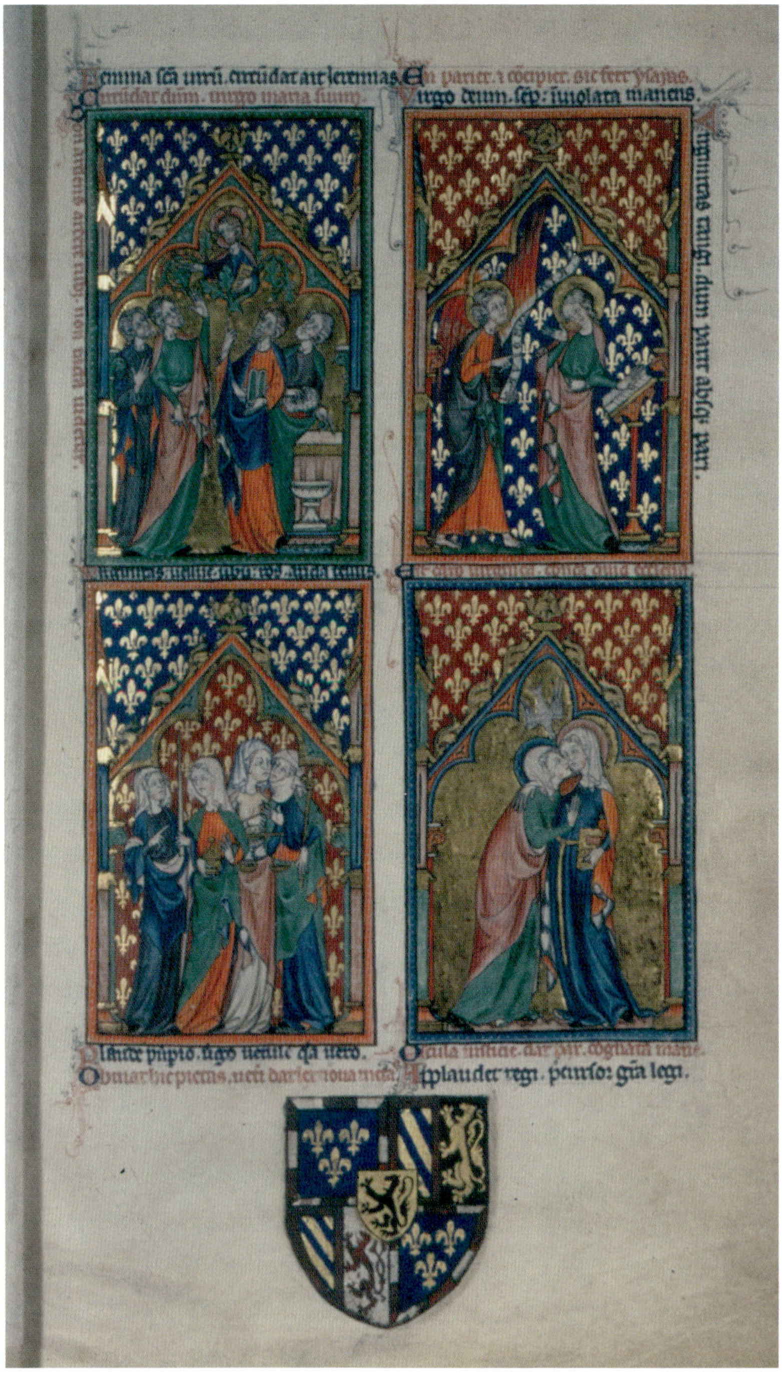

Figure 4 *Peterborough Psalter (MS 9961.2, f. 10). (Photograph © Bibliothèque Royale de Belgique.)*

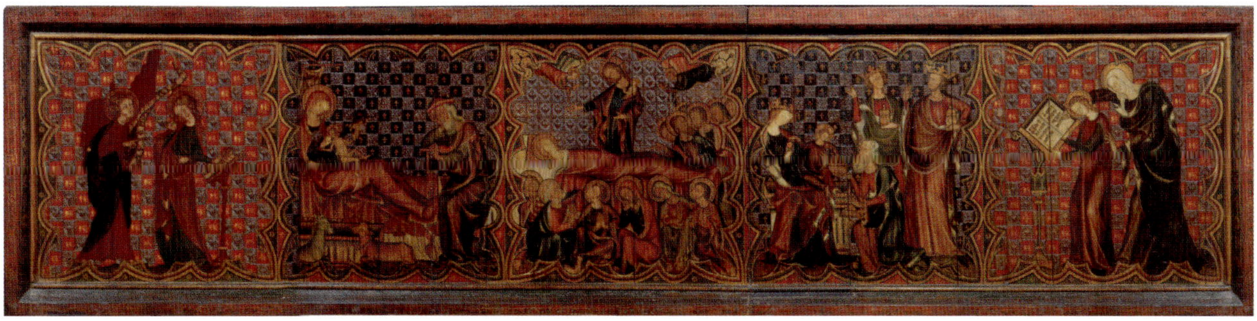

Figure 5 *Digital reconstruction of the frontal.*

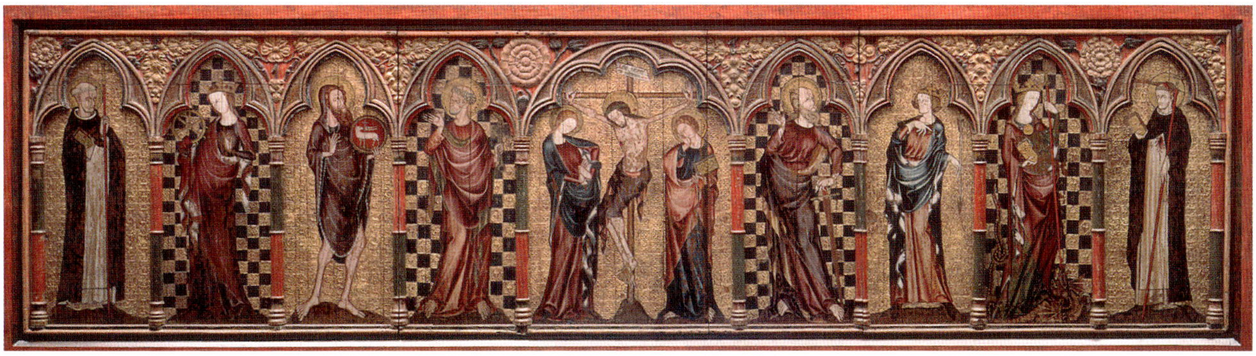

Figure 6 *Thornham Parva Retable, after treatment. (Photograph by kind permission of St Mary's church PCC, Thornham Parva.)*

and lighting of the altar and candlesticks. Taking into account the fact that the retable was recently restored, both were adjusted to give them a more uniform appearance (Fig. 8). The windows above the altar also sparked debate amongst the conservators and Thornham Parva's parishioners. Different opinions existed about windows in the original medieval setting (which no longer exists) and the appearance of the digital reconstruction. In the end, the project's sponsor chose the solution that they felt to be most appropriate (Fig. 9).[1]

The final version of this image is currently on display in St Mary's church, Thornham Parva, Suffolk. There, visitors to the church can enjoy seeing the actual retable along with a visual representation of how it may have looked together with the frontal, based on research available at the time (Fig. 10).

Portrait of Elizabeth I, British, sixteenth century, Westminster Abbey, London

The Westminster Abbey archives showed that alterations to this portrait had been made in the early eighteenth century when the queen's face was changed to give her a younger appearance.[2] The archival evidence was supported by visual evidence of overpaint on the face and hands. After the decision was made not to attempt removal of the overpaint on the portrait it was decided to investigate the appearance of the underlying queen through other means. X-radiography confirmed the presence of the earlier face

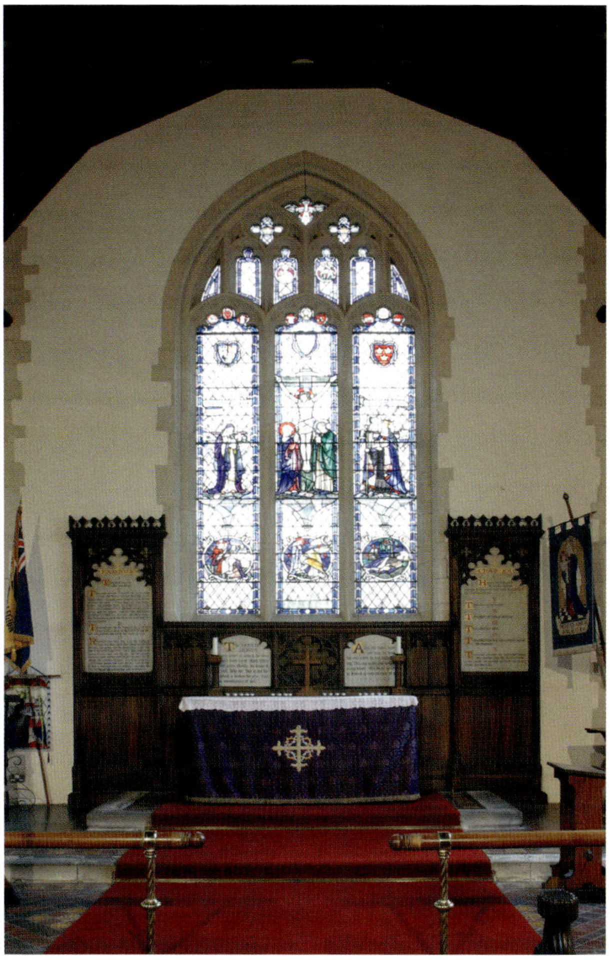

Figure 7 *Interior of St Mary Magdalene church, Ickleton.*

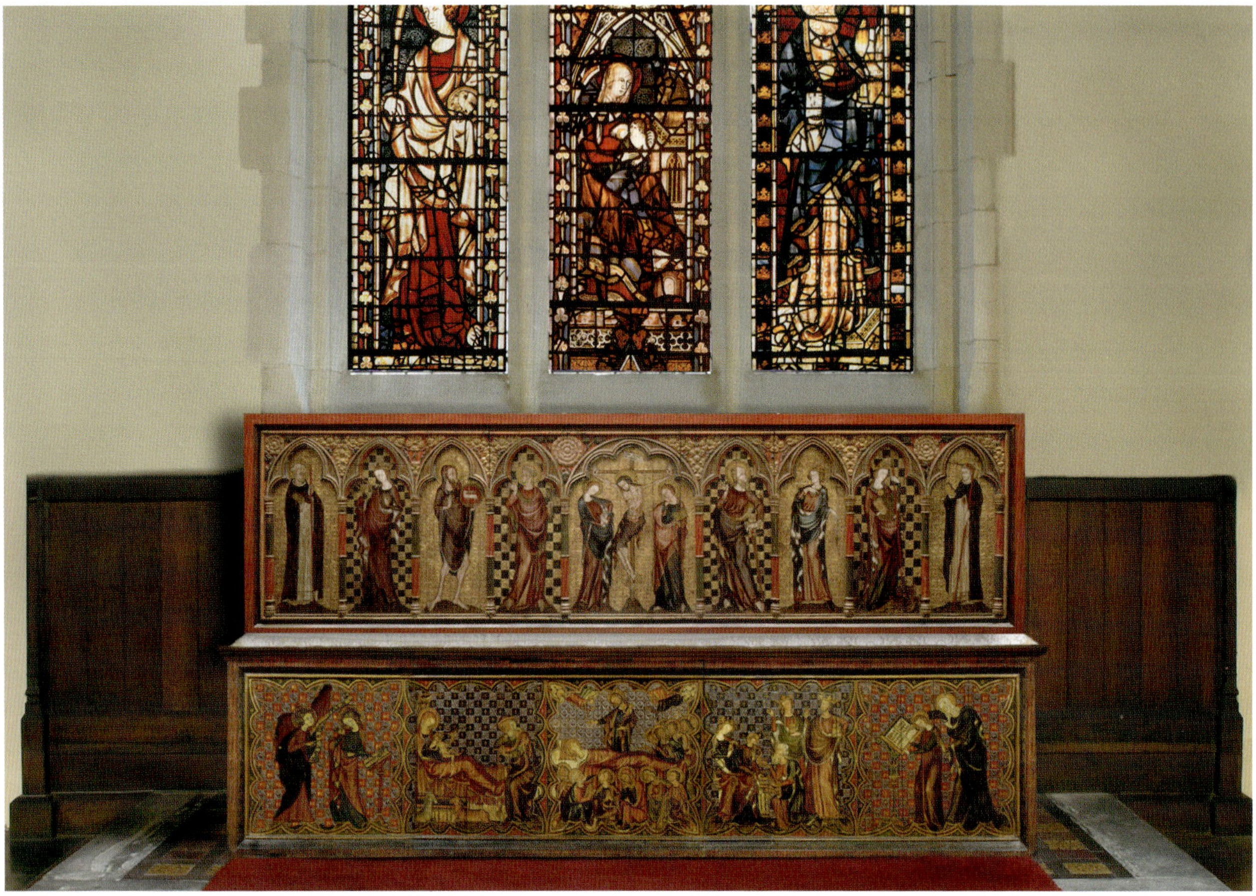

Figure 8 *The Thornham Parva Retable digital reconstruction, with stained glass windows.*

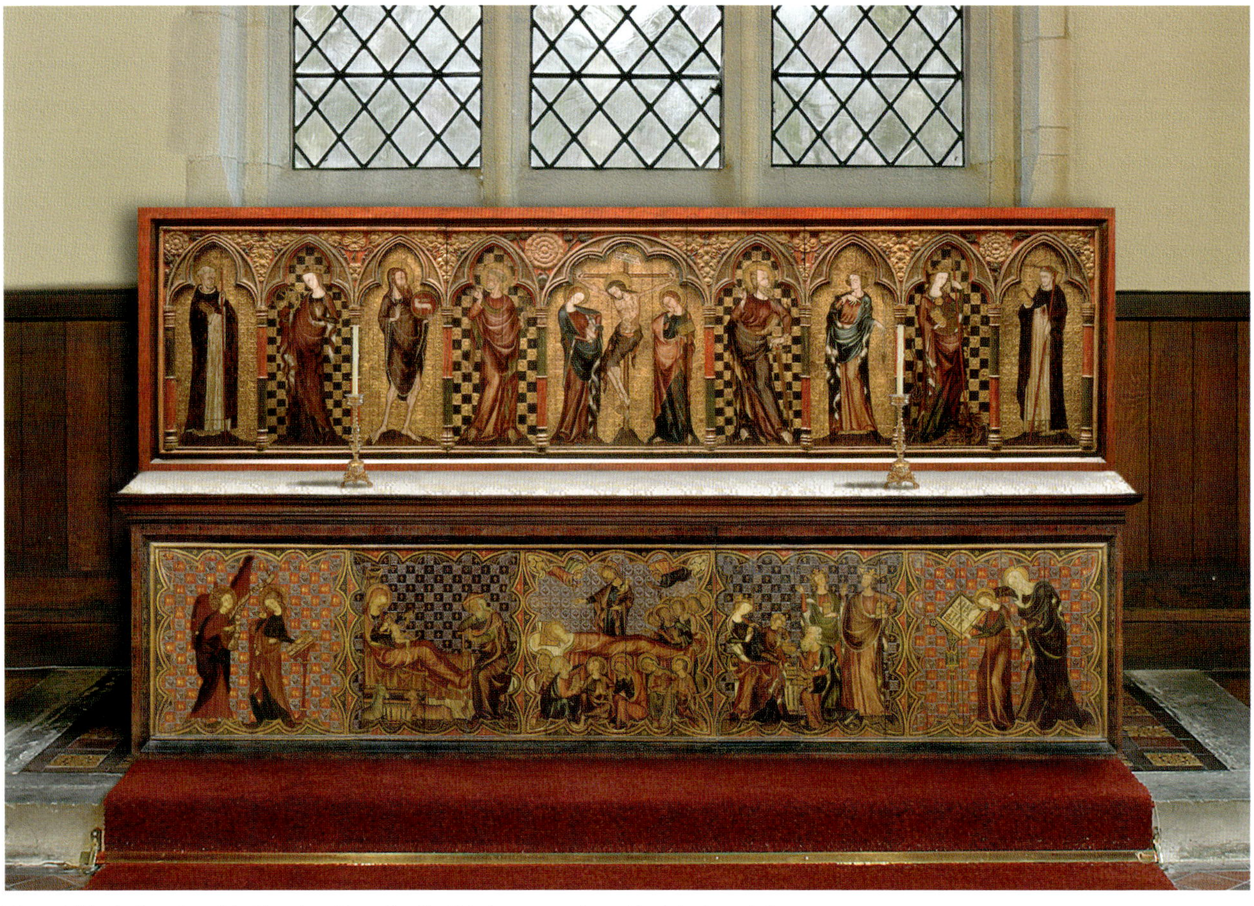

Figure 9 *The final version of the Thornham Parva Retable digital reconstruction, with plain glass windows.*

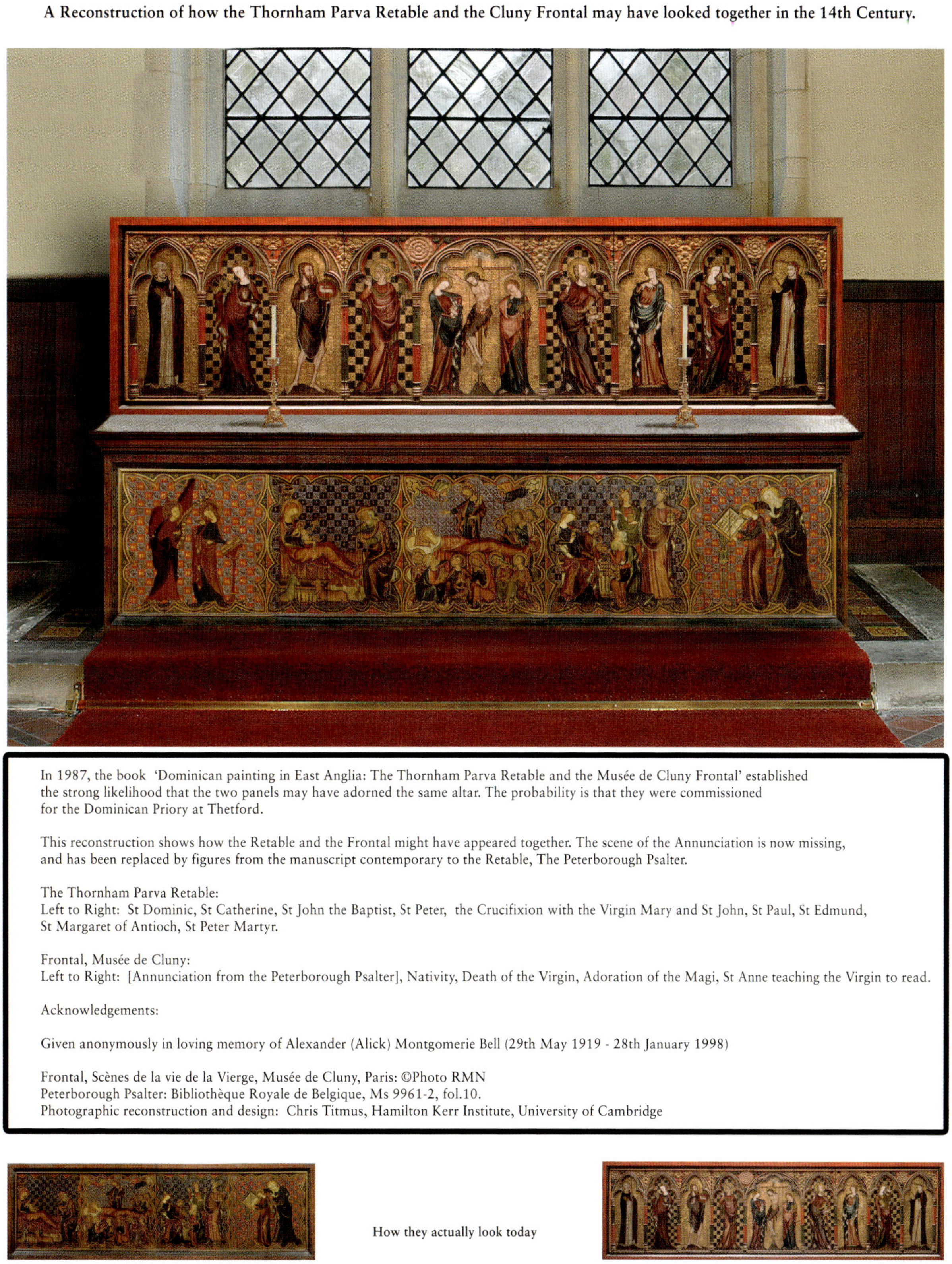

Figure 10 *The graphic used in St Mary's church, Thornham Parva to illustrate the suggested original appearance to the visitors. (Photograph by kind permission of St Mary's church PCC, Thornham Parva. The digital reconstruction was kindly given, anonymously, in loving memory of Alexander (Alick) Montgomerie Bell (29 May 1919 –28 January 1998).)*

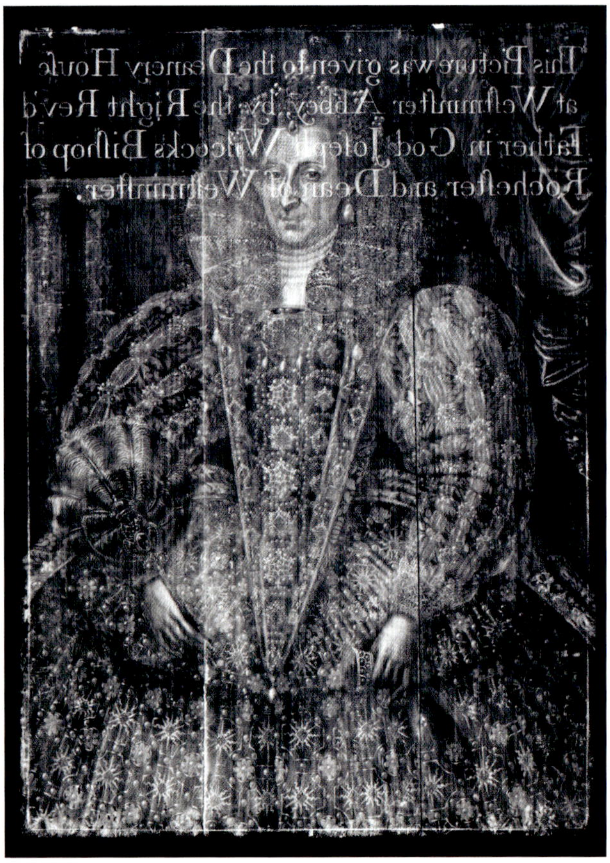

Figure 11 *X-ray of the portrait of* Elizabeth I, *Westminster Abbey. (Image courtesy of the Dean and Chapter, Westminster Abbey.)*

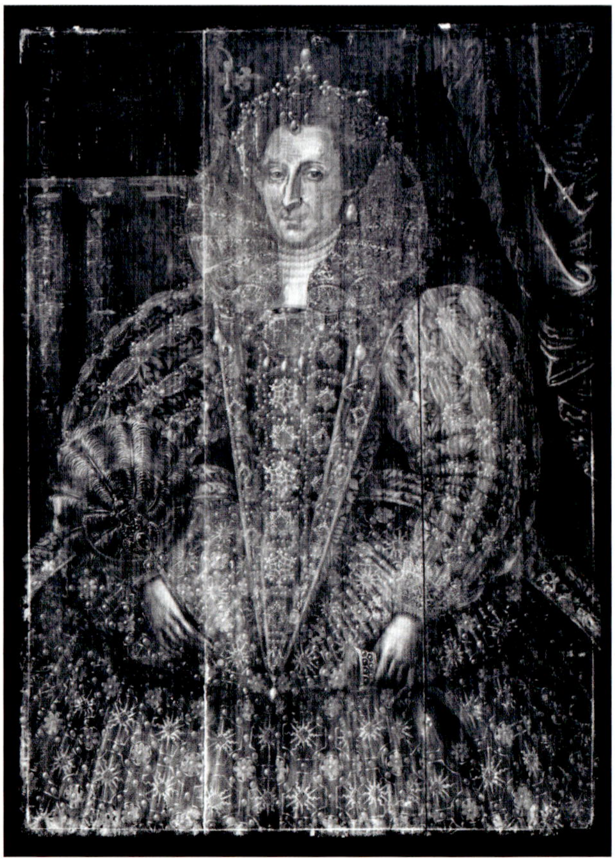

Figure 12 *Digitally retouched X-ray of* Elizabeth I *to remove the inscription on the reverse. (Image courtesy of the Dean and Chapter, Westminster Abbey.)*

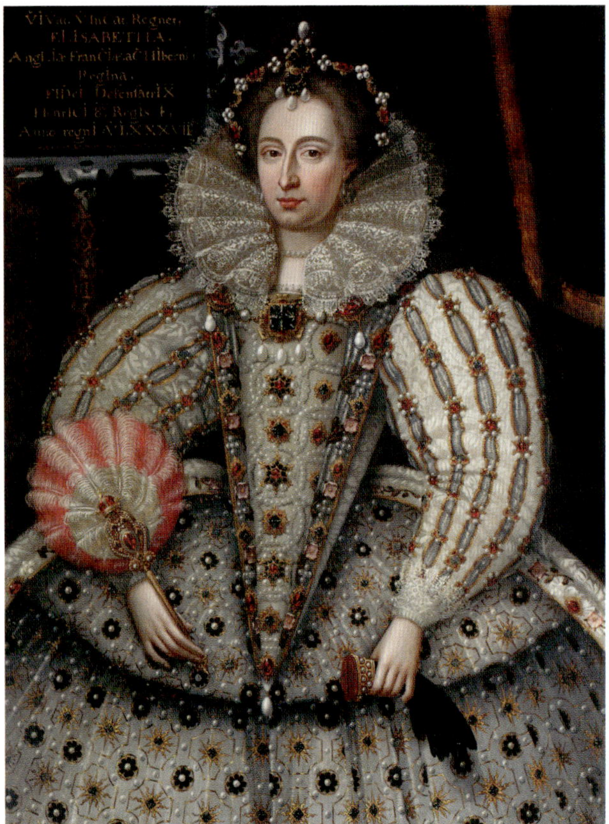

Figure 13 Elizabeth I, *Westminster Abbey. (Photograph courtesy of the Dean and Chapter, Westminster Abbey.)*

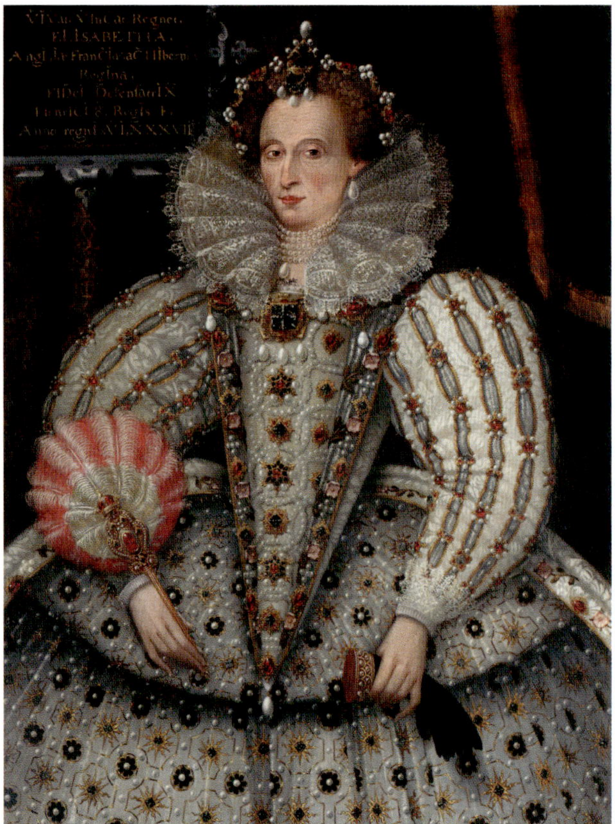

Figure 14 *Digital reconstruction of* Elizabeth I *to illustrate the original appearance. (Image courtesy of the Dean and Chapter, Westminster Abbey.)*

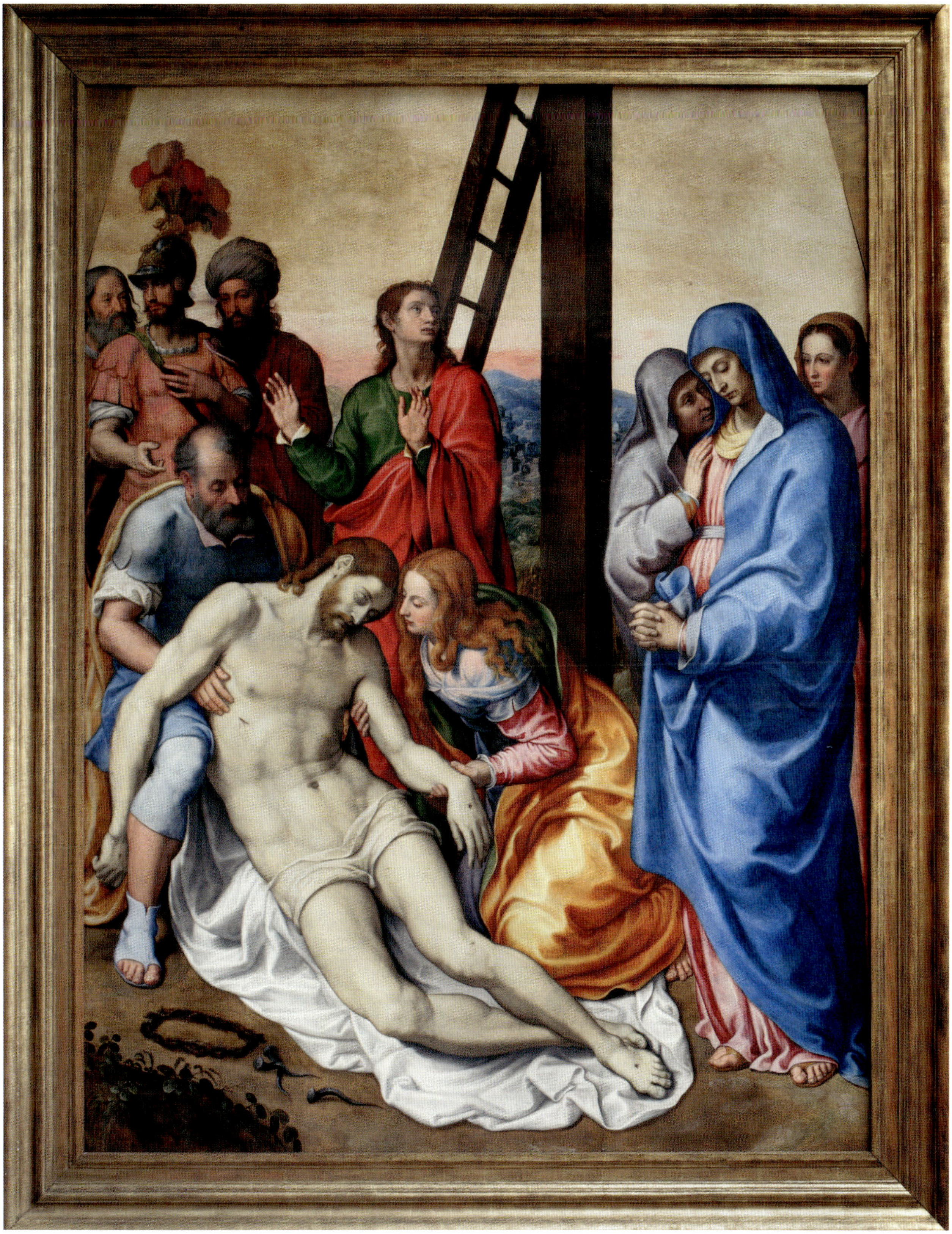

Figure 15 *Siciolante da Sermoneta,* Deposition of Christ, *King's College, Cambridge. (Photograph courtesy of King's College.)*

beneath but unfortunately it was obscured by the presence of an inscription on the rear of the painting (Fig. 11). An initial task was to retouch out this text digitally in order to provide a clearer image (Fig. 12). Research was undertaken to trace a portrait that had a comparable earlier face; good fortune prevailed, since paintings from this date were often copied, and another version of the same portrait was located at Boughton House, Northamptonshire. Through referencing the images to the X-radiograph, it was possible to graft and blend the face and hands from the Boughton

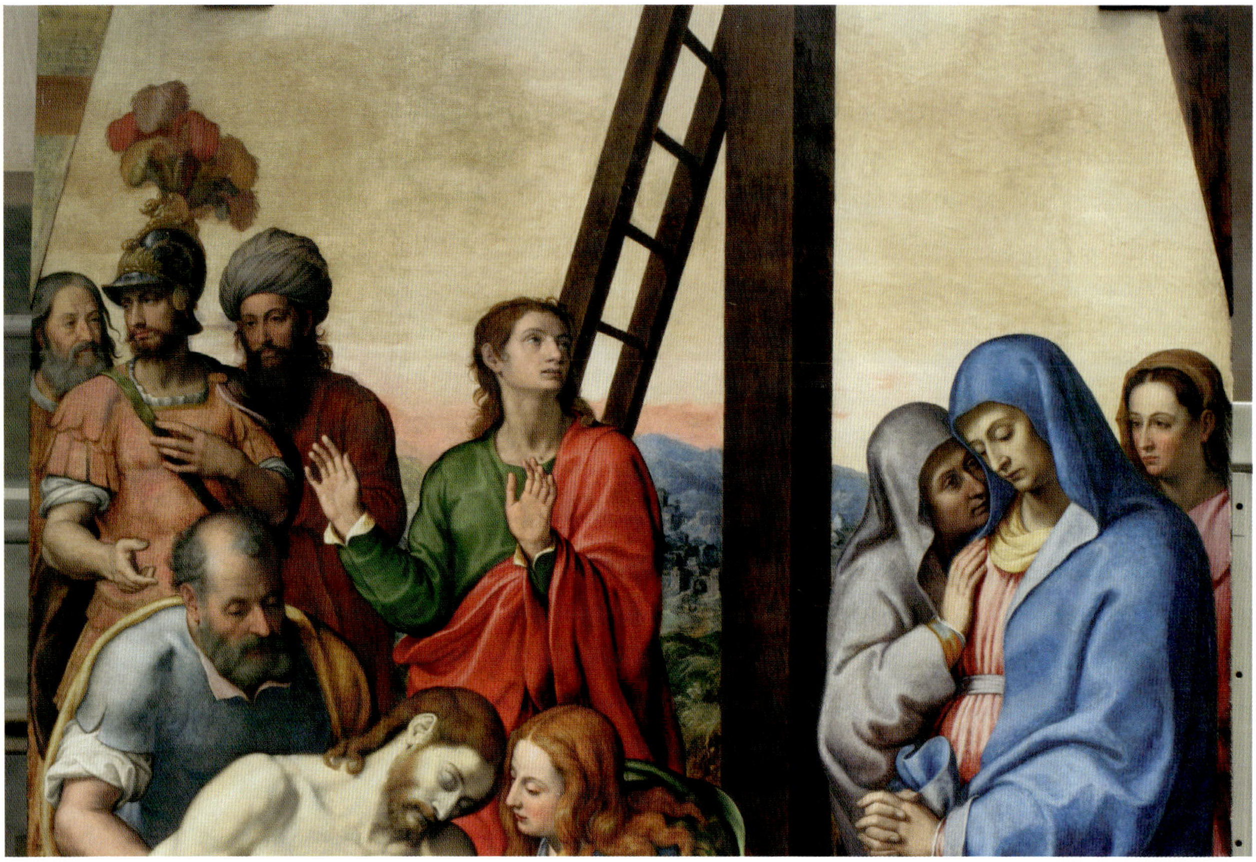

Figure 16 *Detail of* Deposition of Christ *showing cut-away sections on the top corners.*

House image onto the portrait from Westminster Abbey (Figs 13 and 14). With this digital reconstruction it is now possible to give visitors an impression of how the painting once looked. The project was featured in the *Time Team Special* television programme, broadcast in June 2010, on Westminster Abbey.

Siciolante da Sermoneta, *The Deposition of Christ*, King's College Chapel, Cambridge

This painting (Fig. 15), which hangs in the chapel of King's College, Cambridge, now looks quite different from when it was painted in Rome in 1560 (Kempski *et al.* forthcoming). The digital reconstruction was created in an attempt to visualise the painting in its original condition, with its pigments unchanged in colour. The triangular sections added to the top corners suggest that the panel had been squared-off from a previously arched shape (Fig. 16). Research into other compositions by Siciolante and his contemporaries suggested a likely original shape for the top. This was added in Adobe Photoshop using a separate 'layer', incorporating an adapted semicircular mask to provide the basic shape. In order to fill the newly created space, the sky, ladder and upright post of the cross were extended upwards by copying from suitable areas of the existing painting. Additional figures were considered but decided against due to a lack of space. Scanning electron microscopy with energy dispersive X-ray (SEM-EDX) analysis had revealed traces of cobalt, suggesting the sky was originally painted blue with smalt, now discoloured to yellow. The sky was therefore overlaid with a blue tint to match the results of paint mixing trials with smalt that had been carried out as part of the project. A similar illustrative digital reconstruction of discoloured smalt has been undertaken by the National Gallery, London (Spring *et al.* 2001). The faded red lake of the soldier's armour was also enhanced to give the reconstruction a closer match to its original appearance. The final stage, as always, was to carefully blend and adjust all the elements to give the finished result (Fig. 17).

Caravaggio, *The Taking of Christ*, National Gallery of Ireland, Dublin

A physical, painted, reconstruction of *The Taking of Christ* by Caravaggio (Fig. 18) was requested for a television programme in the series The *Secret Life of a Masterpiece*.[3] Caravaggio's technique was particularly economical and efficient, which the programme producers wanted to illustrate with a reconstruction of part of *The Taking of Christ*, necessitating a visit to Dublin to obtain a high resolution image for reference in the HKI studio.

Part of Caravaggio's skill lay in leaving parts of the initial underlayer exposed between, and within, paint passages.

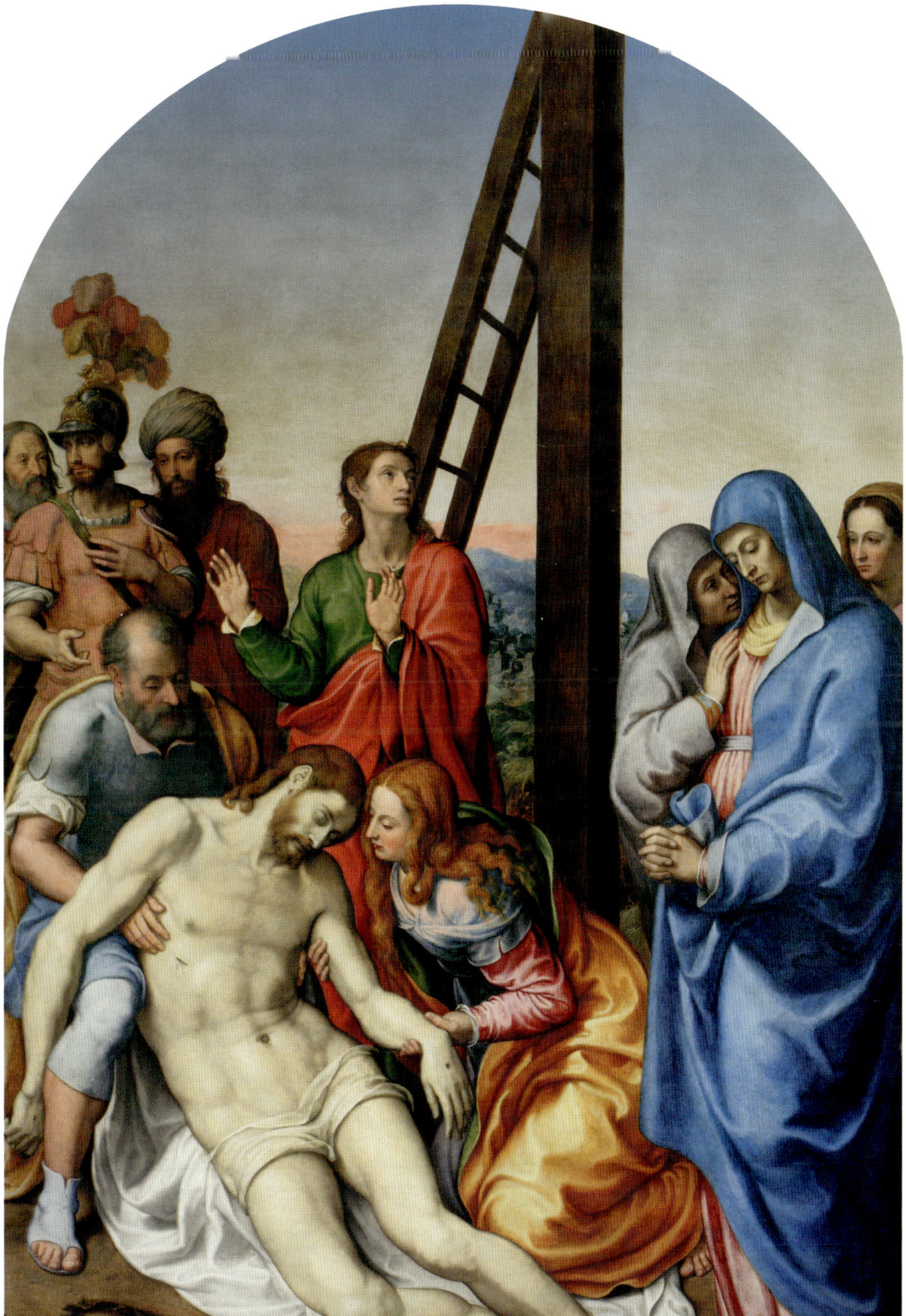

Figure 17 *Digital reconstruction of* Deposition of Christ *to show the suggested original appearance.*

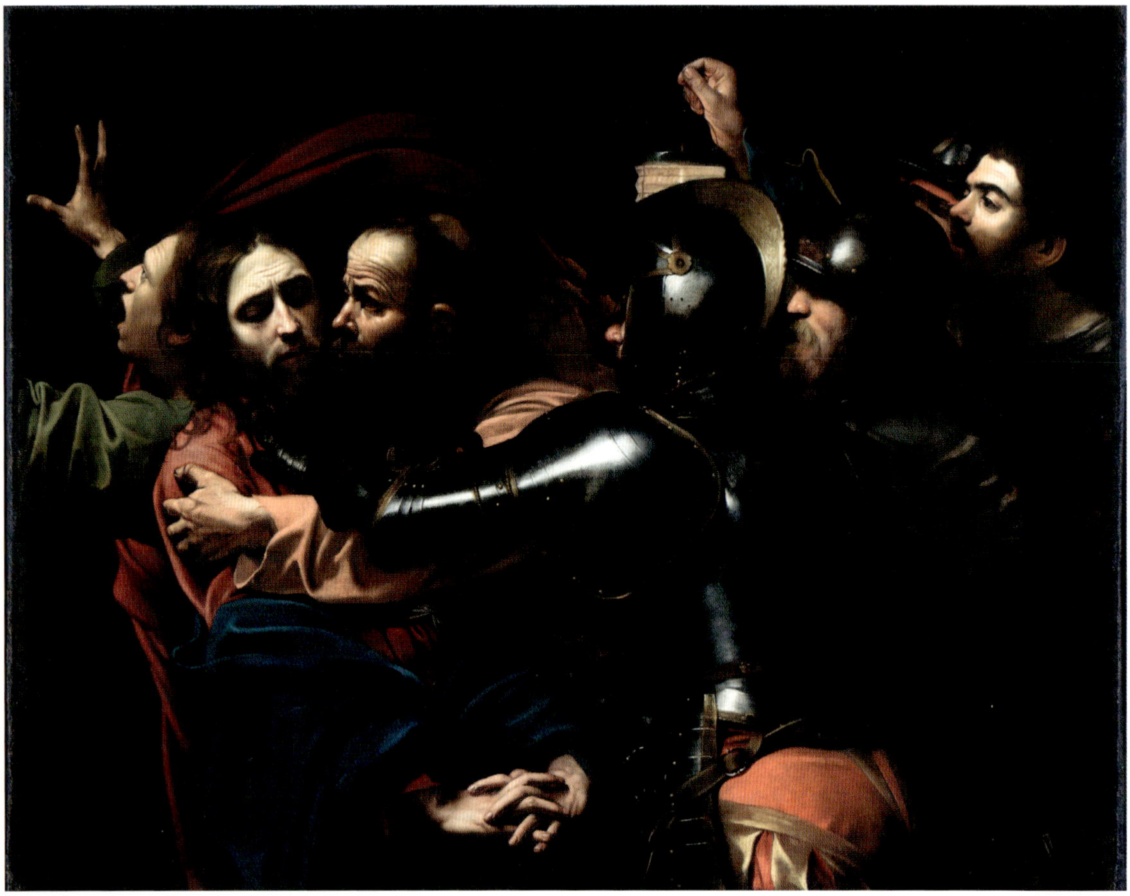

Figure 18 *Caravaggio,* The Taking of Christ. *(Photograph © National Gallery of Ireland, Dublin.)*

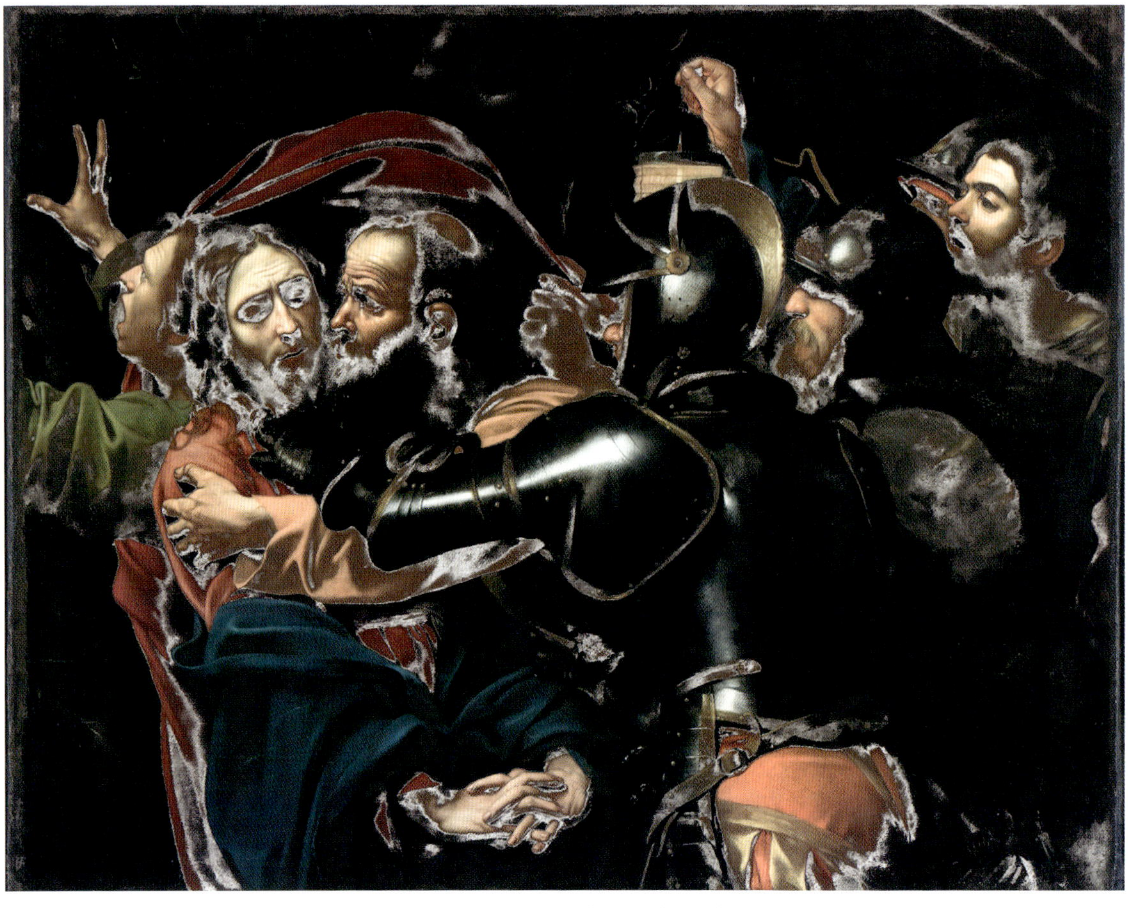

Figure 19 *The digital reconstruction of the painting using a colour change to illustrate the artist's technique.*

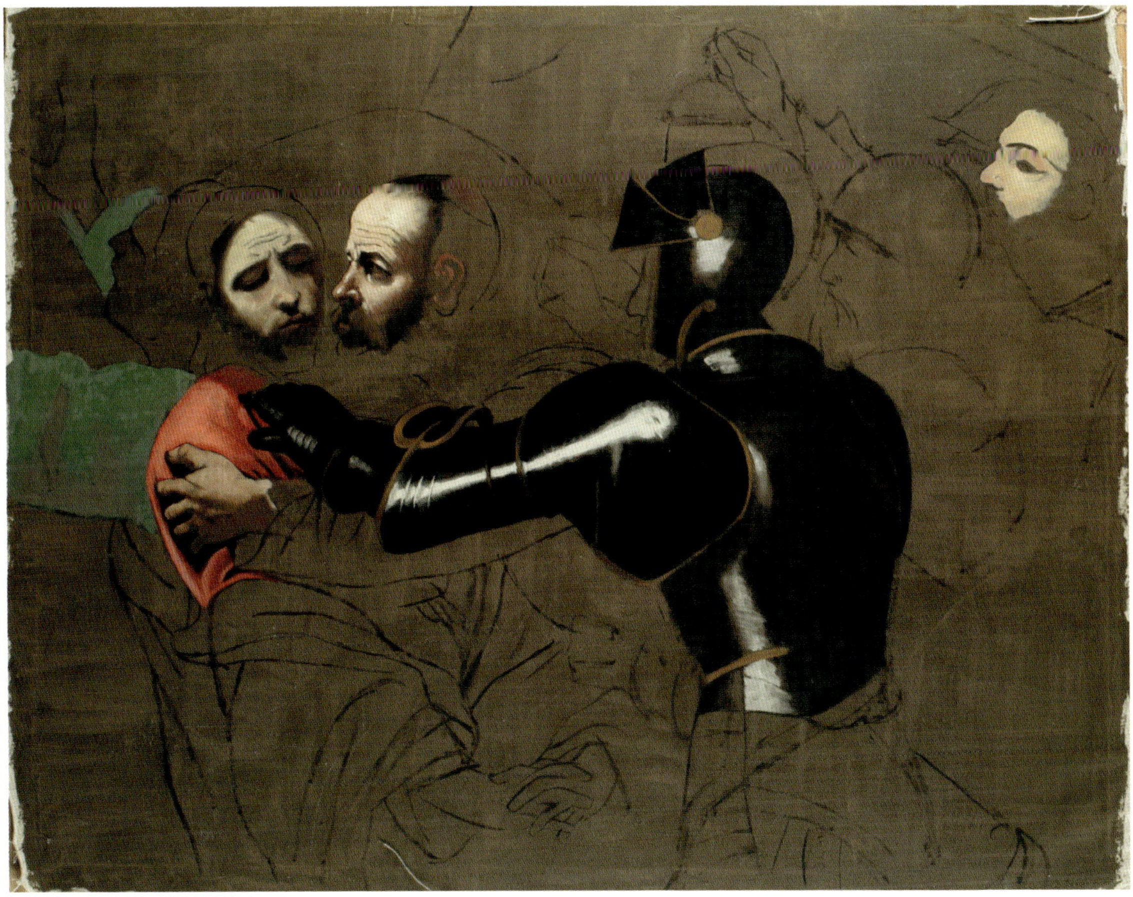

Figure 20 *The painted reconstruction as used during filming.*

This layer is a dark rich red-brown and it contributes to the shadows, with the mid-tones of flesh and drapery blended into it as they emerge into the light. Caravaggio's technique means that the edges of figures are rarely well defined and the same unifying colour is found inconspicuously in many paint passages. It is difficult to identify this underlayer on the original, let alone in a photograph, but knowledge of its presence was important for the reconstruction. An area of clear background around the figures was identified and isolated in the digital image, then the 'change colour' feature in Adobe Photoshop was employed to make it stand out more clearly (Fig. 19). Simply changing the colour of a selected area clarified an important aspect of the artist's technique, and proved a valuable aid in the production of the physical copy (Fig. 20).

Frederick George Watts, *Portrait of Thomas Walker*, Peterborough Museum, Cambridgeshire

The *Portrait of Thomas Walker* by Watts (Fig. 21) is a delightful illustration of a 'reconstruction' made by entirely natural means (Kempski and Noh 2008). In this case a very fine image of the painting had been left on the inside surface of its glazing by free fatty acids that had migrated through the paint layers, evaporated from its surface and then been deposited on the glass. This 'reconstructed image' of the painting was a natural phenomenon that graphically illustrated an aspect of the chemical composition of a nineteenth-century painting and a common process of degradation. Whilst the same painting ingredients and chemical processes are widespread, it is rare that they leave such a clear visible trace.

Documentation of this phenomenon required careful preparation. The image of the portrait, made from a microscopic layer of deposited fatty acids on the glass, was extremely faint under normal lighting conditions. It was evident to the naked eye because the constant movement of the eye and head allowed a mental summary of many slightly different viewpoints to be constructed. This three-dimensional, dynamic information is lost in a photograph.

With the painting removed for conservation work, the glass was re-secured in the frame for safety. A structure was built in the photographic studio to hold the framed piece of glass in front of a black screen. The glass was lit using a selection of spotlights in an attempt to recreate 'dark ground illumination', as it would be termed in microscopy. The frame itself was then lit separately (taking care to avoid light spillage onto the surface of the glass) to enhance the gilding. The aim was to light the glass from behind using a lighting pattern that gave contrast, to make the delicate image more visible. The frame lighting, from the front, needed to be softer, as

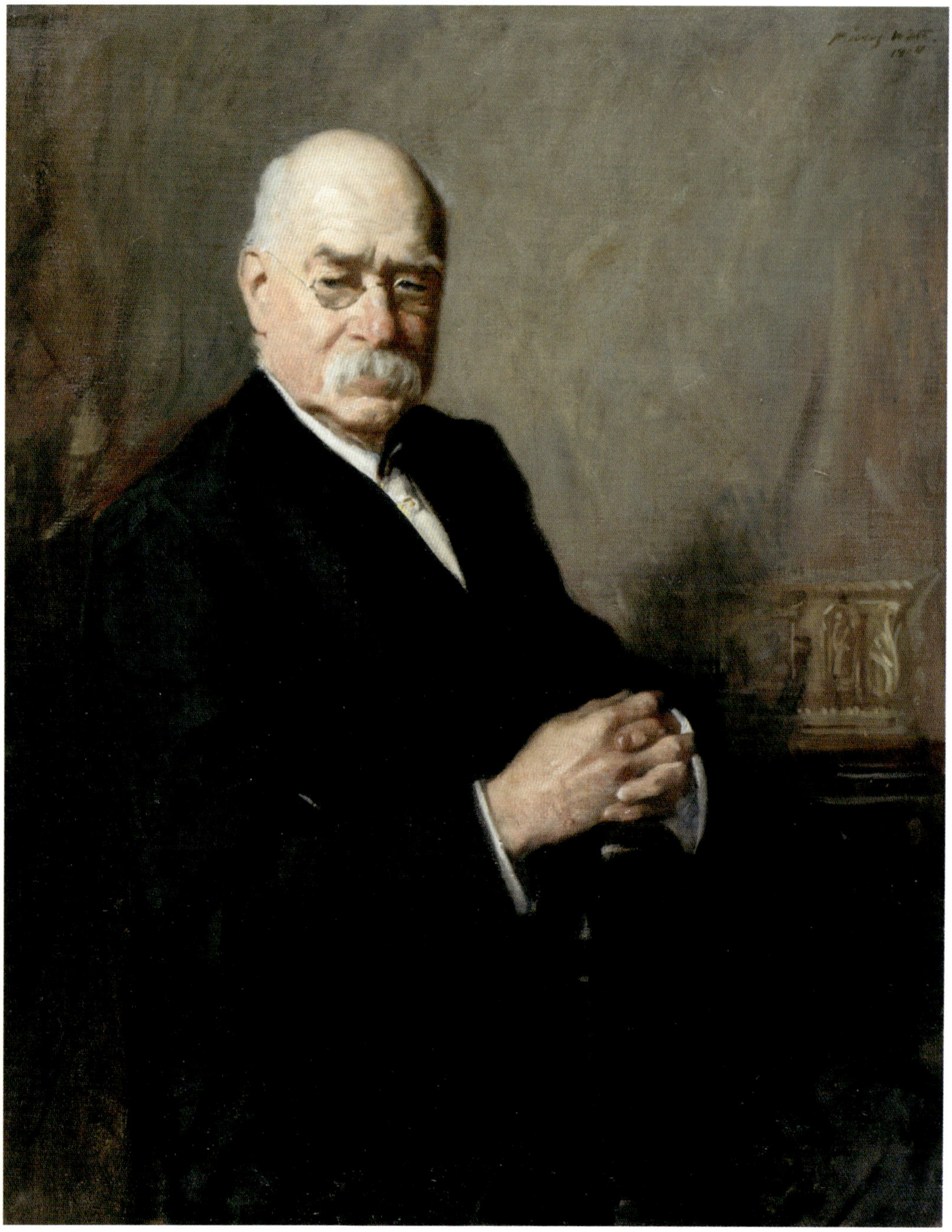

Figure 21 *Frederick George Watts,* Portrait of Thomas Walker, *Peterborough Museum. (Photograph courtesy of Peterborough Museum and Art Gallery.)*

harsh shadows would not enhance the appearance of the gilding. From this point, it was simply a matter of balancing the light levels between the front and the back to give the final image (Fig. 22).

After the photograph was taken, the glass was cleaned, the ghost image disappeared and the conserved painting was replaced in the glazed frame.

Conclusion

Whilst not attempting a comprehensive survey of the use of digital imaging in conservation, this paper has illustrated the utility of digital reconstructions in the context of conserving paintings. A digital reconstruction of the Westminster Retable in its late nineteenth-century state helped conservators to understand changes, which had taken place over an extended time frame, in the physical condition of a complex multicomponent object. Part of conservation involves the balancing of details with an impression of the whole and digitisation and stitching provided the visual context in which to assess historic levels of damage. Physical processes that take place in paintings can have significant visual impact, yet some changes, such as the migration and evaporation of fatty acids from the Watts portrait and their deposition on glass, are almost

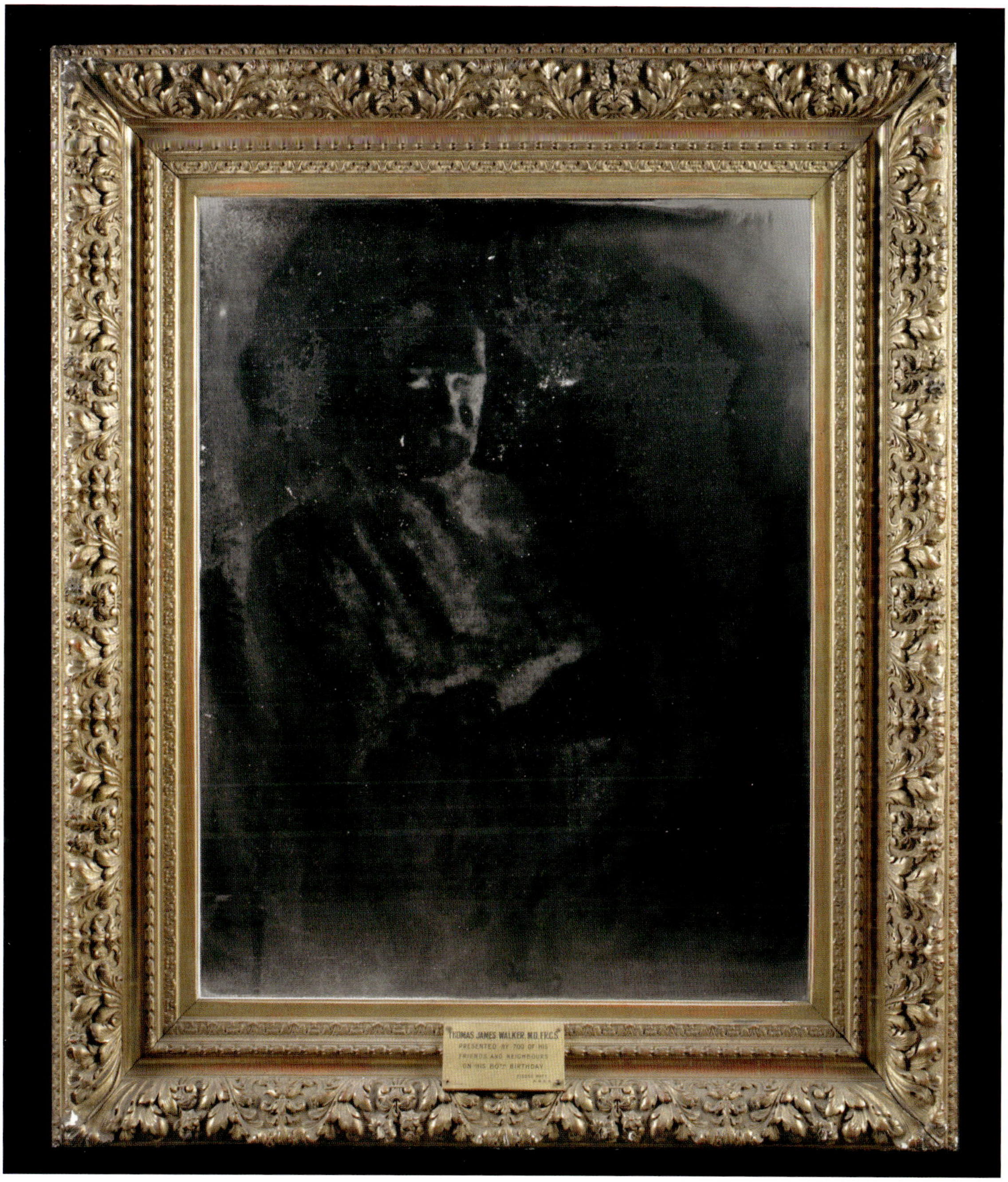

Figure 22 *Image showing the fine residue deposited on the glass by the painting.*

invisible. Any change, which may result in visual alteration of the painting over time, is important to document where possible. Digital reconstructions can also enhance subtle differences in relatively unchanged paintings. The task of reconstructing a painting by Caravaggio that was not physically present in the studio was made easier by digitally manipulating the colour space in a photograph of the original.

However, most digital reconstructions of paintings are undertaken for the purposes of communicating technical ideas to the public. The paintings featured in this paper were aged between nearly 150 and 750 years old, which allows very slow changes to become apparent. One such change is the discoloration of smalt that was evident in the sky of the painting by Siciolante. The format of a digital reconstruction can be changed in order to address the visible effects of both intentional changes as well as the inevitable changes due to chemical degradation. Human intervention changed the appearance of the Thornham Parva Retable and the portrait of Elizabeth I. Digital reconstruction enabled the effects of those changes to be assessed without any physical intervention with the paintings and in this way digital reconstructions are able to address issues of change in a manner that is free from technical risk or ethical dilemma.

Notes

1. The project was funded anonymously in loving memory of Alexander (Alick) Montgomerie Bell (29 May 1919–28 January 1998).
2. The inscription dates the portrait to the 37th year of Elizabeth's reign, which would put her in her 60s, but in the painting she looks more like someone in their 30s; Sauerberg 2010.
3. See Miller and Patrick, in this vol.

References

Binski, P. and Massing, A. (eds) 2009. *The Westminster Retable: History, Technique, Conservation*. London and Turnhout: Harvey Miller Publishers.

Kempski, M. and Noh, Y. 2008. 'F.G. Watts, *Portrait of Thomas Walker*'. Unpublished technical report, HKI 2375, Hamilton Kerr Institute.

Kempski, M., Leonard, D., Boyce, E. R. and Massing, J.M. forthcoming. 'Conservation and technical study of Siciolante da Sermoneta's *Deposition of Christ*, from King's College Chapel, Cambridge', *The Hamilton Kerr Institute Bulletin* 4.

Massing, A. (ed.) 2003. *The Thornham Parva Retable: Technique, Conservation and Context of an English Medieval Painting*. London and Turnhout: Harvey Miller Publishers.

Norton, C., Park, D. and Binski, P. 1987. *Dominican Painting in East Anglia*. Woodbridge: Boydell Press.

Sauerberg, M.L. 2010. '*Portrait of Elizabeth I* from Westminster Abbey'. Unpublished technical report, HKI 2456, Hamilton Kerr Institute.

Spring, M., Penny, N., White, R. and Wyld, M. 2001. 'Colour change in *The Conversion of the Magdalen* attributed to Pedro Campaña', *National Gallery Technical Bulletin* 22: 54–63.

FOUR WEEKS OF WORK FOR FOUR SECONDS OF FAME: RECONSTRUCTIONS FOR TELEVISION

Rose Miller and Christine Patrick

Renate Woudhuysen-Keller made a reconstruction of *The Annunciation* by Jan van Eyck (*c.*1434–1436, National Gallery of Art, Washington, DC) for the television series, *The Private Life of a Masterpiece*, to be broadcast on the BBC as part of a Christmas special in 2006. Her work obviously impressed the production company, Fulmar TV, since it led to a series of requests to the Hamilton Kerr Institute (HKI), resulting in reconstructions playing a part in four festival episodes, from Easter 2009 to Christmas 2010.

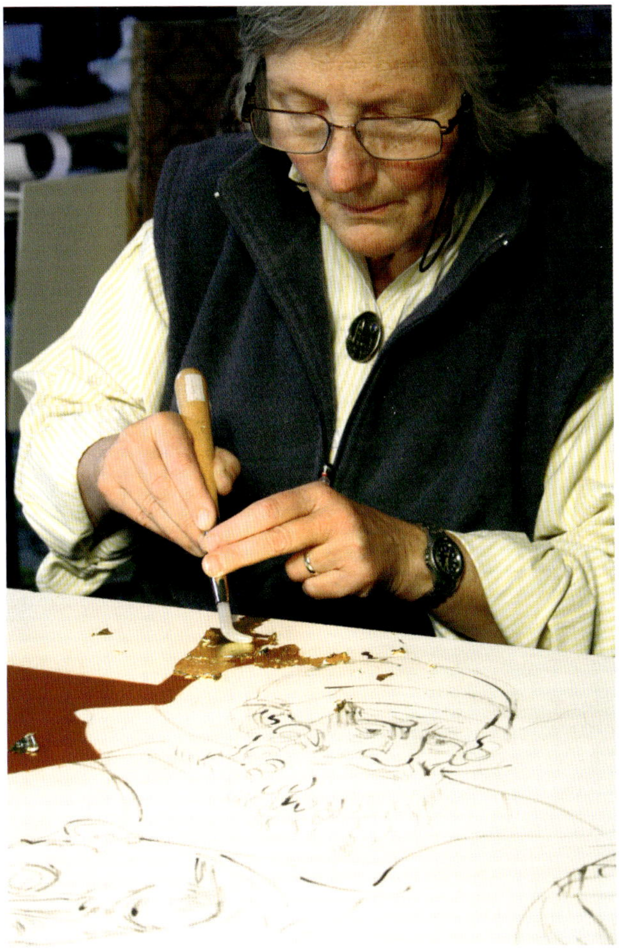

Figure 1 *Renate gilding panel 2 for the reconstruction of Rogier van der Weyden's* Descent from the Cross.

The Private Life of a Masterpiece is the most widely sold and seen arts series the BBC has ever made.[1] The programmes each follow a single painting, from its making, through its history to its perception today. Reconstructing world-renowned paintings for a programme that had UK viewing figures of up to three million held great potential for educational benefits to the general public as well as students, interns and staff at the HKI. The race was on to replicate part of a masterpiece in only a matter of weeks each time. This paper discusses the trials, tribulations, triumphs and revelations of making reconstructions for television and focuses on the reconstructions with which the authors were involved – Rogier van der Weyden's *The Descent from the Cross* (*c.*1435, Museo Nacional del Prado, Madrid) and Filippo Lippi's *Adoration of the Christ Child* (*c.*1459, Staatilche Museen zu Berlin Gemäldegalerie) – but will also draw on the experiences of reconstructing Caravaggio's *The Taking of Christ* (*c.*1602, National Gallery of Ireland, Dublin) and Sandro Botticelli's *The Mystic Nativity* (1500, National Gallery, London). Despite a natural inclination not to be impressed by the glamour of television (having chosen a career that has a history of being behind the scenes), it cannot be denied that the prospect of detailed filming of our (often unrecognised) meticulous work was exciting.

The speedy production of historically informed reconstructions at the HKI is made feasible both by the personal experience of, and the cupboard of materials built up by, Renate during her 30-plus years at the HKI, with help from her multitude of assistants (also known as eager and willing students and interns). This meant the stalks of mare's tail had been dried ready for sanding and the horse's tail hair was washed and ready to be

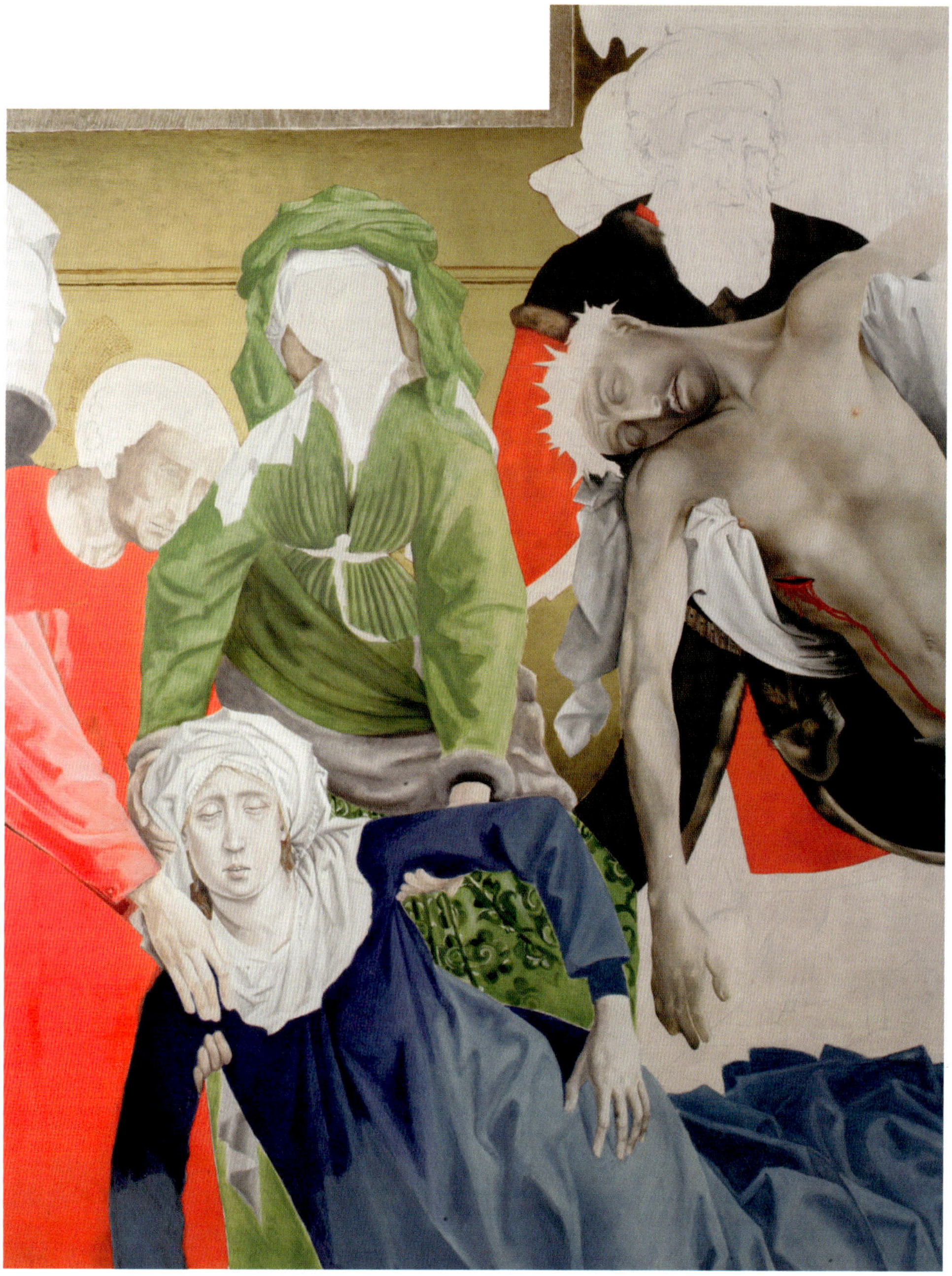

Figure 2 *The reconstruction of Rogier van der Weyden's* Descent from the Cross *(panel 1).*

used for polishing. It was already established that you must wet your brush before dipping it into the pot of warm ground in order to avoid introducing air bubbles. Foundations of technical knowledge have been firmly laid, both at the HKI and across the field, and each of these television reconstructions was able to draw on this, both for wider information regarding the particular period, but also technical analysis specific to the paintings. This is in no small part thanks to the culture of sharing research and images within the conservation profession, leading to high resolution digitised X-radiographs and infrared images arriving via email and on CDs via 'snail mail'.

The first question was how to reconstruct the paintings without having the original in the studio? In the case of Rogier van der Weyden's *Descent from the Cross* (programme broadcast Easter 2010), a laptop and an internet connection provided the answer. Google Earth's add-on function was launched in January 2009 and the *Descent* had been chosen as one of the 14 paintings to be reproduced at a resolution of 14,000 mega pixels.[2] The zoom function allowed us to see the painting in near-microscopic detail, with more clarity than is possible when viewing the picture on the museum wall. The makers of Filippo Lippi's *The Adoration of the Christ Child* (broadcast Christmas 2010) were not so lucky, the lack of access to the original proved to be an obstacle: as much visual information as possible was gathered on a visit to the painting in Berlin. This was hindered to a certain extent by awkward surface reflections from glazing and the ever-present gallery attendants – unfortunately

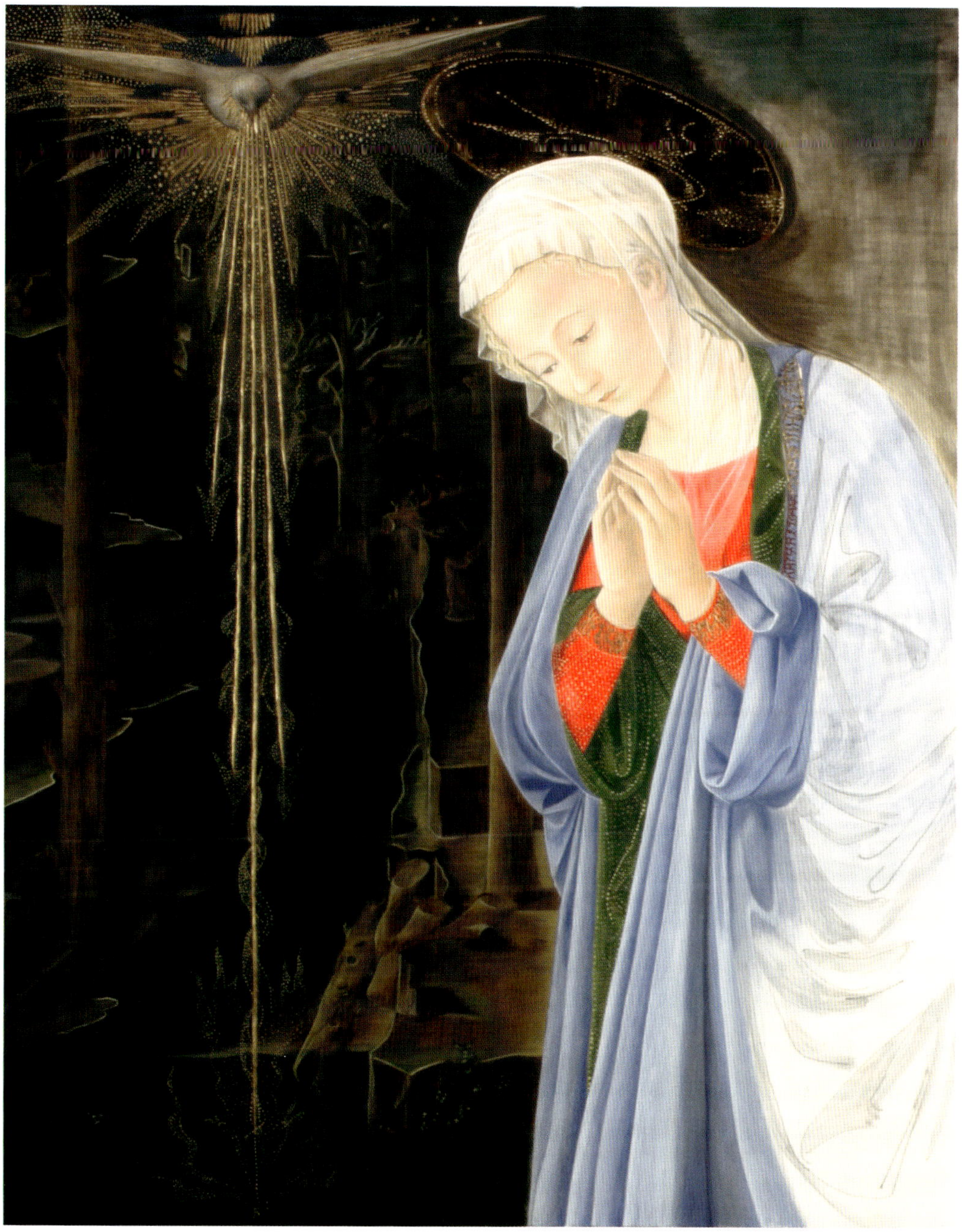

Figure 3 *The reconstruction of Filippo Lippi's* Adoration of the Christ Child.

trained to prevent close inspection! Despite this, the Berlin trip enabled access to conservation records and images of infrared details, revealing important information regarding the original construction of the painting. Stills from Fulmar TV's filming of the picture and life-size prints of digital photographs proved to be very useful.

The visit to Berlin to see Lippi's *Adoration* and a trip to Madrid to see van der Weyden's *Descent* exacerbated the second major problem – time. Practical work on the reconstructions took priority, allowing little extra time for further research. Fulmar TV was extremely helpful in providing bullet point notes on both published and unpublished technical knowledge, resulting from their own research for the programmes. For the *Descent*, the production company requested a focus on blood (of Christ), money (the value of ultramarine) and tears (of the Virgin Mary). A number of picture plans were made in order to ensure the relevant passages of the chosen central area (including the figures of St John, the Virgin Mary, Christ and Joseph of Arimathea) were finished to the appropriate levels. This included areas that we planned to paint live to the camera during filming. The plans inevitably received much revision throughout the process of preparation and painting (Fig. 4). It seemed imperative that the painted panel should at least give an impression of a painting in its final stages, so we blocked-in the main colour fields to show the simplicity an underpainting might have before it receives the upper layers of shading and highlights. For Lippi's *Adoration* there was a wider brief, allowing freedom in the composition and

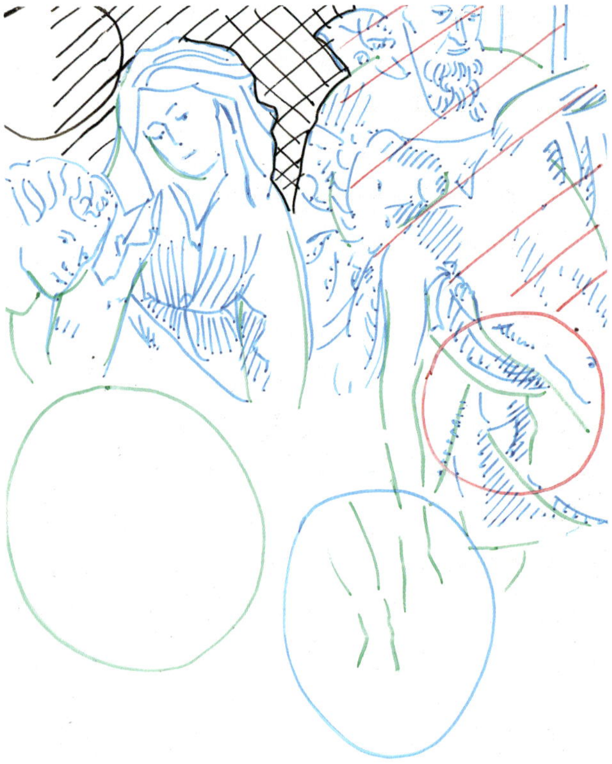

Figure 4 *A plan for the reconstruction of Rogier van der Weyden's* Descent from the Cross.

level of completion of the reconstruction. A section of the painting including the Virgin with the dove was chosen to demonstrate the main technical aspects of the picture. Particular attention was paid to his application of paint, in places involving both egg- and oil-based layers. Lippi's impressive use of gold, applied using various methods, was looked at in some detail.

Although only a section of the original size of van der Weyden's altarpiece was chosen to reconstruct, it was still of far greater dimensions than is usual for student replicas conducted at the HKI. Moreover, it was made twice, to the same dimensions, in order to illustrate the underdrawing, priming and gilding process (panel 2) separately from the final gilding and paint layers (panel 1). This duplication necessitated consistency over large areas, and the scale led to questions such as how best to use the silicaceous mare's tail to sand the chalk-glue ground (in bundles of stalks or cut into a flat but small sheet). It also highlighted the efficiency necessary in both the preparation and handling of the object – lifting an inch-thick, 2 m^2 oak panel is no easy feat. Knowing that it was more important to achieve a highly polished ground in the areas to be gilded saved precious time and elbow grease. However, unlike the Lippi, the size of the painted surface of the van der Weyden made working as a team fairly easy, since two people could work comfortably side by side. It enabled us to move around the painting, building up successive layers at quite a speed. The mahl stick became an essential tool to avoid disturbing very recently painted passages. The smaller size of the Lippi allowed for only one of the two involved to work at a time. Although this permitted some rest whilst the other painted, it was quite a push to complete the work before the filming day, with paint still being applied whilst the production team unpacked.

Between 10 days and four weeks, with one to three people working at a time, was spent on each project. As conservators we all had manual dexterity and a degree of artistic ability, along with the appropriate stamina and passion to work through many lunchtimes, evenings and weekends. The filming deadlines were tight and we seemed to wade into the swamp of historical techniques with only a small amount of experience each – the supervision of Renate and Mary Kempski was invaluable to the projects. When treating a painting a conservator would expect to have a confident grasp on its materials and methods, but the reconstructions required simply getting on with the job. One imagines time pressure would have often played a part in the making of the originals, particularly when painting to the deadline of a commission. It may be that the pressure to finish a picture for the filming date was not entirely dissimilar to the original experience of the painter and/or his workshop members working to fulfill a patron's demand.

The underdrawing of the van der Weyden was traced from a full-size enlargement of a recently captured infrared image taken by the Museo del Prado, Madrid, which had revealed surprisingly free and gestural marks. On panel 1 (final painting and gilding) this information was embellished with many lines taken from the painted surface, given the necessity for this to be a visually accurate copy as well as an emulation of technique; in this situation the balance veered towards the former. After the two large inch-thick oak panels had been cut for the van der Weyden, and their lengthy preparation was under way, the production company suggested we could have used plywood. This was a good illustration of the differences in approach, and also a lesson that was learnt for the following television collaboration: as long as it just about *looks* right, framing of shots and editing can add the necessary authority – an oak panel was considered acceptable for the Lippi, since there was no poplar to match the original support in stock at the time. This is not to say that our aim is usually to re-enact a historically *accurate* painter-at-work. Rather, it is to reconstruct the material object using historically *informed* materials and methods. And of course we cut familiar corners: utilising Melinex, swabsticks, permanent and ballpoint pens, E-cloths, eraser crumbs, wet-and-dry sandpaper, Fome-Cor and the photocopier for enlarging images.

The technique of van der Weyden's *Descent* can be summarised as follows: oak panel with a chalk-glue ground; underdrawing detected; oil-based priming layer present; paint layers in oil with defined areas of water-gilding. The technique of Lippi's *Adoration* can be summarised as follows: poplar panel with a gesso ground, underdrawing detected, painted mainly in egg tempera with

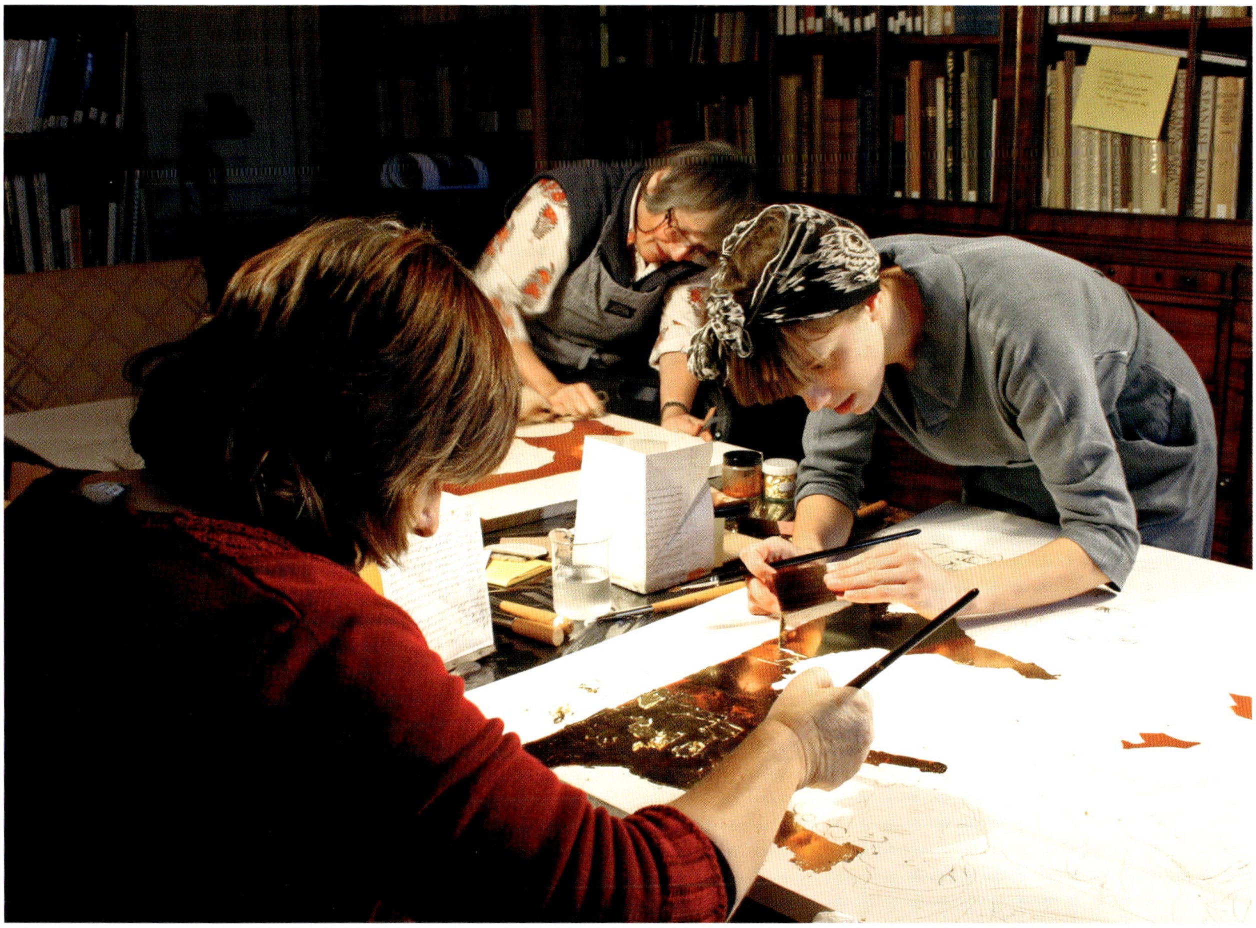

Figure 5 *Mary Kempski, Renate Woudhuysen-Keller and Rose Miller gilding the two van der Weyden reconstructions.*

some oil-based layers; three methods of depicting gold incorporated into the image. The following bullet points contain practical observations resulting from the making of the van der Weyden (V) and Lippi (L) reconstructions. They are points of interest, including the odd revelation, with regard to the techniques of both the original paintings and the reconstructions.

We spotted certain underdrawn marks on the infrared image (kindly supplied by Museo Nacional del Prado) that appeared to show evidence of the use of a quill – these were distinguished by lines that had darker lines running along the edges, and the end of the mark separated into the shape of a swallow's tail, thus indicating the splayed nib of the quill.

V Whilst experimenting with the making and use of a quill, the practical history of the formation of medieval script became self-evident – perhaps emphasised by the absorbency of a chalk-glue ground. It is necessary to hold the quill to the surface and draw it sideways in order to get the ink flowing, creating a flick at the beginning of each stroke or line.[3]

V Conscious of our lack of experience using a quill we decided to employ an imitation rosewood pen, a writing instrument thought to have been in use during this period. Rose branches cut from the HKI garden did not have time to dry, so a swabstick and a chopstick, both cut as with a quill, were used instead.

L The outline of the image (traced onto Melinex and transferred using a charcoal coated paper underlayer) was fixed into position using vine black in gum arabic and water, applied to the panel using a swabstick cut like a quill. The drawn lines appeared strong and it was feared these would show through the final paint layers. A thin layer of egg-tempered lead white was therefore applied over the entire surface, an intermediate layer not seen on the original, but found on the early copy of the painting that hangs in the Magi chapel in the Palazzo Medici-Riccardi in Florence.

V Certain marks on Christ's chest seen on the infrared image did not seem to be relevant to the final painting, instead appearing as mistaken dashes in the middle of areas of flesh. We decided against including them in our version of the underdrawing, thinking that they might remain visible through the thin paint layers of the flesh. During painting it became apparent that these marks seem to have been related to subtle modelling of Christ's chest. They may have assisted in the placing of the initial shadows, which were critical in the creation of the strong sense of form and also the cool and pallid complexion through exploiting the turbid medium effect. The paint, along with the priming,

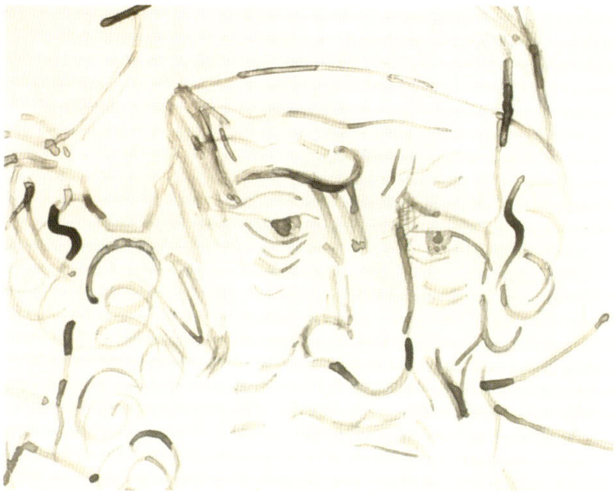

Figure 6 *A detail of underdrawing on the reconstruction of Rogier van der Weyden's* Descent from the Cross *(panel 2).*

in this area of apparent translucency was in fact thick enough to hide the underdrawing.

V Various interlayers were often found to be necessary in the course of preparing and painting. We rubbed a layer of linseed oil, using a rag, into the chalk-glue ground before painting the oil-based priming layer over it. This encouraged better spreading of the paint, since it 'took' more readily to the oily surface.

V With hindsight we regretted not spending a little longer on achieving a smooth surface in this priming layer by smoothing it with a sable brush; when using thin upper paint layers, the texture of the underlayer has a (predictably) distracting effect on the final appearance.

V 'Oiling-out' was also needed during painting if an underlayer had dried overnight and a continuous brushstroke was required. For example, in painting the uninterrupted stream of blood that trickles from Christ's side (Fig. 7).

V Conversely, the effect of oil paint 'beading' when applied to a dry underlayer appeared to have been used (to great effect) by van der Weyden in the depiction of the individual flicked hairs on the trim of Joseph of Arimathea's costume.

V The smoothly blended flesh tones with an oil medium were imitated by painting in four stages. The modelling was established in the first and second layers (at which point the dashed lines in his chest would have been of use). The third layer lightened the lights and deepened the darks. The fourth layer involved small areas of glazing, which appeared on the painting almost as rows of fine dashes. During painting it was found that this effect could be closely imitated by the use of fingers to dab the excess paint. This was an action that came naturally in order to even out the glaze and achieve the subtle marks necessary to maintain the fine modelling.

L Traditionally, due to its nature, egg tempera is applied in a fairly strict manner, often painstakingly stroke by stroke. It was during painting that it became apparent how Lippi had begun to break boundaries in this medium. He painted the imposing forested background in a strikingly free fashion, and this effect was achieved using a fairly heavily loaded flat sable brush. The landscape was then painted on top using small, round sable brushes to apply highlights where required.

V Having already experienced a problem with greying of ultramarine when bound in oil on the reconstruction of Sandro Botticelli's *The Mystic Nativity* (programme broadcast Christmas 2009), high-grade genuine ultramarine was ordered in to be used in the depiction of the Virgin's robe on the *Descent*. Unfortunately our investment did not entirely pay off and an intensity of blue equal to that seen on the original remained elusive, and continues to be studied.

L The blue of the Virgin's mantle was painted with egg-tempered fine grade ultramarine. Due to both the density and irregularity of the particles it was important to the handling properties that the paint was ground using a hard porphyry slab and granite muller – as opposed to the more common glass slab and muller (which are too soft).

L An oil-based layer of copper resinate was applied in two fairly thin layers, again using a flat sable brush, across the painted background, giving depth and saturation. Unfortunately these layers dimmed the painted ochre highlights and these had to be reapplied. This simple mistake is one Lippi would certainly have avoided, and precious time could have been saved if we had too.

L The rays emanating from the Holy Spirit were made using mordant gilding. This was a major aspect where time was not on our side. The copper resinate oil layer had only been applied a few days previously and had not dried. In an attempt to prevent the gold from adhering to it, a glair isolating varnish was employed. Despite this precaution, the gold stuck to a large area of the background and, in consequence, time that we did not have to spare was devoted to careful scraping and swabbing away of the unwanted gilding. A likely explanation for the failure of the glair layer is that the initial egg-tempered malachite was rather granular and absorbent, and with only two copper resinate layers applied, the glair was able to penetrate rather than form a coherent barrier. Furthermore, slight blanching developed in the glair layer over one to two days, probably due to painting it onto an oil-based layer that had not fully dried. This area of the painting was temporarily remedied for the cameras by saturation with linseed oil.

V We found it necessary to varnish the water-gilded areas before applying the painted flecks; otherwise the paint would not 'take' to the metallic surface (in this case the varnish layer was intended to remain on the surface).

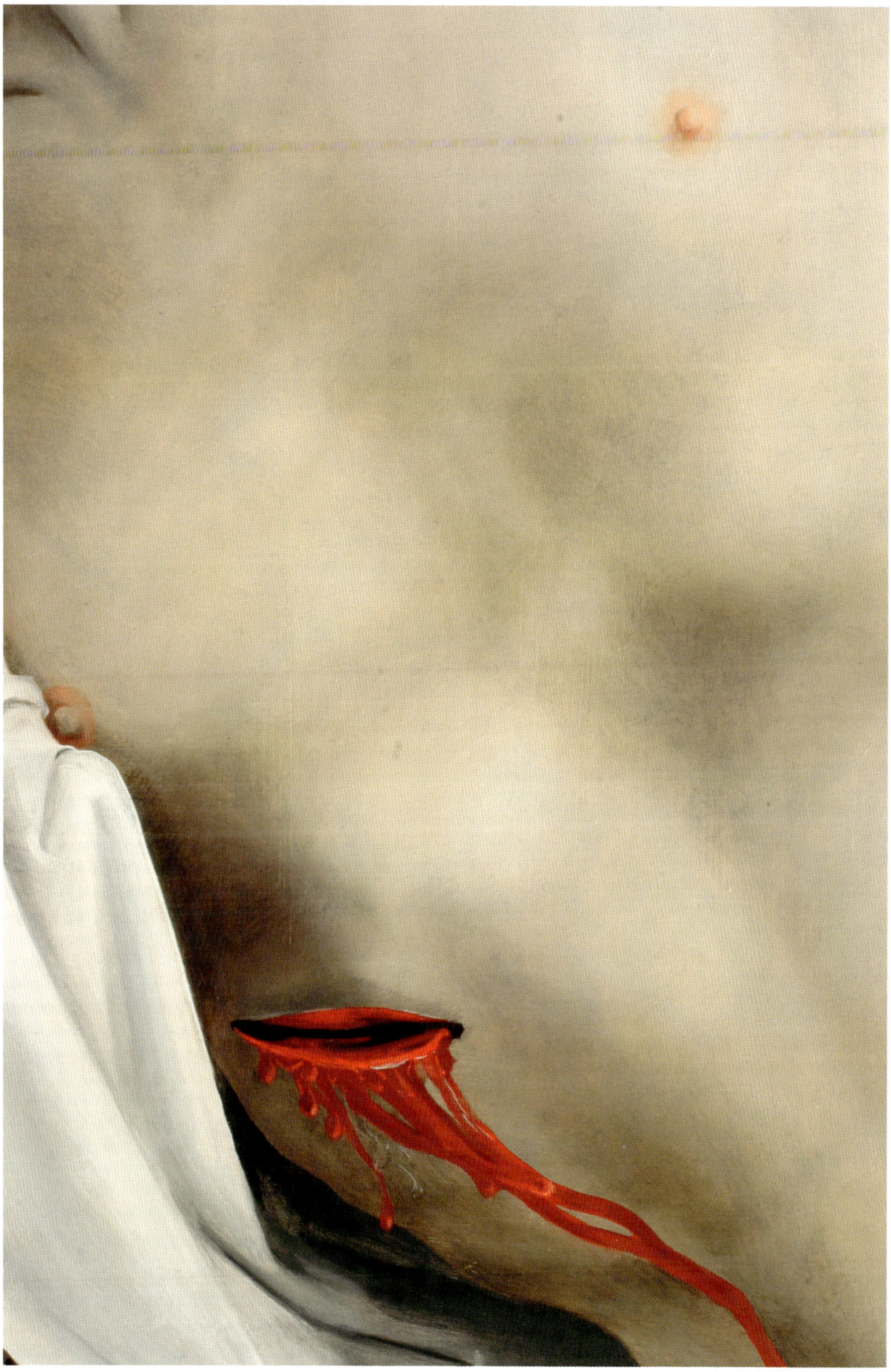

Figure 7 *A detail of Christ's chest on the reconstruction of Rogier van der Weyden's* Descent from the Cross *(panel 1).*

Unfortunately, none of the above observations made the final cut. Despite the detailed planning for the van der Weyden reconstruction, to ensure that the requested areas were left ready to be painted live to camera, the majority of footage used in the final programme was cropped and edited to the extent that the overall impression of the painting was lost. At 2.00 pm on filming day it was decided the blood of Christ was surplus to requirements. A disappointed reconstructor who had spent the last week painting this area fumed in the corner and tried to remember that the painting had, and would continue to have, great educational value. The following points *were* included in the television programmes.

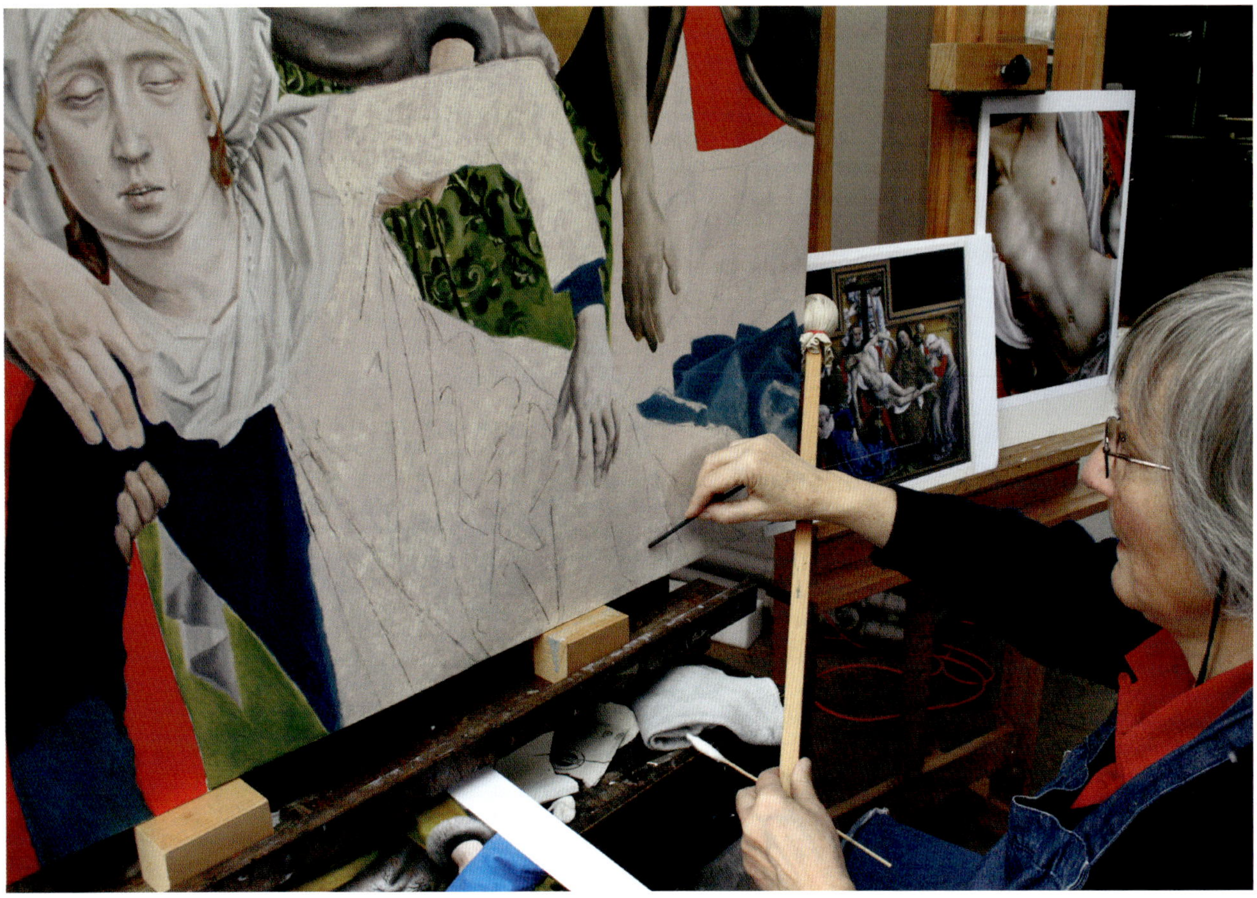

Figure 8 *Renate repainting the Virgin's robe on Rogier van der Weyden's* Descent from the Cross *(panel 1) in the search for illuminosity using genuine ultramarine.*

L The commonly used method of pouncing, which creates a series of dots to form a painting's underdrawing, was described and thoroughly demonstrated to the camera. Although its use is not confirmed on the Lippi, evidence of this method of transfer has been found on the early copy of the picture in Florence, and it was considered to be a good demonstration of a method that was common practice during the period (Fig. 10).

V The preparation of panel 2 (underdrawing and gilding) led to problems not likely to have been encountered on the original. When gilding we found that the incised lines that delineated this area were not sufficient to contain the wetting of the bole, which spread onto the exposed chalk-glue ground. Had the oil-based priming layer been applied on these areas (as would have been the case on the original), the time taken to clean the edges of the gilded passages (using a cut-off hogs' hair brush) would have been saved. Unfortunately, this hasty correcting of our mistake was caught on camera and made it into the final cut.

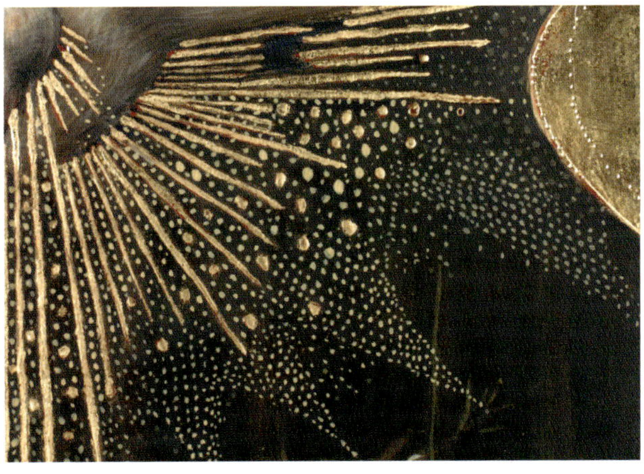

Figure 9 *A detail of the three methods of gilding employed on the reconstruction of Filippo Lippi's* Adoration of the Christ Child.

V The preparation of the panel featured briefly in the final programme, along with shots of the making of initial marks of underdrawing. Unfortunately the ground application was shot on an unprepared third panel, and the underdrawing was filmed carried out on the blank reverse of panel 2, rather than in an area of the front as planned.

L Lippi's use of egg-tempered yellow ochre in imitation of gold (used alongside water and mordant gilding) is thought to have been innovative for the mid-fifteenth century. This, and the glitz, perhaps prompted the inclusion of the gilding methods in the final edit. The overall amount of gilding used on the painting is limited but is applied in a manner that achieves dazzling effects.

L The painting of the Virgin was completed using the traditional egg tempera method with tiny parallel brushstrokes (Fig. 11). Lippi's mastery of the

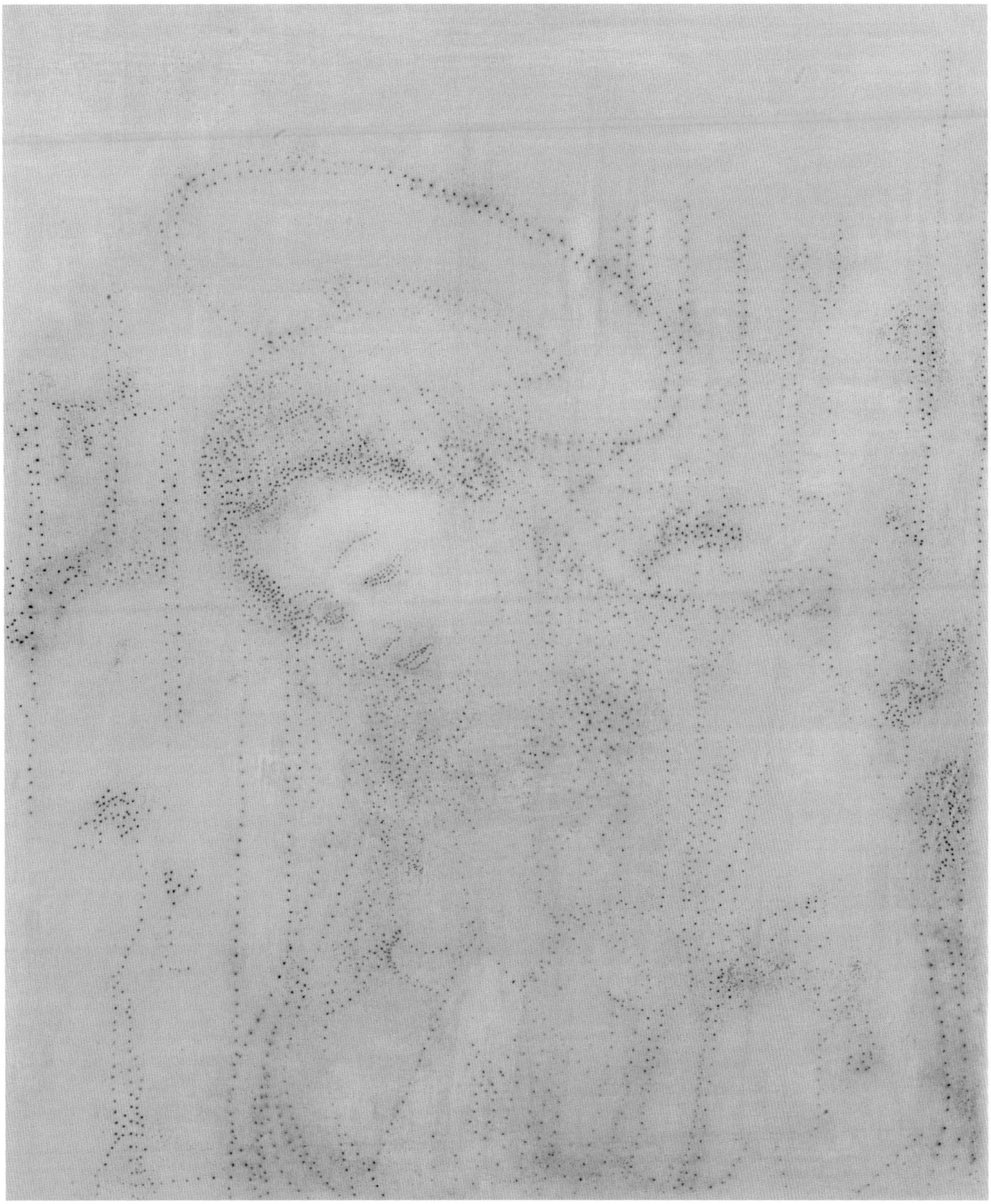

Figure 10 *The pounced underdrawing on the reconstruction of Filippo Lippi's* Adoration of the Christ Child *used to demonstrate the common transfer method.*

medium meant that the smooth and seamless transitions are barely visible, other than on close inspection. Imitation of this technique on the reconstruction was well documented by the film crew, closely showing the gentle stroking of the fine brush hairs upon the smooth gessoed surface in detail – along with some intense close-up shots of the reconstructionists at work (Fig. 12).

V The tears of the Virgin Mary satisfied the camera's want for dramatic skill and one was painted live to the camera on her face, prepared as planned to a near-final finish. A small, moon-shaped shadow was applied first. The highlight was added on the opposite side, with the addition of lead-tin yellow to the lead white in order to counteract the turbid medium effect. Only two or three brushstrokes were necessary to create great realism.

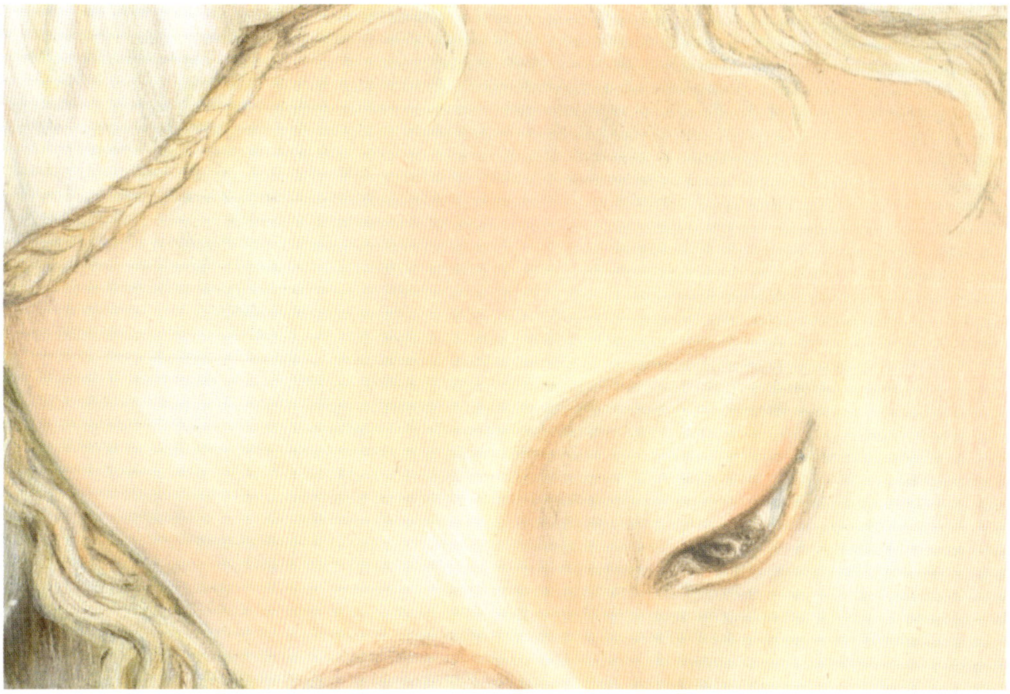

Figure 11 *A detail of the Virgin on the reconstruction of Filippo Lippi's* Adoration of the Christ Child.

There was an underlying feeling when preparing and filming for a television audience that an exciting discovery relating to the artist's materials or methods would be unearthed. However, it was found that the various techniques used by the individual artists were comparatively common practice for their time. An almost nineteenth-century desire (hidden in most of us) for secrets of the old masters to be revealed could not be satisfied because there was none to be found. All four artists knew their materials, how to use basic but strongly refined methods and, most importantly, how to exploit this knowledge – they all had a certain genius for painting.

However, this series of reconstructions has prompted further investigation of the problem we could not solve – the loss of colour intensity of genuine ultramarine when bound in an oil medium. It offers an unappealing grey hue when compared with the intense blue seen in paintings, particularly in admixtures with lead white. This phenomenon was not encountered with genuine ultramarine when tempered with egg as in the Lippi. The problem does not occur when painting with French ultramarine or azurite in oil, and therefore had not become apparent during the years of student copies, when these pigments were often employed as substitutes for the costly genuine pigment. The quality, source and preparation of ultramarine are being considered in the search for luminosity. The physical nature of modern lead white used in mixtures with ultramarine is also being questioned, leading to large jars of oxidising lead sitting in the boiler room of the HKI.[4]

The copy of Caravaggio's *The Taking of Christ* (broadcast Easter 2009) was the quickest to paint (as would be expected) with only 10 hours spent with a brush in front of the canvas. This compares to around 100 hours painting time on the Lippi panel. Using egg tempera as a medium limits the speed at which you can work (however much of a hurry you are in, and even using free brushwork in the underlayers). Time is needed to create carefully the slight variations in tone to make gradual skin transitions or smooth folds in the drapery. When combined with oil glazing and a variety of gilding methods it becomes an even slower process. The experience gained in the four copies reflected changes in the history of painting, from Lippi's innovations in the use of tempera with oil glazes (on a poplar panel), van der Weyden's exploitation of the oil medium (on an oak panel), Botticelli's uncharacteristic use of a canvas laid over panel (a blind stretcher – thought to have enabled the traditional use of gilding despite the canvas support) to Caravaggio's rapid execution using oil on canvas.

The intended purpose of the reconstructions within the television programme was to show how the work of art was made. Each of the broadcasts featured selected methods and working practices of the artist. Every stage of the painting process was included throughout the series, but not necessarily within a single episode. This left unanswered questions relating to individual paintings. For example, although detailed footage of the methods of underdrawing was included with the reconstruction of Lippi's *Adoration*, no mention was made of the support and ground layers of the painting (both of which were covered in the programme on the *Descent*).

The format of the programme on Caravaggio's *The Taking of Christ* was such that the reconstruction and its painter (Rupert Featherstone) made frequent appearances throughout, perhaps due to the focus on Caravaggio's spontaneity and use of live models, leading to film-like

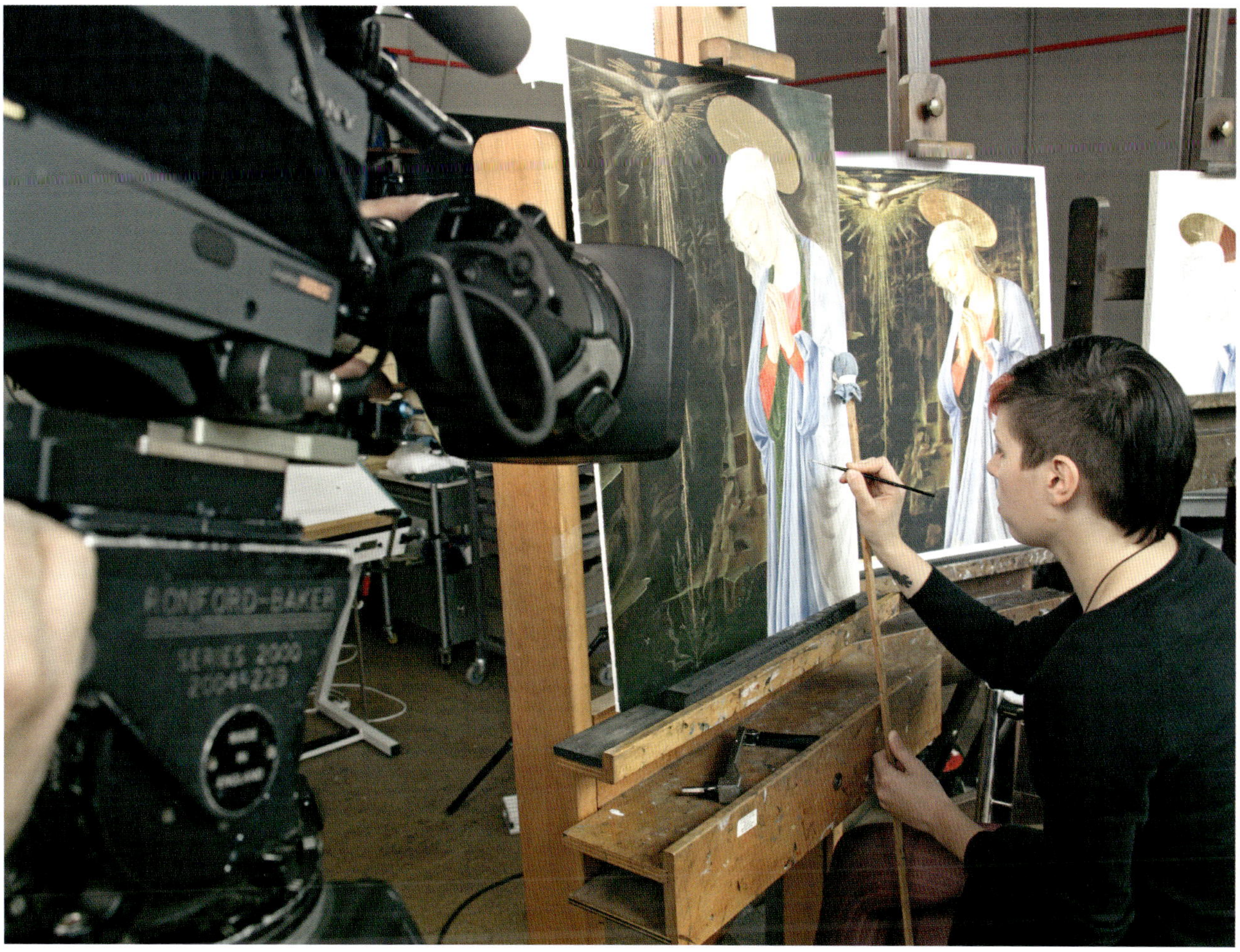

Figure 12 *Christine Patrick during filming, working on the reconstruction of Filippo Lippi's* Adoration of the Christ Child.

sequences of the painter at work. Conversely, the reconstruction that was physically the biggest task of the four featured the least. Despite the detailed planning to allow step-by-step filming of each element of technique, the reconstruction of van der Weyden's *Descent* received 1 minute 50 seconds of airtime in a 50-minute programme. This was equal to the coverage, in the programme, of a piece of video art inspired by the painting, and 30 seconds less than Google Earth. The overall painted panel 1 was in shot for four seconds and the duplicate underdrawing panel 2 did not feature.

Karel van Mander's tale of van der Weyden's *Descent* falling overboard whilst on its voyage from Catherine the Great's castle in Hungary to her nephew Phillip II's palace near Madrid is thought to be an allegory to illustrate the importance and miraculous nature of the painting. It seems we may have participated in today's myth-making surrounding 'masterpieces' – television programmes that proclaim the genius of a single painter, focusing on a single painting. A conflict of interest perhaps came through our aim to elucidate the creation of a painting by making a reconstruction (however tedious the details), and the television company's need to create a narrative.[5]

Those involved with the reconstructions made for television gained invaluable practical experience – preparing the support, making, applying and smoothing the ground, grinding paint and painting with it, using traditional pigments such as genuine high grade ultramarine, madder, malachite, copper resinate and lead white and gilding using a variety of traditional methods. Further to established knowledge, new practical tricks continued to be discovered: during the application of the chalk-glue ground on the van der Weyden panel, Renate found that in order to avoid creating air bubbles not only does the brush need to be wetted before dipping it, but also that a flat-ferruled brush with *short* hairs helps further to avoid the common problem.

Reconstructions lead to observations made only during the act of making and, perhaps more importantly, the act of *painting*; this element is so vital, yet so difficult to define and therefore also difficult to discuss. Further questions and research in the continuing thread of enquiry were generated by these reconstructions. It is hoped that the programme communicated to its audience how the paintings were made, despite some aspects of the reconstructions gaining more airtime than others. Overall, for those involved it was a positive experience and we are very pleased to have played a part in the internationally successful BBC documentary series, *The Private Life of a Masterpiece*.

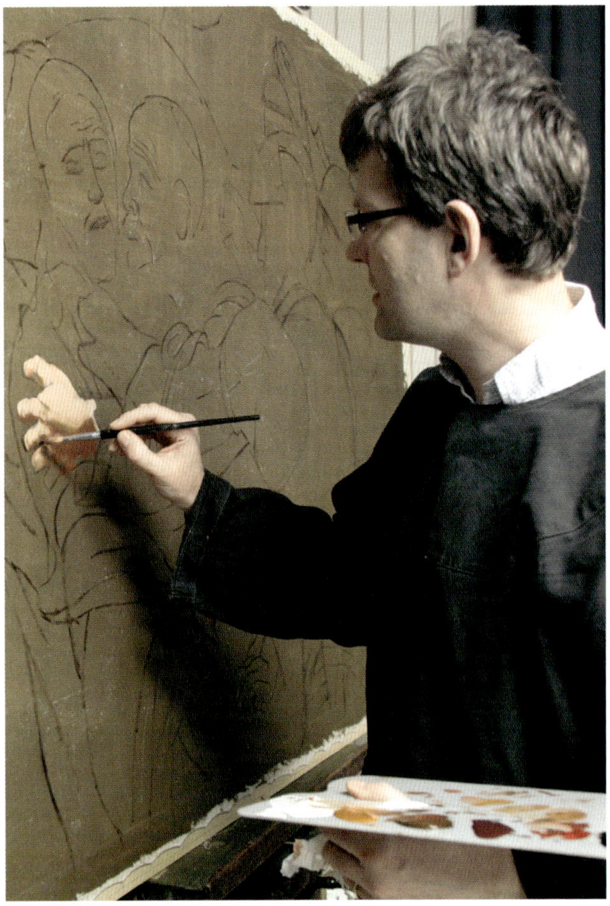

Figure 13 *Rupert Featherstone at work on the reconstruction of Carravaggio's* The Taking of Christ.

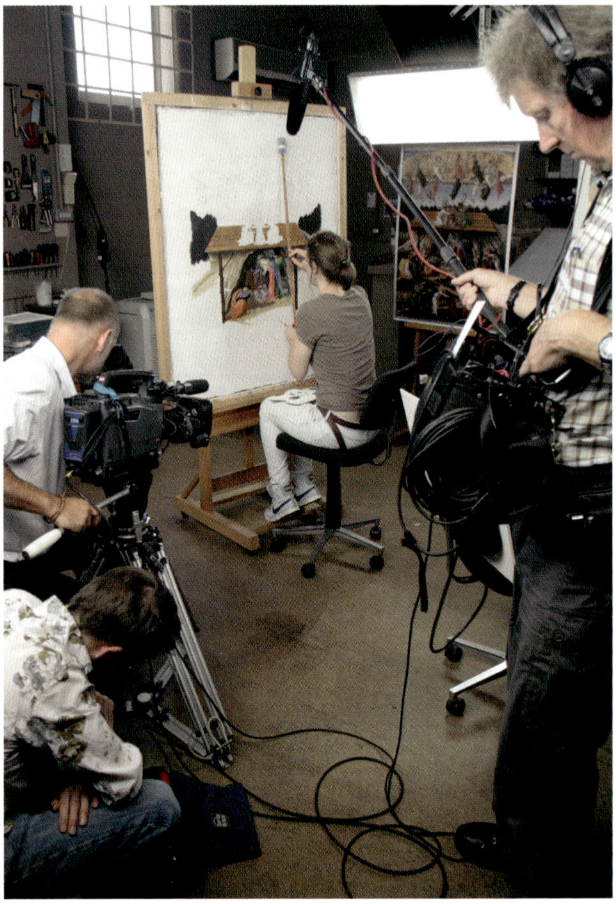

Figure 14 *Victoria Sutcliffe during filming, working on the reconstruction of Botticelli's* The Mystic Nativity.

Acknowledgements

Fulmar TV – particularly Jeremy Bugler and Jake Wilson; Ana Gonzalez Mozo, Museo Nacional del Prado; Babette Hartwig, Staatilche Museen zu Berlin Gemäldegalerie; Sergio Benedetti, National Gallery of Ireland; Conservation Department, The National Gallery, London.

Reconstructionists: Eleanor von Aderkas, Krista Blessley, Rupert Featherstone, Mary Kempski, Rose Miller, Christine Patrick, Victoria Sutcliffe and Renate Woudhuysen-Keller. They would all like to thank the colleagues who helped when needed, including the reconstructionist's panelmaker, Alan Barker.

Notes

1. We thank Jeremy Bugler (Fulmar TV) for drawing this to our attention. The television critic of *The Times,* David Chater, listed it as no. 30 in his top 50 shows of the 'noughties'.
2. www.google.com/earth.
3. Svetlana Taylor, conservator in the Department of Manuscripts and Printed Books, Fitzwilliam Museum, Cambridge is thanked for confirming the origins of this observation.
4. See Kimbriel and Noh, in this vol.
5. 'The programmes are researched in immense detail and with great care and we include nothing in the programme that cannot be verified, or if something cannot be verified as in the notion that the *Descent from the Cross* was rescued from the sea, then the narration makes it clear that this is in the realm of myth. Indeed, most of the programmes include corrective to myths, or sometimes new discoveries'; Jeremy Bugler, Fulmar TV.

RECONSTRUCTION OF THE TIN RELIEF DECORATION ON THE THORNHAM PARVA RETABLE

Alice Tavares da Silva

Applied tin relief decorations are found on the Thornham Parva Retable (*c.*1330–40), filling the background to the eight standing saint figures and the *Crucifixion* scene, both in plain and chequerboard patterns, and also adorning some of the saints' attributes (Fig. 1) (Tavares da Silva 2003a). This now well-documented technique (Nadolny 2001: 129–33; Tavares da Silva 2003b) was the subject of a reconstruction exercise during the period of the conservation of the retable at the Hamilton Kerr Institute (HKI) in 1998. It was thought that attempting to recreate the applied relief decorations would help in answering some practical questions regarding the production of this complex, highly decorative technique, and also contribute to the understanding of the construction of the retable itself.

An immediate initial observation was that within each of the six groups of motifs used, the relief squares were all identical, therefore mass-produced using six different templates or moulds. Questions arose regarding the nature of this template. Would there have been one mould for each motif or multiple identical moulds? How long was the drying time needed between their production and their application (knowing that they are made mainly from oil and pigments) and was this a conditioning factor in the making of the retable? Observation from the original also found evidence for the squares having been applied individually to the panel following a predetermined outline of the figures, and being cut to size and used to fill in small gaps and uneven contours (Tavares da Silva 2003a: 47–8).

Moulds

Reproductions of the six motifs were made using *pastiglia* over a prepared chalk ground with the view of making six positive stamps that could then be used to make one or multiple moulds for each motif (Fig. 2). It was decided that this would be an easier way to reproduce the reliefs instead of learning intricate carving skills to produce a mould directly. Indeed, this proved to be a quick and effective way to make convincing reproductions of the relief decorations, as initial tests showed (Fig. 3). The *pastiglia* was a good way of reproducing the fluid appearance of the motifs' fine detail, and the use of clay was an easy and straightforward way to produce one or many identical moulds. Most important, at this stage, was the observation that the tin foil, used as a release layer for the fill material, was stiff enough to allow its removal from the mould when still soft, whilst keeping all the fine detail of the impression intact.[1] This led to the conclusion that as little as one mould for each motif would have been needed in the workshop to make large quantities of a repeating motif, if their drying was undergone outside the mould.

The possibility that each of the six motifs was originally carved or engraved in a hard durable material (such as hard wood or metal), remains likely. However this exercise has shown that the *pastiglia* stamps and the clay moulds produced convincing reproductions of the original motifs and that, although involving an extra step in the manufacturing process, their use should not be ruled out. They proved to be a very simple and straightforward way of mass producing tin relief decorations in a convenient time frame, avoiding the need for intricate carving skills, as illustrated by the resulting reproductions. Six clay moulds were thus made from six *pastiglia* stamps and used to produce as many relief decorations as desired (Figs 4 and 5).

Making the relief decorations

The process entailed the delicate step of pressing the tin foil into the mould impression. This had to be done gently with a cotton wool pad to avoid tearing the very malleable and

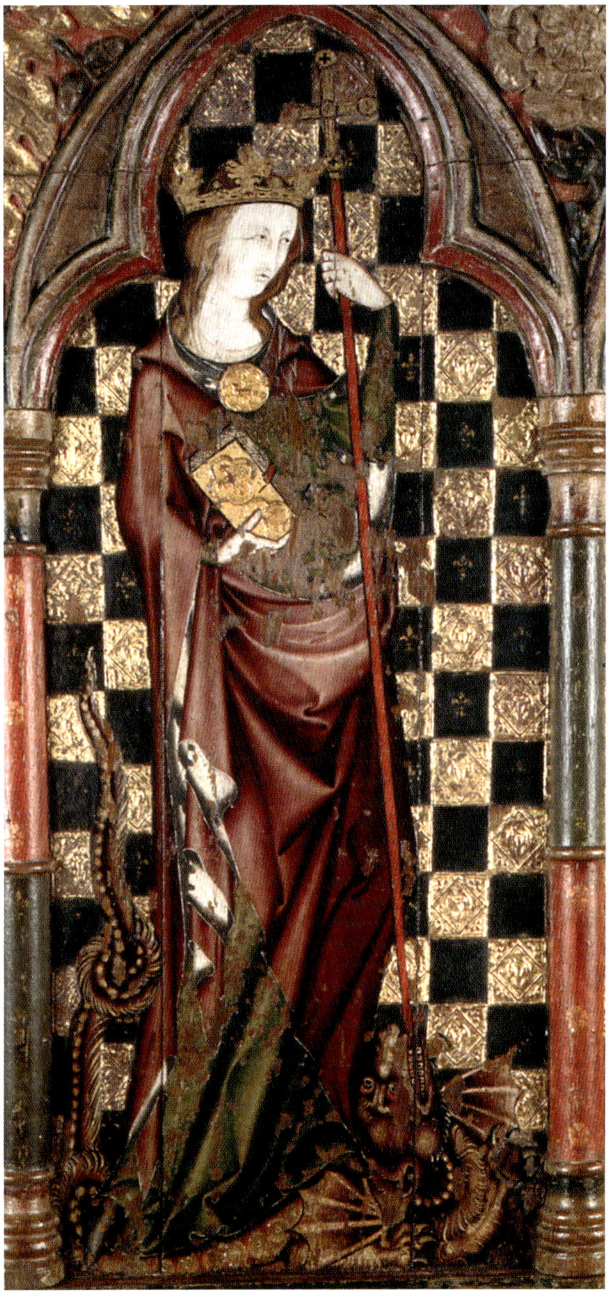

Figure 1 *St Margaret. Detail from the Thornham Parva Retable, after treatment. Here the tin relief was used in a chequerboard pattern around the saint's figure and locally to adorn her book and brooch. (Photograph by kind permission of St Mary's church PCC, Thornham Parva.)*

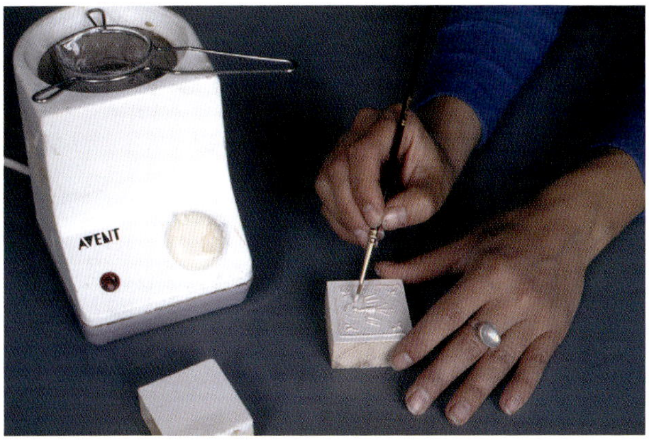

Figure 2 *Making the relief stamps using the* pastiglia *technique.*

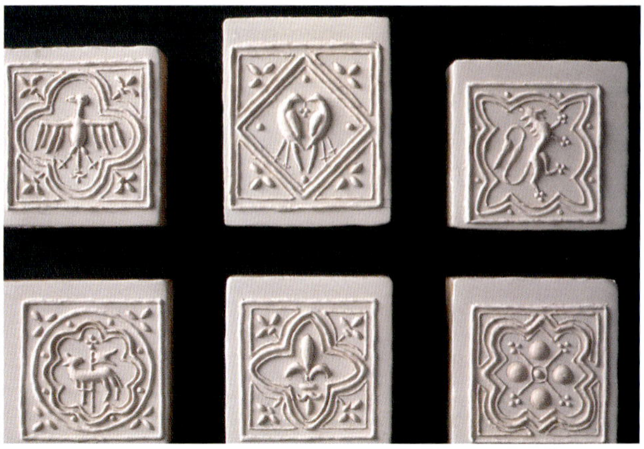

Figure 3 *The* pastiglia *relief stamps for the six relief motifs found on the Thornham Parva Retable.*

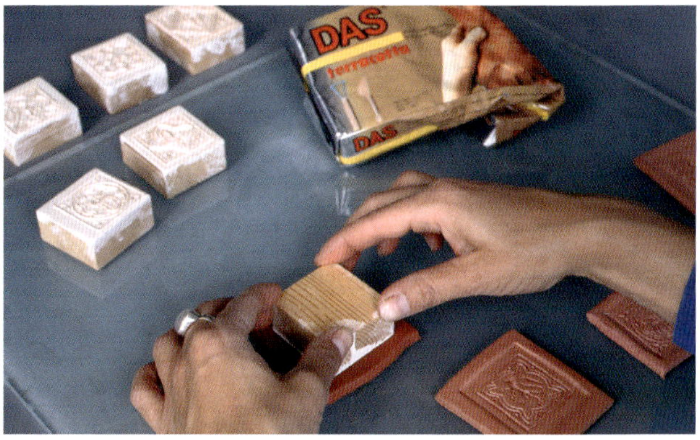

Figure 4 *A mould being made by pressing the clay with the* pastiglia *stamp.*

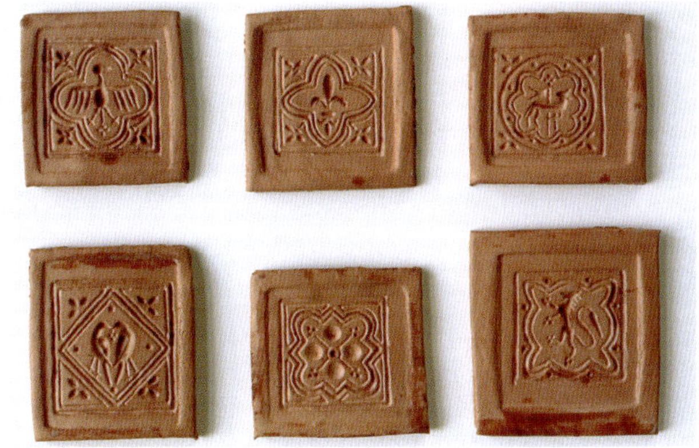

Figure 5 *The clay moulds corresponding to the six relief motifs found on the Thornham Parva Retable.*

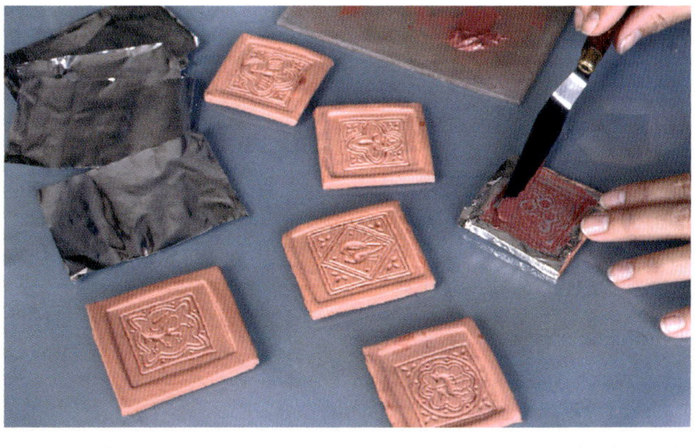

Figure 6 *After lining and pressing with tin foil, the impression is filled with the putty material. The excess material is then scraped off.*

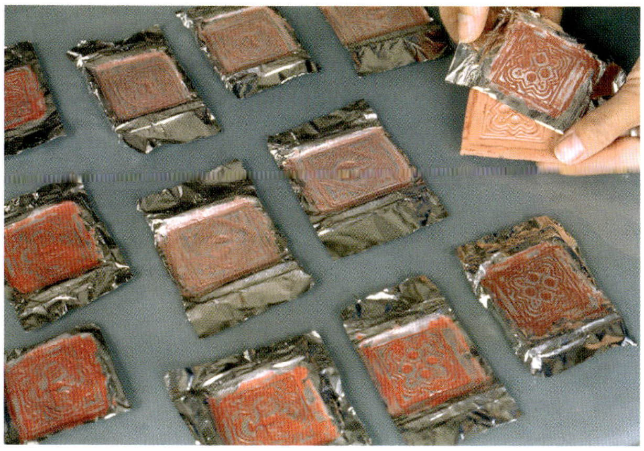

Figure 7 *Production of large quantities of tin relief decorations, left to dry outside the moulds.*

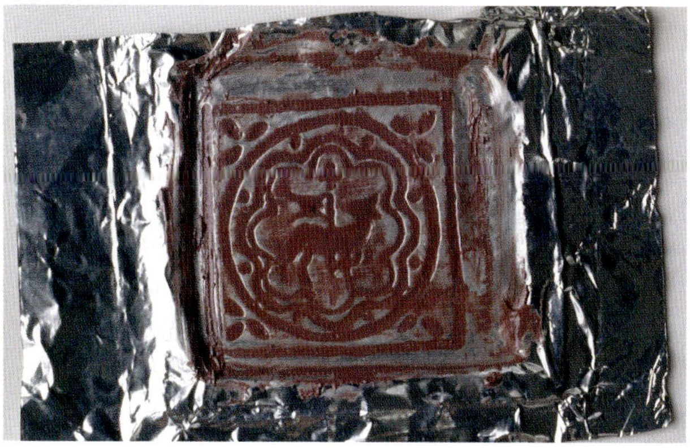

Figure 8 Agnus Dei *relief decoration during drying. Note that the fill material only covers the recesses of the impression, and that some smearing of this material has been left after the scraping of the excess putty.*

soft metal foil. Once lined with tin, the mould was filled with an oil putty consisting of a mixture of fast-drying pigments, fillers and drying oil, ground together to a stiff buttery consistency (Fig. 6);[2] the relief was then released from the mould and placed aside to dry. The same mould was then used for further applications of tin foil and putty until the required number of a particular motif had been achieved (Fig. 7).

It was quickly noticed at this stage that the fill material would dry faster and produce a more even relief decoration if applied to the foil as thinly and sparingly as possible, so that only the recesses of the impression would be filled (as seen in Fig. 6). Levelling the fill material at this stage produced relief squares that were evenly flat on their reverse, ready to be applied to a flat layer of adhesive putty. These observations led to another breakthrough in understanding the production process. The decorations must have been made in two separate steps: first, the filling of the impression in the mould, allowing it to dry thoroughly (since the drier and harder it gets at this stage, the more likely it is to maintain the fine detail intact); second, the application of a similar putty layer but this time to the panel due to receive the applied decorations. This ensures an even distribution of the adhesive layer resulting in a levelled application of the squares adjacent to each other. Cross-section samples taken from the retable had shown the existence of two discrete layers of fill material below the tin foil, with similar colour and composition, their presence now logically explained by these practical observations (Tavares da Silva 2003a: 48).

The relief decorations can thus be made in large quantities, and left to dry as long as necessary, but the adhesive layer is pasted onto the panel only shortly before the relief is applied, when it will still be sufficiently tacky to receive it. This production in large quantities is reliant on batches of fill material that can vary in pigment proportions and therefore have slight variations in colour, as observed on the Thornham Parva Retable during treatment (Tavares da Silva 2003a: 48). It was in fact quite difficult to maintain an exact colour between different batches of putty.

Another interesting observation that also reinforced the conclusion of two steps in the making of the tin relief background was the smearing of putty that is sometimes left on the impression during the scraping of excess material (Fig. 8). This was also observed on some relief squares of the original painting due to the now abraded gilding and tin layers, and easily spotted due to the difference in colour between batches of the putty material as mentioned above (Fig. 9).

Application

Once a large number of relief squares had been made, their application to the test panels followed with further interesting revelations. The test panels were prepared with a chalk-animal glue ground and a lead white-oil priming, as found on the original. A thin adhesive putty layer was applied to the panels with a spatula, taking care to spread it out thinly and evenly level. This layer was allowed to dry for a few hours, but left sticky enough to hold the relief squares (Fig. 10). This initial drying before application was

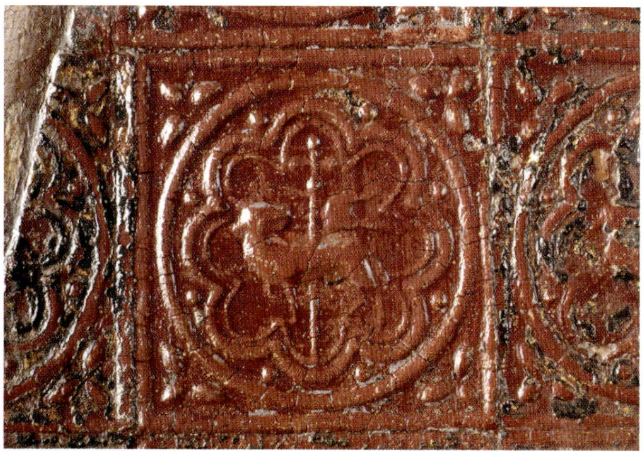

Figure 9 *An original* Agnus Dei *relief square. Detail from the background to St John the Baptist, Thornham Parva Retable. This detail shows the difference in colour between the raised and the flat areas of the decoration. Note also the smearing of the lighter fill material over the flat area. (Photograph by kind permission of St Mary's church PCC, Thornham Parva.)*

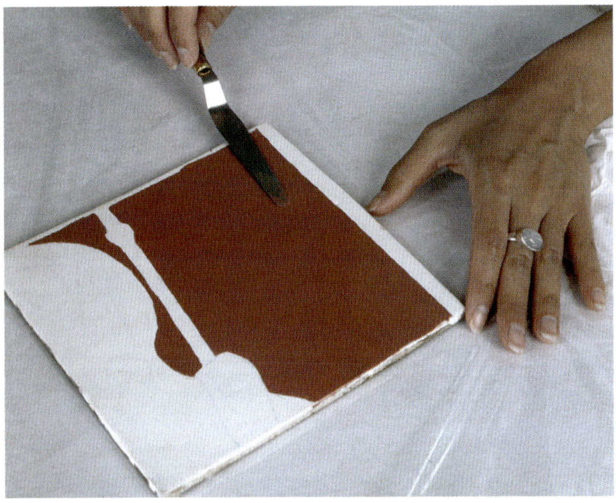

Figure 10 *Application of the adhesive putty layer to a test panel.*

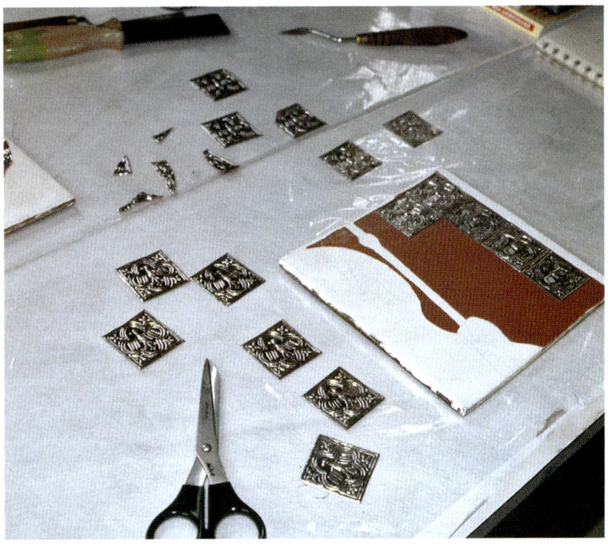

Figure 11 *Trimming and application of relief decorations to a test panel.*

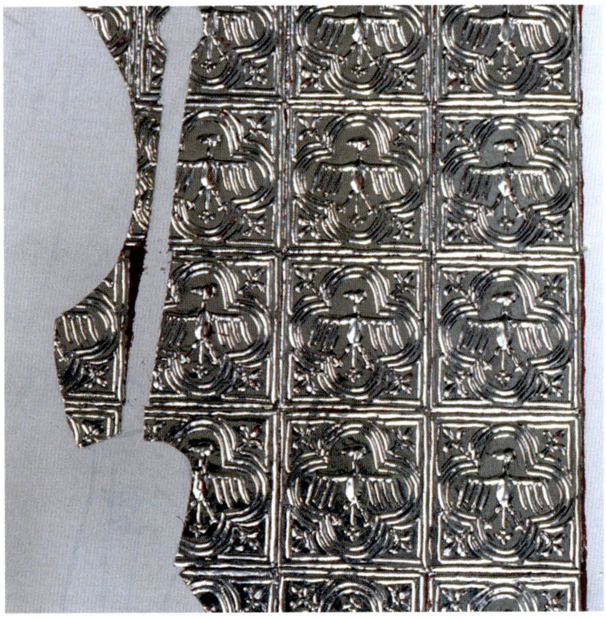

Figure 12 *Application of the eagle motif to a test panel. One relief square was placed inverted, and a fragment from a different motif was also used on this panel.*

felt desirable in order to reduce drying times, thus helping to maintain an even level across the surface. It would have allowed plenty of time for the careful painting of this layer around the contours of each figure, as well as for the planning and application of the relief decorations.

The preprepared and dried squares can be easily handled and trimmed to the required shape and size, and then applied to the tacky adhesive putty layer (Fig. 11). If the application of squares in a line to a straight edge is obviously straightforward, the meeting of the contour of a halo, hand or attribute certainly is not. Here the relief squares had to be cut to meet specific curved shapes to each position and to fill in awkward gaps between fingers and halos (Fig. 12). This of course involves a certain amount of planning and preparation before sticking anything down onto the adhesive, making good use of the needed drying time mentioned above. Even so it was still possible after a few days to return to the test panel and carry out fine adjustments to the contour of the figure by trimming the applied tin relief with a very sharp blade. Again, evidence for similar adjustments was found on the original panel (Tavares da Silva 2003a: 47–8).

With so much preparation and cutting of the already dry tin reliefs, it is inevitable that the work table is at this stage full of small fragments of tin relief. No wonder, then, that during the construction of the Thornham Parva Retable many small pieces of the six different motifs were used to fill in small spaces here and there, not always in the right orientation or indeed around the corresponding saint figure (Tavares da Silva 2003a: 47). The reconstruction made during this exercise contains similar (although intentional) mistakes that can be seen with the naked eye, but interestingly do not interfere with the final appearance and purpose of the gilded relief decoration.

Oil mordant and gilding

With the absence of any medium analysis of the mordant layer, the reconstruction of this paint layer was based on existing recipes from medieval treatises.[3] These describe many different pigmented oil mordants for gilding, with variable compositions and proportions, but in general all making use of pre-treated drying oil, which can be either heat-bodied or boiled with litharge (lead oil). To this a fair amount of *vernice liquida* (liquid varnish prepared by dissolving sandarac resin in boiling linseed oil) is added in quantities that vary from just 'a little' to 'half a painter's pot of varnish'.[4] The pigment content is also variable in these recipes, but usually includes the necessary siccative pigments such as lead white or red lead. This coupled with observations of cross-section samples and elemental analysis, led to the making of an oil mordant containing lead white, chalk, yellow ochre, red ochre, red lead and vermilion.

The pigments were ground in equal amounts of lead oil (as used for the fill material) and liquid varnish made

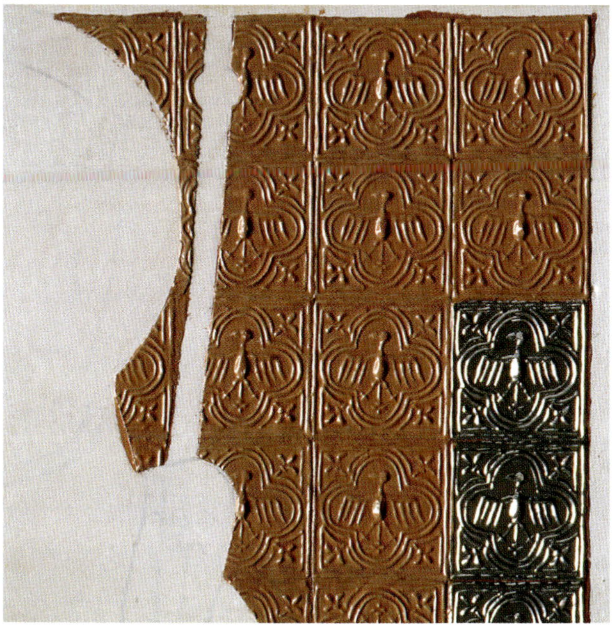

Figure 13 *The eagle motif during the application of the orange oil mordant.*

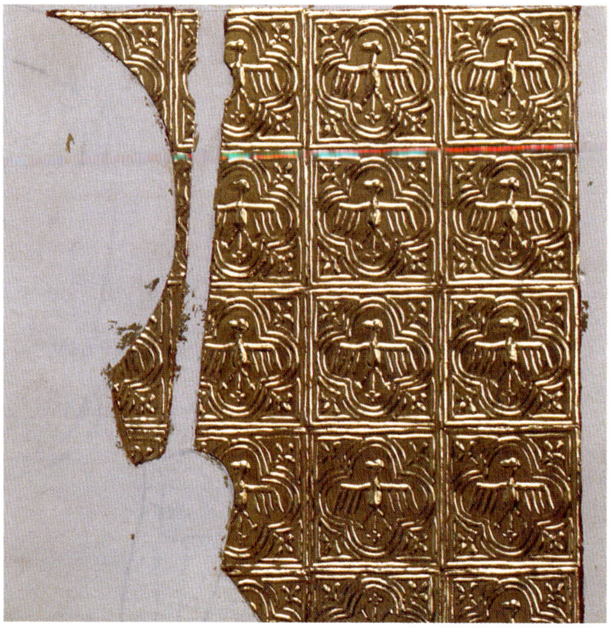

Figure 14 *The eagle motif after gilding.*

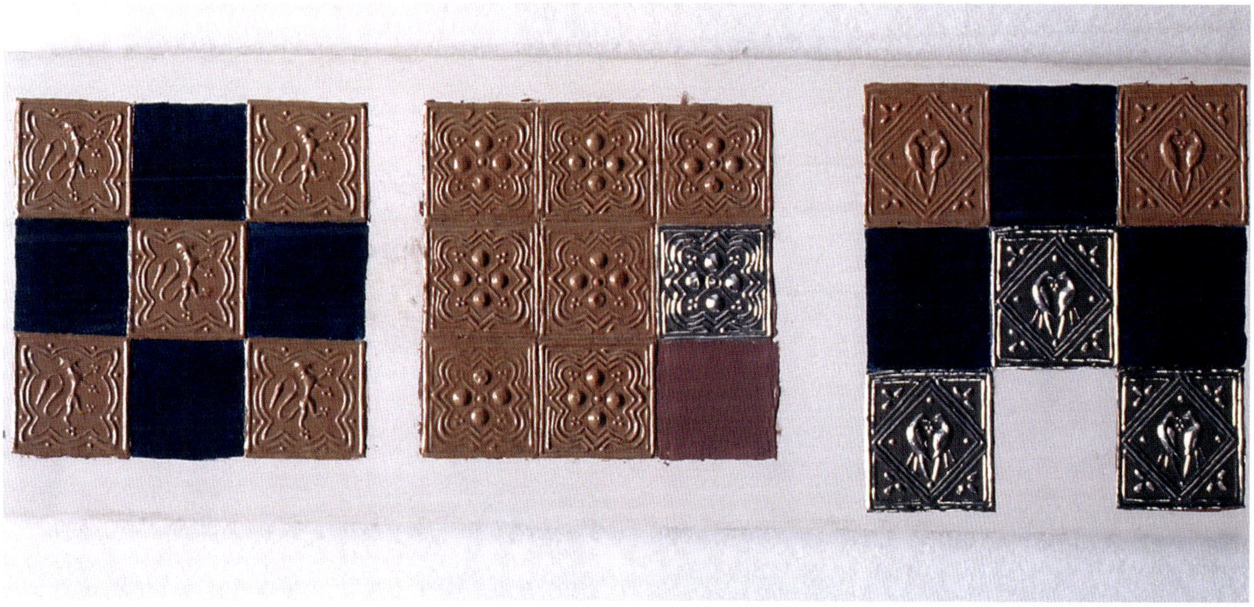

Figure 15 *Relief decorations in a plain and a chequerboard pattern, with the orange mordant and the first layer of azurite.*

by dissolving sandarac resin in hot linseed oil.[5] The resin content, an important element of the composition, gives the mordant its fluidity, allowing it to dry to a very smooth finish, thus creating a paint with a silky sheen, free of brush marks, and consequently producing a better gilding result.[6] The mordant was brushed onto the tin relief squares as evenly as possible and left to dry for about five days (Fig. 13). It was only when almost dry to the touch that it was considered ready to receive the gold leaf. A soft brush and cotton wool were found useful to help the gold to conform to all the detail and for a final polishing of the gilding (Fig. 14).[7] The rather messy edges of the gilding, which contaminate the reserve for the figure, would have been covered during the painting stage.

Chequerboard pattern

As known from the original panel, the blue squares that create the chequerboard pattern were painted in two layers: the first painted after the application of the tin relief but before gilding; the second after mordant gilding, and used for redefining the edges of the squares contaminated by the gold leaf used (Tavares da Silva 2003a: 50). This second layer, being also the base for the stencil gilding, would have been painted during the last stages of the painting of figures (Figs 15 and 16). For the blue paint, a mixture of medium coarse azurite (for the first layer) and coarse azurite (for the upper layer) with small quantities of lead white and chalk was ground in linseed oil.[8]

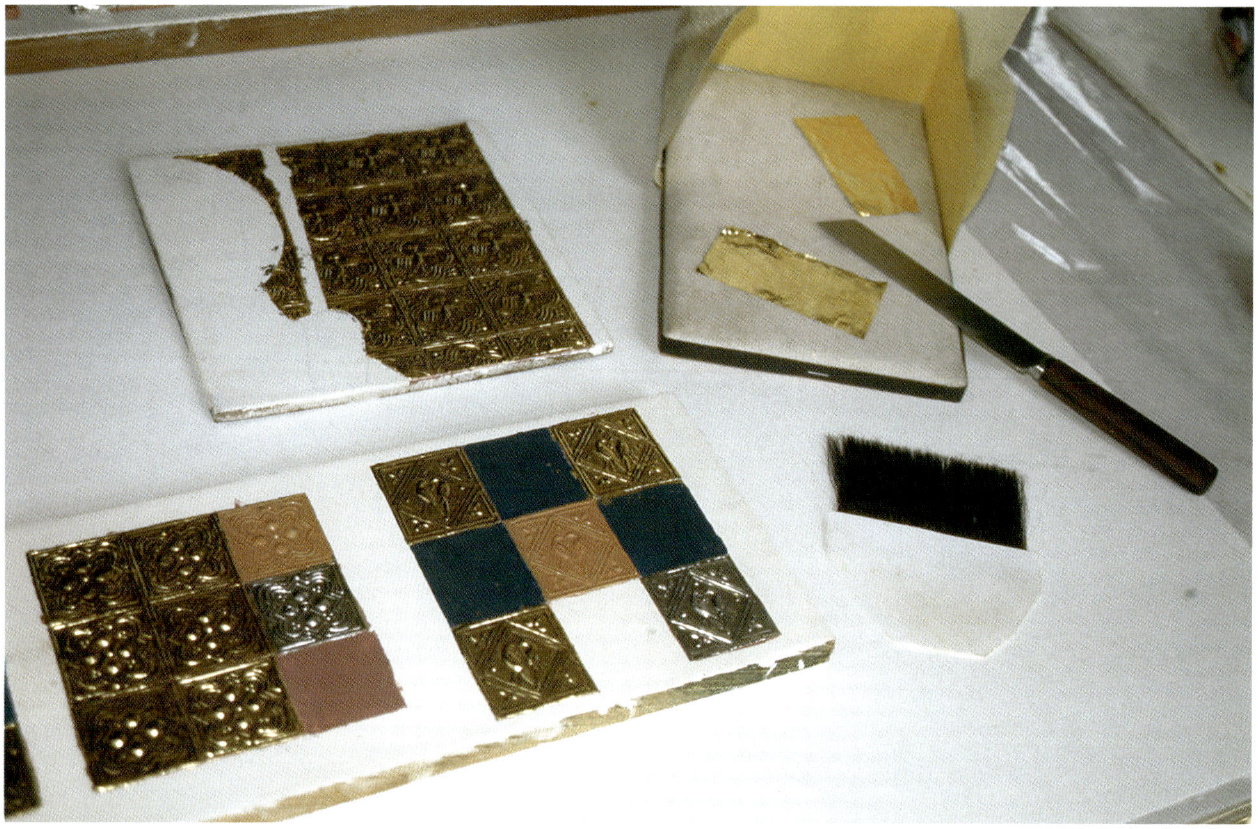

Figure 16 *Relief decorations during gilding.*

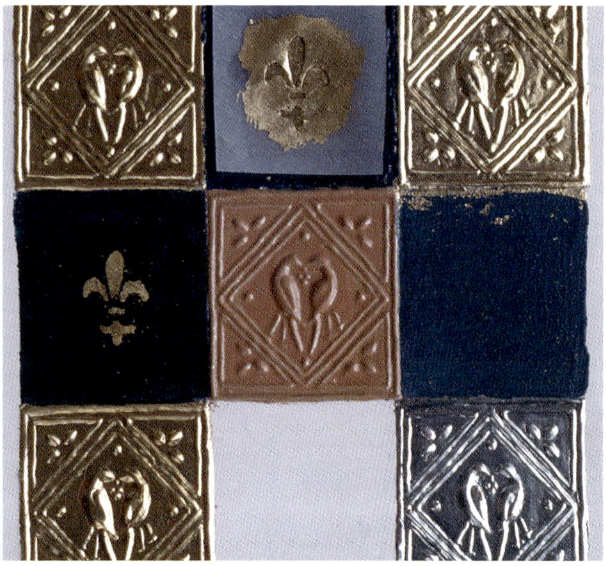

Figure 17 *The addorsed birds motif in a chequerboard pattern at different stages of production, showing the stencil gilding during its application.*

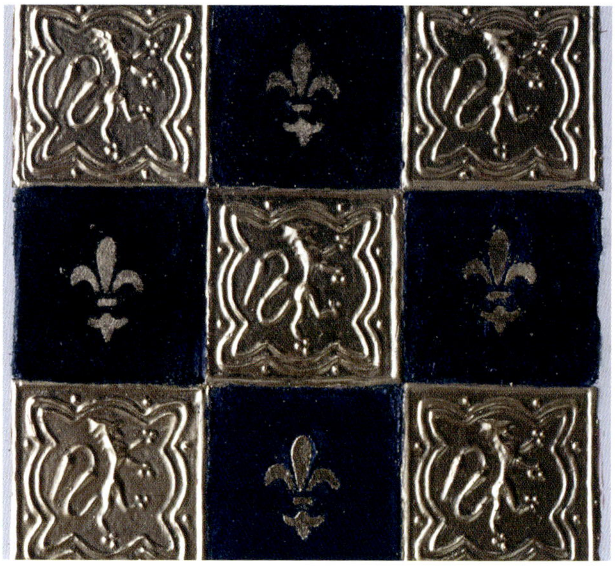

Figure 18 *The lion motif in a chequerboard pattern after gilding.*

Stencil gilding

The stencil gilding was successfully achieved by simply applying the gold leaf through a template directly onto the almost dry second layer of azurite paint. The template was made with tracing paper and reused as necessary. This method, requiring the use of neither mordant nor adhesive, proved to be a very simple and quick process for making the gilded stencils in large quantities, and was based on the observations from the original stencils where no adhesive was found. Had the blue paint been too dry, then a layer of, for example, *vernice liquida,* could be painted on and used as the adhesive for the stencil whilst still tacky (Fig. 17).[9]

Conclusion

The reconstruction of the decorated background of the Thornham Parva Retable, with its applied tin relief technique and gilding, has directed attention to the practical aspects of these decorative techniques, and helped to answer questions regarding their production. It has also been invaluable in clarifying our understanding of the different stages of the construction of the painted retable.

Clearly, it is possible to make tin relief decorations without specialist carving or engraving skills. The reconstruction has explained the presence and function of the two distinct fill material layers through practical observations, as well as the process for applying the stencil gilding. It has demonstrated the fact that the production of large quantities of tin relief decorations is not a time-limiting factor in the construction of an object such as the Thornham Parva Retable; they can be produced in large quantities and set aside to dry, well ahead of when they will be needed for adorning a painting. It seems logical to suggest that they could have been part of a division of labour within the painter's workshop, a task assigned to an assistant or apprentice, and being carried out ahead of time and as part of a larger stock of decorative accessories used by the craftsmen during the making of paintings.

This reconstruction, with its gilded tin relief squares, chequerboard pattern and stencil gilding has also provided an opportunity to visualise the original appearance of a now much damaged area of the painting, and a glimpse into the finished appearance of what was certainly a highly decorated, bright and glittering altarpiece (Fig. 18).

Notes

1. The tin foil used was approximately 25 μm thick and was supplied by Kremer Pigmente.
2. The fill material contained lead white, chalk, quartz, calcite, vermilion, red lead and charcoal black in varied proportions in an attempt to match the original colour approximately. It was ground in lead oil with added colophony resin. I am grateful to Renate Woudhuysen-Keller for her help in the preparation of the lead oil and putty mixtures; see also Tavares da Silva 2003b: 129.
3. For example, see the manuscript of Jehan Le Bègue 107, Bolognese manuscript 171 and Paduan manuscript 96 in Merrifield 1967; see also Borradaile and Borradaile 1966: 61 and Cennino 1960: 96.
4. For references to recipes for making drying oils including lead oil, see Merrifield 1967: ccxxxvi-ccxlv. For recipes for liquid varnish see Bolognese manuscript 206 in Merrifield 1967 and Theophilus 1979: 28–9.
5. One part of resin added to two parts of oil and heated to approximately 240°C for 30 minutes (the resin started to melt at 150°C). It was then filtered to remove impurities and any undissolved resin.
6. I am grateful to Renate Woudhuysen-Keller for these observations and for all the practical help in making our version of the *vernice liquida*.
7. Cennino also describes how mordant gilding can be 'burnished ... to perfection' with cotton wool: Cennini 160: 97. The word 'burnished' should be read here as polished, since burnishing implies water-based gilding and the use of a burnishing stone to achieve a highly polished surface.
8. The chalk content was found to be necessary when trying to disperse azurite in oil, greatly minimising the pooling of oil to the surface after painting. I am grateful to Renate Woudhuysen-Keller for her help with preparing different grades of the pigment and with this practical solution for making the blue paint.
9. Only in one instance was there evidence found for a varnish/adhesive layer associated with a gilded stencil, on one of the half-columns of the carved canopy; see Tavares da Silva 2003a: 53.

References

Borradaile, V. and Borradaile, R. (tr.) 1966. *The Strasburg Manuscript: A Medieval Painter's Handbook*. London: Alec Tiranti Ltd.

Cennini, Cennino, 1960. *The Craftsman's Handbook, 'Il libro dell'arte'*, D.V. Thompson (tr.). New York: Dover Publications.

Merrifield, M. 1967. *Original Treatises on the Arts of Painting*, 2 vols. New York: Dover Publications.

Nadolny, J. 2001. *The Techniques and Use of Gilded Relief Decorations by Northern European Painters, c.1200–1500*. PhD dissertation, Courtauld Institute of Art, University of London.

Tavares da Silva, A. 2003a. 'The decorated background'. In *The Thornham Parva Retable: Technique, Conservation and Context of an English Medieval Painting*, A. Massing (ed.) 47–53. London and Turnhout: Harvey Miller Publishers.

Tavares da Silva, A., 2003b. 'Reconstruction of the decorated background'. In *The Thornham Parva Retable: Technique, Conservation and Context of an English Medieval Painting*, A. Massing (ed.) 129–33. London and Turnhout: Harvey Miller Publishers.

Theophilus 1979. *On Divers Arts: The Foremost Treatise on Painting, Glassmaking and Metalwork*, J.G. Hawthorne and C.S. Smith (tr.). New York: Dover Publications.

BEING PAOLO UCCELLO

Nicola Christie

The art of copying is achieved by such close observation that the copyist approaches a fair degree of understanding of their subject. When the subject is a fifteenth-century painting, then the above applies but the understanding must extend to the pigments, the paint and how they might have looked 500 years ago. The reconstruction can never be more than an interpretation because of this.

I spent many hours looking at Paolo Uccello's *The Hunt in the Forest, c.*1470 (Fig. 1), thinking about layer structure, wondering at tiny details and examining pigment particles at high magnifications (Christie 1988). This close observation of the minutiae led slowly to (mostly) insignificant discoveries but each contributed to the 'understanding' of the whole picture. Of the more significant observations, 25 years later I can still recall the excitement of finding the vanishing point faintly indented in the depths of the forest, pondering the curious, spherical particles of green in cross-sections and the persistent traces of gold, patterning the foliage.

In the mid-late 1980s when I was at the Hamilton Kerr Institute (HKI), we had access to a seemingly wide range of analytical methods to assist our observations but in 2012 they would probably be considered inadequate. Looking at the fuzzy black and white prints photographed directly from the infrared vidicon screen by the dozen, I remember many, many hours printing in the dark room then, holding my breath as I cut each photograph to match the edges of its neighbours, mounting them piece by piece onto Fome-Cor and, finally, photographing the whole, imperfect mosaic. Now, this process would take an hour from start to finish and undoubtedly produce far more information. Nevertheless, my fuzzy mosaic shows the unmistakable ruled, perspective lines through the horn blower's figure and Uccello's elegant contours, tweaked and adjusted in his hunt for the perfect composition. Some initial pigment identification I made by microchemical tests (fiddly and unreliable in my hands), having not yet been introduced to the wonders of rather

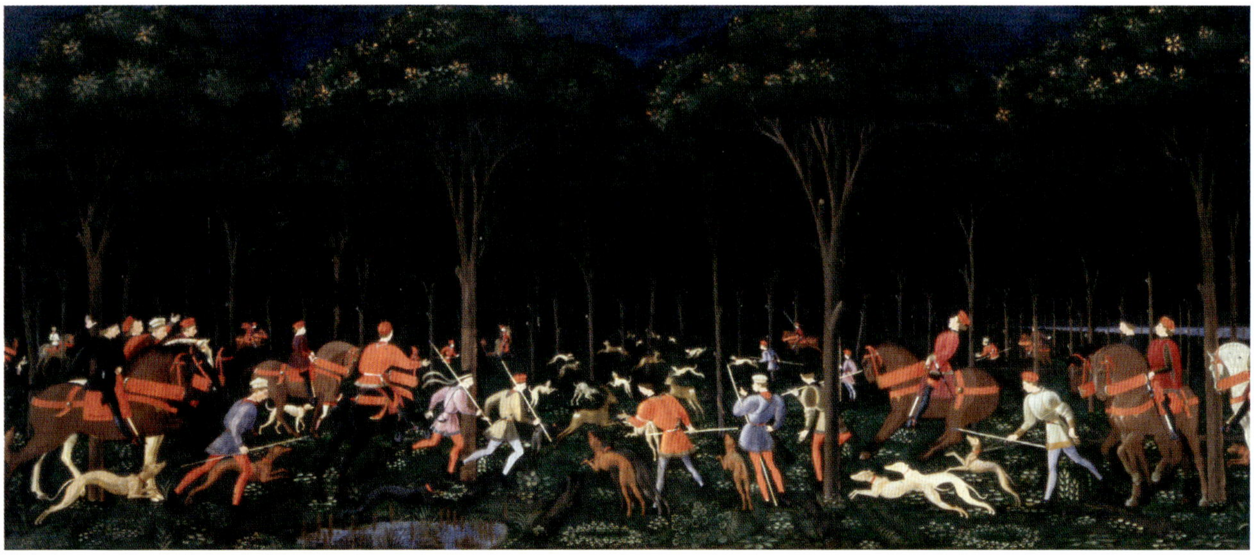

Figure 1 *Paolo Uccello,* The Hunt in the Forest, *c.1470. (Photograph courtesy of Ashmolean Museum, University of Oxford (A79).)*

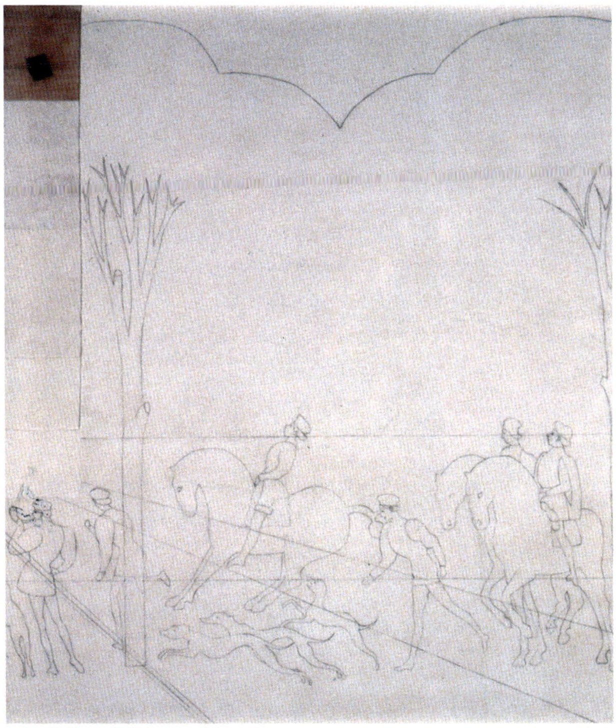

Figure 2 *Reconstructed underdrawing.*

Figure 3 *After painting the dark underlayers.*

more permanent pigment dispersions. Very little medium analysis was carried out 'due to the size of the sample required' whereas now a sample the size of this full stop provides a mass of information.

The making of the reconstruction was immensely enjoyable. Although the close observation never stopped, I believed I had enough understanding of my subject to glue two planks of wood together, coat them in layers of gesso and begin painting. One of the purposes of the reconstruction is to instruct the viewer in how the original was created by revealing the layer structure. At least one fully worked-up area is helpful. The *malrand* was created

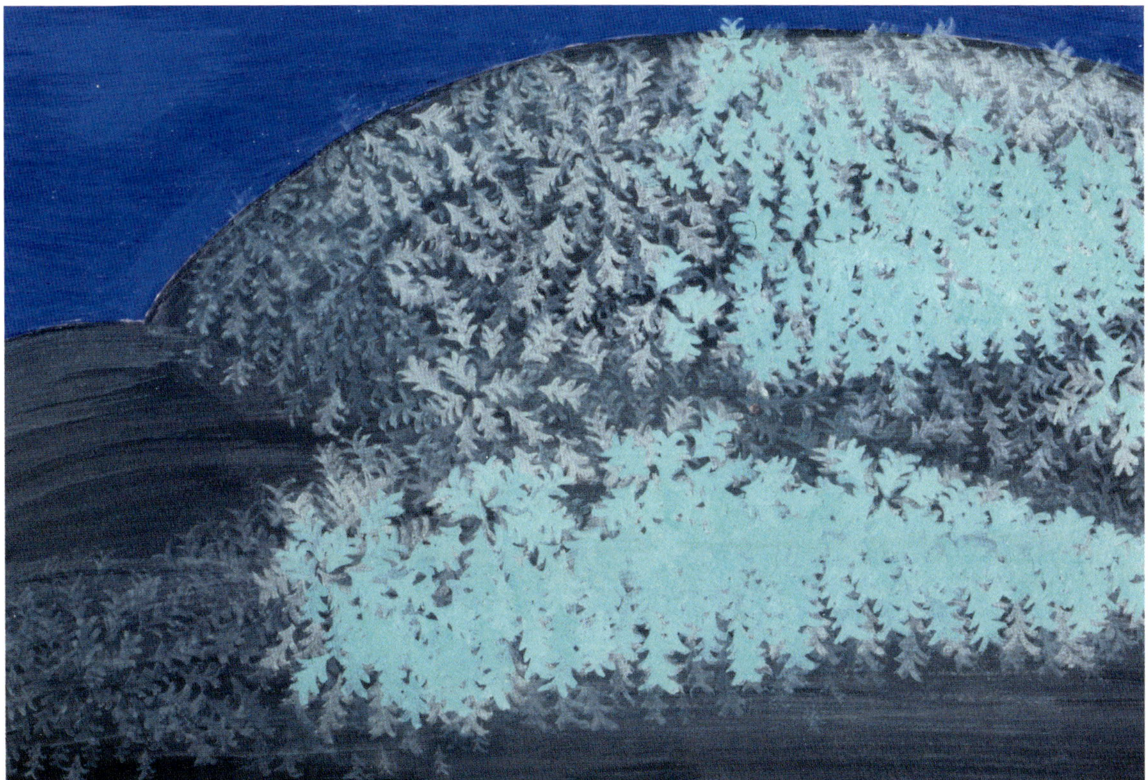

Figure 4 *Detail showing the painting of the oak leaves.*

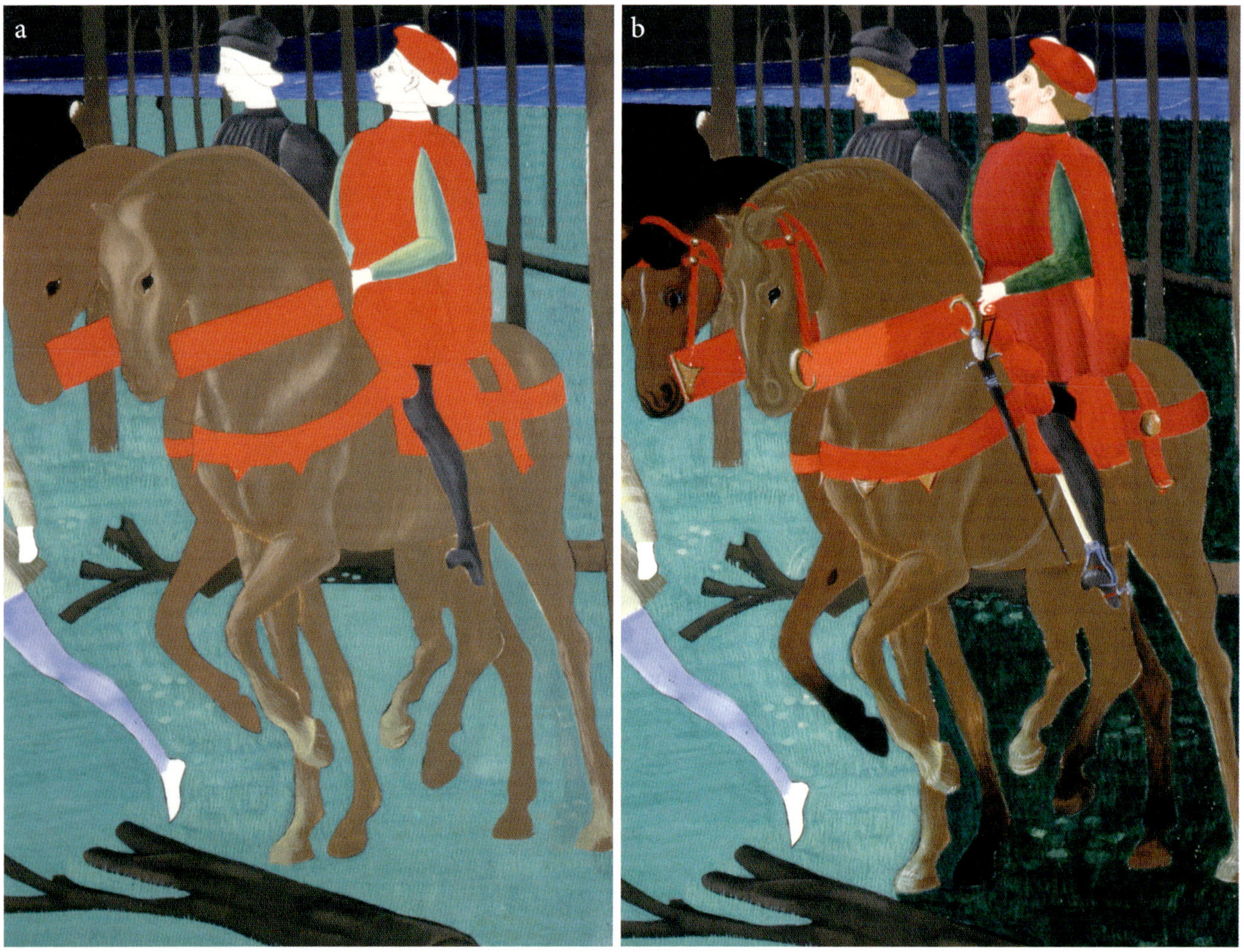

Figure 5 *Detail of the two riders (a) after application of body colour (b) after application of glazes.*

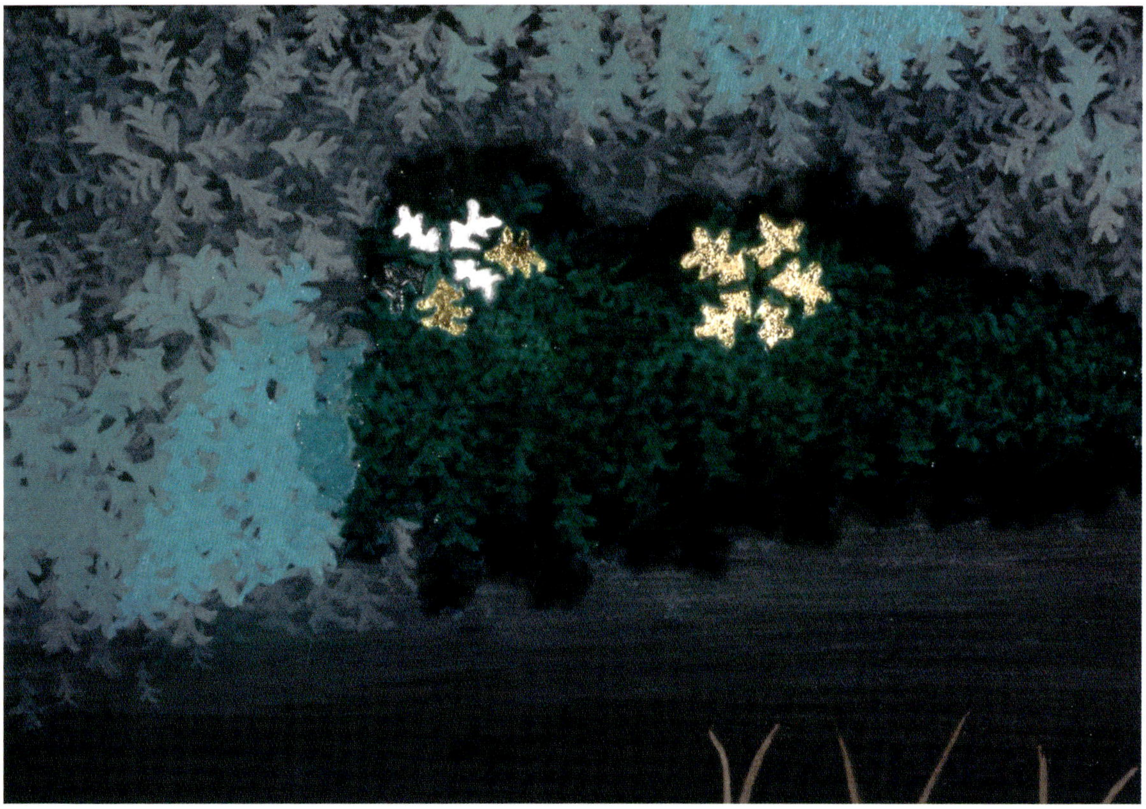

Figure 6 *Detail showing the gilded oak leaves.*

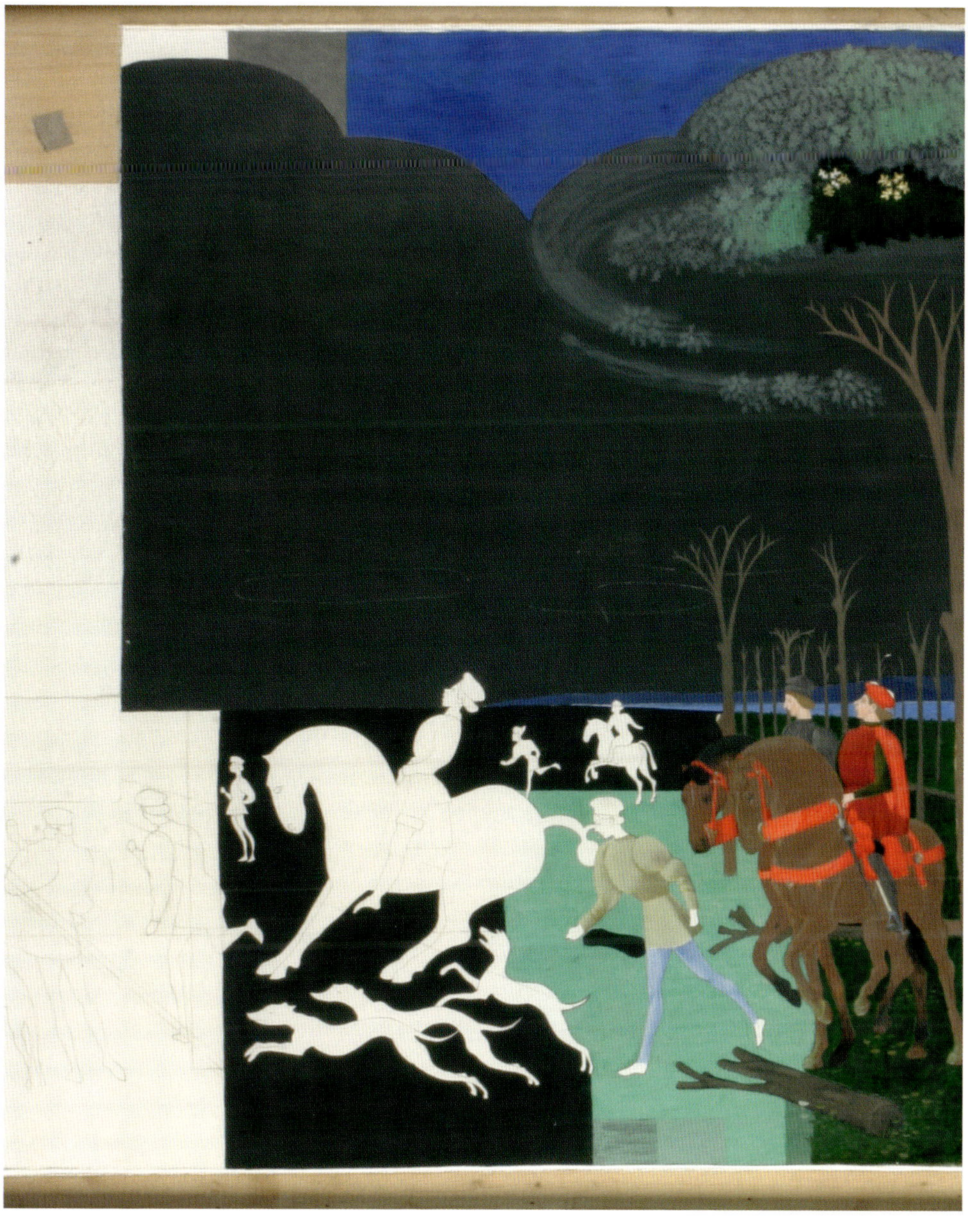

Figure 7 *The completed reconstruction of* The Hunt in the Forest.

by simply attaching two strips of wood to the prepared panel and applying gesso up to and over them: a basic approximation to an engaged frame. Only when I had finished the reconstruction did I remove the wooden strips, producing a satisfyingly clean break along each edge of raised gesso. Underdrawing followed (Fig. 2) and then the first layers of paint: bone black bound in gum arabic as identified by analysis, leaving a pattern of white silhouettes across the surface (Fig. 3). Incisions reinforced key elements of the composition and the perspective framework. Layers of green bound in egg yolk followed: coarsely ground malachite from Kremer Pigmente to imitate the texture and colour of Uccello's artificial malachite. This was possibly the most difficult period of the reconstruction process as I built up layers of slightly too pale a green over black, which looked quite unlike the intense foliage of Uccello's forest. Then, layering jagged curves of oak leaves one over another over another (Fig. 4), the shapes of the trees appeared eventually, afterwards adding lead white and lead-tin yellow for the highlights that dance across the surface through trees and grass. The sky – always provoking a debate over the time of day depicted – is a simple mixture of coarsely ground particles of ultramarine mixed with lead white but in a now deeply discoloured medium. The strong blue of the reconstruction suggests how it may originally have appeared.

The two riders on the right of the composition had always been the passage I intended to work up to completion. Following observations of the magnified surface and cross-sections, I copied Uccello's pigment mixtures for the bay and chestnut horses, particularly enjoying the way I could delineate the green highlights on the fetlocks in the egg medium. Vermilion mixtures for the garments and tackle provided the scarlet body colour that was then enriched with glazes of organic red mixed with white, blues and black to range from cool pinks to crimson. Although the source of the organic red was not identified, I chose to make a glaze of madder (purchased from Kremer rather than made from scratch) ground with heat-bodied linseed oil to produce a wonderful glossy paint. To avoid unattractive pooling, the glaze can only be applied in many thin layers, allowing each to be at least touch dry before the next layer can be attempted. The same technique applies to the copper resinate glazes, but here I did cook up verdigris and Venice turpentine to produce an intense, viscous green that transformed my pale malachite magically as I applied each glaze (Fig. 5). These rich layers are much diminished on Uccello's *Hunt* with much of the browned copper resinate removed mistakenly with discoloured varnish in past restorations, along with many of the organic red glazes.

How the final touches of gold were conceived had never been resolved to my satisfaction. The apparently 'hollowed-out' leaf shapes were inconsistent, with some created intentionally and formed perfectly while others were apparently the result of a technical defect. Traces of gold in the shape of leaves applied directly onto the paint surface are unmistakable but other fragments of gold in the 'hollowed-out' leaves less so. I chose to remove leaf-shaped areas of paint at the end rather than leave them in reserve from the start as this method seemed more practical than planning the highlights before even the underlayers were applied. Some gold I applied onto the gesso exposed within the hollows and some on the paint surface as observed on the original (Fig. 6). Whatever the original intention, this pattern of golden shapes, both decorative and sculptural, complete the painting in a way it would be impossible to imagine it without (Fig. 7).

After a recent visit to the Ashmolean Museum, the *Hunt* continues to intrigue and delight me. I am not certain I found all the 'right' answers to questions of technique, or that Uccello created his painting in precisely the way I laid out on my reconstruction panel. The experience of making a reconstruction affords a privileged view of an artist's creative process and, in my case, fostered a lifelong concern with technique. This process of looking and questioning, encouraged in students, continues to serve us well as conservators.

Reference

Christie, N. 1988. '*The Hunt in the Forest* by Paolo Uccello: Technical Examination and Copy'. Unpublished project, Hamilton Kerr Institute.

RECONSTRUCTING THE PREPARATION LAYERS OF A LATE FIFTEENTH-CENTURY PANEL PAINTING FROM SEVILLE

Lara Broecke

The *Road to Calvary* (Fitzwilliam Museum, Cambridge) is a painting in the Hispano-Flemish style and is thought to originate from Seville (Fig. 1). The names Juàn and Diego Sánchez are inscribed on the painting and documentary and stylistic evidence dates it to around 1497. During conservation treatment at the Hamilton Kerr Institute in 2002–2003 the painting became the subject of historical and technical investigation and a section of it was reconstructed (Fig. 2). The results of the examination of this and other paintings, roughly contemporary contracts and Pacheco's *The Art of Painting* (Véliz 1986) informed the reconstruction. The project demonstrated the complexity of thinking required to create a painting of this sort, something most evident in the reconstruction of the preparation layers, described here.

The panel consisted of two sweet chestnut boards with an iron staple across the join on the face and wooden fillets glued into a gap between the boards; pine battens were

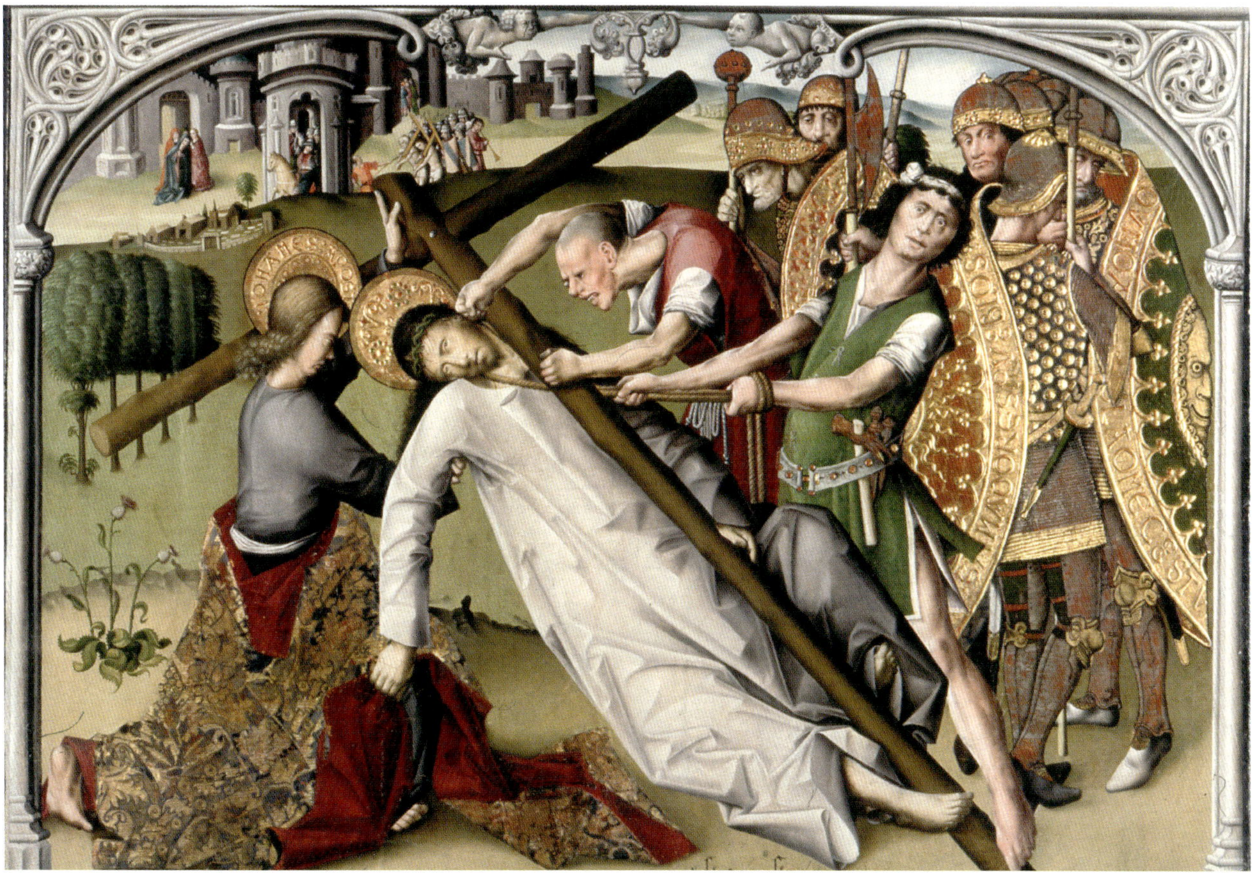

Figure 1 *Juàn and Diego Sánchez,* Road to Calvary, c.*1497, The Fitzwilliam Museum, Cambridge.*

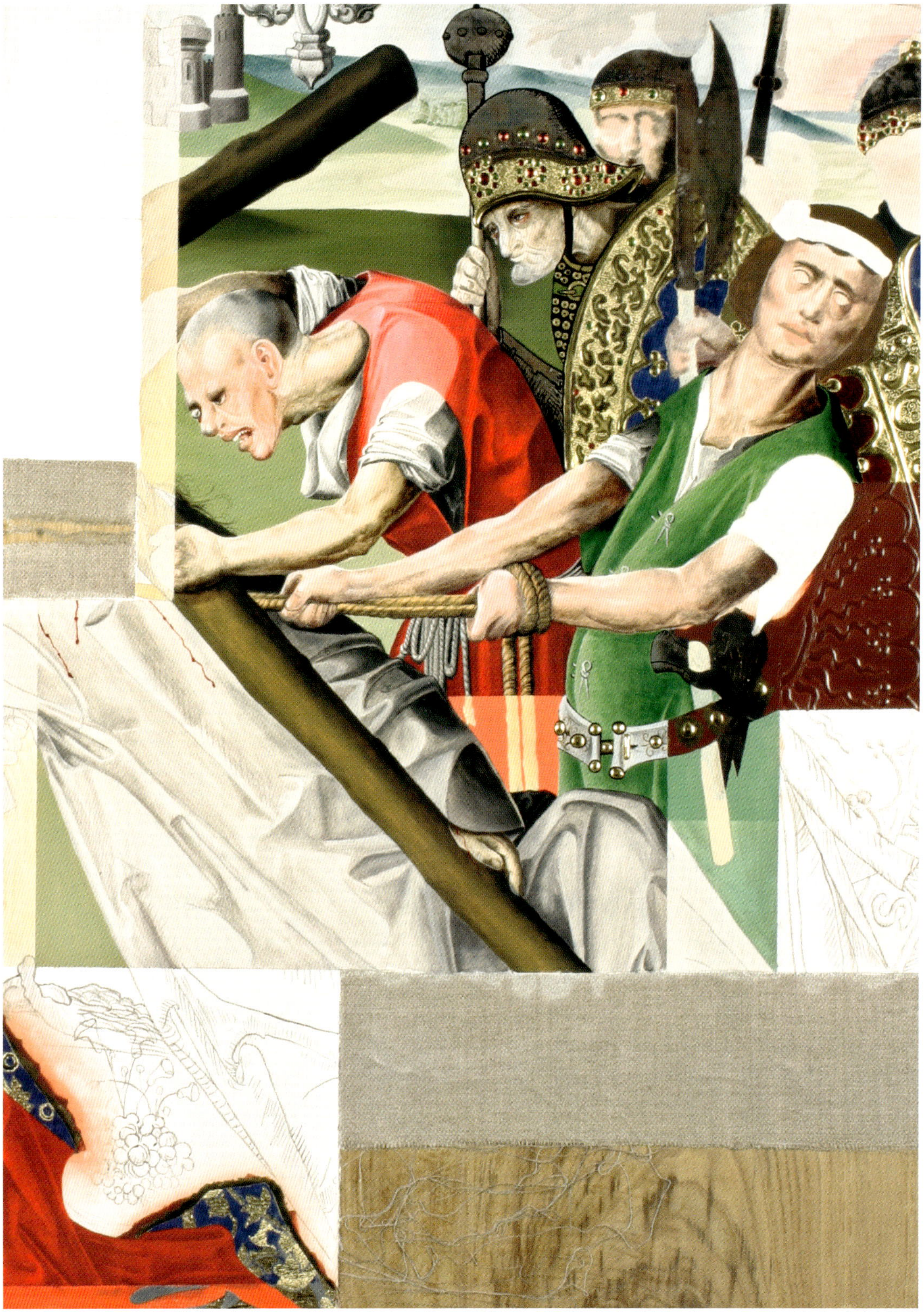

Figure 2 *The completed reconstruction of* Road to Calvary.

nailed on from the front (Fig. 3). The first stage of the preparation was the filling of gaps around the staple and nail heads. In the *Road to Calvary*, a filler found around the metal elements and beneath the canvas that covered the whole panel was identified as *yeso*[1] bound with glue.

For the reconstruction a *yeso* filler[2] was made. Calcium sulphate hemihydrate hardens quickly in water[3] and, while it was observed that the addition of rabbit-skin glue slows this down, the drying time is still quick enough to make this a more convenient filler than the slower drying and softer *yeso vivo*[4] or *yeso mate*.[5] The mixture was heated and stirred until a relatively thick consistency was achieved. Rabbit-skin glue (10%) was first applied around the metal elements and gaps in the fillets to prevent the

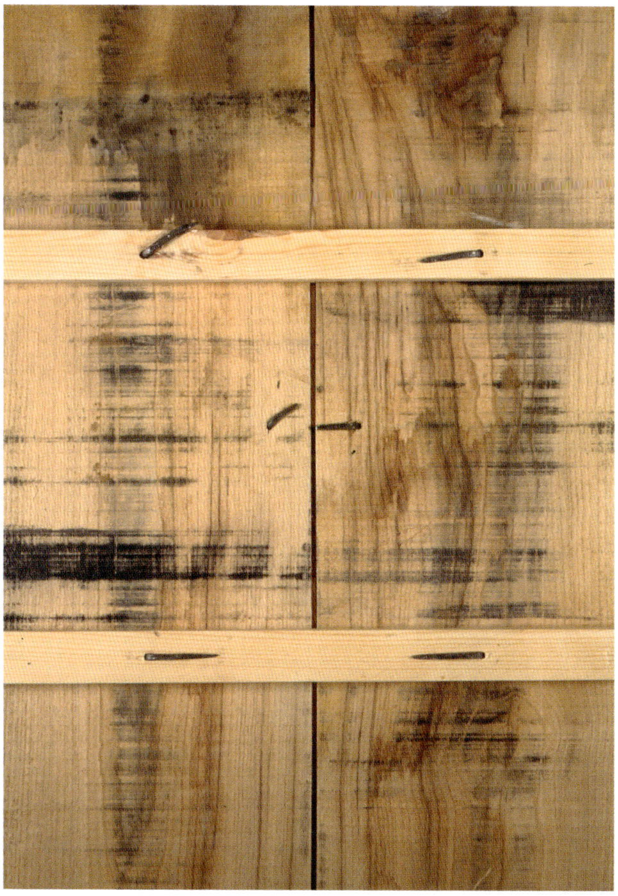

Figure 3 *The reverse of the reconstructed panel, including the use of hand-forged nails.*

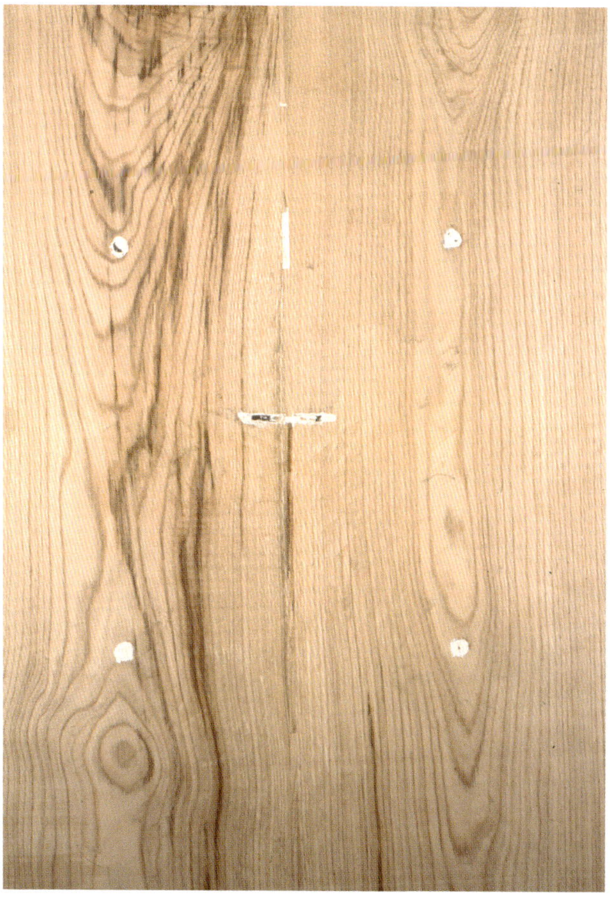

Figure 4 *The smoothed panel, from front, with filled staple and nail holes.*

wood from absorbing the glue from the filler. The filler was then applied thickly and left to dry before the face of the panel was planed smooth (Fig. 4).

An *engrudo* of 5% rabbit-skin glue in water was next brushed onto the panel hot.[6] A relatively weak solution was used in order to give good penetration of the wood, the purpose being to seal the wood to prevent absorption of the size used for the attachment of the canvas and the tempering of the *yeso* ground. When this was dry *giscola*[7] was applied. Pacheco implies that the *giscola* served to coat knots and nails and prevented penetration of resins from the panel into the preparation layers; for this reason, a strong glue might be used for pine panels but with chestnut, which is less resinous, a weaker glue is acceptable (Véliz 1986: 86–7).

For the reconstruction *giscola* was made according to Pacheco's recipe: a quart of water, the juice of three heads of garlic and a little *yeso vivo* added to a strong *engrudo* (Véliz 1986: 87). A quart of water is two pints, which would constitute a substantial dilution if only enough *engrudo* had been prepared to size one average panel, therefore 5% rabbit-skin glue in water seemed suitable. The quantity of garlic suggested by Pacheco was then crushed into the hot size and the mixture passed through a stocking to filter out the pulp. The garlic may have lowered the surface tension of the size layer and acted as a fungicide (Véliz 1986: 142). Pacheco does not specifiy the quantity of *yeso vivo* required so a small amount of sieved *yeso vivo* was used – enough to make the glue and garlic mixture cloudy but not noticeably thickened. The *giscola* was then brushed hot onto the panel (Fig. 5). When dry the surface of the panel was rubbed with a cuttlefish bone in an attempt to smooth it, since the sizing had caused some wood fibres to stand up; this is recommended by Pacheco for smoothing the ground layers (Véliz 1986: 88) but was too soft for use on wood, tending to turn to powder.

In an X-radiograph of the *Road to Calvary* long, twisted threads were observed around the joins and in areas of weakness in the wood on the face of the panel, beneath the canvas; these were presumably intended to reduce movement. Contracts from Seville specify that natural fibres should be spread over the face of the panel and along the joins on the back (Hernández Díaz 1933: 83, 96; 1937: 17); this has been observed on panels from other parts of Spain (Hassall and Cummings 1974–75)[8] and is described by Pacheco for Castile (Véliz 1986: 87). Loose canvas threads were used for the reconstruction, dipped in a *giscola* made with 10% rabbit-skin glue and laid across the board join (Fig. 6).

At this point in the original painting, canvas had been applied over the whole panel. In other regions of Spain it has been unusual to find both fibres or threads and a

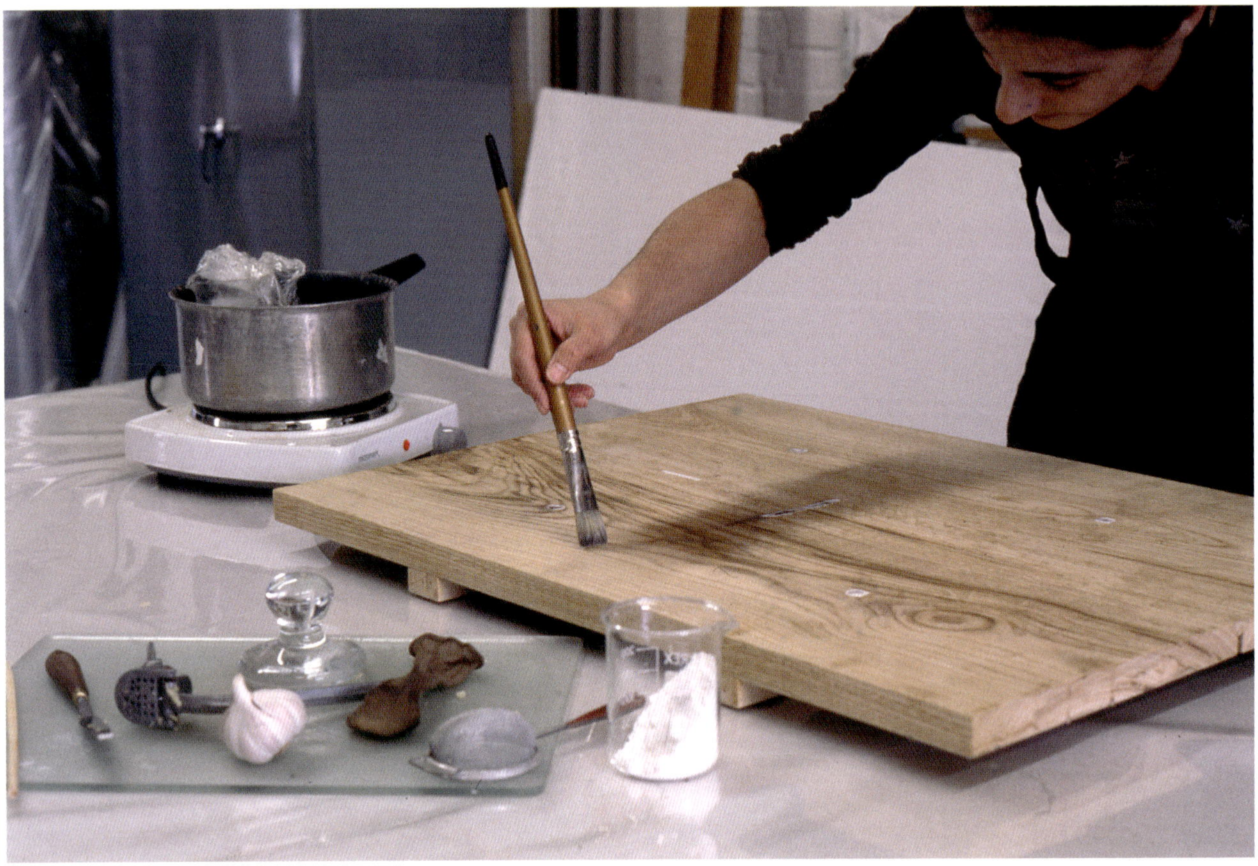

Figure 5 *The* giscola *brushed hot onto the panel.*

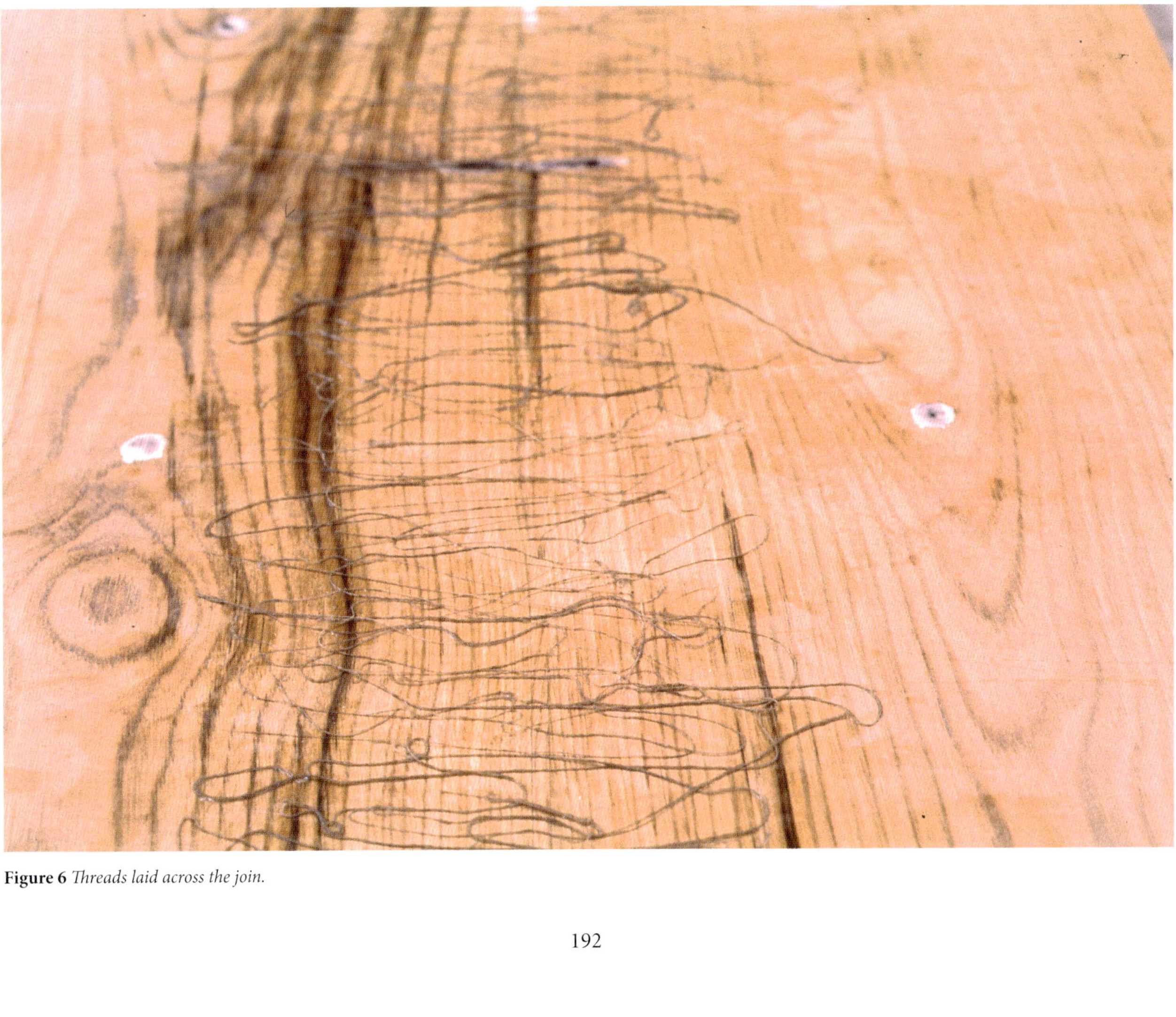

Figure 6 *Threads laid across the join.*

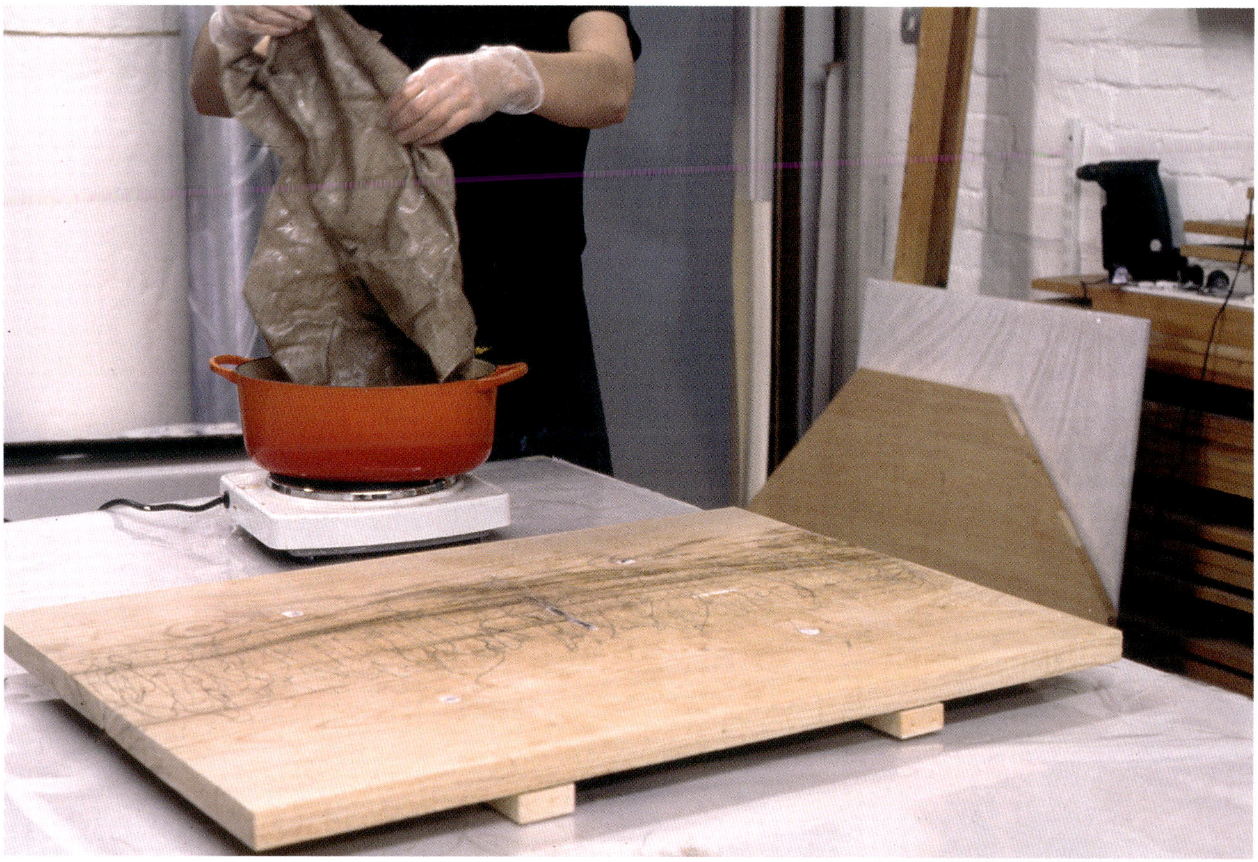

Figure 7 *Saturating the canvas in* giscola.

canvas (Hodge *et al.* 2000: 30; Doménech *et al.* 1998: 23). According to Pacheco, painters before his time 'covered the fibrous strings with linen' but this was unnecessary if cedar or chestnut was used (Véliz 1986: 87); this implies that the canvas prevented penetration of resin into the ground, although Pacheco also states that it stops the board joins from opening. Despite Pacheco's caveat for chestnut, the contracts from Seville, in agreement with the evidence from the *Road to Calvary*, consistently stipulate the use of both fibres and cloth.

When the threads were applied the *giscola* had gelled slightly on the panel, so a weaker consistency (7% glue in water) was used for the canvas to ensure that it would be stuck to the panel rather than resting on gel. The canvas was saturated in warm *giscola* (Fig. 7) and then laid onto the panel. Excess glue was squeezed out at the edges by repeated smoothing of the canvas out from the centre. It was then left to dry. Some small air pockets and lumps of hardened glue formed between the canvas and panel during drying. Together with the underlying threads and one protruding nail head these produced a very uneven surface (Fig. 8).

The next stage was the application of the ground. Samples from the *Road to Calvary* showed calcium sulphate in a coarse lower layer followed by a fine upper layer.[9] Calcium sulphate grounds were typical of Andalucia, while calcium carbonate was favoured in some other parts of Spain (Véliz 1998: 142). Contracts for paintings from Seville specify two

Figure 8 *After adhering the canvas, in raking light.*

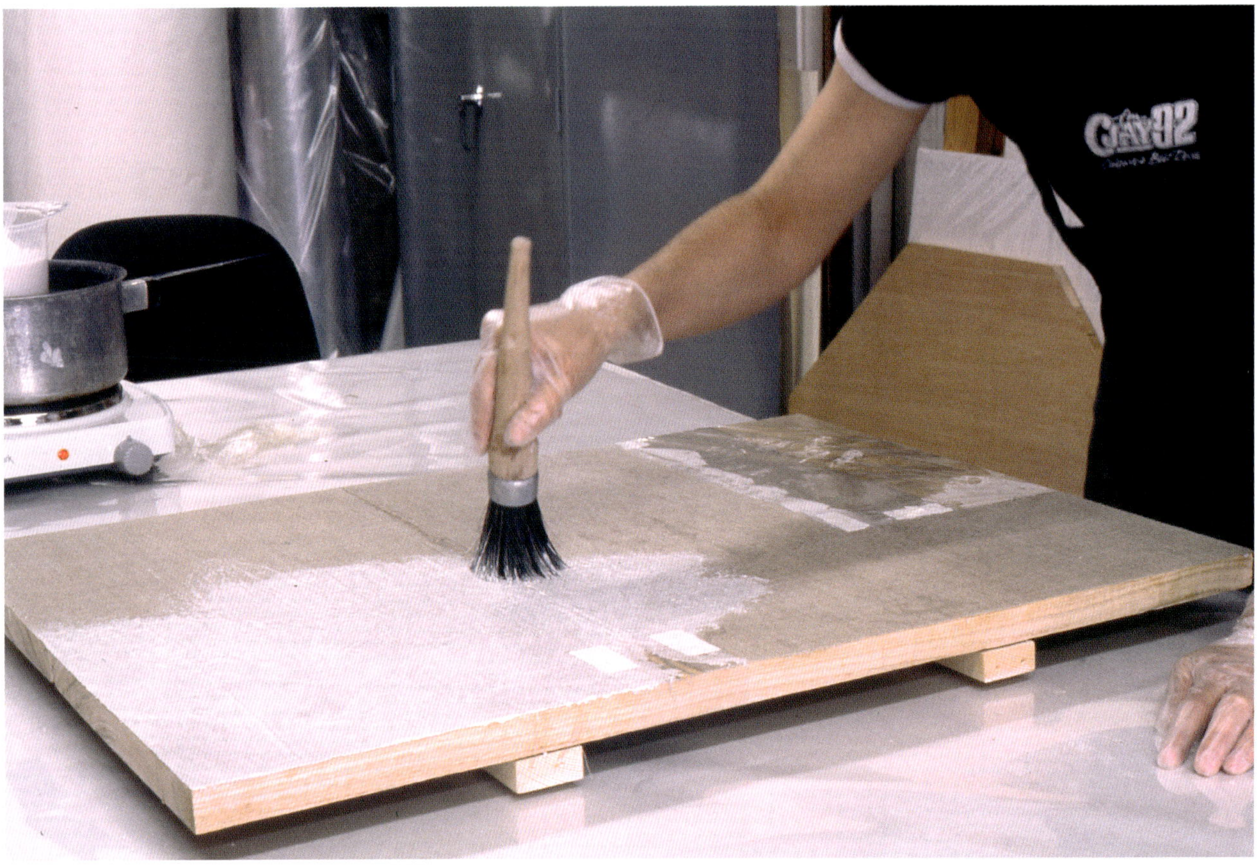

Figure 9 *Stippled application of the thicker layer of* yeso vivo.

Figure 10 *After levelling and sanding of the* yeso vivo *layer, the dark areas are due to the thinner layer remaining over the threads.*

ground layers: the first based on *yeso vivo* and the second on *yeso mate* (Hernández Díaz 1928: 114). Pacheco suggests three to five coats of the lower ground and five or six of the upper ground; in both cases the *yeso* should be tempered with sheep glue and applied hot, in thin coats (Véliz 1986: 66, 87–8). Contracts show that the ground would then be scraped and polished (Hernández Díaz 1928: 114; 1933: 83), a process carried out, according to Pacheco, with a knife or a new cuttlefish (Véliz 1986: 88).

For the lower ground on the reconstruction, the first coat of *yeso vivo* was thin and applied with a stippling action to fill the interstices of the canvas (Theophilus 1979: 27). A thicker *yeso vivo* was then applied, also with a stippling action to ensure good contact with the canvas, when the first coat was touch dry (Fig. 9). Five subsequent coats of *yeso vivo* were applied using a smooth, swift brushing motion with the brushstrokes running in alternate directions in each coat to minimise impressions (Cennini 1960: 72–3). Each coat was allowed to become touch dry before the next was applied to ensure good bonding between the coats but thorough drying.

Once dry, the *yeso vivo* was levelled with a cabinet scraper and sanded. The ground appeared dark where threads ran beneath the canvas since it was thinnest here (Fig. 10). Over the nail heads and staple it was brownish, probably due to impregnation by rust, indicating that the metal components should have had a non-aqueous coating.[10]

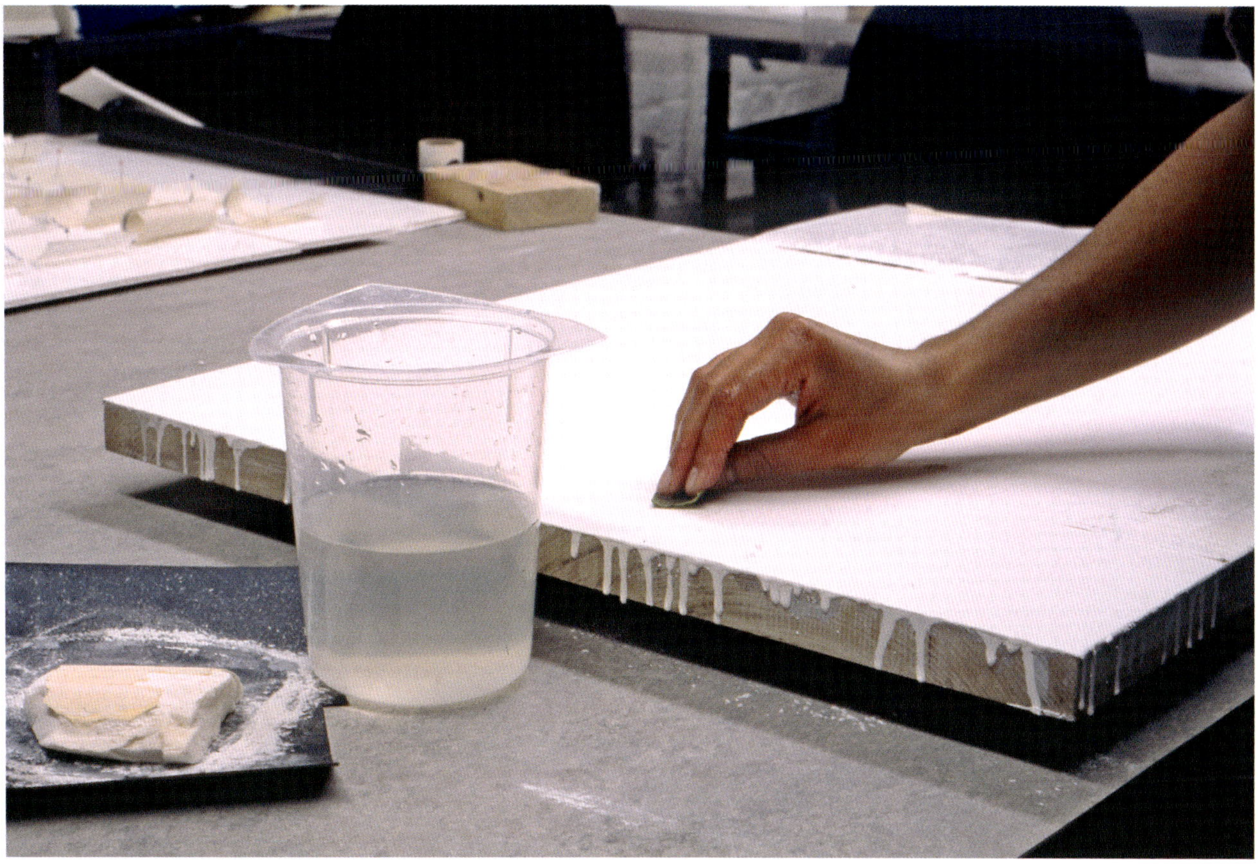

Figure 11 *Smoothing the* yeso mate *layer using wetted pieces of mare's tail.*

Yeso mate, which has a much smoother consistency than *yeso vivo*, was tempered to a creamy texture.[11] The glue for tempering the *yeso mate* should have a similar strength to, or be slightly leaner than that used for the *yeso vivo* so that the upper ground will not flake away from the lower ground due to tension produced during drying. Before the *yeso mate* was applied, the surface of the *yeso vivo* was re-wetted with a damp brush to ensure that it would not absorb the glue from the *yeso mate*. Five coats were applied, each becoming touch dry before the next was added and the direction of the brushstrokes alternating with each coat.

Once the *yeso mate* was dry the surface was smoothed. This was first attempted with a cuttlefish bone, as recommended by Pacheco (Véliz 1986: 88), but unsuccessfully as it crumbled. Possibly the cuttlefish bone was too old (Pacheco specifies that it should be new) or the *yeso mate* was too strongly bound. Instead, a dried piece of mare's tail was re-wetted and used to create a slurry at the surface of the *yeso mate* that could be manipulated as it dried to give a very smooth texture (Theophilus 1979: 27) (Fig. 11).

A sealing coat of 2% rabbit-skin glue in water was next brushed lightly onto the panel to saturate the ground and prevent it from absorbing the medium from the paint layers. A solution weaker than the glue for the *yeso mate* was chosen to prevent tension in the sealing layer from causing cupping in the ground. Once this was dry the panel was rubbed lightly with a dry piece of mare's tail to give an excellent, smooth surface ready to receive the underdrawing and paint layers (Fig. 12).

The array of similar materials and the unfamiliar terms for them in the Spanish literature made the build-up of the ground layers in Spanish paintings of this period appear bewilderingly and, perhaps, unnecessarily complex. However, making a reconstruction imposes a strict discipline, since it is impossible to carry out techniques in practice without first having established exactly what materials are to be used and how. Where studying the literature in theory would have left an impression of a confused and convoluted process, converting it into practice revealed that the materials and techniques used by Spanish painters were very similar to the more familiar materials and techniques used by Italian painters of the same period and, furthermore, that each layer in the build-up of the ground had a specific and logical role to play in the creation of a stable support for the paint

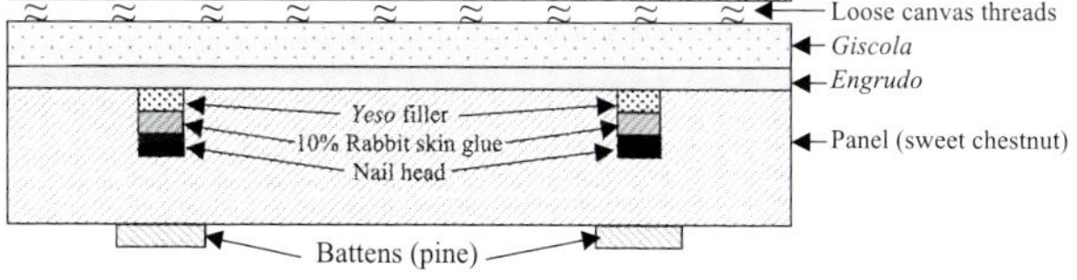

Figure 12 *Diagram illustrating the build-up of the ground layers.*

layers. The paintings made on such supports were most often intended for display against the walls of churches or chapels, where conditions might fluctuate widely with the seasons and with the entry and exit of congregations, therefore the more precautions that could be taken to alleviate the effects of fluctuations in humidity, such as warping, rusting, delamination, cupping and flaking, the longer the painting was likely to survive. It is a testament to the efficacy of these preparations that Spanish paintings of the period can still be appreciated today.

Notes

1. *Yeso*: any form of powdered calcium sulphate, tempered or untempered.
2. *Yeso* filler: artificial calcium sulphate hemihydrate, mixed with 10% rabbit-skin glue in water at body temperature to form a strong crystal lattice.
3. Calcium sulphate hemihydrate is produced by heating natural calcium sulphate dihydrate to drive off some of the water from its chemical structure; when the hemihydrate is rehydrated it forms calcium sulphate dihydrate in a rigid crystal lattice.
4. *Yeso vivo*: natural calcium sulphate dihydrate, unslaked, crystalline (widely varying forms); when tempered for the reconstruction: sifted and mixed with 7% rabbit-skin glue in water at body temperature.
5. *Yeso mate*: artificial calcium sulphate dihydrate, slaked, crystals absent; when tempered for the reconstruction: mixed with 7% rabbit-skin glue in water at body temperature.
6. *Engrudo* glue. All kinds of glue are listed as *engrudo* in the literature and found in this function on paintings (see Hernández Díaz, 1933: 83, 87, 96; Véliz 1986: xvii, 86–7; Hodge *et al.* 2000: 29).
7. *Giscola*: glue with garlic juice and a little *yeso vivo*.
8. Identification of fibres by Simon Bobak and Ray Marchant, September 2002.
9. The nature of southern European calcium sulphate grounds and the processes by which the various forms of calcium sulphate are made have been discussed in, amongst others, Wehlte 1975: 354; Federspiel 1995; Zillich 1998; Woudhuysen-Keller 2008: 166–70 and Broecke 2010: 153–4.
10. Contracts from Seville suggest *sisa olio* (Hernández Díaz 1933: 83, 96).
11. *Yeso vivo* occurs with a wide variety of crystal structures and can contain very large crystals. When *yeso mate* is made the *yeso vivo* is heated to drive off much of the water from the chemical structure and then rehydrated, or slaked, with constant stirring to prevent crystals from forming, so that the calcium sulphate dihydrate produced has a much smoother texture than the natural form.

References

Broecke, L. 2010. 'The reconstruction of an early Italian painted crucifix: method and observations', *Zeitschrift für Kunsttechnologie und Konservierung* 24(1): 149–69.

Cennini, Cennino, 1960. *The Craftsman's Handbook, 'Il libro dell'arte'*, D.V. Thompson (tr.). New York: Dover Publications.

Doménech, M., Mateo, R., Peris, V. *et al.* 1998. 'Analytical study of the evolution of panel painting technique in Valencian workshops from the fourteenth to the seventeenth century'. In *Painting Techniques: History, Materials and Studio Practice*, A. Roy and P. Smith (eds) 22–6. London: IIC.

Federspiel, B. 1995. 'Questions about medieval gesso grounds'. In *Historical Painting Techniques, Materials and Studio Practice*, A. Wallert, E. Hermens and M. Peek (eds) 58–64. Los Angeles: Getty Conservation Institute.

Hassall, C. and Cummings, A. 1974–75. '*SS. Cosmos and Damian*'. Unpublished condition and treatment report, London, Wellcome Trust.

Hernández Díaz, J. 1928. *Materiales para la historia de arte Español. Documentos para la Historia del Arte en Andalucía.* Universidad de Sevilla, Laboratorio de Arte (10 vols), vol. 2. Seville: Facultad de Filosofia y Letras.

Hernández Díaz, J. 1933. *Arte y artistas de renacimiento en Sevilla. Documentos para la Historia del Arte en Andalucía.* Universidad de Sevilla, Laboratorio de Arte (10 vols), vol. 6. Seville: Facultad de Filosofia y Letras.

Hernández Díaz, J. 1937. *Arte hispalense de los siglos XV y XVI. Documentos para la Historia del Arte en Andalucía.* Universidad de Sevilla (10 vols), vol. 9. Seville: Facultad de Filosofia y Letras.

Hodge, S., Spring, M. and Marchant, R. 2000. 'The Santa Marina Retable from Mayorga, attributed to the Master of Palanquinos, *c.* 1490s', *The Hamilton Kerr Institute Bulletin* 3: 7–34.

Theophilus 1979. *On Divers Arts: The Foremost Treatise on Painting, Glassmaking and Metalwork*, J.G. Hawthorne and C.S. Smith (tr.). New York: Dover Publications.

Véliz, Z. 1986. *Artists' Techniques in Golden Age Spain: Six Treatises in Translation*. Cambridge: Cambridge University Press.

Véliz, Z. 1998. 'Wooden panels and their preparation for painting from the Middle Ages to the seventeenth century in Spain'. In *The Structural Conservation of Panel Paintings*, K. Dardes and A. Rothe (eds) 136–48. Los Angeles: Getty Conservation Institute.

Wehlte, K. 1975. *The Materials and Techniques of Painting*. New York: Van Nostrand Reinhold.

Woudhuysen-Keller, R. 2008. 'Reconstruction of tempera painting techniques: some examples, including *gesso sottile*'. In *Art Technology: Sources and Methods*, S. Kroustallis, J.H. Townsend, E. Cenalmor Bruquetas, A. Stijnman and A. San Andres Moya (eds) 166–73. London: Archetype Publications.

Zillich, I. 1998. 'Der Gipsgrund und seine Verwendung im Bilde', *Zeitschrift für Kunsttechnologie und Konservierung* 1: 99–107.

PREPARING A COPPER PANEL FOR PAINTING: A LATE SIXTEENTH-CENTURY RECONSTRUCTION

Alison Stock

This paper concerns a reconstruction of *The Adoration of the Shepherds* attributed to Hendrick van Balen (1575–1632) from the Fitzwilliam Museum (Fig. 1).[1] I undertook the reconstruction simultaneously with the conservation of the painting, and therefore worked on this project in front of the original with reference to technical analysis (Figs 2 and 3).

Having never painted on metal before, this was an opportunity to experience the feel of painting on this slippery surface and explore the effects achieved. However, what proved most interesting were the questions that arose regarding the preparation of the copper for painting. This involved scoring the surface and applying garlic juices, which are methods described in the conservation

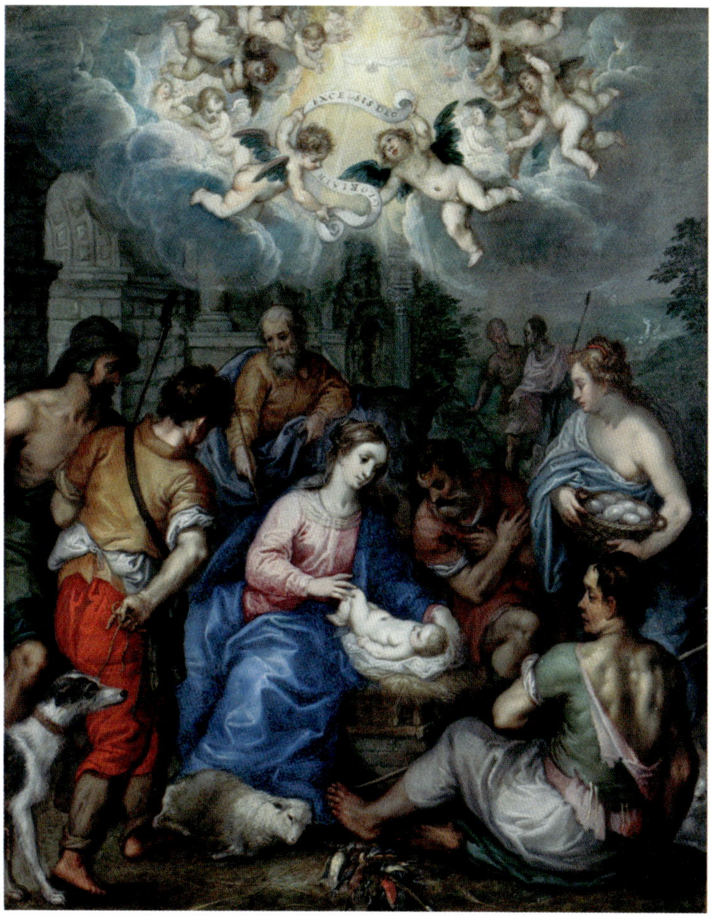

Figure 1 *Hendrick van Balen (attrib.),* The Adoration of the Shepherds, *The Fitzwilliam Museum, Cambridge. After conservation.*

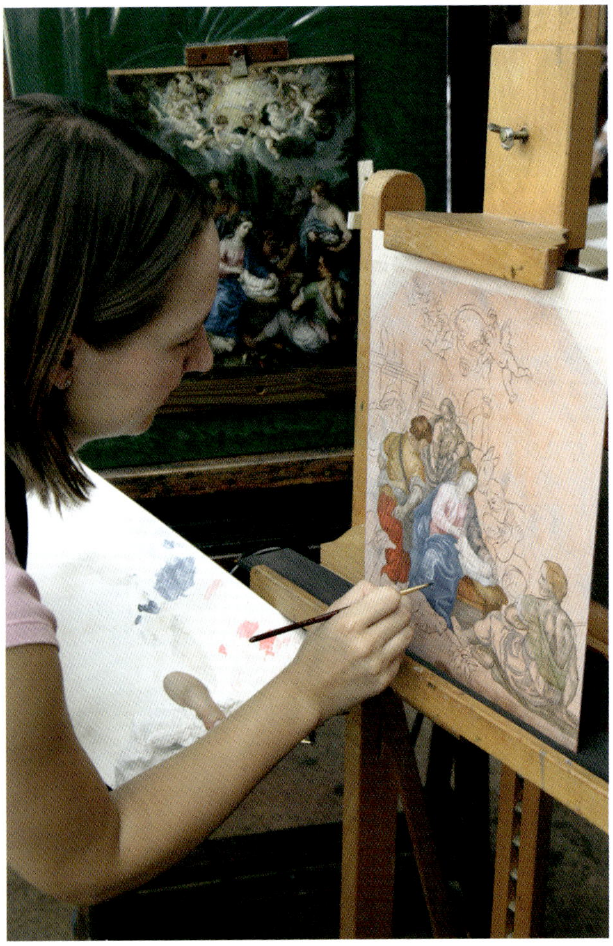

Figure 2 *The reconstruction in progress.*

literature and painting treatises. I speculated as to whether a layer of oil may also have been applied prior to the pigmented ground. Whilst trialling these methods, observations were made on the effect of each stage on the next, raising questions as to whether artists really did use garlic, and the possible links between printmaking and painting.

Scoring

Horovitz (1999: 68) acknowledges that probably the most important requirement of preparation was that the copper had to be roughened to provide a 'tooth' for the paint. There was evidence that this was done in *The Adoration*, as prominent vertical and diagonal scratches – interpreted as scoring marks – were visible through areas of exceptionally thin paint (Fig. 4). This preparation seems contradictory with Pacheco, writing in 1649, who advises using a clean and smooth plate (Véliz 1986: 69). Watin's manual from 1773 expresses concern about the paint adhering to the metal, which he overcomes not by scoring, but by adding a little turpentine in the first layers, which 'helps the oil to penetrate' (Watin 1773: 83). Perhaps it was not worthwhile for these authors to comment on roughening, either because this stage was an obvious procedure that did not need describing, or because it was a result of the manufacturing of the plate, rather than the painter's preparation.

In order to imitate the scoring observed on *The Adoration*, I undertook tests with sandpaper, a sharp pointed engraving tool, and a pumice stone, on a small sheet of copper. Surprisingly, the pumice stone made the most comparable marks to those found on the original, in the form of thick irregularly spaced scratches.[2] I had anticipated actually 'scoring' into the metal with a sharp tool.

A new sheet of copper was selected for the reconstruction, and after scratching with a pumice stone I was concerned that the marks would still be visible through the paint layers (Fig. 5). With some satisfaction it was discovered that subsequent preparatory methods (described below), filled the grooves and they were not visible upon completion of the painted sections.

Garlic juices

Palomino, writing from 1715–24, suggests 'plates should always be rubbed first with garlic because they tend to have some slight concavities in which the *imprimacíon* is slow to dry' (Véliz 1986: 152). De Piles (1776: 137–8) suggests that the only preparation needed for copper is to cut a clove of garlic in two and rub it onto the plate. Horovitz explains how garlic juice 'wets the surface and provides a sticky mildly grainy base over which a thin film of paint is easy to control' (Horovitz 1999: 70).

It was impossible to determine whether the artist of *The Adoration* had used garlic, but I decided to do so on the basis of its approval in the literature. After some trials I found that applying crushed garlic cloves through a bag made from silk achieved a thin and even application.[3] The panel was then positioned vertically lest dust should settle (Fig. 6). As I continued with the preparation I did not see the benefit of this layer and it ultimately had a detrimental effect on the ground (see below).

Layer of oil/resin

In most of the cross-sections taken from *The Adoration* a green layer between the support and ground was observed, commonly identified as a layer of copper oleate formed from a reaction between the copper surface and the oil medium in the paint (Fig. 7).[4] This next stage of preparation aimed to investigate whether this discoloured layer is a discrete layer of oil applied to the panel before the ground. Such a layer may have been applied for various reasons: a considered application by the artist for ease of handling subsequent paint layers; a 'cleaning' stage with linseed oil to remove remains of ashes from roughening (Horovitz 1986: 45); an imitation of the tradition of etching where a hard ground was sometimes used consisting of linseed oil and colophony;[5] or oil may have been used to remove ink from a plate.

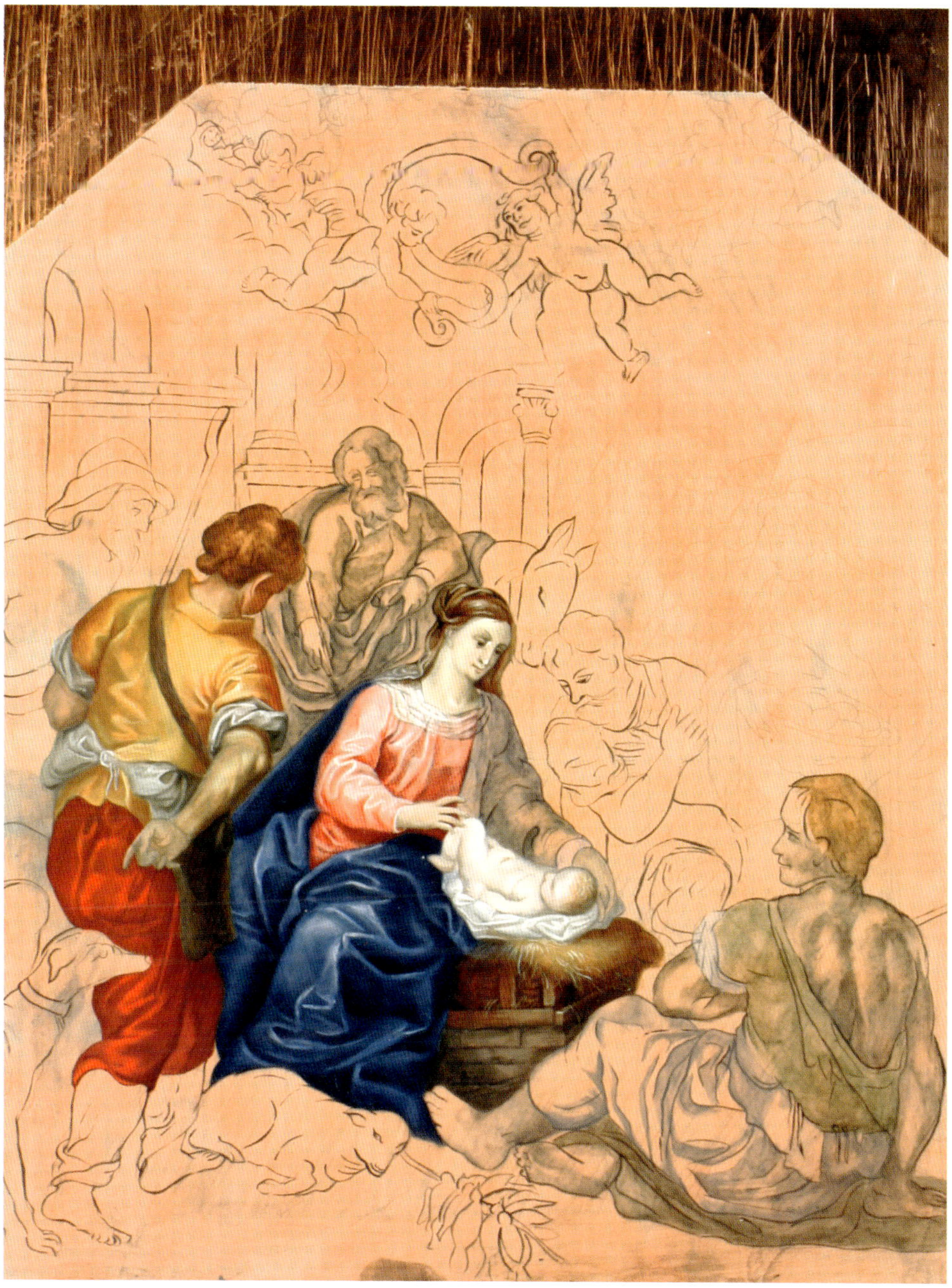

Figure 3 *The completed reconstruction of* The Adoration of the Shepherds.

There is likely to have been an overlap between painting, etching and engraving, so for this reconstruction an 'etching ground' of oil/resin was applied. This took the form of *vernice commune* (linseed oil and colophony) and was applied hot to the pre-warmed copper panel, the heat facilitating the flow of the oil/resin.[6] However, after one week of drying tiny pieces of crystallised colophony had formed and the layer was still very soft and sticky. I decided that the layer was too thick so the sticky excess was wiped away with a silk cloth, resulting in a thinner layer that was rubbed into the surface with fingertips. Despite thinning, I was pleased to see that this layer filled all the grooves created by the pumice stone.

Having carried out this process I questioned whether artists would have been inclined to undertake this step, considering the heating involved, long drying time, and risk of dust settling. This all seemed quite complicated and contrary to De Piles' description (above), which gives an impression of simplicity. Acknowledging my inexperience with this procedure led me to carry out further research and it was found that Symonds' Italian notebooks describe an easier method of applying an oil/resin etching ground, which would have resulted in a much thinner layer.[7]

Ground

The ground was barely visible in *The Adoration*, but cross-sections indicated a very thin grey layer varying between approximately 10 and 20 μm containing vine black and

Figure 4 *Detail from the sky showing scoring in the support.*

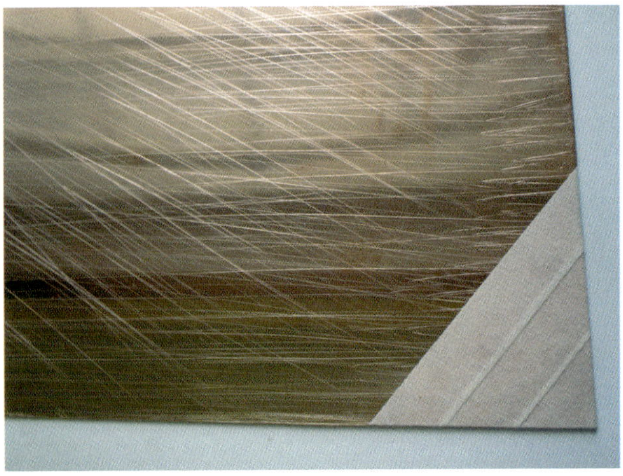

Figure 5 *Detail of the copper plate used for the reconstruction after scratching with a pumice stone.*

lead white. The thinness of the ground would have allowed the colour of the copper to show through, thus creating a 'ready-made' double ground. Brushwork relating to ground application was visible through the thinnest paint passages, and fingerprints were also detected.

The treatises describe the use of a brush and fingers to apply, spread, and even out the ground layer. Pacheco describes how the panel should be primed only with one very thin layer, spread with the fingers and not the brush (Véliz 1986: 69). Palomino also describes how smoothness and polish is achieved by thoroughly grinding the

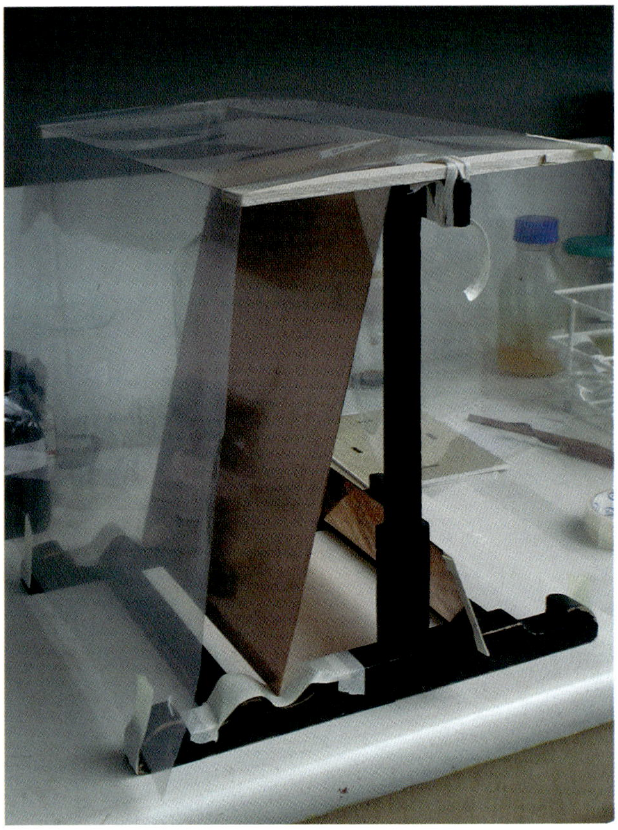

Figure 6 *The copper plate drying vertically under a cover.*

ground, spreading with the brush, evening with the thumb or the palm of the hand, and finishing with a soft brush (Véliz 1986:152).

The reconstruction was primed with a pigmented ground three weeks after the oil/resin layer had been applied, which felt dry to the touch. The ground was the consistency of toothpaste and prepared from pigments (1 part lead white to 2 parts chalk, and a small amount of vine black) and a fast-drying lead oil.[8] A small drop of spirit of turpentine was added according to Watin's instructions (see above). I applied the ground with a stiff hogs' hair brush, but this was difficult to brush out and achieve an even application. This was probably due to the thick consistency, coupled with the slow drying oil/resin layer below, which when worked upon became slightly tacky. To imitate the original, I also used my fingers to spread the paint and rub it into the oil/resin layer underneath. Interestingly my own fingerprints were not imprinted contrary to evidence found on the original, probably because of the slow drying oil/resin layer beneath. The effect of this thin grey layer on top of the red copper was a warm pink ground – the colour of the copper resonated through.

Reflections on the methods

Having completed the preparatory stages of the reconstruction and begun painting, I noticed that the ground had blackened in various places, probably caused by a

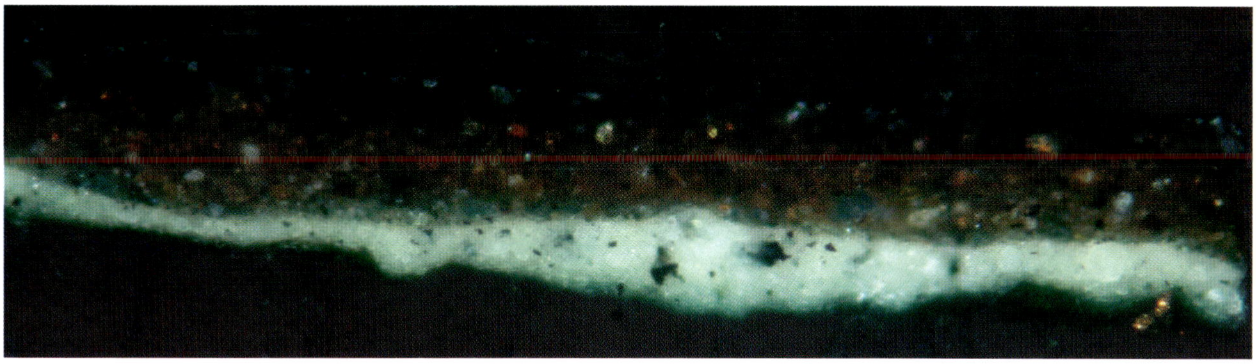

Figure 7 *Cross-section from the red trousers of the figure at the left.*

reaction between the sulphur in the garlic juice and the lead white pigment. This was investigated further on a test strip of copper.[9] It was found that a ground (composition as described above) applied to the copper prepared simply with garlic, blackened within hours, and within a week had also turned the ground noticeably greenish. Interestingly discoloration did not appear when the surface prepared with garlic was also prepared with an oil/resin layer prior to application of ground, providing an isolating layer.[10]

Considering this aesthetic change so soon after application does make one wonder whether artists really did use garlic. If so, could this be detected by looking for pigment deterioration in lead-based grounds? If artists were intent on using this material would they have also applied oil/resin to mitigate the deterioration effects? Did artists paint their image on top of the ground before the discoloration became visible, or did they get to know their materials so well that they knew how long to leave the garlic layer before painting in order that the sulphurous gases completely evaporated? In terms of the conservation of these paintings it would be interesting to ascertain how the build-up of layers of garlic, oil/resin and ground influences the durability of paint layers. This reconstruction, and others made on copper at the Hamilton Kerr Institute (HKI), could be monitored for changes over time (Izat 2001; Spring 1991).

Conclusion

There are obvious limitations to this investigation.[11] However, were I to prepare a copper sheet for painting again, I would do so without either garlic or oil/resin layers. It was noticeably easier to apply the ground directly to a smooth bare copper surface, which painted out with ease as the brush slid effortlessly over the metal surface, and fingers could be used to dab and even out the paint. When prepared in this way, the fingerprints remained in the ground layer, much like in *The Adoration*. The question arising from this is whether a painting prepared in this way may deteriorate quicker than one prepared with scoring, garlic and oil/resin.

Finally, I found this reconstruction to be an important learning curve in the sensibilities of a practical project – identifying problems, overcoming difficulties and reflecting on the processes and results. These skills are translated by a conservator into any conservation project, and this exploration of artists' methods and materials has continued to inform my work as a conservator.

Acknowledgements

I would like to thank the following for their involvement and support with this project: Ian McClure for his ideas and help with selecting a painting on a copper support from the Fitzwilliam Museum, and David Scrase for kindly agreeing to my choice; Spike Bucklow for his advice regarding taking cross-sections and analysing them; Renate Woudhuysen-Keller for practical advice during the reconstruction (especially with the *vernice commune*, madder lake and drying oils), and for help with the written report; Chris Titmus and Chris Hurst for help during photography; and Christine Kimbriel who completed the conservation of the painting.

Notes

1. The reconstruction was carried out to scale. The original painting measures 34.6 × 27.3 cm, and the average depth of the panel was measured at 0.94 mm.
2. The same method was tested and preferred in a previous reconstruction carried out on copper at the HKI; Spring 1991.
3. This was left to dry for two hours before applying the next stage of preparation.
4. Research is still in progress regarding the reactions between copper carboxylates and mixed linseed oil fatty acids; Pavlpoulou and Watkinson 2006.
5. Two types of ground – hard and soft – were used for etching. The soft grounds had wax added. After applying the ground it was passed over a burning candle until the soot from the candle turned the ground black. The etcher could then score into the surface exposing the bright red copper beneath. When the image was completed the plate was then exposed to acid in order to etch into the exposed copper. The ground was then removed, and ink applied to the surface, which would sit in the etched lines and be rubbed off from the parts of copper that were covered with ground. A print could then be made.
6. The *vernice commune* was made by melting 120 g colophony in 60 g linseed oil.
7. The oil/resin is first made into balls the size of walnuts by pouring it, whilst hot, into cold water; the balls are then wrapped in silk and applied to the plate; Beal 1984: 205–6.

8. The fast-drying oil was chosen for efficiency (traditionally it is more likely that linseed oil was used). The drying oil was 'lead oil' made by Renate Woudhuysen-Keller from a recipe given to de Mayerne by Van Dyck: 20 g lead oxide was stirred into 300 ml linseed oil and heated to 110°C. At this stage the mixture was opaque orange, and after a day it separated rendering a copper-coloured translucent oil. After 18 days it turned light yellow, having gone through a red phase, and at this stage it was ready to use.
9. It should be noted that this test strip of copper was soiled before use and was therefore 'cleaned' by rubbing with grade p1000 sandpaper. This was so fine that it did not leave too many scratches, rendered the copper bright orange and presumably removed a layer of red copper oxide. Horovitz (1999: 68) describes the importance of removing this layer of red copper oxide.
10. The blackening of the pigment or appearance of a greenish colour did not happen on this test strip while I was a student at the HKI, but may have done since. Spring's copy (carried out in 1991) had been prepared with garlic, followed by a layer of drying oil mixed with cold-pressed linseed oil, prior to the ground application. When examined in 2007 it was possible to detect blackened 'brushstrokes' through the isolating layers of oil, perhaps indicating where the garlic was applied. These blackened brushstrokes are also evident in the white ground, but do not show through the paint layers.
11. Some limitations include the inexperience of the novice copyist, deviations from historically accurate materials (such as the use of drying oil for efficiency), the use of a modern sheet of copper, and the fact that the experiments conducted were not carried out with scientific control.

References

Beal, M. 1984. *A Study of Richard Symonds: His Italian Notebooks and their Relevance to Seventeenth-century Painting Techniques*. PhD dissertation, Courtauld Institute of Art, University of London.

Horovitz, I. 1986. 'Paintings on copper supports: techniques, deterioration and conservation', *The Conservator* 10: 44–8.

Horovitz, I. 1999. 'The materials and techniques of European paintings on copper supports'. In *Copper as Canvas: Two Centuries of Masterpiece Paintings on Copper 1575–1775* (Phoenix Art Museum exh. cat.) 63–92. Oxford: Oxford University Press.

Izat, A. 2001. 'Reconstruction of *St Dominic Receiving the Rosary from the Virgin Mary* HKI 2048/2'. Unpublished third-year project. Hamilton Kerr Institute.

Pavlopoulou, L. and Watkinson, D. 2006. 'The degradation of oil painted copper surfaces', *Reviews in Conservation* 7: 55–65.

de Piles, R. 1776. *Elements de Peinture Pratique*. Paris.

Spring, M. 1991. 'A copy of the painting *Pan and Syrinx in a Classical Landscape* by Martin Ryckaert from the Fitzwilliam Museum, HKI 1584'. Unpublished third-year project. Hamilton Kerr Institute.

Véliz, Z. 1986. *Artists' Techniques in Golden Age Spain: Six Treatises in Translation*. Cambridge: Cambridge University Press.

Watin, J.F. 1773. *L'art du peintre, doreur, vernisseur*. Paris: Grangé, Durand et l'Auteur.

PERSPECTIVE: CONSTRUCTING A SEVENTEENTH-CENTURY DUTCH INTERIOR

Daniela Leonard

The painting selected for this third-year student reconstruction project comes from the collection of the Fitzwilliam Museum. By the Dutch artist Dirck van Delen, it depicts a church interior and is signed and dated 1628 (Fig. 1). During this period there was a great deal of interest among intellectuals in theories of linear perspective; however, the extent to which theory influenced the working practice of artists is far from clear. The intention in reconstructing this painting was to determine van Delen's procedure as one example of the construction of a seventeenth-century perspective painting.

Dirck van Delen (1605–1671) was born in the village of Heusden and later settled in Arnemuiden, near Middleburg, in the south of the Dutch Republic. According to an inventory made after his death, he owned a substantial collection of drawings and prints, which he appears to have made use of in his own works.[1] Throughout his painting career he specialised in 'perspectives', architectural compositions of invented churches and Italianate palaces. Such works of art were very highly valued in this period because of the technical skill involved in their construction, and fetched high prices (Liedtke 1982: 16).

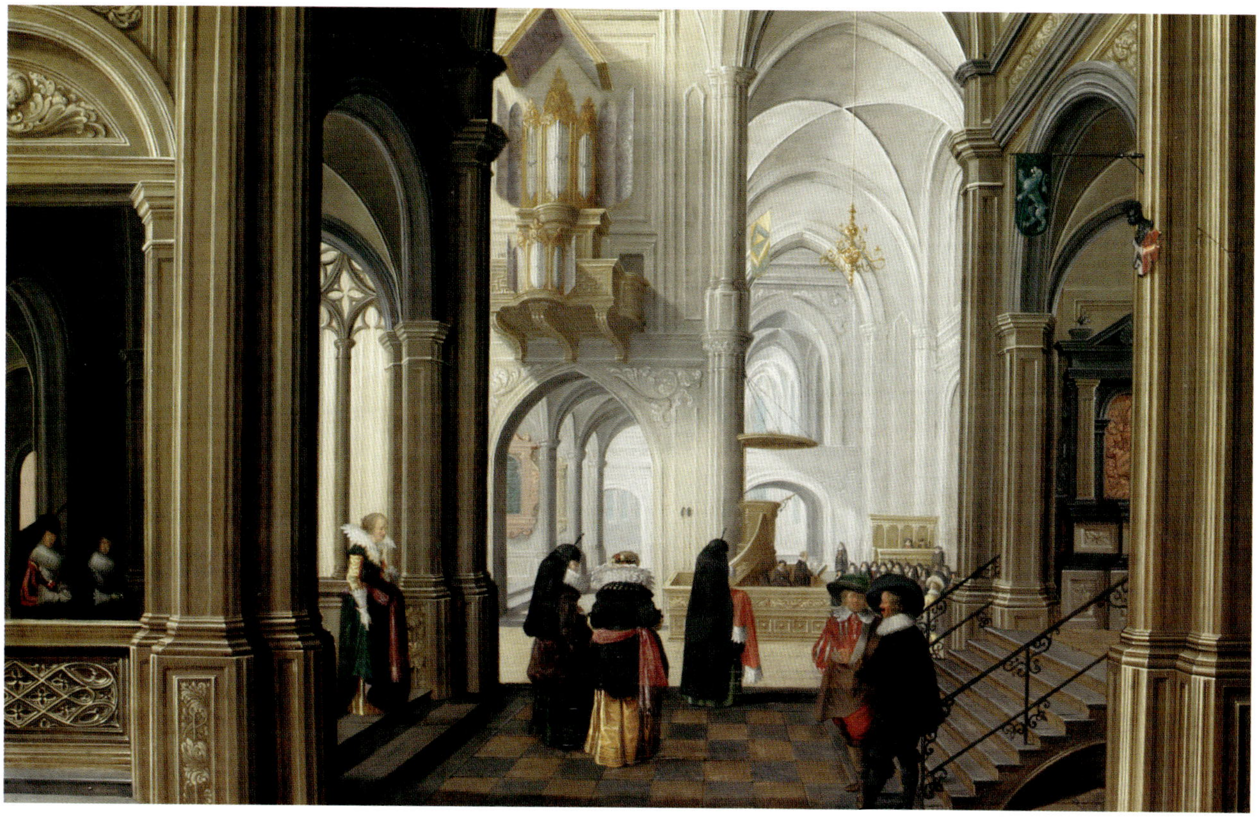

Figure 1 *Dirck van Delen,* Interior of a Church, *1628, 36.9 × 58.1 cm, oil on panel, The Fitzwilliam Museum, Cambridge (30).*

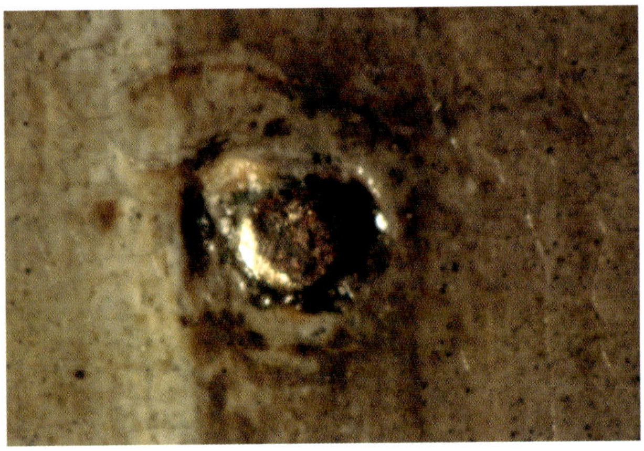

Figure 2 *Microphotograph showing the embedded pin.*

The roots of perspective paintings begin in the Italian Renaissance and the invention of linear perspective as an empirical means of constructing a convincing three-dimensional space on a flat plane (Kemp 1990: 9). Although Albrecht Dürer is cited as the first Northern artist to make consistent use of perspective techniques, it is the Dutch artist Jan (or Hans) Vredeman de Vries (1527–*c.*1604) in the middle of the sixteenth century who is considered to be the first to focus exclusively on the representation of architectural perspective scenes (Kemp 1990: 53). In 1604 de Vries published *Perspective* (de Vries 1964), a handbook that contains a series of engravings exhibiting the use of linear perspective. De Vries' book was widely read by artists in the first half of the seventeenth century and it is possible that van Delen owned a copy and made direct use of it in the design of his architectural paintings (Giltaij and Jansen 1991: 9). It has also been suggested that he was influenced by the circle of architectural painters in Antwerp, including the Steenwijcks and the Neeffs, followers of de Vries (Macandrew 1984: 7).

The Fitzwilliam Museum's church interior is one of the earliest works in van Delen's oeuvre. He presents us with a generic scene of daily life in a fanciful, but believable architectural space. A procession of women, part of a christening party, enters the church from a set of arches on the left. Two male figures converse on the right, next to steps leading to a chapel with an arched entrance that mirrors the left side. Behind the principal figures, the congregation is placed in the middle distance listening to a sermon. The composition of the scene creates the impression of a stage set with two wings and a backdrop. This is in contrast to the majority of church interior paintings from the period, which typically depict an open space receding to a distant vanishing point located at the centre of the nave. In this case, van Delen placed his vanishing point on a column to the right of centre, effectively blocking the viewer's sight down the length of the church. The viewpoint is from above, as if the viewer is on another set of stairs looking down on the scene presented by the artist. The figures are placed on a chequered floor separated from the rest of the church by a step. The sharp contrast between the light and dark areas of the floor acts as a visual barrier, making the background beyond the step appear disconnected from the foreground. All of these

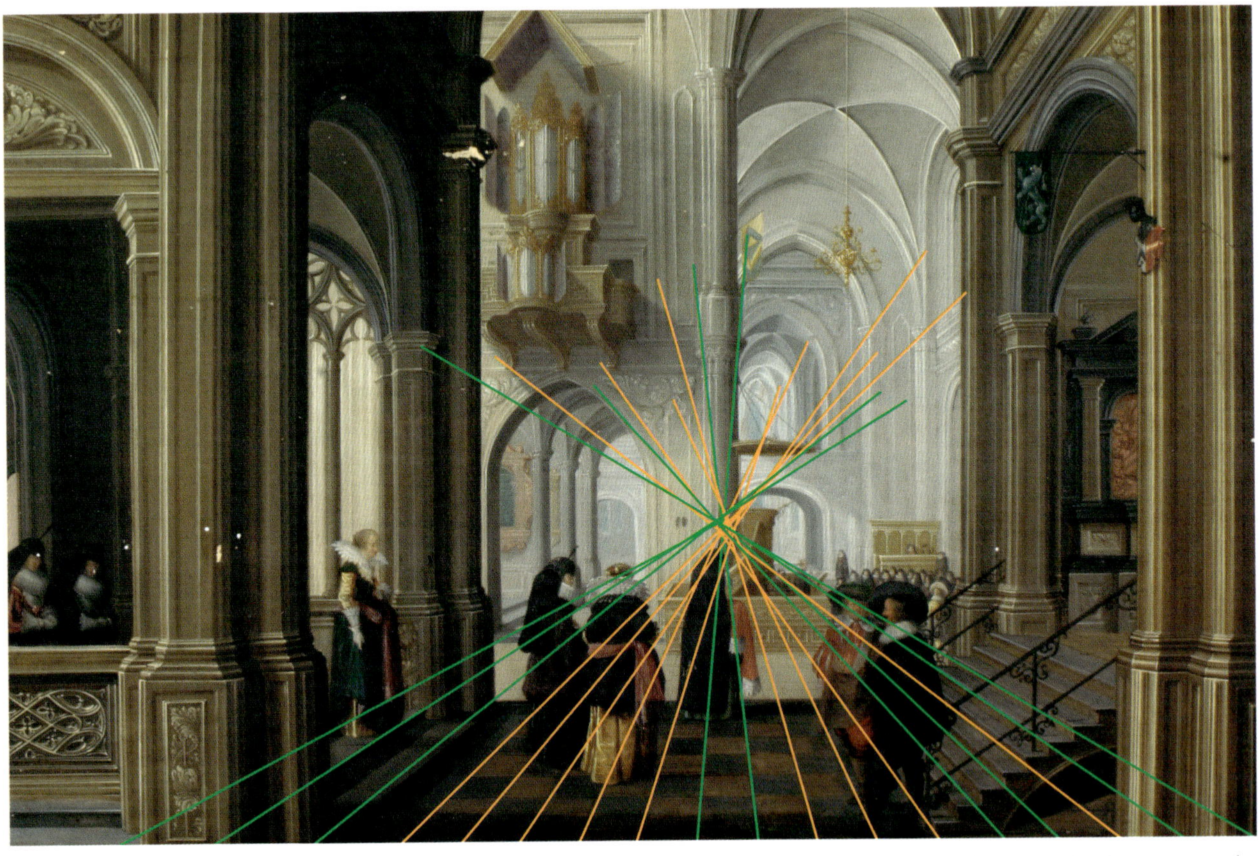

Figure 3 *Image highlighting the orthogonal lines in the floor. The green lines meet the vanishing point, the orange lines miss it. (Photograph taken during treatment.)*

compositional elements serve to separate the viewer from the interior of the church; we are invited to be spectators of the scene, but are denied access onto the stage.

This painting is the first of several identified from the period in which van Delen reused the same architectural elements in different combinations. In 1629 he executed a much smaller painting on copper with a similar composition, including nave, organ, side arches, columns and chequered floor in more or less the same positions as those of the Fitzwilliam painting, along with many of the same figures. In 1630 he painted a representation of the 1566 iconoclasm that includes part of the same nave and floor. A year later he painted a panel of larger dimensions in which the nave, organ and chequered floor, as well as the side aisle and many of the figures, are almost identical to the Fitzwilliam's painting. The stairs on the right side are also similar, but are seen from a different angle, leading out towards the viewer from a tomb. Finally, in 1632 he painted another small copper panel with the same scene, but in this case the position of the viewer has been moved to the left of the organ and rotated 90° so that the congregation faces the viewer and the christening party enters from the right.[2] Again, many of the elements are repeated, with the nave still receding into the picture plane and the side aisle reversed to the right side. This series of paintings confirms that van Delen was not trying to create a faithful image of a specific church. In fact, with the notable exception of Pieter Saenredam, it was common practice for perspective artists of this period to paint imaginary scenes, selecting elements from the drawings and prints of other artists and rearranging them to form new compositions (de Vries 1992: 52).

Conservation treatment and analysis of the Fitzwilliam's church interior revealed several clues that suggest van Delen combined the use of linear perspective with printed sources in the construction of his architectural space. During the removal of overpaint from the surface of the painting, a pin embedded in the wood was discovered at the vanishing point of the composition (Fig. 2).[3] Such a pin would have been used to construct a perspectival plan directly onto the surface of the panel. Either a string coated in chalk can be tied to the pin, pulled taut and then released to leave a mark on the surface, or the pin can be used as an anchor point for a ruler. The lines that are visible on the painting and in infrared appear very straight with crisp edges; therefore, if van Delen used a coated string it was probably only as a temporary guide followed by a more permanent underdrawing with a ruler. Many of the orthogonal lines running from the tiled floor do not quite hit the vanishing point, which suggests that a ruler was used, as a string tied to a pin could not fail to meet at the centre (Fig. 3).

Equally, many of the orthogonal lines in the architectural elements on either side and in the background do not converge exactly at the vanishing point. Considering van Delen's continued reuse of these elements in his paintings, it is likely that they derive from multiple sources and that he made use of linear perspective for the tiled floor and the stairs in the foreground as a means of tying the pieces together into a single composition. Nail holes discovered

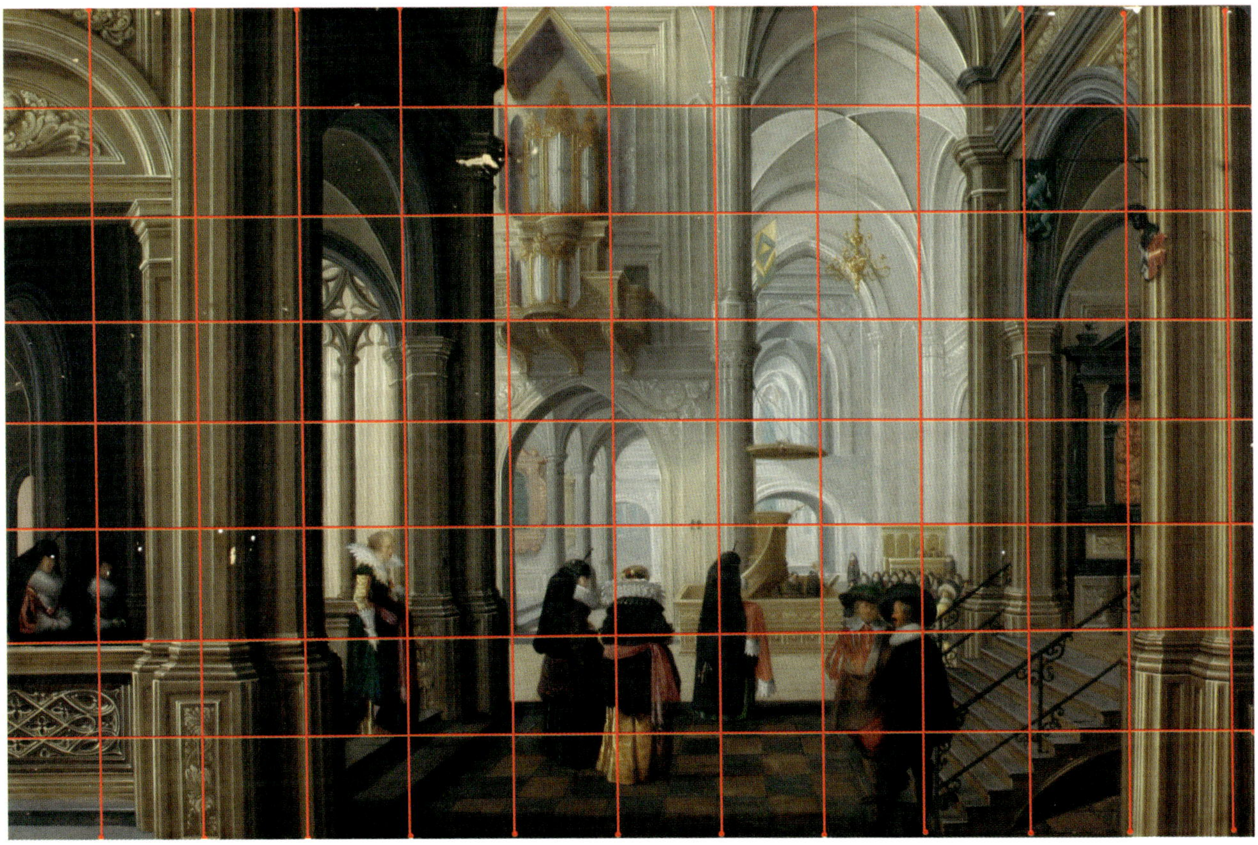

Figure 4 *Image showing the grid pattern made by matching up nail holes found on reverse. (Photograph taken during treatment.)*

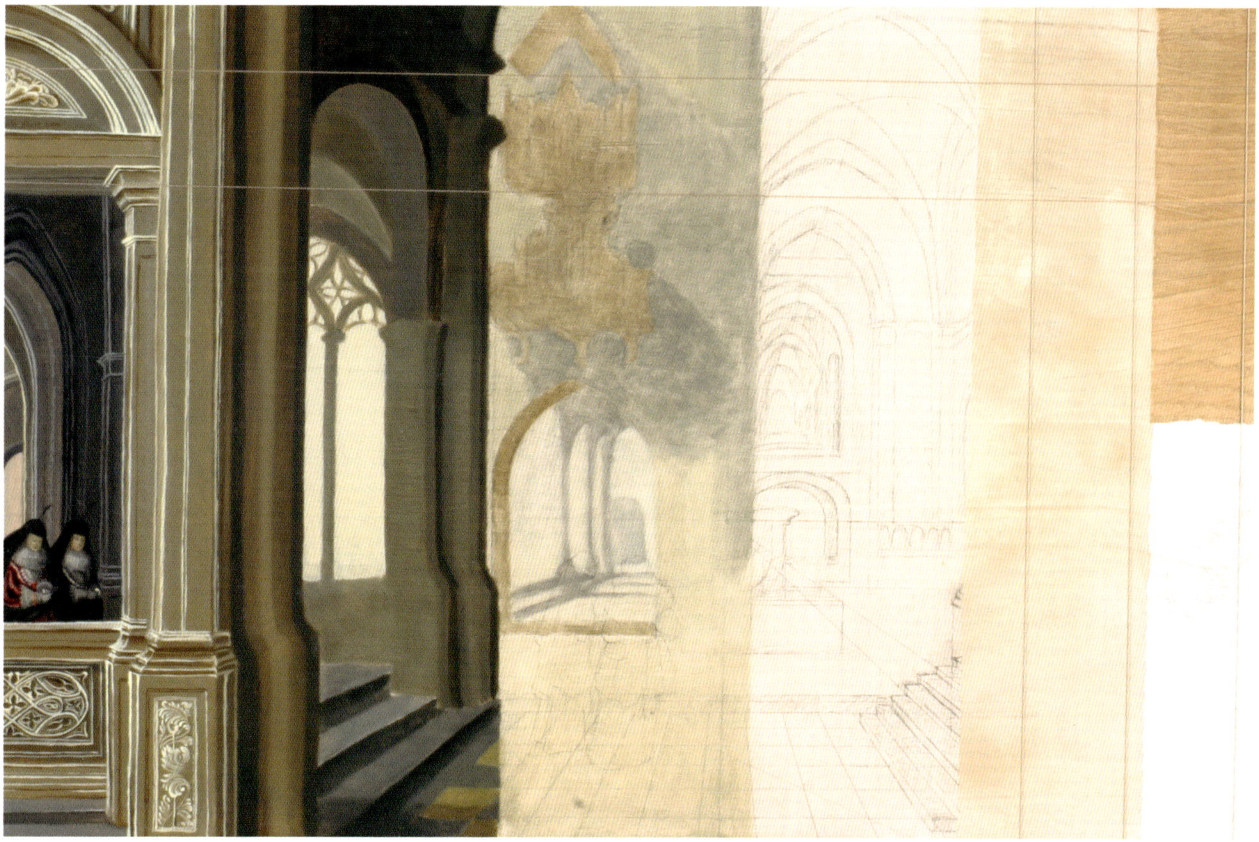

Figure 5 *The completed reconstruction of* Interior of a Church.

on the reverse of the panel provide a clue as to how van Delen transferred his composition from drawings. The holes are evenly spaced and appear to have been used to loop a string across the front of the painting in a grid pattern (Fig. 4). This could be done as a means of copying a design.[4] The presence of both pin and nail holes suggests that van Delen compiled his compositions directly onto the panel rather than making a single cartoon on paper for transfer. The fact that some elements do not precisely fit into the perspectival construct was not necessarily important, as long as the general impression of a continuous space was achieved. It has not been determined whether van Delen was particularly concerned with any of the theoretical discourses regarding the perfection of linear perspective; his paintings indicate that his priority was to produce believable compositions rapidly and with relative ease.

The reconstruction of van Delen's church interior (Fig. 5) helped to determine which procedures seemed the most likely, practical means of executing such a painting. Technical analysis provided useful clues, not only to the materials used, but also to van Delen's process. The support was identified visually as a single piece of hand-sawn oak of near-radial cut. Although no size layer could be seen in samples, several layers of rabbit-skin glue at 2.5% and then at 5% were applied to the reconstruction panel as a means of preventing the medium of subsequent layers being absorbed into the wood. The paint layer is in sound condition and the underlayers are not exposed. Cross-sections revealed that van Delen applied a chalk ground and two priming layers, the first also primarily of chalk and the second of lead white with a scattering of red pigments thought to be a mixture of red earth and vermilion or red lead.[5] In the reconstruction it was found that chalk mixed with a linseed oil medium creates a translucent tan paint that brings the white ground back to the colour of the wood support. The second pink ground layer lends a warm tone to the composition throughout, subtly altering the sense of atmosphere in the church.

Infrared photography revealed a carbon-based underdrawing consisting of several elements (Fig. 6): a basic central perspective plan with a vanishing point, horizon line and several orthogonals; the architecture of the church interior, including design elements and the organ; and the figures, which would have been added after the space was laid out. A cross-section taken from an orthogonal line shows that van Delen did not compose his underdrawing onto the chalk ground layer before painting. Instead, he applied at least the initial part of his drawing on top of the second priming layer. There is no evidence in the infrared photograph that van Delen deviated significantly from his drawing when applying his paint. It is difficult to determine how much architectural detail visible in the image was executed at the drawing stage. He must have transferred enough of his design to guide him in the application of the dead colouring, but whether it was necessary to make further additions would depend on how much of the underdrawing was visible

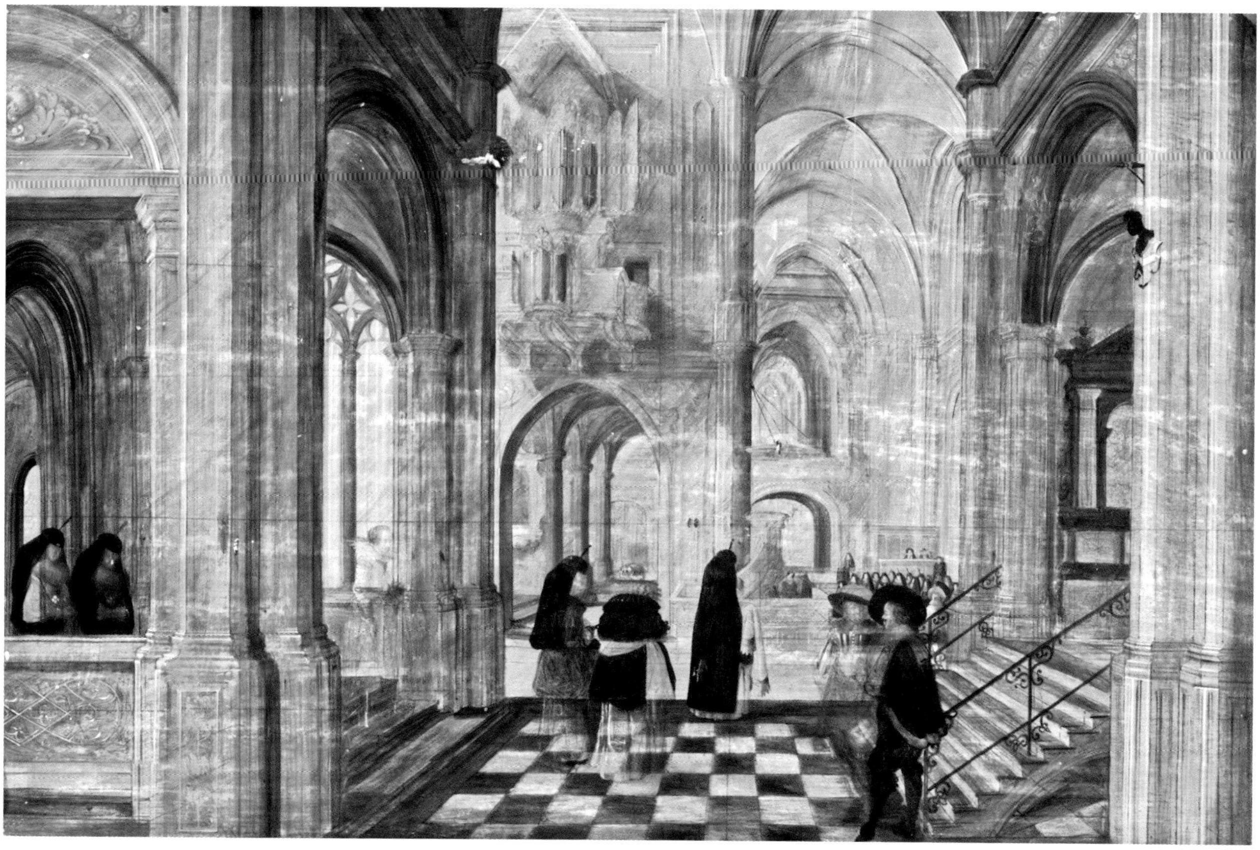

Figure 6 *Infrared image of* Interior of a Church.

through the main paint layers. It is quite possible that the advantage of using strings rather than drawing a grid is that strings can be reattached after the dead colouring has been applied so that details in the architecture can be added that will be visible through the main paint layer. In the reconstruction the drawing could not be seen after the dead colouring and main paint layers were applied. It is almost certain that at least the figures were sketched in at a later stage, as it is possible to see parts of the design through the final paint layers of the original.

For the reconstruction, tests were made with a variety of drawing materials to select the one that best matched what was found on the original painting. It was determined that van Delen used a dry material, as the lines can be seen to skip across the fine *impasto* of the first priming layer. He must have been able to apply the underdrawing on top of an oil layer and then cover it with a second layer without smudging.[6] A number of materials fulfilled this requirement, in particular graphite, and to a certain extent charcoal.[7] In fact, almost all of the materials performed better when sandwiched between two oil layers than when applied to the chalk ground. It was thought that van Delen would have used a natural black chalk, as this was a very common drawing material, but the natural chalk tested did not leave clear marks on top of an oil layer.[8] It was decided that graphite was the closest match.

The precise order in which the various elements of the underdrawing were executed remains uncertain. It was initially assumed that van Delen began with the perspectival plan, as it would be logical to lay out the horizon line and central vanishing point of the composition at the start. However, the fact that the horizon was found to correspond with one of the grid lines indicates that the grid was laid out first. The perspectival plan was undertaken on the copy following both the infrared photograph of the painting, and the instructions of Rob Ruurs in his book, *Saenredam: The Art of Perspective* (1987: 15–16). Measurements were taken from the painting in order to place the vanishing point and the distance point on the reconstruction panel. Then a horizontal and a vertical line were drawn through the vanishing point, as seen in the infrared photograph. After the horizon line was drawn, marks were made at the bottom edge, corresponding to the placement of the tiles. A second horizontal line was drawn to mark out the top edge of the tiled floor. The orthogonals were created by lining up a ruler between the vanishing point and the marks on the bottom edge. Only three lines visible in the infrared photograph extended all the way to the vanishing point; most of the orthogonals appear to have been drawn only in the tiled section of the foreground, below the second horizontal line. Using a ruler to draw lines in this lower section of the painting, it was found to be quite easy accidentally to move slightly away from the pin, which may explain why many of van Delen's lines were found to be inaccurate. Finally, a diagonal line was drawn to the distance point, and horizontal lines drawn wherever it crossed the orthogonals, resulting in a receding chequered floor pattern.

As no evidence of van Delen's method of transfer could be found other than the holes on the reverse of the panel, the reconstruction was used to test the viability of a string grid for copying. The painting was held against the reverse of the reconstruction panel in order to mark out the location of each hole. Small nails were then hammered into place, and a string tied to one corner and looped around each nail, passing across the front of the panel to form a grid pattern. The same grid was marked out onto the infrared photograph, which then served as the initial cartoon to be copied. The underdrawing was undertaken freehand with a graphite pencil, following the squared design seen in the infrared photograph. The strings were found to be a minor nuisance, but did not greatly hamper the drawing process, even when a ruler was used to draw straight lines across the panel.

Once the design was completed, van Delen set out the general tones of his composition with a dead colouring.[9] He then applied his paint layers thinly and lightly smoothed the surface to eliminate brushstrokes. In cross-sections the dead colouring was found to be similar to the main paint layers in thickness and in composition, containing many of the same pigments, but in different proportions. By altering the ratios of his pigments van Delen varied his tones, and then by blending his paint layers he created subtle transitions between light and shade, giving a three-dimensional effect to his architecture that when juxtaposed with the dark, crisp lines in the foreground increases the sense of space within the composition. All of the paint layers were applied thinly, to allow the priming and the dead colouring some influence in the final effect, resulting in a sense of luminosity that permeates the entire image.

The infrared photograph reveals scratches to the dead colouring, running almost horizontally across the composition. These marks are visible on the painting, but are clearly not affecting the upper paint layers. Considering the smooth surface of the painting, it seems possible that van Delen chose to polish his dead colouring in preparation for subsequent paint layers. This polishing could have been executed with a pumice stone, which would be abrasive enough to cause such damage to the underpainting.[10] The layers of dead colouring contain carbon black, making them visible in infrared. The areas that have been rubbed away reveal the priming below, and appear white in the infrared photograph.

The details that describe the architectural design were added in the final stages of painting. Van Delen executed a series of virtuoso vertical lines, applied with absolute precision along each facet of the columns in the composition. It is not known exactly what method he employed to accomplish this feat of dexterity, but he is likely to have had a setup in his studio such as a draughtsman's table built at an angle with a straight edge that could be easily secured in place when required (Wadum 1995: 152). The highlights appear to have been applied with a brush, but the thinnest dark lines have harder edges and may have been made with a quill. Resting the side of the brush handle against the edge of a mounted ruler greatly facilitated the straightness of the line and the pressure of the brush then controlled its thickness. Maintaining an even line width was found to be the most difficult aspect of reconstructing the final touches.

Scanning electron microscopy with energy dispersive X-ray (SEM-EDX) analysis of a highlight on one of the columns confirmed the presence of lead-tin yellow and an earth pigment. Visual analysis of the shadows suggested the use of raw umber. Tests with these pigments in lead oil demonstrated the difficulty of applying long, thin, unbroken lines of paint. With the help of Renate Woudhuysen-Keller, several different media were tested in an attempt to improve the extendibility of the paint.[11] It was found that a generous drop of colophony mixed into the lead oil created a stringy texture that allowed the paint to flow much more smoothly from the brush.[12] The lines formed with this mixture were full and rounded when applied, but did spread slightly in test samples before drying (most likely, the ratio of colophony to lead oil was not quite correct). On the reconstruction, a dry sable brush was passed lightly over the lines to smooth them out and prevent them from spreading, as well as to ensure a proper adhesion between the layers. Inspection of the original painting suggests that van Delen may have done the same.

The figures were painted at the very last stage, and in areas can be seen overlapping the highlights in the architecture. Yet, as previously mentioned, van Delen included sketches of the figures in his underdrawing. Close inspection reveals that he avoided painting highlights where he planned to place his figures. The well-dressed men and women in the foreground have been clearly and carefully defined, whereas the congregation in the background is loosely described with abbreviated strokes that provide only a suggestion of bodies and faces in the crowd.

The process of reconstructing Dirck van Delen's church interior has revealed a significant amount of information about the artist's methods, highlighting the complexity of his procedure and the role that each step plays in the quality of the final image. It is clear that such paintings could not be executed rapidly, but required preparation to ensure a smooth surface, careful planning to achieve the desired visual effects, and a great deal of manual dexterity to apply the details that bring the final composition together. If the painting appears more than a little formulaic, as evidenced by the repeated use of the same elements in subsequent works, this only hints at the practicalities of painting such labour-intensive works of art. Although contemporary painters were to expand on the uses of linear perspective in more accurate representations of real spaces, the evidence of transfer and of the simplest of perspectival plans in this painting demonstrate that this was not van Delen's aim. Perhaps he was more concerned with constructing his own unique reality, and although he has almost certainly borrowed aspects of his composition from other sources, as was standard practice, he did not copy by rote. Even at this early stage in his career, van Delen exhibited ingenuity and great skill in the construction of a detailed and convincing interior space.

Notes

1. Information on the contents of van Delen's inventory accessed online: www.ottonaumannltd.com/delen.html (accessed July 2009). For the original source see Blade 1976.
2. Sotheby's Sale L08036, Lot 19. Dirck van Delen, *The Interior of a Gothic Cathedral, with Numerous Elegant Figures, and Women Listening to a Bible Reading*, signed and dated 1632, oil on copper, 20 × 24.7cm.
3. Once the reconstruction was begun, a distance point (used to alter the angle of recession in the grid) was determined to be in a loss on a column on the left side. No evidence of diagonals leading to this point could be found in infrared.
4. No evidence of a drawn grid was found in infrared, though it is possible that van Delen used an easily erasable material such as charcoal. It has also been suggested that the holes may have been made at a later date by an engraver wishing to copy the painting; however, one set of holes was found to correspond exactly with the horizon line, visible only in infrared, which indicates that the grid was indeed used during the construction of the composition. Rupert Featherstone, pers. comm., July 2009.
5. The medium used by van Delen was not analysed. Cross-sections showed that the chalk ground was water-sensitive and so whiting mixed with a 10% solution of rabbit-skin glue was used in the reconstruction. Linseed oil was chosen for all subsequent paint layers based on its common use in Dutch paintings from the period.
6. Fels (2001: 79) suggests that coal and natural drawing chalks were used because they would not smudge.
7. The following materials were tested: modern pencil, graphite pencil, charcoal, oil crayon, modern black chalk and silverpoint, as well as the liquid media of iron gall ink and carbon ink (in a medium of gum arabic).
8. Natural black chalk can vary greatly in composition, therefore it is quite possible that another type of chalk would have performed better on an oil layer; see Bomford 2002: 34.
9. In his manuscripts, Théodore Turquet de Mayerne (a contemporary physician with an interest in artists' techniques) refers to the first paint layer as 'the dead colours'; Fels 2001: 148.
10. Renate Woudhuysen-Keller, pers. comm., July 2009.
11. The following materials were added to the lead oil medium for testing: boiled oil, stand oil, egg yolk and colophony.
12. The paint brush chosen had long, thin bristles intended for fine details; however, it was found to be too thick for painting the fine lines required for the reconstruction so was altered by cutting away most of the bristles, leaving only a few to apply the paint.

References

Blade, T.T. 1976. *The Paintings of Dirck van Delen*. Dissertation, University of Minnesota.

Bomford, D. (ed.) 2002. *Art in the Making: Underdrawing in Renaissance Paintings*. London: National Gallery.

de Vries, J.V. 1964. *Perspective* (1604). New York: Dover Publications.

de Vries, L. 1992. 'Saenredam and seventeenth-century architectural painting: Rotterdam', *The Burlington Magazine* 134(1066): 51–4.

Fels, D. Jr. 2001. *Lost Secrets of Flemish Painting: Including the First Complete English Translation of the De Mayerne Manuscript. British Museum. B. M. MS. Sloane 2052*. Hillsville, VA: Alchemist.

Giltaij, J. and Jansen, G. 1991. *Perspectives: Saenredam and the Architectural Painters of the 17th century*. Rotterdam: Boymans-van Beuningen Museum.

Kemp, M. 1990. *The Science of Art: Optical Themes in Western Art from Brunelleschi to Seurat*. London: Yale University Press.

Liedtke, W.A. 1982. *Architectural Painting in Delft: Gerard Houckgeest, Hendrick van Vliet, Emanuel de Witte*. Doornspijk: Davaco.

Macandrew, H. 1984. *Dutch Church Painters: Saenredam's Great Church in Haarlem in Context*, exh. cat. Edinburgh: Pillans and Wilson.

Ruurs, R. 1987. *Saenredam: The Art of Perspective*. Amsterdam: Benjamins/ Forstens Publishers.

Wadum, J. 1995. 'Johannes Vermeer (1632–1675) and his use of perspective'. In *Historical Painting Techniques, Materials and Studio Practice*, A. Wallert, E. Hermens and M. Peek (eds) 58–64. Los Angeles: Getty Conservation Institute (1995).

THE RECONSTRUCTION OF *THE YARMOUTH COLLECTION*

Jessica David

Introduction

The Yarmouth Collection (*c.*1665) portrays a resplendent assortment of curiosities, luxury and novelty items, the skilful handling of which has been markedly altered by time and treatment (Fig. 1). A partial reconstruction of the 165 × 246.5 cm painting was made in 2007 in an effort to understand compositional and illusionistic devices that have been distorted by age and degradation – specifically, the extensive fading of red and yellow lake pigments. Close observation of the paint layer alongside analytical techniques – X-radiography and infrared photography, microscopy and elemental analysis of paint cross-sections – were used to study the unknown artist's painting practice and tools.[1]

When the reconstruction was made, before the painting's conservation, dramatically faded passages were

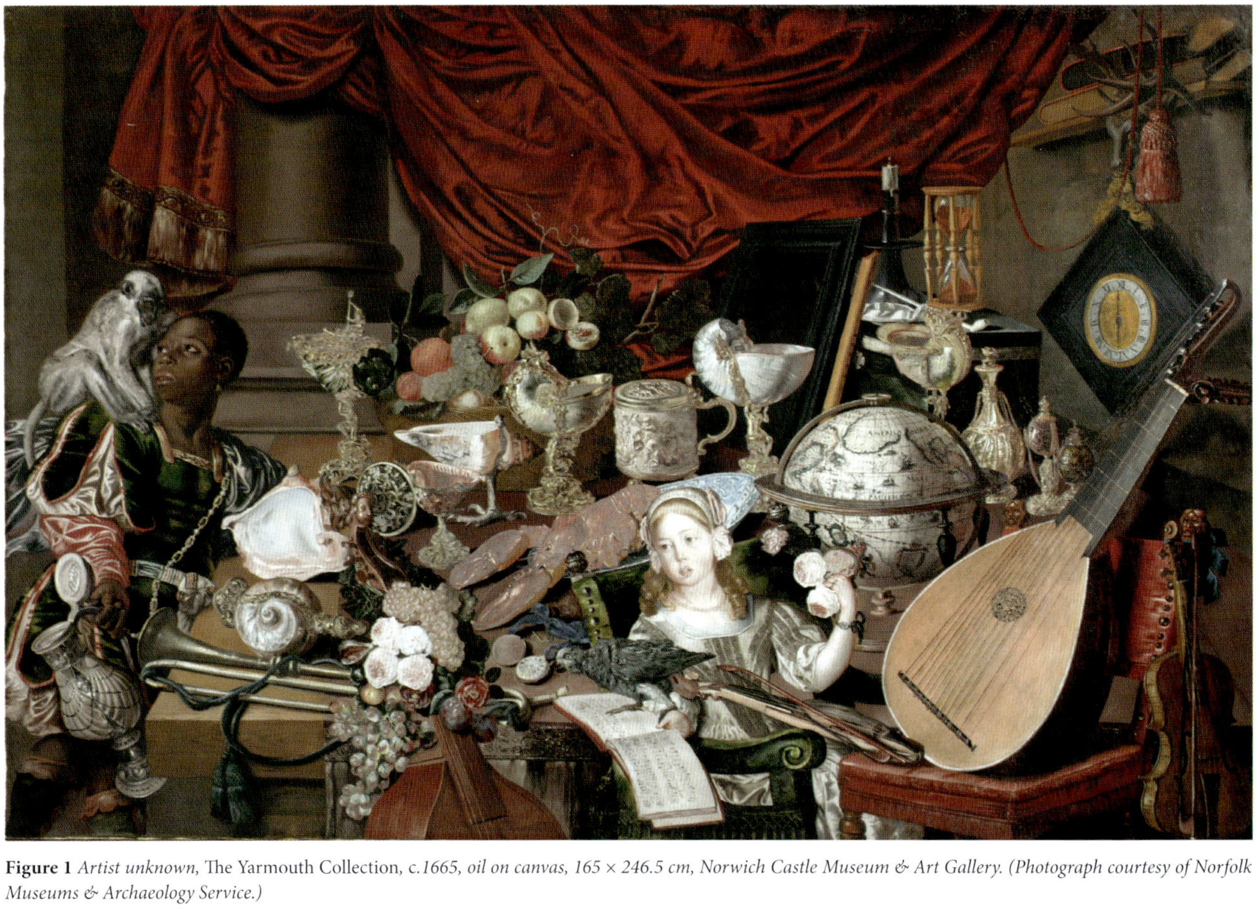

Figure 1 *Artist unknown,* The Yarmouth Collection, c.*1665, oil on canvas, 165 × 246.5 cm, Norwich Castle Museum & Art Gallery. (Photograph courtesy of Norfolk Museums & Archaeology Service.)*

further distorted by a thick, discoloured varnish. Certain objects in the still-life – such as the Wan-li bowl and African parrot – rely upon the faithful representation of hue to convey their significance. The area of reconstruction was strategically chosen to encompass areas of notable colour shift including the parrot, bowl and lobster at the centre of the composition, in order to elucidate the painting's meaning and the reason for its appearance today. By retracing the artist's creative process, from the preparation of the canvas to the application of final *impasto* highlights, the function of the painting became clearer, along with a sense of its original presence.

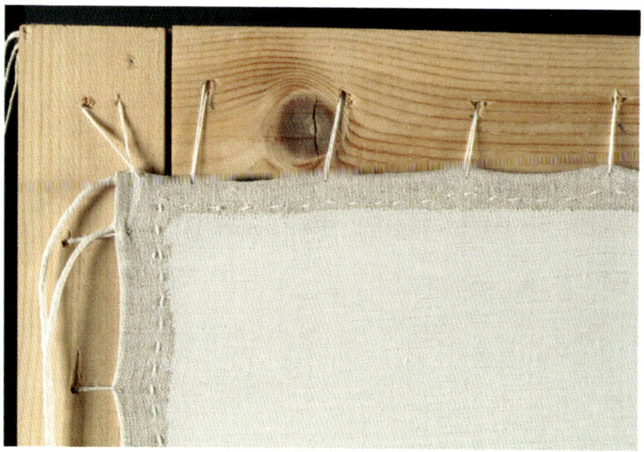

Figure 2 *Upper left corner of the reconstruction canvas laced taut on the loom.*

A personal painting

Also known as the Paston Treasure, *The Yarmouth Collection* was commissioned by Robert Paston between 1660 and 1670 from an unknown (but likely) Dutch painter. The objects portrayed in the painting represent a small selection of treasures and curiosities owned by the Paston family of Oxnead Hall, Norfolk. The bulk of the collection was likely assembled by William Paston (Robert's father) during his travels to Italy, Cairo and Jerusalem (Ketton-Cremer 1957: 212–22; Wenley 1991).[2] By 1679, the combination of Robert's poor health and tremendous debt prompted the liquidation of the Pastons' valuables, at least five examples of which are pictured in the painting (Wenley 1991: 121; 2005: 98; Anon. 1679). The timely portrayal of the collection suggests that the still-life was specifically commissioned as an artistic inventory to document possessions that would soon be lost. As such, the painting can be read as intensely personal and entwined with the family's turbulent history.

The reconstruction

The objective of the reconstruction was not replication but a recreation of the painting's original production guided by contemporary texts, technical analysis and observation. The result is not a completed section of the original painting but a document of how it was constructed, with emphasis paid to passages of particular virtuosity.

The support

First, a loom or strainer was constructed on which to stretch the canvas. A thin channel, about 3 mm wide, was gouged from the outer perimeter of the loom to house and protect the lacing threads that pulled the canvas taut. Holes for the lacing threads were drilled at an angle from the channel at the loom's outer edge through the face of each member.

A 90 × 70 cm section of the painting was selected for reconstruction. This area happened to overlap the seam in the original canvas and was therefore included in the reconstruction. Two pieces of linen were cut to the requisite dimensions, the thread count and weave comparable with the original canvas. With a fine needle and linen thread, the two pieces of canvas were joined; the weft running horizontally. All four edges were then hemmed and a piece of linen string 'piped' through the hem on all sides.[3]

Next, the canvas was stretched. A long length of linen thread was stitched through the edges of the canvas, just catching the string within the hem. The needle was then threaded through the face of the loom, out of the top edge and down again to catch the canvas, and so forth. Each side of the canvas was laced independently. The threads were carefully pulled through the drilled holes until the canvas was fairly taut and then tied off at the corners (Fig. 2).[4]

Sizing and priming

In keeping with contemporary manuals on painting technique and microscopic observation of *The Yarmouth Collection*, the reconstruction canvas was sized and primed in preparation for the upper paint layers. A 2.5% rabbit-skin glue size was applied, slightly warm, with a wide bristle brush. In his manuscript on painting (*c*.1620–46), Théodore Turquet de Mayerne refers to this process as 'undercoating' and suggests '[a size layer] of not too weak scrap glue or [common] glue', pressed in with a muller (Fels 2001: 148). Consistent with de Mayerne's treatise on painting, a pumice stone was used to gently smooth the surface of the canvas after the glue had dried. The priming was prepared with a 1:1 ratio of lead white pigment to chalk, ground in oil.[5] This stiff-bodied paint was spread across the canvas with the edge of a large palette knife. The knife was held at an angle almost perpendicular to the canvas, encouraging the priming to fill the interstices of the canvas and obliterate the canvas seam. Broad spatula marks visible in the X-radiograph of *The Yarmouth Collection* suggest that it was primed using a similar technique. A portion of the priming was left exposed at the upper left corner of the reconstruction.

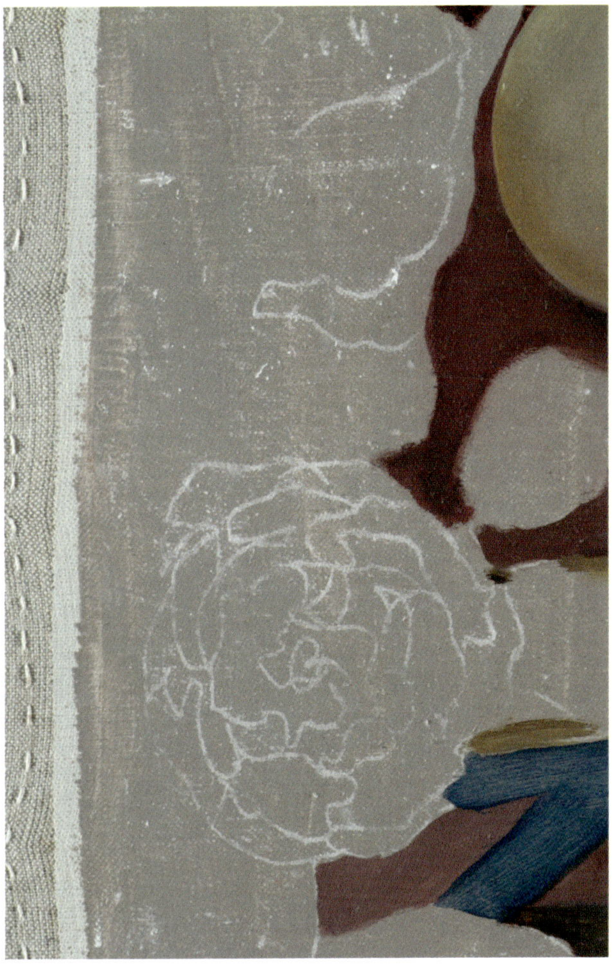

Figure 3 *The white chalk underdrawing was transferred on top of the ground layer. A section of the white priming layer was left exposed at the upper left of the reconstruction.*

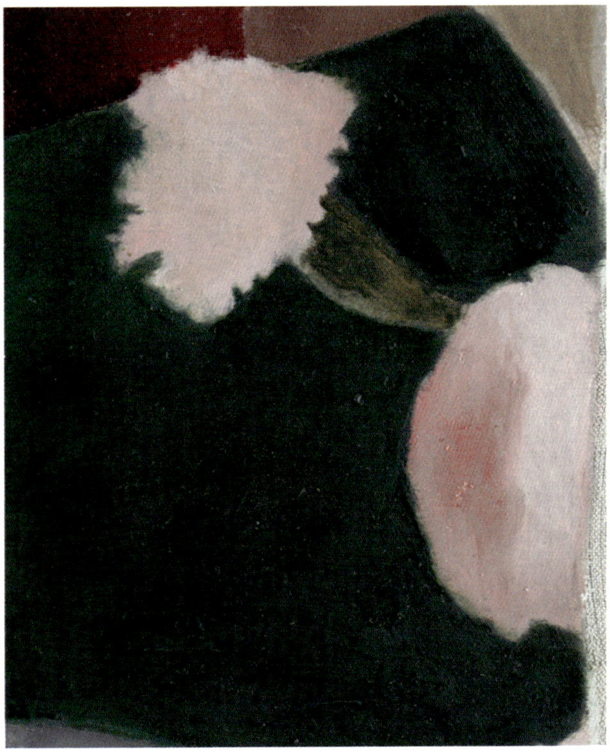

Figure 4 *The dead colouring was applied thinly, blocking in areas of shape and colour.*

The ground or *imprimatura* layer

The Yarmouth Collection has a light greyish pink ground layer that was left exposed intentionally in many areas of the painting: as a mid-tone on the nautilus shells and their mounts; on the body of the cylindrical ivory tankard; on the globe and young girl among others. Elemental analysis of that layer confirmed the presence of lead white, charcoal black, vermilion, Van Dyck brown, brown ochre, glassy lead-containing particles and chalk.[6] The chalk was probably added as a bulking agent while the lead glass acted as a siccative. A mixture of these pigments was made for the reconstruction and once a satisfactory match was reached, pulverised lead glass was added.[7] The ground layer was applied with the same method as the priming: sparingly, with a palette knife.

The underdrawing and image transfer

Infrared study of the painting revealed no carbon-containing underdrawing and microscopic examination eliminated the possibility of dark drawing lines beneath the relatively thin paint layer. Therefore, a tracing of the original painting was transferred to the reconstruction using white chalk. On the topic of underdrawing, de Mayerne states, 'The painting should be drawn out with chalk … Trace the pieces and press them through using paper rubbed with chalk' (Fels 2001: 222). Following this system as closely as possible, the opposite side of the tracing was covered with white chalk and then, chalk-side down, the lines were retraced with light pressure, resulting in a perfect replication onto the ground (Fig. 3). Despite reservations about transferring the entire drawing at once, the chalk proved surprisingly robust, withstanding inadvertent contact during the painting process.

Dead colouring

The oil-bound dead colouring on *The Yarmouth Collection* varies significantly between paint passages. Some areas, such as the table to the left of the little girl, were described with a flat colour, whereas others were modulated in value and hue. Two cross-sections taken from the Wan-li bowl, for example, reveal disparate proportions of black pigment in the dead colouring layer, suggesting that the bowl was modelled. In his treatise, Marshall Smith recommends that some subjects, particularly fruit, are 'finished well in the dead colour' or their softness and roundness will not be emulated, subsequent layers consisting only of glaze pigments (Smith 1692: 76; Wallert 1999: 21).

Guided by visual examination and cross-section analysis, the dead colouring of the table, bowl, parrot and lobster was rendered as a simple, almost topographical interpretation of shape (Fig. 4). The gilt nautilus shell mounts were addressed with warm and cool strokes of shadow

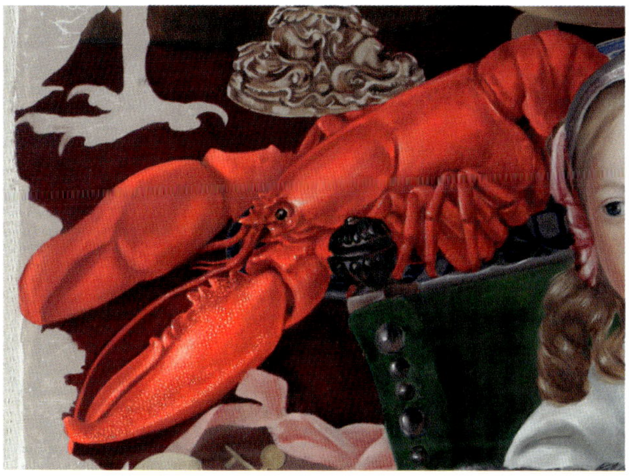

Figure 5 *Detail of the lobster, its left claw articulated with* impasto *dots of paint for three-dimensional effect.*

(consisting of azurite, brown ochre, yellow ochre and bone black), the ground colour acting as the predominant mid-tone as it does on the ivory tankard between them. The little girl, parrot, pocket watch and flowers were articulated with minimal modelling. No *impasto* brushwork was employed at this stage; the paint applied was very lean in keeping with the ubiquitous 'fat-over-lean' rule.

Working up

The level of technical accomplishment demonstrated in *The Yarmouth Collection*, the tactility of the subjects and illusion of space can partly be attributed to a sparing and systematic application of paint. Typical of seventeenth-century Dutch still-life practice, each layer from the ground upwards contributes to the ultimate appearance of the composition. Lower paint layers are not completely obscured by subsequent applications but appear in various guises, as mid-tones or highlights. By permitting each layer to dry thoroughly before adding another, lower paint layers are not adulterated. The technique is, therefore, not purely additive but represents forethought and economy that visually knits the composition together.

Sections of the reconstruction have been left unfinished to illustrate the stratigraphy of the paint build-up. The pigments identified through analysis conducted at Tate and the Hamilton Kerr Institute (HKI) include the following: ultramarine, azurite, smalt, vermilion, red lead, cochineal lake, lead-tin yellow, orpiment, yellow lake, yellow ochre, copper resinate green, raw sienna, Van Dyck brown, brown ochre, lead white and bone black.[8] All pigments were ground on a glass plate in a linseed-based lead oil and mixed on a palette to the desired hue. The paint was applied with a small bristle brush and blended with a dry sable brush.

Wan-li bowl

The contours of the bowl were already laid in with dead colouring, leaving only the blue pattern to be applied. Pure strokes of ultramarine blue and smalt were used to delineate the decorative pattern; the smalt applied wet-in-wet over the ultramarine in areas of shadow. The smalt had a tendency to pool in areas, creating the impression of a true ceramic glaze. Though more difficult to manipulate than ultramarine, the choice of that pigment carries significance as Wan-li bowls were traditionally glazed with cobalt glass pigment (Dillon 1908: 5; Watt 1979: 68). The true-to-life effect is lost in the original painting as a result of the smalt's discoloration.

Lobster

Like the porcelain bowl, the lobster was loosely modelled in the dead-colouring stage with varying proportions of vermilion, cochineal lake, lead white and a small amount of ivory black.[9] Over this, a thin, uniform layer of cochineal was applied with the exception of one claw that was preserved to demonstrate the layer build-up. The lobster had undergone extensive analysis in an effort to understand the optical effect which, before restoration, distorted its form with a veil of blanched and discoloured paint.

Above the flat application of cochineal a layer of vermilion was scumbled to capture the lighter tones of the lobster's shell and describe the turbid intensity of its colouring. Deep shadows along the joints of the shell were reinforced with several more layers of cochineal lake. The gritty texture of the lobster's claw is a result of tiny dollops of paint consisting of lead-tin yellow and lead white pigment. The original lobster shell was covered with several campaigns of these *impasto* dots, some covered with vermilion paint and others left as a light yellow. Although the reconstruction of this technique proved time-consuming, the effect was gratifyingly crustaceous and three-dimensional (Fig. 5).

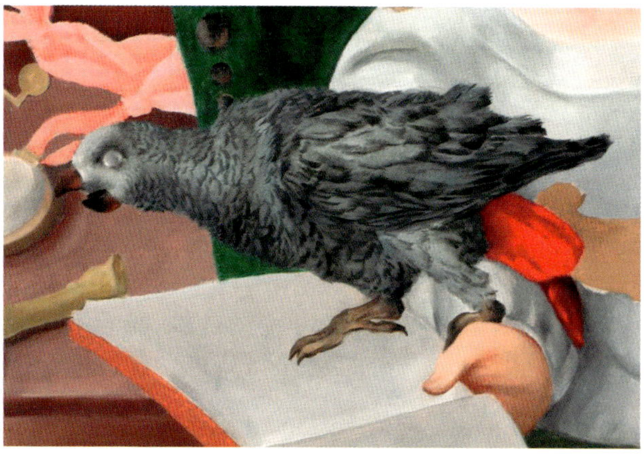

Figure 6 *Detail of the African parrot's busy pattern of feathers during the working-up stage.*

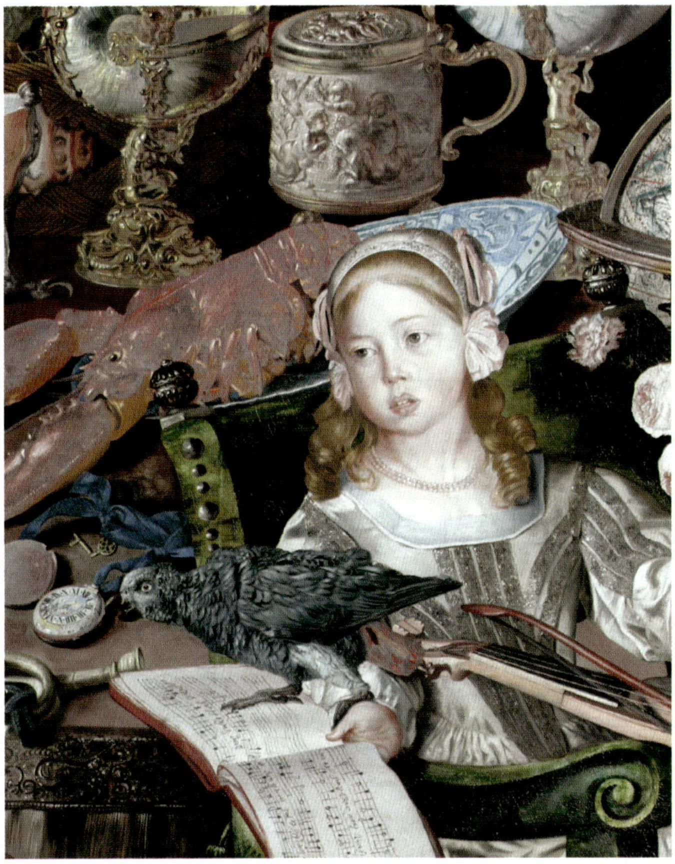

Figure 7 *Detail of the area chosen for reconstruction from* The Yarmouth Collection.

African parrot

The feathers of the parrot appear dizzyingly complicated in the original painting, but the intricacy is achieved through a systematic layering of brushstrokes. Over the slightly modulated dead colouring, the contours of each feather were articulated with a thin brush and a mixture of lead white, ivory black and azurite paint. The result was a busy pattern of hatched lines across the parrot's body (Fig. 6). Its signature red tail feathers, a visual symbol of its species and ability to mimic speech, are completely lost in the original painting. Similar to the lobster, the layers of cochineal pigment are dramatically faded. On the reconstruction, each tail feather was defined with strokes of pure cochineal over the vermilion dead colouring. This stage is one step short of the final illusion: the careful placement of highlights on each of the feathers to articulate their sheen and softness.

Young girl

The little girl's flesh appears faded and cool in the original painting, a result of degraded yellow and red lake pigments. Most of what is visible today is dead colouring – a wet-in-wet application of lead white, vermilion, raw sienna and bone black. The working-up stage of the reconstruction offered an opportunity to recreate her original vitality. Above the dead colouring, freshly ground weld and cochineal glazes were brushed thinly over the girl's flesh. Once dry, a mixture of weld, cochineal, raw sienna and lead white was added to define the warm mid-tones of her complexion.[10] Her lips were glazed with a veil of cochineal and highlights added to her forehead, nose and chin. Her satiny dress was captured with the strategic placement of highlights and shadows of lead white, bone black and azurite applied over the grey dead colour of her gown and cap. With these sparse materials, blended wet-in-wet to a smooth finish, the appearance of a steely blue satin was achieved.

Finishing touches

The finishing touches on *The Yarmouth Collection* adjust the balance of values in the painting and bring choice objects into focus (Figs 7 and 8). Final highlights and shadows required more than one campaign; for example, the lead-tin yellow highlights of the girl's hair were carefully blended with a sable brush and then individual hairs were picked out with crisp ridges of paint. The deep shadows around her eyes and mouth were laid first, followed by neat dashes of white on her eyes and lips, lending animation to her previously vacant stare. The lobster's prickly shell was finished with additional dabs of lead white paint, emphasising its roughness against the smooth contours of the girl's satin cap and the Wan-li bowl.

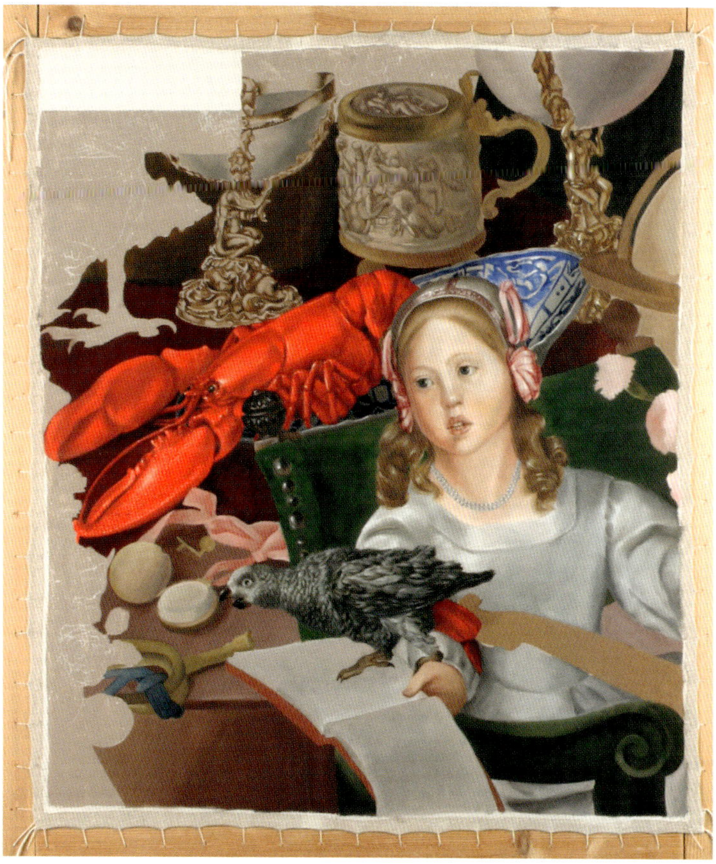

Figure 8 *The finished reconstruction after the application of final highlights.*

Conclusion

The Yarmouth Collection bears testament to the aspirations and misfortunes of the Paston family by documenting their diminishing collection of treasures. A studied and one-time successful interplay of artistic invention and stoic realism, the still-life is a perfect vehicle for capturing a moment of transience in the lives of its patrons and the individual objects portrayed. The technical study and reconstruction of this complex painting have supplied a better understanding of its function and original appearance. At the time the reconstruction was made, extensive pigment degradation and layers of old restoration hindered the perception of its quality and success as a composition. Following its recent restoration at the HKI, *The Yarmouth Collection* has returned to its home at Norwich Castle Museum, Norfolk, where it can be appreciated in a greatly improved state.

Acknowledgements

Warm appreciation to everyone at the HKI with special thanks to Renate Woudhuysen-Keller for her patience and enthusiasm, Spike Bucklow, Chris Titmus, Chris Hurst, Alan Barker, Rica Jones, Kate Stonor, Robert Wenley and Norwich Castle Museum.

Notes

1. The painting was X-rayed at Tate Britain in 2005. Cross-section analysis using scanning electron microscopy with energy dispersive X-ray (SEM-EDX) analysis and pigment identification using polarising light microscopy (PLM) was conducted by Rica Jones and Kate Stonor at Tate and Spike Bucklow and the author at the HKI.
2. For a complete inventory of objects sold, see Pembroke College, University of Cambridge, MSS, LC.II 230. A number of the objects portrayed in the painting are extant: the tankard held by the servant (one of a pair: private collection, London; Metropolitan Museum of Art, New York); the nautilus cup to the left of the globe (Rijksmuseum, Amsterdam); the overturned enamelled 'Surrey' cup with strombus shell (Norwich Castle Museum); the nautilus cup to the right of the globe (Museum Het Prisenhof, Delft); the mother-of-pearl perfume flask to the left of the composition (private collection, London).
3. The string inside of the canvas hem prevents its accidental tearing during stretching, when a great deal of stress is placed on the edges of the canvas.
4. There is no evidence of the original stretching method visible on the lined canvas today. The system described above is based on historical accounts and the likelihood that the original canvas was stretched on the strainer in which it would ultimately be framed, eliminating the logistical inconvenience of restretching a very large canvas at Oxnead Hall.
5. The binding medium was not analysed but the texture and solubility of the layer suggests it is a drying oil. The drying oil used in the reconstruction is a mixture made by Renate Woudhuysen-Keller: a 'lead oil' comprising heated linseed oil and lead oxide.
6. In their earlier examination of the painting, Rica Jones and Kate Stonor identified two types of brown: Cologne earth or Van Dyck brown, and sienna (Jones and Stonor 2005: 5). These results were

confirmed during additional sampling at the Hamilton Kerr Institute.

7. Large shards of lead glass were pulverised using a mortar and pestle until almost a powder and then ground with a muller in water until a fine consistency. When the water had evaporated, the slurry of particles was scraped off the plate and added to the paint.
8. Cochineal was identified by Jo Kirby of the National Gallery, London using Fourier transform infrared spectroscopy (FTIR) and high performance liquid chromatography (HPLC); Kirby 2007.
9. The cochineal lake was produced by Renate Woudhuysen-Keller at the HKI. It was precipitated on alum and ground several times in water prior to use. Ground in oil, it was extremely viscous and resistant to brushing out evenly but when chalk was added the consistency became far more workable. This may explain the large quantities of chalk found in samples of cochineal from the original painting.
10. The weld was also produced by Renate Woudhuysen-Keller, precipitated onto alum and ground twice in water before being used in the reconstruction. Two drops of modern siccative were added to speed its drying in oil.

References

Anon. 1679. 'Inventory of Rebecca Paston's closet'. Pembroke College, University of Cambridge, MSS LCII 230.

Dillon, E. 1908. 'Some notes on the origin and the development of the enamelled porcelain of the Chinese', *The Burlington Magazine* 13(61): 4–7.

Fels, D. Jr. 2001. *Lost Secrets of Flemish Painting: Including the First Complete English Translation of the De Mayerne Manuscript. British Museum. B. M. MS. Sloane 2052*. Hillsville, VA: Alchemist.

Jones, R. and Stonor, K. 2005. 'Examination and condition report, *The Yarmouth Collection*'. Unpublished technical report, Tate Britain X03693.

Ketton-Cremer, R. 1957. *Norfolk Assembly*. London: Faber & Faber.

Kirby, J. 2007. 'Dutch School, 17th century, *The Yarmouth Collection*, Norwich Castle Museum and Art Gallery, on loan to Tate Britain, X03693; sampled 6.5.2005'. Unpublished technical report, National Gallery, London.

Smith, M. 1692. *The Art of Painting According to the Theory and Practice of the Best Italian, French and German Masters*. London.

Wallert A. (ed.). 1999. *Still Lifes: Techniques and Styles: The Examination of Paintings from the Rijksmuseum*. Amsterdam: B.V. Waanders Uitgeverji.

Watt, J.C.Y. 1979. 'Notes on the use of cobalt in later Chinese ceramics', *Ars Orientalis* 11: 63–85.

Wenley, R. 1991. 'Robert Paston and *The Yarmouth Collection*', *Norfolk Archaeology* 41(2): 113–44.

Wenley, R. 2005. 'The Paston Treasures: portrait of a seventeenth-century collection', *Silver Studies* 19: 131–6.

RECONSTRUCTION OF A FRUIT AND FLOWER PIECE BY JAN VAN OS

Spike Bucklow

The painting *Still Life with Fruit and Flowers*, by Jan van Os (1744–1808), is in oil on panel (Fig. 1). It is currently in the Fitzwilliam Museum, one of five by the same artist in the collection. The painting is signed but was not dated. Upon examination at the Hamilton Kerr Institute (HKI), the original painting was covered in a soiled modern polymeric varnish, which lay on top of a pigmented natural resin varnish. Both were removed and the painting was revarnished (Bucklow 1993). Some glazes had faded, but otherwise the painting was in excellent condition. No samples were taken and the reconstruction proceeded based upon close observation of the paint surface (Fig. 2). Other paintings by Jan van Os (at the Fitzwilliam Museum and National Gallery, London, as well as watercolours at the British Museum, London) were also examined in detail.

The reconstruction was made in 1993 and took approximately 100 hours to make, from preparing the panel to the final highlights and shadows on dewdrops. The execution was relatively quick because Jan van Os' ephemeral subject matter required a very methodical approach. Before the era of temperature-controlled transport, the flowers and fruit depicted on the panel could not have been assembled at any one time. Another flower and fruit painting by van Os (National Gallery NG 1380) is dated both 1777 and 1778, acknowledging the limited availability of his subject matter over a number of seasons. The grapes would have been depicted in the autumn of 1777 and the tulips in the spring of 1778. This implies that van Os worked from nature, as early flower painters claimed to do,[1] although he may also have used watercolour sketches as models for some parts of the display, since numerous such model books survive (Segal 1992:17).

The original panel was a single piece of mahogany. The reconstruction was made from two pieces, joined with animal glue. The panel was prepared with chalk in rabbit-skin glue applied in three layers over a period of two hours and thinned the following day to remove evidence of brushstrokes. A priming of equal volumes of lead white and chalk in linseed oil was applied in two layers and, in an unfortunate oversight, I failed to smooth the second layer so brushstrokes are visible in some final passages. The priming was dry after two days and the pencilled design was transferred from a thin sheet of paper. This proved to be more intrusive than the original, presumably because the copied design was heavier.

The original painting was executed in poppy oil but this detail was not forthcoming until after the reconstruction had begun. The reconstruction was made with linseed oil. Although this has the disadvantage of yellowing more than poppy oil, it does dry more quickly, enabling the reconstruction to be completed within three weeks. The following pigments were used: lead white, chalk, lead-tin yellow, yellow ochre, orpiment, buckthorn lake, Indian yellow,[2] raw sienna, burnt sienna, minium, vermilion, red lakes, terre verte, ultramarine ash, ultramarine, indigo, Prussian blue and carbon black. Jan van Os' systematic technique was most evident in the paint layers. Each passage was executed in a different manner and the manner of each was consistent across other paintings. Different fruits, flowers or leaves could have up to four paint layers. The first, flat, blocking-in layer was invariably high key, but thereafter the layer sequence was specific to the particular item depicted.

A formulaic approach to each depicted item would have been essential if the subject matter was indeed captured from life. This is because each paint layer took about two days to dry, so the elapse time for painting a bunch of grapes in four layers,[3] for example, would be a minimum of six days.[4] One of the painting's themes is *vanitas*, acknowledging the transience of life, and Jan van Os was careful to put a single mouldy grape at the heart of the white bunch. However, if he had not painted the first couple of layers before getting the grapes into the studio, then the whole bunch would have been mouldy by the time he got to the

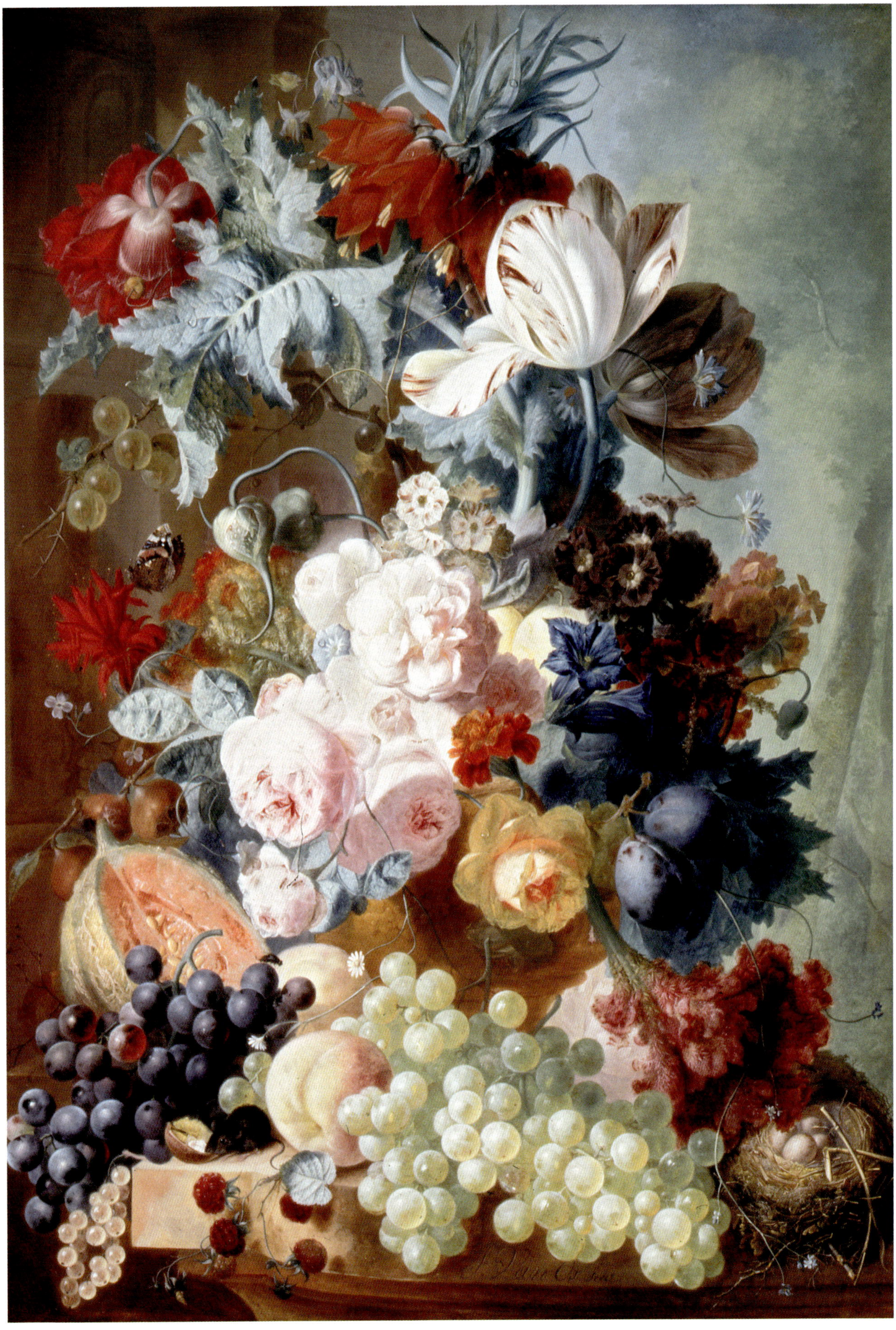

Figure 1 *Jan van Os,* Still Life with Fruit and Flowers, *oil on panel, 787 × 587 mm, The Fitzwilliam Museum, Cambridge (PD82-1973).*

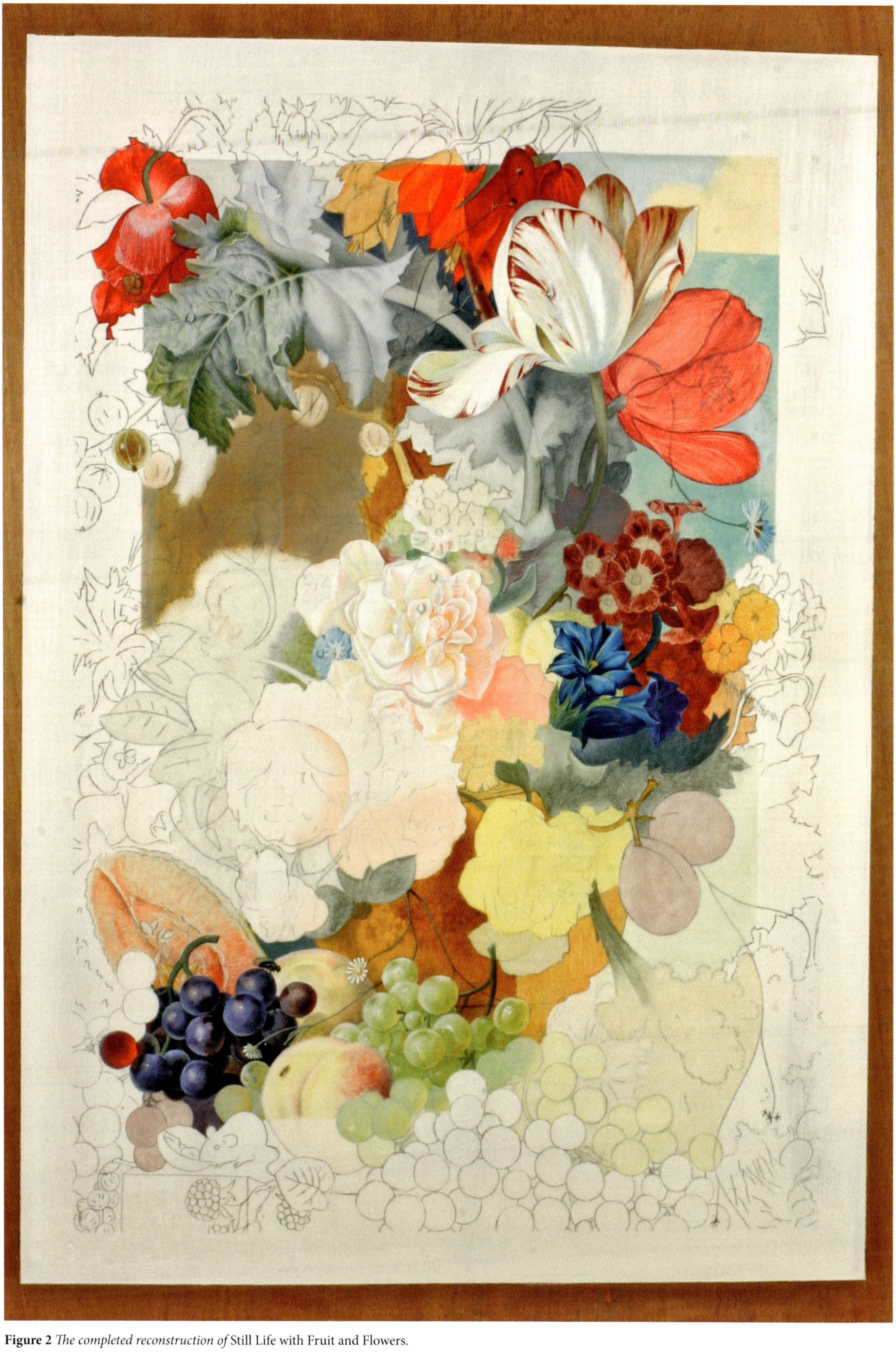

Figure 2 *The completed reconstruction of* Still Life with Fruit and Flowers.

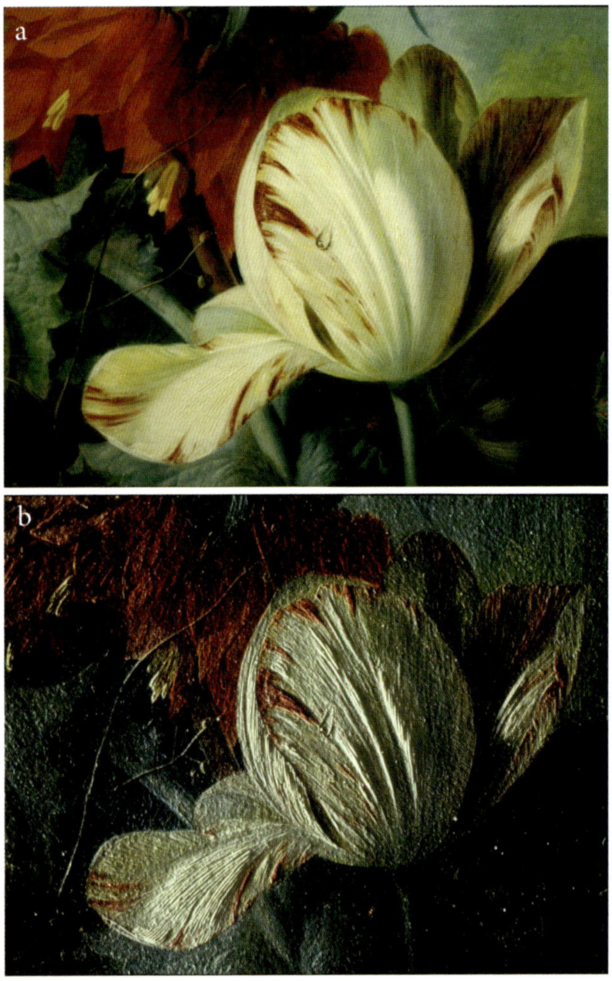

Figure 3 *Detail of the tulip in (a) diffuse light and (b) raking light.*

final touches in the fourth layer. This suggests multiple models for different aspects of each depicted item – one bunch of grapes may have provided the overall structure whilst another bunch provided surface details, for example. Certainly, different paintings seem to feature the same tulip with petals at differing stages in the process of wilting.

Jan van Os had a very detailed vision of the final painting months in advance of being able to finish it. The composition was defined at the drawing stage, but the lighting was determined by the first or second layer of paint, before being able to see the complete ensemble that was to be depicted. The original had very few *pentimenti*, showing that the artist's initial vision was followed faithfully, but one change occurred in the black grapes. The grapes to the left of the peach were originally all black, but van Os realised that the mouse eating a walnut would be lost in shadow, so he added three white grapes to increase its visibility.[5] Jan van Os' formulaic black grapes were first all pale purple, then, the backlit ones were bright opaque red, followed by a blue glaze and a white scumble.

Dutch flower painting in the seventeenth century was a self-conscious celebration of technical prowess in observation and execution (Alpers 1983: 112–18). Jan van Os' approach to flower painting continued in the same highly finished tradition but no longer pursued the realistic imitation of three-dimensional space, being influenced instead by the two-dimensional designs of Japanese woodcuts and Islamic art. His compositions defy the rules of physical flower-arranging (smaller on top and larger below, for example) and their coherence relies upon graphic arabesques and the distribution of light and shade. Lighting effects are therefore crucial.[6]

When photographing the original painting after its treatment, Chris Titmus pointed out that the lighting for the arrangement of fruit and flowers was impossible. For example, some parts of the poppy leaf are lit from the left, whilst others are lit from above and some individual grapes have their own unique light sources. By using lighting to fragment large entities and draw attention to particular parts, Jan van Os created a two-dimensional image that satisfied the eye but which referred to something that could never exist. Consummate skill was required to make the viewer accept the impossible without question, and this self-conscious game-playing is part of the painting's appeal, along with its inbuilt tensions due to simultaneous references to *spronk*, the celebration of worldly luxury, and *vanitas*, the acknowledgement that all worldly things are transient.

Many of the painting's elements allude to the passage of time. The bird's nest full of eggs, the mouse gnawing a walnut, a butterfly in the shadows, an ant on the peach, a rotting grape, a wilting petal and evaporating dewdrops all have symbolic significance. The painter's skill freezes ephemera for all to see. But the act of trying to reconstruct the painting, and then seeing the reconstruction as an everyday object (as opposed to a museum object), drew attention to other ways in which Jan van Os played with light and time.

At first glance, it looks as if the painter has devoted hours of painstaking attention to the white tulip. Each petal looks as if its radiating anatomical ribs have been carefully picked out to help define the flower's curvature. However, copying the way it was made told another story. The first layer was mainly lead white and the flat shape was painted in less than two minutes. Two days later, another mainly white layer was painted on top of the first white. The only difference between the layers was the medium: the first was linseed oil and the second was an emulsion made from linseed oil and glue. The first white paint flowed to make a nice, thin, smooth film whereas the second white paint was mayonnaise-like and retained its shape as it came off the bristle brush. The tulip's petal ribs were ridges of white paint and their curvature was due to swift calligraphic strokes executed with a flat stiff brush that was used like an italic pen. The ribs took another couple of minutes. Two days later, some red lake was blended in from the edges. Finally, a black shadow and white highlight were placed on a part of the petal where the white ridges of paint had earlier been flattened with a touch from the end of the brush. Spread over one working week, the tulip took less than 10 minutes to paint.

Of course, Jan van Os' tulip is vastly superior to the one in my reconstruction. His calligraphic brushstrokes were much more assured and, critically, he knew how to mix a thixotropic emulsion with exactly the right flow properties. His 10-minute tulip, spread over a week, was only possible because of decades of practice after training by a master, Aart Schoumann (1710–1792), who had inherited centuries of accumulated knowledge about paint media (Mitchell 1968:12). This knowledge has now been lost and our only insights are through reconstructions.

After finishing the reconstruction it was hung in a corridor and I walked passed it for many months barely paying it any attention. The corridor was quite dark and had small, low windows providing a strong directional light that varied with time of day and year. In other words, it was hung somewhere that was similar to the original Dutch domestic setting. When the sunlight bounced off the opposite wall in the corridor, the tulip looked as it would in the diffuse lighting of a museum or gallery. But when the sunlight came at an angle and shone down the corridor, it looked very different – the ridges of paint cast deep shadows and the petal ribs became very pronounced. Eike Friedrich has created an interactive digital reconstruction of the effect using the reconstructed tulip and polynomial texture mapping (PTM) software. This can be seen on the HKI's website (Fig. 3).[7]

One day, when walking past the obliquely lit reconstruction, I caught a movement out of the corner of my eye. I stopped, looked at the tulip and retraced my steps. As I walked passed the tulip, it changed, just as a ploughed field can change (looking towards the sun, you only see the shaded sides of furrows and the field looks dark, but moving on and turning back, you only see the furrows' sunlit sides and the field looks brighter). One or two steps either side of the tulip made a big difference. In one position I saw paint ridges and the petal looked light, and in another position I saw shadows cast by the ridges and the petal looked dark. The paint ridges are not parallel so the effect is more complex than a ploughed field; the shaded areas run up and down the petals and around the tulip, giving an illusion of volume.

Jan van Os' extraordinarily efficient way of painting tulips not only enabled him to work quickly on many paintings simultaneously using the same slowly wilting flower, it also created an understated but highly dynamic side to the painting that would have given much pleasure to the original Dutch owner, but which most museum visitors miss.

Notes

1. See, for example, statements by Brueghel in Crivelli 1868; Hairs and Finet 1985.
2. The pigment was a modern substitute rather than the authentic material.
3. My layer structure for black grapes was: (1) ultramarine, vermilion, lead white, (2) ultramarine, vermilion, (3) ultramarine, red lake, black, (4) lead white, ultramarine. For white grapes: (1) lead white, lead-tin yellow, (2) terre verte, lead-tin yellow, (3) Indian yellow, terra verte, (4) lead white. Pigments listed in order of decreasing quantity in each layer. For further details about the materials of flower painting see Murray and Groen 1994.
4. Poppy oil would have dried slower than linseed oil but there may be a difference between modern refined oils and artists' oils. The question of siccatives in the original was not addressed.
5. Paint becomes more transparent with age, so the original black grapes are now visible through the later white grapes.
6. The National Gallery painting and three of the Fitzwilliam paintings (PD 848-1973, PD 83-1973 and M67) have pineapples at the top of the flower arrangements. Pineapples grow on the ground, weigh about a kilo and have very short stalks. Their placement in the arrangement underlines how far these paintings depart from reality, whether considered as three-dimensional or four-dimensional, when the conflation of seasons is also acknowledged.
7. www-hki.fitzmuseum.cam.ac.uk/research/painting/van_os.html.

References

Alpers, S. 1983. *The Art of Describing*. London: Murray.

Bucklow, S. 1993. Treatment report HKI 1768, Hamilton Kerr Institute.

Crivelli, G. 1868. *Giovanni Brueghel, pittor fiammingo sue lettre e quadretti esistenti*. Milan: Presso l'Ambrosiana.

Hairs, M-L. and Finet, D. 1985. *Flemish Flower Painters of the Seventeenth Century*, E. Grzelak (tr.). Brussels: Lefebvre et Gillet.

Mitchell, P. 1968. *Jan van Os*. Leigh on Sea: Lewis.

Murray, S. and Groen, K. 1994. 'Four early Dutch flower paintings examined', *The Hamilton Kerr Institute Bulletin* 2: 6–20.

Segal, S. 1992. *The Tulip Portrayed*. Amsterdam: Museum voor de Bloembollenstreek.

COPYING ALFRED STEVENS' *LA LISEUSE*

Rebecca Kench

During my third year at the Hamilton Kerr Institute (HKI) I chose to copy Alfred Stevens *La Liseuse*, a mid-nineteenth-century canvas painting, from the Fitzwilliam Museum's collection, of a woman sitting in a chair reading a book. The painting is signed but not dated, although, judging from the sitter's costume, it was probably painted in the mid-1860s (Gerson 1960: 123).

The painting (Fig. 1) is typical of Stevens' work of this period. *La Liseuse* is painted with spontaneous but carefully controlled brushwork. Interestingly, an X-radiograph of the painting (Fig. 2) revealed a different painting below the present one, which I was able to identify.[1] For the purposes of the copy no attempt was made to reconstruct this earlier composition. As the paint layer was in very good condition with no cracking or losses it was not possible to take cross-sections to determine the layer structure, although I was able to take a pigment dispersion to determine the pigments used in the ground layer; these were lead white and gypsum.

Stevens' painting was executed on a pre-primed canvas of fine, plain weave and high quality, representative of the finest canvases sold at the time. So my first task was to attempt to emulate this. First, a canvas was loomed in the Dutch method using string. The vertical tacking edges in Stevens' painting are primed suggesting the canvas was cut from a larger pre-primed canvas and not primed on the stretcher.

After much reading and discussion about the possible ground layers, I adhered to a mid-nineteenth-century treatise (Mérimée 1839: 219). A first preparatory layer of hot animal size was applied with a sponge to both sides of the canvas because the artist had used a fine closed weave, and this was considered the best way to saturate the canvas. On top of this the ground layer was applied using a mixture known as 'ceruse', which seems to have been the most commonly used ground layer at the time. It was difficult to research the exact composition of 'ceruse'; the literature revealed only that the main component was lead white and the most usual addition to this was chalk. So after consideration, three parts of chalk were made up with one part lead white mixed in linseed oil and applied with a large knife. Four days later a second layer was applied. A week later, once dry, the canvas was gently pumiced to smooth the surface then removed from the loom. However, when I attempted to attach it onto a stretcher it cracked readily, presumably from the addition of too much chalk. The canvas was pumiced further and a new ground layer applied using lead oil with equal quantities of lead white and chalk. A week later, once this was dry, I attempted to restretch it. The initial ground layer had set up an inherent problem in the painting and it cracked once more. Considered discussion followed and it was decided that I should proceed with this canvas so I attached it to the stretcher and lightly pumiced it once more. The canvas was fatty and excessively shiny, so it was carefully washed with a damp, soapy cloth, cleared with water and dried with tissue.

In attempting to recreate the ground layer, I had read various treatises and taken advice on the best way to prime the canvas but this just resulted in a flaking ground layer. My failed attempts at recreating a colourman's pre-primed canvas highlighted the importance of experience. I had found very few written sources on a specific method of priming a colourman's canvas and was unable to determine the exact quantities used, presumably because it was considered a routine job.[2] Renate Woudhuysen-Keller's help was invaluable in directing me towards the relevant literature and advising me on the application, and also in allowing me to make these mistakes. Trial and error would have eventually revealed the quantities and methods needed to recreate this priming layer.

An *imprimatura* of yellow ochre and raw sienna was applied over the ground and thinned with a small amount of turpentine. Stevens used this layer as an integral part of the composition, allowing it to show through in many areas, mainly in the darks of the clothing and the highlights in the background.

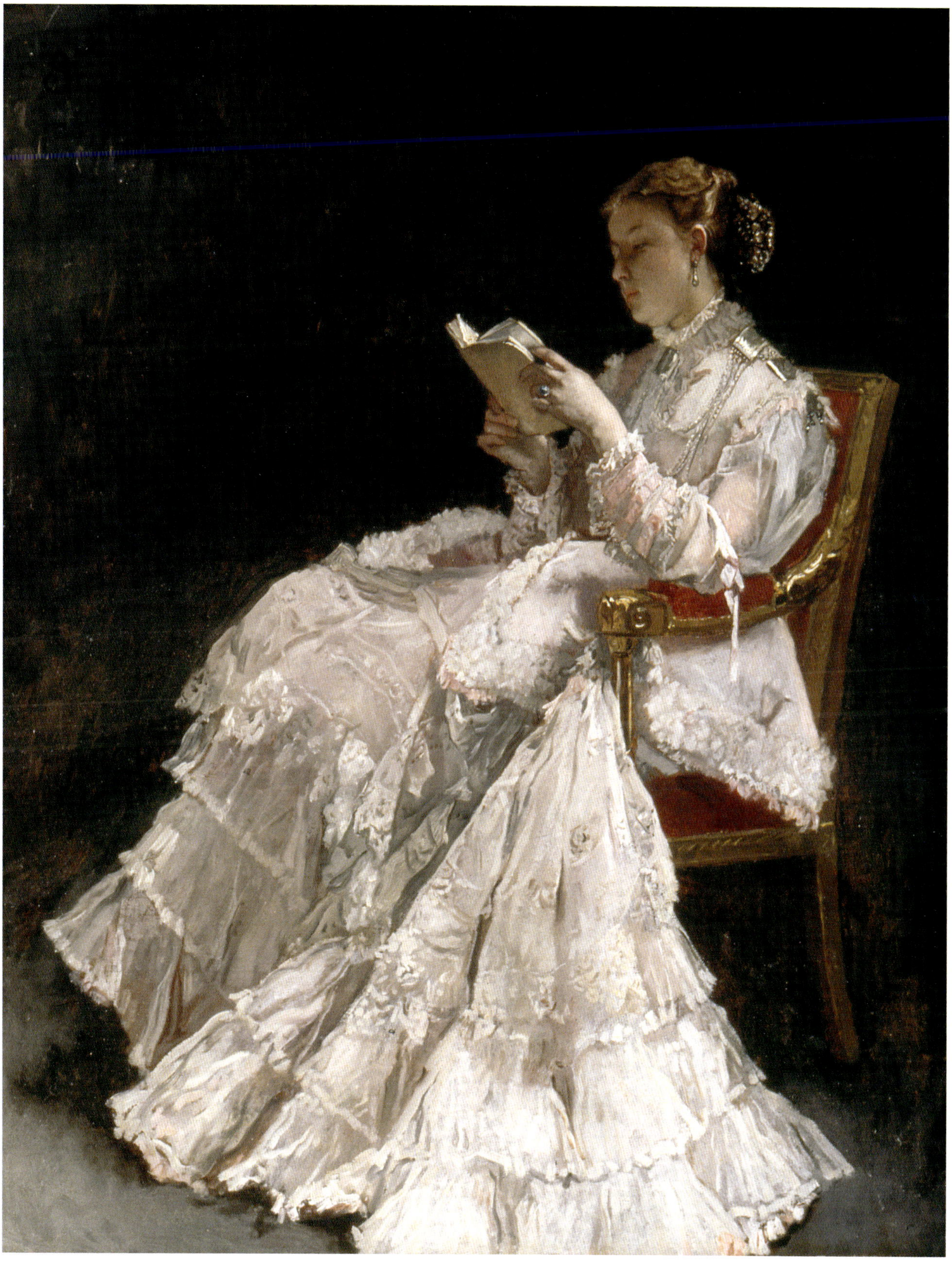

Figure 1 *Alfred Stevens,* La Liseuse, c.*1866, The Fitzwilliam Museum, Cambridge.*

The outline of the painting was traced and transferred with charcoal onto the canvas, then strengthened with a wash. The paint layers were mostly applied from a tube as this was thought to be the most authentic method. Any modern paints not considered sufficiently authentic were prepared from dry pigment using a lead oil prepared by Renate, diluted in equal parts with cold pressed linseed oil (Keller 1973). Stevens painted using transparent

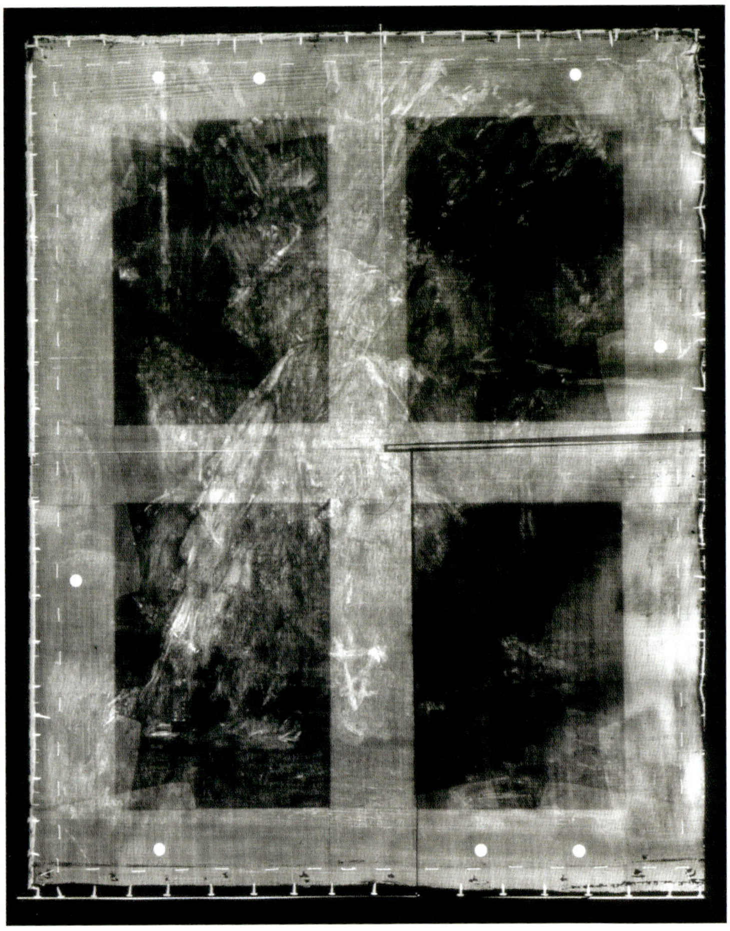

Figure 2 *X-ray of* La Liseuse.

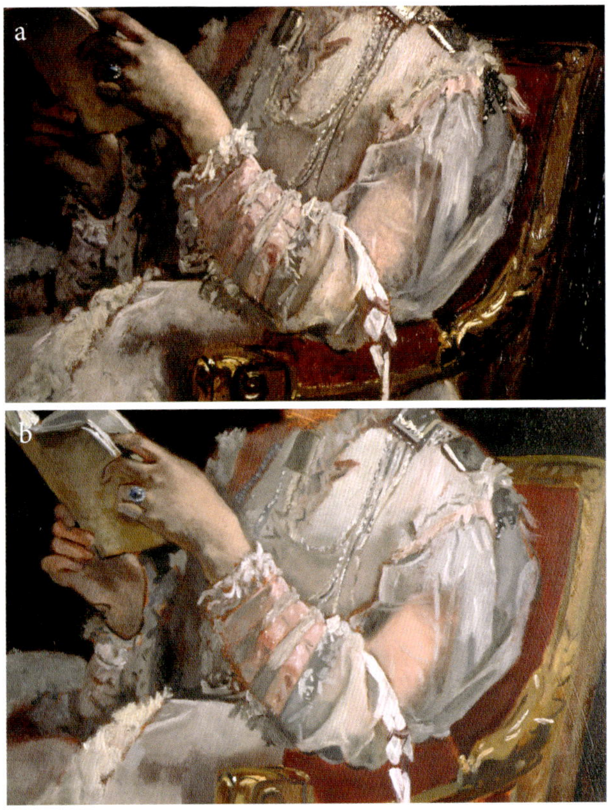

Figure 3 *(a) Detail of the hands and dress on* La Liseuse *and (b) corresponding detail on the reconstruction.*

colour in the darks, opaque in the lights. Some of his paint layers were applied over a dry layer beneath; some were applied wet-in-wet.

The highlights and folds of the dress had been painted quickly with a confident hand and the face and hands had by contrast been meticulously painted. Initially I had assumed that the meticulous paintwork would prove to be the most challenging and was surprised to find that this was not the case. The seemingly freer brushstrokes were much harder to recreate (Fig. 3). Every stroke had been considered and calculated to achieve the final effect. The use of *imprimatura* as shadow emphasised how carefully the painting was thought out and rendered from the initial brushstroke. I found copying the brushwork difficult and at times felt defeated by it. Renate was very reassuring and always persuaded me that anything was possible.

Studying and attempting to emulate Stevens' painting was an invaluable lesson. This copy (Fig. 4) showed me primarily how important it is to look beyond the initial impression given by a painting and to carefully consider all its aspects before starting. The exercise caused me a number of problems and without Renate's patience and advice I would have struggled to complete it. She always had faith in me and taught me the value of perseverance.

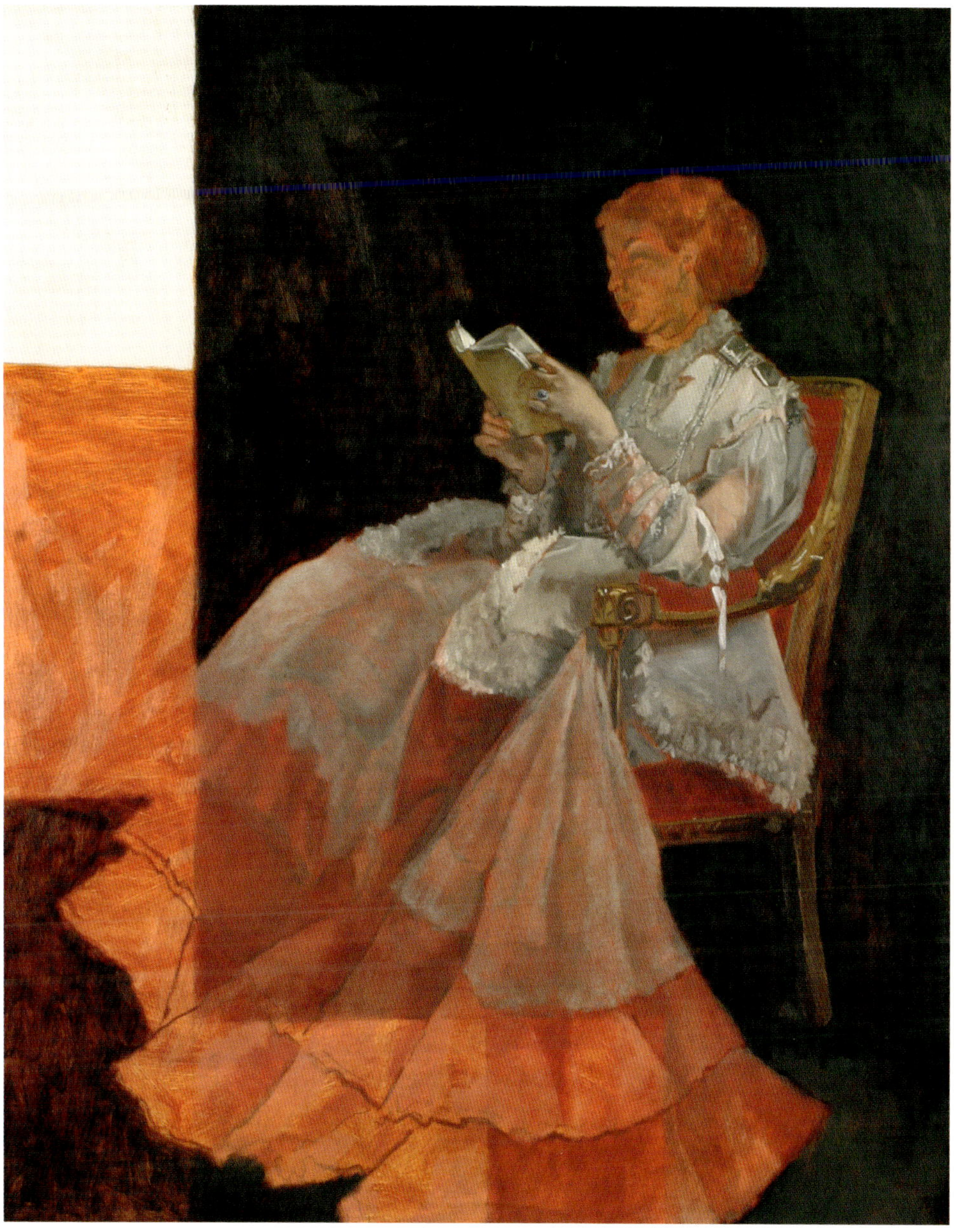

Figure 4 *The completed reconstruction of* La Liseuse.

Notes

1. The painting beneath the current composition is upside down. It is of a woman standing and seems to be very similar to Stevens' painting *Miss Fauvette* (*c.*1862), now in a private collection.
2. The reconstruction was undertaken before the publication of Carlyle (2001) and before the HKI's acquisition, in 2011, of the Winsor & Newton archive that documents such technical details.

References

Carlyle, L. 2001. *The Artist's Assistant*. London: Archetype Publications.

Gerson, H. 1960. *Catalogue of Paintings in the Fitzwilliam Museum, Cambridge*, vol. 1. Cambridge: Syndics of the Fitzwilliam Museum, Cambridge.

Keller, R. 1973. 'Leinöl als Malmittel', *Maltechnik Restauro* 2: 74–105.

Mérimée, M.J.F.L. 1839. *The art of painting in oil, and in fresco; being a history of the various processes and materials employed, from its discovery, / by Hubert and John van Eyck, to the present time: tr. from the original French treatise of M. J. F. L. Mérimée. With original observations on the rise and progress of British art, the French and English chromatic scales, and theories of colouring, by W.B. Sarsfield Taylor*, W.B. Sarsfield Taylor (tr.). London: Whittaker and Co.

LIST OF CONTRIBUTORS

Lara Broecke
Visiting Scholar (2008–2012), Hamilton Kerr Institute, The Fitzwilliam Museum, University of Cambridge, UK

Spike Bucklow
Senior Research Scientist, Hamilton Kerr Institute, The Fitzwilliam Museum, University of Cambridge, UK

Charlotte Caspers
Artist and Specialist in the Reproduction of Old Master Painting Techniques, Amsterdam, The Netherlands

Nicola Christie
Senior Paintings Conservator, The Royal Collection, UK

Sue Ann Chui
Associate Conservator, Paintings Conservation, The J. Paul Getty Museum, Los Angeles, CA, USA

Jessica David
Assistant Paintings Conservator, Yale Center for British Art, New Haven, CT, USA

Rupert Featherstone
Director, Hamilton Kerr Institute and Assistant Director (Conservation), The Fitzwilliam Museum, University of Cambridge, UK

Tine Frøysaker
Associate Professor, Institutt for Arkeologi, Konserverung og Historie, University of Oslo, Norway

Anne van Grevenstein-Kruse
Emeritus Professor in the Practice of Conservation, University of Amsterdam, The Netherlands

Sarah Herring
Isaiah Berlin Assistant Curator of post-1800 paintings, The National Gallery, London, UK

Madeleine Katkov
Independent Conservator, Oxford, UK

Mary Kempski
Assistant to the Director and Senior Conservator, Hamilton Kerr Institute, The Fitzwilliam Museum, University of Cambridge, UK

Rebecca Kench
Painting Conservator, National Museums Liverpool, UK

Christine S. Kimbriel
Conservator, Hamilton Kerr Institute, The Fitzwilliam Museum, University of Cambridge, UK

Daniela Leonard
Andrew W. Mellon Fellow in Paintings Conservation, Art Institute of Chicago, USA

Mirjam Liu
Paintings Conservator, Institutt for Arkeologi, Konservering og Historie, University of Oslo, Norway

Ann Massing
Assistant to the Director Emerita, Hamilton Kerr Institute, The Fitzwilliam Museum, University of Cambridge, UK

Ian McClure
Susan Morse Hilles Chief Conservator, Yale University Art Gallery and Yale Center for British Art, New Haven, CT, USA

Karen Mengshoel
Paintings Conservator, Institutt for Arkeologi, Konservering og Historie, University of Oslo, Norway

Rose Miller
Paul Mellon Research Curator, Hamilton Kerr Institute, The Fitzwilliam Museum, University of Cambridge, UK

Youjin Noh
Conservator, Hamilton Kerr Institute, The Fitzwilliam Museum, University of Cambridge, UK

Christine Patrick
Conservator, Hamilton Kerr Institute, The Fitzwilliam Museum, University of Cambridge, UK

Alan Phenix
Scientist, Getty Conservation Institute, Los Angeles, CA, USA

Jenny Rose
Assistant to the Director and Senior Conservator, Hamilton Kerr Institute, The Fitzwilliam Museum, University of Cambridge, UK

Karin and Manfred Schoeller
Private Collectors, Switzerland

Alison Stock
Independent Conservator, Kent, UK

Kate Stonor
Scientific Department, The National Gallery, London, UK

Alice Tavares da Silva
Conservator, Hamilton Kerr Institute, The Fitzwilliam Museum, University of Cambridge, UK

Chris Titmus
Imaging Specialist and Tutor, Hamilton Kerr Institute, The Fitzwilliam Museum, University of Cambridge, UK

Hayley Tomlinson
Assistant Restorer, The National Gallery, London, UK

Abbie Vandivere
PhD Researcher for Impact of Oil project/Freelance Conservator, Amsterdam, The Netherlands

Johanneke Verhave
Independent Conservator, Rotterdam, The Netherlands

Ernst van der Wetering
Emeritus Professor, University of Amsterdam, The Netherlands

Margreet Wolters
IRR Specialist, Rijksbureau voor Kunsthistorische Documentatie, The Netherlands

Paul Woudhuysen
Keeper, Manuscripts and Printed Books (1974–1999), The Fitzwilliam Museum, University of Cambridge, UK

Lucy Wrapson
Conservator and Research Associate, Hamilton Kerr Institute, The Fitzwilliam Museum, University of Cambridge, UK

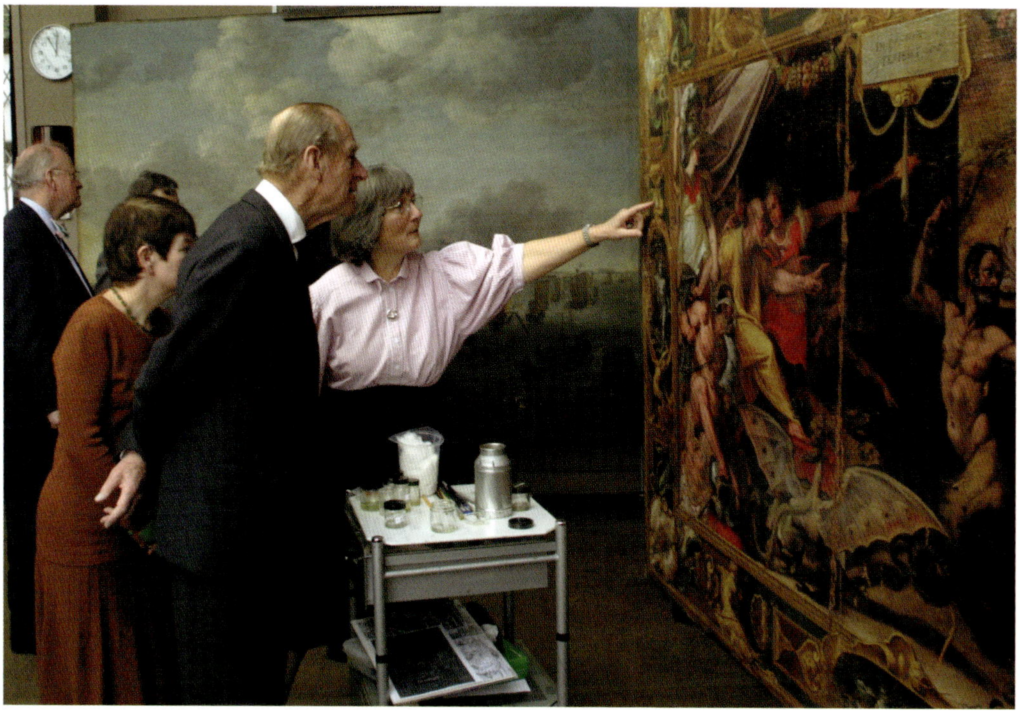